The Origin and History of the Primitive Methodist Church Volume 2

You are holding a reproduction of an original work that is in the public domain in the United States of America, and possibly other countries. You may freely copy and distribute this work as no entity (individual or corporate) has a copyright on the body of the work. This book may contain prior copyright references, and library stamps (as most of these works were scanned from library copies). These have been scanned and retained as part of the historical artifact.

This book may have occasional imperfections such as missing or blurred pages, poor pictures, errant marks, etc. that were either part of the original artifact, or were introduced by the scanning process. We believe this work is culturally important, and despite the imperfections, have elected to bring it back into print as part of our continuing commitment to the preservation of printed works worldwide. We appreciate your understanding of the imperfections in the preservation process, and hope you enjoy this valuable book.

THE ORIGIN AND HISTORY

OF THE

PRIMITIVE METHODIST CHURCH

BY THE
REV: H. B. KENDALL, B.A.

Vol. II.

224576

London:
EDWIN DALTON: 48—50 ALDERSGATE STREET, E.C.

THE LIBRARY
BRIGHAM YOUNG UNIVERSITY
PROVO, UTAH

PRIMITIVE METHODIST CHURCH.

VOL. II.   BOOK II. CONTINUED.

CHAPTER XII.

THE BEMERSLEY BOOK-ROOM, 1821-43.

EXPERIENCE, temperament and policy all combined to make Hugh Bourne publisher and pressman. His character had been shaped and a new direction given to his life by the printed word. Though naturally taciturn and, like Moses, "not eloquent . . . but slow of speech and of a slow tongue," he was communicative through another medium than that of speech. All along he obeyed a pretty steady impulse to express himself in manuscript and type—to externalise his own convictions and his impressions of the facts before him, as his life-long journalising, and his innumerable memoranda respecting past and current events clearly show. In all this he was the direct opposite of William Clowes, who was averse from the use of the pen. For him the inside of a printing-office had few attractions, yet, like Aaron, he was naturally eloquent, and could "speak well." Moreover, as a practical man, Hugh Bourne knew what power there was in the press as an instrument of propagandism; and, as one of the founders and directors of a new denomination, he may have had the ambition to copy, in his own modest way, the example of John Wesley—whom he so much admired—who was one of the most voluminous authors and extensive publishers of his own, or indeed of any, time. So Hugh Bourne's publications ranged from a somewhat bulky Ecclesiastical History to a four-page collection of "Family Receipts," which tells how to relieve a cow choked with a turnip, and how to provide a cheap and wholesome travelling dinner for fourpence. Whence, it will be seen, that the doings of Popes and Councils as well as the small details of domestic and personal economy, alike came within the purview of his printed observations.

These characteristics and habits may be seen at work in Hugh Bourne even before 1811. In proof of this, note the printed account of the first camp meeting, hot from the press, that was scattered by thousands; the "Rules for Holy Living" distributed on camp-grounds, and even slipped through the broken panes of Church windows; his

"Scripture Catechism," 1807—not half as well known as it deserves to be; and his tract on "The Ministry of Women," 1808. Note, above all, in this introductory period, his adaptation of Lorenzo Dow's Hymn Book, 1809, of which, until 1823, edition after edition was published, being bought so eagerly, especially on new ground, that the revenue derived from its sale helped largely to sustain some of the new missions. Some of the provincial printers—wide-awake men—soon discovered the value of this little Hymn Book as a marketable commodity, and issued pirated editions, sometimes making trivial alterations, and then having the effrontery to put "Copyright secured" on the title-page. We ourselves have met with no less than eight such pirated editions issued before 1823, bearing the imprints of local presses at York (two), Leeds, Gainsborough, Selby, Burslem, Bingham, and Nottingham.

After the establishment of the Connexion in 1811, Hugh Bourne pursued the same policy. Printed tickets superseded written ones. In 1814, the rules of the new denomination were carefully edited and published; Sunday Schools were with much labour furnished with Bibles and reading-books, and other requisites; Tract Societies were organised and equipped; a large Hymn Book was compiled and published in 1812, but it met with little favour among the societies. It was too heavy to float, and it must be regarded as having been one of Hugh Bourne's publishing ventures that failed. The same fate befell the quarterly *Magazine*, projected and launched for a very short voyage in 1818.

To all intents and purposes, there *was* an Editor and Book Steward before the offices were officially created and the officers appointed. If, at first, Hugh Bourne practically combined both offices in himself, it must not be overlooked that his brother James was always at his back ready to share his monetary responsibility; and, to the honour of both, let it also be remembered that, though at their initiative the societies might authorise these early publishing ventures, the brothers did not appropriate any profits that might accrue, but surrendered them to the Connexion, while they took all the risks of loss. Thus, one thinks, it was a foregone conclusion that when the first Conference found it necessary to appoint an editor Hugh Bourne should be designated to the office, and receive instructions to complete the suspended issue of the *Magazine* of 1819—which he did in the manner already described. But when at the next Conference the question of appointing a Book Steward was mooted, the case was different; there were evidently two opinions both as to the person to be appointed and as to the *locale* of the Book-Room already looming on the Connexional horizon.

HUGH BOURNE, CONNEXIONAL EDITOR.

"60. Q. Who shall be Book Steward?

A. If the *Magazines* are printed in Hull Circuit, E. Taylor. If in Tunstall Circuit, J. Bourne."

If there were any rivalry between the two circuits for the honour of having the book-room within its borders—as we strongly suspect there was—it was soon ended in favour of Tunstall; for, at the Conference of 1821, in answer to the question: "How shall the Book Concern be managed?" it was resolved:—

"James Steele, James Bourne, Hugh Bourne, Charles John Abraham, and John Hancock, are elected as a Book Committee to manage the concerns for the ensuing year. These are to receive and examine all matters to be inserted in the *Magazine*, and all other matters which it may be necessary to print. H. Bourne is appointed Editor, and J. Bourne Book Steward; and the Committee are at liberty to receive matter from W. O'Bryan, and to insert in the *Magazine* from time to time, such of it as they may think proper. The Committee are empowered to establish a General Book-Room, and a printing press for the use of the Connexion."

This incidental reference to the founder of the Bible Christian Church is historically interesting; and, with his usual acuteness, Hugh Bourne points out in the *Magazine* for 1821, the remarkable similarity between the two denominations as regards their practical recognition of the ministry of females. Referring to Joel's prophecy (ii. 28-29), he says:—

"In the latter part of the promise which respects daughters and handmaidens prophesying, or preaching, a remarkable coincidence has taken place in ou Connexion, and in the Connexion which arose in Cornwall. It is really surprising that the two Connexions, without any knowledge of each other, should each, nearly at the same time, be led in the same way, as it respects the ministry of women. Both Connexions employed women as exhorters, and as local and travelling preachers. When the two Connexions became acquainted with each other, and found so striking a similarity in their proceedings with regard to female preachers, it became a matter of desire to know by what steps each Connexion had been led into the measure. This produced a request on the subject, to which the following letter was sent as an answer, etc."

But to return to the Book Committee. Hull had lost the Book-Room, and was to develop itself in its own splendid way, while Tunstall was, for some years to come, to become more and more the directive centre. Yet, though Hull acquiesced in the arrangement, its delegates, we are told, asked that, until the necessary printing plant had been acquired for the Connexion, the *Magazines* might be printed by "their own printer" at Hull—probably J. Hutchinson. The Conference granted the request and hence, H. Bourne says: "he had to attend at Hull and bore his own expenses." But this arrangement certainly did not last long, for the last number of the 1821 *Magazine*, at least, was printed at the Connexional printing-office at Bemersley: so that the work of printing the first two volumes of the *Magazine* was executed by five different printers, residing in as many different towns—to wit: Leicester, Burslem, Derby, Hull, and Bemersley! What is now the *Aldersgate Primitive Methodist Magazine* has had a long and, on the whole, a prosperous voyage, but at the outset the sea was choppy and unkindly, and the bark had its mishaps.

While the brothers Bourne are looking after the purchase of printing-presses and founts of type and a suitable place to put them in, we will just glance at the members of the Book Committee and its functions. As to the latter: Here, as everywhere, there has been evolution, so that it were indeed an error—though one easily fallen into—to suppose that our ecclesiastical courts must have been from the beginning just what they are now. At first the Book Committee was a General Committee as well; and for a year or two, in conjunction with the General Committee at Hull, it had to give advice and counsel to the circuits, and send a deputation to settle matters when desired. The Conference Minutes of 1822 even go on to say: "If the two committees think that there is a providential opening, they shall institute, or take steps to institute,

J. HANCOCK'S HOUSE AND ENGRAVER'S SHOP.

a missionary establishment for sending out missionaries in a general way." The mode of editing the *Magazine* prescribed was certainly a peculiar one. Communications were not to be addressed to the Editor personally, but to the Book Committee, which had to decide upon the suitability or otherwise of the contributions sent. Contributions from the circuits had also to receive the endorsement of their Circuit Committees; so that the *Magazine* was to be both supplied with matter and edited by committees. As the contributions chiefly desired and expected were memoirs, preachers' *Journals*, and revival intelligence, this curious arrangement was evidently designed to prevent puffery and self-advertisement, and to secure authentic reports. These regulations were soon relaxed so far as contributors were concerned, but there is evidence to show that, throughout the Bemersley period, the Editor edited through his committee, and John Flesher found this out when he entered upon his new duties at Bemersley, which is a later story. In 1824, we read:—"The Book Committee have now nothing to do with the general concerns of the Connexion." Further, it is to be noted of the Book Committee, that for many years it was also the Committee of Privileges; small in the number of its members, and appointed separately from the other committees. In 1850 the Committee of Privileges is the same as the General Committee, and in 1863 we have the significant statement: " The Book Committee shall be composed of the General Committee." This arrangement obtained until 1894, when again a special Book Committee was appointed. Though this chapter deals with the Bemersley Book-Room period, we have thought it better, for the sake of gaining a connected view, to follow the Book Committee in its latest evolution.

As to the *personnel* of the first Book Committee: John Hancock and C. J. Abraham are the only members of the Committee we are not already familiar with. Both were leading men in the Tunstall Circuit through the whole of this period, and the former especially, as the corresponding member of the General Committee, for many years wielded considerable influence. He was a member—and an active one—of the Book Committee until his death, which took place on January 2nd, 1843. Born in 1796, he was an engraver by trade, though later on in life he became largely interested in the manufacture of pottery. He is said to have been savingly enlightened by reading Thomas Aquinas, "The Angelic Doctor"—probably a unique experience for a Primitive Methodist. He was converted in 1814, and joined the class of James Steele. The society at Pitt's Hill was his special sphere of labour, and after his death it was frequently remarked: "He was the first leader of Pitt's Hill, the first in raising the old chapel, he laid the first stone of the new chapel, preached the first sermon within its walls, and was the first whose mortal remains were interred in its burial-ground." *

C. J. Abraham is already known to us as the druggist of Burslem who, probably about this time, became the husband of Ann Brownsword. The names of both stand on the Tunstall Plan, and Ann Abraham, especially, was much esteemed as a deeply pious and acceptable preacheress. C. J. Abraham, like J. Hancock, was, both locally and connexionally, a leading official throughout the whole of the Bemersley *régime* being an active member of the General as well as of the Book Committee. He was a trustee of the first Burslem Chapel in Navigation Road, as well as of Zoar Chapel, acquired in 1842, though it was not used by the Burslem Society until two years later. It was the trust responsibilities connected with these two properties which were the cause of so much anxiety to Hugh Bourne in his later years, when the affairs of his brother and of C. J. Abraham had become hopelessly involved.

Bemersley Farm, the home of the Bournes, was the place selected for the first Book-Room. We would like to picture Bemersley as a whole, and Bemersley Farm in particular. We naturally feel an interest in a place which, for twenty years, was one of the foci—we may even say *the* focal point—of our connexional life; the spot where the central wheel of management was set up. As though, then, we were one of those many pilgrims, who during those twenty years visited for the first time a spot they

* "A Memoir of Mr. J. Hancock, of Tunstall," by Frederick Brown (Tunstall, 1843).

had long heard of but had never seen, we approach it from a distance, and take in the general features of the landscape before we seek to gain a nearer and, if we can, an interior view of the Connexional Book Establishment. The description given by the local historian may help us to this general view of the hamlet of Bemersley and its surroundings; for, although it is Bemersley as it was at the end of the eighteenth century he describes, its main features must, in 1822, have undergone little alteration.

"Bemersley is about a mile north-west of Norton Church, and near three miles from Tunstall—almost entirely moorland. Old Bemersley Farm stood on a hill that overlooked the landscape on either side, and many a dale and valley and wood did this ancient house command from its eminence. Looking at the scenery to-day, it requires little discernment to perceive how wild and rugged the place must have been in 1772. On one side lay the Valley of the Potteries, but the smoke and the bustle were hidden in the distance; and on the other the view stretched away over the great moorlands. There were three or four farm-houses dating from the sixteenth century, about the same number of cottage houses, and at the remote part of the hamlet stood Greenway Hall. Round this old house there was a large park and extensive game preserves."

BEMERSLEY FARM AND THE FIRST PRIMITIVE METHODIST BOOK-ROOM.

Bemersley Farm stood by the roadside some little distance from Bemersley. The visitor saw nothing in the outward aspect of the building to give it any distinction above other buildings of its kind. "It had nothing of the world's glory." It was but an ordinary farm-house with the usual appurtenances—fold-yard, barn, and stables. Here lived the Editor and the Book Steward, who had to adapt the buildings to their new purposes. James Bourne, therefore, laid out before May, 1823, the sum of £373 8s. 10d. in the purchase of a printing-press, type, and other printer's plant, and bookbinder's tools and materials as well, as we may infer from the entry in the Conference Minutes: "That it be recommended to the circuits to get their binding done at the Book-Room, if the Book-Room can get it done as well and as cheap as elsewhere." In one of the farm-buildings adjoining the house, the printing-press and a few cases of type were set up, and the Conference "Minutes" of 1822 have the imprint: "Bemersley near Tunstall:—Printed at the Office of the Primitive Methodist Connexion, by J. Bourne;" whereas the Minutes of 1821 say: "J. Hutchinson, Printer, Silver Street, Hull"

The Book-Room proper consisted of a detached rectangular building of the Barnic order of architecture, and plain even for a barn. As shown in our picture, it was pierced with few windows and sparsely provided with doors. Some of the walls of this building were lined with shelves divided into pens, in which the magazines and hymn books, small pamphlets and books—of which the most popular was the "Journals of John Nelson"—were stowed until the bi-monthly packing-day came round, when a gentle ripple of excitement went through the establishment. The bulk of the parcels were conveyed in carts to the canal-quays and shipped in boats to the various circuits.

Besides the two chief officers, there were resident a bailiff of the small farm, a journeyman, and an apprentice, and the son of James Bourne, who it is said worked in the printing-office, saying nothing of Mrs. Bourne and two maids. About the year 1836, John Hallam was added to the establishment. His position was a somewhat peculiar one; for, after 1836, his name is not found on the stations for a term of years, though he is one of the members of the Book and General Committees. The explanation is, that by his hearty acceptance of Hugh Bourne's views and methods of work, and by his laborious and successful ministry, he had ingratiated himself with the Editor, and he being now in 1836 in very indifferent health, Hugh Bourne had installed him at Bemersley as his assistant, and had induced his brother to make him his assistant also, Mr. Hallam's salary being paid out of the private purse of the brothers. In this way John Hallam acquired great influence at the Book-Room and in the administration of Connexional affairs, even before the year 1843, when he was officially appointed Book Steward. It should also be said that Mr. George Baron, of Silsden, who often acted as Connexional Auditor, frequently paid visits to the Book-Room during this period, and that his business aptitude proved of great assistance to James Bourne. In 1840, the late Rev. Thomas Baron went to Bemersley to take the place of his brother for a short time, and, in his interesting reminiscences of that visit, he tells how it was his duty, early each weekday morning, to carry the post-bag with the Book-Room's letters for dispatch, two miles distance, to Norton, and to call at a public-house for letters which were left there for the Book-Room. Mr. Baron gives us a pleasant glimpse of the interior economy of the establishment: of the regular and reverent daily devotions, of the meals in common, of the hospitality afforded to the ministers who frequently visited the

MR. G. BARON.

Book-Room, and even to the goodly number who came from other societies to attend the Quarterly Lovefeast. What is still more interesting, we get a glimpse into the Editor's own room, where, when back from his not infrequent journeys, he attended to the duties of his office.

"When at home he was generally busily engaged in editing or writing matter for the *Magazines* and in Connexional correspondence. His study was a good-sized room, fitted with shelves for his library. Among the books in it there was a complete well-bound set, from the beginning, of the *Arminian* and *Wesleyan Magazines*. The first volume contained a somewhat lengthy preface, neatly written and signed by John Wesley in his own handwriting. It is to be feared that the volumes have been scattered or lost. Had they been kept together they would now have been an interesting and valuable relic. Among other books in the library were a number of Wesley's and Fletcher's Works, Adam Clarke's Commentary, Gillie's "Historical Collections," Finney's "Lectures," Hebrew and Greek Lexicons, etc. [and these were for use, not ornament]. In the cold weather, a screen was placed in this room, behind which the venerable man was often quietly seated before a writing-table, busily seeking to stir up others in the work so near his own heart—that of the conversion of sinners." *

REV T. BARON.

Such, then, was our first Book-Room. Thomas Bateman was a passing pilgrim here in May, 1824. He was on his way with George Taylor to attend the District Meeting at Ramsor to be held in Francis Horobin's house. The District Meeting was expected to be an unusually important one, as the rules had to be revised, and far-reaching changes introduced specially relating to district formation and representation. Hence, Thomas Bateman had been pressed to attend. He had stopped the night with James Nixon, whom he had accompanied to his class with much profit to himself. Then, John Hancock—whom he now met for the first time—had looked in, and read him a lecture for having declined to preach special services at Pitt's Hill—John Hancock's own favourite society—alleging that ordinary services must always give way for special ones. And now, the wayfarers—for they walked the whole distance to Ramsor—had called at Bemersley, having noted all the places of historic interest to Primitive Methodists as they went along. At Bemersley a short time was spent in looking round, and Thomas Bateman indulged in "numerous reflections on the place and its surroundings on which an angel might pause and wonder."

Sentimental reflections are here pardonable enough; but the most obvious reflection called up by the view of the Bemersley Book-Room is that which Thomas Bateman himself suggests. That the important District Meeting of 1824—which we may

* See appendix to second edition of "Life of Hugh Bourne," by Dr. W. Antliff and the *Aldersgate Magazine* for 1900, pp. 751-4.

venture to say was a rehearsal of the proceedings of the Conference—was held in the room of a farmhouse in a secluded hamlet in one of the most secluded parts of Staffordshire, was a fact just as remarkable as that the Connexional Book-Room should be located in the farm-buildings of another Staffordshire hamlet. Both facts were remarkable, and yet natural; for they show in a very striking way, what other consentient facts also show; that we were as yet largely a village community and, further, that considering the area up to this time occupied by Primitive Methodism— embracing the country we have already surveyed—the location of the Book-Room was fairly central, and not inappropriate. By 1843 this will be no longer true, as John Flesher will soon learn when he comes to take up his editorial duties at Bemersley.

But why was Thomas Bateman never a member of the Book Committee, and not even a member of the General Committee until 1839? This question is worth considering in its relation to the Bemersley period of our history. It is fortunate that we can here let Thomas Bateman answer for himself. Writing of this same Ramsor District Meeting of 1824, he says:—

"There was much business—all peaceable; but I did not feel in my proper element. I believe at present God has not sent me either to baptise or legislate, but to preach the Gospel. And though much deference was shown to me by the brethren, I feel no wish ever to attend another such meeting: and after much thought, believing as I did that my friend Taylor had a special call and was well qualified for such work, I resolved never to attend another District Meeting or Conference so long as he lived and could attend, unless I had some special call to do so. [And he kept his resolve and was not present at District Meeting or Conference until after 1837, but made up for it afterwards.]"

Writing fifty-seven years after, he repeats the statement here made, but further adds what is germane to our purpose:—

"From this cause [the keeping of this resolve] my name seldom appeared in the Minutes or otherwise as affecting Connexional movements. *Still, no change of any moment took place without my being consulted*, and I was always ready to give the best advice I could, which was always received with the greatest cordiality."

We believe the words we have italicised to be true to their very last iota, and that, though Thomas Bateman was apparently in the background through the greater part of the first period, *we* must put him in the very fore-front of the men—most of whom we know—who guided the revolutions of the central wheel of management. We do not forget such prominent Tunstall District men as Thomas Wood, the Brownhills, R. Mayer, the first Primitive Methodist Mayor of Newcastle-under-Lyne, and others already mentioned. Even before he was fully committed to the Connexion, Hugh Bourne was drawn to young Bateman. He read him portions of the History of the Connexion he was then busy with. He opened his mind freely to him concerning the forthcoming *Magazine*, and asked him to become a contributor; and to the very end of Hugh

THE LATE R. MAYER, first Primitive Methodist Mayor of Newcastle-under-Lyne.

Bourne's life, there was no man who had more influence with, and over, him than the quiet, sagacious, forcible-speaking farmer and surveyor of Chorley.

We must now proceed to chronicle some of the more important transactions of the Bemersley Book Committee. First in order among these, were those relating to the Hymn Book. It seems gradually to have been borne in upon the mind of Hugh Bourne that the Revival Hymn Book was a valuable property worth preserving. Therefore, in 1821, he resolved to copyright the book. To enable him to do this he himself composed some original hymns, and Poet Sanders was asked to do the same—for a consideration. There exists a curious document, worth giving *in extenso*, in which William Sanders, in precise legal form, contracts to furnish twenty-five original hymns for the same number of shillings.

"Received March 1821, of Hugh Bourne, the sum of twenty-five shillings, for twenty-five hymns, which by contract were composed by me for his use, and which I have made over to him in the fullest sense of the word, and which from this time become and are in every sense his own absolute property. The first line and metre, and number of verses of each are as follow:—1st. C.M., four verses, beginning—'Alas! how soon the body dies'; and so it continues to the 25th, P.M.— eight verses—Camp-meeting Farewell—'Dear Brethren and Sisters in Jesus, Farewell.' I say received by me,

"WILLIAM SANDERS."

"Signed in the presence of C. J. Abraham."

The wisdom of the protective measures taken was seen in 1823, when a printer at York named Kendrew, who had infringed the copyright of the Hymn Book, was brought to his knees. The law was set in motion, but Kendrew capitulated before the case went into court, and signed an agreement pledging himself not to repeat the offence, to pay all the costs incurred, and to surrender all copies of the unauthorised edition in his possession. The Committee having gained its object, which was to vindicate its rights and safeguard the interests of the Connexion, could now afford to be generous. Hence the stringency of the last condition was somewhat relaxed, and it was agreed to pay Kendrew a certain sum on each surrendered copy of the Hymn Book. The Conference held at Leeds this same year (1823) directed that "a large standard Hymn Book should be prepared and printed at the Book-Room, for the general use of the Connexion." Evidently it was felt that even the improved edition of 1821, with its one hundred and fifty-four hymns, was inadequate to meet the growing demands of church-life. A book was called for which should "contain Hymns for the sacraments and for the general varieties of meetings and worship." The Minutes of 1823 go on to say that "the new book is expected to be got ready by the close of the present year, or early in the next year." With 1824, then, began the reign of the Large and Small Hymn Book (bound together) which served the uses of the Church until 1853, when John Flesher was instructed to compile a new Hymn Book. The Preface to the Large Hymn Book claims that it has been "compiled from the best authors, and enriched with original hymns," and that "the original hymns were of a superior cast." With his eye on this alleged "superior cast" a friendly critic has written—evidently with regret:—

"We look in vain among the original hymns . . . for one that has survived the test of three-quarters of a century's wear; posterity, we grieve to say, did not find in them the etherial quality of an immortal hymn. We wish that there had been at least one sweet singer for all Churches, and for all time, among the band of consecrated single-hearted men, who did so much for British working men at the beginning of this century."*

Now, though it scarcely falls within our province to discuss the literary merits or demerits of our early hymn books, a word or two may be said. It may be that no one has given us a hymn dowered with immortality, and which has made its way into almost every Hymnary. That may be conceded. But there are two hymns—both said to be the joint production of Hugh Bourne and W. Sanders—we would speak up for, or rather, let them speak for themselves—"My soul is now united," which first appeared in the 1821 Collection, and especially, "Hark! the gospel news is sounding," in the Large Hymn Book. These have worn well, and are not worn out yet. For open-air purposes there is no better, more stirring hymn than this latter; it has well been called, "The Primitive Methodist Grand March." These, and others that might be named, are incomparably better than some of the jingles that have had considerable vogue in these later days. The best defence, however, we have to offer for the old hymns is, that "they served their generation by the will of God," and some of them at least, like the two named, have not yet fallen on sleep. They had the power to arouse attention and nourish the spiritual life. "Hark! the gospel news is sounding," was once being sung, at the dusk of eventide, in a little hamlet.

Suffer little children to come unto me. Luke xviii. 16.

The Primitive Methodist
CHILDREN'S MAGAZINE.

No. 1.]   OCTOBER, 1824.   [Vol. 1.

INTRODUCTION.

WE are now entering on a new work: a work designed for you, ye children of praying Parents; of Parents who bear you up before the Lord; and who strive, to bring the guard of heaven upon you by prayer. You already inherit a blessing; for the generation of the upright is blessed. You hear the words of piety from the lips of your parents. Your hearts are moved with a desire to love God, to be the children of your heavenly Father, and to serve him as long as you live.

Sometimes you view the creation in all the beauties of spring; and consider that it is your heavenly Father who causes the grass to grow,

"A young man, full of spiritual anxiety, was leaning on a wall in the distance, and heard the joyous strains of the refrain: 'None need perish.' A responsive faith awoke in his soul; peace came; he dedicated his life to Jesus, and is now a minister of the Connexion. Again: 'By the singing of this soul-stirring hymn ['My soul is now united'] at a lovefeast near Pocklington, in 1822, eighteen souls surrendered to Jesus Christ and found peace!"†

Could even "Lead, kindly Light" do more than this?

---

* Rev. J. O. Gledstone, "Primitive Methodist Hymn Books," in *The Puritan*.

† See "Lyric Studies: A Hymnal Guide," by Revs. J. Doricott and T. Collins. An admirable compendium to which the author would express the obligations of years.

In 1824, the *Children's Magazine* was begun. Though this venture was entered upon with no little anxiety, it proved from the very first a signal success. The demand greatly exceeded expectations; so much so, that several impressions had to be printed, until seven thousand copies had been struck off, and the monthly circulation reached six thousand. We have pleasure in giving a reproduction of the first page of the first number of this excessively rare publication.

As we all know, "Take care of the children" was the life-long solicitude and dying charge of Hugh Bourne. In his case it amounted to a passion, and became one of his most strongly-marked characteristics. Nor was he slow in urging upon others the same solicitude for bringing the young under the influence of Christian truth. Age wrought no abatement of his zeal; and hence, probably the last separate production that came from his pen, bore the title:

"The Early Trumpet: A Treatise on Preaching to Children. By Hugh Bourne, Bemersley, 1843."*

What has been said of the early Hymn Books equally holds good of the early Magazines: they were suitable for their time and for the purpose they had to fulfil. This may safely be said, as it also may, that what sufficed in 1823 had its obvious shortcomings twenty years later, and would never do now. Other times; other Magazines. Undoubtedly the Magazines of the Bemersley period helped to cement the circuits of the Connexion together, and to promote the work of God. The revival intelligence they contained, the biographies, the occasional articles on "Providence," "Faith," "Conversation-gift" etc., would do much to stimulate and to inform their readers. It is wonderful, considering his many journeyings, and the amount of other work he did, that Hugh Bourne fulfilled his editorial duties as well as he did fulfil them. We cannot help remarking, too, how widely divergent have been the estimates formed of his intellectual capabilities and performances. Our own opinion is that, as to these, he has been often under-rated. He had his oddities and weaknesses, and especially in later years, his infirmities of temper, but he had an alert and vigorous mind, and he could write in a way that made it impossible for any one to mistake his meaning. By choice he habited his thoughts in homespun. Some gifted men, who clothed their thoughts in Johnsonian garb, have interpreted his homespun as a sign of intellectual poverty. Never was there a greater mistake. His thought's expression was not cast in the customary moulds of verbal form. It was rugged, even uncouth, as though hewn from granite: but there it is—outstanding, clear, and unmistakable.

Even the ablest and most heaven-sent editor may find his work a difficult one, just because so many of his readers think it so easy. Allowing for this, and also allowing for the advancing intelligence of the Connexion through the 'Twenties and 'Thirties, which went on creating wants not fully satisfied, we are not surprised to find in the old Minute Books evidence that the *Magazine* was sometimes criticised, and that proposals were made for its improvement. Especially was this so in such centres of light and

---

* The only copy we have seen is one given by H. Bourne himself to Rev. W. R. Widdowson.

leading as Nottingham and Hull. In proof of this take the following resolutions passed at the Nottingham Circuit Quarterly Meeting, 1827 :—

"*March 19th.* Res. 59. 'That there be an improvement in the *Magazine.* That it be an octavo size, price sixpence and improved in matter.

"(60). That every preacher be required to write four pages per year.

"(61). That there be three editors." [And then the 'three' is crossed out and 'two' over-written.]

So also at Hull, in March, 1830, the Quarterly Meeting discussed the *Magazines* and came to the conclusion that "they ought to contain more original articles," and requested "each preacher [in 1830 there were twenty-four in Hull Circuit] who could, to write at least one page per month."

As we turn over the leaves of the old Conference Minutes, we meet with many reminders of the changed conditions which time has brought about, and we get the impression that the first Book Committee was composed of careful, managing men who were fertile in resource. The Conference of 1823 recommended that a depository of books obtained from the Book Room should be formed in every circuit. The money in the first instance was to be taken out of past profits and supplemented, if need be, by subscriptions. A circuit with one preacher was to take three pounds' worth of goods; a circuit with two preachers, six pounds worth, and so on in proportion. The Station Book Steward, who it must be remembered was not necessarily a travelling preacher, was to see to the carrying out of this recommendation. In 1824, Hugh Bourne felt it necessary to ask the Conference to allow him four pounds a quarter as salary, and ten shillings a week for board and lodging—a young man's salary. History says that there was one person of considerable talking-power at the Conference who thought it his duty to oppose this modest request; but it was granted notwithstanding, the objector being in a hopeless minority. In 1827, a scheme for the starting of a "Preachers' Magazine," on which Hugh Bourne had set his heart, was broached. In answer to the question, "What shall be done in relation to the *Magazine?*" it was resolved :—

"One number in duodecimo shall be published, and if it does not pay its way, Hugh Bourne has agreed to bear the loss. But if it take so large a circulation as to do more than pay its way, the profits must not go to H.B. but to the Connexion. Also a succession of Nos. may be published if there be an opening."

A succession of numbers sufficient to make up one volume did appear, but there were no profits for the Connexion; and Hugh Bourne was permitted to make up the deficiency.

In 1833, what in the Minutes is usually termed "the cross-providence" overtook the Book-Room. On Good Friday Eve, 1833, the Book-Room took fire. How it originated no one knew; "whether from the fire that dried the paper or from the snuff of a candle." Damage to the extent of £1,900 was caused, involving, about equally, the private property of the Book Steward and that belonging the Connexion. At that time, James Bourne was a man of considerable means, and it is recorded: "J. B. desires nothing for that portion of the loss which belonged to him; but hopeth that in time, by the kind providence of God, he may surmount it." A levy of one penny per member was imposed in order to make good this loss of Connexional property. Sixty years after, the Book-Room, then standing, as it now stands, within the "conflagration area" of Central London, was within measurable distance of having a second experience of the like kind, but tenfold worse in degree. But this time a favourable Providence saved the goodly pile from disaster. While anxiety was reflected on the flame-lit countenances of the Book Steward and his staff, a change in the direction of the wind averted what seemed to be the impending catastrophe.

How and why the Book-Room got from Bemersley into the roar of Central London must be told later on.

CHAPTER XIII.

MANCHESTER AND THE ADJACENT TOWNS UNTIL 1843.

MANCHESTER was made an independent circuit in 1821 by the same Quarterly Meeting which made Burland a branch. Because of its derivation from Tunstall, the original circuit, it was placed fourth in order amongst the sixteen circuits which at that time constituted the entire Connexion.
Looking merely at the order of circuit formation, Manchester would rightly claim to come under notice before Burland, which was not made a circuit until 1823; but, having special regard to the geographical direction and spread of Primitive Methodism, the right is reversed. We have seen that north-west Cheshire was being inundated by the revival movement twelve months before its wave had reached the city on the Mersey. The extension of Tunstall Circuit to Manchester was one result of that great revival which may be said to have begun by John Wedgwood's mission to Staffordshire in 1819. We propose, therefore, in this chapter, to present the facts, so far as they can be ascertained, relative to the introduction of Primitive Methodism into Manchester, and to show what position the denomination had attained in that city and the neighbouring towns to which its labours had extended, by the year 1842.

Hitherto, it seems to have been thought almost hopeless to recover the names of those who had the honour of being the very first pioneers of the Connexion in Manchester. We would fain hope, however, that, even with the scanty data available, the nameless ones may yet be identified. There is a long-standing tradition to the effect that Primitive Methodism was first carried to Manchester by "a local preacher from Macclesfield; that he had a wooden leg; that he walked from Macclesfield on the Sunday morning to Manchester; that he preached at the New Cross after dinner; and that he walked home after preaching in the evening, thus performing a journey of *thirty-six miles* on foot!"[*] Now tradition is often very tenacious in its hold of essential fact, especially when the fact is such as to make a strong appeal to the imagination; and the mental picture of the unknown missionary with his artificial limb, stumping his way to Manchester and back, has stamped itself on the imaginations of men. Who else should the hero of our tradition be than "Eleazar Hathorn of the wooden leg"—the convert of Lorenzo Dow, active participant in the first Mow Cop Camp Meeting, the fellow-labourer of John Benton in the East Staffordshire Mission of 1814, and the instrument in the awakening of John Ride? We had reached the conclusion that the man we were in search of was no other than Eleazar Hathorn, when we found unexpected and pleasing confirmation of such conclusion in an obscure footnote of Herod's "Sketches," in the words: "This said Eleazar was the first Primitive that

---

[*] The Introduction and Spread of Primitive Methodism in Lancashire, in "Anecdotes and Facts of Primitive Methodism." By Rev. Samuel Smith, p. 91. For other References to Eleazar Hathorn, see vol. i. pp. 68; 192.

entered Manchester."* We may therefore reasonably conclude that the identification holds; and although Manchester bulks largely in the eye of the Connexion, and is sure to bulk still more largely in the future, it has no need to look otherwise than complacently on the figure of the old soldier determinedly plodding his way to deliver his message at the New Cross. We can think of no more fitting precursor and prototype of that community which had, with slender and imperfect appliances, and against heavy odds, to win its way step by step to an assured and honourable position in Cottonopolis. The war-worn veteran was a herald quite as worthy as though he had rushed there on his own motor-car, or been able to speed to the big city with the swiftness of an Elijah forerunning the chariot of Ahab.

But if Eleazar Hathorn was the herald of the Connexion to Manchester, who was its apostle—its sent one? To whom, of official status, does Hugh Bourne allude in the explicit statement: "Manchester was visited and preaching established about March, 1821"?† This statement is not at variance with the tradition already referred to; rather do tradition and statement confirm each other. Eleazar Hathorn who, in keeping with his habits, had gone to Manchester to do a little independent missioning, in the time of Macclesfield's fervour, would naturally report his doings, and probably urge upon the "heads of houses" (and we know that Hugh Bourne visited him) to follow up officially these visits of his. We light upon a clue as to the person selected to "open" Manchester, in an entry in Hugh Bourne's *Journal*. Writing under date, January 18th, 1821, he tells how he came to Belper and saw Thomas Jackson, and then goes on to say: "We agreed for him to go to Manchester, to be there on *Sunday*, March 9th." Unfortunately, there is an evident error here as to the date; for March 9th was Wednesday, and not Sunday. Probably March 6th was the date intended. In order that T. Jackson might be at liberty to give this Sunday to Manchester, some re-arrangement of appointments was necessary; so H. B. was to get R. Bentley to preach at Rocester at that time, and H. B. was to preach at Rocester on the 20th of March. This arrangement was carried out so far as Hugh Bourne was concerned, and, doubtless, Thomas Jackson fulfilled the duty assigned to him, and on the 6th March, officially opened Manchester. Here is the "apostle" we are in search of.

Let us briefly recall the "form and pressure" of the time when we made our entry into Manchester. George the Third had but recently died, and in a few months (July 27th, 1821) the coronation of his graceless successor would be celebrated. One notable feature of the celebration was to be a procession, two-and-a-half miles long, from Peter's Field to Ardwick Green, and the night was destined to close with a drunken orgie in Shude Market, qualified by a retributive disaster. Peterloo, with the rankling memories it had left, was only just behind. At New Cross, where our first missionaries so often took their stand, not many months before, cannon had been planted to sweep the streets and overawe the populace. Nor were those cannon placed there merely for dumb show. Manchester was like a caldron in which conflicting elements were seething. They were indeed sad times, as may be gathered from the fact that another Thomas Jackson,

---

* Herod's "Biographical Sketches." Footnote, p. 461.
† *Magazine* for 1821, p. 77.

though a duly ordained Methodist minister whom the highest Connexional honours awaited, was at this time "forced by the magistrates even after the public services of the Sabbath-day (in Oldham Street) to walk the streets through the night, in company with others, for the purpose of reporting any suspicious movements that might appear."* With Peterloo in the near background, and the struggle against the Corn-laws and for the Charter in prospect, who will say that the former times were better than these, or question the statement that there was room in Manchester for any corrective and ameliorative influences Primitive Methodism could bring?

We are told that the first meetings of the newly formed cause in Manchester were held "in a loft over a stable in Chorlton-upon-Medlock, somewhere about Brook Street, also in a cottage in London Square, Bank Top." Very soon "a top room over an old factory up an entry in Ancoats," locally known as "the Long Room," was acquired; and on July 30th, 1820, Ann Brownsword preached several times in this room and also at the New Cross. She speaks of crowded services in the room and of having had ten converts on two successive week evenings. At this time she reports that there are five classes and eighty members. On the 27th and 28th of August Hugh Bourne preached at New Cross and in the Long Room. He renewed the tickets to the society and arrangements were made for the first camp meeting, which from another source we learn was held on the Ashton Road, on September 17th. This camp meeting was conducted by James Bonsor, fresh from his experience at the Stafford Sessions, who had been brought from Darlaston Circuit in exchange for Ann Brownsword. James Bonsor's labours were not confined to one locality, but pretty well distributed as the following entry shows:—

"*Sunday, October 1st, 1820.*—At eight preached in Cropper Street. At ten Bro. Smith preached at Salford Cross, and I gave an exhortation. A many seemed affected. At half-past eleven I preached at another place in Salford. At half-past one, Bro. Smith and I preached in Castle Field. Many people and a good time; sinners cried much for mercy. At half-past three I preached in another part of Manchester to a large congregation. Near five, I preached at Salford Cross, and at half-past six, at Manchester New Cross."—*Magazine*, 1821, p. 20.

Thus on one Sabbath he took part in seven services in different parts of Manchester. No wonder that from the committee meeting, held on October 6th, he reports that things are in a very flourishing state; that there are nearly one hundred members, and that they had agreed to take another room in a different part of the town. The room here alluded to would probably be the same as that more explicitly referred to by Hugh Bourne (*Magazine* 1821) in the report of the Michaelmas Quarterly Meeting of the Tunstall Circuit, wherein he says of Manchester: "They have a very large room in New Islington, and they have had the courage to take another large room in Chancery Lane. This example may be followed with advantage in most towns."

As early as James Bonsor's short mission in Manchester two names that should not be forgotten came before us for the first time. Samuel Waller, a cotton-spinner in

---

* "Recollections of My own Life and Times." By Thomas Jackson, p. 173. Mrs. Linnæus Banks deals with this precise time in "The Manchester Man." The work contains much local colour and word-sketches of contemporary persons and localities.

partnership with his brothers, was at this time a Methodist class-leader. He was brought in contact with the Primitives and felt drawn to them by reason of their methods of doing good and their plainness in dress. With the concurrence of his brother, who was also a Methodist class leader, he joined the infant society. His first public effort was made on September 25th, 1820, at what was called a watch-night service in the Long Room, when he and Walton Carter each gave an exhortation, and James Bonsor "made a statement as to the work of God." Before twelve months were over, he suffered imprisonment for preaching in the open air, and Samuel Waller shares with Thomas Russell the honour of having endured the longest and most trying imprisonment recorded in our Connexional annals. A subordinate constable, a renegade Methodist, made himself obnoxiously busy in interfering with the service held on the evening of June 17th, 1821. There was no disturbance, and no clear case of obstruction, yet Mr. Waller was committed to take his trial at the Salford Sessions, charged with: "Having in the King's highway, in Ashton-under-Lyne, unlawfully and injudiciously caused and procured a great number of persons to assemble together, obstructing the said highway, to the great damage and common nuisance of the liege subjects of our Lord the King; and with making a noise, riot, tumult, and disturbance; and with making such riot by shouting and singing; and wholly choking up and obstructing the street and highway." Mr. Waller was sentenced to be imprisoned for three months in Manchester New Bailey, and, on the expiry of his term, he was re-committed for six days in order to make up the three calendar months. So far as the North of England is concerned, we shall meet with no other incident like this in the history of Primitive Methodism. Yet no inference can be drawn from the incident to the discredit of the people of Lancashire. On the contrary, their sense of justice was outraged by the treatment meted out to Mr. Waller, and there was no lack of sympathy with the prisoner, who was seriously ill during his confinement. The prison doctor showed himself either indifferent or incompetent; but by the good

THE "LONG ROOM," NEW ISLINGTON, MANCHESTER.
The entrance is through the Archway, now partly closed, at the right end of building. The Long Room is the top story.

offices of friends the best medical aid was procured, and the governor of the jail acted in a most humane manner. It is clear that political animus had more to do with this travesty of justice than ought else. The magistrates had lost their heads. They saw signs of possible riot and disturbance everywhere. The bias of the chairman of the Quarter Sessions was revealed by the observations he dropped during the course of the trial; and, if what is alleged be true, that the chairman was the vicar of Rochdale, who had been "military leader" on the black day of Peterloo, much is explained.

"The day after Mr. Waller's discharge, Wednesday, October 17th, 1821, a meeting was held at Chancery Lane, when it appeared this imprisonment had been the means of stirring up many to hear the Word, and on the whole that it had served greatly to advance the Redeemer's kingdom."* No doubt at this significant service there would be sung some of those special hymns "On the Releasement of S. Waller from Prison," we find in the *Magazine* for 1822. We do not catch, in these hymns, the triumphant note that strikes us in those called forth by John Wedgwood's Grantham experiences. In these the pervading sentiment is one of chastened thankfulness, as is seen in the chorus of one of them :—

"Releas'd from bondage, grief, and pain,
We meet with this our friend again."

One of the best of these hymns was written by Walton Carter, already referred to. He too encountered the "backsliding Methodist constable," who pulled him down at Ashton Cross and tore his clothes. But though Carter was brought before the magistrates at Oldham, he and his companion were dismissed. Of Walton Carter's antecedents we can glean nothing; but he became a noted missioner in Manchester and its neighbourhood, and was our Connexional pioneer in several towns which are now the head of important stations. In fact he seems to have fulfilled the duties of a travelling preacher in the Manchester Circuit during the years 1821-2, although his name does not appear on the official stations; so that, although Manchester Circuit in 1821 has only John Verity down for it, with the words "for six months" appended, we need not suppose that Manchester was left without a preacher for half the year. Walton Carter was on the ground. His well-written *Journals* appear side by side with those of Verity in the *Magazine*, and when Verity has left, Carter is still actively engaged in the circuit, and as late as May, 1822, sends an account to the *Magazine* of the first Oldham camp meeting. In 1823 his name appears on the stations for the first and last time, in connection with Halifax. He retired from the ministry, and subsequently became the proprietor of a day and boarding school at Bucklow Hill, near Knutsford. The breach with the past was not complete. He still kept in touch with Manchester; for amongst his boarders were several youths belonging to Primitive Methodist families resident in the city in which he had once rendered good service. There is reason to fear, however, that his last days were not the brightest and the best.

Before the close of 1821, there were, as the books show, in Manchester alone

* There is a full account of the trial of S. Waller in the *Magazine* for 1822, pp. 259, 281. See also S. Smith's "The Introduction," etc., already cited, p. 98.

two hundred and eleven members. The progress of the Society in other respects than in numbers was marked by the building, in 1823-4, of Jersey Street Chapel, which, right through and beyond the first period of our history, was the well-known centre of our work in Manchester. The superintendent at the time was Thomas Sugden, whose name disappears from the stations in 1824. He was not, however, lost to the Connexion, but settled down in Manchester, and made himself useful in various ways. "Thomas Sugden, confectioner, Manchester," was one of the original signatories of the Deed Poll, who took their seats, for the first time, at the Conference of 1832. Ralph Waller (the brother of Samuel Waller), cotton-spinner, Mellor, near Manchester, was another of these original members; and when, by the death of George Taylor, the first vacancy occurred on the Deed Poll, the Bradford Conference elected Stephen Longdin, of Manchester, to the office. Stephen Longdin's election to this office, together with the fact that his portrait is to be found amongst those of the early Presidents of Conference, along with the very few laymen, such as George Hanford, Joseph Bailey, and Thomas Bateman, who are credited with having attained to that unusual distinction, proves that at the time of his election to the chair in 1849, he was widely known as a Connexional man. Born in 1795, he survived until 1878; and, as early as 1824, he had become a useful class leader, and was giving proof of the possession of unusual preaching ability and of special aptitude for the administration of affairs, all which made him, through a long course of years, a leading figure in Manchester Primitive Methodism.

OLD JERSEY STREET CHAPEL, MANCHESTER.

The opening services of Jersey Street Chapel, in which Hugh Bourne took part, were held in the early part of 1824. The building was spacious; the gallery alone having accommodation for five hundred people. "Unfortunately the attendance at the subsequent services was not so large as had been anticipated. The interest on the heavy mortgage and the costs of maintenance pressed seriously on the limited resources of the Society, and in the end it was felt that the liabilities were too heavy to be carried. The trustees, therefore, determined on an alteration of the building. A floor was inserted across the well of the gallery, and in the lower portion of the building dwelling-houses were constructed, the rents of which materially helped the trustees to carry the financial burden. After these alterations the public religious services were well attended, and several persons who attained distinction in public life became regular hearers. Alderman Walton Smith, Mr. Joseph Nall, Councillor

THE PERIOD OF CIRCUIT PREDOMINANCE AND ENTERPRISE. 21

PRESIDENTS OF CONFERENCE UNTIL 1849, AS FAR AS RECORDED.

Gregory Alcock, and the Waller family were for a long period among the stated worshippers."*

The structural, brick-and-mortar history of Jersey Street, of Canaan Street, of West Street, or any other of the historic chapels of Primitive Methodism is the least important part of its history to be recalled. The main thing to be recognised is the body of rich and constantly multiplying associations that for so many people gathered round the building; the large place it filled in the better part of the lives of so many; the memories and the talks by the fireside of the men who ministered or were ministered unto within its walls; the historic meetings, the notable texts and sermons, the remarkable conversions, the rousing prayer-meetings, the inspiring hymns, the love-feast experiences; the institutional Saturday-night band-meeting, for which even the country people would steal an hour from their marketing; even the traits and oddities and outstanding features in the characters of the habitual frequenters of the sanctuary, remembered all the more vividly when they are gone—all this constitutes the true history of the plain old building now no more, and explains the hold it got on the hearts and imaginations of men, and yet all this has to be conceived rather than described in relation to Jersey Street, which was the ganglion—the nerve-centre of our denominational life in Manchester for so long a term of years.

Two Conferences were held in Jersey Street—that of 1827, of which we know a little, and that of 1840, of which we know next to nothing. At the former there were five o'clock morning preachings, a procession through a large part of the town to the camp-ground near the workhouse, and in the evening there was held what may be called an *In Memoriam* service for James Steele, who had died but a few days before the opening of Conference. W. Clowes would have taken a leading part in this service but for the fact that he was then, and had been for some time, in an indifferent state of health. As it was, it fell to the lot of Hugh Bourne and Thomas King to speak of the life and death of this honoured servant of God. In his *Journal*, however, Clowes tells how he had visited James Steele—whom he designates "one of the founders of the Primitive Methodist Connexion"—only a few minutes before he expired. He records how, though the sands of the hour-glass were fast running out, the good man "entered freely into conversation respecting the work of the Lord," and how, when asked if his faith stood firm, he replied in the words of the Psalmist, "I will not forsake thee when thy faith faileth."

An administrative change of some importance was effected at this Conference. A new district was formed out of some of the frontier stations of Tunstall, Nottingham, and Hull Districts, and of this new district Manchester was made the head. Towards the formation Nottingham gave New Mills, and a year after Bradwell; Hull gave Preston, Blackburn, Clitheroe, and Keighley; while the mother-district contributed Preston Brook, Liverpool, and Chester, together with Manchester and its daughter-circuits Oldham and Bolton, and Bolton's own child—the Isle of Man. Thus it will be seen at a glance, that Manchester District was made rather than grew. A new district was created, as it were by a stroke of the pen, for administrative purposes,

* Communicated by Mr. W. E. Parker.

out of circuits of diverse origin. It is not, therefore, with the beginnings of the Conference-created Manchester District of 1827 this chapter has to do, but rather with the Manchester district of to-day, made up, as for the most part it is, of circuits of which Manchester was the nucleus. If the time should come, as possibly it may, when the circuits which grew out of Hull's North Lancashire mission shall become a separate district with, say, Preston as its titular head, then there will be something like a reversion, and district arrangements will in a striking way conform to the facts of our history, which show how the ground now covered by the present Manchester and Liverpool Districts was first missioned by a triple agency.

"The Remissioning System" and "The Pious Praying Labourers" of Manchester.

The four years following 1832 were for Manchester, as they were for the Connexion generally, a period of remarkable numerical increase. During this period the membership of the Manchester Circuit rose from five hundred and eighty-four in 1832, to one thousand three hundred and twenty in 1836, and the circuit more than doubled the number of its travelling preachers. Doubtless, the same general causes that wrought for improvement in other parts of the Connexion produced their salutary effects here also. The Church was all the healthier and stronger for service because of the time of trial and sifting through which it had passed. Over and above these widely distributed causes, however, there was a special cause largely accountable for local success, to which Hugh Bourne thus alludes in his *Journal*:—

"*July 30th, 1832.*—Came to Manchester, ten miles by the railway. Saw brothers Butcher, Brame, and Gibson [the travelling preachers], and was thankful to hear of there being an excellent revival at Rochdale, in this Circuit; and that the converting work is on the move in the Jersey Street Chapel in Manchester. I was also thankful to hear that the pious praying labourers in Manchester have entered on the open-air system with vigour and effect. I do trust that this system will find its way into all the circuits."

Who were these pious, praying labourers, and what was the open-air system they practised? First in order amongst the names "to be had in respectful remembrance" must be placed the venerable Thomas Hewitt, in whose house in London Square, Banktop, the first class met in Manchester, and from whose doorstep the first missionary preached. He remained firm to the end of life, and zealous in his attachment to the Connexion; and his eldest son, who likewise bore the name of Thomas, was for some time the efficient superintendent of the Sunday School.

Of Jonathan Heywood, whom S. Smith describes as "a mighty man in prayer," we have a short pen-and-ink sketch by Mr. W. E. Parker:—"Jonathan Heywood, an old man, full of song, a joyful Christian, exerted a strong religious influence during many years. He was somewhat diminutive of stature, but showed much quickness, alertness, even nimbleness. He was always ready for the spiritual fray. When speaking or singing he seemed as though set on springs, and with a thin, shrill voice, but with intense fervour and power he sought to help men by holy song into the kingdom of

God. For many years before his death he was a complete invalid, and a great sufferer, but in all his affliction he witnessed a good confession, and died in triumph."

Another member of the goodly fellowship of workers was Thomas Holden, who, Mr. Parker tells us, at an early date in the history of the society, came from Todd Hall, near Haslingden, and was, for thirty years, a most successful class leader. "His was a constant and conspicuous figure in the congregation of Jersey Street. His fine, manly form and his sweet but powerful voice made him a desirable leader in open-air work. A prayer meeting without his presence or without his prayer was not to be thought of." When James Holden, his eldest son, at last yielded to the convictions he had long resisted, that son's demonstrations of joy at his new-found liberty were like those of the healed paralytic, or like theirs whose captivity was turned. Others rejoiced with him in song and shouts of triumph. The scene was one not easily to be forgotten, and was often recalled. James Holden retained his active connection with Jersey Street until his lamented death in 1896.

MR. JAMES HOLDEN.

As recently as 1901, there passed away one whose life more than covered the entire history of Manchester Primitive Methodism. As a girl, Mrs. Hannah Mc Kee received her first class-ticket in 1824, and was thus the contemporary of them who formed the remissioning bands, and she may well have assisted in their efforts. Not on this ground alone does she merit reference here, but because, for sixty years, she was a teacher in Jersey Street and New Islington Sunday Schools; a contributor on a somewhat large scale to the funds of the Church; at the time of her death the oldest Primitive Methodist in Manchester; and because she has left descendants, even to the fourth generation, who are closely associated with our denomination.

Jonathan Ireland was undoubtedly the leader of the band. It was from him Hugh Bourne learned the facts about the "remissioning system," which he gave at length in the *Magazine* for 1835; and though no names are mentioned (by J. I.'s own request, it is said) it is clear that Hugh Bourne regarded him as the "founder" and leading spirit of the movement. Jonathan Ireland was by aptitude and preference "a determined street-preacher," as he has been well called. He began his religious life in association with the Church of England, in "gay Preston." But even then his native bent showed itself. He was restive under restrictions. The contemplative life had no charms for him; nor could the observance of routine, however decorous, satisfy. He must *do* something, and something out of the common. So he rang the church bells, and planted shrubs in the churchyard. He even took part in house prayer meetings, where each one read his prayer out of the book; and once, when he made a burst into free prayer, he chastised himself by self-reproaches for having given way to what was Methodistic and improper. But he broke free from his fetters, and became a Methodist and a successful class leader, and an active sick visitor. Then he

MRS. HANNAH MCKEE.

came to Manchester, and found his true vocation when he joined the Primitives. This was in November, 1823, when Jersey Street Chapel was a-building.

When, in 1832, Manchester, like so many other towns and cities, was being ravaged by the cholera, Jonathan Ireland was moved to put forth special efforts to carry the gospel of salvation and consolation into the "streets and lanes of the city." He was nobly seconded by Jonathan Heywood, Thomas Hewitt, and others like-minded. Their method was, beginning at the house-door of one of the band, to go singing through the streets to a suitable stand in some populous quarter, and then halt, while a short, pointed exhortation was given. The like procedure was repeated again and again, until the time for morning or evening service had come, when they sang their way to the chapel. These remissioning efforts were continued all through that fateful summer with good results; but—and this is the noteworthy thing—they were not laid aside when the cholera had ceased its ravages. Each time the cholera has visited this country it has swollen our annual returns on the right side. An increase of 7120 stands to the credit of 1833; and the increase for 1850, following upon the fearful visitation of 1848-9, when more than five thousand persons perished, was still higher, amounting to 9205, a figure never reached before or since. But closer scrutiny would show that in some localities, the year of ingathering was followed by a year of wastage; that re-action followed revival; that many whom the cholera had frightened into the Church rather than driven to Christ, withdrew; and that even the Church itself, now that the scourge was overpast, too frequently relaxed its efforts to save men. But, as we have said, it was not so in Manchester; rather was remissioning carried on more energetically than before.

The planting of our Church in Salford grew out of the unremitting efforts of Jonathan Ireland and his co-workers. The first headquarters were in a room in Dale Street; then, in 1844, King Street Chapel was opened (afterwards Blackfriars Street, and now Camp Street, Broughton). One cannot read Jonathan Ireland's "Autobiography"* without being impressed with his tireless zeal and, no less, with his tact and resourcefulness. He was a true disciple of Hugh Bourne in never failing to notice the children. Even the slatterns and viragos of a "mean street" were mollified, as they saw the preacher shaking hands with the bairns at the close of a service. When he went into an Irish quarter, he knew better than to lead off with a denunciation of the Pope and all his works. He sought rather to begin by finding some common ground of agreement with his hearers. One quotation we will give, to show his methods and the kind of work that was being done during those earlier years:—

"One Sunday morning at nine o'clock (it was the Sunday following the races, and so drunkenness was peculiarly prevalent), I went into Wood Street, which runs out of Brown Street, to mission, several friends being with me. When I got up to preach I looked at the people, and cried out: 'You are a sorry set, without comfort and character; no credit, for nobody will trust you a farthing. Now, I'm here as your friend; and I'll tell you a way in which you may, in twelve

* "Jonathan Ireland, the Street Preacher. An Autobiography." Edited by Rev. J. Simpson, his son-in-law.

months have a good suit of clothes, goods in your home, money in your pockets, and comfort in your families.' This got hold of their minds; and I held them fast while I preached Jesus unto them. I had to preach that same morning in the room [in Salford]. When I had finished in the street I invited all to go with me just as they were. Many yielded, so I gave them a second edition. But while I had been engaged outside a man came up, and calling one of the members to him, he said : 'I'm glad I've met with you this morning. Your singing attracted me; for I was on the way to the old river, where, in some secret spot, I might end my miserable life by cutting my throat. Take this,' said the man, handing forward a razor, 'for if you have it I shall have one temptation less to grapple with.'"—(p. 41).

But even before the establishment of the Salford mission there already existed another mission-centre in Oxford Road. First a small cottage, then a small cellar, then a room over some stables, next a larger room once used by the Tent-Methodists. Such was the order. On the opening of this room, while Thomas Sugden was leading the love-feast, the floor fell in, and the story goes that the mishap occurred while all were lustily singing, "We are going home to glory." One man was injured, and many were frightened. The next remove was to a building in Ormond Street, vacated by the Wesleyans for their new chapel in Oxford Road. Ultimately this was exchanged for Rosamond Street Chapel, which for many years stood as the head of Manchester Second Circuit, now Moss Lane.

Yet a third mission was begun in these formative years, in a room over three houses in Ashton Street, London Road—now swept away by the London Road Station. The friend who had leased the room to the society at a low rental, at his death left the sum of £130 for a new chapel, "if a new chapel should ever be required by the Primitive Methodist denomination in Manchester"!—another proof of the doubt as to the perpetuity of the Connexion that crossed and troubled the minds at that time, even of those who were friendly disposed. Mr. Chadwick's legacy came in useful as a kind of nest-egg. More chapels *were* built in Manchester, as our full-page illustration shows, and there are more to follow. Ogden Street Chapel, opened in 1850, superseded Ashton Street room, and from this has grown Manchester Fourth and Ninth Stations, with the exception of Droylesden, taken from Stockport Second and attached to Manchester Ninth, on its formation in 1893. Good Mr. Chadwick's doubts as to whether the Primitives would ever build a new chapel in Manchester, have had their answer in Higher Ardwick Church, opened in 1878; and there was a natural sequence between the £15,000 expended on that stately pile and the £130 he somewhat timorously put down in his last will and testament. Thus, while a survey of the denomination's advance in Manchester during recent years, especially in its relation to ministerial education and training, will naturally challenge our attention later on, it was right that we should, even at this stage, at least indicate the thread of continuity running through our Connexional life in this great city. What we now see is largely the outcome of the missionary efforts carried on so vigorously during the first period

We began with Manchester at the New Cross, and, so far as Manchester itself is concerned, we may fittingly end there. "The New Cross (open air)" stands as the second place on a plan for 1832, and a Sunday afternoon service was held where the old

THE PERIOD OF CIRCUIT PREDOMINANCE AND ENTERPRISE. 27

MANCHESTER CHAPELS

- G^T CLOWES S^T
- UPPER MOSS LANE
- HIGHER ARDWICK
- NEW ISLINGTON
- KING S^T
- G^T WESTERN S^T
- HALL S^T
- CHORLEY R^D
- HIGHER OPENSHAW

pillar once stood, right on until the days of the Chartist agitation, when the authorities put their veto on *al fresco* meetings—political or religious—at that favourite stand. The magisterial mind of that epoch could not make subtle distinctions.

It was by lingering at one of these New Cross services when returning from Oldham

REV. T. HINDLEY.    RACHEL WHITEHEAD.    MR. NATHANIEL NAYLOR.

Street Wesleyan Chapel, which they attended, that Nathaniel Naylor and his wife fell in love with the Primitives. They thought it right to join the denomination, and became active workers and liberal supporters of the Jersey Street and New Islington societies. The youngest daughter of the house became the wife of Thomas Hindley, so widely known and respected as a minister in the Manchester District. There are other names of early workers, that ought to be more than names to us, but space forbids little more than the mention of them. There were: John Turner, for many years the courteous, prudent, efficient choir-master; Thomas Sharrock, an early Sunday School superintendent, much beloved, though he had an awe-inspiring presence and the reputation of knowing more than most; W. Williams, Thomas Sugden's successor in the confectionery business, circuit secretary and afterwards steward, a thoughtful, acceptable preacher, and a good District and Connexional man, at whose house, in Ancoat's Lane, ministers and friends from a distance would drop in for rest and talk; Samuel Johnson, a local preacher for many years, a man of wide reading and large outlook, whose discourses were listened to with interest and profit by many Lancashire congregations; Barnabas Parker, Charles Malpas also, and Job Williams, and Rachel Whitehead, and John Crompton, and Charles Taylor, who, in their several spheres, lived the Christian life and served the interests of Jersey Street Society.

This brief chronicle of departed worth may pleasantly end with a reference to good but eccentric David Bailey, of whose devotion and oddities tradition still loves to speak. He would "shut to the door" even of his shop while he retired for prayer, and so immersed himself in evangelistic work that his brethren feared his business would suffer; he was a dealer in earthenware near Shudehill Market, and his superin-

MR. S. JOHNSON.   MR. C. TAYLOR.

THE PERIOD OF CIRCUIT PREDOMINANCE AND ENTERPRISE. 29

tendent was appointed to admonish him. "David," said Rev. W. Antliff, "are you never afraid you'll break?" "Break?" said "Pot" David; "not till the fiftieth Psalm breaks at the fifteenth verse, 'Call upon Me in the day of trouble, and I will deliver thee.'" The answer was distinctly good, though it is to be feared David put a strain upon the promise it was never intended to bear.

SALE; WALKDEN MOOR; MIDDLETON.

Though, for the time being, we have done with Manchester city, we have not quite done with Manchester Circuit. At first, as has already been intimated

SALE CHAPEL AND SCHOOLS.

MR. JOHN E. WRIGHT.

Manchester Circuit was almost the first rough draft of the Manchester District of to-day. Important circuits were formed from it at an early date; but at present our concern is not with these, but rather with one or two places that were missioned at an early date and continued to be an integral part of the Manchester Circuit all through the first period, though now, in nearly every case, they have become heads of circuits.

Sale, we are told, was missioned as early as 1824-5. At that time the people around were "uncommonly rough and ignorant," and being chiefly employed in market-gardening, domestic work was left over until the Sunday. The mission to Sale was opened by a notable camp-meeting held in a hired field. Early in the day the converting work broke out, and the number of mourners was so great that a corner of the field was set apart for the holding of a continuous prayer meeting while the camp-meeting was still going on. This corner, appropriately named "the hospital," was placed under the superintendence of Thomas Buttler, a man of experience, who single-handed did much successful pioneer work in the country-side. "This day's labour led to results which were felt all over the neighbourhood. A visible reformation of manners followed." A Primitive Methodist society was formed, and "the Wesleyans were quickened and became prosperous."* A school chapel was erected in 1839, and the present church and school in 1872. The greater part of the manual and team labour involved in the taking down of the old building was undertaken by those most deeply interested in the work, amongst whom may be named, the Bollis family, Messrs. James Oakes, Samuel Derbyshire, and John E. Wright. The last named, from the time of his joining the Church, to his death in 1890, conscientiously fulfilled the duties of his various offices.

REV. JAMES GARNER.

Sale will always be associated with the memory of James Garner, one of the most massive and outstanding figures of the Manchester District. By virtue of a rare combination of qualities he was equally eminent in the pulpit, the committee room, the floor of Conference, the presidential chair, and the author's desk. Thirty-four out of the thirty-six years of his circuit ministry were spent in the old Manchester District, and about one half of these in the cities of Liverpool and Manchester. He began his ministry in 1830 as the junior colleague of his brother, John Garner, in the Oldham Circuit, and it was at the Oldham Conference of 1871 he was superannuated. He spent the remainder of his days at Sale, where his son-in-law, Mr. James Greenhalgh, accountant and Connexional auditor, resided. He was superintendent at the time the first chapel at Sale was built, and he took a deep and practical interest in the building of the present church. Before the end came, December, 1895, in a momentary lapse, he was heard to say: "Well, Mr. Bourne, I am glad to see you. *How is the Connexion doing?*" Consciousness had harked back to the early times, and the master-passion of life was strong in death.

MR. J. GREENHALGH.

On the Manchester Circuit plan for 1832 we find, amongst other places, Mosley Common, Walkden Moor, Middleton, Unsworth, and Stretford; and, now and again,

* See "Jonathan Ireland, the Street Preacher," for the quotations given in this paragraph.

an incident can be recovered having its value as illustrating the missionary activity going on in these localities. At Walkden Moor, one of the first trophies of grace to be won was H. Gibson. Ill at ease under what seems to have been incipient conviction of sin, he had enlisted into the First Life Guards, thinking that surely so complete a change as this would give him peace. But he was no happier at Whitehall than at Walkden Moor, and he was glad when, his father having purchased his discharge, he was free to return to his home. His old acquaintances welcomed him effusively, and he was soon enticed to match his bird at a cock-fight for ten shillings a side. His bird lay dying on the floor and, as he knelt before it, it came to him in a flash how he had knelt in the stable at Whitehall and promised God that if He would deliver him from soldiering he would lead a better life. He had broken his vow; but perhaps it was not yet too late. He would keep it now. He rose, threw down his money, and fled from the pandemonium. His pals pursued him with entreaties to return, but, like Pilgrim escaping from the City of Destruction, he hastened away, crying, "No, no! Farewell, cock-pit!" Not even yet did Gibson find peace. Like John Oxtoby, he was a Churchman of a kind, and Mr. Cry, the curate, prescribed for him: "Attend the church and sacraments regularly"; for is not that the whole duty of man? Then, hearing that J. Verity was to preach at "old Charlotte's" at Waterbeach, Gibson went to the service, but instead of Verity he heard a labouring man "with blue hands," who showed him his own heart, and what it was that really ailed him. H. Gibson was converted, held on his way, and became a local preacher.

At Middleton (since 1872 the head of a circuit), the first chapel-keeper was John Taylor, who had been a notorious pigeon-flyer and "hush-seller," *i.e.*, keeper of an unlicensed beer-house. He was reached by some straight talk at an open-air service, at the outskirts of which the pigeon-flyers were standing discussing to-morrow's match. Jonathan Ireland, who delighted in facts, was telling the story of this man's conversion, at a missionary meeting in Jersey Street some time after, when Taylor rose up before him in the congregation and shouted, "I'm the man."

The way into Gatley (now in the Stockport Circuit), we are told, was opened by Thomas Buttler, whom we have seen superintending the "hospital" at the first camp-meeting at Sale. Buttler went about the country prospecting, seeking the most likely places in which to open a mission. As he rode his ass from village to village, he claimed exemption from paying toll on the ground that he was doing the Lord's work. If, on the Sabbath, he heard the loom at work in a house as he went along, he would enter and rebuke the Sabbath-breaker. Buttler found his way to Gatley; and the result of our labours there was a great reformation, which led the farmers to say: "These people deserve encouragement, for since they came our apples are not stolen, nor our hedges broken down."

Our Early Hymns: their Popularity with the Masses.

Such missionary anecdotes as these show the kind of work that went on in the early days, and the kind of work that, above all, needed to be done; and here in Lancashire we are struck, as we were in writing of the Leicestershire revival, with the prodigious numbers the missionaries got to hear them, and with the almost entire absence of persecution. At Bolton—at the stocks and in the wood-yard where the first services were held,—at Ashton Town Cross, at Astley, at Oldham,—in fact wherever the missionaries went, they had no difficulty in gathering congregations. In the estimates of numbers given the word thousands occurs much more frequently than hundreds. "Preach! preach!" was the cry raised at Ashton Cross when, for a moment, the backslidden constable had silenced Walton Carter. The people were hungry for the Word and would not be denied, so that Carter had to gather himself together and preach, despite his torn coat and the constable's threats. Here too, as elsewhere, facts go to show that the hymns the missionaries sang counted for much in making

PREACHING AT BOLTON MARKET CROSS IN THE OLDEN TIME.

REV. HENRY HIGGENSON.

their street-missioning and open-air services acceptable and effective. Our fathers knew the power there is in a taking melody, and were not slow to avail themselves of this power. Like William Jefferson, they did not see why the devil should have all the best tunes, and so did their best to carry off the spoil. "The Lion of Judah" was only one of many tunes thus requisitioned. One evening, when the eccentric Henry Higgenson was on his way to a tea meeting at Walsall, he heard a lad singing a song which attracted him. "Here, my lad, sing that again, and I'll give thee a penny." The lad did as he was told, more than once. "Here you are, my man," said Higgenson, throwing him the penny; "I've got the tune, and the devil may take the words." The policy, if it were policy and not rather a sure instinct, was justified by its results, and perhaps nowhere more than in Lancashire, as Jonathan Ireland clearly admits. The admission may well be given in his own words, as the remarks show considerable acuteness, and contain a kindly reference to Richard Jukes, who, although he was a prolific and popular hymn-writer of his day, is in some danger of being forgotten:—

"Before the Primitive Methodists came to this city [Manchester], and for some time after, it was very common to hear lewd or ribald songs sung in the streets, especially on the Lord's day. *But our movements drove them away by putting something better in their place.* We used to pick up the most effective tunes we heard, and put them to our hymns; and at our camp-meetings people, chiefly young ones, used to run up to hear us, thinking we were singing a favourite song. But they were disappointed therein; nevertheless, they were arrested and often charmed by the hymn, which at times went with power to their hearts. And so the words of the hymn put aside the words of the song. It will show the utility of singing lively hymns in the streets; yea, more particularly, it will show the use to society in general of our hymn-singing in the streets, if I here relate a fact which was told me by a friend on whose veracity and accuracy I can place reliance. He said: 'I was one day in a hair-dresser's shop in a country village, when a man came in to be shaved, having a handful of printed hymns, which he had been singing and selling in the streets. I entered into conversation with him, in course of which he said: "Your *Jukes* has been a good friend to us street-singers; I have sung lots of his hymns, and made many a bright shilling thereby. People generally would rather hear a nice hymn sung, than a foolish song,—and his hymns are full of sympathy and life. Depend on it, the singing of hymns in the streets has done a deal of good; for children stand to listen to us, and they get hold of a few lines, or of the chorus; and with the tune, or as much of it as they can think of, they run home, and for days they sing it in their homes, and their mothers and sisters get hold of it, and in this way, I maintain, our hymn-singing is of more use than many folks think. I shall always think well of Jukes," concluded the man."

What Primitive Methodist will not heartily concur in this conclusion of the philosophic street singer? "Jukes' hymns have been sung from one end of the Connexion to the other, by tramps in the street and Christians in the chapels; and the late Dr. Massie says, the hymn entitled, 'What's the News,' &c., has been sung and repeated in the great Revival in Ireland."* George Herbert told us long since that:—

"A verse may find him who a sermon flies."

And popular, sacred songs are the most volatile and penetrating agents of religious propagandism, the more powerful because their power is unsuspected. They float on the breeze like the thistle-down, and like it they carry their seed with them. It is a simple yet sufficient illustration of this far-reaching, penetrative power of the *verse* which John Coulson relates. When, in 1819, on his way to Hull to seek out W. Clowes and the Primitives, he called at a house of entertainment at Mansfield. A sweep was

REV. R. JUKES.

* Rev. J. Harvey, "Jubilee of Primitive Methodism," 1861.

sitting turning over the leaves of a dingy pamphlet, to whom presently came the hostess, with the words: "Robert, you must sing that hymn with the hallelujahs at the end of it; for the children will not go to school until they hear it." The sweep stood up and sang:—

>"Come, oh come, thou vilest sinner;
>Christ is ready to receive;
>Weak and wounded, sick and sore,
>Jesus' balm can cure more.
>Hallelujah, hallelujah,
>Hallelujah to the Lamb!"

We are not sure whether a still higher claim cannot be put forth for the open-air hymn-singing of Primitive Methodism from sixty to eighty years ago. Not even yet can England be called with the same truth as can other countries that might be named— the land of song. One of the impressions the foreigner gets of London is that, despite the constant roar of traffic, the people are strangely silent. But, if we are to believe Thomas Mozley,[*] the England of 1820 was distinguished neither for its songfulness nor for its silence, but for a vocal expression which had no gladness in it, and which he himself thus describes :—

"I will content myself with one point of contrast between England as it now is and England as it was two, indeed I might now say three generations ago. It has forced itself upon me so often that I should hardly do justice to myself if I did not declare it. In my younger days there was heard everywhere and at all hours the voice of lamentation and passion, not always from the young, not always even from the very poor. In towns and villages, in streets and in houses, in nurseries and in schools, and even on the road, there were heard continually screams, prolonged wailings, indignant remonstrances, and angry altercations, as if the earth were full of violence, and the hearts of fathers were set against their children, and the hearts of children against their fathers. No doubt it was so in the time of the poet who filled the vestibule of hell with squalling children. But, as I have said, these were not all children who brawled or lamented in the open air and in the mid-day, filling the air with their grievances, and resolved, as they could not be happy themselves, none else should be. Such a picture would be pronounced at once utterly inapplicable to the times we now live in, but I leave it to almost any octogenarian to say whether it be not a true account of England as it was sixty or seventy years ago."

The picture drawn by Mozley of England as he knew it in 1820, dark though it be, is not, we are convinced, overcharged with sepia. "Merry England" was a designation sadly inappropriate to our land before the repeal of the Corn Laws. What the Psalmist so much deprecated had befallen us; there *was* "complaining in our streets." Hence the open-air songs of the new evangel breathing hope and promising deliverance

---

[*] See the chapter on "England in 1820 and England in 1884," in Vol. II. of his "Reminiscences, chiefly of Villages, Towns, and Schools." Thomas Mozley was a brother of Canon Mozley, the theologian, a relative of Cardinal Newman, and a prolific leader-writer on the *Times*. He died in 1893, in the eighty-third year of his age, so that, in giving his impressions of the England of 1820 (the year Primitive Methodism was introduced into Manchester), he was writing of what was well within his own knowledge.

THE PERIOD OF CIRCUIT PREDOMINANCE AND ENTERPRISE. 35

came as a startling novelty, and no wonder men flocked to listen. And if now Mozley's picture held up to the present would appear the veriest caricature, we should rejoice that our Church has greatly helped to destroy its verisimilitude. As we pass along the streets of the working-class quarter of our towns and cities we hear the Salvation Army band, and from many a lighted window we catch the sound of familiar hymn. Sacred song, like bread, is cheap and common now, we say. It was not always so, and we have done something to give sacred song its vogue.

LATE MR. E. LOMAX, BOLTON.

THE MANCHESTER GROUP OF CIRCUITS. "WE ARE SEVEN."

By 1843 the Manchester Circuit of 1821 had come to be represented by a group of direct and indirect descendants—seven in number. As the result of a process of division and sub-division *plus* extension, the original circuit had developed into the Bolton, Oldham, Isle of Man, Stockport, Bury, Rochdale, and Stalybridge Circuits. Let us rapidly follow the main lines of this development.

Bolton was granted circuit independence, June, 1822. J. Verity was here on June 24th, 1821, when he writes of preaching to three thousand people, joining twenty to the society, and notes that there is "an appearance of a great work." Just a month after he is at a camp-meeting, and leads a love-feast in the Cloth Hall. On August 19th he preaches three times in the open air, having, it was said, a congregation of five thousand people. Two days after, he is collecting for the fitting up of a large room, and meets with "amazing success." He is greatly encouraged by a gift of sixteen shillings from a number of mechanics. They were just about to have a "footing" carouse, when an "influence which could only proceed from Almighty God caused them to deny themselves," and devote the money to the "poor Ranters," as they called them. Verity closes his labours at Bolton by forming a Leaders' Meeting, and at this time, August 24th, reports that there are nine classes and one hundred and sixty members. Progress is marked by the opening, on September 3rd, of the large room by Walton Carter as preacher, and though it was a week evening, he had a congregation of eleven or twelve hundred people. It is noteworthy that when Bolton was made a circuit no other place was associated with it, hence, as two preachers are on the station in 1823, and five hundred members are reported, it is clear that other adjacent places must soon have been missioned.

In this same year, 1822, a brick chapel was erected in Newport Street, and a congregation continued to worship there until 1865, when a chapel was purchased from the Baptists in Moor Lane, now the head of Bolton Second. The present Higher Bridge Street Chapel, the head of Bolton First Circuit, was erected in 1870 at a cost of £6,588. It occupies the site acquired as far back as 1836 by Samuel Tillotson, on which a plain, substantial building was erected, flanked on either side by a house (in one of which the preacher resided), and having

LATE MRS. BEBBY.

c 2

a burial-ground in front. In 1868 a school was built in the rear of the chapel, and the years brought other changes to the property, the most serious being decrepitude—a tendency to fall. The insecurity of the structure led to the erection, during the vigorous superintendency of the Rev. James Travis, of the chapel shown in our picture. In 1893 the school premises were entirely re-modelled.

All the facts go to show that from the first, Bolton, like other Lancashire towns, took kindly to Primitive Methodism. "Took kindly" is scarcely the word. It would be nearer the truth to say—it eagerly, almost fiercely welcomed it. Bolton and Primitive Methodism gripped each other. The first Minute Book of the Manchester

HIGHER BRIDGE STREET CHAPEL, BOLTON.

Circuit shows that before the close of 1821 there were more members in Bolton than in Manchester itself, the numbers being 321 and 211 respectively. The young circuit was vigorous and enterprising. Probably the story is mythical which tells how the Bolton Quarterly Meeting having, when all expenses were met, a balance of sixpence, forthwith resolved, on the strength of that sixpence, to call out an additional preacher, who was none other than James Austin Bastow. But the Bolton Circuit officials, some of whose portraits are given, were just the men to venture much and win, as they assuredly did, if the story of their calling out

THE PERIOD OF CIRCUIT PREDOMINANCE AND ENTERPRISE. 37

Mr. Bastow be true. But, be this as it may, the Bolton Circuit had the courage of faith in resolving, six months after its becoming a circuit, to send John Butcher as a missionary to the Isle of Man. Probably it is without a parallel that mother and daughter-circuits should come on the stations together, as was the case with Bolton and Castletown, Isle of Man, in the Conference *Minutes* of 1823.

John Butcher landed at Derby Haven, and "opened his mission in nearly the first house he came to." A Mr. Kelly, we are told, received him into his house, for which act of good-will he was unchurched by the denomination to which he belonged. The missionary's *Journal* shows that he began his labours at Castletown on Friday, January 10th, 1823, and that he went on holding services at Colby, Ballasalla, Howe, Port John, and other places in the south-west of the island.

MISS JANE CROOK.

MR. J. PENDLEBURY.

In this Manx Mission of the Bolton Circuit we have an early and normal example of the Circuit-mission. By this is meant that the circuit has looked beyond its own doors and, assuming the functions and responsibilities of a missionary executive, has conceived the plan of sending its accredited agent to some more distant sphere. The mission is the outpost to which the circuit serves as the base. Thus regarded, the mission to the Isle of Man was the boldest thing a Primitive Methodist circuit had as yet attempted. It anticipated the Irish missions by ten, and the Edinburgh and Glasgow missions by four years. Leeds' mission to London, which took place about the same time, is the only instance we can recall that can be compared with it for boldness. The London mission was a venture that failed; the Manx mission succeeded. And yet, in some respects, the latter was the bigger venture; for the Isle of Man, though not far away as mere miles count, was oversea, and Mona was then, much more than it is now, a little

PRESENT CHAPEL AT HARWOOD, BOLTON.

kingdom apart, with its own customs and laws and even language, so that it was something of the nature of an experiment whether Primitive Methodism would commend itself to these islanders of Celtic race, and take hold of their rich and fervid nature. The experiment succeeded. The evangel the two Butchers—the son soon joining the father—had to offer fitted the Manx people as perfectly as the ball fits its socket. There was scarcely the shadow of persecution, unless the occasional exhibition of suspicion and prejudice may be counted such. "As we sang through the town some cried, 'Shame! shame!' We get nothing much worse than this. And on the other hand, we hear many more saying, 'It is like the old times, when the Methodists first came to the Island.'" They recognised and welcomed the primitiveness of the Methodism brought them. How the work spread in this corner of the island during these first months of the year may be gathered from a joint-letter written on May 5th from Kirk Arbory, and addressed: "Dear brethren and fathers in the Gospel." The letter, of which unfortunately only the initials of the signatories are given, is a document that cannot well be omitted.

"We have the pleasure of informing you that the preachers you have sent over to us have, by their preaching and the blessing of Almighty God, been rendered instrumental in the salvation of many souls. We have now in society about two hundred members, and the work appears to be prosperous, and as if it were just beginning; for the people flock to hear them, 'as doves to their windows,' from the distance of four or five miles, and are crying, 'Come, preach for us.' But as we have but two preachers, they can only compass about twelve or fourteen miles in length, on one side of the Island. And as we have no local preachers, we cannot reach the places as we could wish. We have some who are nearly ready for exhorters. We have begun to have some prayer meetings, and they are a great blessing unto us.

"We have begun preaching at Douglas; one of our preachers has preached there at the market-place these five Sabbaths last past, and the services have been attended by amazingly large congregations.

"We remain, in the bonds of love and fellowship,

"A. C.; J. G.; J. C.; C. C."

At Midsummer, Henry Sharman was added to the staff of preachers, and from his *Journal* it is clear that already the towns of Douglas and Peel had been fastened upon and made the strategic points for further evangelistic labours. During the remainder of the year, Sharman had his "rounds," foreshadowing the branches and circuits of a later time. First, we find him labouring on the Castletown side, and then, after a time, he goes into the Douglas "round," which included Laxey. It is interesting to note that Thomas Steele was very helpful to Sharman while he was in this part. He records that "he has been

PEEL OLD CHAPEL.

made a blessing to our society in the Island," and that "we preachers believe the Lord sent him." Finally, Sharman goes for a month to more distant Peel, "a place noted for its wickedness and hardness, which gave him some concern." Land had already been secured for a chapel at Douglas. Just before the Christmas of 1823 Castletown chapel was opened; four other chapels are said to be in course of erection, and the number of members in the Island is reported as six hundred and forty-three.

For two years only Castletown stands on the stations, then it is simply "Isle of Man." Evidently Douglas soon began to take the lead, and became the residence of the superintendent. In 1842, differentiation began to show itself. We have Douglas; Ramsey Branch; and Peel Mission. In 1849, Ramsey is a circuit, with Peel as its branch; later, Peel is re-absorbed. In 1851, Castletown is a branch; and, in 1868, both Castletown and Peel have become independent stations. Finally, when, in 1887, Laxey was made a station, the present number and order of stations were arrived at. These changes reflect the vicissitudes through which our Church in the Island has passed, and the numerical returns bear similar witness. In 1832, the number of members given is 339; next year the number is 1,000, which is also that of 1842; but, in 1837, the number had sunk to 756. It is singular that our present numerical position in the Island is practically the same as in 1842, viz., 1,089, while the number of ministers is also the same. Seasons of spiritual declension alternating with seasons of revival do not altogether, or perhaps even mainly, account for these fluctuations. Of course they *have* operated and left their mark on the periodic returns. But the chief explanation will probably be found in the action, more or less acute, of economic and industrial conditions determining the flow of emigration from the Island, which has right along been a serious hindrance to the steady advance of the societies. Yet, despite this hindrance, the Isle of Man still contributes one-ninth part of the total membership of the Liverpool District, and it has strongly rooted itself in the religious and social life of the Island, as the advance the Church has made on the material side during late years strikingly shows. Illustrations of this later phase of our history we hope to give hereafter; but, even confining ourselves to the earlier period, Bolton's mission to the Isle of Man must be pronounced a success both in its direct and indirect results. Names which at once betray their Manx origin are found on the muster-roll of our workers, past and present, both in the Isle and out of it. They stand side by side with the plain Saxon patronymics we know so well. The blend and association of racial qualities in Christian communion and service thus indicated has been all for good. Names such as Clucos, and Quayle, and Cain are unmistakeably Manx, and they are the names of some out of many who might be named, who served the interests of our Church in the Island during the earlier days. Philip Clucos (born 1809, died 1885) was a noted pioneer worker and evangelist in his day, and as such he traversed the Island, winning many converts. The hospitality of the Quayles, of Glenmaye — of which society Mrs. Quayle was the first member—is reported of to this day. Of John Cain, of Rinshent, Foxdale,

MR. PHILIP CLUCOS.

it is said he opened his house for services, and when the farm-kitchen was too small he fitted up his barn. He was the leading spirit in the erection of the first chapel at Foxdale. His house was always open to the servants of God, and his horses at

GLENMAYE OLD CHAPEL.

their disposal to lighten their journeys. Through the biographies in the *Magazines* we get glimpses of other early workers and befrienders of the Cause. There are Jane Cubbon, who welcomed John Butcher to her father's house at Colby; Patrick Cannal, one of his first converts at Kirk Michael, and trustee and steward of the chapel built in 1824; Ann Quirk, who united with the first class at Douglas, and Ann Kaown, "whose house was unspeakably valuable in the introduction of Primitive

MR. W. QUAYLE.    MRS. W. QUAYLE.    MR. JOHN CAIN.

Methodism into Douglas; John Corlett, local preacher, who, as a sailor, during ten years preached in the Shetland Isles, at the ports of Scotland and Ireland, and was afterwards for three years a devoted town missionary at Douglas; John Clague, of Ramsey Circuit, who preached for twenty-one years in his native Manx, and Robert

Tear, also of the same circuit, "whose addresses, principally given in his native tongue, were full of originality, pointed, homely and pious, aptly illustrated by references to agricultural customs."

Returning to Bolton Circuit. In December, 1823, Henry Sharman writes: "We were enabled to send the money we owed to Bolton Circuit, and were very little short in paying all besides." So that not only was Bolton nothing out of pocket by its venture, but it had also the satisfaction of knowing that by its enterprise it had added a miniature kingdom to the Connexion, and set a worthy example before other circuits. Besides the Isle of Man, other circuits have, during the course of years, been formed from Bolton, viz., Bury, Bolton Second, Darwen, Leigh, Heywood, and Horwich. Of these successive changes in internal administration, the first only falls within the first period. In the first Minute Book of the Manchester Circuit, Bury has only six members, from which fact it may be inferred that at the close of 1821 Bury had but just been missioned. In 1835, Bury stands on the Bolton plan as a branch with some fifteen places, including Edenfield, Ramsbottom, Heywood, Chadderton, Summerseat, and Ratcliffe. At the Conference of 1836 it became an independent station, with one minister and two hundred and sixty-two members.

Oldham.

Oldham was missioned about the same time as Bolton, and here also "thousands crowded to hear the Word of life in the open-air." There is no need to discount these words of Verity's as though they were merely a rhetorical exaggeration. Unless everybody has conspired to deceive us, Oldham camp-meetings down to, and even beyond, the middle of last century were noted for the immense throngs attending them. The Rev. W. Antliff, who spent five of the most influential years of his ministry in Oldham (1857-61), tells us that the Oldham Whitsunday camp-meeting, held on Oldham Edge, was one of the largest in that part of the kingdom. He gives the probable numbers present in 1861 as ten thousand; for that of 1858, his predecessor, Miles Dickenson, gives the estimate of fifteen thousand. But it is only fair to say that the traditional estimates of the numbers brought together at some of these annual gatherings go far beyond these figures. It almost seems as though the first Oldham camp-meeting of May 19th, 1822, had set the pattern for all subsequent ones. The site of the Oldham gathering on this famous camp-meeting Sunday—of which we wish we could have had a census of attendance and the number of professing converts—was at Bardsley, in a field lent by Mr. Brierley, of the Fir Trees Farm. The services were carried on entirely by Manchester men, of whom Walton Carter was the leader. Fourteen thousand people were said to have been present; there were two preaching-stands, five praying companies, and two permanent ones. Carter says of this notable gathering: "People of all denominations received it with approbation; while the attention of the multitude was arrested, and the hearts of many were inspired with zeal for the Lord of hosts."

This Pentecostal day, however, did not found the church at Oldham though it did strengthen it and add to its numbers. A class had previously been formed at Brook, near Bardsley, with James Wild and R. Ashworth as its leaders; and a second

42 PRIMITIVE METHODIST CHURCH.

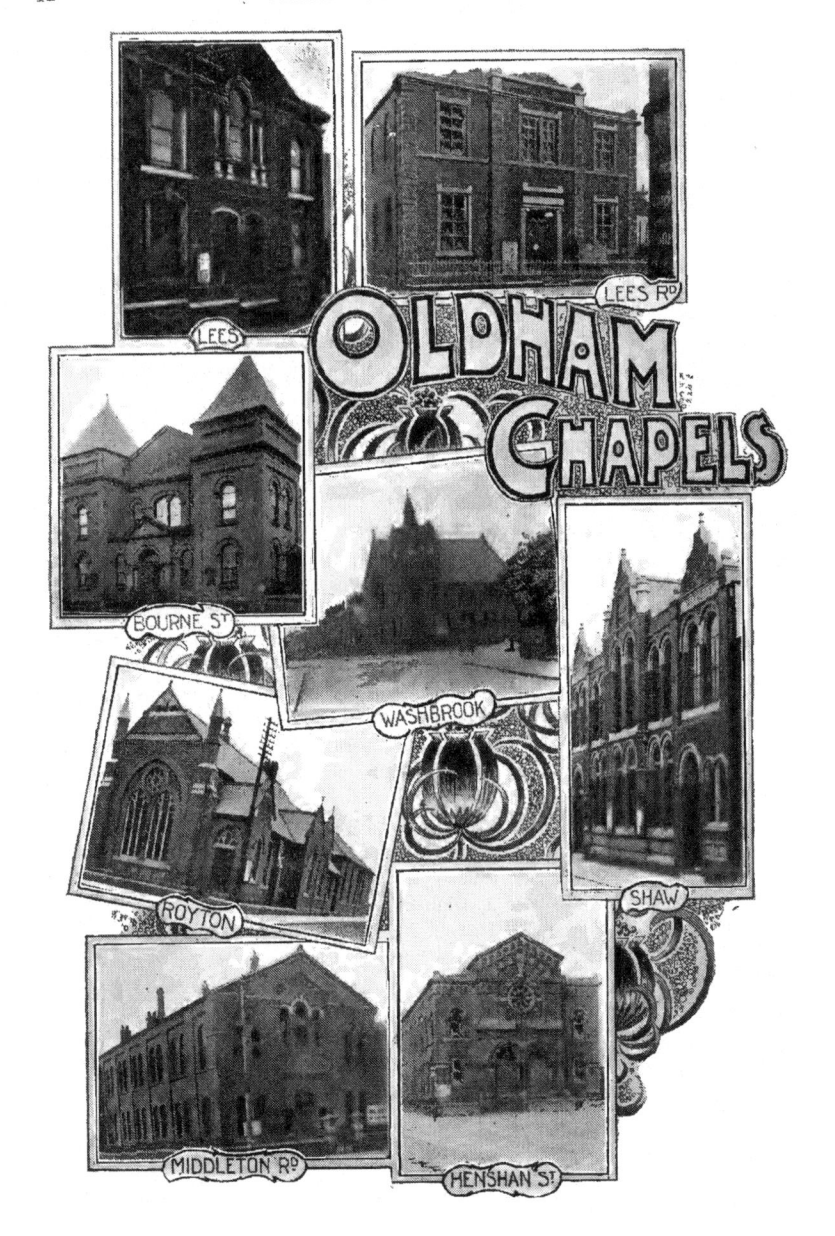

Oldham Chapels

LEES
LEES Rᴅ
BOURNE Sᵀ
WASHBROOK
ROYTON
SHAW
MIDDLETON Rᴅ
HENSHAN Sᵀ

THE PERIOD OF CIRCUIT PREDOMINANCE AND ENTERPRISE. 43

at Oldham, of which Peter Macdonald and F. Mannock were put in charge. Peter Macdonald graduated for the position of first leader through Roman Catholicism and Methodism. If Jonathan Ireland had, for his soul's good, rung the church bells; Peter Macdonald had, as an acolyte, tinkled the bells at the celebration of mass, in his native county of Carlow. But he got his mind enlightened when he came to England to follow his trade, abjured the errors of Romanism, and, like others hereabout, passed through Methodism to join the new revival movement, which both suited him well and, as he thought, needed what help he could give. His life, culminating in a triumphant death in 1835, was written by Samuel Atterby, and might profitably be reprinted by Oldham Primitives. Besides the officials of the first generation already named, mention may be made of James Taylor, a convert of Thomas Aspinall in 1823, "one of the first and fastest friends of Primitive Methodism in the town"; J. Kent, Circuit Steward from 1829 to 1838; and W. Winterbottom, of Shore Edge, who was present at the first camp-meeting, and a local preacher from 1828 until his death about 1880.

It was in 1862 that Oldham was divided into Oldham First and Second Circuits, the latter with Lees Road as its head, including also Lees, Bardsley, Waterhead, Elliott Street, Delph, and Hollinwood. Regarding this as our goal for the time being, two lines of development as leading up to it are distinctly traceable as early as 1821. These are set before us in the entry in the first Minute Book of the Manchester Circuit: "Mumps and Oldham 160 members." The Oldham line is comparatively simple and direct; the other, starting from Mumps and ending in Lees Road, is as zig-zag as pictured lightning. Oldham's first humble domicile was a stable in Duke Street; the next, a room in Grosvenor Street, which, becoming too small, was vacated for a small chapel in the same street, built about 1826; then in 1832, during the superintendency of William Taylor, a much larger building was erected in Boardman Street, which for a good many years was Oldham's principal chapel. As for the other society, like Moab, it seems to have been emptied from vessel to vessel and not allowed to settle on its lees. From whatever causes, it had to shift its quarters several times before it acquired a location with anything like fixity of tenure. This was in a measure accomplished when, in 1830, a room in Vineyard Street was acquired, which for ten years served for public worship and Sabbath School teaching.

MR. J. LONGLEY.
Oldham Second Circuit.

1825 and 1826—"those years the locust hath eaten"—seem to have been at Oldham, as they were elsewhere, a time of trial and waste. There are eight preaching-places fewer on the plan than before, and the number of local preachers is reduced by six. But under the vigorous and methodical ministry of F. N. Jersey and his colleagues, the aspect of things somewhat brightened, and the two years—1829-31—John Garner spent in the circuit were remarkable for their prosperity. He was then in the bloom and vigour of his manhood, and at the zenith of his ministerial power. James Garner was called out as an additional preacher. Not only was Vineyard Street acquired, but in 1831 a chapel was opened at Hollinwood. Just thirty years after, a second chapel was built at Hollinwood, and since 1880 it has stood at the head of Oldham Third Circuit. We gather that the revival which resulted in adding two hundred members to the circuit membership during these two years was marked by certain "peculiar features," not clearly specified by John Garner's biographer. Writing with an almost provoking reticence, he says: "Certain peculiar features of the work excited, in his observing mind, a degree of apprehension. He narrowly watched the movements of the parties who acted prominent parts in the public religious services. And as he believed them to be persons of real worth, and influenced by sincere motives, he honoured them with his confidence, and was thankful for their hearty co-operation." In these words, the biographer rather timidly glances at some of those physical manifestations of highly-wrought religious feeling that not unfrequently showed themselves in early Methodism, and were not altogether unknown in the beginning of our own Connexional history. Sometimes these manifestations took the form of fallings; at other times their subject would go into trance conditions, or, yet again, would leap or dance. The "peculiar features" of the Oldham revival took the form last named, as Jonathan Ireland tells us. They in Manchester heard rumours of what was going on in Oldham, and determined to see for themselves whether rumour spoke truly. Probably they timed their visit so as to be present at the quarterly love-feast held December 13th, 1829, at which, says John Garner in his *Journal*, "many from Manchester and other places attended; the chapel [Grosvenor Street] was crowded, and sixteen persons professed to have been made happy in the Lord during the day." Ireland speaks without reserve of the manifestations reported of at Manchester. "We had not been long in the chapel when the jumping began. It soon spread, and became general all over the chapel. But Mr. John Garner said: 'If you don't like this sort of work, you can take your hats and leave us.'" It should be noted as a fact of much importance that Ireland distinctly states this saltatory habit was "confined to the best and most devoted members of the society." No doubt Mr. Garner would rather have had the gracious influences without these accompaniments; but he was a shrewd man, and, though he had kept careful watch, he could detect neither imposture nor characterless fanaticism in these phenomena. Hence he was chary of rebuke, lest haply he should root up the wheat with the tares.

On February 14th, 1836, the streets of Oldham saw a busy and every way primitive sight, interesting to us as showing that the traits so characteristic of Hugh Bourne were as strongly marked as ever, though he was now in the sixty-fourth year of his age. In the morning he had led a class, shaken hands with all the Sunday school scholars, and then preached to them in Boardman Street Chapel; and now, in the afternoon, he was heading a procession after his own heart. There were seven stoppages for prayer, and H. B. preached seven one-minute-and-a-half sermons, plain, pointed, and, for the sake of the children, containing references to the power of divine grace as able to 'take the naughty out of their hearts, and to save them from Satan and his blue flames.' All this he describes with evident zest,

MR. LUKE NIELD.
Oldham Second Circuit.

and the description is blended with counsel as to the right ordering of such services, and models of the right kind of one-minute sermons are given; and then he turns to tell, with wonderful naïveté and simplicity, the incident of the child that was his companion throughout this processionary service:—

"A little matter took place, which drew great attention. When we had been moving for some time, I happened to turn my head, and was aware of a little girl, of about three or four years of age, having hold of my coat, and walking by my side in an orderly manner. This a little surprised me. I put her on the foot-path to walk with some other girls; but she was immediately at my side again as before. And, however dirty the streets, or difficult, she kept her place. After we had stopped at any time to pray and speak, she was at once at her place again; and when the street was very dirty, I occasionally took her by the hand. I felt a little anxiety lest the little creature should be hurt. But all went well; and when returning to the chapel, the street being very dirty, I put her on the foot-path, and had the satisfaction to see her come safe to the chapel. And I afterwards found this little girl's conduct had drawn the attention of many."

There is something of the didactic and prophetic about this incident, which we may be sure Hugh Bourne did not, after all, consider "a small matter." Hugh Bourne and the child hand in hand, heading the procession through Oldham streets, was a lesson, and a parable of the future as well as a pleasing picture. It said : "Take care of the children. Do not repulse them and say, 'Trouble not the Master.' Have them with you. Lift them out of the dirt, and keep them from falling." And it anticipated these later days, when the young are ungrudgingly welcomed into the van of the Church's forward movements.

The picture, as thus given, is scarcely complete without a reference to Hugh Bourne's engagement on the morning following the multifarious labours of the Sabbath, which might well have brought "blue Monday" in their train. If it came, it found him still following his bent—caring for the young life. After a night's rest at his old friend James Wild's, he went with S. Atterby to Lees, to inspect the Infant School taught in the chapel S. Turner had built in 1834. H. B. compared notes with Brother Watts, the teacher, and suggested certain improvements he himself had projected, and finished up by holding a service with the children.

We close our notice of Oldham by calling attention to the portraits, which will be found in the text, of some, out of many that might have been given, of tried and faithful officials who may be considered to have been the makers of Oldham Second Station.

MR. D. CLEGG.
Oldham Second Circuit.

On the Sunday before the Coronation, July 15th, 1821, John Verity formed societies at Newton, Stalybridge, and Ashton-under-Lyne. Despite the opposition met with at the last-named place, the work prospered; indeed, so much favour did the missionaries find with the people, that they came forward willingly to furnish the preaching-room, as Verity thankfully and even exultantly records. From the evidence supplied by an old plan, it would seem that Ashton stood as a circuit in 1824. But, if so, its name does not appear on the Conferential stations as such, and, in 1825, Ashton, together with Hyde and Dukinfield, were transferred from Manchester to Oldham; and in 1838, these and other places became the Stalybridge Circuit.

Ashton made full amends for the rough treatment of our early missionaries by some of its inhabitants. It has paid a large indemnity, by which the Connexion has been enriched. As a set-off to the hustling of Walton Carter and the imprisonment of S. Waller, it has sent forth some of its sons who have done splendid service. The Ashton society was instrumental in the conversion of three young men who were companions. One of these was James Austerbury, now spending a quiet evening after serving the Church at home long and faithfully; the second was Edward Crompton, who after spending some years in the ministry in this country, entered that of the Primitive Methodist Church of the U. S. A.; the third was John Standrin, who prior to his being sent out in 1857 by the G. M. Committee to Australia, travelled in the Knowlwood Circuit—1854-55. During revivalistic services which he conducted at Summit, on the Lancashire side of the Pennine range, a group of young men were won to the Church, some of whom were to carve their name deep in the history of our Church during the middle and later periods of its history. When we say that one of these was James Travis, another John Slater, and a third Barnabas Wild, long esteemed in the Sunderland District as a solid preacher and an upbuilder of the churches, it will be seen that Ashton is an interesting link in the chain of causes which, in the providence of God, have produced far-reaching results.

ROCHDALE; STOCKPORT.

Rochdale was part of the Manchester Circuit until 1837, when it became the head of a station with five hundred members. We know the exact date when our missionaries first lifted up their voice in this important town. It was July 15th, 1821, when Walton Carter "went to open Rochdale," as he himself has told us. "Three of our society," he says, "went with me. We sang up the street at one o'clock, and collected a good many people. But heavy rain coming on, I was obliged to desist; but resumed my place at five, and preached to a very large and attentive congregation. Some were affected, and I have heard since were brought to God."

The heavy rain here referred to may have been the identical rain-storm which, as Jonathan Ireland avers, led Jenny Bridges to take pity on the missionary, and offer him the shelter of her cellar in Cheetham Street for the service. Anyway, the cellar was Rochdale's first lowly preaching-place. The tenants of the cellar, John Bridges, the carrier, and his wife, must be numbered among the eccentrics of our Israel, yet one trait in Jane's character may be recalled to her credit. Reverence may show itself in cellar as well as in cathedral; and for that particular flag in her own cellar whereon Jane knelt when she found peace through believing, she had ever a feeling akin to reverence. She kept it clean. She pointed it out to visitors. To her it was a spot as sacred as an adorned altar.

From the cellar, a remove was made, in 1825, to a room in Packer Meadow, off Packer Street. The remove was a step upward in the scale of respectability; for we are told that Packer Street (of which we give a view, taken from an old print), was, in those days, considered one of the important streets of the town. Though very narrow, many business and professional men had premises here; and at the top of this street was the ascent to the parish church by a flight of one hundred and twenty-one steps; while at the bottom of the steps, to the right, was the famous "Packer Spout," a well noted for its cool, clear, pure water.

The room over the cloth-dresser's in Packer Street served the uses of the society until 1830, when Drake Street Chapel was built, at first without a gallery. This, in its turn, lasted until 1862, when the present chapel was built at a cost of £2,500. Thus, for a generation—right through the mid-third of the century—"old" Drake Street was the Church's centre in Rochdale for worship and service. Many worthy people, of whom one or two only we may recall, gradually grew old and grey in attending upon its ordinances and fulfilling their varied ministries.

Edmund Holt was, for many years, the choirmaster of Drake Street. Here any Sunday he might have been seen, surrounded by other instrumentalists and singers, manipulating a huge concertina. This good though eccentric man, it is said, was equally at home on the platform as in the singing pew, and by his public addresses could play on the feelings of men, by turns evoking tears and laughter. His name-sake, Thomas Holt, was of different type; quiet, modest in speech and act, a "son of consolation." Both survived until 1877. James Whitehead was another official who rendered long and important service. He threw

PACKER STREET, ROCHDALE.

EDMUND HOLT.    THOMAS HOLT.    THOMAS WHITEHEAD.

much energy into the discharge of his varied offices—Circuit Steward, Sunday School superintendent, class leader, and local preacher, and yet, when done, had a surplus of energy left to draw upon. When he died in 1865, it was to the general regret of the townsfolk of Rochdale, as well as of his own people. The portraits of these and one or two other early workers are given in the text.

STOCKPORT: WOODLEY.

Stockport and the places thereabout for some years formed part of the Manchester Circuit. One of the early workers tells how he and his fellow "locals" used regularly to walk from four to twelve miles on a Sunday morning, preach indoors and out-of-doors, pray with penitents, and then tramp back again. When they went southward to Stockport or beyond, they would meet in the evening on the Lancashire Bridge and journey home. The first word said by one to another would be, "How many souls to-day, lad?" and often they rejoiced together over the spoil they had taken.

To some appreciable extent Primitive Methodism had been influenced by Stockport "Revivalism." The Revivalists (amongst whom probably were Ebenezer Pulcifer and

PRESENT CHAPEL, WELLINGTON ROAD, STOCKPORT.

James Selby of Droylesden) had carried the fire to Congleton, at which Hugh Bourne's zeal was kindled afresh. They set causes to work which turned James Steele into a Revivalist, and resulted in the conversion of William Clowes and others of the fathers. So that when Primitive Methodism entered Stockport to stay, Stockport was only getting its own with usury. From this time onward, Stockport is a good deal to the fore. It has frequent incidental mention in the records of the time, as though it were a place which lay right in the track of the Church's movements. Our founders not unfrequently came this way, and passed through or tarried here. Thus William Clowes tells us that just after the District Meeting of 1828, he came to assist in the opening of a new chapel at Stockport (Duke Street), and found that his congregation had gained admission to the service by the presentation of purchased tickets. The same monetary arrangement obtained in 1833, when he preached the school sermons. This time he was the guest of "friend Beeston," and it had taken him two days to get from Silsden, riding, as he had to do, through heavy rains, behind an unmanageable horse. The present chapel, "Ebenezer," Wellington Road, S., was built in 1882, at a cost of £6000.

It was in 1831 that Stockport became an independent station, with John Graham and R. Kaye, a native of Bolton, as its preachers and "one wanted." Samuel Smith and Jesse Ashworth are names closely associated with Stockport's early days. The former was born at Denton, a village near Stockport, and though he removed to Leeds to serve his apprenticeship, he returned in 1834 to superintend the station for two busy and successful years. The religious services of the District Meeting of 1835, held at Stockport, resulted in the conversion of more than forty persons. Samuel Smith must be regarded as having been one of the makers of the original Manchester District. He travelled in Manchester itself and the principal stations of the District, and finished his useful life as a supernumerary-assistant at Stockport, January, 1878, aged 80 years. More than most, Samuel Smith was a preacher for the people, and he had their social and political welfare at heart. It was Stockport which first sent Richard Cobden to Parliament, and the crusade of which Cobden and Bright were the leaders had Samuel Smith's full sympathy. True, the Consolidated Minutes might say: "He, *i.e.*, a travelling preacher, must not deliver speeches at political meetings or parliamentary elections," but Samuel Smith and a few others probably interpreted this to mean that they were only prohibited from making speeches in the Tory interest, and so reading the rule they took care to observe it strictly. S. Smith's ardent and early advocacy of Total Abstinence will be referred to when we come to deal with Preston, but in proof of his practical sympathy with the ameliorative movements of his day, it is said that he was elected as one of Lancashire's representatives on a deputation to Sir Robert Peel, and that he was one of those who pressed upon the great commoner the total and immediate abolition of the corn laws.

REV. SAMUEL SMITH.

It was during his term in Stockport that Samuel Smith took kindly notice of Jesse Ashworth, then a youth of fourteen. He succeeded in creating in his young mind the thirst for knowledge, and especially the thirst for Biblical knowledge. He took him with him to Gatley, where the youth gave his first exhortation. He proposed him for the plan, and the same year young Jesse found himself at sixteen years of age

REV. J. ASHWORTH.

a travelling preacher. This was in 1837, and the duty of placing on record the facts and an estimate of his long and useful life will fall to the lot of the Conference of 1904.

In the roll of Stockport Circuit's early worthies the following names should have honourable place:—J. Penny, first Circuit Steward, and local preacher, W. Cheetham, sen., Circuit Steward, and his present successor, W. Cheetham, jun.; J. Ashton, the first Sunday School Superintendent; Thomas Dunning, a noted "local" and street preacher; John Harrison, local preacher; and J. Peckston, Chapel Treasurer and a generous supporter of the cause.

W. CHEETHAM, SEN.

Woodley, in the near vicinage of Stockport and, since 1887, a circuit in its own right, has had a long and interesting history. It was opened in 1822, in the usual way, by the holding of open-air services. It much needed missioning. The candle lighted by Wesley had all but gone out. What religion it had was mainly of the formal inactive type; "dog-fighters, cock-fighters and man-fighters," on the contrary, were too active, and our missionaries had to contend with persecution of the rude and mischievous kind. Two houses that were successively offered were as quickly closed to us because of this activity of the sons of Belial. Whereupon the preacher for the day made an appeal to his out-door audience, and one Israel Burgess felt the force of that appeal. He feared lest the missionary should, after the manner of the apostles, shake the dust off his feet and depart, and hence he agreed, if his family were willing, to lend his house for the services. So much in earnest were they, that his wife walked to Stockport to announce to the preacher their acquiescence. Services were held here for a time, until a room in a warehouse was taken, and then in 1835 a chapel with schools below was built. Young Jesse Ashworth was present at the opening services which were conducted on successive Sabbaths by Thomas Holliday, J. A. Bastow and John Flesher, the last of whom thrilled his audience as he preached two of his great sermons—the Penitent Thief, and the Raising of the Widow's Son.

REV. S. STAFFORD.

A blessing rested on the house of Israel Burgess. A Burgess was the mother and grandmother of the Staffords, five of whom served for some time at least in the Primitive Methodist ministry; the most widely known of these being Samuel Stafford (1854-90), and his nephew, Luke Stafford, whose name is associated with the origin of the Prayer and Bible Reading Union. Henry Stafford, the father of the latter, was for forty-five years a local preacher in the Stockport Circuit, and an active supporter of the cause at Woodley. Bramall too is a name to be mentioned with respect in any notice of the early history of our Church in Woodley.

REV. LUKE STAFFORD.

It was Edward Bramall who began the Sabbath school in his own house. For two Sundays only was it held here, being then removed to the ware-

THE PERIOD OF CIRCUIT PREDOMINANCE AND ENTERPRISE. 51

house, which served until the schools below the chapel of 1835 could be utilised. In 1861 separate schools were built. Since the day when E. Bramall improvised seats for his scholars by planks placed on bricks, progress has been made. Thomas Bramall, now retired from the active ministry, was one of the band sent out by Woodley.

In or about the year 1849, the Church at Woodley was strengthened by the accession of John Lees Buckley to its ranks. By dint of perseverance he overcame initial difficulties that would have daunted a weaker man, and gained an honourable position among the manufacturers of his district. But success did not spoil him. He never lost his prayerfulness or his relish for spiritual things. Primitive Methodism in Woodley and the district owes much, especially on the material side, to the beneficence and steady connexional attachment of John Lees Buckley and his family. For twenty years he was superintendent of the Sunday school, a local preacher, a patron of the Manchester Institute, a working member of various district and connexional committees. He died January 21st, 1880, aged 65 years.

MR. HENRY STAFFORD.

MR. J. LEES BUCKLEY.

WOODLEY PRIMITIVE METHODIST CHAPEL, BUILT 1868.

CHAPTER XIV.

The Missioning of York and Leeds.

IT is time we returned to Hull to see what that Circuit was doing for the extension of the Connexion. An authentic document of the time ready to our hand may help us here. It is a letter sent to Hugh Bourne by Richard Jackson, the energetic steward of Hull Circuit. The letter, dated March 20th, 1822, reads like a dispatch from the seat of war—as indeed it was. We shall have to refer to this important letter again when we come to speak of Hull's mission to Craven and to Northumberland; that part of the letter which more immediately concerns us here is this statement: "It is two years and nine months since Hull was made a circuit town . . . . and we have since made seven circuits from Hull, viz. :—Pocklington, Brotherton, Hutton Rudby, Malton, Leeds, Ripon and York Circuits." The formation of the first three circuits named in this list has already been described, and what this and the next chapters have to show is the direction and degree of the geographical extension made as registered by the formation in 1822 of the York, Leeds, Malton and Ripon Circuits. What we have now to watch and discern the meaning of is the establishment of strategic centres in the wide county of York, and the organised endeavour to occupy for the Connexion a tract of country which now forms a considerable part of the Leeds and York, and Bradford and Halifax districts.

York.

The continuous and commanding part the ancient city of York has played in the civil and ecclesiastical history of England has very largely been the outcome of its unique geographical position. Lying as it does at the entrance to the vale of York, the city has held the key to the Great North road along which armies and travellers and merchants and merchandise were bound to pass. It is no accident that the mediæval city has renewed its youth as a great railway centre. York has always had to be reckoned with, and even Primitive Methodist missionaries had very early to reckon with it. They could not have given it the go-by without making both a physical and moral detour which would have meant bad strategy and personal dishonour. To evangelise Yorkshire and omit York would indeed have been to play Hamlet, and to leave Hamlet himself out. Hence, within six months of Clowes' entry into Hull, we find him confronted with the task of entering York. As though he himself were fully aware of the significance of the event, he not only gives its exact date, but a graphic description of his feelings at the time, and of the circumstances of his entry which were not without a certain dignity and picturesqueness. The account must be given in Clowes' own words; nor will the reader fail to notice his feeling of the inevitability of the duty that lay before him as evidenced by the narrative. As Christ "must needs go through

THE PERIOD OF CIRCUIT PREDOMINANCE AND ENTERPRISE.   53

Samaria," so Clowes felt there was a needs-be that he must deliver his testimony in York.

"Being now in the immediate neighbourhood of the city of York, I formed a resolution, in the name of the Lord God of Israel, to lift up my banner in that far-famed city of churches. Accordingly, I sent a notice to the city crier to announce to the citizens of York that a 'Ranter' preacher would preach on the Pavement. But the crier sent me word that he durst not give public notice of my purpose, unless I first obtained sanction of the Lord Mayor. Here I soon found I was in a measure locked in a difficulty. It occurred to me that if I waited upon his lordship to solicit permission, he would very probably refuse me liberty; and

OLD PAVEMENT, YORK, FROM AN OLD PAINTING IN THE POSSESSION OF W. CAMIDGE, ESQ.

were I to attempt preaching after a denial, very likely he would order me to prison; and then if I should pass by the city without bearing my testimony in it, my conscience would remonstrate, and my duty to God and my fellow-creatures would be undischarged; consequently, I determined to proceed and preach the gospel in the streets of the city, in conformity with the instructions which I had received from Jesus Christ, without asking permission of any one.

"Accordingly, on Monday, May 24th, 1819, at seven o'clock in the evening, I stood up on the Pavement in the Market-place, in the name of the Lord who had so often supported me in similar enterprises. I commenced the service by singing the fourteenth hymn in the small hymn-book:—

"Come, oh come, thou vilest sinner," &c.

In a short time the people drew up in considerable numbers, and the shop-doors and other places were crowded. All was very quiet until I had sung and prayed, when a man in the congregation became rather uproarious; but I got my eye upon him, and he was checked. When I had proceeded about half-way through my discourse, a troop of horse came riding up, and surrounded the congregation and the preacher. The devil immediately suggested to me that the Lord Mayor had sent the soldiers to take me, under the idea that I was a radical speaker, inciting the people to rebellion; but I rallied after this shot from the enemy's camp, and went on exhorting sinners to flee from the wrath to come. I accordingly concluded my sermon without molestation; the soldiers and people retiring in proper order. Some asked me who I was, and what I was; I told them my name was William Clowes, and that in principle I was a Methodist, and that I would preach there again the next fortnight. Accordingly, I took up my staff and travelled seven miles to sleep that evening accompanied by a few friends."

W. Clowes' promised second visit to York was not paid in a fortnight as announced; nor it would seem until some six weeks after. But before the summer was over, not only Clowes, but his colleagues, Sarah Harrison and her husband at separate times preached in the Thursday Market (St. Sampson's Square), this spot being probably chosen as better adapted for the purpose than the Pavement. Each of these services had features in common. Behind the missionary, on each occasion, we can discern the now somewhat shadowy figures of village friends and abettors especially belonging to Elvington, some seven miles distant. Here lived the brothers Bond, well-to-do farmers, whose names frequently occur in the early journals as extending hospitality to God's servants and in other ways helping to establish our cause in these parts, and notably in York. Elvington was in a sense the base for the mission to York. Clowes took his staff and travelled on to Elvington to sleep after his first visit to the city. It was while at Elvington the friends urged Sarah Harrison to enter York. The villagers by the Ouse and Derwent were proud of their county-capital, as well they might be. They were ambitious that *their* missionaries and *their* chief city should be on good terms with each other. To them York with its twenty thousand inhabitants was the big city. With its churches and minster, its Lord Mayor and soldiery and Judges of Assize, it stood for all that was distinguished and impressive. If only W. Clowes and Sarah and John Harrison would go up in the name of the Lord and take York, who could tell what great things might follow? So not only did the missionaries go, but the villagers went with them for company and support—only they went with diverse feelings. For it is very noticeable how in each case these leading missionaries of Hull Circuit went to York with a weight of anxiety resting upon them that could not be concealed, and that it was difficult to account for. It seemed as though the dread of the city rested upon them. So it was with Sarah Harrison who was the next to go. At first the cross appeared too heavy for her to take up. She was however encouraged by a promise from several to accompany her, and she accordingly went. When she was entering the North Gate and having a first view of the city her courage was shaken, and for some time she felt as if she could not preach. So it was with Clowes: "On my way [from Elvington to York] my spirit became greatly exercised; heavy trouble pressed upon me; I had an impression of fear and uneasy apprehension

THE PERIOD OF CIRCUIT PREDOMINANCE AND ENTERPRISE.   55

respecting my mission to the city. However, as I proceeded, I recollected I had counted the cost, and however I might be called to suffer, truth would win its way and God would be glorified." John Harrison's experience was almost identical with the experience of his colleagues who had preceded him. "Tuesday, July 6th, I and my friend left for York. We entered the city, but the thought of having to preach was to me a great trial: I trembled with a great trembling." These reminders that our pioneers were after all men and women of like passions with ourselves, and had their seasons when duty which they would not flee from looked formidable, are not to be disregarded, for, despite the tremors of the flesh, God was with them and enabled them to deliver their testimony in Thursday Market with power and success.

ST. SAMPSON'S SQUARE, YORK, THEN CALLED THURSDAY MARKET, WHERE THREE OPEN-AIR SERVICES WERE HELD.

Sarah Kirkland preached to an immense crowd at the corner of the Thursday Market from a butcher's block, obligingly placed at her disposal by its owner who was a Methodist. As for Clowes, thousands gathered round him as he preached, but though some had said "they would be taken up," to his surprise "not a tongue of disapprobation was lifted up, all was quiet, and all heard the truth of God proclaimed with the deepest attention." John Harrison too had a large congregation and the people "gave evidence of their approval of the truth by their tears."

As the result of these memorable visits of the pioneers, a society of seven members was formed, and with the help of the friends at Elvington a room was secured in a building near St. Anthony's Hall (Blue Coat School), Peaseholme Green, for the holding of services. The society's occupancy of this room was but a brief one, lasting only a few months. Not only had the room little to offer in the way of comfort or cheerfulness, but as the society grew its inadequacy became more and more apparent. Looking round for more eligible quarters, attention was turned to an unoccupied chapel in Grape Lane, originally built for the Rev. William Wren who had seceded from Lady Huntingdon's Connexion in 1781. After his death, three years after, it had been hired by the Congregationalists, and then in turn occupied by the New Connexion, the Wesleyan Methodists, the Particular Baptists, and Unitarian Baptists; * so that in the thirty-nine years of its existence as a building it had changed hands and denominations no less than half-a-dozen times. Many old Nonconformist meeting-houses have had

GRAPE LANE CHAPEL. THE FIRST PRIMITIVE METHODIST CHAPEL IN YORK.

a strange, eventful history, but one thinks it would be hard to find one with a more chequered record than Grape Lane. Something of the outward appearance of the building, which for thirty-one years served as our denominational centre in the city of York, may be gathered from our picture. However defective it might be according to our modern standards of beauty and convenience, Grape Lane was a decided advance on Peaseholme Green, and so the building was secured, G. and A. Bond of Elvington,

* I am indebted for these facts to " Primitive Methodism. Its Introduction and Development in the city of York," by Wm. Camidge, F.R.H.S. The monograph is a model of what such works should be.

S. Smith tells us, becoming surety for the rent. It was opened on July 2nd, 1820, by John Verity, John Woolhouse—both of whom had just been taken out as preachers by the Hull Circuit—and by W. Clowes, who preached in the evening. The opening services coincided in time with the formation of York as one of the branches of Hull Circuit.

From the manuscript journals of Sampson Turner now before us we find George Herod, Sampson Turner and Nathaniel West labouring together at the beginning of 1822 in the York branch, which became a Circuit in March of the same year. As this is the first time N. West's name comes before us, and we shall hear much of him until 1827, a few words respecting this remarkable man will be in place. He was an Irishman, and when we first see him in 1819, he wears the King's uniform and is known as Corporal West of the King's Bays. He was a man every inch of him; of splendid physique, more than six feet in height, and with good natural parts sharpened by discipline. Altogether he was a man to impress and look at admiringly. When his regiment was stationed at Nottingham he was drawn to the room in the Broad Marsh and got soundly converted. He soon began to preach, and became very popular. In Leeds, to which town the King's Bays shortly removed, Corporal West attracted great crowds by his preaching. While at Leeds he talked so much of the Primitives—of their zeal, their methods, their success, that the desire was awakened in many to see and hear this wonderful people for themselves. A pious young woman, a Methodist, fell in love with the handsome soldier and offered to find the whole or greater part of the money to purchase his discharge from the army. The offer was accepted, and N. West showed his gratitude by marrying his benefactress. But before this the King's Bays had removed to York, and Corporal West may have been one of the troopers who encircled William Clowes when he preached on the Pavement on May 19th. Before the summer was over he was certainly connected with the York Society, for Sarah Harrison expresses her pleasure at meeting with him on her third visit to the city just after the preaching room had been taken. By May, 1820, ex-corporal West was a travelling preacher and, as we have seen, at the beginning of 1822 we find him one of the York staff. Beyond this point we need not at present follow him.

Grape Lane acquired some notoriety at first from the persistent attention bestowed upon it by a band of miscreants—not of the lowest rank in the social scale—who resorted to all the familiar devices for annoying and intimidating the preacher and his congregation, which we need not stay to specify. Unwilling at first to invoke the law for their own protection, the Society through its officers seems to have approached Lord Dundas, who at that time was the chief city magistrate. To his credit, be it said, the Lord Mayor cast his influence on the right side and personally attended a service at which John Hutchinson was the preacher. No preacher could have wished for a better behaved congregation than John Hutchinson had that night, and it was thought that the action of Lord Dundas would have a wholesome, deterrent effect. But the persecution soon began again, and when George Herod summoned two of the ringleaders at the Christmas Sessions of 1821 for disturbing public worship, he lost his case, and was saddled with the costs, amounting to £16. "Everything appeared clear against them, yet when the trial came on, they somehow or other got brought through, which very much injured our temporal concerns," says N. West. Naturally enough the freemen whom the authorities were reluctant to punish as they deserved, now felt freer to carry on their malpractices. On the eve of holding a great love-feast in York, N. West had to get the tickets of admission printed at a distant town and withhold their distribution until the morning of the love-feast, in order to hinder the would-be disturbers from getting access to the meeting by the presentation of tickets they had themselves got printed. By this precautionary measure " we kept a great mass of unbelief away" says N. West. This love-feast of the 24th February, 1822, was a memorable one. Though Mr. Herod was conducting a second circuit love-feast at Easingwold at the same hour, the country societies sent such large contingents that some eleven hundred persons were present, and the meeting, which was carried on for several hours until Messrs. Turner and West and the other labourers were quite exhausted, resulted in some forty conversions. It was just about this time, as S. Turner tells us, that the rebels broke the vestry window-shutters all to pieces while he was preaching, and three young men were taken up and committed to the Sessions for trial. This time the disturbers were convicted, and the reign of lawlessness was shaken though it did not end until some considerable time after. *

The first plan of the York Circuit, April—July, 1822, shows twenty-two preachers all told, and thirty-two preaching places. Of these, with the exception of York, only Easingwold has, since 1872, become the head of an independent country station. The lines of development to be followed by York as a Circuit were already in 1822 laid down. All round, at no great distance, the ground was occupied or earmarked by branches or circuits belonging to or formed from Hull—Pocklington, Brotherton, Tadcaster, Ripon and Malton. Unless it had attempted distant missions, York Circuit could only do as it has done—strengthen and extend itself within the progressive city and keep firm hold of the adjacent agricultural villages. It could not, like Scotter, Darlaston or Manchester, hope to become the fruitful mother of circuits. At the close of 1824, Tadcaster Branch was attached to York Circuit, and so continued until 1826. Probably, never before, or since, has the Circuit covered so wide an area as it did then, when four preachers were on the ground, two of whom were Thomas Batty and J. Bywater.

One of the makers of York Primitive Methodism was William Rumfitt. When he came to York in 1822, a young man of nineteen, he was already a local preacher. He at once joined the Society in Grape Lane which he found "in a low and feeble condition." This testimony finds incidental confirmation from the contemporary *Journals* of Sampson Turner, the first superintendent

MR. W. RUMFITT.

* "Afterwards I suffered great annoyance. They came into the room—smoked, talked, let sparrows fly to put out the lights, etc. So I went to law and won. For there was another Lord Mayor who was favourable to us. He told them he would imprison every one of them on a repetition of the offence." Notes of a conversation with S. Turner taken down in 1874, with which his *Journal* agrees.

of the York Circuit. It would seem there were difficulties and drawbacks, having their source both within and without the Church, which retarded progress; and now and again the records betray the writer's misgiving that the whilom branch had been granted independence before it was quite ready for it. This ink-faded script in which Sampson Turner confides to us his exercises of soul, is but a sample of the superabundant evidence to hand showing that our earliest societies were peculiarly exposed to the intrusion and governance of men of mixed motives and unsanctified temper. From the very nature of the case the danger was inevitable. Sharp discipline was necessary to purge "out the old leaven;" but to keep it from creeping in again nothing availed more effectually than a few strong, righteous, far-seeing officials, always on the spot—for "the presence of the morally healthy acts as a kind of moral deodorizer." So true is this that those circuits which steadily won their way to an assured position, as York ultimately did, were, we may be sure, blessed with a certain number of these moral deodorizers—natures antipathetic to the old leaven.

REV. J. RUMFITT.

William Rumfitt's period of Church activity spanned the first and intermediate periods of our Connexional history. As we have seen he joined the York Society in 1822, and it was in 1879 that devout men carried him to his burial. He was a local preacher during the whole of that long period, and a class-leader during a considerable portion of it, besides filling other offices. Two nights in each week were devoted by him to the public exercises of religion. In 1857 he was elected a deed-poll member, and so seriously did he take this trust that for twenty-one years in succession he was never absent from his place in Conference. While his house was a kind of "pilgrim's inn" he took care that it should also be a Church in which Bible-reading, praise, prayer, and talk about good things formed the constituents of the domestic atmosphere. It was according to the fitness of things that the children nurtured in such a home should carry on the family tradition; and John and Charles Rumfitt (now LL.D., and a clergyman of the Established Church) both entered the ministry, the former travelling for forty-one years (1852-93) with great acceptance. He first began to preach about 1845 in association with Mr. George Wade who also from 1835 to 1871 was a useful class-leader and prominent official of the York Circuit. John Rumfitt's biographer intimates that at this time—that is in the "Forties"—Grape Lane was at its best, and York Circuit one of the most prosperous and flourishing circuits in the Connexion.

Perhaps the very success of Grape Lane in these closing years of the first period was one chief cause of its undoing and final supersession. Though the Church improved, Grape Lane and its locality did not improve, but rather degenerated as time went on. The approach to the building and its environment were equally objectionable; and its structural shortcomings seriously interfered with comfort and the efficiency of church-work. Many schemes for securing a more eligible centre were

MR. W. CAMIDGE,
F.R.H.S.
The Historian of York Primitive Methodism.

canvassed, but with little practical result until, under the vigorous leadership of Jeremiah Dodsworth, what had been deemed almost too much to hope for was achieved. A family mansion in Little Stonegate was bought for £800, and on the site of the demolished building Ebenezer Chapel was erected and opened in November, 1851, by Jeremiah Dodsworth; two famous divines, Dr. Beaumont and James Parsons, also preaching sermons in connection with the notable event. A new era in York Primitive Methodism began by the dedication to the service of God of Ebenezer, which right through and beyond the middle period of our history was the recognised centre of Primitive Methodism in York. How many old Elmfieldians retain vivid recollections of the march to and from the plain chapel in Little Stonegate hard by the venerable Cathedral! With it, too, are inseparably associated recollections of Sir James Meek, as yet our only Knight and man of title, who it must be confessed wore his honours meekly and discharged his civic and Church duties with true gentlemanliness and modesty. H. J. McCulloch had his title too, being almost invariably known as "Captain," and he was for some years actively associated with Little Stonegate; at one time indeed having charge of the service of praise. It was in 1853 that Alderman James Meek transferred his membership from the Wesleyans and brought his class with him. As a leader, he was conscientious in the discharge of his duties. It was no uncommon thing for him to travel from Scarborough, or wherever he might happen to be at the time, for the express purpose of meeting the members of his class. Though we thus couple Sir James Meek and "Captain" McCulloch in the same paragraph, because Providence made them contemporaries and fellow-citizens and colleagues in church-work, it is none the less true that they were very different men. Propinquity showed them to be a pair of opposites. Not only were they marked off from each other by external differences in appearance, tone, manner, but these differences ran down into still deeper underlying differences. Yet both were identified with Ebenezer and interested in its prosperity, and both, though in contrasted ways, played their part in those wider connexional movements, near the vortex of which York was brought by the founding in 1854 of Elmfield school with its rudimentary ministerial training college, and by the establishment in 1866 of the Primitive Methodist Insurance Company with its managerial office at York. To these we shall return in considering the origin and development of our Church institutions. Meanwhile, let it be noted that the fact of the Conferences of 1853 and 1864 being held at York seems to indicate that by this time York had come to be regarded as one of the leading circuit-towns in our Israel.

Jeremiah Dodsworth, the builder of Ebenezer, deserves more than a passing reference here, and this for various reasons, one such being that from the year 1839 to 1864, during which period his active ministry extended, he laboured in Leeds, Malton, Keighley, Burnley and other Circuits with which we must shortly concern ourselves. Mr. Dodsworth was the most eminent scion of a family which both in its parent stock and its offshoots—in Hull, at Aldershot, and even at the Antipodes, has done much for Primitive Methodism. John Dodsworth, the father, who died in 1860, aged 84, was a fine specimen of patriarchal piety, and the mother was equally distinguished for her feminine graces. Their irreproachable character gave reality and lustre to the village church of Willoughby, five miles from Hull; indeed, it may even be said to have owed to them its very existence and continuance. For their dwelling for many years did double duty as a place of public worship and house of entertainment for the preachers, and when at last the chapel was built, it stood at the corner of John Dodsworth's garden, the site being a deed of gift from his master by whom he was highly esteemed. Something of the old saint's character may be gathered from one of his dying utterances: "I am climbing up Jacob's ladder on my hands and knees, and there is not a spell from bottom to top that *I* have put there. It was built by mercy—all mercy."

It may not be generally known that even before Jeremiah Dodsworth had become a most effective and popular preacher, he had already proved himself a Free Church stalwart and champion of the down-trodden agricultural labourer from which class he sprang. As such he figures somewhat prominently in Cobbett's "Legacy to Parsons," of all books in the world, the reason being, that Jeremiah Dodsworth was one of the last to refuse payment of tithe on labourers' wages—one of the most obnoxious forms of impost soon after swept away by the legislative besom. He was charged a tithe of four shillings and fourpence on his wages by the Rev. Francis Lundy, rector of Lockington, whose living was of the annual value of £532; and on his refusal to pay, two Justices of the Peace, the Rev. J. Blanchard, another pluralist clergyman, and Robert Wylie, sentenced him to pay the four shillings and fourpence and the costs of prosecution. He, still refusing to pay, the same two magistrates issued a warrant of distress against his goods and chattels. But he had no goods and chattels to distrain; so Rev. John Blanchard as magistrate committed him to the House of Correction at Beverley, there

REV. J. DODSWORTH.

to be kept for the space of three calendar months as punishment for not paying his "offerings, oblations and obventions." * This "village Hampden" and hereafter successful chapel-builder and popular preacher has yet stronger claims for remembrance here, as having in his later years become one of the most popular writers our Church had as yet produced. At this epoch, as we know, many very earnest and clever people were making it their special business to popularise the advancing Puseyite theology. This was their mission and they fulfilled it sedulously; and so tales and biographies and histories poured from the press, subtly flavoured with sacramentarian and high-church sentiment. In like manner, Jeremiah Dodsworth, in his own way, sought to popularise the old Evangelical theology. The theology was there in its substance and essence, but, above all his books were readable, written in a pleasing, flowing style, and making strong appeal to the indestructible feelings of men. "The Eden Family," and "The Better Land" especially, like James Grant's kindred book, "Heaven our Home," and our own John Simpson's "The Prodigal Son" were good exemplars of the popularised Evangelical theology and sentiment, and had a vogue far beyond their writers' own churches.

Great an advance as Ebenezer was on Grape Lane, the time came when "Tekel"—"Thou art found wanting"—was seen to be written on its broad front. For many years the impression deepened that after a half century's occupancy, the time had come for this honoured sanctuary to make way for a successor that should worthily mark the attainment of a further stage of Connexional advance. The ampler school and vestry accommodation so sorely needed could then be provided, and the new building might be so located and planned that it would serve as the pro-college chapel and in other respects fittingly

MONKGATE CHURCH, YORK.

---

* "Cobbett's Legacy to Parsons." The facts are also referred to in "Methodism as it should be," 1857, p. 249. Neither of these authorities gives the slightest hint that Mr. Dodsworth did not serve out his sentence. But Rev. H. Woodcock in his "Primitive Methodism in the Yorkshire Wolds" (p. 113) says: "But he was released, and we believe Mr. B. paid him £20." If the clergyman paid the fine and costs it should be put down to his credit. But as yet diligent inquiry has not enabled us to verify this point.

represent the oldest interest of the denomination in the metropolitan city. Accordingly preparations were cautiously made to effect the desired change. In advance, a block of property in Monkgate was bought for £1,000, and the rents of this in time enabled the trustees to redeem the cost of purchase. The debt on Ebenezer was cleared and the building sold for £2,000, and in 1902 the "John Petty Memorial Church" was opened. We give an illustration of this building as well as of Monk Bar contiguous thereto; "Bar" being the local name for the gates by which the walls of York, 2¾ miles in extent, are pierced.

But even this does not complete the story of York's enterprise in chapel-building. Forty years ago a mission was started across the river on the south-west part of the city. The mission prospered, and in 1864 a room was opened in Nunnery Lane to serve as a chapel and Sunday school. "Ultimately," says Mr. Camidge, "the people of the Nunnery Lane Mission Room built Victoria Bar Chapel as it has always been called. It is situate just within the opening in the Bar walls, which opening gives access to and from Bishophill and Nunnery Lane." * The chapel was opened in the spring of 1880, and in 1883 York Circuit was divided, Victoria Bar becoming the head of York Second Circuit.

MONK BAR, YORK.
(Our Chapel just through the Bar.)

LEEDS.

We are fortunate in knowing the exact date when Primitive Methodism was introduced into Leeds, as also the events which led up to it. It was on November 24th, 1819, when Clowes "opened his mission" in the already growing West Riding town "by the direction of the providence of God." In these carefully chosen words Clowes may be supposed to refer to those seemingly detached and fortuitous events he does not stop to detail which, in the hand of Providence, had become a chain to draw him to Leeds, as before he had been drawn to Hull. "By the direction of the providence of God!" so might Peter have spoken of his arrival at the house of Cornelius, or Paul

---

* "Primitive Methodism: Its Introduction and Development in the city of York."

of his first landing in Europe to publish the gospel. Our chief source of information as to these preparatory conditions and happenings accounting for Clowes' entry into Leeds, is a communication addressed to George Herod by the Rev. Samuel Smith, who was one of the most prominent actors in the events he describes. It may be claimed for the facts detailed by S. Smith, that they are not only interesting in themselves as throwing light on the origins of Leeds Primitive Methodism, but that they have a still higher value, as serving to relate Primitive Methodism to that type of religious activity and phenomenon of the time we have called "Revivalism." After all that has been written, we need not once more indicate what is sought to be conveyed by that word, or stay to show again that Revivalism was largely a survival and recrudescence of primitive doctrine and experience, and of old-time methods of evangelisation. It will be enough to remind ourselves that, right along our course thus far, from Mow Cop to the Humber

VICTORIA BAR CHURCH, YORK.

and back again by the Peak to the Mersey, we have seen this fervid aggressive type of religious life manifesting itself, in ways regular or irregular, banned or tolerated. It would be strange indeed were we to miss in Leeds, of all towns in England, what we met with in Nottingham and Hull and Manchester. We think of Leeds as a freedom-loving town. At this particular time it was a stronghold of Nonconformity. Methodism had struck its roots deep in the life of the people. Not many years before, the town and neighbourhood had been set on fire by William Bramwell's ministry of flame. In such a town one would naturally expect to find those whose proclivities lay in the direction of Revivalism to be, not less but rather more numerous than elsewhere, and a knowledge of the ecclesiastical history of Leeds would but justify the expectation. But narrowing our view: it was a band of Revivalists, Primitive Methodists in spirit, though not in name, who were responsible for W. Clowes' coming to Leeds. Through them Providence lifted the beckoning finger and the signal was obeyed.

The Rev. S. Smith tells us that in 1818—the year William Bramwell suddenly expired in Leeds—"he commenced a mission in the low places of Leeds and the vicinity, and in a little time he was joined in it by John Verity and thirteen young men—all zealous to employ their spare time in the work of visiting and preaching to the low, degraded and neglected dwellers in yards, alleys, back streets and cellars. Not one of them, except John Verity, was connected as a preacher with any religious community, but upwards of one hundred persons were through their labours brought to God and joined some religious society." As yet they had not as much as heard of Primitive Methodism as an organised form of aggressive religion; but they were soon

LEEDS IN 1830.

to hear. First of all, during the summer of 1819, Corporal West of "The Bays" was billeted with his troop in the town. He did not hide his light under a bushel. Alike in his preaching to which he zealously gave himself, and in conversation, he spoke of his recent conversion at Nottingham through the instrumentality of the Primitive Methodists, whose preachers he extolled, awakening the desire in many to see and hear them for themselves.[*] Then in the columns of a certain Hull newspaper called the *Rockingham*, there were occasional notices of a strange people who had made their appearance in that town and were carrying all before them. Of course the notices were

[*] See Memoir of Rev. John Hopkinson in the *Magazine* for 1859, p. 386, where however the writer, Rev. H. Gunns, speaks of "a Mr. West, an officer of a regiment of cavalry," evidently with no knowledge that this person was identical with the soon-to-be Rev. Nathaniel West.

both facetious and spiteful. They were described as "wearing brown coats, strong shoes and corduroy small-clothes; as having all things in common, and also that they had eaten up the whole substance of several farmers." These paragraphs were read with interest, for though the notices were coloured and even distorted by the prejudiced media through which they had passed, these Leeds Revivalists were still able to perceive several points of similarity between the "Ranters" and themselves, one being that they were both "spoken against" for trying to do good in unconventional ways; so that what they read only inflamed their desire to know more of the community jibed at by the *Rockingham*. Finally, the rumour went that the "Ranters" had now reached Ferry Bridge, whereupon counsel was taken, and it was arranged to send John Verity and J. Atkinson, "Esq.," of Hunslet, to get to know all they could respecting the people about whom there were such strange reports. The deputation seems to have proceeded to Ferrybridge early in September,* and what success it met with, together with the rest of S. Smith's story, he shall be allowed to tell in his own words :—

"Mr. Atkinson called on Mr. Joseph Bailey, who kept a boarding-school, and with whom he had been partially educated. Messrs. Atkinson and Verity were much surprised to find that Mr. Bailey was a member of this new community. He introduced them to the preacher for the day, the late Samuel Laister, of Market Weighton, who preached in the open air, and published for John Verity to preach in the afternoon; with which appointment the latter complied. While J. V. was engaged in the preaching service, a passenger on the London and Leeds coach—'The Union'—saw him, and, knowing him, reported the circumstances to the Methodist Leaders' Meeting on the Monday following. Action was taken upon it, and John Verity, in his absence, was suspended from his office as a leader, and a Mr. Brooks was appointed to attend his class on the Tuesday evening. When John Verity returned on the Tuesday, I made him acquainted with the doings of the Leaders' Meeting as far as I had heard. His class met in the Wesley Chapel vestry in Meadow Lane. I accompanied him to the meeting where we found Mr. Brooks, who stated his case, and absolutely refused John Verity permission to pray with the people; but he did pray, and Mr. Brooks sang during the time. I begged J. V. to retire, as such doings could be of no service. We retired to his house and talked matters over, and agreed to write to Hull, inviting the 'Ranters' to visit Leeds, and promising we would join them. We that night wrote a joint letter, addressed to 'The Ranter Preacher, Hull.' The contents of the letter were to the effect that, if a preacher were sent to Leeds, we would provide for him board and lodgings for three months in order that he might make a fair trial. The parties agreeing were John Verity, J. Atkinson, Esq., J. Howard, surgeon, and Samuel Smith. To this letter we received an answer in a few days signed 'R. Jackson, Circuit Steward,' saying :—'We will send a preacher as soon as we have one at liberty; in the meantime we advise you to go on, plan your preachers, open new places, and form classes,' etc. They also sent three hundred hymn-books and one hundred rules which had been drawn up at the Nottingham Preparatory Meeting a few weeks before. On the Thursday following I formed a class in Mrs. Taylor's [house], at the top of

---

* S. Smith says about the last Sabbath in August. But as they had previously read in the *Rockingham* of the opening of West Street Chapel, which was not opened until September 10th, it cannot well have been before the 17th September.

Kirkgate, and John Verity formed one at Mrs. Hopkinson's, in Hunslet Lane. We made a plan, and on it we had seven preachers; and we then proceeded to open places, being known only by the name of 'Ranters.' We opened Mrs. Taylor's cellar for preaching, and Mrs. Hopkinson's house—both in Leeds. We entered the villages of Armley, Busten Park, Hughend, Hunslet, Woodhouse-car, and Wortley. In each of these places we formed a class."

So much for the series of occurrences which led to Clowes' first visit to Leeds. S. Smith then goes on to speak of the circumstances of the visit itself. The account he gives is in substantial agreement with that Clowes himself gives twice over in his *Journal*, although, when the two accounts are compared, we recognise differences in detail, reminding us in an interesting way that our knowledge of the simplest event of history is, after all, only relative and approximate; that no two persons will quite independently write of what they once saw and took part in without their narratives exhibiting variations. What seems clear when we compare and harmonise the two versions is, that Clowes was accompanied to Leeds by Mr. John Bailey, the schoolmaster of Ferrybridge, and that, indirectly at least, through him, the Thursday evening service was held in the schoolroom in Kirkgate belonging to Mr. Bean. Clowes remarks that as some of the people left this service, they were heard to say that what they had been listening to was "the right kind of stuff." Next day Clowes went on to Dewsbury and preached there for the first time in the house of Mr. J. Boothroyd. For the Sunday services Messrs. Smith and Verity secured a large room in the third story of Sampson's waggon warehouse, in Longbaulk Lane, used by a dancing master on the week day; and Clowes also employed the bellman to go round the town announcing that "A Ranter's preacher from Hull would preach in Sampson's warehouse, on Sunday morning, at ten o'clock." When Sunday came, the first service ended without any special incident, but in the afternoon, while a Mr. Hirst was conducting the service, an interruption occurred. The redoubtable Sampson himself, whom Clowes graphically describes as bent on opposition and full of subtlety, came to the top of the stairs and cried that the building was falling, and a stampede began, which was only stopped by Clowes striking up the hymn: "Come, oh come, thou vilest sinner." After an exhortation by Mr. Bailey, it was given out that another service would be held in the evening, and the congregation dispersed; but when the hour for evening service came, it was found that Sampson had hung a padlock on the warehouse door, and they were fain to hold their service in Mrs. Taylor's cellar instead of in "the upper room." Clowes admits that Sampson and his padlock had for the moment nonplussed him; but he thankfully records that, as usual, the devil had outwitted himself, for a man came late to the warehouse, expecting a service, and, finding the "door was shut," was led to reflect that so also it might be at last when he came up to heaven's gate if he did not there and then repent, which, happily, he did. S. Smith records that during this visit Clowes met the members—fifty-seven in number, in Mrs. Hopkinson's house, and incorporated them with the Primitive Methodist Connexion.

W. Clowes always claimed to have been Hull Circuit's leading missionary to Leeds and its neighbouring towns and villages—and with good reason. It is evident from his published *Journal*, as well as from private documents in his hand in our possession, that the experiences he met with during these pioneer visits made a deep impression on his mind and were often recalled. He knew what it was to endure privation and suffer inconvenience. At first accommodation was poor and not always available, except when paid for, and it behoved him to be careful in spending the circuit's money, in view of possible embarrassments. Hence, he was sometimes in straits and had to lodge where he could—occasionally in rather strange places. But a change for the better soon took place, and we find him thankfully recording: "I now had my home with Mr. Smith at the top of Kirkgate, whose family offered to shelter me at all times of my need. I cannot help reflecting on the change that I have experienced in these circumstances. When I first came to Leeds I lodged in public-houses, and went supperless to bed."

Still, Mr. Clowes' visits to these parts, though pretty frequent, were only flying ones, and, unless there had been some reliable men on the ground, a permanent interest could scarcely have been built up. But there were such reliable men who, as personal factors in the upbuilding of Primitive Methodism in Leeds and around, demand recognition. Messrs. Verity and S. Smith almost immediately entered the ministry, but their places were taken and their work carried on by others. Two of these also became travelling preachers—John Hopkinson and John Bywater—but not until they had rendered effective service locally, while John Reynard remained on the ground until his death in 1854, and was a tower of strength to the societies.

REV. JOHN HOPKINSON.

John Hopkinson, born at Ardsley near Wakefield, in 1801, was the son of the Mrs. Hopkinson in whose house W. Clowes enrolled the members of the first class. He received his first spiritual good amongst the Wesleyans, but when John Verity was expelled for complicity with "Ranterism," he joined the new community. His reasons for doing so, as stated by himself, are worth giving. They were:—(1) His strong attachment to J. Verity, who was his guide, philosopher, and friend. (2) The simple, pointed style of their preaching was congenial to his taste. (3) Their open-air movements he cordially approved. (4) Their field of action found employment for talents of the humblest order. So, under the stress of these views and considerations, he became a Primitive Methodist. He undertook the leadership of the society at Dudley Hill, though it was eleven miles from his residence. In 1820 he began to preach, and three years after he entered the ministry, and for thirty-five years he continued in active service. In summing up his character and work his biographer has stated: "He was an exemplary Christian and a laborious minister. . . . He was connected with the admission of 3700 members into society; his prayers were pointed; his sermons well arranged and powerful; he travelled on twenty-five stations. He faithfully served God and his generation, and his end was peace."*

REV. JOHN BYWATER.

* Memoir in the *Magazine* for 1859, p. 391.

John Bywater is a name that calls for rehabilitation. He has received but scant recognition and fallen into undeserved neglect. Until the late Dr. Joseph Wood chivalrously vindicated his name,* little remained to show the kind of man he was, and how worthy to be remembered by the denomination he served so well. True: there is the official memoir in the Conference *Minutes* of 1870, but there is little else; and that memoir is so short that it can be given here in its entirety without making undue demands on our space. Says the official penman:—

"John Bywater was a native of the town of Leeds, Yorkshire. In his youth he was converted to God and united with the Primitive Methodists. He commenced his itinerant ministry at the Conference of 1825, and subsequently laboured in and superintended some of the most important circuits in the Connexion. For five years he was General Missionary Secretary. He was superannuated by the Conference of 1860, and died at Cote Houses in the Scotter Circuit, October 12th, 1869, aged 65 years."

Between the facts here stated and the shortness of the notice there is a striking disparity. We need not go into the reasons for this studied brevity and speedy relapse into silence. The reasons—if reasons there were, hold good no longer, and it is time we saw the man in his true perspective and proportions. If he did through inexperience and shattered health fail comparatively as a farmer, on his enforced and somewhat early retirement, he had not failed as a chapel-builder, as an administrator, as a preacher, as a friend, as a Christian minister. Thus much is due to his name. In Leeds, young Bywater was true and loyal. During the early troubles which overtook the society, we are told that John Hopkinson and John Bywater were true comrades and yoke-fellows; "they stood firm for Connexional rule, and almost laboured themselves into the grave to save the cause from wreck; and success crowned their efforts."

The allusion here made to the storm-cloud which burst over Leeds Primitive Methodism in the early days, calls for a little fuller reference before we go on to glance at one or two other workers. "Revivalism," as we have defined it, did Primitive Methodism some good; it also did it some harm. So Leeds, like other places, found to its cost. Revivalism helped to found the Leeds Society, and it all but succeeded in shattering it. We have, in writing of Hull, referred to the group of preaching and praying women—notably Ann Carr, Miss Williams, and Miss Healand—who carried on evangelistic labours in Lincolnshire and the East Riding of Yorkshire. There is evidence to show that the Misses Carr and Williams were counted as Primitive Methodists, and not merely accepted as unattached auxiliaries. At the March, 1820, Quarter Day of the Hull Circuit, a letter was sent to Miss Carr asking if she were willing to enter the ministry. Ann Carr was born at Market Rasen in 1738, and died June 18th, 1841. In Leeds she and her friend Williams laboured hard and formed many friendships. There was a good deal of the masculine in Ann Carr's composition, and neither she nor her colleague took very kindly to the yoke imposed by a regularly organised Connexion. They preferred to hold a roving commission and to take an erratic course, letting fancy

* "Recollections of John Bywater and Early Chapel-building in the town of Hull by J. Wood, D.D." *Aldersgate Magazine*, 1898.

or circumstances determine their direction and procedure. It is intimated by Mr. George Allen that they had no predilection for the plan, but were quite willing on invitation to take the pulpits of those who *were* planned, and that misunderstandings and collisions were the natural result. Being called to account for irregular movements associated with officiousness, they took offence and, parading their grievances, made a division. A chapel was ultimately built by the separatists in Leyland, which became known as Ann Carr's Chapel. This interest was sustained with varying success for a long period. At length signs of physical and mental failure began to show themselves in the once vigorous woman, and a short time before her death Ann Carr went back to her first love and reunited with the Wesleyans, who purchased her chapel. A "Life" of her was published, peculiar in this that it is almost silent as to her former connection with our Church. Any one unacquainted with her career would never suspect on reading the book that she was at one time so prominent a Primitive Methodist. The memoirs in God's book are written with greater impartiality.

When the clouds rolled by, John Reynard was found at his post. Born in 1800, Mr. Reynard was converted through hearing Gideon Ousley (the famous Irish evangelist), on one of his visits to Leeds. He united with the Wesleyans and remained with them until 1820, when he was invited by S. Smith (whose sister he married) to attend the preaching service then held in a house in Hill-house Bank.

"He acceded to the invitation and was edified and blessed; so much so that he said to his friend: 'I shall walk into the country this afternoon, and if the society be as lively there as it is in Leeds I shall join you.' The two walked to Armley for the afternoon service. Mr. J. Flockton preached, and the same Divine influence attended the Word as had been felt during the morning service in Leeds. Mr. Reynard, therefore, decided to cast in his lot with our people, and on May 16th, 1820, he joined Mr. J. Dutton's class. When Mr. Dutton was taken out to travel he was appointed to take charge of the class, and continued its leader for many years."—Memoir in *Magazine*, 1855, pp. 193-4.

MR. JOHN REYNARD, OF LEEDS.

The estimate of Mr. Reynard's character, as given by Mr. Petty in his "History," needs no revision. It is just and discriminating, and hence worthy to be handed down as a carefully written judgment based on personal knowledge.

"Mr. Reynard, says Mr. Petty, soon became a useful and distinguished member. Possessing promising talents, he was speedily called to exercise his gifts in public speaking, in which he proved to be more than ordinarily acceptable and useful. He had a sound judgment, clear views of evangelical truth, a retentive memory, a ready command of language, a distinct utterance, and considerable power over an audience. His pulpit and platform efforts were highly estimated everywhere, and were frequently in requisition, both in his own circuit, and in numerous other stations. For thirty-four years he devoted his energies to the work of a local preacher, and reaped a large measure of success. He was an enlightened and ardent friend of the community

THE PERIOD OF CIRCUIT PREDOMINANCE AND ENTERPRISE. 71

of which he was an ornament, and took a large share in its most important transactions. He was not only a leading man in his own circuit, where his influence was great, and beneficially exerted; but was likewise raised to the highest offices of trust and responsibility which the Connexion could confer upon a layman, being constituted a permanent member of Conference, which he regularly attended, and at which he rendered valuable service. He pursued a sound course in matters of Church business, and studied to promote the best interests of the Connexion. For some time previous to his death, it was evident to his friends that he was ripening for the garner of God. He became increasingly dead to the world, and more spiritual and heavenly in his temper and disposition. His removal to the celestial country was affectingly sudden. On Sunday, December 17th, 1854, he attended his preaching appointment at Kippax, near Leeds, and while engaged in prayer in the congregation, his voice began to fail, and the last words he was heard to utter, were, 'Lord Jesus, bless me! O God! come to my help!' A paralytic stroke deprived him of speech, and of the use of his right side. He lingered until the Wednesday following, when he expired without a lingering groan, aged fifty-four years. On December 24th, 1854, 'devout men carried him to his burial in Woodhouse Cemetery, and made great lamentation over him.' He died comparatively young; but he had been permitted to perform a large share of useful service in the Church of Christ, and to the glory of his Saviour's name."

MRS. BROGDEN.

It is pleasing to know that fifty years after Mr. Reynard's death the family has still its representatives in Leeds Primitive Methodism. We give the portrait of his amiable daughter, the late Mrs. Brogden, whose husband, Mr. Alexander Brogden, was an earnest worker in our Church, and for many years superintendent of Quarry Hill Sunday school; while Mrs. Brogden herself (*obiit* December, 1902) was for ten years a class-leader, and also a successful Sabbath school teacher at Quarry Hill and Belle Vue.

If John Reynard was the Primitive Methodist bookbinder, John Parrot was perhaps for a considerable time its best-known printer. His imprint is to be found on "The Primitive Pulpit" and many other books and pamphlets printed in the 'Fifties and 'Sixties. A native of Hull and connected with Mill Street Society he removed to Halifax in 1835, where he became a local preacher. Two years after he settled in Leeds, where he lived and worked until his death in 1871. He was a hard worker, and what was less common in those days—a lover of fun and frolic. He filled and fulfilled many offices, but probably the best and most lasting work he did was his Bible-teaching. There are those occupying important positions in the Church to-day who will be ready to express their obligations to the genial printer.

JOHN PARROTT.

In 1820 Leeds was made a branch of Hull Circuit, and it is an interesting coincidence that Samuel Laister, the first Primitive preacher the deputation heard on their visit to Ferrybridge, was one of the first preachers of the Leeds Branch. Samuel Laister was a native of historic Epworth, and was of Methodist parentage. In the *Methodist Magazine* for 1784 there is given a remarkable dream of the Last Judgment dreamed by the father of Samuel, to which his conversion and that of his four brothers was directly attributable. He removed to Market Weighton and became a Primitive Methodist local preacher, and in September, 1820, went out to travel. We shall soon meet with him again at Malton, and especially at Darlington, where he finished his course. From a branch Leeds became a circuit in 1822, having no fewer than ten preachers down for it on the stations, of whom John Coulson is the first. The same year Quarry Hill chapel was built, which through many changes still survives as one of the historic chapels of Primitive Methodism. This year was also notable for the action taken by the December Quarterly Meeting in sending two missionaries to London, of which we shall have to speak more fully in another connection. In 1823 the fourth Conference was held at Leeds. Apart from the action taken in regard to the new hymn book,* perhaps the most noteworthy transaction of this Conference related to the establishment of a Preachers' Friendly Society. It was ordered that one preacher from each circuit should attend a meeting at Hull, on August 24th, for the purpose of making the needful arrangements, but with the fettering proviso that "the preachers shall not be allowed to beg for the establishing of the fund." We are not surprised to learn that this restriction, felt to be so galling, was removed the very next year. Though the religious services in connection with the first Leeds Conference are said to have been powerful and fruitful, and the hospitality of the Leeds friends exceedingly hearty, yet, we are told by W. Clowes, there were several matters of a trying nature to occupy the attention of the delegates. As a whole, considerable progress had been made during the year, but some of the circuits had become embarrassed, and the Connexion was entering within the penumbra of its temporary eclipse. The Conference over, Hugh Bourne thought it his duty to write an admonitory letter to the preachers,† at the same time asking them to contribute towards the relief of the embarrassed circuits. The appeal met with little response—four pounds, which included one pound given by himself, being the net result. This moved him further to address "A Private Communication," reflecting strongly upon certain "runners-out of circuits," and pointedly calling attention to particular cases of irregularity. The drastic character of this "private communication" naturally created heart-burnings, and ensured warm discussions at the annual meeting at Halifax. Of the second Leeds Conference—that of 1818—of which Thomas King was the President, and Emerson Muschamp, of Weardale, the Secretary, little need be said, as it does not appear to have been concerned in any weighty matters.

Let some of the administrative changes through which the original Leeds Circuit has passed be briefly chronicled. First, Bradford (to be hereafter referred to) was made a Circuit in 1823, then Otley was taken from Leeds, and for two years (1824-5) ranked as an independent circuit. Dewsbury also stood on the Conference Minutes— 1824-8—as a circuit in its own right. Afterwards both Otley and Dewsbury reverted

* See *ante.*, vol. ii., p. 10.

† "A number of our Yorkshire circuits, with one in Derbyshire, and some of the Lancashire circuits, are considerably embarrassed; and some of them are grievously embarrassed."—H. Bourne's Letter to the Preachers, June 6th, 1823.

THE PERIOD OF CIRCUIT PREDOMINANCE AND ENTERPRISE.   73

LEEDS CHAPELS

- HAREHILLS AVENUE
- BEESTON HILL
- REHOBOTH
- JOSEPH ST
- MORIAH
- SOUTHFIELD
- CARDIGAN RD
- BELLE VUE

to Leeds. Then, in 1840, Otley again acquired independence. In 1849, when that capable minister, Richard Davies, was the superintendent, Leeds was still one circuit, though a powerful one with 1162 members. It comprised the Home Branch and the South Leeds and Dewsbury Branches. In 1850 South Leeds became a separate station, and three years later was called Leeds Second. Dewsbury remained a branch until 1857, when it was granted autonomy. In 1862 the West Branch of Leeds First became Leeds Third or Rehoboth. These dry, though necessary, details are of some significance as showing how modern and even quite recent has been the development of Leeds Primitive Methodism with its existing eight circuits. Statistics not just herein place would confirm the impression that the story of this development—of which on its material side some idea may be gained from our page illustration of Leeds chapels—belongs to the later period of our history.

MR. GEORGE ALLEN.

Information respecting the history of Primitive Methodism during the first period is regrettably scanty. We are, therefore, all the more beholden to Mr. George Allen for his published jottings on our history in Leeds.* Mr. Allen became a scholar in the Sunday school, then conducted in Shannon Street, as early as 1823, and afterwards an active and useful official of the Leeds First Circuit. To him we are indebted for a few facts relating to the genesis of the Leeds Second and Third Circuits which shall be given in his own words:—

"A Mr. William Armitage, who lived in Wheeler Street, Bank, Leeds, about 1833, removed to Park Lane, and carried his religious influence with him. A prayer-meeting was held at Mrs. Blakey's, Hanover Square, afterwards. On Sunday nights a preaching service was held at Mr. Tyas', in Chatham Street, and in a short time a class meeting was held on Monday afternoons at Mr. Tyas'. Thus the work spread until they took a room in Park Lane, which had been a joiner's shop. Then Rehoboth chapel and the houses connected with it were built (1839), the Lord being their helper. But before this, preaching services had been commenced in a yard in Meadow Lane. After that they built a chapel in a yard because, I suppose, they could get the land there at a cheap rate. . . . The chapel at Holbeck was parted with in about 1836 and Prince's Field Chapel built, which is now in Leeds Second Circuit; Park Lane (Rehoboth) being in the Third."

The facts here given may usefully serve as *points de repère*, but we want something more. Fortunately we get some side-lights illuminating the facts here barely given from the lives of Thomas Batty and Atkinson Smith, who were the ministers of Leeds Circuit from 1831 to 1833. In these two years they made full proof of their ministry, with the result that there was an increase of three hundred to the membership of the Church. We have already indicated what were the outstanding features of Atkinson Smith's character and ministry. These were never more conspicuously in evidence than during his two years' term in Leeds. His biographer, who travelled in the Leeds Circuit in 1842 and took his bride, Sarah Bickerstaffe, to the preacher's house at

* "A History of Primitive Methodism in Leeds (1819-1888)," by George Allen.

Quarry Hill, adduces the testimony of a Leeds class-leader to the influence of Atkinson Smith's prayers and labours. When we know that the class-leader in question was John Reynard, and that it was in his house the young preacher resided, the testimony is weighty indeed.

"'Leeds Circuit,' says Mr. Reynard, 'owes its rise in a great measure to the prayers of Atkinson Smith.' And then, pointing to his chamber floor, he observed: 'I have known him be on these boards for four hours together, agonising in prayer.' I [C. Kendall] found many who owned him as their father in Christ. . . Among many others to whom his labours were made a blessing was Mr. Thomas Ratcliffe, who became a well-known minister of our Church."

In 1832 Leeds suffered severely from the visitation of the cholera. As in Manchester, so here, during the ravages of this fell disease, special attention was given to open-air services. '"The preachers were set at liberty from their week-night appointments that they might concentrate their efforts on the living masses of the town." Atkinson Smith did not shrink from visiting the cholera hospital to "rescue the perishing and care for the dying."

Here is an extract from A. Smith's *Journal* relating to Bramley, now Leeds Fifth Circuit, with which we close, for the present, our notice of Leeds.

"*September 13th, 1831.*—I went to Bramley, a place containing five or six thousand inhabitants. We have only ten members, and seldom more than twenty hearers. I resolved to re-mission the place; Wm. Pickard joined me. We took a lantern, went to the bottom of the village, and began to sing 'We are bound for the Kingdom,' &c. Three hundred people accompanied us to the chapel. I preached to them, but not with my usual liberty; yet the revival began that night, and in a short time forty or fifty persons found the Lord.' 'To this day,' adds the biographer, writing in 1854, 'the people of Bramley speak of Smith's seeking a revival with a lantern and candle.'"

CHAPTER XV.

THE YORKSHIRE MISSIONS AND MALTON AND RIPON CIRCUITS.

"WHEN I look at the work in Yorkshire, it is amazing! Many chapels are built, and the land generally spread with living Churches, and hundreds of souls brought to God." So Clowes wrote in March, 1821, and the purpose of this chapter is, if possible, to convey the impression that the wonder expressed by Clowes concerning "the work in Yorkshire" was natural and justified by current events and by what resulted from them: in other words, it is to be attempted to show that the wide and rapid extension of Primitive Methodism through the agency of Clowes and his fellow-workers of the Hull Circuit in 1820-1 is, so far as this side of our island is concerned, the outstanding fact to be noted and made to yield its impression.

Rigid adherence to the chronological order of circuit formation would, for once, fail to do justice to the facts of our history and gain from them the right impression. York, Leeds, Malton, Ripon were the only circuits in this part of Yorkshire made in 1822; yet, by that time, all the country lying between these towns was overrun and as it were pre-empted for the Connexion. Tadcaster, Driffield, Scarborough, Bridlington, might not permanently become Circuits till long after, probably because they were comparatively close to Hull and under its fostering care and guardianship; none the less, these and other Yorkshire towns, with the villages they served, were once for all won for the Connexion by the movement of 1821-2. Primitive Methodism paid no transient visit, but entered to stay. It was only when Yorkshire had been thus traversed and practically secured, that the North was almost simultaneously reached by two distinct lines of advance—the one *via* Brompton and Guisboro', the other *via* Ripon and Darlington. We propose then in this chapter to show how this base was secured, and in doing so, the most natural course will be to begin with Tadcaster—whose borders marched with those of Leeds on one side and with those of York and Brotherton on the other—and then to follow the geographical spread of the movement which swept Yorkshire in what Clowes, who was in the midst of it, thought an amazing manner. This method is all the more necessary as, even after June, 1820, when branches were formed, their boundaries were often crossed. What with frequent interchanges and sallies and excursions it is difficult to locate the preachers. They are now here, now there, pursuing the work of evangelisation. Practically the East and North Ridings were during this period one big Circuit.

TADCASTER.

We begin then with the ancient and interesting town of Tadcaster, lying on the direct road between Leeds and York, from which towns it is fourteen and nineteen miles distant respectively. It is also on the Great North Road and, with its ancient bridge crossing the Wharfe, it was as the postern-gate to the city of York. Its position accounts for the fact that the two most decisive and bloody battles recorded in English history—Towton and Marston Moor, were fought within a few miles of the town, while, in 1642, Sir Thomas Fairfax and the Earl of Newcastle contended in the streets of Tadcaster itself for the possession of the all-important bridge.

Primitive Methodism was introduced into Tadcaster as early as June 1820 by Nathaniel West who, like John Flesher, began his ministry here. So successful was N. West's Tadcaster mission that, by September, he could report that one hundred and thirty-nine members had been enrolled in the town and neighbouring villages which were

OLD TADCASTER CENTRE.
Clowes held Open-air Services here in 1825.

TADCASTER—APPLEGARTH.
Scene of First Camp Meeting, and where Camp Meetings were held for fifty years, in field behind trees on the left of picture, and right on the banks of the river Wharfe.

assiduously visited. His three months' labour resulted also in the acquisition of a chapel, by which we are probably to understand the renting and fitting up of the room in Wighill Lane, shown in our picture. Tradition says that this had formerly been used by a sweep, and that at this early stage of the society's progress three soldiers, whose duty it was to serve as escort to the post from York to Wetherby, rendered good service. Before leaving Tadcaster for the Malton Branch, N. West took part in the opening services along with J. Farrar and Mrs. H. Woolhouse, of Hull, and her travelling-preacher son. After being in use for two years, the first chapel was built in Rosemary Row. This building, we are told, ultimately fell into the hands of the Roman Catholics who, in order to erase the words "Primitive Methodist Chapel," had a cross cut in the stone-work between the windows. If the old chapel was thus perverted, the "Applegarth," the old camp meeting site, picturesquely situated by the river Wharfe, where for fifty years camp meetings were wont to be held, was interdicted to the society. Here, in 1825, W. Clowes took part in a famous camp meeting. But Tadcaster is a brewery town, and, on the field being let to a brewer, its owner stipulated that no more camp meetings should be held therein. The present chapel, it may be mentioned, was built in 1865, at a total cost, with schoolroom, of £1008.

We cannot linger on Tadcaster. It is now a small and, numerically, feeble station; but its history shows that, relatively, it was formerly of much greater importance than it is to-day. The town has held, and more than held, its own. Some places have been given to Selby Circuit; but there has been shrinkage in relation to the village interests, which old journals and documents show were once numerous and comparatively vigorous. The towns and large urban centres had not begun, like the fabled Minotaur, to deplete and devour the village populations. It may be worth while to indicate in a separate paragraph (which the reader can skip if he choose) the vicissitudes through which the Tadcaster Circuit has passed. The record may be regarded as typical of many that might be given, and as not being without historical value as suggesting the difficulties which the retention of our village circuits has involved.

TADCASTER FIRST MISSION ROOM WIGHILL LANE.

TADCASTER FIRST CHAPEL.
End building, Rosemary Row.

The Tadcaster mission of Hull Circuit, opened by Nathaniel West, June, 1820, became a branch of Hull Circuit in September of the same year, and so continued until the close of 1824, when it was attached to York Circuit. In 1826 it was constituted part of the "Tadcaster and Ferrybridge Circuit." It stood on the Minutes as an independent station from 1827 to 1837, in which latter year it had

214 members. Henceforward, until 1850, it was once more a branch of Hull. It assumed circuit rank again in 1851-2. From 1853 to 1863, inclusive, it was a branch of Scarborough. Lastly, in 1864 it was again made a circuit, and as such has continued.

During its long and somewhat chequered history, Tadcaster has had a succession of staunch adherents who have stood by the cause in sunshine and shade. We find the name of John Swinden figuring in documents of the early 'Thirties. He and his wife Elizabeth were converts of W. Clowes in 1825, and ever since 1835 there have been two of this name on the plan. The Rev. John Swinden, a scion of this family, is one of the goodly number Tadcaster Circuit has sent into the ranks of the regular ministry. Of these the Rev. Wilson Eccles is another modern representative. Three of the aforesaid Elizabeth Swinden's brothers—Atkinson by name—became useful local preachers, while a fourth was class-leader. Thus we see again the hereditary principle at work.

RIPON.

When Ripon is mentioned, we are not to think merely of the pretty though somewhat sleepy city on the Ure, with its ancient Cathedral of St. Wilfrid, together with its adjacent villages, which represents the Ripon Circuit of to-day. Rather are we to figure to ourselves a tract of country stretching from the borders of Leeds and Tadcaster Circuits to Middleham, and from the valley of the Nidd to Thirsk, comprising what are now the Harrogate, Knaresboro', Pateley Bridge, Thirsk, Ripon, Bedale, and Middleham Circuits. They took seizin of this country for the Connexion, though as yet all of it might not be effectively occupied. The Ripon Circuit, formed in 1822, ultimately grew to be with its branches one of the most extensive Circuits in the Connexion, and, after 1824, when it was incorporated with the newly formed Sunderland District, it was travelled by some of the best known and most capable ministers of that District.

W. Clowes opened Knaresbro' as early as October 24th, 1819, by preaching "abroad" amid wind and rain at nine o'clock in the morning, and in a dwelling-house in the evening. On the Tuesday following, he preached in a different part of the town and formed a society of four members. Two other visits to Knaresbro' were paid before the year closed, and kindly mention is made of an old Scotchwoman, Mary Brownridge, who bade him welcome to what her house afforded. At already fashionable Harrogate "the uncircumcised fastened the door of the house he was in" to prevent his egress; but he got out at the back of the premises. At Killinghall, hard by, he preached in a joiner's shop and in the Wesleyan Chapel, and while at family prayers next morning at the house of Mr. Swales, two of his servant-men cried out for mercy. It was while tramping through the snow from Harrogate to Leeds that Clowes had his encounter with a gentleman riding a very fine horse, who proved to be the Vicar of Harewood. The long discussion between them led Clowes to indulge in sundry reflections, one of which was that, notwithstanding all his privations and sufferings, and the toil and persecution he suffered as a missionary of the cross, he would not exchange situations with the Vicar of Harewood, "for," adds he, "my religion makes my soul happy." Mr. Clowes also visited Whixley, the home of the Annakin family, and Burton Leonard, where a good society was formed, and especially Marton-cum-Grafton. Here Mr. Mark Noble, a Wesleyan, incurring censure for countenancing and aiding and abetting the missionary, felt constrained to join the society that was formed, and henceforth freely extended hospitality to the preachers. In the revival which took place at this time, Mr. Thomas Dawson, by far the ablest and most influential official of the Ripon Circuit in the early days, was brought to God. He entered the ministry, but was obliged to relinquish it after eighteen months' trial, his strength not being equal to the heavy demands of the work. He located in the Ripon Circuit, and as an evidence of the respect entertained for him by his brethren, who well knew his loyalty and the value of his counsel, he was elected a deed poll member at the Conference of 1856. The Rev. Colin C. McKechnie, who knew him intimately, has left a pen-and-ink sketch of Mr. Dawson, which we have pleasure in quoting.

MR. THOMAS DAWSON.

"Mr. Thomas Dawson was, beyond question, the most gifted of all our laymen. He was well-informed, had a keen perception, and a logical mind. Nothing pleased him more than taking part in a debate; and if he had anything like a good case in hand, he was almost sure to win. Indeed, if the case were bad, the chances were in his favour, for he had the faculty of making the 'worse appear the better reason.' He delighted in the society of the preachers, and in meeting them at his house. Afflicted with asthma, he was at times compelled to sit up at nights, as he could not lie. At such times if a preacher happened to be with him, he would spend hours in discussion, the subjects often being of an abstruse and metaphysical nature. One night I spent with him was devoted almost entirely to the discussion of

'Fixed fate, free will, foreknowledge absolute.'

And he seemed to forget all his ailments in the polemical ardour with which he repelled the Calvinistic views taken of those high subjects. Mr. Dawson was a thoroughly good man, upright, devoted, zealous in Christian work, and an out-and-out Primitive." *

Mr. Clowes entered the city of Ripon for the first time on March 4th, 1820. A local preacher being planned at the Wesleyan chapel on this Sabbath whose face was almost unknown to the congregation, Clowes was privately pressed to take his place, and at last consented. The service was a powerful one, and either the preacher's matter or manner betrayed him, for, when the congregation were dispersing, one said, aloud : " If these be 'Ranters,' then I am a 'Ranter.'" The evening service, we are told, was held in the house of Mr. B. Spetch, in Bondgate, and in the prayer meeting which followed, William Rumfitt and Moses Lupton, afterwards General Missionary Secretary, and President, were two out of fourteen who professed to find the Saviour. A strong society was almost immediately formed, which received numerous accessions from the somewhat frequent visits to Ripon paid by Clowes during the year, as noted in his published *Journal*. As early as June, 1820, Ripon was made a branch, and in September three preachers were stationed to it, viz., James Farrar, Robert Ripley, and John Garbutt.

* Rev. C. C. McKechnie's MS. "Autobiography," in the possession of the author.

A month after we find W. Clowes taking part in the opening of a new chapel at Martin-cum-Grafton, and once more we meet with Mrs. Woolhouse assisting in the services.

Amongst those who travelled the extensive Ripon Circuit in the first period were several with whose names and work we shall become familiar in writing of the Northern District; men like John Lightfoot, John Branfoot, William Lister, W. Dent, John Day, Thomas Southron. Nor should we omit mention of Mary Porteus, who was on the circuit's staff of preachers from 1828 to 1830. On the intellectual side she must be regarded as taking a high place amongst our female itinerants. She did not come behind any of them in piety and zeal, and she excelled most of them in preaching power. The Rev. W. Dent—a competent judge—has said of her, "that it was really a privilege to hear her preach, for she had both the requisite gifts and grace." Mary Porteus was a native of Gateshead and entered the ministry in 1826, taking circuit work until 1840, when enfeebled health compelled her retirement.

MOSES LUPTON.

For one of her sex and constitution Ripon was an exacting station. Some idea of the physical toil involved in the working of such a Circuit may be gathered from the statement of the Rev. W. Lister that, during the three years of his superintendency of the Ripon Circuit, 1835-8, he had walked 2,400 miles.

In speaking of the early history of the Ripon Circuit it would be almost unpardonable to make no reference to Joseph Spoor, who had so much to do with the shaping of that history. In a very real sense he made his mark on the Circuit, and it was equally true that the Ripon Circuit left its mark on him, for it was while labouring, as he only could, in the Middleham Mission of this station—forty-seven miles in length and twenty in breadth—that he broke down in health, and had to superannuate for a time. Yet he was no weakling. Indeed, when Thomas Dawson secured him at the District Meeting of 1835 for the Ripon Circuit, well knowing he "could toil terribly," he was in the full vigour of his powers. He had a compact, sinewy, agile frame. He was courageous as a lion, and yet he could show on occasion of an emergency much tact and resourcefulness. He made no pretension to learning or eloquence. He spoke out in plain Saxon, and the themes on which he discoursed presented little variety; but his own soul kindled as he spoke, and the old themes were all aglow like Moses' bush that burned unconsumed in fire. Added to all this, there was at times a dash of eccentricity about his movements both in and out of the

MARY PORTEUS.

F

pulpit which attracted the attention of men and made him popular. Many of the well-known incidents associated with his name occurred during his term of labour in Ripon and its various branches, which term was remarkable for a great revival of religion—one that was not restricted to a few places but spread over nearly the whole Circuit. New societies were raised in several places, and others that had seriously declined were revived. It was just after this revival that the Circuit was formed into branches.

In 1837, Mr. Spoor was appointed to labour on the Thirsk and Bedale Mission. At the village of Langthorne the outlook was at first exceedingly unpromising. But he was told there was hope for the place if only John Hobson, the tallest man in the village, could be won for Christ. Thereupon Mr. Spoor and his colleague, W. Fulton, covenanted to pray at a given hour each day for the conversion of this village champion and son of Anak. Shortly after this, John Hobson was drawn by some irresistible influence to a service conducted by Mr. Spoor. Unmistakably enough it was he; for, like Saul, he towered head and shoulders above the rest. John Hobson was converted and became the leader and staunch supporter of the village society.

JOSEPH SPOOR.

In December, 1837, Mr. Spoor was appointed to open a Mission at Boroughbridge. It was while preaching on a village-green near this old town that he had his encounter with the Anglican priest who in his wrath threatened to stop him. To this Mr. Spoor replied: "There are several ways of stopping you, but there's only one way of stopping me. Take away your gown, and you dare not preach; take away your book, and you cannot preach; and take away your rich income, and you won't preach; while the only way to stop me is by cutting out my tongue." Of course the retort was not original; but it leaped forth on occasion like a trenchant impromptu and shows the readiness of the man.

Mr. Spoor and Fulton were dragged before the magistrates by an officious policeman for a service which they held in Ripon Market-place. It seemed that despite all they might say they were to be sent to prison. Spoor rejoiced at the opportunity of suffering for the sake of the Gospel and shouted: "Glory be to God! the 'kittie' for Christ!" but a prominent citizen came into Court, expostulated with the magistrates and put a new face on the matter. It is said that a long and able letter appeared in the newspaper insisting upon the right to conduct worship in the open air, and reflecting upon the conduct of the policeman and the magistrates, and that the letter was from the pen of Dr. Longley, then Bishop of Ripon, and afterwards Archbishop of Canterbury.

But, to our thinking, an incident narrated by Rev. C. C. McKechnie shows Mr. Spoor in a still more attractive light. Mr. McKechnie had as a lad of seventeen just arrived from his distant home in Paisley to begin his labours in the Ripon Circuit. Rather cruelly, his superintendent had made him preach in the city on the very evening of his arrival, and the service had been to him a trying one. The next day as he sat in his lodgings he was much cast down. The rest of the story shall be told in Mr. McKechnie's own words:

"Something like despair settled upon me, and it seemed to grow thicker and faster. In the early afternoon, as I sat in my room brooding over the past, present and future, I wrote all sorts of bitter things against myself for having ventured upon such an enterprise, so unfurnished for my work, and so ignorant of what I was doing. Whilst thus depressed and desponding the tears coursing down my cheeks, my room-door opened, and Mr. Joseph Spoor walked in. And here let me say with thankfulness, his coming was like the visit of an angel of God. His presence brought a blessing with it. A more peaceful, spiritual, brotherly face

MARKET-PLACE, RIPON.

I had never looked upon, and the tones of his voice had a healing and reviving influence upon my poor bruised heart. He seemed to comprehend my case in a moment. I cannot express the fulness and sweetness of his sympathy, or the gentle but effectual way in which he swept away my brooding fears. 'Oh, dear, no! I had no reason to be despondent; that was the work of the enemy. I might be sure my way would brighten. Get on? Oh, yes! I would get on beyond doubt. I must look up and trust and pray and work, and all would turn out well. I would meet with many kind-hearted people who would help and cheer me in every way.' With such words as these, backed by a few mighty words of prayer, Mr. Spoor exorcised the evil spirit, and left me a new man. Yes; I may truly say I was made a new man; a new life inspired me. I now felt ashamed of my cowardly fears. No; I would not succumb to the difficulties of my lot. I had come out into this field of labour in response to what I believed to be a divine call, and I would, by the help of God, prove myself worthy of it."—(*MS. Autobiography.*)

MALTON AND PICKERING.

We give, below, the ministerial fixtures for September–December, 1820, made by the Hull Circuit authorities:—

"*Hull.*—William Clowes, John Hewson, Edward Vause, and John Armitage.
Brotherton.—John Woolhouse and John Branfoot.
Pocklington.—John Verity, John Harvey, and William Evans.
Ripon.—James Farrar, Robert Ripley, and John Garbutt.
Tadcaster.—Thomas Johnson, John Abey, and Samuel Smith.
Leeds.—Samuel Laister and Thomas Nelson.
Malton.—Nathaniel West and John Lawton.
Driffield.—Robert Howcroft.
Bridlington.—John Coulson."

Rightly regarded, this prosaic-looking record is full of significance. It illustrates yet again W. Clowes' judgment as to the "amazing work" carried on by Hull in 1820-2. It is only one year and nine months since Primitive Methodism was introduced into Hull, and yet no inconsiderable portion of the broad-acred county has been divided up and allotted to the preachers of the Hull Circuit. Still, this record is manifestly incomplete, for it leaves out York, where, as we have seen, a chapel was opened in July, 1820, and several preachers whose names stand on the Minutes of the first Conference have no mention in this table. Another thing we may learn from this record: It shows that the towns and slices of country we are writing of are not to be regarded as isolated and independent, but as parts of one whole to be operated upon by a simultaneous movement directed from Hull.

At this early period the preachers were usually changed every three months, and sometimes even oftener than that. They were transferred from one branch of the circuit to another like Salvation Army captains by the head-quarters staff. They are all Hull Circuit preachers, but are shifted from branch to branch like pawns on a chess-board. Was the shortness of the term of service conducive to concentration and intensity of labour? Perhaps so. With three months only available to justify his appointment or otherwise, the days were precious and not to be let pass without crowding them with work. Hull Circuit had a long arm, and held its preachers with a tight hand. At each quarter day inquisition was made of a minute and searching kind, embracing not only inquiries as to the preacher's success as a soul-winner, but extending even to the cut of his hair and coat, and the correctness of his deportment. As late as 1832, a preacher, whom it may suffice to name J. P., was suspended, "for being late at Easterington Chapel, lying late in the morning, speaking crossly at Preston to some children when taking breakfast, and, finally, for eating the inside of some pie and leaving the crust!" The charges were on the face of them petty enough, but probably there lay, behind, the conviction that the brother was unadapted and unadaptable to the work he had undertaken.

The record given above may also serve as a recapitulation and forecast. Hull home-branch, together with Pocklington, Brotherton, Hutton Rudby, York, Leeds, and Tadcaster, have been referred to. Now, by 1820, we see that a beginning has been made with Driffield and the Wold-towns. "Bridlington" means that the sea-coast of the East and North Ridings, over and above Holderness, has to be missioned; while "Malton" means that the country lying north of Pocklington and the Wolds and between the Hambledon Hills and the sea-coast, and stretching northwards to the Cleveland Hills, has to be attempted. Nor must we forget that Hutton Rudby is already an independent circuit, and, by 1822, will have reached Guisborough. So, although the discovery of the rich beds of hematite are still in the future, and no one as yet dreams of the busy iron-towns which one day will stand on the flats by the estuary of the Tees, still in that direction the country, such as it was, had by 1822 been penetrated by our missionaries.

Speaking generally, the work of Hull Circuit at this time was carried on and its successes gained in a country possessing few towns of any magnitude. Of necessity, it was mainly village evangelisation that was carried on, and the *Journals* of the missionaries show that in the East and North Ridings scores of villages were entered, converts won, and causes established in the short space of two or three years. Once more we may question whether we have not lost ground, and have not to-day fewer village interests than we had in the pioneer days.

All important is it for us to know what was the religious condition of this district at the time of its first missioning, and what ameliorative influences were brought to bear upon the people by the new evangel. Even yet there are parts of the North Riding which are wild and thinly populated, as any one who has walked from Pickering to Whitby will know. Eighty years ago the inhabitants of these moors and dales were indeed a people remote and secluded. Our missionaries penetrated into scattered villages that were sadly neglected. We are not without reliable evidence on this head. The late Canon Atkinson* tells us that, when he became parish clergyman of Danby in 1846, the days were but lately passed when one clergyman had charge of three, and in one case he knew, of four parishes, making one service a Sunday and a modicum of visitation on week-days a thing to be desired rather than actually enjoyed. Yet, though what would be called pluralists, these clergymen were but poorly paid, their pittance barely reaching the proverbial forty pounds a year. Mr. Carter, the Vicar of Lastingham, got only £20 a year and a few surplice fees. True: he was an expert angler, and caught sufficient fish with his line and hook to serve his family, and to effect a change in kind with his neighbours. Still, he felt the pinch of poverty and, to add to his income, he hit upon the expedient of having refreshments served up between the services in the Saxon crypt. At the archidiaconal visitation he told his ecclesiastical superior that "he took down his fiddle to play a few tunes, and then he could see that no one got more drink than was good for him, and if the young people proposed a dance he seldom answered in the negative."† So the church, which was the earliest seat of Scoto-Irish Christianity, was turned into a public-house! We know we are

---

* "Forty years in a Moorland Parish."
† "Slingsby and Slingsby Castle," by Rev. A. St. Clair Brooke.

describing a state of things, as regards the Church, long since gone by. But our point is, that the poverty and helplessness of the State-Church in those remote parts must have created a condition of things needing a powerful remedy. If the official clergymen were not merely overworked and underpaid, incompetent or spiritless but, as was too often the case, lax in conduct, still more urgent was the need of heroic measures in order to reach the dull and alienated minds of the people. It was of a clergyman in Cleveland, lying intoxicated in the ditch, that one said to another, contemptuously: "Let him lig [lie]; he'll not be wanted till Sunday."

That Methodism kept Christianity alive in these northern dales Canon Atkinson handsomely concedes. He might probably hold that Methodism was only acting as the *locum tenens* until the Church should return to take up her assigned duty. But be this as it may, he admits the fact that, in the parts he knows so well, Methodism and Primitive Methodism had conserved the gospel. When, prior to his institution into his benefice, he saw what was to be his church, littered, ill-kept, with its shabby altar, he says:—

"I could understand the slovenly, perfunctory service once a Sunday, sometimes relieved by none at all, and the consequent sleepy state of Church-feeling and worship. I could well understand how the only religious life in the district should be among and due to the Wesleyans and Primitive Methodists."*

Some of the first travelling-preachers on the Malton Branch sent pretty full *Journals* of their labours to the *Magazine*. From these we take an item or two that may help us to understand how and wherefore the Word of God spread so rapidly in these parts. One of these early workers and journalisers was William Evans. He was one of eight who were taken out to travel by the September Quarterly Meeting of 1820, and began his labours in the newly-formed Malton Branch. He was so zealous a missionary that he did not stint his labours to the fulfilling of his planned appointments. Measured by the standard of the plan he performed works of supererogation. He records in his *Journal:*—

"*Saturday, October 6th, 1820.*—Had no appointment, but being informed that the people at Hayton were desirous to hear us, I travelled fourteen miles and preached to them, and the Word did not fall to the ground: three were brought to the Lord, and one drunkard went off with the solemn inquiry, 'What must I do to be saved?'"

With a spirit like this, so alien from all that was perfunctory, actuating the pioneer workers, one can the more readily understand why village societies on the Upper Derwent and in the Vale of Pickering should multiply as fast as the cells of the yeast plant, and that by May, 1821, N. West should be able to record that in six months four hundred members had been added to the Malton Branch.

Another excerpt from the *Journals* gives us a picture of a camp meeting of the olden time—a picture worth preserving, because, like the camp meetings held on the Wrekin, Scarth Nick, and Mow Cop itself, it was staged and framed amid grand and impressive scenery. God can work His "greatest wonders" in souls renewed and sins forgiven in

* *Op. cit.*, p. 48.

a disused brick-field or on a bleak moor, but when the wonders of grace are wrought among the wonders of Nature both become the more impressive. So S. Smith felt when he wrote:—

"*August 19th, 1821.*—Attended Pickering Camp Meeting. We opened at half-past nine. We sung and prayed; and brother Hessey preached. The praying companies then drew out and took up five stations, and the scene was beautiful and interesting—five large companies wrestling with God in a pleasant valley. On one side was an ancient castle, with its cloud-capt towers, the ruins of which were awfully grand. Another side presented a distant view of the town of Pickering. Another view gave the lofty quarries of limestone. On another side was a large plantation of lofty and majestic trees of different kinds. Through the valley ran a winding brook, calling to mind these lines:—

'Our time, like a stream,
Glides swiftly away.'

But at the important moment the sound of prayer and praise was heard through the valley, and five large companies pleaded with God for precious souls. One soul got liberty in this time of prayer, and when the usual time had been spent, the companies were called up by the sound of a horn to the waggon. When we had gone through the services of the day we concluded the field-labours, and retired to hold a lovefeast in the chapel, where, after two or three had spoken, the work of the Lord broke out on every hand. Thirty or forty souls were crying for mercy; others were praying with them. I never before was eye-witness to so glorious a work. Twenty-two souls professed to receive pardon of all their past sins, and a determination to flee from sin for the time to come. At the same time we had preaching on the outside to those who could not get in. Glory, glory to God and the Lamb for ever."

The opening of the chapel referred to in the preceding extract had taken place four months before (April 22nd), and was of such a character as to show that the occasion was regarded as a notable event in the town and district. N. West, in his sanguine way, estimates the number brought together at five thousand. No less than seven preachers took part in the services held simultaneously within and outside the chapel. Jane Ansdale (afterwards Mrs. Suddards) had now begun her useful ministry, and to her was assigned the honour of preaching in the chapel both afternoon and evening.

R. CORDINGLEY.

Other chapels built at an early date in this part were Swinton, opened August 13th, 1820; "John Oxtoby was with me," says S. Laister, the opener, "and the Lord gave us many souls;" Malton, opened October 13th, 1822, by John Verity, then travelling on the adjoining Pocklington station; and Kirby-Moorside, the lowly building acquired in 1824 serving until 1861, when it was superseded by a better one. But Leavening Chapel, opened by John Verity, October 8th, 1820, has more frequent mention in the early *Journals* and documents than any other, probably because of its association with the eccentric Robert Coultas, the correspondent and frequent travelling companion of John Oxtoby, and also because the pious clergyman of the neighbouring parish of Acklam occasionally worshipped within its walls.

The best account we know of Robert Coultas is a brightly-written memoir from the pen of the veteran Rev. Richard Cordingley, who travelled at Malton in 1826, and at Pickering in 1856. In that memoir—worth disinterring from the *Magazine* and printing *in extenso*—Robert Coultas is rightly described as "an extraordinary man." He would never consent to stand higher than the first on the list of exhorters, but yet having ample means, he would go on extensive religious tours and evangelise in his own peculiar way—much prayer interspersed with conversation-preaching. "When Robert had worked his body down, he used to return home, tarry awhile, and then commence again in some neighbourhood whither he thought Providence called him, with a companion or without, as the case might be. He laboured with great success in various villages and towns, still following his old habit of returning home to rest when exhausted with excessive toil." He was present at the Pickering Annual Camp Meeting of 1856, and though Mr. Cordingley had not seen him for thirty years, he knew him at once by his loud and unmistakable "Amen." He laboured in the prayer meeting after the lovefeast with all his heart and strength. "Souls, as *usual*, were converted; for never," said he, "had we a camp meeting at Pickering without souls being converted." He quietly fell on sleep, June 13th, 1857, aged 86 years.

As early as 1819, W. Clowes notes hearing "a truly gospel sermon by Mr. Simpson" in the church at Acklam. The same evening Clowes himself preached in a house, and he records with satisfaction, not untinged with surprise, that Mr. Simpson came to the service and gave him the right hand of fellowship. Sampson Turner, too, when preaching in Leavening Chapel, October 9th, 1822—"as compact a little chapel as ever I saw"—had Mr. Simpson as a hearer, and notes in his *Journal* that "he is favourable to our people, and I believe a truly converted man." We meet, during the course especially of our earlier history, with so many clergymen of the type of the parson of Brantingham, who "advanced in a very menacing attitude" towards Clowes when the latter was preaching, and then "suddenly turned to the right-about and wheeled off the ground," that it is a relief at last to come upon one clergyman in the East Riding of quite another spirit.* Our first missionaries were menaced with the clenched fist of the parochial clergyman much oftener than they were offered the right hand of fellowship. All honour then to him of Acklam who, if well-accredited stories be true, went to such lengths of friendliness to our Church as got him into trouble with the ecclesiastical authorities. What would the archdeacon say when told that parson Simpson not only frequented conventicles and welcomed itinerant preachers to bed and board, but had actually caused a notice to be put up in the church-porch, which read: "No service. Gone to the camp meeting"? Of course he was censured and prohibited from attending any more conventicle services, and so we have the further picture of the

* Rev. W. Garner speaks of Brantingham as "a place noted for rabid opposition to religious liberty." It was here Mr. Garner first met with vicar John Gibson's notorious pamphlet against the Primitive Methodists. To this he gave a trenchant answer in his "Dialogues between the Rev. J. Gibson, B.D., the Vicar of Brent, with Furneux Pelham, Herts, and Martin Bull, Primitive Methodist."

clergyman taking his stand, sometimes even amid frost and snow, by chapel door or window, to listen to the sermon.*

As a circuit, Malton has had a continuous and steady-going existence since 1822. Until the formation of the Leeds District in 1845, it stood in right chronological order on the stations of the Hull District, just after Pocklington and Brotherton, *i.e.*, Pontefract, Circuits. Though Pickering was made a circuit in 1823, the arrangement was premature, lasting for that year only, and it had to wait until 1842 before it was again granted circuit independence. The parent circuit was left with two preachers and 470 members, while Pickering began its course with 347 members and three preachers, of whom, it is interesting to note, John Fawsit was the third.

It would be unpardonable were this history to contain no further reference to one who, as an ardent and gifted Bible-student and author, deserves to be ranked with J. A. Bastow and Thomas Greenfield. They are few indeed still surviving who remember his bright personality and his enthusiasm for learning; for he died in 1857 at the early age of thirty-seven, just when his literary powers were ripening. But though J. Fawsit died comparatively young, his application had been so intense that several books came from his pen that deserve to live. The best of these are "The Sinner's Handbook to the Cross" and "The Saint's Handbook to the Crown," the latter revised for the press on his death-bed. These books are written in a devout practical spirit, give evidence of wide reading, and in the allusiveness and occasional quaintnesses of their style remind us of some of the lighter Puritan writers. J. Fawsit was born at Scotter, and entered the ministry in 1841, the same year in which J. Bootland, J. R. Parkinson, D. Ingham, and J. T. Shepherd, well-known preachers of the old Hull District, began their toil. After travelling at Retford, Leeds, Malton, London, and Bradwell, he settled down at Wellow in the pleasant Dukeries, and did good service to the Connexion to which he was so attached. To no one whom we have known—certainly to no Primitive Methodist—would the title, "The Earnest Student," be more appropriate. He was not born to affluence. He had to labour for the support of his family, and, next after his religious duties, he made *that* his chief business, but books he would have. One of the most vivid impressions of our boyhood is the mental picture of his large library, with Sir Walter Raleigh's "History of the World" standing out among the rest (a title that struck our youthful mind as a tolerably large order).

REV. J. FAWSIT.

* The strange story of how John Verity won a chapel from the squire by his preaching seems too well authenticated to be summarily dismissed; but it is not given in the text, for the simple reason that, when the above was written, no reliable evidence had been obtained as to the name and situation of the village in question. We, however, were inclined to locate the village in the neighbourhood of Malton, because the story is linked in time and locality with Verity's introduction to the clergyman, whom we took to be Mr. Simpson. Just before going to press, the Rev. W. R. Widdowson informs us he has come across a note of the late Rev. S. Smith, which states that the village was Scagglethorpe, near Malton, and that the chapel thus strangely acquired continued to be used by us until the demise of the squire, when it passed out of our hands. The story is told at full length by the late Rev. Jesse Ashworth, *Aldersgate Magazine*, 1899.

But J. Fawsit was no mere book-worm: he was a student. The writer of his memoir says truly:—

"His love of knowledge was a passion, and it never cooled. . . His application was most intense and protracted. At three o'clock in the morning, in the depth of winter, his lamp might have been seen burning; indeed, till weakness compelled him to desist, he spent very few hours in bed. He was a self-taught man, and did honour to that class of individuals who undertake to educate themselves. He travelled much, and had acquired the habit, not only of reading as he walked, but of writing too; the first draft of much that he published was first put on paper in this way."

Earnest students of the type of John Fawsit are sparingly sown and rare in any community. But it so happened that the newly-formed Pickering Circuit could show two such uncommon growths. Besides its junior minister, it had for one of its leading officials John Lumley, whose life affords another striking example of self-help and strenuous mental culture. Robert Coultas and John Lumley were both products of the pleasant Vale of Pickering, and yet they differed as widely as any two sincere Christian men of the same community can possibly do. One lived largely in the world of books and thought, of which world the other knew little and for which he cared still less. While Fawsit would appreciate the good points of the extraordinary strolling evangelist, he would be drawn to the thoughtful druggist of Kirby-Moorside by force of strong affinity. He would find in him a kindred soul, and by congenial intercourse the already strongly-marked bias of each would be confirmed. Men like John Lumley, George Race, John Delafield, and others who might be named, are as genuine products of Primitive Methodism as John Oxtoby, Robert Coultas, or W. Hickingbotham. They always have been, and will be still more in the future, an indispensable element in its growth and strengthening. Hence they claim our recognition, and all the more, because their tastes and pursuits being "caviare to the general," their lives devoid of startling incident and their characters of eccentricity, they may so easily be passed over.

John Lumley began his career at thirteen as a farm labourer, but gave himself with such ardour to the acquisition of knowledge, that he became a schoolmaster, and ultimately a druggist. Neither mathematics nor pharmacy, however, could wean him from Biblical study. He early laid a good foundation by reading the New Testament through once a month, and set himself to master the points at issue between Calvinism and Arminianism, as part of his equipment for that controversy, committing to memory the whole of the Epistle to the Romans. In 1838, he lost his official position in connection with the Wesleyan Methodists owing to his refusal to pledge himself not to preach for other communities. In 1840, he joined the Primitive Methodists and became a local preacher, school superintendent, and class leader. John Lumley, like Matthew Denton and Thomas Church, must have an early place in the list of Primitive Methodist laymen who ventured into the field of authorship; for, in 1844, he published a work on "The Necessity, Nature, and Design of the Atonement," which received very favourable notice. In 1845, he removed for the second time to the United States, and died there in 1850. His interesting memoir was written by W. Thompson Lumley,

THE PERIOD OF CIRCUIT PREDOMINANCE AND ENTERPRISE. 91

who for the long period of sixty-three years was associated with the Pickering Circuit as one of its most prominent and capable officials, and died as recently as 1897.

The family of Frank has had a long and honourable connection with the Pickering Circuit, dating back to 1833, when Ann, the fair daughter of the house, was converted, and, despite the bitter opposition of her parents and brothers, joined the Church. In the end her firmness and tact overcame all family opposition, and she had the joy of welcoming parents and most of her brothers into the same fellowship. Soon she was pressed to speak in public, but entered on the work with extreme diffidence. Her first effort, however, proved so remarkably successful in its spiritual results, that all scruples were set at rest, and for sixty long years her name stood on the plan as a local preacher. Her tall and slender form, her resonant voice bespeaking intense conviction, and her womanly tact rendered her ministrations very acceptable, and she preached far and wide in the villages round Pickering and Kirby-Moorside. For three or four years after beginning to preach she was accompanied by a young lady-friend, Alice Jane Garvin, who was gifted with an excellent voice and sang the gospel while the other preached it. The two sometimes went on foot, but at other times, we are told, each rode on a smart well-groomed donkey; and the picture thus called up is not at all an unpleasing one. When Ann Frank entered into the marriage state with Mr. Swales her chosen work suffered little interruption. In their home at Pickering cheerful hospitality was dispensed, and the godly pair had the satisfaction of seeing their only son enter the ranks of the ministry in which he has faithfully served upwards of thirty-six years.* Mrs. Swales died February 4th, 1895.

MRS. ANN SWALES.

Our sketch of the past history of Pickering Circuit would be incomplete were it to contain no reference to Messrs. J. Frank, J.P., of Pickering, and W. Allenby, of Helmsley. Both happily survive as veterans, with a record of more than half a century's faithful service, that has been of untold advantage to the district in which they reside. Mr. Frank is the Circuit Steward, and has been connected with the Pickering Sunday School for fifty years. Mr. Allenby is also a Sunday School Superintendent, and became a local preacher in the early fifties, along with his life-long friend, Rev. Joseph Sheale.

THE WOLD CIRCUITS: DRIFFIELD AND BRIDLINGTON.

Both Driffield and Bridlington are "in the Wolds." The two towns were missioned about the same time, and, as heads of branches or circuits, their relations with each other have been close and intimate; indeed, for some years Bridlington was a branch of Driffield Circuit. Hence, as geographically and historically the two go together, they may be fittingly considered under the common designation of "the Wold Circuits."

MR. W. ALLENBY.

---

* Their daughter, too, it may be noted, is married to the Rev. W. A. Eyre.

By the Wolds we are to understand that well-defined upland tract, which, like a great crescent of chalk-hills, sweeps round from Flamborough Head to the Humber, and is bounded on the east by the low ground of Holderness, on the north by the Vale of Pickering, and on the west by the Vale of York. From time immemorial Driffield, planted at the foot of these oolitic uplands, has been the chief town—the capital of the Wolds. With its clear sparkling trout-streams, its flour mills, its clean, pleasant streets, its air of prosperous comfort, it has yet had a long history. Driffield embalms the name of Deira, a subdivision of the ancient kingdom of Northumbria. Alfred of Northumberland had his castle here, and the Moot Hill is still the name of the eminence on which the folk-mote assembled, and a tablet in Little Driffield Church commemorates Alfred's death in 705. Busy and thriving as Driffield is, it still clings

MIDDLE STREET SOUTH, DRIFFIELD.

to some of the old-world customs. Its parish clerk still rings the harvest-bell at five o'clock every morning for twenty-eight days during harvest; for the Wold country is nothing if not agricultural, and Driffield is its emporium.

This interesting district has, from a Primitive Methodist standpoint, been more fortunate than many other parts of the Connexion, in that its story has been well and fully told in a work easily accessible. We chiefly confine ourselves, therefore, to the first missioning of the Wolds and its chief circuit towns, Driffield and Bridlington, referring our readers to Rev. H. Woodcock's "Primitive Methodism on the Yorkshire Wolds" for fuller details.

When and by whom was Primitive Methodism introduced into Driffield? Perhaps we may not be able to arrive at absolute certainty on these points; but there is a passage in the *Journals* of W. Clowes which may at least yield a strong probability. In the passage in question, Clowes reflects, for him, rather strongly, on the action of certain members of the Hull Circuit Committee, who interfered with the arrangements for placing the preachers, made September, 1819. Quite illegally, he maintains, and ill-advisedly, Samuel Laister was sent on *a mission to the Yorkshire Wolds*, which, says he, "turned out as I fully expected—a complete failure." Be it said, Clowes finds no fault with S. Laister. On the contrary, he affirms: "He was greatly in the doctrine of a present salvation, and had a burning love for the souls of men."* But he *does* find fault with the Committee-men for not suffering themselves to be guided by men of riper experience than themselves; and he roundly tells them that they ought to have known better than to send an unseasoned missionary to an untried country like the Wolds, and in the winter time too. It is evident then that S. Laister did attempt the Wolds mission, and, if so, he would not be likely to miss Driffield; and we have his own statement that he was taken out by the Hull Circuit in 1819, and the first printed record of his labours we have relates to Malton Circuit in 1820. So far, then, as the records go, S. Laister may have attempted a Wolds mission in the Fall of 1819; nor, so far as we are aware, has tradition anything to say against it. S. Laister may have been "the aggressive preacher from Hull whose name is unrecorded,"† who took his stand on the Cross Hill and preached to the curious crowd; and, though under the conditions prevailing at the time, S. Laister's mission may have been a *comparative* failure, just as Paul's mission to Athens was, like that also, it may not have been *altogether* a failure. The probable conclusion arrived at, then, is that the nucleus of a society may have been formed as early as 1819.

The first society, we are told, met on Sunday evenings at a bakehouse in Westgate, and had for its leader Thomas Wood, "the little shoemaker." Thus early we come across the name of the man who, until his death in 1881, was as the main-spring of Driffield Primitive Methodism. We have already noted his conversion in the Pocklington Circuit, and how he never rested until he got his companion and life-long friend, W. Sanderson, converted. In 1819, we find him removed to Driffield, and though but a young man of twenty-two, he begins to take upon him the care of the freshly-formed society. Though living in lodgings himself, he found the unmarried preacher bed and board; but as this arrangement was not without its difficulties, he one day said to his betrothed: "We must get married soon and make a home for the preacher." Further illustrations of what Thomas Wood was as a man, and of what he did as an official for the Driffield

THOMAS WOOD.

Circuit during his service of sixty years, will be found in Mr. Woodcock's book. What strikes us in reference to the man is the aptness of the description applied to him— "a man of double-distilled common-sense." And there was no element of bitterness in the distillation. He had the Yorkshireman's plod and pertinacity. He had too, the

---

* Clowes' *Journals*, pp. 166-7.
† "Corners of our Vineyard: Driffield Circuit," in *Christian Messenger*, p. 189.

Yorkshireman's cheery optimism. That he was no crier up of the past and crier down of the present, may be gathered from one or two of his *acuta dicta*, which also have their value as generalisations of our history by one who had long experience to go upon.

"Modern Primitive Methodism, with its Schools, its Bands of Hope, and its Missionary Institutions, is a nobler thing than early Primitive Methodism, with its excitement and its songs.

"Many of our early members were refugees from other Churches; now we have a good society of our own creating.

"Fifty years ago, when we laid hold of a talented man like 'Willie' Sanderson, we were never puzzled to know what to do with him; and when we could not get the man we wanted, we made the best use of those we *could* get. Some of the least promising turned out the most successful."*

GEO. BULLOCK.
Deed-poll Member.

Another early and valuable acquisition to the cause of Primitive Methodism in the Wolds was George Bullock, of Wetwang, a man of vigorous mind well-furnished by reading, skilful in debate, and sagacious in counsel. For sixty years he never missed an appointment except in case of sickness, and when in his prime he was one of the most popular and hard-working local preachers in the East Riding. His worth was fittingly recognised by his election as a member of the Deed Poll by the Conference of 1875. He ceased from labour in 1887 at the age of 83 years.

A reference to the record already given of the ministerial fixtures made September, 1820, by the Hull Quarterly Meeting, will show that at that date a footing had been got both in Driffield and in Bridlington. Then, in January, 1821, Clowes visits Driffield, and on Thursday, the 18th, he notes in his *Journal:* "I preached at Driffield in the Play House, our Society having taken it for a preaching-place." The building here referred to was known as the Hunt Room, and was used for balls, concerts, and theatrical entertainments.

DRIFFIELD OLD CHAPEL.

In 1821, the erection of a chapel in Mill Street was begun. The undertaking was a weighty one for the society, and the pressure of monetary and other difficulties

---

* "Primitive Methodism on the Yorkshire Wolds," p. 44.

led some to predict the chapel would never get finished, while others feared if finished it would never be paid for. The extrication of the society from its embarrassments is traditionally attributed to the prayers and efforts of John Oxtoby, who was sent down by the Hull Circuit to render help at this juncture. One of the first fruits of his visit was the conversion of Mr. W. Byas, a wealthy retired farmer, for whom John Oxtoby had worked in former days. He was one of those who heard Oxtoby's first sermon preached in Driffield, and after it spent a restless prayerful night. His state of mind being made known to Oxtoby and T. Wood, they visited Mr. Byas at his home, with the result that he found peace. He gave a liberal donation towards the building fund, and advanced the sum of £350 on mortgage, which at his death was willed to the trustees, and the bequest placed them in an easy financial position.* The chapel, we are told, was originally only seventeen feet from the floor to the ceiling, yet some years after, a gallery was put in four pews deep; in 1856, the walls were raised considerably, the gallery enlarged, more lights inserted, and the accommodation increased by 130 lettable sittings. † The present noble chapel was built in 1876, under the superintendency of Rev. T. Waumsley, and the circuit owns also two good preachers' houses erected the same year.

DRIFFIELD NEW CHAPEL.

* "To the infant cause at Driffield, W. Byas, Esq., was a nursing father. He was brought to God by the simple but powerful instrumentality of John Oxtoby. After his conversion he often invited the preachers to his hospitable and plentiful table. Driffield was the first station to which we were appointed forty-five years ago [1823]. Mr. Byas gratuitously entertained us with board and lodgings; and his kindness was seconded by his housekeeper, Mrs. Hall, and his servant Margaret Easingwood, now Mrs. Vokes. The chapel, too, which he liberally assisted to build, he placed in easy circumstances before his demise." Rev. W. Garner, "Life of W. Clowes, 1868," p. 273.

† The particulars here given, relative to the first chapel and its subsequent alterations, are found in an article by Rev. H. Knowles, *Primitive Methodist Magazine*, 1857, p. 11.

From the very beginning, Driffield was rightly considered a strong branch. This being so, one may naturally wonder why it was not granted circuit independence until 1837. Aspirations for self-government evidently were not wanting; for, in 1832, a meeting of circuit officials, consisting of Messrs. Bullock, Reed, Huntsman, Panton, Cobb, Sellers, and the three travelling-preachers, Messrs. Garbutt, Eckersley, and John Sharp, was held to consider the question. A resolution in favour of circuit independence was arrived at, but the project did not then mature. The Hull Circuit authorities were against it, and the branch reluctantly, or otherwise, acquiesced. An explanation of this long retention of a strong branch in a subordinate position—an explanation, which explains more than this particular case, is suggested by Rev. W. Garner's remarks to the effect that, under the influence of impaired health and increasing infirmities, W. Clowes became somewhat timorous in chapel-building, and showed little or no readiness to convert branches or missions into independent stations. He adds, to quote his precise words:—

"Without the guiding and sustaining hand of Hull, he was afraid to let them try to stand and walk alone. Through this timorous policy, several branches, for example Driffield, Brigg, Whitehaven, Barnard Castle—were retained in connection with Hull long after they were qualified to support and govern themselves. By these stations large surpluses were often remitted to the parent branch, not indeed for its individual use, but to aid it in its general missionary operations. ('Life of Clowes,' p. 406)."

But "the day of freedom dawned at length," and in 1837, Driffield was granted circuit autonomy. Its first bulky plan has on it the names of five travelling-preachers and some fifty distinct preaching-places. The next year its reported membership was 816. Bridlington remained a branch of Driffield until Christmas, 1857, and Hornsea in Holderness until 1861. To-day Driffield is one of the widest, and numerically, the strongest country circuit in the Connexion, reporting to the Conference of 1903 a membership of 1082; indeed, there is only one large-town circuit which is numerically stronger—viz., Leicester Second, with 1100 members. Driffield has the area of a diocese rather than that of an average circuit. The situation of some of its places, and their distance from the circuit-town, involve some difficulty in working and considerable expense, yet it is not easy to see how the circuit can be divided. For a few years the experiment was tried of making Nafferton the head of a station, but the arrangement does not seem to have worked satisfactorily, and in 1880 there was a reversion to the old arrangement.

Almost every one of the thirty-four places on the Driffield Circuit Plan has its story to tell, as Mr. Woodcock has shown in his interesting volume. Langtoft—"the village of floods and water-spouts"—has already been referred to as the scene of one of the earliest English camp meetings.* If the churchyard of Kilham holds all that is mortal of Capt. Edward Anderson, that of Beeford shows the tomb of probably the most popular boy-preacher of Primitive Methodism. Thomas Watson, a native of Beeford,

* *Ante*, vol. i., pp. 66 and 68, where a view of Langtoft Church is given, as also the tombstone of Capt. Anderson.

was only nineteen years of age at his death in 1837, and yet he was a travelling-preacher six years. Contemporary documents show that he was in constant request for special services, and as his epitaph records: His slender age, deep piety, and extraordinary abilities, render his death a subject of deep and lasting regret. Beeford can also cite its instance of clerical animus, which took the form of a vexatious law-suit. When in 1873 the chapel was in course of erection, the late Canon Trevor entered an action against the trustees for an alleged encroachment on certain glebe-land which he held in trust. The reverend plaintiff valued the land in dispute at four shillings, while the defendants' solicitor stated its real value to be about fourpence The Canon lost two trials, and had to pay some two hundred pounds in costs.

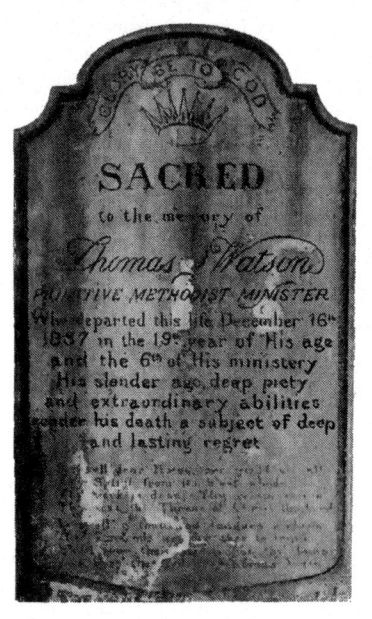

Driffield Circuit has been prolific in men and women of sterling character, whose worth finds due recognition in the pages of Mr. Woodcock's book, so often referred to. Besides Thomas Wood, Driffield has had such officials as Messrs. Thomas Jackson, Isaac Miller, and David Railton, the "man greatly beloved," who happily still survives. At Middleton-on-the-Wolds lived and died (August, 1850) Mr. F. Rudd, the father of Rev. F. Rudd, who for thirty-one years was a local preacher, second to none in the East Riding. At Hutton Cranswick, amongst many striking characters, Thomas Escritt, familiarly and affectionately known as "the Bishop of Cranswick," was the outstanding figure. As you saw him seated in the chapel, clad in his Sunday best, with his long snowy locks and venerable form, he looked like a country clergyman, though he was only a farm-labourer. But "he was the most beautiful specimen of a farm-labourer I ever met with or heard of," says Rev. J. Scruton, himself a native of the village. "He was a genius and a natural orator, though coy and shy. He was a man of the Bible, a man of eloquence, and a man of God." Thomas Escritt loved his employers, and was beloved in return, and his wish that he might be buried by the side of his old master was readily granted. For fifty years, as he went to his daily work, he was accustomed to turn aside to a particular spot to pray for grace and help to do his duty; and in the evening, as he returned from work, standing on the same spot, to thank God for His vouchsafed presence during the day. In this way, through half a century, Thomas Escritt celebrated matins and vespers, until in the course of time the trodden grass showed a well-defined path. At this sacred trysting-place an annual camp meeting was held, called by the villagers "Thomas Escritt's Camp Meeting," as a token of respect for the saintly old man, who died January, 1885, aged 87 years.

A man of quite another stamp was Robert Belt, blacksmith, of West Lutton, honest, sturdy, fearless. One Sunday morning, as he was going to his appointment, he observed Sir Tatton Sykes doing what he thought ought not to be done on the Lord's Day, and he went up to the baronet and told him so. The rebuke, though it was taken with ill-grace at the time, in the end procured for Robert Belt Sir Tatton's respect, and patronage as well. And here, it should be said to the credit of Sir Tatton, one of the great land-owners and magnates of the Wolds, that, despite his training and associations, and in the teeth of the clerical pressure brought to bear upon him, he was not slow to recognise the value of Primitive Methodism. He gave land to erect three chapels— Wansford, Wetwang, and Sledmere. The grant for the last-named was largely due to the pluck, persistence, and personal solicitation of Rev. C. Leafe, who, while he travelled the Driffield Circuit, also achieved the task of building chapels at Beswick and Watton. Sir Tatton Sykes is credited with having expressed the following judgment concerning the influence of Methodism in the Wolds. Though Methodism has no need to seek for testimonials to the value of its work, it cannot but be agreeable to have the findings of its annalists and historians confirmed by an outsider, who is at the same time a resident hereditary landlord of the district.

"If it had not been for the Dissenters the English people would have been heathens; and they are worthy of a site on which to build a chapel in every village in the land. *Most of the religion between Malton and Driffield is to be found amongst the Methodists.*"

The most pertinent facts belonging to the introduction of Primitive Methodism into Bridlington can soon be given. John Coulson has the honour of being the Connexion's pioneer labourer in Bridlington and its vicinity. His name stands in connection with Bridlington on the plan of ministerial fixtures made September, 1820. Tradition tells that he walked over from Driffield one Saturday afternoon so as to be in time for the close of the Bridlington Market, and that his first service was interrupted by the constable. It gives also reminiscences of his visits to Flamborough and Filey. Before the close of the year W. Clowes made his way from Preston-in-Holderness to Bridlington, in order to survey the land and have a consultation with Mr. Coulson as to the prospects of the mission already begun. He speaks of finding already thirty members at Bridlington, and of assisting Mr. Coulson to draw up a plan for the working of the mission. The next quarterly meeting of the Hull Circuit appointed Clowes to reinforce and still further extend this east-coast mission; and his *Journals* show that from January to March, and again in July, 1821, he was engaged in the work of opening up the coast and its hinterland from Bridlington to Sandsend beyond Whitby. Remember, it was winter-time, and that the cutting north-easters on that high and rock-bound coast search to the very marrow, yet Clowes and his helpers preached at Bridlington on the Quay, on Scarborough Sands and in the Castle-Dykes, in Whitby Market-place, and on the beach at Robin Hood's Bay, as well as in barns as at Ayton and Seamer, in school-rooms and houses. The mission was strengthened by the drafting in of other labours, and the result of their joint toil laid the foundation of what are now the Bridlington, Filey, Scarborough, and Whitby Circuits. Clowes, as we know, was a man who habitually expected great things from God, yet he says: "When I look at the work in Yorkshire it is amazing to me." *Our* amazement is called forth by the sight of the labour performed no less than by its results.

Owing to its position Bridlington quite naturally had many of the characteristics of a Wold circuit. These characteristics it still retains, with others due to its proximity to the sea. In Bridlington old town and its offshoot, Bridlington Quay, these features may be seen in contrast almost side by side. If Bridlington, with its fine old Priory Church, reminds us of Driffield, only that it is a little more quiet and sleepy, the Quay, only a mile away, would rather suggest Scarborough or Whitby. This, in 1820, was an old-fashioned sea-port, and not unknown even in those pre-railway days as a modest watering-place. At the Quay the scene was often animated enough; for

BRIDLINGTON QUAY.

sometimes the noble bay—bounded on the north by the lighthouse on Flamborough Head which Clowes visited—would be crowded with vessels lying becalmed, or seeking shelter from rough or contrary winds. The residents of the Quay were of the amphibious kind one might expect to find in such a place—a few fishermen, shipowners, or those concerned in the unloading, refitting, or victualling of ships, with a few visitors and retired persons whose tastes brought them to the sea. Primitive Methodism early got a footing both in Bridlington and the Quay. Here lived Mr. Stephenson, an early befriender of the cause, whose vessel John Oxtoby, when standing on the pier, singled out from a number of others, though his eye had never rested either on the vessel or its picture before. It had been feared the vessel was lost, but Oxtoby had prayed about it, and it had been revealed to him that the ship he now identified would come safe to port. The first unpretentious chapel at the Quay was built in 1823. In the bight of Bridlington Bay the sea has made sad encroachment on the land, and in course of time the first chapel stood so near the cliff that when the north-easters blew it shook again, and was wet with the flying spume and spray. Not before time a second chapel was built on another site in 1870, still further enlarged in 1879.* In the old town a building was acquired and fitted up as a chapel capable of accommodating two hundred hearers. This was opened by W. Clowes and Atkinson Smith in 1836.

With the conspicuous exception of Flamborough, soon to be referred to, the landward villages of Bridlington, like the rest of the Wold villages, are agricultural, inhabited chiefly by farmers and labourers, and the small tradesmen and craftsmen who minister to their simple wants. Amongst these Primitive Methodism made its way. Some of its converts were men of strong individuality, and rendered long and effective service—men like Jonathan Goforth, of North Burton, local preacher, natural philosopher, antiquarian, and intermeddler in all sorts of out-of-the-way knowledge. Jonathan Goforth was of the same craft as Thomas Wood, of Driffield. Writing in 1821, William Cobbett says that shoemaking is "a trade which numbers more men of sense and of public spirit than any other in the kingdom."† The fact, vouched for by Rev. H. Woodcock, that at one time there stood on the two plans of Driffield and Bridlington Circuits the names of no fewer than twenty-one persons who followed this trade, speaks well for the degree to which Primitive Methodism had got hold of "the men of sense and public spirit" in the Wold country. Bridlington Circuit too, like Driffield, has had its peasant stalwarts; such as Mark Normandale, of Thornholme, whose sturdy attachment to Methodism was a thorn in the side of Archdeacon Wilberforce. Happily, Lady St. Quintin had more tolerance than her clergyman, and declined to bring pressure to bear upon her employé. Bridlington Circuit has given to the ranks of the ministry G. Normandale, H. Woodcock, the well-known writer and historian of Wold Primitive Methodism, W. R. Monkman, W. Hall, W. Sawyer, W. Mainprize, and T. R. Holtby.

Quite early Bridlington had close relations both with Driffield and Scarborough, but in the end its natural connection with the Wolds prevailed, and Flamborough, where the horn of the crescent of the Wolds projects into the sea, became the limit of the circuit. But in 1827, we find the "Bridlington and Scarborough Union Branch of Hull Circuit"—"Bridlington to have the priority." In 1833, Bridlington and Driffield are together a branch of Hull. In 1843, it becomes a branch of Driffield, and in 1859 an independent circuit.

THE FLAMBOROUGH AND FILEY FISHERMEN.

We have no intention of writing the history of Flamborough or Filey Primitive

---

* "The entire street in which my mother was born, and in which she passed her early years [at Bridlington], has long since been swallowed up by the ever-encroaching sea."—T. Mozley's "Reminiscences," vol. i., p. 148.

† Cobbett's "Rural Rides," vol. i., p. 55.

Methodism. That has already largely been done.* What concerns us here is, the significance of that history as an episode in the larger history of our Church's advance and mission. The capital fact demanding notice is that Hull's Bridlington Mission for the first time brought the agents of our Church into direct, close, and permanent contact with a distinct class—the fishermen who ply their hazardous calling around our coasts. With what result? We have seen what the new evangelism did for the folk of the Yorkshire Dales and Moors; did it succeed in moralising and sweetening the lives of the fisher-folk dwelling on the cliffs and in the coves "between the heather and the northern sea"? It made a determined attempt to reach them. Did the attempt succeed? Let us see.

FLAMBOROUGH HEAD.

Flamborough, on its bold head-land crowned with the well-known lighthouse, with its cliffs and caves and sea-birds, and the famous entrenchment of the Danes' Dyke running from the North Sea to Bridlington Bay, and cutting off the huge cantle of land on which the village stands, is one of the most interesting spots in England, and its hardy inhabitants, chiefly fishermen, are equally interesting, possessing as they do many distinctive traits. A thousand years ago or so the predatory Danes took possession of this natural stronghold, which, perhaps, the Britons had dug out a thousand years

* See especially "Our Filey Fishermen," by Rev. G. Shaw, 1867. "God's Hand in the Storm," by Rev. C. Kendall, 1870. "Life of John Oxtoby."

before. This stronghold the new-comers fortified and continued to hold. They intermarried, and lived so much a people apart, that their home got the name of "Little Denmark." To this day, it is said, the Flamborians give evidence of their Scandinavian origin in build and gait and complexion, as also perhaps in the deep religiousness of their nature, which, largely if not wholly, purged from the superstition of the past, made them take so kindly to Methodism, that this coigne of Yorkshire has now become one of its strongholds. From the very first, Primitive Methodism found ready acceptance in Flamborough. W. Clowes was frequently here, and as early as January 14th, 1821, he notes in his *Journal*:—

> "I preached again at Flamborough at two and six. It was a very gracious day: two souls got liberty. Fifty in society, and I joined five more. Monday, 15th, brother Coulson preached, and I gave an exhortation. One soul got liberty."

The Flamborians are now largely a sober, chapel-going and God-fearing people. What they were at the beginning of the nineteenth century was something very different, corresponding rather to the couplet:—

> "A wretched church, and a wooden steeple,
> A drunken parson, and a wicked people."

Very suggestive in this regard is the statement, made on good authority, that it was not with the goodwill of many of the people of these parts that the noble lighthouse was erected. One of the first converts of Primitive Methodism in Flamborough was Leonard Mainprize. Considering what the family, of which he was the head, has done and is doing for the interests of our Church in Bridlington Circuit, the winning of such a man must be reckoned a good day's work. One of Leonard's sons was Vicarman Mainprize, for many years a typical working fisherman, who in following his calling had many hairbreadth escapes. Comparatively late in life he became a rich man through the coming to him of a legacy. The change in his circumstances made no difference to the simplicity of his Christian character, though it greatly augmented his power for doing good, and the Bridlington Circuit reaped the benefit of his beneficence.

Midway between Scarborough and Whitby stands Filey, fronting its noble bay. Now it is widely known as a beautiful health-resort, but at the time of which we write, it was little more than a fishing-village. One who was there in 1823, speaks of its "one short row of small cottages, like a coast-guard station, built for visitors who did not come." Hard as it is for us to realise it now, Filey was then "noted for vice and wickedness of every description." So says Mr. Petty in his *History*, and all the evidence goes to prove the truth of the indictment. The Sabbath was disregarded; if anything, the Sabbath was the busiest day of all the week. There was plenty of superstition, the dark survival of Pagan times, but of real religion there was little enough. Methodism was struggling for existence, and the influence of the Church was almost a negative quantity.

MR. V. MAINPRIZE.

True, there was an ancient fabric—St. Oswald's—which stood on the other side of the ravine that divides the North and East Ridings, but according to the testimony of the visitor already mentioned, it was "a dreary and not quite weatherproof building." Both the situation and condition of the parish church were emblematic of the aloofness of the people from the religion it stood for. So far from exerting any practical influence on the lives of the bulk of the fishermen, it might as well have been in another world as in another Riding. "Like priest, like people," says the adage, and what both priest and people were like may be judged by an incident which took place at the bedside of a dying parishioner, who had asked that he might receive the last sacrament :—

"Parson *(loquitur):* 'Do you swear?' Sick man: 'No.' 'Do you ever get drunk?' 'No.' After other questions of a similar kind, the parson asked: 'Do you owe any debts?' 'No.' 'Well, then, you are all right. But you owe me my

FILEY.
From a photo by Walter Fisher and Sons, Filey.

fee for your father's gravestone, and I cannot give you the sacrament until you have paid me.' The dying man settled with the clergyman, received absolution, and died satisfied."*

There is pathos about the life of the fisherman—an undertone of sadness like the moaning of the harbour-bar Charles Kingsley speaks of :—

"For men must work, and women must weep;
And there's little to earn, and many to keep,
Though the harbour-bar be moaning."

* "Filey and its Fishermen," Thomas P. Mozley, who was at Filey in 1823 and 1825, and in the latter year attended "The Fishermen's Chapel," *i.e.,* the Primitive Methodist Chapel, refers to this clergyman, "Reminiscences," vol. i., p. 444.

That pathetic undertone was distinctly to be heard in Filey and many another fishing-village eighty years ago. You could catch the sound of it beneath and despite the rude sports, the loud ribald song, the boisterous merriment. There were the daily toil, the hazard of storm and disaster, the anxiety of women waiting and watching at home. The stones in the old churchyard bore the silent record of many such lowly domestic tragedies. There is a passage in one of Mary Linskell's books as true of Filey and Flamborough as of more northern Robin Hood's Bay or Staithes:—

"The two women with whom Genevieve had come down from Thurkeld Abbas were the daughters of a drowned man, the widows of drowned men, the sisters of drowned men. All they possessed—the means of life itself—had come to them from the sea; the self-same sea had taken from them all that made life worth living."*

Such was Filey, and such, thank God! it soon ceased to be. It needed vital religion to moralise the people. The men needed it to give them strength to cope with the storm and the imminent danger. The women—bread-winners, too—needed it to help them to bear the strain of anxiety, and to comfort them in the time of their desolation. And vital religion came. How and with what results we must briefly tell.

Filey was not so easily won as Flamborough and other places along the coast. It was tried again and again, but the stolid indifference of the people seemed impenetrable. But for John Oxtoby, Filey might have been left to its fate. The tradition is, that when the question of continuance or discontinuance was under serious discussion at the Bridlington Quarterly Meeting, held at the house of Mr. Stephenson, Oxtoby, who had kept silent hitherto, was appealed to, and unhesitatingly gave his judgment in favour of prosecuting the mission. Abandon Filey? It was not to be thought of for a moment. God had a great work to do in Filey; and Oxtoby declared himself ready to engage in that work, whatever privations it might involve. This ended the discussion, and it was resolved to give Filey *one* more trial. Oxtoby had got as far as Muston Hill, on his way to attempt what many regarded as a forlorn hope, when the sight of Filey in the distance drove him to his knees. His audible petitions were not only intensely earnest, but so familiar as almost to suggest irreverence, did we not know the man and the essential reverence as well as intimacy of his intercourse with God. He—John Oxtoby—had given a pledge that "God was going to revive His work at Filey," and He must do it, or His servant would not be able to hold up his head. He put God on His honour; He would not allow His servant to be discredited: "That be far from Thee, Lord." He received the assurance that God would verily keep His word, and rose from his knees, saying: "Filey is taken! Filey is taken!" To the foresight of faith, the work not yet begun was already accomplished. Oxtoby, on Muston Hill, pleading for Filey, recalls William Braithwaite's wrestling for souls at East Stockwith,† and both incidents have their counterpart in John Ride's and Thomas Russell's victorious conflict on Ashdown for the salvation of Berkshire. They make companion pictures. "Give me souls, or I shall die;" "Filey is taken!" "Yonder country's ours!" are only short

---

* "Between the Heather and the Northern Sea," p. 77.
† *Ante*, vol. i., pp. 369 and 419.

sentences, and easily rememberable; but they are, in their way, as significant for Primitive Methodist history as some of the sayings of great captains, like Nelson, are significant for English history.

Filey *was* taken. The remarkable revival of 1823 was morally revolutionary and lasting in its results. It laid the foundations of a strong cause in Filey, and before the year ended a chapel was built, which, after two enlargements, was in 1871 superseded by a handsome and commodious edifice. The Wesleyan Society shared in the labours and success of the revival, and was much quickened and largely augmented, and even the parish church began to look up and to be better attended. The morals of the village rapidly improved. Religion wrought for sobriety, thrift, softening of manners, social peace, and domestic concord. It was Filey fishermen who led the way in abandoning Sunday fishing. At first the innovators were a small minority, and met with the usual difficulties experienced by reformers. Even if they had been losers by their Sabbath observance, the obligation to keep the Sabbath would have been the same; but, as a matter of fact, they were not losers, but caught more lasts of herrings in six days than others did in seven; until even the small fisher-lads would observe: "If there were twea (two) herrings in the sea Ranter Jack would be seaär to git yan (one) on them." The good example, honoured by Providence, was infectious. Gradually other skippers and owners fell into line with the reformers, until Sabbath observance became the rule. In short, compared with what it had been, Filey became a model fishing-town, so that in 1863 the Rev. Edwin Day, Wesleyan minister, could declare: "He had considerable knowledge of the fishermen on many parts of our coast, but he knew none equal to the Filey fishermen, and he declared, with the greatest freedom, that their superiority was entirely owing to the successful labours of the Primitive Methodist Connexion."

FILEY CHAPEL.

All the credit—if any credit at all belongs to the human agents—must not be given to J. Oxtoby for the remarkable revival of 1823. Not forgetting the pioneer labours of

J. Coulson, we find that J. Peart, B. Morris, W. Howcroft, and W. Garner, all took part in it, and it was under a sermon, preached by J. Peart, that the revival may be said to have begun. But even if we could have wished it otherwise, the rustic evangelist, whose prayers and homely exhortations were couched in the broad East-Riding dialect, is the chief outstanding figure. Tradition persists in associating Oxtoby's name with the revival as its main instrument; and those who have closely studied the history of Filey Primitive Methodism, and are best acquainted with the spirit and prominent features of its Church-life, are the readiest to admit that, in this instance, tradition has not erred; that Oxtoby's influence was not only great and formative at the time, but also procreative of its like, shaping the lives of those who were to become, in their turn, the shapers and directors of the society and circuit. We may here, with advantage, adduce the testimony of the Rev. R. Harrison:—

"Primitive Methodism is very much what it is in Filey through the prayers and faith of 'Praying Johnny.' Those who have thought much respecting the history, methods, and spirit of our Church in Filey, see to what extent he has been, and is reflected and reproduced. It has always been marked by Christian simplicity, strong faith, and direct, earnest prayer. It would be under rather than over the mark to say that as many souls have been saved in the class meetings as after the preaching services. There has always been a strange social element in the Church-life of Filey, and a marked domesticity in its devotions."

Foremost among the converts of Oxtoby, who became the originators and shapers of the society, may be named Mrs. Gordon, John Wyville, and William Jenkinson. The first-named was the wife of a coastguard officer, a woman of education, who had travelled and seen the world, and was ready to be led into the light and repose of faith by Oxtoby. Mrs. Gordon was one of the most remarkable and useful women Primitive Methodism has produced, nor must the fame she afterwards acquired as "the Queen of Missionary Collectors," and the work she did in London, be allowed to obscure her claim to have been one of the nursing mothers of our cause in Filey. She, in her turn, was instrumental in the conversion of Ann Cowling, afterwards Mrs. Jenkinson, who became second only to herself as a missionary collector, and, as such, excited the wonder of W. Clowes as to how she contrived to raise so much money, until he learned that there was an agreement between the fishermen and herself that they should give her for the missionary cause a certain percentage on all the fish they caught above a certain quantity, on condition that she prayed for them while they were fishing.

John Wyville, who survived until 1866, was another of the "old standards" of Filey. He never forgot John Oxtoby's placing his hand on his shoulder and saying: "Thou must get converted, for the Lord has a great work for thee to do." The saying was prophetic and fulfilled to the letter. He soon after joined the society, attended to reading and the cultivation of his mind, and became a laborious and efficient local preacher. William Jenkinson (*obit.* 1866) was yet a third convert of Oxtoby's, who lived to see one hundred of his relatives members of society.

The godly succession has been kept up by such men as the brothers Jenkinson and Matthew Haxby, whose portraits appropriately have a place in our pages. Their evangelistic labours as "the Filey Fishermen" have made them widely known, but how much good they have exerted by their example and leadership and personal influence cannot be told here. Jenkinson Haxby happily still survives, and was honoured in 1902 by being made a permanent member of Conference.

In closing our observations on the Flamborough and Filey fishermen, we are again reminded of the toils, anxieties, and hazards of the fisherman's life. We still hear the sad undertone, as of the moaning of the harbour-bar. The biographies in our *Magazines*, through a succession of years, show how many of our adherents have been engulphed by the sea from which they sought their livelihood. It is pleasing to know that religion, as presented by our Church, makes the fisherman none the less hardy, brave, self-sacrificing. In the terrible storm of October, 1869, Richard Haxby, sen., said to his crew: "Now, some of you have a wife and young children dependent upon you; I have a wife that I well prize, but no young children, therefore, you should seek every precaution to shun risk and escape death. Besides, you are not ready for another world; Frank and I are insured for eternal life; *therefore, lash us to the tiller, and you go below where there is less danger.*" * This is no solitary instance. In that same storm Matthew Haxby, referred to above, caused himself to be lashed to the tiller, and steered the vessel during most of the seventy hours, for said he: "If a wave comes and washes me overboard, I am all right. I shall go straight to heaven, where there is no more sea."

MR JENKINSON HAXBY.

Religion, in the form of Primitive Methodism, suits the fisherman well, and the fisherman at his best has done Primitive Methodism infinite credit. That, we trust, is what this *History* shows; for after all, while for obvious reasons we have spoken much of Filey, it is taken as a type and object-lesson. While writing of Filey and Flamborough, we have found our thoughts turning to Scarborough and Staithes, to Cullercoats, and to fishing-towns and villages in East Anglia and Cornwall, and elsewhere, where our Church has done a similar work, in kind if not in degree, amongst the fishermen as it has achieved at Flamborough and Filey.

SCARBOROUGH AND WHITBY MISSION.

"On Saturday, January 27th, 1821, by an unexpected providence, my way was opened to preach at Scarborough." So stands the record in the *Magazine*. How providence opened Clowes' way we are not distinctly told. Possibly he may have had an invitation to visit the town, backed by the offer of the use of Mr. Lamb's schoolroom. Be this as it may, on the date mentioned, Clowes, accompanied by his friend Coulson, walked to Scarborough, and found on his arrival a few persons whose minds, stirred by a ripple of excitement, were already in a state of expectancy. Some one had dreamed the night before that he saw two "Ranters' preachers" going up the streets of Scar-

MR. MATTHEW HAXBY.
By permission of W. Fisher and Son, Filey.

---

* "God's Hand in the Storm," p. 30.

108   PRIMITIVE METHODIST CHURCH.

borough with an intention to preach the gospel. The dream would naturally help on its own fulfilment, and Mr. Clowes preached in the schoolroom and Mr. Coulson elsewhere. Three full Sundays out of the six yet available for this mission were devoted by Clowes to Scarborough, and two to Whitby, while the remaining Sunday was divided between Scarborough and Seamer. At Scarborough, his practice was to preach twice in the schoolroom and once on the sands, and he notes with satisfaction that the people who came to the seaside services in such multitudes, behaved with decorum and listened attentively to the Word. The first society class in Scarborough was formed by Clowes on February 11th, and before he returned to Hull, by way of Flamborough and Bridlington, in order to attend the March Quarterly Meeting, the nine members had been increased by later converts.

From Scarborough Clowes pushed on for Whitby, but as he passed through Robin Hood's Bay, the fishermen "got wit" that a "Ranter preacher" was amongst them, and Clowes was fain to preach in three houses opening into one another. This plural place of assembly was packed with people. When, soon after, Clowes paid a return visit to Robin Hood's Bay, and held a service by preference on the beach, he was assisted by J. Branfoot, and had as one of his hearers William Harland, the young schoolmaster of Stainton Dale, who then and there resolved to lead a Christian life. At Whitby, Clowes followed the same method of procedure as at Scarborough. Both on the 11th and 18th of February, one of the services of the day was held in the market-place. At the first some unruly spirits were present disposed for mischief, but "a man of weight, for duty done and public worth," was on the ground in the person of the Chief Constable, and his presence exerted a restraining influence.

WHITBY TOWN HALL.

The man of authority had met with Clowes when conveying prisoners to York, and had listened to his preaching in the open-air. He had then assured Clowes of a hospitable reception, should he ever find his way to Whitby. To his honour, be it said, the Chief Constable made good his word. Fryup in the Dale, Lyth, Sandsend, besides Ayton and Seamer, were also visited by Clowes during his mission.

The mention of Rev. W. Harland's name above, may remind us that in the persons of John and Thomas Nelson—who are said to have come from a village near Whitby,—of Henry Hebbron and of William Harland, the North Riding of Yorkshire gave Primitive Methodism four men who, in their day, were extraordinarily useful and popular. Had the Hutton Rudby and East Coast Missions together done nothing more than send forth these early workers, it would have yielded an abundant return for the toil and self-sacrifice involved in prosecuting the missions; since in the formative period of the Connexion—just when it was ready to take the shaping and impress of strongly marked personalities, these men gave their zeal and strength, their wit and humour and popular gifts to the work.

Mr. Hebbron and the Nelson brothers we shall meet again in the Sunderland District; but a further word may be permitted in reference to William Harland who, with William Garner, William Sanderson, and George Lamb, lived to be reckoned one of Hull District's "grand old men." William Harland was a native of Newton near Pickering, and was born in 1801. He was educated for a schoolmaster, and hence, from a scholastic point of view, was privileged beyond most of his brethren. Those who came in contact with him were impressed with his amiability no less than with his intelligence. On a subsequent visit to these parts, Mr. Clowes had some conversation with the young schoolmaster, who set him on his way to Cloughton after preaching at Stainton-Dale, and found him to be "a young man of considerable information and kindness of disposition, and capable of doing much good in his day and generation." Yet Mr. Harland did not for some time identify himself with the new movement, though he lent his schoolroom for preaching services and duly attended them. At last, however, he made up his mind. Mr. W. Howcroft had given an invitation to all who desired to become members to remain after the service and he would give them a ticket on trial; whereupon Mr. Harland stepped up to his own desk and asked if the preacher would give him a ticket on trial. "No; I won't"; said Mr. Howcroft, "but I will give you one as an approved member." Mr. Harland preached his first sermon at the opening of Newton chapel, which was a converted cart-shed, and he lived to preach the opening services of the chapel subsequently erected in 1850. At the Hull Quarterly Meeting, September 1838, Bro. J. Harrison was appointed "to consult him respecting his willingness to enter our ministry." Mr. Harland *was* willing, and for forty-three years he rendered good service on the platform, where he was at his best, and in the pulpit. He was elected President of the Conference of 1862, and filled the editorial chair from 1850 to 1862. He was made a deed-poll member in 1870, and retained that office till 1879, when growing physical infirmities compelled him to resign. Mr. Harland died October 10th, 1880.

No agent better suited for carrying forward the work already begun could have been found than N. West, who was now borrowed from Malton for a month. He made his way to Whitby, where, on the 25th March, he preached twice in the market-place and once in a house, and next day formed the new converts, numbering fifty-five, into three classes. At Robin Hood's Bay there were, he notes, already twenty-eight in society.

Two Sundays N. West laboured at Scarborough. On April 1st, he "stood up" at the Castle Dykes and preached to a large congregation, made up of all sorts of people— "quality, poor, soldiers, sailors," &c. "At half-past five," says he, "I stood up in the name of the Lord again; but was much disturbed by Satan, who opposed very much by his slavish vassals; however, through God we got through, and at night held a prayer meeting. After all, we were more than conquerors through Jesus, for fifteen fresh members joined." On the following Sunday he preached twice on the sands. In the morning, many were observed to weep who had despised religion before, and at the afternoon service there were supposed to have been no less than three thousand present who "paid great attention."

Nathaniel West went back to Malton, and R. Abey came on the ground. In his *Journal* he notes the opening of the first chapel in Scarborough, May 13th, 1821. This home-made structure was designed and built by brother Luccock, and stood on the site of an ancient Franciscan Convent in St. Sepulchre Street. A Sabbath school being urgently needed, the western wing of the building was appropriated to the purpose. To save expense, the work was done by amateurs. George Tyas laid the bricks for the partition wall, and James and William Wyrill fixed the doors and window-frames. These two brothers became the first superintendents of the school, and James Linn became its first scholar. A melancholy interest attaches to the name of James Wyrill. In the terrible storm of February 24th, 1844, the yawl he commanded was struck by a heavy sea when making for the harbour, and went down with all hands in sight of the multitude lining the pier and foreshore. James Wyrill's body was recovered after being in the sea one hundred and twenty-nine days. This sad incident is recalled to show, that ever since Clowes and Nathaniel West numbered fishermen among their auditors, our Church in Scarborough has succeeded in attaching some of those who live by the fishing industry of the town to its fellowship, and has found among them some of its most earnest workers. In this connection the names of Sellars and Appleby should not be omitted.

R. Abey, who opened the first chapel, tells us that during his eleven weeks' term of service on the Scarborough Mission he saw one hundred and ten added to the societies. Then, according to the arrangement made at the first Conference, he and Thomas Sugden were to be transferred to the Tunstall District, while S. Turner and J. Garner were to be drafted to fill their place in the Hull District. When Abey took his departure, a number of the Scarborough friends accompanied him a couple of miles on his way, and then by prayer commended him to the grace of God. R. Abey, having travelled eight years with acceptance, settled down on a small farm at Snainton, and continued a useful local preacher. Bridlington and Scarborough (with Whitby) were now in June, 1821, made the heads of distinct branches, and John Garner was appointed to the former and S. Turner to the latter, the two young men walking from Hull to take up their respective charges. By September it was reported that the work was going steadily on in the Bridlington Branch, and that it had three preachers and 390 members. Scarborough, too, must have made some progress, since in 1823, it was made a separate circuit. Such, however, it remained only for one year. When, in 1824, Whitby was taken from it to form a new circuit, the membership of Scarborough

THE PERIOD OF CIRCUIT PREDOMINANCE AND ENTERPRISE. 111

Circuit was reduced to 160, and it became once more a branch of Hull, and as such it remained, either conjointly with Bridlington or separately, until finally, in 1852, it became a circuit with 654 members. Apart from Scarborough's claim to be the queen of watering-places, there are other considerations, which make all that relates to the beginning and development of our Church in the ancient borough of some interest to Primitive Methodists. To name but two of such considerations: Scarborough is, next to Hull, the largest town in the Hull District, and it is a recognised popular Conference town: sure sign that the denomination has, like Grimsby—with which it has many points of affinity—attained to considerable strength and influence. The history of Scarborough Primitive Methodism has had its two dispensations—the old and the new—rather sharply marked off from each other. The contrast between the Scarborough of 1820, with its primitive Spa, and the Scarborough of the present day, with its

OLD SCARBOROUGH, 1820.

magnificent Spa Saloon and all else that is the outgrowth of recent years, is great indeed, as our illustrations show. But the contrast between the Primitive Methodism of the old epoch and the new in Scarborough is scarcely less noteworthy; and yet how comparatively recent these more impressive developments have been! It is with a feeling of surprise we realise that, as late as 1860, the only chapel the denomination could show in Scarborough was the one standing on the original site in St. Sepulchre Street. True, the building had been enlarged in 1839 to hold seven hundred hearers, but still, we who worshipped there can recall now how the lengthening shadows of the old dispensation rested upon the building. Good work was done in the old sanctuary. There were worthy men—men of intelligence and character, and of Connexional loyalty—

men like Messrs. Boreman, Fenby, Linn, Sellars, Appleby, and especially John Yule, shrewd, quaint, who knew both the outside and inside of books almost as well as he knew men. There were seasons of revival, and much enthusiasm and success in the 'raising of missionary money, but for all that, one can see now that, until the building of Jubilee Chapel in 1861, the good old dispensation reigned. This enterprise was a turning-point and new departure, and, historically, rightly belongs to the chapel-building era, that seems to have been inaugurated by the erection in Hull of Jarratt Street Chapel. There were those of the old dispensation, however, in Scarborough as there were in Hull, who did not understand or sympathise with the new movement then having its beginning. Men shook their heads and prophesied disaster, but,

SCARBOROUGH, PRESENT DAY.

happily, lived long enough to see their lugubrious predictions falsified.* The *vis inertiæ*

* If any proof is needed of the statement here made, it will be found in a letter of warning and remonstrance written to the superintendent at the time by Rev. J. Flesher then resident in the town. That letter is printed in the memoir of C. Kendall, *Magazine*, 1882, and remains to show how even the great and good may have their limitations of view. This reference is due to the dead, and would, one cannot but think, be approved by them; for Mr. Flesher closes his letter which had to be read to the "go-a-heads" with the words: "I keep a rough draft of these views for future reference, and should unexpected facts prove them to be ill-founded, I shall, if alive, rejoice that the superior prudence and zeal of these brethren who think and act differently from me, have been crowned with complete success."

THE PERIOD OF CIRCUIT PREDOMINANCE AND ENTERPRISE. 113

to be overcome was so great, that the superintendent, who had gone some way in pushing on the project for the new chapel, resolved to leave the circuit and let some one else come to it who could bring the undertaking to a successful issue, and then enjoy the fruition of the work. He exchanged circuits with Hugh Campbell, whom

JAMES LINN.

W. BOREMAN.

J. SELLARS.

REV. T. WHITEHEAD.

J. YULE.

W. APPLEBY.

REV. H. CAMPBELL.

we may justly regard as one of the great chapel-builders of the Hull District, since sixteen chapels and two unfinished ones, besides schools at Louth and ministers' houses at Scotter, stand to his credit. Mr. Campbell came fresh from building Victoria Street Chapel, Grimsby, but, unfortunately, he lost his life as the result of a street-accident

H

before the Aberdeen Walk Chapel was opened in 1861. Another notable advance was marked, combining all that was best both in the old and new, when a new chapel, handsome and commodious, was built in 1866 in St. Sepulchre Street, under the superintendency of the Rev. Thomas Whitehead. Since then, as our own view of Scarborough chapels shows, still further chapel extension has taken place in the borough. For Scarborough the chapel-building era has done great things, as it has done also for Grimsby.

CHAPTER XVI.

THE MAKING OF SUNDERLAND DISTRICT.

THOUGH we begin a fresh chapter, it is but to resume the narrative of Hull Circuit's missionary efforts at the precise point the two preceding chapters left it. These further advances, both in a westerly and northerly direction, resulted in the formation, in 1824, of a new district made up of those branches that were deemed sufficiently strong to stand alone. These new intakes from the outlying field of the world were called the Sunderland District, because the largest and strongest circuits of the district were found along the lower reaches of the Tyne and the Wear, and were the outcome of the Northern Mission. But it is observable that in the Sunderland District, as originally constituted, the Silsden and Keighley Circuits also have a place, the reason being that, besides its Northern Mission, Hull Circuit had also a mission in the West Riding beyond Leeds, among "Craven hills and Airedale streams," and Silsden and Keighley, the first-fruits of this line of evangelisation, were incorporated with the newly-made Sunderland District. This Western or Craven mission had extensions into Lancashire, even as far as the Ribble, and the fact that Preston, Blackburn and Clitheroe stand on the stations of 1824, shows that this evangelistic movement did not spend its force this side the Pennine range. For the time being these Lancashire circuits are attached to Tunstall District, but they will naturally fall to Manchester District when that is formed in 1827. Nor is this all; while moving west and north, Hull Circuit was also at the same time, with Darlington and Barnard Castle Branches as a convenient base, pushing on vigorously in the north-west, and by 1824, Hexham and Carlisle were fit for self-government, and accordingly have their place among the stations of the Sunderland District. Looking at their result, we may regard these three lines of evangelisation as parts of one movement. We have Sunderland District in the making.

HULL'S WESTERN MISSION: SILSDEN IN CRAVEN, AND KEIGHLEY.

Primitive Methodism went into Craven, to Darlington, to Newcastle, to North Shields, just as it had gone to Hull and Leeds—by invitation. In each case, before he went, the missionary had heard the cry—"Come over and help us." But the cry came not from those who wanted saving but from those who wanted to save, and had their own ideas as to how the salvation could best be brought about. One anticipatory observation we cannot forbear making once for all: it is remarkable how in almost every successive district into which Primitive Methodism came, there was the repetition on a small scale of what had taken place in Staffordshire at the beginning of its history. The fact points to the prevalence of similar conditions of church-life—to conflicting ideals of Christian worship, duty and service. To some in the same church "revivalism" was not wanted any more than fire or fever; while to others it was the thing above all others they wished to see. Differences which have disappeared, or if they have not, no longer serve to divide men, then seemed formidable and unadjustable. These differences were not lessened by the fact that what one class regarded as innovations in practice, the other class claimed to be "according to Wesley"—original and "primitive." So brethren did not quite see eye to eye, and got to be at cross-purposes. These differences ever along tended to differentiate themselves so as to become cognisant to sense, and it has taken three-quarters of a century to disentangle these differences and to bring the estranged brethren together again. Reflections such as these will be obvious enough as we follow the narrative through this new chapter.

Silsden, in Craven, whence came one of these Macedonian cries, was, in 1821,

REV. JOHN FLESHER'S HOME, SILSDEN.

a village of some 1300 inhabitants, who were chiefly engaged in nail-making and wool-combing. As to higher matters, the place, we are told, was notorious for "ignorance, rudeness and crime." And yet, it hardly should have rested under such a stigma, for Silsden was not far distant from Haworth, where Grimshawe had preached and prayed. Six miles away was Skipton, the capital of the Craven district, with its historic castle and its memories of the Cliffords. At this time, John Flesher was living in Silsden at the house of his father, the village schoolmaster. Though but a youth of twenty he had been a Wesleyan Methodist five years, and already had preached his trial sermon before the Rev. Joseph Fowler, of "Sidelights" fame.* As is the case with the many,

* "Side Lights on the Conflicts of Methodism. Taken chiefly from the Notes of the late Rev. Joseph Fowler," etc. By Benjamin Gregory, D.D.

the young "local" might have been content to tread the beaten path of routine; but he was not. He spent much time in visitation; he made personal, pointed appeals to his friends and neighbours on soul-matters; he even went the length of preaching from his father's doorstep. We need scarcely wonder if some of his proceedings were little relished by his co-religionists. "How forward! How indiscreet! So young a man, too!' There were head-shakings, and non-committal, critical looks and whisperings. Still there were not wanting those who approved, although they might not share his zeal. One who had been down in Lincolnshire buying wool, brought back glowing accounts of the doings of the Primitives in those parts, and finished with the observation that the young schoolmaster might do worse than invite these people into Craven: they would suit him to a nicety. Whether the suggestion were seriously meant or not, it was seriously taken and soon bore fruit.

Meanwhile, another Wesleyan local preacher in the neighbourhood of Skipton was led to take the same step as John Flesher—to invite the Primitives to enter Craven. John Parkinson, a local preacher since 1812, was what Hugh Bourne would at once have described as a "Revivalist." He had taken part in beginning and carrying on a Sunday school in his father's barn; he did not confine his labours to places set apart for public worship, but preached in the streets and lanes and on village-greens; he had what he called his 'mission,' comprising several villages he regularly visited. The criticism and discouragement, which came in due course, led him seriously to "ponder his ways." Was he right or wrong? After conference with a friend, the two adjourned to an enclosure leading to Silsden Moor, and there they believed they received a divine intimation that they must go on in their chosen line of activity. At this juncture, tidings reached them that hundreds of sinners were being converted in Leeds and its neighbourhood through the labours of the Primitive Methodists, and their "Come over and help us" was duly sent. Their resignations were handed in to the authorities and reluctantly accepted, and they were now free to throw in their lot with the missionaries when they should arrive.

In response to this double invitation, Samuel Laister, whom we have already seen on the Wolds, at Leeds, and at Malton, was sent to Skipton and Silsden, March, 1821, and, soon after, the devoted Thomas Batty came on the ground, and laboured some nine months in Craven before going on the north-western mission at Barnard Castle. Thomas Batty (born 1790) as a child came into close touch with Joseph Benson, Joseph Entwisle and other eminent Wesleyan ministers who were entertained at his father's house. William Bramwell's hand had often been fondly placed on his head. Batty entered the navy and got his discharge in 1813. He became a Wesleyan local preacher at North Frodingham, but having preached at two camp meetings in the Driffield Branch, he had to make his choice between ceasing to attend camp meetings or ceasing to be a Wesleyan local preacher. He chose the latter alternative. This was in the spring of 1820, and just a year after, he began as a hired local preacher in Driffield Branch, and

REV. THOMAS BATTY.
Aged 45 years.

was soon transferred to Silsden Mission. The second service at Silsden was held in the house of Mr. Flesher, sen., and for some little time the society had the use of his barn for religious services. One of Mr. Flesher's cherished recollections was of a certain evening when "forty-four sinners were pricked in their heart under one sermon." One of the forty-four was the late Mr. Joshua Fletcher, for many years a leading Connexional official in Yorkshire. Messrs. David Tillotson and William Newton were also among the first converts in the old barn, and rendered eminent service to the cause, while Silsden was the birth-place, natural and spiritual, of Revs. W. Inman, T. Baron and S. Bracewell, and the home of Mr. G. Baron, whose connection with the Bemersley Book-Room has already been referred to.*

Needless to say, John Flesher not only invited the Primitives to Craven, but when they came united himself to them. Soon, however, he removed to a school in Leeds, and by June, 1822, he had entered the ministry, his first appointment being to Tadcaster. Later, we shall see something of what he was as legislator, re-organiser of the Book-Room and Editor: what he was in his prime as a preacher and platform speaker we can now but imperfectly picture. But one who knew him well, has declared that "he surpassed every other speaker it had been his fortune to listen to, 'in the matter of *passion*,' as Foster phrases it, which he infused into all his discourses." He calls him "the Bradburn of Primitive Methodism," and avers that "he might have been its Watson, if he had not preferred *immediate* to *more remote* results." †

OLD BARN, SILSDEN, WHERE THE FIRST SERVICES WERE HELD.

MR. JOSHUA FLETCHER.    MR. DAVID TILLOTSON.    MR. WILLIAM NEWTON.

* See vol. ii. pp. 7—8 for portraits and further references to the brothers Baron.

† "United Methodist Free Churches' Magazine," 1859. We judge the writer to have been the Editor, Rev. Matthew Baxter, who for two years, 1829-31, was in our ministry. Mr. Flesher had a high estimate of Mr. Baxter's talents.

As a pioneer worker in the Craven district, John Parkinson deserves a further word or two. He is said to have missioned Braildon, and to have been among the first to publish the glad tidings at Keighley, Shipley and Bradford. He, too, was not wanting "in the matter of passion." He evidently had all the intensity and perfervidness of the West Riding temperament, as the following description of an actual camp meeting scene in Craven at which he figured, will show. Mr. Flesher himself is the writer, and while the passage is worth giving as a fair specimen of Mr. Flesher's prose, of which we have so little, it may have its use as going some way to show us—what we are so anxious to know—what sort of preaching it was which in those far-off days produced those immediate and tremendous effects which excite our wonder, and our envy too, as we read.

"He figures in my recollection as I saw him addressing a crowd from a waggon at Silsden. Every eye and heart of the vast assembly seemed riveted on the speaker, and deep feeling was betrayed on every countenance, as if struggling for an outlet. The doom of the finally impenitent was under review at the time, and terribly did the preacher portray it. Suddenly he paused, as if to let his hearers weigh their destinies. This heightened the effect, and many a stone-hearted sinner sighed under the weight of his guilt. As tears were flowing fast, mingling with the moanings of the broken-hearted, brother Parkinson, in apparent triumph, while his countenance, gesture, voice, and feeling harmonised with his address, opened the gate of mercy so effectually that some immediately entered it, and were saved, some clung to the wheels and shelvings of the waggons to avoid being borne down to the ground under the load of guilt, while the praises of the pious poured forth from all parts of the assembly. Jubilant were angels that day over many sinners repenting and turning to Christ."

That John Parkinson missioned Shipley in 1821 is confirmed by Rev. Richard Cordingley, who tells us that meetings were held in the houses of Mrs. Emanuel Hodgson and Mrs. Cordingley. Richard Cordingley joined the class that was formed, and when barely fifteen years of age, came on the Silsden plan, having as his fellow-exhorters Solomon Moore, of Keighley, and Jabez—afterwards Dr.—Burns, whom we shall meet again. Of later worthies of Keighley Primitive Methodism, respectful mention must be made of the two remarkable brothers, Messrs. F. and Addyman Smith.

An untoward event that might have proved a huge disaster happened on the occasion of the holding of the first lovefeast in Keighley, September 16th, 1821, and was deemed of sufficient public interest to be chronicled in the current issue of "The Times." The lovefeast was held in the topmost story of a wool-warehouse. Thomas Batty, as the leader, had just pronounced the benediction, when the floor gave way. With shrieks, and amid dust and broken beams and flooring, the crowd fell into the rooms below. The preacher, by his sailor-like agility, managed to save himself by leaping into the embrasure of a window; but many were hurt, and one woman died next day from injuries received. Some said the event was intended as a judgment on the "Ranters"; nevertheless the cause prospered, and, in 1824, Keighley was made a Circuit of the Sunderland District. One of the first to open his house for religious services was the father of Rev. J. Judson, who began his more public labours by becoming a hired local preacher in Keighley, his native Circuit. His ministry of forty-one laborious years began in 1833 in the Silsden Circuit, where he stayed three years, the last year being devoted to Grassington Mission under the auspices of Keighley. Mr. Judson travelled in most of the leading circuits in the Manchester District, and died at Oldham, June 28th, 1876.

Before leaving the neighbourhood of Keighley, a reference may be permitted to the opening of Haworth by F. N. Jersey, who spent two months on the Silsden Branch. Writing under the date of April 25th, he says:—

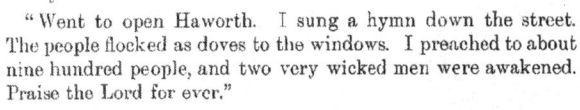

"Went to open Haworth. I sung a hymn down the street. The people flocked as doves to the windows. I preached to about nine hundred people, and two very wicked men were awakened. Praise the Lord for ever."

The Rev. Patrick Brontë became curate of Haworth and removed there in 1820. When F. N. Jersey sang down the streets of the moorland village, Charlotte Brontë was a girl of six. One likes to think that the girl who was to make that village famous heard the singing, and may even have looked on the unwonted scene.

REV. JOHN JUDSON.

Silsden Branch included not only the Craven district, but also some places in the adjoining county of Lancaster, such as Barley, lying under Pendlehill, where there was a vigorous society, and Trawdon, the native place of Robert Hartley, uncle of Mr. W. P. Hartley, whom also this district was afterwards to nurture, to the great advantage of our Church. Born in 1817, Robert Hartley entered the ministry in 1835, and in 1859 went to Australia, "becoming the most widely-known and most generally respected minister of the gospel of Central Queensland." He could count among his friends such men as Canon Knox Little and Dr. A. Maclaren, and at his death, in 1892, the citizens of Rockhampton erected a public memorial to his "noble character, godly life, and untiring benevolence." It was at Barley that John Petty preached, November, 1823, his first sermon, and it was at Trawdon where he began, and fell in lasting love with the practice of open-air preaching. John Petty's home was at Salterforth, a village on the western border of Yorkshire. It was first missioned by F. N. Jersey, who preached in the village street during the dinner-hour. The next to follow was Thomas Batty. In the character of this minister, whom his father entertained, John Petty found the most powerful persuasive to the Christian life. The sermons Batty preached in the barn were not so telling as the sermon he preached by his daily life and conversation. So this thoughtful youth felt. Hence, without any great spiritual shock or struggle, he went on to know the Lord, being "drawn by the cords" of a Christ-like man. Mr. Petty lived to write the biography of his captor for Christ, and he tells how, as a youth of fifteen, "he was deeply moved, and his heart graciously drawn out after God." Mr. Batty, he adds: "Seemed to be always happy, constantly joyful in the Lord, practically presenting religion in a most attractive and winning form. He could converse, sing,

ROBERT HARTLEY.
Aged 43.

preach, and pray almost all day long; and greatly did he charm and profit the domestic circle."* Mr. Petty, sen., became the leader of the first class at Salterforth, while his son was soon to enter on wider service. Two years to a day after preaching his first sermon at Barley, "John Bowes fetched me to help him in Keighley Circuit," says Mr. Petty, and in 1826, when not yet nineteen, he was sent to distant Haverfordwest.†

The missionaries now pushed on still farther into Lancashire. Blackburn and Preston were reached, and these towns became almost at once the head of a new branch. The late Rev. W. Brining affirms that Thomas Batty missioned Preston in 1821. The statement is confirmed by Jonathan Ireland, who tells us that Mr. Batty preached in a cottage, in which some of the more zealous Wesleyans held one of their prayer meetings; that in a short time the members were forbidden to receive the Primitives into their houses, and that some of the members resisted the interdict, Mr. W. Brining, a Wesleyan local preacher, being one.‡ So far Jonathan Ireland. Mr. Brining himself states, that his father and he joined the Primitives in January, 1822, and took a large room, for the rent of which his father became responsible; also that he and three others were appointed local preachers, and that the March Quarterly Meeting of the Hull Circuit "took him out to travel," and that he began his labours on the Preston Branch along with Mr. G. Tindall. There is also evidence to show that John Harrison, too, was an early pioneer labourer in this district. According to the late Rev. S. Smith, Mr. Harrison made his way to Preston, and was entertained by Mr. Shorrocks (afterwards a leader in Manchester), and was also taken before the Mayor of Preston as a suspicious character, but was courteously entreated and dismissed with "a glass of wine!" §

WM. BRINING.

Mr. Batty also opened Blackburn, Wigan, Padiham, and Accrington. From the *Journals* and memoirs of the time, we cull one or two references to these and other places connected with this early mission. We are told that at Blackburn Mr. Batty preached his first sermon standing on a dunghill! Be this as it may, one man that day was, metaphorically, lifted *from* the dunghill; for a certain James Chadwick, one of the worst men in the town, was converted, and became a useful member of society. At Wigan, on May 6th, 1822, he sent the bellman round the town, and in the evening preached to about a thousand people. At Chorley he spoke at the Cross to an immense concourse of people, and in the evening preached in the room which the players had occupied. Mr. Brining made his way to Haslingden, and a class was formed at "Manchester Mary's." Mr. G. Tindall

J. HARRISON,
Aged 42, 1838.

* "Memoir of the Life and Labours of Thomas Batty, 1857," p. 44.
† See *Ante*, vol. i. p. 344.
‡ "Jonathan Ireland, the street-preacher," p. 26. See also for Mr. Ireland's Preston experiences *Ante*, vol. ii., p. 24.
§ "The Introduction and Spread of Primitive Methodism in Lancashire;" in "Facts and Incidents," p. 103.

enters in his *Journal*, on April 25th, 1822 : "Went as a missionary among the small villages to search for places to preach at." On May 6th, he spoke at Clitheroe Market-cross to a large concourse of people, and formed a class of ten members. On June 16th, he spoke at Padiham, Oakenshaw, and Accrington, and adds : "I had to oppose drunkards, formal professors, Unitarians, and almost all other characters of sinners."

The progress made by both branches was such that, in December, 1823, they were granted self-government ; Silsden starting its career with five preachers and Preston with three. At the same time Clitheroe, with Burnley, Accrington, Barley, Colne, and other places were detached, and constituted a branch of Silsden. 1824 saw both Blackburn and Clitheroe raised to the status of circuits. But, ere long, Clitheroe found it difficult to maintain its position, so much so that Keighley, Blackburn, and Bolton Circuits were in succession asked to take it under their wing; but in each case the overture was declined. Then, Daniel-like, the circuit determined "to stand alone ;" only, as Clitheroe Society had for the time being become extinct, Burnley was made the head of the circuit.

Burnley is a typical Lancashire town, largely the creation of the new industrial era. Its position, in a basin-like depression among the hills, has helped it. The humid atmosphere of the valley is just adapted for cotton-spinning, and manufacturers have been quick to seize their advantage, so that now Burnley is a busy centre of the cotton-spinning industry. Hence, if not exactly a town of yesterday, Burnley has made its most notable advance within recent years, as may be gathered from the fact that, at the beginning of the last century, its population was little more than

BETHEL CHAPEL, BURNLEY 1ST CIRCUIT.

five thousand. Our Church has thriven with the thriving of the town. Burnley is understood to be the "Lynford" of Mr. Joseph Hocking's story, "The Purple Robe," and amongst the hard-headed, strenuous folk there depicted, our ministrations have met with much acceptance. When, in 1896, Burnley for the first time welcomed the Conference to North-East Lancashire, any one who saw the commodious and substantially-built chapels in the town and neighbourhood, would have learned with some surprise that, up to 1834, the society of but fifty members had not as yet got its chapel, but had to make shift with rented rooms, four of which were occupied in succession before Curzon Street Chapel was opened in 1834. This "setting-up house" took place during the superintendency of Rev. M. Lee, whose term of service in the Burnley Circuit seems to have begun the era of progress. In 1852, Bethel Chapel was built, and certainly not before time, since Curzon Street Chapel did not provide seatage for much more than half the members who formed the society. This chapel of 1852, since greatly improved and added to, is all that is left to represent the original Burnley Circuit. New interests have been created, and by division and subdivision Burnley Second, Colne, Barrowford, and Nelson Circuits have been formed—the first division taking place in 1864, when Colne started on an independent career.

The historian of Burnley Primitive Methodism has rightly recalled the names of many of its worthies past and present.* We borrow his references to two or three of the early workers. First in order comes John Lancaster, who, as a youth, received lasting good from John Petty when he preached at Burnley in knee-breeches, and standing on the slop-stone. "He was for thirty-three years one of the most devoted and earnest men ever given to a Christian community." Stephen Tattersall "was long a useful and zealous official;" Jonathan Gaukrodger, "ever ready by toil and purse to help the cause;" John Marsden, "cheerful, generous, 'given to hospitality,' an efficient and devoted superintendent of the Sunday School;" W. Thornber, for fifty-five years a local preacher; and John Baldwin, "who may be described as the successor of John Lancaster; for more than thirty years a class-leader, and who for more than half a century filled, with much acceptance, the office of local preacher."

BRIERFIELD CHAPEL, BURNLEY 2ND CIRCUIT.

The head of Burnley Second is Colne Road, Brierfield, with its chapel, erected 1864,

MR. JOHN LANCASTER.   ALD. J. SMITH.   MR. J. CLARKSON.

and its splendid school premises built twenty years after. Connected with this cause, to which he has rendered most efficient aid, is Alderman J. Smith, who was Chairman of the Metropolitan Tabernacle Missionary Meeting in 1902, and who is well known for

* "Bethel Primitive Methodist Chapel, 1852-1902. Jubilee Souvenir," by Rev. George King.

the interest he has taken in the Connexional Orphanage and other institutions. The late James Clarkson was to the Brierfield Society pretty much what John Lancaster was to Bethel. When he was arrested by grace he was a beer-seller; but he pulled down his sign, poured his unsold liquor down the sewer, and never rested till he found forgiveness. "By his diligence, zeal, piety, and abundant labours he became one of the most useful officials in the Connexion."

After Blackburn was made a circuit the same process of "multiplication by division" went on which we have seen at work in the case of Burnley, its earliest offshoot. The one circuit has become at least five; for Blackburn is now represented by Haslingden, formed as long ago as 1837; Foxhill Bank and Accrington, made from Haslingden in 1864, and the three Blackburn Circuits. With Haslingden Circuit was connected Mr. James Whittaker, for many years a prominent Lancashire official. Precisely the same kind of intensive growth has gone on in the Preston Circuit since its formation in 1823. But what it concerns us more just now to note is the fact, that Preston, by its early missionary labours, helped to extend the borders of the Connexion. It pushed forward into new territory—into certain parts of North Lancashire the first missionaries from Hull had not reached. This not very thickly populated country lay to the north by the Lune and Morecambe Bay, and curved round to the Ribble, where, on one side of the estuary, in the Fylde district, were Fleetwood and Blackpool, and on the other Southport, rising among its sandbanks. Here and there in this district Preston succeeded in establishing societies which abide and flourish. Notably Preston began those tentative efforts which ultimately secured a footing for the Connexion in the two popular watering-places, even then fast growing in size and public favour. We must briefly notice these aggressive efforts which were a continuation of Hull's Western Mission, and carried the evangel from the Humber to Morecambe Bay and the sand-dunes by the Irish Sea.

We have before us a plan of Preston Circuit for May–July, 1832, when S. Smith, J. Moore, and J. A. Bastow were its preachers. Halton beyond the Lune and Lancaster are two places on this plan regularly supplied with preachers. At Lancaster the Preston missionaries sometimes experienced rough usage, and occasionally made acquaintance with the interior of Lancaster Castle.* (Parenthetically it may be mentioned that as late as 1874 the Rev. Thomas Wilshaw was summoned by the Chief Constable for preaching from the Town Hall steps. The costs of the defence were generously paid by Mr. James Williamson, jun., afterwards Lord Ashton, and the magistrates dismissed the case). A Missionary Meeting was held at Lancaster in 1829, interesting to us because it brought together Hugh Bourne and a Preston youth who was just about to begin a ministry of unprecedented length and influence. A camp

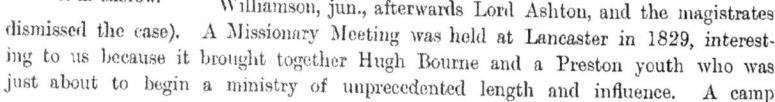

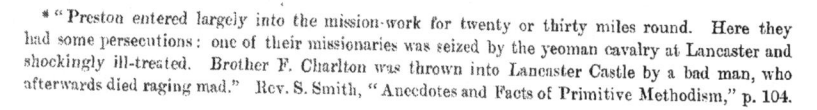

J. A. BASTOW.

* "Preston entered largely into the mission-work for twenty or thirty miles round. Here they had some persecutions: one of their missionaries was seized by the yeoman cavalry at Lancaster and shockingly ill-treated. Brother F. Charlton was thrown into Lancaster Castle by a bad man, who afterwards died raging mad." Rev. S. Smith, "Anecdotes and Facts of Primitive Methodism," p. 104.

meeting and lovefeast he attended at Preston in 1826 had powerfully impressed George Lamb. He joined the society, and improved his talents so markedly that his profiting appeared to all; and now, it would seem, Hugh Bourne had set his heart upon being the medium of conveying to the young man the call of the Church to wider service, and had come to Lancaster for that very purpose, as well as to assist at the Missionary Meeting. The two had conference together, and then Hugh Bourne thoughtfully gave the young man, just putting on the harness, a letter of recommendation to the friends at Halifax, Leeds, and York, the towns he must pass through on his way to Pocklington, his first circuit. Fifty-seven years after this informal ordination service, Mr. Lamb was still in harness. Old age had but mellowed his character, while there was little appreciable decline of vigour or industry in his service; and then the word of dismissal came, February, 1886. Mr. Lamb was twice President, 1866 and 1884, General Book Steward, Conferential Deputation to Canada, 1876, Member of the Deed Poll, 1880. A mission, that in its first eight years gave John Flesher, John Petty, and George Lamb to our Church, as Hull's Western Mission did, has strong claims on our remembrance.

At Lancaster, an old coach-house in Bulk Street was, in 1836, fitted up as a chapel. Through the spread of "Barkerism" this building was for a time lost to the society. Afterwards, however, it was recovered, made Connexional, and served the uses of the society until 1854, when Ebenezer was built. Meanwhile, Lancaster had been separated from Preston and made part of the Settle and Halifax Mission of Halifax Circuit. In 1837, the writer's father "travelled"—in the full sense of the word—on this mission, which stretched some forty miles, from Bellbusk in Craven to Heysham by the seaside. As he was wont to say: "It constituted a first-rate promenade for creating an appetite, but was remarkably scanty in supplying the wherewithal to appease it. *That* had to be got how and when it could." We need not follow the history of Lancaster after it was taken over by the General Missionary Committee, except to notice that it was again separated from Settle, and after a period of barrenness and struggle it gradually improved, and in 1868 was granted circuit independence, Morecambe being formed from it in 1901. A document in our possession brings home to the mind in a realistic way the amount of toil, voluntarily and cheerfully undergone in the past by the local preachers of some of our most unproductive fields of labour. But for their loyalty and tenacity, what are now comparatively vigorous circuits, such as Lancaster is, might have been abandoned. The document in question is an analysis of the Lancaster Plan for the quarter April to June, 1844. It shows that the twelve local preachers, whose names stand on this plan, took amongst them one hundred and seventeen Sunday appointments, and thirty-nine week-evening services, exclusive of prayer meetings and class meetings, and that the number of miles they walked to their appointments amounted in the aggregate to seven hundred and sixty-two.

Three of the twelve whose names stand on this plan bear the name of Bickerstaffe— William and two of his sons. The former was the carrier of the mails between Settle and Lancaster. He was a Wesleyan local preacher, and in those pre-railway days found a home for the travelling-preacher and stabling for his horse. But he joined the Primitives, "thinking he could be more useful amongst them." He did not regret the choice he had made, but did all for the new community and more than he had done for the old one, with which he had no quarrel. His son, Henry, was for many years a leading official of the Lancaster Circuit, while *his* son, Mr. T. Y. Bickerstaffe, is its present Steward, and a local preacher of the fourth generation bears the old name. The reference to the Bickerstaffes may be pardoned as, in 1843, the father of the writer took a daughter of this house from the Bulk Street Society to be the companion of his ministerial toils.

On that same Preston Plan of 1832, to which we have referred, we find Chorley, besides Wrightington, Wheelton, and Standish, in the direction of Wigan. To this period and district belongs the story of Mr. Bastow's imprisonment for preaching in Wigan Market-place. An occupant of the same cell, struck by his respectable appearance, wanted to know what he had done to get himself put there. "Preaching the gospel" was the answer. "And I," said the man, "am here for not attending divine worship. They are a strange people here, and how to please them no one knows.

HOOLE FIRST CHAPEL.

You are sent to prison for being good, and I for being bad. We are a strange pair— both to be imprisoned by the same man and the same laws!" We note that in the process of consolidation, Chorley was made from Preston and Wigan from Chorley, in 1837 and 1867 respectively.

Hoole, which also stands on this plan, formed the base for the missioning of Southport and its vicinity. Here, somewhere about 1824, a two-floored house was rented, the partitions were removed, and a flight of stone steps, built on the outside, led to the upper room, which formed a fair chapel, while the room on the ground floor was used as a school. Two chapels have since been built at Hoole, and in the graveyard, attached to the first of these, lie the remains of one at least of the three men who, with the Preston ministers, had much to do with the missioning of Southport—Thomas and Richard Hough and John Webster, who for many years were abundant in missionary labours. The first services at Southport, we are told, were held in a barn at Churchtown—likewise on this plan—and a chapel and school were built in 1833 and enlarged in 1853, and Southport, with 186 members, became a circuit in 1864. It is interesting to note that the plan of 1832 announces a camp meeting to be held "in the North Meols," near Southport, on June 10th.

Preston, too, missioned the Fylde district. Rev. S. Smith has an anecdote, from internal evidence belonging to an early period, relating to "our Fylde missionary," who after preaching at night in the streets of Poulton—"a sadly wicked place"—found himself eighteen miles from home without the prospect of supper or bed, but who providentially found both. There is reason to believe that Freckleton was made the base for opening up the Fylde, in which are now the Blackpool and Fleetwood Circuits. At this place a pious widow, named Rawstorne, lent her thatched cottage for services, and provided accommodation for the missionary. Then, in 1848, the Rev. B. Whillock, the Superintendent of Preston Circuit, in conjunction with the afore-named John Webster, took a factory, and became responsible for the rent. This building was used for worship until 1862, when a small chapel was opened, and this served until superseded in 1892 by a worthier building. The Rev. B. Whillock entered the

THOMAS HOUGH. 　　　J. WEBSTER. 　　　REV. B. WHILLOCK.

ministry in 1830, and in 1870 removed to the United States, where he is a permanent member of the Primitive Methodist Eastern Conference. As his letters show, Mr. Whillock retains a lively interest in the Church of the homeland, and is full of reminiscences of its past.

Besides helping to enlarge the geographical area of the Connexion, Preston also did something towards enlarging the scope of its endeavours. It led the way in one branch of social reform—that which seeks by organised effort to war against intemperance. It showed how this kind of social service could be undertaken religiously, and temperance meetings be made to further the interests of the kingdom of God. No historian of the Temperance movement in this country can overlook the part played by "proud Preston" in the beginnings of that movement. He will point to that town and show how, from 1832 to 1835, the new sentiment in regard to strong drink not only grew in strength, but in clearness of purpose. It became surer of its ground, and more militant and altruistic. Nor can the historian of our Church omit all reference to these things; for, if now we not only have a Temperance Department within the Church, but belong to a Church which is very largely a Temperance Church, it is partly owing to the fact that, seventy years ago, the ministers of Preston Circuit, and some of the members of old Lawson Street, as after of Saul Street, were heart and soul in the new movement, which speedily drew others within its vortex. Probably, not even before 1831, was our Church one whit behind other Churches in regard to the question of intemperance; rather was it ahead of them. To say this, however, is not to say a great deal; and it is safe to affirm that when this plan of 1832 came from the press, Preston was in advance of the Connexion generally in temperance sentiment. True; there were here and there convinced individual abstainers. The Rev. James Macpherson signed the pledge as early as 1828, and Hugh Bourne was practically a teetotaller before either Moderation or Total Abstinence Societies had an existence. But what Preston did was to afford an object-lesson, showing how to mobilise the forces of the Church against the drinking customs which preyed upon society, and even threatened the Church itself. It made a beginning in combining individual temperance men in a league against the common foe —offensive and defensive. Let us give the briefest summary of events relating to the early stages of the Temperance movement in Preston—so far at least as our Church was concerned in those movements. We give this summation in paragraphs, and those desirous of fuller information may consult with advantage the Rev. J. Travis' articles on "Primitive Methodism and the Temperance Reformation in England."*

SAUL STREET CHAPEL, PRESTON.

"*March 22nd, 1832.*—Preston Temperance Society formed on the basis of the 'moderation pledge.'

"*April 13th.*—Committee appointed, of which Rev. S. Smith was a member. Its first meeting was presided over by Rev. J. A. Bastow. The second memorable meeting was held on May 3rd in Lawson Street Primitive Methodist Chapel, at which Mr. Livesey, in a forcible speech, took the line of total abstinence.

"*July 11th.*—First Temperance Tea-party, at which 574 persons were present, and Messrs. Livesey, S. Smith, and several Preston working-men spoke. Next day

* *Aldersgate Magazine*, 1899.

a Field Meeting of the Society was held on the Moor, at which Messrs. Livesey, Smith, and Teare gave addresses.

"*September 1st, 1832.*—A special meeting was held for discussing the question of the total abstinence pledge. No decision was arrived at, but several tarried after the meeting, and seven signed the total abstinence pledge. Of these 'seven men of Preston,' three were Primitive Methodists, viz., John King, Joseph Richardson, who was wont to say, 'I am the happiest man alive, for no man can be happier than a teetotal Primitive Methodist;' and the third was Richard Turner, who is credited with having originated the word 'teetotal.' At his funeral in 1846, the Saul Street Sunday School, and four hundred teetotallers from different parts of the country, attended.

"*April, 1834.*—Mr. George Toulmin,* the Secretary of the Lawson Street Sunday School, and Mr. Thomas Walmsley, moved the resolution, which resulted in the formation of the *first* Sunday School Total Abstinence Society, inaugurated April 18th. It was not till 1835 that the Preston Temperance Society became a strictly Total Abstinence Society, so that the Juvenile Society formed by the Primitive Methodists was the first society on a 'teetotal' basis in Preston, and, it is believed, the first Juvenile Teetotal Society in England."

MR. J. KING.
One of the
"Seven Men of Preston."

MR. GEORGE TOULMIN, J.P.

We conclude our notice of Preston by giving the portrait of Rev. George Kidd, whose ministry in Preston, 1864-7, was signalised by his heading one hundred and twenty stalwarts who refused to pay the Easter Church Dues, and secured their abolition : also that of Mr. William Salthouse, born at Roseacre, in the Fylde District, in 1834, who for half a century has stood by Preston Primitive Methodism, and served its interests preferably in the quieter ways of service.

REV. G. KIDD.

MR. W. SALTHOUSE.

HULL'S NORTH-WESTERN MISSION.

As already said, Darlington and Barnard Castle furnished the base for the prosecution of Hull's North-Western Mission. The immediate fruits of this mission are seen in the inclusion of Hexham and Carlisle in the Sunderland District, at its formation in 1824, and, by 1842, in the addition of Westgate, Alston, and Whitehaven to its roll of stations. This mission was already being vigorously carried on when the large towns on the Tyne

* Mr. Toulmin became proprietor of the *Preston Guardian,* and other Journals, member of the Town Council and Borough Magistrate, and his son, who also is an ardent temperance man, is the Member for Bury in the present Parliament.

and Wear were entered. Naturally, this is just what from geographical considerations one would expect to find; since Darlington lies on the great North Road, and, from time immemorial, travellers have taken Darlington on their way to Newcastle and Berwick. Though, therefore, neither Darlington nor Barnard Castle is among the primary circuits of the Sunderland District, we still must, for reasons both chronological and geographical, glance at the introduction of Primitive Methodism into these Durham towns, and the lines of evangelisation that went out from them, before looking at "the Northern Mission," which, strictly speaking, did not begin until March, 1822.

This section of our history is not without its obscurities and difficulties, largely created, one cannot but think, by the method followed by W. Clowes in his published *Journals*. That method was not rigidly to adhere to the chronological order in his narrative of events, but to group together incidents which occurred on his various visits to the same place. Little harm need have resulted from this method of grouping had the dates of these various visits also been given; but often dates are wanting, and hence the difficulties which have led some previous writers astray. Fortunately, as in the case of Darlington, Newcastle, and South Shields, the *Journals* and memoirs published in the contemporary Magazines furnish us with a clue to guide us on our way with some degree of confidence. It was needful to say thus much, in order that the occasional variations between our narrative and preceding ones may be prepared for and explained beforehand.

As the wind carries the seed in its fairy parachute, so the breeze of rumour had much to do with disseminating Primitive Methodism. The "fame" of the missionaries went through the countryside, bringing men or missives asking for a missionary to be sent to other ground. That is how Primitive Methodism got here and there in the county of Durham, as elsewhere. William Young, whom we take to have been at the time an earnest Wesleyan, had heard of the stirring doings at Knaresborough, and sent Clowes a pressing invitation to visit Ingleton eight miles from Darlington. Our reading of the available evidence is that the visit was duly paid on Sunday, June 4th, 1820. From the Ripon branch, Clowes made his way to Darlington. Here his coming may have been prepared for and welcomed; for, from the memoir of Rev. Jonathan Clewer, we learn that, after his marriage in 1820, he removed to Darlington, laboured as a local preacher, and "rendered great help towards establishing the infant cause." So well did he acquit himself that it was felt he was fitted for a wider sphere, and in 1822, Jonathan Clewer began his labours at Tadcaster, and continued them until his superannuation in 1851. Whether, on June 4th, Jonathan Clewer had already begun his useful labours in Darlington, we cannot be sure, but on that Sunday W. Clowes took his stand in Northgate and preached.

REV. J. CLEWER.

The situation selected was not without its significance. The street is part of the great North Road leading on to Durham, and in a house in this street, not far from Bulmer's Stone and the new Technical College, Edward Pease lived, and in a room in this house occurred a memorable interview between George Stephenson, Nicholas Wood, and Edward Pease, which resulted in the construction of the first railway—the Stockton and Darlington line. After preaching he went to Ingleton, where he was welcomed by Messrs. Emerson and Young. They sang through the streets, Mr. Clowes giving an exhortation, and then a prayer meeting was held in Mr. Young's house. We take it, that before July 16th (when Clowes went on the Hutton Rudby Mission) two Sundays more were divided between Darlington and Ingleton. On one of these Sundays he preached at Darlington twice, having for his second congregation a thousand people, and then walked to Ingleton, where he also preached and led the class! On the other Sunday he preached in Bondgate, and the same evening renewed tickets to twenty members at Ingleton. During this visit he preached more than once at Cockfield, and formed a society of four members at Evenwood. With Jonathan Clewer already, or soon to be, at Darlington, with Messrs.

BULMER'S STONE IN EDWARD PEASE'S TIME LYING IN FRONT OF THE
OLD COTTAGES, NORTHGATE.

Emerson and Young steady adherents of the cause, and some twenty members at Ingleton, and with a small society at Evenwood, we have already the beginning of a branch in these parts; and so, May 6th, 1821, Samuel Laister began his labours in Darlington Branch, and continued them unremittingly until his lamented death on Christmas Day of the same year. At first, he could not but feel the contrast between the congregations he had been accustomed to in the West Riding, and the feeble cause he found in the Quaker town. Speedily, however, the prospect brightened, and it "begins to remind him of the branch he has left."

The missionaries preached at places as far removed as Wolsingham and Stockton-on-Tees. The former was visited in response to an appeal personally made by Mr. W.

Snowball and two others who, having heard of the work being done in South Durham, came over to Cockfield to see Mr. Laister. Mr. Snowball lived to become the Steward of the Wolsingham or Crook Circuit, as it afterwards got to be called, and from 1821 to the day of his death, his house was always open to the ministers of the Connexion. In a similar way, Mr. Laister was invited to Witton-le-Wear by Messrs. Littlefair and Pyburn. Stockton was visited as early as May 13th, by S. Laister, who writes in his *Journal:* "I spoke at Stockton: a cold, hard place. No Society." By March, 1822, Stockton and the places thereabout were formed into Hull's "Stockton Mission," and reported seventy members. Later, we shall find it formed the southern part of the Sunderland and Stockton Union Circuit.

Meanwhile, Darlington itself—then a small town of some 5,750 inhabitants—was not overlooked. The society grew in numbers, and likewise, it would seem, in public favour, which has never been wanting in this town of progressive ideas. This may be inferred from the fact that, as early as October 16th, the foundation of the Queen Street Chapel was laid. At first, Mr. Laister and his colleague, W. Evans, preached in the market-place, then a room in Tubwell Row was taken, and afterwards services were held in the Assembly Room of the Sun Inn, at the corner of Northgate, where most of the important meetings of the town were then held. But even this room soon became too small, and the young society found itself committed to chapel-building.

Darlingtonian Primitives should do their best to keep green the memory of Samuel Laister, who died in their midst, probably a martyr to excessive toil. As a pioneer worker, he did much for Primitive Methodism in various parts, as our narrative has shown. S. Laister was not spared to see the opening of Queen Street Chapel on March 3rd, 1822, when, according to Sykes' "Local Records," one thousand persons were present, and a collection amounting to £17 2s. taken. The preacher on the occasion was W. Clowes, who had been appointed to the Darlington Branch in January. But while Mr. Clowes preached in the chapel, F. N. Jersey had an overflow congregation of two hundred persons outside the building which, until the erection of Greenbank Chapel in 1879, under the superintendency of Rev. Hugh Gilmore, was to serve as the head of the Darlington Circuit. Mr. Clowes' station in Darlington was a short one, amounting to not more than eight Sundays, three of which were devoted to an evangelistic excursion to North Shields, which will shortly engage our attention. "My appointments in the Darlington Branch," says Mr. Clowes, "were filled up while I was away, by F. N. Jersey, a sailor, who undertook to travel with me one quarter for nothing, that he might have my company. He, however, had but little of it, for I left him, and made this excursion to North Shields, and it has not been in vain." From first to last, Clowes gave three Sundays to Darlington town, including the Sunday of the chapel-opening. One of the remaining Sundays was devoted to Bishop Auckland, where, as was usual where Clowes was, something happened. This time it was a *mishap*. The props that supported the upper room in which the service was being held, being somewhat decayed, gave way, to the alarm of many though, providentially, to the hurt of none. The other available Sunday was given to Barnard Castle, February 24th, where he found a society of one hundred and twenty had been raised up.

From this time Barnard Castle becomes an advanced post—a fresh base for extensive

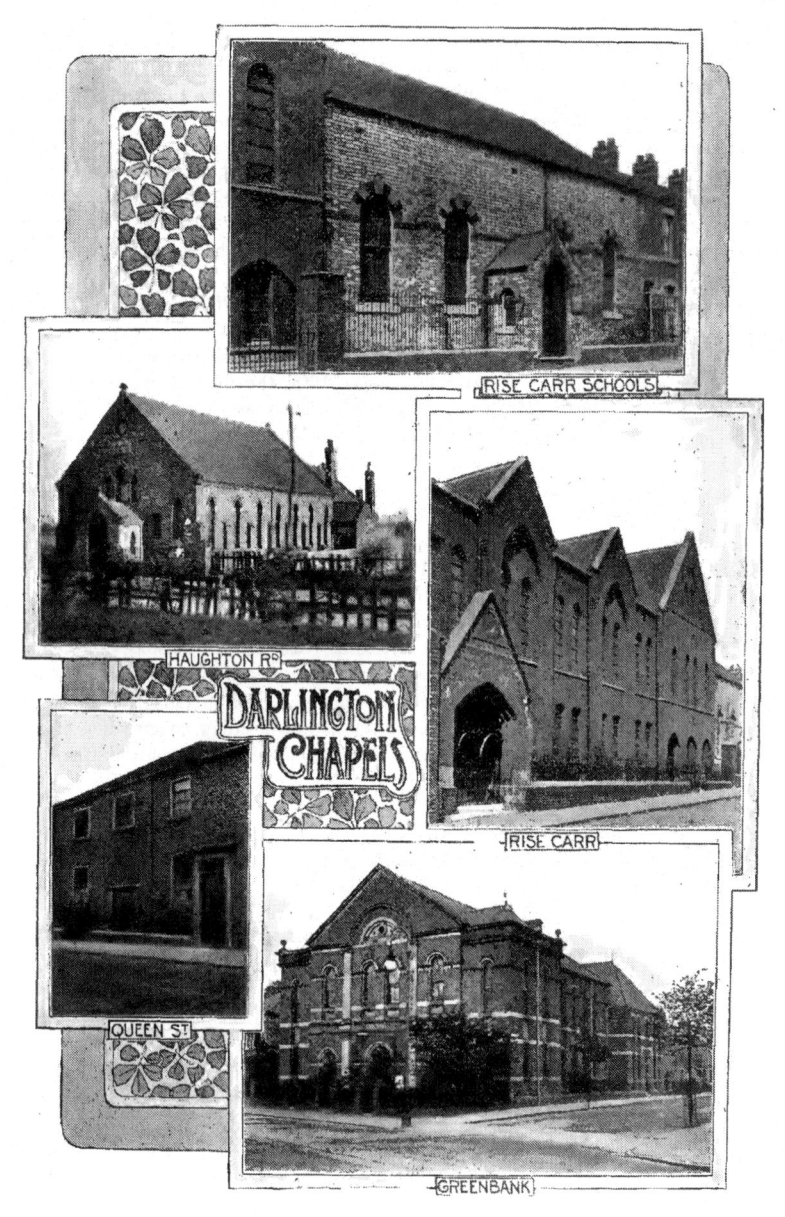

DARLINGTON CHAPELS

RISE CARR SCHOOLS
HAUGHTON RD
RISE CARR
QUEEN ST
GREENBANK

missionary effort. Our attention must therefore be directed to this old-world town which has so much of interest, both for the lover of the antique and the lover of nature in her fairest aspects. How did we secure a footing in Barnard Castle?

While the Darlington friends were full of their new chapel project, and discussions on plans and specifications and ways and means were rife, Samuel Laister "thought they would make a push to take Barnard Castle." As usual, invitations had come, and Bro. W. Evans, a good prospector,* was commissioned "to see what kind of an opening there was." He therefore went and preached in the market-place, and announced that S. Laister would follow a fortnight after; accordingly on a day in late August, S. Laister went to Barnard Castle and "spoke to many hundreds of well-behaved people," and formed a society of nine members. In two months the nine had increased to eighty, and in four months, as we have seen, the number had risen to one hundred and twenty.

We may here conveniently add a few further particulars as to the town of Barnard Castle's after history kindly supplied by Rev. B. Wild. "The Society first worshipped in a room in Thorngate, but afterwards removed into the Gray Lane. In 1822, a Mr. Hempson was stationed here, who by his indiscretions caused a division in the fold which considerably reduced the membership. Mr. W. Summersides was sent to superintend the Circuit in 1828, and under his ministry the numbers increased. The erection of a chapel now began to be discussed, and preparations for the building were forthwith commenced. 1829 saw the consummation of the work begun in 1828, and the chapel was opened by the Revs. W. Sanderson, G. Cosens, and J. Flesher, then the superintendent of the Circuit. In 1836, the side-galleries were put in, and in 1851, the vestry adjoining the chapel was built."

Shortly after Mr. Clowes left the Darlington Branch, Barnard Castle was separated from Darlington and formed into a new branch called "The Barnard Castle and Wolsingham Branch of Hull Circuit." On the 18th March, Clowes left for the North Mission which Hull Circuit had agreed to take over from Hutton Rudby. Clowes, as the leading missionary, went on in advance, and was speedily followed by the brothers Nelson. F. N. Jersey had already opened Crook (January 30th), and formed a society, and the very day Clowes left for the North, Jersey preached at Stanhope, it being "a fine starlight night." We also find him at Satley and Shotley Bridge. These references are significant as to the degree and direction in which the work was spreading. Still more significant is the fact that Clowes, on his way to North Shields, called at Wolsingham and Barnard Castle, evidently to oversee the North-Western Mission. He visited Satley "on the hills," Stanhope, where he found seventeen members, Hamsterley, Barnard Castle, and other places, and "directing Bro. Jersey to take up Westgate" he went on to his own special field. Westgate *will* soon be taken, but scarcely by F. N. Jersey, as he left almost immediately after for Silsden, where we have already seen him hard at work.

From a minute in an old Barnard Castle Circuit-book it would almost seem as though Shotley Bridge had itself become a kind of sub-branch as early as 1822. The minute in question says: "That if Shotley Bridge does not see its way clear to send a missionary to Hexham during the next quarter, we will send one." This minute confirms the

* See *ante* vol. ii. p. 86.

interesting account already given by Mr. Petty, of the way in which Primitive Methodism was introduced into Hexham. As the account is circumstantial and evidently based on first-hand information, we reproduce it here, simply suggesting that by Weardale we are probably to understand the lower part of the dale.

"A native of this town [Hexham] had been employed in his secular calling in Weardale, and, on visiting his parents at Hexham, he gave exciting accounts of the introduction of Primitive Methodism into that dale, and of the zealous and successful labours of the missionaries. His statements, together with the hymns and tunes he sang, excited considerable interest among his friends and acquaintances, many of whom expressed a desire to hear the preachers of this new denomination. And a Mr. John Gibson attended their religious services in connection with the opening of the Butchers' Hall, in Newcastle-on-Tyne, on October 20th, 1822, and invited the preachers to Hexham. As the preachers of Newcastle could not comply with his request, he applied to Shotley Bridge, in Barnard Castle branch, and a preacher from that town visited Hexham on the 26th of the same month. A place was provided for preaching, and a society of five members was formed in the evening. The bellman was sent through the town to announce that a Primitive Methodist Missionary would preach in the Old Kiln, on the Battle Hill, the following day. The excitement this announcement produced was very great, and long before the time appointed for the service to commence the Old Kiln was crowded. The services of the day were very powerful; the missionary preached with 'the Holy Ghost sent down from Heaven'; many stout-hearted sinners trembled, and five more persons united with the infant cause. The Old Kiln was speedily fitted up so as to make it more convenient for public worship; and despite serious persecutions, bricks and stones being often thrown

BATTLE HILL, HEXHAM.
The old Malt Kiln was entered through an opening on the left at the top of the street.

by the ungodly, the good work continued to prosper, and many souls were turned to the Lord."*

Hexham Circuit comprised a goodly portion of South-Western Northumberland. The fact, thus barely stated, is quite enough to show that Hexham must have been one of the widest circuits in the Connexion, and when the characteristic physical features of this border district are recalled, one can readily understand that the circuit was wild and toilsome as well as wide. Such it was even in 1842, when the late C. C. McKechnie was one of its ministers. He had already travelled in the Ripon and Brompton Circuits, but neither of these in respect to width and wildness could stand comparison with Hexham, though Ripon was thirty-one miles by thirty, and Brompton was not much less in area, seeing that it took in the greater part of Cleveland. In 1842, Hexham Circuit stretched from Rothbury on the north to the borders of Allendale and to Derwent Head on the south, and from Greenhead on the west to Corbridge on the east. There had, however, been a time in its history when the circuit covered even more ground than this; for Blaydon and Shotley Bridge, Wickham and Swalwell, are on its plan of 1826. These and other places seem to have been grouped together to form the forgotten circuit of Winlaton, which stands on the Conference Minutes from 1827 to 1829 inclusive. After this date, these places were taken over for a time by Newcastle, so that with the extinction of Winlaton as a sort of buffer circuit, Hexham again joined hands with Newcastle. In missionary enterprise, too, Hexham Circuit played no mean part in the early days, having at one time, as Rev. J. Lightfoot tells us, employed and sustained three missions—Morpeth, Rothbury, and Jedburgh, in Roxburghshire. It was very largely through the influence of Squire Shafto, of Bavington—of whom we shall have to speak—that the Rothbury Mission was begun. John Coulson secured Joseph Spoor as the first missionary to "break up" this new ground. It was a rough beginning even for this muscular and intrepid Tynesider. So hard and apparently unproductive did he find the soil, that he lost heart, and one day took the road homeward, in a mood like that of Elijah when he fled from Jezebel; but as he sat under *his* juniper tree, thinking, he took heart again and resolved to go back to his work. It was during this mission also that Spoor had his memorable encounter in Morpeth market-place with Billy Purvis, the once-time famous Newcastle showman. When the tug-of-war between the showman with his drum and horn, and Spoor with his praying and singing, had ended in a victory for the latter, Purvis shouted a parting salute through his speaking-trumpet: "Ah war'n thou think's thysel a clever fellow noo!" However brought about, it is to be regretted that the Connexion has little to show for its early toils in Upper Coquetdale. It is true that in later years extension has taken place in North-Eastern Northumberland, but we have lost hold of the less populous and more rugged interior of the county.

When, in 1824, Hexham appeared as one of the circuits of the newly-formed Sunderland District, it abutted on Carlisle Circuit, which also formed one of the first circuits of the district. Therefore, in following the trend of evangelisation, we have now to inquire how we came to get a footing in Carlisle. The story cannot be told

* (pp. 186-7).

THE PERIOD OF CIRCUIT PREDOMINANCE AND ENTERPRISE.

without reference to a special independent mission, which Hull Circuit began in May, 1822, when, acting upon instructions from head-quarters, F. N. Jersey set out from Silsden on a mission to Kendal, in Westmoreland, and its neighbourhood. This mission concerns us here chiefly because one of its indirect results was the establishment of a cause in Carlisle, and also, secondarily, because of the fierce persecution the missionary met with in prosecuting his mission. Jersey laboured hard, and not altogether in vain. Many of the people heard him gladly—one good Quaker at Sedburgh saying: "The days of John Wesley are come again." An aged woman, near Kendal, who had received spiritual benefit, was so delighted with the small hymn-book she had got, that she walked to Carlisle, some forty-four miles, to show her treasure to her relative, Mr. Boothman, and to tell him of that other treasure of inward peace she had gained. Mr. Boothman was deeply interested in what was told him. He was evidently another of those "Revivalists"—sympathisers with aggressive Christian work—who welcomed our advent into their neighbourhood. He requested his son-in-law, Mr. Johnson, to accompany his aunt to Kendal and make full inquiry as to the doctrines, polity, and practice of the new community. Mr. Johnson returned, well satisfied with the result of his inquiries, and bearing a copy of the rules of the society. The issue was that these two resolved to apply for a missionary; open-air preaching was at once begun, and a society formed. Such was the link of connection between the Kendal Mission and the establishment of our cause in Carlisle. At this point we return for a moment to follow F. N. Jersey, who from Kendal went in March, 1823, to open Ulverstone, Broughton, Dalton, and other places in the Furness district. Here the ground was flintier than at Kendal. At Ulverstone he thus bemoans himself: "What a hardened, wretched place I am stationed in!" At Dalton he writes: "This is the hardest place that ever I was in. In this town they have a market every Sunday, during the harvest, for the purpose of hiring, and fight and get drunk." While holding a service at the Market Cross at Dalton, he was called upon to face a storm worse than any he had met with at sea. Three horns and a watchman's rattle made a din in his ears while he tried to sing and pray, and then he sprang from his knees and shouted: "Glory to Jesus! I can praise Thee amidst all the din of hell." The end of it was, that he was haled before two magistrates and committed to Lancaster Castle for four months. The sentence heard, he was leaving the room when the lawyer said: "Mr. Jersey, remember you'll have to pay all your expenses to Lancaster Castle." "Indeed, sir," replied Jersey, "I'm very glad of that, because if that be the case I shall never get there, for I'll never pay a farthing." "Well," said the man of law, "that will not keep you out of the castle. We will get you there." When he was lying in the castle, like the veriest rogue and vagabond, Mr. G. Herod, who was then labouring in the town, showed him no little kindness, and was allowed to take him food. One old lady, good soul! took the prisoner a pillow. We think we can see her on "kindly offices intent," wending her way with the precious burden under her arm. Jersey, however, did not serve out his full time: on receiving instructions from the Hull authorities, who were much concerned at the incident, he at last consented to give bail, and was liberated after eighteen days' confinement. He preached that night at Lancaster, next day went on to Kendal, and the day after called at Ulverstone to "see after his little flock." Soon we shall find him taking part in the great revival in Weardale. Peace to F. N. Jersey's memory! He was a capital evangelist, but a poor administrator. Rough mission-work he did well; but he was ill-adapted to govern a large circuit like Nottingham, to which he was sent in 1834. Trouble overtook him. His peace was disturbed, and his usefulness dwindled. He became a Baptist minister, and finally emigrated to America. As for Kendal Mission, though in 1823 it reported one hundred and eighty-nine members, it was for a time abandoned, probably because its retention was found to be financially burdensome. Rev. R. Cordingley, however, recommenced the mission in 1829. Penrith was taken up as a mission by Hull, and united to Kendal in 1831. Afterwards Kendal became a mission of Barnard Castle Circuit, and so continued until it attained circuit independence in 1857, while Penrith became a branch of Alston, until it, too, became a circuit in 1876. After all its vicissitudes, Kendal Mission was privileged to rear and become the training-ground of John Taylor and his fellow-apprentice, and almost foster-brother, John Atkinson, who was destined to be one of the men of 'mark and likelihood' of the middle and later periods of the Connexion's history. John Atkinson was converted under a sermon preached at Staveley by Edward Almond in 1851. He soon came on the plan, and was engaged in preaching almost every Sunday, sometimes walking thirty miles to a single appointment. He entered the ministry in 1855, and the first four years of that ministry were spent in the Shotley Bridge and Wolsingham Circuits, that owed their origin to Hull's North-Western Mission. Rev. C. C. McKechnie was John Atkinson's superintendent at Wolsingham, and it is interesting to note that at their very first interview he was struck with his "uncommon force of mind," and already discerned that there were "intellectual potentialities in him such as he had rarely met with."

Returning to Carlisle: Some few weeks after a missionary had been applied for, Mr. Clowes made his way across the country from the North Mission and began a month's successful labours in Carlisle and places adjacent thereto. His first services were held at Brampton on November 1st, 1822, where the house of Mr. William Lawson—our Connexional pioneer in Canada—was placed at his disposal for the holding of a prayer meeting.* Here also resided John and Nancy Maughan, "distinguished and never-failing friends of the cause." At the time of their death, in 1831, Mrs. Boothman and Mrs. Maughan are spoken of as being the oldest members in the Carlisle Circuit. On examination, Clowes found fifty-five adherents at Carlisle and twenty-five at Brampton. He organised the societies, appointing leaders and other officers, and formed a small society at Little Corby. The services at Carlisle were held in Mr. Boothman's hat-warehouse. A burlesque advertisement inserted in the local newspaper apprising the public "that a collection would be made to support some fellows who had gone mad, like the Prince of Denmark," drew a large and disorderly multitude together; but lampoons were as ineffectual as Mrs. Partington's mop to stay the progress of the work. Nor did Mr. Clowes limit his labours to the holding of public religious services, but he and Mr. Johnson, before mentioned, visited in the city from house to house. Few men could do so much work in little time as Mr. Clowes,

* For portrait and further reference see vol. i. p. 438.

and when, on December 3rd, he set out, one hundred and eighty miles, to attend the Hull Quarterly Meeting, he penned certain reflections which show that his month's mission in Cumberland had, as usual, been productive. "The ground," he writes, "is all broken up between Hull and Carlisle. Where it will go to next I cannot tell. . . . During this quarter the ground has been broken up from Newcastle to Carlisle. Our circuit extends from Carlisle in Cumberland to Spurn Point in Holderness, an extent of more than two hundred miles. What is the breadth of the circuit I cannot tell; it branches off various ways. From Carlisle the work seems to be opening two ways; one to Whitehaven, the other to Gretna Green in Scotland."

From this point the progress made by Carlisle Mission—soon made into a branch—was so steady and encouraging as to justify its being made into a circuit. This was done in December, 1823, and in 1824 Carlisle duly appeared on the list of the stations of the newly-formed Sunderland District. Thus, in 1824, the Carlisle and Hexham Circuits abutted on each other, as did also Hexham and Newcastle. In the *Magazine* for March, 1825, we find a communication, signed J. B. [John Branfoot] and J. J. [James Johnson?], Sec., still reporting progress, financial and numerical, in the most northerly circuit of the Connexion. "That part of our circuit," the *communiqué* goes on to say, "is doing particularly well which lies on the Scottish borders. We preach at two or three places within two or three miles of Scotland. On these the cloud of God's presence particularly rests, *and it appears as if it would move into Scotland*. But this is with the Lord. However, some who out of Scotland have come to hear, are saying, 'Come over and help us.' Others of them who have got converted among us, and have joined us, are saying, 'Oh, that you would visit our native land.'"

It was not long before the cloudy pillar *did* move Scotland way. Three months after Messrs. Oliver and Clewer walked from Sunderland to open their mission in Edinburgh, Carlisle Circuit, whose superintendent was then John Coulson, sent James Johnson—whom we take to have been the Mr. Johnson already several times referred to—to begin a mission in Glasgow, July 13th, 1826. Open-air services were held in various "conspicuous places" in the big city, and by October one hundred persons had united in Church fellowship, and a preaching-room, capable of accommodating seven hundred persons, had been secured. The mission, thus unobtrusively begun in the commercial capital of Scotland, seems to have made quiet headway, and to have been largely self-sustaining. Glasgow appears on the stations of the Sunderland District for the first time in 1829. Glasgow soon in its turn established a cause in Paisley, and, ere long, a room connected with the old Abbey Buildings, called the Philosophical Hall, was taken for services, and a minister was resident in the town. Though Paisley was attached to Glasgow Circuit, and received considerable help therefrom, it would seem that Carlisle had a hand in the development, if not in the first establishment, of our cause in Paisley, since the Rev. John Lightfoot, writing as the superintendent of Carlisle in 1831, observes: "The circuit considerably improved in its finances, so as to be able to send a missionary to Paisley."

In the year 1834 there was a youth living at Paisley who is of some account to this history. The names he bore—Colin Campbell McKechnie—betokened the Highland clan to which he belonged. His eldest brother, Daniel, had been converted amongst the Primitives, and was a sort of factotum in the little church—leader, local preacher, steward, superintendent of the Sunday school, and what not. But Daniel had now a home of his own, and the McKechnies were nominally, at any rate, adherents of the Kirk. But, probably through his brother's agency, Bella McNair was servant in the household, and in the providence of God she was used to attach this youth, whom high destinies awaited, to Primitive Methodism. If it be asked how this was done, we answer: the small hymn-book was a chief factor in the process. The early hymns were a powerful instrument of propagandism—all the more powerful because, as in this case, it could be employed in cottage or workshop as well as on village-green or market-place. That Mr. McKechnie was sung into the kingdom seems hardly too strong a way of putting it, if we may judge by his own words:—

REV. C. C. MCKECHNIE.

"Bella McNair was a thorough Primitive, devout, zealous, and with an excellent voice for singing, which she freely used. Aware of her rare gift of song, and of its power as an instrument of usefulness, she often—I might almost say—she incessantly, used it in singing the charming hymns so commonly sung by our people in those days. Some of them were very touching, so at least I thought and felt. They acted upon my religious nature like the quickening influence of spring, and evoked in my heart strong yearnings after God and goodness. I was led to talk to Bella about her pretty hymns, and the kirk to which she belonged, and she very warmly and earnestly invited me to the services."

When Colin went for the first time to Sunday school he was warmly received and felt himself in a new world. After a mental struggle, he received the sense of pardon and joined the Church. While yet in his early teens he was made leader and local preacher, and in the year Paisley became a circuit—1838—began his ministry at Ripon, where we have already seen him. Those who are interested in tracing the strange interdependence of events, may see how the aged woman, who carried the small hymn-book from Kendal to Carlisle, was an essential link in a "peculiar chain of providence," which reached to Glasgow and Paisley, and back again to Wolsingham, where C. C. McKechnie and John Atkinson met as colleagues on ground won by the North-West Mission. Had that link been wanting!—but it is needless to speculate. With the plain facts of history before us, the Kendal Mission can hardly be pronounced a failure—though the history-books may say it was—since, as one of its direct and indirect results, two such shapers of the old Sunderland District were brought together.

Coming back to the further missionary efforts put forth by Carlisle Circuit, reference may be made to Wigton, now the head of a circuit, which was first missioned by Mary Porteus on August 5th, 1831. On that date she preached at the Market Cross, as John Wesley had done before her. The day before she undertook this task, she had read, at Bothel, an account of Wesley's service at the Cross, and the thought that she—a frail woman—was about to attempt what that great and gifted man had done, pressed upon her as she went forward to discharge her trying duty. On September 2nd she took her stand at the Cross again, but when next she went, in November, she found some kind friend had taken a large schoolroom for the services.

Even before the close of 1822, W. Clowes had noted that Primitive Methodism was tending in the direction of Whitehaven. Shortly after this, Messrs. Summersides and Johnson visited this town, thirty-eight miles from Carlisle. Then Clowes himself, in August, 1823, came on the ground and began a campaign in this district, which lasted until November 9th. He visited Harrington, Cleator, Workington, Parton, Cockermouth, St. Bees, and other places. As usual, there was no lack of incidents in this campaign. At Cleator an old man who was hearing him, exclaimed: "Why, I never heard such a fool in my life!" The preacher retorted that the remark was not original, for that precisely the same thing had been said of Noah by people who changed their mind when the flood came; but all too late. At St. Bees he had as one of the fruits of his mission, David Beattie, a native of Dumfriesshire. Beattie did good service as a minister until his lamented death in 1839. He was one of the earliest of that small but distinguished band which Scotland has furnished to our ministry. At this time, too, a camp meeting was held on Harris Moor, near Whitehaven, which, from being the first of its kind ever held in the district, made a stir. At this camp meeting a number of partially intoxicated Papists interrupted the service, whereupon Clowes transfixed them with his eye, and solemnly warned them that, ere twenty-four hours should pass, many of them might be hurried into eternity. And it was so; for by an explosion in the pit, which occurred next day, many of these disturbers lost their lives. This startling event so alarmed Hugh Campbell, that he, with others, was led to join the society. This truly honest man began his ministerial labours at Hexham in 1830. Another of Clowes' Whitehaven converts was Andrew Sharpe, a man of local note on account of his physical prowess. John Sharpe, his grandson, entered the ministry in 1848; went out to Australia in 1855, where, until 1876, he did splendid service. "He was a fine specimen of the strong Cumbrian character: a splendid borderer of clear and decided convictions, held with Spartan firmness;" a man of vigorous and well-stored mind. After his retirement he settled at Hensingham, where he passed away, May 27th, 1895.

As Whitehaven remained a branch of Hull Circuit for so many years, it was from time to time privileged with the labours of most of the best-known ministers of that circuit. John Garner and John Oxtoby were here together during the September quarter of 1824. Despite the trouble caused by a deposed minister, who remained on the station after his deposition and tried to foment mischief, the work still rolled on. "We had," says Mr. Garner, "a great and powerful work, and we took a large church to worship in called Mount Pleasant Church." It had been built for the worship of the Episcopal Church, but its consecration being refused, it fell into the hands of Dissenters, apparently not one iota the worse for the lack. For more than thirty years Mount Pleasant Church was used by Primitive Methodists for the purposes of public worship.

Whitehaven was made an independent station in 1840, so that by the end of the first period we have, as the development of the Kendal, Carlisle, and Whitehaven Missions, the nucleus of the present Carlisle and Whitehaven District, with, however, the addition of Alston, Brough, and Haltwhistle, these being the outcome of Hull's North-Western Mission. Since 1842, consolidation has gone on apace in West Cumberland. Maryport was made from Whitehaven in 1862, and Workington in 1884; and Cockermouth from Maryport in 1893.

THE GREAT REVIVAL IN THE DALES: WESTGATE AND ALSTON MOOR.

One is surprised to find that in 1832 Westgate and Alston had actually more members than the Hull home-branch itself. In a tabular report of that year of the various branches of Hull Circuit, "Westgate and Alston" are credited with 751 members, while Hull has 631, and Driffield 469. It confirms what has already been stated as to Hull's retention of a branch long after it was strong enough to stand alone. It was "a long cry" from Westgate to Hull, and yet it is Hull Quarterly Meeting which, in 1831, by resolution, makes George Race and William Lonsdale exhorters! Though, therefore, Westgate and Alston were not made circuits until 1834 and 1835 respectively, they had long been numerically powerful, and not wanting in officials who knew their own mind, and had a mind to know.

These two strong branches were molten and cast in the fire of a great revival— a revival, take it for all in all, greater perhaps than any we have thus far had to chronicle. And, what is still more remarkable, great revivals have, at ever recurring intervals, swept over Weardale, Allendale, Alston Moor, and Cumberland, one or two of which we may glance at before closing this section. As insurance offices speak of a "conflagration area," so the districts just named, and especially the dales, may almost be termed "the revival area." "Well, then, the people who inhabit those dales must certainly be of a highly emotional temperament, easily stirred to excitement, and perhaps just as easily relapsing into indifference." No, no; the reader has quite missed the mark; he has not pierced the centre of the sufficient reason. Never was truer word written of the Northmen, and especially of the Dalesmen, than that in which the Rev. J. Wenn describes them as "anthracite in temperament." "Northerners," he continues, "are not exactly comparable to carpenters' shavings, soon alight and quickly extinguished; rather do they resemble anthracite in the slowness of its combustion and the retention of its heat . . . capable of sustained religious fervour could they but once be kindled."*

WESTGATE CHAPEL AND SCHOOLS.

The first great Weardale Revival, alike in its inception and progress, illustrates the truth of these remarks. It was a work of time, and a work requiring infinite patience, to kindle the inhabitants of the upper part of the dale, but, when once they were kindled, the fire burned with a glowing intensity and spread amain. By common consent Thomas Batty is acknowledged to have been the "Apostle of Weardale." This does not mean that he was the pioneer missionary of the Connexion in the dale;

* Rev. J. Wenn's MSS. Kindly lent.

THE PERIOD OF CIRCUIT PREDOMINANCE AND ENTERPRISE. 143

for he was not. That honour probably belongs to George Lazenby, who is said to have preached the first sermon at Stanhope in a joiner's shop in October, 1821, and he was speedily followed by others. Nor does the word "apostle," accorded to Thomas Batty, prejudice the claim of Jane Ansdale, F. N. Jersey, Anthony Race, and others, to have taken a foremost part in the movement. What makes the title "apostle" as applied to him so eminently appropriate is the fact that, in the preparatory stages and in the conduct of the revival, we see concentrated and embodied in Thomas Batty the very spirit of the revival. It would be difficult to find anywhere a more moving picture of what we understand by "travailing in birth for souls" than the picture Batty has drawn of himself in his *Journals* of the time.

When Thomas Batty came to Barnard Castle Branch from Silsden in the autumn of 1822, others had already been some time at work in the dale, which stretches, some

IRESHOPEBURN.
Home of the Boyhood of Rev. J. Watson, D.D.

fifteen miles, from Lanehead to Frosterley. At Westgate, and in the lower part of the dale, the people had been in a measure receptive of the word from the very first. Jane Ansdale's ministrations hereabout had proved acceptable, and a notable convert had already been won in the person of J. Dover Muschamp, a man of some standing in the dale. Curiosity drew him to Westgate to hear Jane Ansdale, who, because of the unfavourable weather, preached in the Wesleyan Chapel, kindly lent for the occasion. As he listened, the arrow of conviction was lodged, and he went away stricken and mourning. Not for some time, however, did he find peace—not even though he attended a camp meeting at Stanhope, and stood bare-headed under the hot sun listening to the word. But when he had retired to his room for the night, healing and forgiveness were experienced, and at once Mr. and Mrs. Muschamp gave themselves heart and soul to the new cause. But though this conversion was a notable, and by no means a solitary one in the neighbourhood, yet it is evident that no extraordinary work had as yet begun. Figures, and Thomas Batty's own explicit statements, show this.

Meanwhile, the burthen pressed heavily on Mr. Batty. How he did labour! And yet it seemed to him he was spending his strength for nought. Crowds—and often weeping crowds—attended the services, "but they could not be got to join the society." They let hearing and weeping suffice. He speaks of one unforgettable night, when he was returning from an apparently fruitless service at Ireshopeburn. As he waded through the snow and water and slush, his depression was extreme, and almost insupportable. He could not talk to his companion; he "could only sigh and groan and weep." His tell-tale countenance seemed to say, "I am the man that hath seen affliction," and that sad countenance was long remembered in the dale. The sequel of this journey is worth telling in Thomas Batty's own words, only that we may premise that Westgate was Batty's destination, and that his home was to be with Joseph Walton, "who was a class-leader and a mighty labourer in prayer."

"When I arrived at Joseph Walton's I was so sorrowful that I could scarce eat any supper. Joseph and I entered into some conversation on the subject that distressed me. I stated to him that if we could not succeed soon, I thought we should be obliged to leave and go to some other people, among whom we should probably do better. He said: 'Nay, don't do so; try a little longer.' I replied: 'Well, I have been at the far end before now, and when I got to the end the Lord began to work, and He can do so again.' This conversation cheered and revived my spirits, and my faith began to rise. Praise the Lord."

When some little time after this, the Ireshopeburn preaching-house was closed to them, Batty did indeed seem to have "reached the far end." But Anthony Race said: "If the devil shuts one door, the Lord will open two." And so it literally came to pass. Of the two houses now offered them, they chose the better one for their purpose, and there, in March, 1823, while Batty was preaching, a man fell to the ground. That night a small society was formed, and the revival began, which swept the dale and led Mr. Muschamp to say exultantly: "I think all the people in Weardale are going to be Ranters."

The laws which govern the origin and course of great revivals are obscure and difficult to trace. It is perhaps impossible to say how far Thomas Batty's mental distress was really "travail of soul"—the very birth-throes of the revival, and how far it was the result of imperfect knowledge of the Weardale type of character, and therefore uncalled for. It was reserved for an observant toll-gate keeper to hint that Thomas Batty did not understand the anthracite temperament of the dalesmen as well as he understood it, and to give him advice, which he followed with advantage.

"I lodged with a friendly man one night, a little after this had happened, who kept a toll-gate in the dale, between St. John's Chapel and Prize. This man said to me on the following morning: 'If you will come and preach about here every night for a week, you will soon have a hundred people in society.' I replied: 'Well, if I thought so, I would soon do that.' The man said: 'I am sure of it: the whole country is under convictions. *You do not know the people as well as I do;* they often stop and talk with me at the gate. I hear what they say about 'the

Ranters,' and I am sure if you would come and preach every night for a week, you would soon have a hundred souls.' This toll-gate keeper was not at that time converted, neither did he make any profession of religion; but he was an open-hearted, well-disposed man, and had taken a liking to our cause. As early as possible, I got my regular appointments supplied by a preacher whom Hull quarter-day sent us. He entered into my labours as appointed on the plan, and I enlarged our borders by missioning entirely new ground. But I previously attended to the advice of my friend, and preached about his neighbourhood every night for a week; and at the quarter's end we had just added one hundred souls." (Memoir of Thomas Batty, pp. 54-5.)

The irrefragable evidence of the numerical returns for successive quarters remains to

NENTHEAD, NEAR ALSTON.

confirm Mr. Batty's statements, and to witness to the magnitude of the revival. In March, 1823, when the revival began, the membership of the branch was 219; in June, 308; in September, 625; in December, 846, when there were five preachers on the ground. There is a blessed sameness in the personal and more far-reaching effects wrought by every great revival such as that which affected Weardale. On these we need not dwell. But the revival was not without its incidents of a less familiar, and some of even a novel, kind. Amongst the latter must be reckoned the eagerness for hearing the gospel, which, as at Wellshope, led the people to economise every inch of available space by removing all the tables and chairs from the room except one chair, on which the preacher stood, and then some stalwart miner would come forward and stand with his back to the preacher, so that he—the preacher—might find support by resting his arms on the man's shoulders! There was competition for the honour of fulfilling this office; and who shall say that such a living reading-desk was not as pleasing in God's sight as the eagle lectern of polished brass?

Before the close of 1823 the Revival had spread to Nenthead. The missionaries had been urged to extend their labours to this district, and, in response, Anthony Race is said to have crossed over and preached at Nenthead for the first time on the Lord's day, March 23rd, 1823. Anthony Race was the grandfather of the late George Race, sen. He had been a Wesleyan local preacher, and as such had taken long journeys— sometimes walking as far as Durham, Hexham, Haydonbridge, and Appleby in Westmoreland. Anthony Race entered the ministry this same year—1823—but his term of service was short, as he died between the Conferences of 1828 and 1829. Thomas Batty soon followed his colleagues to Nenthead and Garrigill. By some they were regarded with suspicion as "outlandish men," or Political Radical Reformers under another name, but the generality of the people waited eagerly on their ministrations and wanted to pay for them by taking up a collection! Batty promised them they should have the opportunity of showing their gratitude on the occasion of his next visit, when the quarterly collection would be due. On this visit, Mr. Batty took his stand on a flag by the door of Mr. Isaac Hornsby, an official of the lead-works. On that flag Mr. Wesley had once stood to preach. When the collection was named each man sought his pocket, and it was as though a body of drilled troops were executing a military movement at the word of command. The precision with which the thing was done was such as to draw forth the admiration of the ex-man-of-war's-man. Although it was a week-night, three pounds were taken up at that collection. In six months one hundred members had been enrolled at Nenthead.

At this point, Westgate was detached from Barnard Castle to become a separate branch of Hull Circuit, with John Hewson as its superintendent, and G. W. Armitage, a youthful but acceptable preacher, as its junior minister. When to these was added John Oxtoby, who in September, 1824, walked from Whitehaven to Westgate, the revival, which had somewhat flagged, gained fresh impetus. The sanctification of believers as a definite work of grace was a prominent phase of the revival at this stage, as well as the conversion of sinners. During these months very remarkable scenes were witnessed in the Dales. Of these scenes we get glimpses in the full *Journals* of Messrs. Oxtoby and Armitage, and the late Rev. W. Dent has also supplied us with some reminiscences of what he himself saw and took part in. Mr. Dent was converted at Westgate in 1823, entered the ministry in 1827, and travelled thirty-three years with great acceptance. After his retirement he settled in Newcastle-on-Tyne, where his spare form, ascetic, spiritual looking face, and his quick bodily movements, which at once responded to and registered the feeling within, made him a familiar figure to our churches. Mr. Dent had a wide acquaintance with Methodist theology, and was an able exponent and defender of the doctrine of Christian perfection. He died March 16th, 1864. Mr. Dent was a keen

REV. W. DENT.

observer of the phenomena of Oxtoby's revival, and his remarks on the "fallings" which were so noteworthy a feature of that revival are worth preserving:—

"There were many cases of prostration in connection with that great work. I have seen more than fifteen at one meeting, some of whom were sober-minded Christians, as humble as they were earnest. And what was very observable, there was nothing in the voice or manner of the preacher to account for such effects; no vociferation, no highly impassioned address. He (J. Oxtoby) stood as steadily, and talked as calmly, as I ever witnessed any one do. But he was fully in the faith—clothed with salvation; having *in many instances, got to know substantially in his closet what was about to take place in the great congregation.* He did not take a falling down as a certain proof of the obtaining of entire sanctification; but ascribed much to physical causes—to nervous weakness. I do not recollect that there were *any* cases of the kind proved to be hypocritical mimicry. It was wonderful how some persons so affected were preserved from physical harm. I remember seeing men fall suddenly backwards on stone flags without being hurt, and on one occasion, in a dwelling-house, a man fell against the fire-place, the fire burning at the time, without being injured."

In September, 1825, John Garner became superintendent of Westgate Branch; and now a wave of the great revival, which may be said to have been going on ever since March, 1823, reached Alston and Allendale. Allenheads, Nenthead and Garrigill are names found in the early books of Barnard Castle Branch. They had been visited by its missionaries, as we have seen, and already had shared in the revival. But the books make no mention of Alston. That place, there is reason to believe, as well as lower Allendale, was first visited by missionaries from Hexham. Now, however, in the autumn of 1825, they are included within the area of Westgate Branch as the following report of the progress of the revival, taken from the *Journal* of John Garner, shows:—

December 19th, 1825.—"I went to Alston, and was glad to hear that one hundred and upwards had united with our Society within the last three months, and that the work of sanctification had been going on all the time. But this glorious, extraordinary and important work, is not confined to Alston. It has spread through the whole branch. According to my best calculation, I think two hundred and fifty, at least, have been converted to God, within the time above specified. The Lord is extending our borders, and opening our way in Alston-Moor, and East and West Allendale. Truly, these are the days of the Son of Man with power, and we are willing to hope for greater things than these; for nothing is too hard for the Lord."

REV. J. GRIEVES.

A year after this the revival had not spent its force. Joseph Grieves had come to the Westgate and Alston Branch in June, 1826. He himself was a trophy of the revival, having been delivered from "drunkenness, profane swearing, and poaching," by his signal conversion at a lovefeast at Westgate in May, 1824. Grieves was at Alston on January 21st, 1827, where he tells of holding a service by invitation in a farmer's house, at which service several were converted, including the farmer himself, who had taken refuge in his own dairy, where Grieves found him on his knees crying for mercy. "Twenty-five joined the society; and a publican declared that the revival had lost him a pound a week."

Our mention of the name of Joseph Grieves leads us to mark yet another sweep of the revival movement, which resulted in planting our Church in Upper Teesdale and the Eden Valley, thus geographically rounding off the North-West Mission. Occasional visits had been made by the missionaries to the neighbourhood before the conversion of Joseph Grieves, who lived at Aukside, near Middleton: but "the harvest was great and the labourers were few," and no provision could as yet be made for Sunday services. Characteristically, therefore, Grieves set to work himself. He established a series of house prayer-meetings, to which the people flocked, curious to learn how these former

MAIN STREET, BROUGH.

ringleaders in wickedness would pray. Under this humble agency a revival began, and one of its earliest gains was Mr. John Leekley, afterwards the founder of Primitive Methodism in the Western States of America. Now a recognised exhorter, Mr. Grieves, along with Messrs. Leekley, Rain, and Collinson, missioned Bowlees, Harwood, Forest, and other places in Upper Teesdale, where societies were established which continue to this day. After giving such indications of zeal and courage, we need hardly be surprised that, in March, 1826, Hull Quarterly Meeting should appoint Mr. Grieves to begin his labours as a travelling-preacher in Barnard Castle Branch. He laboured for thirty-eight years, and the impression the Rev. Philip Pugh's ably-written memoir leaves on the mind of the reader is, that our Church has had few men who have served its interests more faithfully and successfully than did this revival-born dalesman.

And now, as the formation of the Westgate Branch set Thomas Batty at liberty, the Barnard Castle Branch sought compensation for its diminished territory and reduced membership, by sending Mr. Batty to mission Brough in Westmoreland and other places in the Eden Valley. He set out from Middleton on his journey of fifteen miles, commended to the grace of God by his kindly entertainers. He had a long and toilsome journey before him; but, when he stood on the last eminence and looked down on the fair valley beneath, with the Eden like a ribbon of silver winding through, he was not too tired or too much engrossed with the duty that lay before him, to "feast his eyes with the beautiful scenery, and to rejoice at the goodness of God to man."

The gentry of Brough were hostile; the generality, and especially the common people, heard him gladly. Mr. Batty, on that first evening, took his stand on a horse-block before a public-house, which the landlady had obligingly allowed him to use, adding, as she consented, the gracious remark, "that she could have no objection to anything that was good." The bellman's announcement had drawn together a curious crowd, and Batty was suffered to preach without molestation. He slept at Brough Sowerby, where a society was soon formed, and at Brough a friendly farmer lent his barn for services. Meanwhile, the Committee at Hull had officially appointed Messrs. Batty and Thomas Webb to this new mission, and processioning and out-door preaching became the order of the day. The "gentry" now thought it time to bestir themselves. Two of them invaded the barn, where a prayer meeting was being held, and irreverently discussed, to their own discomfiture, the legal bearings of the service they were interrupting. The rumour went that if the preacher persisted in holding a service at the Cross the next Sunday, as he had announced he would do, he was to be pulled down. He was not to be intimidated. A strong band from Brough Sowerby and Kirby Stephen body-guarded Batty as he preached his fourth sermon that day, and the "gentry" watched the proceedings from the outskirts of the congregation. As they crossed the green to the barn for their prayer meeting, Mr. Batty was followed, and asked to show his license. Under protest, the license was produced and handed round, and scrutinised and fingered as though it had been a bank-note of doubtful antecedents and value. "Was it counterfeit or genuine? If good for Yorkshire did it hold good for Westmoreland?" "For all England," said Mr. Batty. At this point the ire of a respectable tradesman of the town was roused by this high-handed procedure. Said he, hotly: "You think to run them down, a parcel of you! You think they are poor people, and cannot stand up for themselves; but I have plenty of money, and I'll back them." And the tradesman was as good as his word. Next morning the "gentry" met at the head inn to consult as to what should next be done in the present serious state of affairs. The plan they hit upon was to send the bellman round to proclaim as follows:—
"This is to give notice, that a vestry meeting will be held this evening at seven o'clock to put down all midnight revelling and ranting." When the bellman had "cried" the town, another commission awaited him. The respectable tradesman aforesaid, with the aid of his brother and sundry Acts of Parliament, drew up a counter-proclamation,

which the bellman went round the town again to cry. It ran as follows:—"This is to give notice, that the laws against tippling and riotous midnight revels at public-houses, gambling, buying and selling, and other evil practices on the Sabbath Day, cursing and swearing, and other laws for suppressing vice and immorality, will be put in force, and notice duly given to churchwardens and constables who, in case of neglect, will be presented at the Bishop's Court or Quarter Sessions." The townsfolk listened, then laughed and said: "That's right; that's right!" Thus, so to say, fizzled out amid laughter this fussy, spit-fire attempt on the part of the "gentry" to frighten the missionary and keep Primitive Methodism out of Brough; and the story is told here because this would-be persecution was the last instance of its kind we shall meet with so far north, and because this persecution that failed was the precursor of a revival such as we have been describing, of which, indeed, it was part and the continuation. "A glorious work," says Mr. Batty, "broke out immediately, and in a fortnight we added thirty-eight souls to our society; and the work was both genuine and deep. Some of the most wicked characters, and others less so, were brought to the knowledge of the truth: "And there was great joy in that town." Mr. Batty adds, that the old gentleman who allowed the use of his barn for services was himself one of the converts. The first chapel, which long stood on the banks of the Augill, and under the shadow of the old castle, was built on a site of land given by him. In 1877, a new chapel was built, which unfortunately was burnt down three years after; but the society energetically set about the work of restoration, and since that time a good school and class-rooms have been added. Brough has been an independent circuit since 1849.

OLD PRIMITIVE METHODIST CHAPEL AND BROUGH CASTLE.

PRIMITIVE METHODIST CHAPEL, BROUGH.

Thus the churches around these northern hills and dales were established by revivals, and again and again have these same churches been replenished and refreshed by similar visitations. No wonder that, in the localities thus visited, these bygone revivals should be often talked of. When such is the case, we are told it is customary for the speaker to distinguish the particular revival he wishes to recall, by attaching to it the name of the person

THE PERIOD OF CIRCUIT PREDOMINANCE AND ENTERPRISE. 151

who, under God, was the chief agent in carrying it forward. Thus they will speak of Batty's or Oxtoby's revival, of McKechnie's or Peter Clarke's—the list is a long one. We can but barely allude to one or two of these revivals which were after the original type. There was the Stanhope revival of 1851-2, which Rev. C. C. McKechnie described in the *Magazine* at the time—a revival which he says "has transformed the character of our little church. It is no longer weak, sickly, emasculate, but full of life, vigour and enterprise." There was the revival which began at Frosterley in 1861, and spread through Weardale; which in two months increased the membership from 68 to 147, and led to the voluntary closing on the Sabbath of seven public-houses. Indeed, the whole period from 1860 to 1866 seems to have been a time of ingathering in Westgate Circuit, for the membership which had been 600 when the Rev. H. Phillips entered the circuit in the former year, had risen to 975 when the Rev. P. Clarke left it in 1867. Allendale, too, which had gained its independence in 1848, had its visitation of power in the years 1859-61, which, after making good all losses, more than doubled the circuit membership. About the same time and onward, a great revival swept over West Cumberland from Whitehaven to Carlisle. In this revival the late Mr. Henry Miller was brought to God, whose active and useful connection with our Church in the Carlisle Circuit has only recently been terminated by death. The names of Rev. Adam Dodds—Nathaniel-like in his guilelessness—and John Taylor —then in the vigour of early manhood and full of revival zeal—will always be associated with this spiritual movement. Nor must the prominent part taken in the revival by Joseph Jopling of Frosterley—a simple, devout, unmercenary lay-evangelist—be forgotten. Himself the fruit of a revival, he in some sort links together the revivals of Weardale and Cumberland. In this suitable connection we give the portrait of Mr. Joseph Collinson, another Frosterley local preacher who showed himself an active promoter of revivals.

MR. HENRY MILLER.

REV. ADAM DODDS.

JOSEPH JOPLING.

MR. J. COLLINSON.

SOME SIDELIGHTS ON THE NORTH WESTERN MISSION.

Barnard Castle and Whitehaven were branches of Hull Circuit until 1840, and Westgate and Alston until 1834 and 1835, respectively. Thus barely stated, this fact of the intimate relations with Hull Circuit, so long sustained by the branches named, seems simple enough. But it is not enough merely to state the fact, which had as many reticulations as the veining of a leaf, and some of these need following if we are to get a true idea of the state of the societies, which must have been largely conditioned and complexioned by this dependence on Hull. We have only to remember that all the affairs of the branches—financial, administrative and disciplinary—were regularly supervised by the parent circuit, in order to see that this must have been the case. Hull sent its preachers, and of these some of its very best, to work these distant branches. Messrs. Flesher, W. Garner, Harland, Sanderson, even Clowes himself—they were all here at one time or another. The societies would fall into the habit of looking to Hull rather than as yet to Sunderland, to know what was being thought of and determined in reference to themselves. The Hull Committee would come to be regarded as a powerful, if somewhat mysterious entity, to be spoken of with respect; so that Thomas Batty could clinch his argument with the "gentry" of Brough by first affirming: " I am sent by our Committee at Hull," and then by asking: "Do you think they have sent me here without legal authority?" The frequent change of preachers in these branches, and the obligation the preachers were under to attend the quarterly meetings at Hull, were regulations which, in practice, would create variety and incident in the societies from Whitehaven to Barnard Castle. The *Journals* of the time are punctuated by references to these recurring quarterly meetings. You read the details of a spell of work, and then are suddenly brought to a stop by some such sentence as: "I then proceeded to Hull in order to attend the quarterly meeting." The preachers seem to be always either going to the quarter day or returning therefrom. Now, as we have written in another place: "It is easy to write that the missionary, Mr. Clowes, for instance, proceeded from Carlisle to Hull to attend the quarter day. A moment's reflection, however, will serve to make it sufficiently obvious, that seventy years ago this was no light journey. It probably enough meant rising with the lark, and with the mission or branches quarterly income in his pocket, and staff in hand, trudging along over bleak fells, and passing through town and village and hamlet. Now and again, it may be, he gets a lift in a carrier's cart or passing vehicle, and then, towards the gloaming, turns tired and travel-stained into some hospitable dwelling, the home of some well-known adherent of the Connexion or of some colleague in the ministry. Then the frugal meal, seasoned with pleasant talk of the work of God, and all sanctified by prayer; the sleep which needed no wooing, preparing for the next day's journey. Many such days must have been, when as yet Whitehaven, Alston Moor, and other distant places were branches of Hull Circuit, and we have listened to the description of some such journey as this from those whose lips are now sealed by death."[*]

Perhaps the thought may occur to us that these long journeys and frequent absences must have involved much toil and loss of time, and have been a serious interruption of labour. Likely enough it was so; but we are writing of things as they were, and not of things as we think they ought to have been. Besides, one can on reflection see that these "journeyings oft" would have their compensations both for preachers and people. We have already, in speaking of Hugh Bourne's incessant perambulations during the time he was general superintendent, compared them to the movements of the weaver's

[*] Smaller "History of the Primitive Methodist Connexion," 2nd Ed. pp. 76-7.

shuttle by which the interlacing threads of the woof are added to the warp, and the tissue slowly put together. Similar would be the effect of the constant going to and fro of men who had not lost the taste or tradition of conversation-preaching. Intercourse would tend to knit together the various societies, and have a positive value for evangelisation. As for the preachers themselves, the stimulus derived from association with so many of their brethren assembled in Hull, would conduce to their greater efficiency, and they would return to their stations like iron that has been sharpened by iron. It is no fancy picture we draw. It so happens that both our arch-founders made "religious excursions"—to use their own phrase—in these parts, and in their *Journals* we can see that, even by the head-waters of Tyne and Wear and Tees, and by the coast of the Irish Sea, we are still on Hull territory. We can also gain glimpses of some early befrienders of the cause in these parts, who kept open house for the servants of God and were recompensed by receiving back from them good into their own bosoms. W. Clowes speaks of being able to preach without intermission, night after night, on his way to Hull. It was not in his line, unfortunately, to give an account written with all the circumstantiality of a log-book, of such a journey. But once—only once it would seem—Hugh Bourne preached his way from Whitehaven to Darlington, and, as usual, his *Journal* is not wanting in that welcome particularity which helps to illumine the past. The one journey he describes may stand for many of which no record survives. What Hugh Bourne once did was often repeated by W. Clowes and other leading missionaries when *en route* for Hull.

On the 4th of August, 1831, Hugh Bourne landed at Whitehaven and spent the remainder of the month in traversing, chiefly on foot, but with occasional helps by the way, the district, excluding Carlisle and Hexham, whose first missioning we have already described. He found W. Garner in charge of the Whitehaven Branch. He visited many families in company with Mr. Garner, and took part in services at Whitehaven, Harrington, Distington, and Workington. Then he took coach to Penrith and looked up Bro. Featherstone. A congregation was got together and Hugh Bourne preached. Next he walked twenty miles to Alston, through "a tract of country more dreary than any I saw in any part of the country." He jots down some particulars as to the violence and freaks of the "helm-wind," peculiar to that part and, in his careful vein, notes how a cheap kind of fuel is made in the district by means of "slack" (coal) mixed with clay and formed into fire-balls. Now he is on the Alston and Westgate Union Branch of Hull Circuit with W. Sanderson as its superintendent, and along with him he again visits many families. He sees Bro. Walton, and is the guest of Mr. Muschamp at Brotherlee one night, and going to and fro he visits most of the places we have had occasion to mention—Allenheads, Allendale Town, Middle Acton, Wearhead, Westgate, and Frosterley. "The pious, praying labourers are diligent," he observes, "and the work has been and is rather extraordinary." A revival is evidently again afoot in these parts. Then he walks to Middleton—ten miles—and finds twenty-one members have recently emigrated, one of these being Bro. Raine, who has become a preacher in Pennsylvania, U.S.A., and a letter from whom he reads. Assisted with a horse he now goes to Brough, where the quarterly meeting of the Barnard Castle Branch is being held, and he spends the night at Mouthlock with Bro. Hilton. Barnard Castle is his next stage, which he reaches partly by riding Bro. Hilton's horse, and partly by walking. He has another diet of visitation here in company with Bro. Harland, the minister in charge of the branch. "In this branch," he notes, "there is a great spirit of prayer, and the work is in a good state." He takes Staindrop on his way, and next day sets out for Darlington, taking care to call at Ingleton in order to share the hospitality of Bro. Emerson. They cross over to Bro. Young's and have a bout of prayer, and Brother Young takes him forward a little way in his conveyance. Their talk is not about beeves or crops, but about camp meetings. Bro. Young tells him of "a confused, unsteady, inefficient camp meeting he had lately attended in a neighbouring circuit;" and Hugh Bourne has his own remarks to make on the cause and cure of this. "The travelling preachers ought to be called to their answer for cutting off the praying services." So he comes to Darlington and Hurworth for Sunday, August 28th, having, in his religious excursion of twenty-four days, preached twenty-eight times—thrice in the open-air—besides attending prayer meetings and visiting and walking an indefinite number of miles. Finally, because the Ripon coach was full, he takes the coach to Thirsk and walks to Ripon, and then by Leeds and Manchester makes for home, but falls ill just before he reaches it—which we cannot much wonder at.

During his itinerary through Hull's North-Western Branches Hugh Bourne, it may be remembered, had met with Joseph Walton and Mr. J. D. Muschamp. The latter was helpful to the Westgate Society when its first chapel was erected in 1824. The land for the site was given, and the miners in their spare time cheerfully assisted in the erection. Mr. Muschamp might have been seen hard at work among the rest. Thirty days he devoted to stone-getting or walling, and twenty to soliciting subscriptions. But presently the work was brought to a stand. It was alleged that the stones in the bed of the burn served to break the force of the "spate," and that their removal would endanger the bridge; hence the person in charge of the bridges of the district, issued his prohibition against the taking out of any more stones for chapel-building purposes. In some way the matter came under discussion before certain magistrates and gentlemen at Durham. "Who are these Ranters?" was the very natural inquiry. Some one well informed as to the facts of the case and well-disposed too, it would seem, stated what had been the moral effects of the entry of the Primitive Methodists into the dale, especially in having done more to put a stop to poaching than gamekeepers, magistrates and prisons together had been able to effect. On hearing this, permission to take as many stones from the bed of the burn as might be necessary to complete the chapel was readily granted. Once more Mr. Muschamp is said to have shown himself a friend in need. When the trustees were straitened for money and unable to meet the payment due to the builder, he went home, sold a cow and gave the proceeds to the building fund. For thirty years he was Circuit Steward and Chapel Treasurer, dying in 1858, at Brotherlee, on the small patrimonial estate where he had lived for eighty-three years.

It was just two months before Hugh Bourne preached at Westgate that George Race had been made an exhorter. It is likely enough the novice both observed and heard the veteran attentively, though they might not have speech the one with the other. But though Hugh Bourne does not mention Mr. Race's name, if he could have foreseen the figure this new-fledged exhorter would afterwards become in the dale and beyond, he would certainly have referred to him, as we are bound to do. It would be rash and invidious to affirm that George Race, sen., was the ablest layman Primitive Methodism has yet produced. It is quite permissible to affirm that, for sheer mental force, there have been few to equal him. He was a dalesman and made no pretension, even in speech or manner, to be anything else. The miners and crofters felt that this village store-keeper was one of themselves, and yet they knew that mentally he was head and shoulders above themselves, and were proud and not jealous of his bigness, of which he seemed hardly aware. For there was in the man a fine balance of brain and heart; his homeliness and companionableness drew men to him, so that the relation between him and his friends and neighbours was like that of a chieftain to his clansmen—familiar, but respectful. He had read much, and he had pondered and explored and discussed with his friends the underlying problems of philosophy and religion. In later years his mind was greatly drawn to geology in some of its aspects—to stratification and denudation, and the rest. He tried to find out how these valleys and hills amongst which he loved to wander had become what they were; how the valleys had been scooped out, and the course of the torrent scored, and the hills uplifted, and some of his doubts on the accepted conclusions relative to these matters, and his own excogitations thereon, were given to the world. Meanwhile he 'knew whom he had believed.' To him, "conversion was the abiding miracle" and Christian experience the basis of certitude. Few could preach with the same power and acceptance as he could, yet he was easily pleased with the preaching of others, for his faith being simple, his heart responded to the ring of sincerity in the utterance. We know our sketch of George Race, sen., is imperfect, but it is an honest attempt to hand down what may serve faintly to recall some of the features of this dalesman *in excelsis*.

MR. GEORGE RACE.

George Race, jun., worthily fills the place his father occupied so long. Heavily weighted as he is by the responsibility of sustaining and carrying onward the traditions and memories associated with the name he bears, that responsibility is being bravely and steadily borne. More would we say were he not, as happily he is, still amongst us.

In this upland region where the rivers have their rise, Methodism in its two branches, old and Primitive, has long been, as it were, the established religion. These moors and dales have received much from Methodism, and it is just as true to say that they have given much to Methodism in return. So far as our own Church is concerned, the mere enumeration of those who have gone forth into its ministry from these parts would occupy more space than we have at command. Were we to add to these the dalesmen born who have, like their own rivers, found their way to the lowlands and populous centres to enrich the life of our churches, the roll would be a long one indeed. We have only to think of the Watsons, Pearts, Clemitsons, Elliotts, Featherstones, Gibsons, Reeds, Emmersons, Gills, Phillipsons, Prouds, and

MR. GEORGE RACE, JUN.

the bearer of other Northern names—to be reminded of our indebtedness. The few portraits we give are only "on account." One of these is that of Joseph Gibson, of Brotherlee, who did such good work in Liverpool and, humanly speaking, died all too

REV. J. GIBSON.    MR. RALPH FEATHERSTONE RACE.    MR. J. RITSON.

soon, in October 1866. Elsewhere will be found that of Dr. John Watson, of Ireshopeburn, who had what was probably the unique distinction of travelling the whole of his probation in his native circuit. As representative laymen of this interesting district we give the portraits of Messrs. Joseph Ritson, of Allendale, Ralph Featherstone Race, of Teesdale, J. Gibson, and J. Elliott, of Weardale.

Mr. J. Ritson, of Ninebanks, West Allen, was intimately associated with the work of Primitive Methodism in the west part of the Allendale Circuit. Converted in Keenley under the ministry of Thomas Greener, he shortly afterwards removed to Ninebanks where he commenced business as a joiner and cartwright. This was in 1833, and at that time we had no chapel in West Allendale. Largely through Mr. Ritson's efforts land was obtained and a chapel built at Carry Hill, three-quarters of a mile further up the Dale. For the next forty years he was a leading figure in the society and laboured indefatigably for the advancement of the cause. His house was the home of the preachers. His eldest son was for many years Circuit Steward; his second daughter became the wife of the Rev. R. Clemitson, and his youngest son is in the ministry of our Church and vice-editor. Retiring from business in 1872, he removed to the neighbourhood of Allendale Town, and took a leading part in the erection of the present chapel. He died July 26th, 1878. Mr. Ritson was a profoundly religious man; "he carried his conscience into the construction of a cart wheel, the roofing of a house, the making of a piece of furniture—each must be a sound piece of workmanship."

MR. J. GIBSON.    MR. J. ELLIOTT.

The two honoured ministers named above may be taken as good specimens of that type of men of which this interesting region is the matrix. The type is one not difficult to recognise. You find in it a pronounced sobriety and thoughtfulness, in perfect keeping with the austere and solemn beauty of the outward things their eyes first looked upon. It has a temperament capable of quiet and sustained enthusiasm. It is hard and solid to look at and handle, but it can kindle and enkindle. In short it is the anthracite temperament. The dalesmen—using the word generally—have the temperament and the tradition of revivalism, and they will be wise for themselves and for the Connexion, if they yield to their temperament and conserve and carry on the tradition.

Some account has already been given of the establishment of our cause in Hexham, and reference has also been made to the extensive area of the circuit and the part it took in early missionary operations. Contemporary journals serve to complete the picture, by giving us glimpses of some of the more notable men and women who in their time contributed to the working and maintenance of the Hexham Circuit.

REV. HENRY HEBBRON.

Invaluable in this regard is the manuscript Autobiography of the late Rev. C. C. McKechnie, who was on the station in 1841-2—just at the end of the first period. Occasionally we shall borrow from his graphic characterisations, and by so doing enrich our pages.

After a time the old Malt-kiln was left for the chapel in Bull Bank, with the preacher's house at its side. This served the uses of the Hexham Society until 1863, when the "Hebbron Memorial Chapel" was opened. Now, after other forty years have passed, a remove is again about to be made to a splendid site at the junction of four principal streets, not more than one hundred yards from the original Malt-kiln. The mention of the "Hebbron Memorial" naturally leads to a reference to the Ridley family of which Mrs. Hebbron was a member. At the time Primitive Methodism was first brought to Hexham, the brothers Ridley occupied a good position and were deservedly held in respect in the town. Though associated with the Congregational Church they showed a very friendly spirit to our newly-planted cause. Their only sister was induced to attend the services, and under a sermon by Rev. W. Garner, Miss Ridley was led to make the great decision, and to cast in her lot with our people. A little romance now began : Miss Ridley became the betrothed of Rev. W. Garner ; her friends disapproved of the match, and took their own method to ensure its being broken. Each thought the other false and each was wrong. But Miss Ridley was destined after all to be the wife of a Primitive Methodist preacher. The Rev. Henry Hebbron became her suitor, and a successful one. He was a gentleman by birth, and unmistakably one in appearance and manner, and with expectations. This time the fates interposed no bar. In their union there was a convergence of several ancestral lines associated with the

MRS. E. HEBBRON.

evangelical succession. Miss Ridley belonged to a family which could boast of its connection with the Ridleys of Williamswick—a family to which belonged the martyr Ridley, while on the maternal side she was related to Thomas Scott the commentator. On his side, Mr. Hebbron was the cousin of the Rev. David Simpson—the author of the once well-known "Plea for Religion." Being left with ample means Mrs. Hebbron thought to carry out the wishes of her husband, who died in 1860, by building a chapel for the denomination in Hexham. On the day—June 24th, 1863—the chapel should have been opened, Mrs. Hebbron died, and her remains were brought from Potto and were interred by those of her husband in Hexham cemetery.

Besides the Ridleys of Hexham, reference must be made to Mr. James Davison of Dean Row. Mr. McKechnie thus speaks of him :—

MR. JAMES DAVISON.

"In the west part of the Hexham Circuit we had some most interesting people, among the rest James Davison, schoolmaster of Dean Row, stood prominent. Mr. Davison was a remarkable man, slow and somewhat hesitant of speech, but clear and penetrating in his judgment, consecutive and forcible in his reasonings, and withal of a generous, ardent, passionate temperament. He contributed largely to the building up and consolidating of the Hexham Circuit, and often attended district meeting and conference as circuit delegate."

As everybody knows, Dr. Joseph Parker was a "Tynechild"—born and brought up at Hexham. Probably neither he nor his father was at any time actually connected with our Church, but they frequently attended its services, and it is about certain that much of young Parker's early preaching was done in connection with our agencies, and that he delivered his first temperance address in a Primitive Methodist chapel. Several of our ministers were frequent visitors to the home of the Parkers, and with the Rev. R. Fenwick he kept up an intermittent correspondence almost to the end. Though therefore we may not be able to claim so large a part in Dr. Parker as in C. H. Spurgeon or Dr. Landells, we may fairly claim to have had some small share in his early development. Dr. Parker, however, is brought in here mainly because of his early relations

REV. C. HALLAM.    MRS. HALLAM.    REV. HENRY YOOLL.

with Mr. James Davison. Something of the calibre of the latter may be learned from the famous preacher's juvenile estimate of him. In a letter of the most intimate kind addressed to the schoolmaster of Dean Row, he says: "Mr. Davison has been a name ever associated in my mind with boundless kindness, cultivated intellect and open straight-forwardness." * "Mr. Davison and Primitive Methodist Camp Meetings!" was the exclamation with which he greeted his old friend on the occasion of a visit paid to Haydonbridge long after he had become famous. Evidently memory still retained in her niche the image of Mr. Davison as the representative figure of Hexamshire Primitive Methodism.

In Mr. McKechnie's manuscript pages we get pleasant glimpses of his colleagues in the Hexham Circuit in this year—1842. Two of these bore names which their sons have perpetuated and made familiar to Primitive Methodists of a later generation. Christopher Hallam, "warm-hearted, genial," was one of these, and Henry Yooll, "a man of devout spirit, who attended well to pastoral duties and was well received as a preacher," was another. Mrs. Hallam might have been reckoned as yet another colleague, for she frequently preached in the Hexham Circuit, as she did in all the circuits in which her lot was cast, and always with much acceptance. Indeed, though Mrs. Hallam was not a travelling preacher in the technical sense, she was known throughout the northern counties as a woman of special gifts and usefulness. Especially was this the case, as we shall see, in Scotland where Mrs. Hallam left enduring memories of herself. Mr. McKechnie speaks of her "wide, intellectual outlook," and claims for her that she had a mental equipment that would have been creditable to any minister of the gospel.

Mr. McKechnie makes grateful mention too of the kindness and connexional loyalty of the Lowes of Cowburn and Galisharigg, and draws an interesting picture of some of the Sunday afternoon services at Cowburn. These had certain features all their own; for the congregation was largely made up of stalwart shepherds from the hills who, as a matter of course, came accompanied by their collies. The dogs were expected to behave themselves, and usually did so, lying quietly under their masters' forms. But sometimes what began in provocative growls would end in a downright fight, and the preacher had to pause till order was restored. Mr. McKechnie had his turn on the Rothbury Mission, and has a good word for the steward of Brinkburn Priory on the East Coquet, who was a warm-hearted and devoted friend of the cause; and especially of Mr. Thomas Thornton, an extensive sheep-farmer of Cambo, some twelve or fourteen miles south of Rothbury. Mr. Thornton had gathered much worldly substance, but subordinated everything to religion. He was a loyal-hearted Primitive, entertained the preachers bountifully, and in other ways supported and helped to extend the cause.

For twenty years Hexham Circuit enjoyed the distinction of having within its borders the owner of an ancient name and of an ancient demesne, who was as thorough a Primitive Methodist as any one could wish to meet. Even in Northumberland, where pedigree counts for much, Robert Ingram Shafto's claim to belong to a good, old, county family was unimpeachable. Now, though our early preachers in their incessant journeyings to and fro often saw the stately homes of England, they usually saw them through the park palings, or from a distant eminence. They seldom came in contact with the owners of these mansions except at Quarter Sessions. It was indeed

* See the article "Dr. Parker" in "Primitive Methodist Quarterly Review," April, 1903, written by Rev. M. P. Davison, the son of Mr. James Davison. The date of the letter is May 14th, 1850.

a novel, if not a unique, experience to be able to feel that the owner of Bavington Hall was a brother Primitive; that, notwithstanding his long pedigree and his rent-roll, he had his name in the class-book; that he liked nothing better than to have Primitive Methodists on his estate and round his table, and enjoyed a camp meeting with as much zest as his shepherd or ploughman. But so it was; and we need not be surprised if Squire Shafto and Bavington Hall rather impressed the imagination of our people, and if, even yet, the names are invested with a certain glamour. Mr. McKechnie was, of course, in his turn a guest at Bavington Hall, and as we know of no better description of it than the one he has given, we shall here borrow from it.

"Bavington Hall stands about twelve miles north of Hexham, on the borders of a rugged tract of country mostly moorland, which stretches away in monotonous dreariness towards the Cheviot Hills. The estate to which it belongs, though not one of the largest in Northumberland, covers a considerable extent of country, and has been the property of the Shafto family for many generations. The Hall itself is not a specially attractive object in the landscape. It is a spacious but heavy-looking building, with little or no ornamentation, evidently constructed more for comfort and convenience than for beauty of appearance.

"Seventy or eighty years ago Bavington Hall was well known to the Primitives in the North of England. Such of them as had not seen it had often heard of it. It had indeed become among them a sort of household word. It was, perhaps, the only house in England where Primitive Methodism had obtained a vital connection with the gentry of the country. The Squire then in possession was a younger son who, after finishing his course of education at Cambridge, had settled at Sunderland as a solicitor. There he came under the influence of our early preachers, experienced the regenerating power of God's grace, and united with the Society. On succeeding to the Bavington estate, he did not hide his light under a bushel. In a simple, unostentatious way, without noise or parade, but not the less effectually, he made it pretty widely understood that he was a Primitive, and intended his life to be in harmony with his religious profession. He opened a communication with the authorities of the Hexham Circuit, invited the preachers to the Hall, and made arrangements for the formation of a Society and Sunday school for the holding of regular preaching services, and the erection of a chapel. The work of evangelising the neighbourhood on Primitive lines also commenced in good earnest. Not only in the surrounding hamlets, but in several outlying farmhouses, this good work was vigorously carried on. Mr. Shafto himself became a local preacher, and had his name on the preachers' plan, though he did not preach much. He considered the Sunday school his proper sphere, and for many years he rendered much devoted and loving service as school superintendent. To strengthen the infant cause and increase its working power, members and local preachers from a distance were, at Mr. Shafto's instance, offered inducements to settle on the estate; and Bavington soon became noted all round the country-side as a centre and stronghold of Primitive Methodism. While liberally supporting circuit and connexional funds, Mr. Shafto took special interest in our Rothbury Mission. For a while, at least, it was chiefly sustained by himself; and the preacher stationed there was encouraged to ask him for any special help he might require in working what was then a much-neglected and semi-barbarous region. The gentry around Bavington, though much shocked with Mr. Shafto's proceedings, prudently abstained from breaking with him openly, thinking, probably, opposition would have the effect of increasing rather than abating the annoyance. Mr. Shafto kept little company, none at all of a gay or worldly character.

He restricted himself almost entirely to the preachers and other prominent members of the Connexion. The Hall was seldom, for any length of time, without company of this kind. On special occasions, when preachers of note were present, the clergyman of the parish would probably be an invited guest; but it was noteworthy that, though treated with perfect respect, no greater deference was paid to him than to our own preachers. To all intents and purposes they were treated alike . . . .

"Mr. Shafto was a modest, warm-hearted, unpretending gentleman, who might be approached and conversed with by the humblest person with the utmost freedom. His personal appearance was not impressive. He was somewhat under the middle size; his countenance, though pleasant, had no striking features; his dress was plain, and his manners, while perfectly correct, were simple and homely. Nature had not gifted him with the higher qualities of mind; but he had good sense and a sound judgment, and his University education gave marked propriety and polish to his speech. . . . . I often noted he never seemed to tire talking about Primitive Methodism. So completely had the Connexion filled the orb of his vision that he seemed to take little cognisance of other churches. The Church of England he regarded as a fallen Church hastening to extinction; nothing could save it—so he thought and said. Primitive Methodism, on the other hand, would, beyond all doubt, grow and multiply and fill the land. More than once I have heard him say it was sure to take the place of the State Church; and the wonder to him was that everybody did not see this as clearly as himself. Such sentiments would be set down now-a-days as foolish extravagance; but it ought to be remembered that when Mr. Shafto dreamt these dreams and saw these visions, the Church of England was at its nadir, while Primitive Methodism was like a young giant, full of life and blood, prodigal of its strength, and marching on exultingly from conquering to conquer."

HUGH BOURNE AT BAVINGTON HALL.

Hugh Bourne, as well as others of the fathers, was an occasional visitor at Bavington Hall; and stories are not wanting of the way in which its mistress, pleasant hostess though she was, would take note of his idiosyncrasies, and would engage him in discussions in which the advantage was not always on his side. For Mrs. Shafto loved an encounter of argument and wit and was a woman of strong convictions. She rallied him on his extravagance, plain to see in the tell-tale sediment at the bottom of his cup! His alarm and contrition when the peccadillo was brought home to him was one of her cherished recollections. She vanquished his scruples as to signing the pledge, and though he claimed "the teetotallers had joined him," he came out from that entrenchment and admitted the cogency of her arguments. Many a scene like that our artist has tried to picture was enacted in the drawing-room of Bavington, and perhaps imagination may be able even to improve upon the picture the artist has drawn. But there was to be an end of them. Squire Shafto died April 5th, 1848, and a new Squire came into possession who knew not the Primitives. The chapel was alienated and a blight came over the fair prospect.

"So sleeps the pride of former days,
So glory's thrill is o'er."

CHAPTER XVII.

THE MAKING OF SUNDERLAND DISTRICT (*continued*).

III.—THE NORTHERN MISSION.

THE story of the Northern Mission has now to be told. The success of this mission was in every way remarkable—so remarkable indeed as evidently to have been beyond expectation, and even somewhat embarrassing. How the new territory thus gained and added on to the Connexion was to be apportioned and administered, raised some problems which had at once to be dealt with. Pre-existing arrangements were modified. A new District unthought of at the Conference of 1823 was extemporised. Five new northern circuits, which had been made during the year, had to be represented at some District Meeting. The district to which they geographically belonged was Brompton, which, in 1823, included North Shields; but, as we see from the Minutes of 1823, no district was supposed to comprise more than six circuits, whereas, if Hexham, Carlisle, North and South Shields, Newcastle, and Sunderland sent their representatives to Brompton District Meeting, that District would have eleven circuits instead of six. So the six northern circuits were provisionally formed into an entirely new District, which had its first meeting at South Shields on Easter Monday, 1824. The Conference Minutes make no mention of this fresh grouping of the northern stations; but that it took place, and that there was for one year a South Shields District, is clear from an interesting entry in N. West's *Journal*, which is worth giving, as bringing before us in a vivid way the progress the Connexion had made in the north-eastern counties in two short years.

"*Monday, April 19th.*—Went with brothers Anderson and Peckett (delegates from Sunderland) to South Shields District [Meeting], where we met the delegates from North Shields, South Shields, Newcastle, Hexham, and Carlisle. The District Meeting lasted till Friday the 23rd. Much peace prevailed. The state of each circuit was prosperous, the whole number in the District amounted to twenty travelling preachers, sixty-one local preachers (not including exhorters), and 3,632 members. We have great reason to thank the Lord."

Our method hitherto has been to relate the particular history of a circuit to the general history; to try to show how that circuit was but a link in a chain, one of a series of stepping-stones, a brick in a building, supported and lending support to others. Agreeably to this method, the missioning of the populous towns on the Tyne and Wear must be regarded as being, in its beginning, the continuation and natural development of Hull's Hutton Rudby and East Yorkshire Missions. In 1821, Hutton Rudby sent Messrs. J. Branfoot and J. Farrar to establish a cause in Guisborough, which for a time proved very successful. After this, Mr. Branfoot found his way to

Newcastle, where, in all these northern parts, the human grain stood thickest and ripest. We say he "found his way" advisedly; for, whether he had a roving commission to go where he thought he could do most good, and so, in the spirit of a true Christian knight-errant, bent his steps to the capital of the North; or whether the Hutton Rudby Circuit gave him a definite commission, the phrase "found his way" will, in either case, suit the fact. Though as yet there was no Primitive Methodist Society in Newcastle, there were those resident in the town who had been Primitive Methodists, and who were still such in sympathy, though for the time being they were attached to a sister community. Among these were Mr. William Morris, whose name stands on the first printed plan of the Tunstall Circuit, and Mr. John Bagshaw, also a local preacher of a later date, and who was shortly to become a travelling preacher in the Newcastle Circuit. These two early adherents had removed from Staffordshire to the North for the sake of employment, but still kept in touch with their old friends. It may even have been that when Mr. Branfoot entered Newcastle, Mr. Clowes had by him an invitation from these two old comrades to visit them, and was only waiting the opportunity to accept it. The visit was duly paid in the autumn of this same year, and the probability is that it was paid when Mr. Clowes was in the Hutton Rudby neighbourhood. It was during this visit that Clowes preached on "the Ascension of Christ" with telling effect. He was better advised than Mr. Branfoot in fixing upon the Ballast Hills rather than the end of Sandgate as the locality for his service; for it was in the Pandon or older eastern district of Newcastle that Primitive Methodism was destined to strike its earliest roots. It chanced, too, that on this first of August, when Mr. Branfoot attempted to preach near Sandgate, there had been a boat-race on the Tyne; and what that means every Tynesider will know. Mary Porteus was there, and she has told us that, as she saw Mr. Branfoot standing on a stool, with the rabble crowd surging round him—some swearing, and others setting dogs on to fight—she thought gospel-preaching was needed there and then just as much as when John Wesley preached on the same spot eighty years before. But as she witnessed the good man struggling to preach, and at last obliged to content himself with words of warning and exhortation, she thought again: "Surely the preacher must think that the people in these northern parts are little better than heathens." The service broke up in confusion, though not before Mr. Branfoot had announced his intention to preach in Gateshead on the following evening. This he did, standing beneath some trees on the very spot where Wesley had once stood to declare the word of life. This time the service was orderly, and the preacher spoke with power from, "I am the resurrection and the life."

It should be noted that during his visit to Newcastle, Mr. Branfoot was the guest of Mr. John Lightfoot, who is said to have been converted at Durham through the agency of William Bramwell, and through his good offices placed in a business-house in Newcastle.

JOHN LIGHTFOOT.

Mr. Lightfoot was the leader of two classes, and an active worker in the Wesleyan Church. Mr. Branfoot's visit, though a brief and apparently abortive one, would have its influence. Later in the day of this same first of August, Mary Porteus was surprised to receive a visit from Mr. Lightfoot and his guest. She counted it an honour to have the good missionary under her roof, and to take part in the prayers which, as a matter of course, marked the visit. Newcastle made ample return to Cleveland for sending her its first missionary; for Mary Porteus began her ministry in the Guisborough and Whitby Union Circuit in January, 1826, and laboured there two and a half years, while in 1827 John Lightfoot also in the same circuit began his useful ministry of thirty-seven years. Thus was fulfilled Christ's saying: "Give, and it shall be given you; good measure."

When next we get an authentic glimpse of John Branfoot he is holding a service in the spacious market-place of South Shields, which has long been a favourite pitch for those who have something to sell or tell. He himself has given us the date of this

SOUTH SHIELDS MARKET-PLACE.

first service: "It was on the 17th of December, 1821," he says, "when we first opened the place." The Market Square, as Mr. Branfoot saw it in the dubious light of that winter's evening, would present much the same appearance it does to-day, except that the fronts of the shops that line three of its sides have been modernised. In the middle stood the Town House, and the fourth side of the square was flanked by the old church and its graveyard. This service was in every way a contrast to that which Mr. Branfoot had attempted to hold in Newcastle. The goodly number that gathered round—pilots, fishermen, miners, coal-heavers, glass-workers—were used to criers and vendors of all sorts, but this one was different from the rest, and must be listened to. So tradition tells, that as they stood there nothing broke the silence save the preacher's voice, and when he had done, men and women still lingered as though loath to leave the spot.

For a time services were of necessity held in the open-air; then two houses in Waterloo Lane, now Oyston Street, were thrown into one, and the room thus formed served as a shelter and home for the small society. This room was a workshop also, as well as a shelter, and in it work went on which made less work for the police-court and public-houses, and ensured better work being done in the mine and glass-works. Some who had led vicious lives were reformed, and their reformation was manifest in the town. Those who had known their former manner of life recognised the change, and had the candour to acknowledge that "good work was being done in the Ranters' room." So the society soon outgrew its first habitation, and a remove was made to a sail-loft in Wapping Street, hard by the river. The third and topmost story of this building was the preaching-room. It was reached by a flight of stairs, dark and steep; the room was open to the ridge of the roof, and dimly lighted by small windows eked out by a few slabs of glass inserted here and there among the tiles. This room was opened for worship by W. Clowes on October 20th, 1822. "The room," he says, "is nearly thirty yards long, but more came than could get in. At night the congregation seemed to be all on a move. There was a cry out for mercy, and two got liberty. This meeting, I conceive, will never be forgotten." There was no persecution met with at South Shields worth speaking of. A few youths might now and again put out the lights on the stair-way of the sail-loft, or let sparrows loose in the room itself; but this was only their way of finding amusement, and these youths were the very material out of which promising converts were made. Indeed, persecution found no favourable soil for itself in these northern towns. There was no territorial influence or popular sympathy to foster it, and employers of labour were disposed to favour rather than to discourage a movement which, in its first evangelistic phase, was so plainly working to their advantage. So the sail-loft was crowded and converts multiplied, until, by the spring of 1823, we find the society deep in chapel-building. A piece of glebe land, near the old graveyard, was obtained on a long lease, and on April 21st, 1823, the foundation-stone of the Glebe Chapel was laid, and a collection of £3 14s. 3d. taken! The amount suggests that the society was financially but poorly equipped for the formidable task to which it was committed; for, with the exception of two or three tradesmen, such as Messrs. Edward Nettleship, Joshua Hairs, and John Robinson, the members were worth no more than their weekly wage. The building of the chapel was not contracted for; it was done by the day, and paid for as the work proceeded. The first service was held in August, when it was a mere shell of a building, and even when it was formally opened in November, it was still unfinished, and remained so for some years. It would seem that the Glebe might have been lost to the Connexion in this time of searching and trial, had it not been for Mr. John Robinson, who was better off than the rest. By diligent trading he had got together means which his careful and inexpensive habits of life made it easy for him to keep together and increase. He came to the rescue of the trustees just at the time of their direst need, when they could do little more than pray for deliverance. He advanced £460, and some smaller amounts were advanced by others, which gave a measure of relief. In the end, Mr. Robinson took upon him the whole financial responsibility and much of the practical management of the trust estate, and bore the burthen until the society was in a position to shoulder

THE PERIOD OF CIRCUIT PREDOMINANCE AND ENTERPRISE. 167

the responsibility. No wonder our fathers were firm believers in a Providence, and had a special "Providence Department" in their *Magazine*. It was by such experiences as these the conviction was inwrought that God had interposed on their behalf. That conviction was recorded on the front of the sanctuary which, in no conventional sense, was regarded as their "Ebenezer"—their "God's Providence House." "What building

MR. JOHN BRACK.    MR. ALEXANDER THOMPSON.

is this?" asked a man of his companion as they passed the Glebe. Before the other could make reply, a boy, who was playing among the rubbish, broke in: "It's the 'Ranters'' Chapel." "Why, how in the world have these folk got such a building as this?" was the exclamation of this "man of the street," expressing a surprise natural in

MR. GEORGE BIRD.    MRS. ROBINSON.    MR. J. ROBINSON.    MR. WILLIAM OWEN.

one not aware of God's partnership in the venture. "If you will go round to the other side you will see," said the boy. They went and read: "Hitherto the Lord hath helped us." Joseph Spoor used to tell this little anecdote with zest. But, indeed, it is more than an anecdote; it is also a parable, with an obvious moral, setting forth the history of many of our early chapels—notably of the Glebe. Despite all the changes of the years, that chapel has had a continuous history. There is still the Glebe Chapel as there is still St. Sepulchre Street. Eighty years have but served to impart a richer suggestiveness to the old name, and to make the pious legend, "*Hitherto* the Lord hath helped us," still more pertinent.

Meanwhile, during this prolonged crisis, the spiritual side of the Church's work was diligently attended to by the few faithful men who stood to their posts. The whole of Werewickshire—the district lying between the Tyne and Wear—was missioned as far west as Chester-le-Street, Ouston, Pelton, and the collieries by the Wear beyond Washington. The places thus opened were made into a circuit in September, 1823, Joshua Hairs being the first Circuit Steward. "A short time before the circuit was formed, a few members from the sail-loft missioned the colliery at the west end of the town and established services there. A class was soon formed, the leader of which was a publican. This society [Templetown] met in cottages and other places, till circumstances favoured the erection of a small place of worship."* At the first Circuit Quarterly Meeting, held December 9th, 1823, there were twenty-three places with 552 members; three months later the membership was 760, the quarter having witnessed an increase of 208.

Our space will permit us to do little more than allude to one or two out of the many officials who have contributed to the extension and upbuilding of the South Shields Circuit. Unfortunately no portrait is procurable of Mr. John Robinson, whose praiseworthy efforts to preserve the Glebe to the Connexion have been referred to; but we give the likenesses of his son—Mr. John Robinson, shipowner, and late Circuit Steward, and of his excellent wife, whose life was full of good works. Other faithful men and active officials were Messrs. George Bird, Richard Bulmer, Alexander Thompson, son-in-law of Rev. John Day, and father of Rev. J. Day Thompson, J. Brack, a most estimable man, and William Owen, a once very familiar figure to the riverine inhabitants of both the Shields, who could preach a sermon, and steer his ponderous ferry-boat across the Tyne, with equal skill.

North Shields.

On Tuesday, February 5th, 1822, W. Clowes crossed over from North to South Shields, and heard J. Branfoot of Hutton Rudby Circuit preach. Referring to South Shields, he writes: "If he had not taken it, we [the Hull Circuit] should now have taken it. So we are shoulder to shoulder. I think we are now likely to spread through the North." Only three days before, Clowes had arrived from the Darlington branch in order to begin a mission at North Shields. He had come at the invitation of Joseph Peart who, four years before, had left his native Alston Moor and was now a schoolmaster at Chirton. Why a Wesleyan local preacher in good standing, as Joseph Peart was at the time, should have taken such a step as this, he himself has told us. The explanation he gives shows that, at North Shields as elsewhere, there existed, side by side, two variant and competing types of Methodism which found it difficult to live and work together without friction. The experience—so common as

* Notes by the late Rev. John Atkinson.

to be a characteristic of the time—goes far to explain and justify the rise and spread of Primitive Methodism.

"One day I was alone in my room, studying how I could best glorify God in supporting His blessed work ; for there had frequently been antagonists to great outpourings of the Holy Spirit even amongst the professed members of the Church. They could not endure the natural results of such visitations, but looked upon it as wildfire, disorder, confusion, enthusiasm, etc. I had a very strong debate with a professor of the dead languages who, as well as myself, belonged to the society of the Old Methodists. While contending with him in vindication of the rationality and great utility of such a work as had been effected in North Shields, about five years previous to that time, by an extraordinary outpouring of the Holy Ghost, he, by way of derision, said, 'You should have been a "Ranter"' It powerfully wrought on my mind, as I sat in the room, that it was my indispensable duty to send for the 'Ranters' (so called). The circumstance was very singular ; for I had never heard and never seen any of them. 'I was not disobedient to the heavenly' call, but wrote for William Clowes, who shortly arrived at our house, and stopped till the cause got established."

Mr. Clowes had preached at North Shields in the autumn of 1821, when he visited his Newcastle friends. He had always his "seed-basket" with him ; and he had preached during this flying visit, on the principle of "sowing beside all waters," even when he was not likely to enjoy the fruits. Now, however, he was here for the double purpose of sowing *and* reaping. February 3rd, 1822, is reckoned by him as the date when North Shields as a new outfield was first opened. On that Sunday evening he preached at the lower part of the town, in a schoolroom belonging to Mr. Webster, who had granted them the use of it for a month, rent free. The town-crier was sent round to let the public know what was afoot, and the room was thronged. Next night, after a preaching service in the same room, the first class was formed consisting of three members, two of whom became travelling preachers before the year was out. One of these, and the first to have his name enrolled as member and leader, was Joseph Peart, who began his fourteen years' ministry in Hull's north-eastern branches. The other was William Summersides, the missioner of Carlisle and Whitehaven, one of Hull's first missionaries to the United States, and, on his temporary return in 1838, the advocate and promoter of Protracted Meetings. When, at the end of three weeks, W. Clowes returned to Darlington, he had formed a second class at the upper part of North Shields ; had preached at Howden Pans "to a thousand of a congregation, in general well behaved" ; and visited Blyth, "where there appeared to be an opening for the work of the Lord."

With an improvement in its "temporal concerns," and influenced by the representations of W. Clowes, the March Quarterly Meeting of the Hull Circuit decided to take over the Northern Mission from Hutton Rudby. After his three weeks' experience, W. Clowes was more confident than when, at the end of three days, he had written : "*I think* we are now likely to spread through the North." Now he was persuaded that the work only needed to be pushed forward and followed up vigorously in order to be a signal success, and it is evident he brought his brethren to see as he did and to share his confidence. So, in a communication to the *Magazine* sent by Mr. R. Jackson on the morrow of the Quarterly Meeting, we are told: "Brother Clowes left Hull on the 18th inst. for Newcastle-on-Tyne, Sunderland, Shields, etc. We are going to send three preachers into Northumberland this quarter." Then follows an allusion to the favourable opening presented by Blyth, on which, no doubt, Mr. Clowes had dilated: "There appears to be a good opening in one town, near the sea-side, which is about 140 miles from Hull."

The Hull authorities had faith in the future of the Northern Mission, and gave bond for their faith by appointing to it John and Thomas Nelson as the fellow-labourers of W. Clowes. The brothers, who sprang from a village in the neighbourhood of Whitby, rendered unforgettable service to the Connexion in its early days. In the North their names are deservedly held in high esteem. Contemporary journals, biographies, and tradition, bear concurrent testimony to the quantity and quality of the work they did in pioneering Primitive Methodism in the eastern parts of Northumberland and Durham. Of the two brothers, Thomas Nelson was slightly the elder, and by a few months was first in the field. He had a good share of natural ability, and a more than common zeal in winning souls. He preached almost exclusively in the open-air when in the North, and often to immense congregations. Whether in this as in other cases which have come under our notice, "the fiery soul o'er-informed the house of clay," and subjected it to a strain that could not long be endured, we know not; but this is certain—Thomas Nelson travelled only seven or eight years. His last circuit was Birmingham. Here, in 1828, his health failed, and he settled down at Rothwell, near Leeds, where he died February, 1848, aged 51 years. The model minister, John Wesley tells us, should have "gifts, grace, and fruit." Thomas Nelson shaped himself after this pattern.

John Nelson entered the itinerant ranks in December, 1820.

JOHN NELSON.

He had the advantage of his brother as to physique, being tall of stature and strongly built, his countenance pleasing, and his presence commanding. In him were united zeal and industry, considerable intellectual power and fluent utterance—a combination of qualities which naturally rendered his ministry popular and attractive. John Nelson entered, too, the ranks of authorship; but he took his place there as the precursor of J. A. Bastow, John Petty, James Garner, and Thomas Greenfield, not as a Biblical scholar or systematic theologian, but as a preacher still. The volume of "Sermons and Lectures" he published—the bulkiest and highest-priced book as yet given to the press by a Primitive Methodist preacher—was a souvenir of his ministry in Hull in 1828—9. It consisted of a series of discourses—doctrinal, practical, and experimental—delivered on Sunday evenings when, in his turn, he occupied the town pulpit. Unfortunately for our Church and unfortunately for himself, too, we believe, John Nelson afterwards withdrew from the Connexion. But this withdrawal did not take place until some years after the time of which we are writing, and does not concern us here.

Close upon a year after their appointment to the North Mission, the three yoke-fellows met at North Shields, for the purpose of attending the preparatory Quarterly Meeting. They slept under Dr. Oxley's roof, which for once failed to afford a safe shelter. A tragedy like that which, in the night of February 27th, 1903, was fatal to the estimable W. R. de Winton, was all but rehearsed. Seldom are men brought so near death and escape scathless. Well might W. Clowes prefix to his account of their common deliverance the words of the Psalmist, "He shall give His angels charge over thee;" for death brushed them with his wings as he passed, and yet no harm befell them. It was the early morning of Monday, March 3rd, 1823. W. Clowes was roused from sleep by the noise of the wind, which had risen to a perfect hurricane. Scarcely had he dressed when a stack of chimneys crashed through the roof and broke in the floors. When he and his alarmed companions made for the stairs they found them blocked by the fallen roof. How under these circumstances they contrived to escape is not very clear; but escape they did. The local chronicler notes the preservation of Dr. Oxley and his family, but he does not know—as how should he?—what the preservation of Dr. Oxley's guests meant for Primitive Methodism. The loss of Messrs. Branfoot and Hewson by misadventure on the Hetton waggon-way on February 26th, 1831, was a heavy blow; the loss of W. Clowes and the Nelson brothers in the great storm of 1823 would have been a disaster.*

The preparatory Quarterly Meeting held, as we have said, on the day of this hair-breadth escape, proposed that North Shields should be made a circuit. Considerable progress must have been made during the year to warrant the taking of such a step. So late as June, 1822, the membership of the Northern Mission was but seventy. Since then the Mission had been divided into the North and South Shields branches, with an aggregate membership of 681, almost equally divided between the two branches. In addition to these, Stockton Mission, which since June had increased its membership from 79 to 114, was soon to be incorporated. What was more, a footing had been gained in the important towns of Sunderland and Newcastle, under circumstances shortly to be narrated. The outlook had appeared so promising that the Hull December Quarterly Meeting determined to send reinforcements, and eight missionaries were now at work—three North of the Tyne, three at South Shields, and two on the Stockton Mission, of whom N. West was one. The *Journals* of the missionaries show that these results had not been accomplished without hard work, often performed under trying conditions. A six weeks' storm in the first two months of 1823 had blocked the roads with snow-drifts, so as to make travelling hard and risky. For a whole week no Western or Northern mails had entered Newcastle, and the inhabitants saw with astonishment the South mails carried on the backs of thirteen saddle-horses. Travellers found themselves storm-bound in country inns and running short of provisions, as though they were in a beleaguered fortress. Clowes speaks of having witnessed distressing shipwrecks on South Shields sands, and having, at Sunderland,

---

* Sykes' "Local Records" refers to this incident of the great storm. Clowes' words are: "We therefore contrived to escape by the top of the roof, which lay then on the stair-case, holding ourselves by the wall." Some years later than this a Dr. Oxley befriended our cause in London. Whether we have here a mere coincidence of name we are unable to determine. The good doctor might have removed in the interim.

offered public thanksgiving on behalf of several sailors who had escaped with their lives. And yet, "fair or foul, snow or shine," the missionaries went on with their work. We get glimpses of Clowes preaching at North Shields, in New Milburn Place and on the New Quay. We see him, in conjunction with John Nelson, visiting Newbiggen and Morpeth. Newbiggen was so little accustomed to the Gospel that it hardly knew what to make of the evangelists: "Some few gathered round, but others stood at a distance as if frightened." At Morpeth they sent the town-crier round, and then preached at the Town Cross. "Several did not behave well;" one man in particular raised a clamour, and, from his movements, seemed to be intending an onset on the preacher, but Clowes "endeavoured to fix him with his eye, and waited upon God." Already we see there were good societies at Percy Main and Benton Square. Still, the great ingathering was yet to come. Clowes and John Nelson both moved off after the Conference of 1823, and Jeremiah Gilbert, of prison fame, was for two years the leading missionary of North Shields Circuit. He speaks of "our noble chapel," in which he began his ministrations. Union Street Chapel was centrally situated and well attended, but an adjective more appropriate than "noble" might have been found to hit off its appearance and character. In the end it came to be a burden and an embarrassment. So much was this the case that, when Mary Porteus was stationed to the circuit in 1836, leave was obtained for her "to take an extensive tour to collect funds through Yorkshire, Lincolnshire, and elsewhere where Providence might direct." Union Street was happily superseded by Saville Street Chapel, opened March, 1861, when the Rev. Thomas Smith was superintendent.

SAVILLE STREET CHURCH, NORTH SHIELDS.

Shortly after J. Gilbert's arrival—July 20th, 1823—a notable circuit camp meeting was held on Scaffold Hill, at which more than twenty persons were converted.* Thomas Nelson and George Wallace were two of the six travelling preachers who took part. Wallace was a native of the district, who ran his short course from July, 1823, to March, 1824, and probably died a martyr to excessive toil. Only a month before his death he walked from Wingate to Kirkwhelpington, a distance of seventeen miles, in snow and rain, and preached at night. "It put me forcibly in mind," says he,

* The "Extracts from the Journals of Jeremiah Gilbert" was printed in 1824, at North Shields, by J. K. Pollock, Camden Street.

"of some of the first Methodist preachers and the missionaries. There were great mountains, and crags, and burns to go over, which sometimes nearly exhausted my strength." When, in December, 1823, Newcastle became an independent circuit and Morpeth a branch of North Shields, there were seven preachers on the ground instead of three, and near 800 members where, in March, there had been 335. The anthracite had fairly caught fire. From this time Newcastle and North Shields went each its own way, and the missionary efforts of the parent circuit had necessarily to be confined to the north—to the country lying between the Blyth and the Tweed. In this part of Northumberland the Connexion has now six stations, all of which can trace their descent from North Shields Circuit, viz., Seaton Delaval, Blyth, Ashington, Amble, North Sunderland, Lowick, and Berwick. Had success been at all proportionate to the amount of toil expended, Morpeth and Alnwick would have been found in this list; for both were early branches of North Shields, though they never grew to be circuits, and after a time ceased to be even branches. Morpeth has had a chequered history. Beginning as a branch of North Shields, it was afterwards served by Hexham. In 1836, with its twenty members, it reverted to North Shields. Much later it was remissioned by Blyth, and is now included in Ashington, one of the new progressive circuits that owe their rise to the sinking of collieries further north. As for Alnwick, the capital of the county, we have nothing to show for some years of labour. We may visit the Duke of Northumberland's famous castle, said to be one of the most magnificent baronial structures in all England; but we shall look in vain for a Primitive Methodist chapel or preaching-room. And yet, W. Lister, Mary Porteus, and other missionaries lived here in the 'Twenties and 'Thirties, and made Alnwick the centre of earnest evangelistic efforts.

Mr. Lister was on the Alnwick branch from January to April, 1829, and again for two months in 1830. We give an item from his *Journal*, which shows that the future President and Book Steward could cheerfully endure privations:—

> "During the months of July and August (1830), I missioned about a dozen of the villages. I often had long journeys, much hard fare, made my breakfast and dinner at times by the side of a spring of water, with a pennyworth of bread bought at some village shop. Yet these were trifles to what my Master had to go through in preaching among the villages. The prosperity of the work sweetened all."

The same *Journal* speaks of a crowded Missionary Meeting held in the Town Hall of Alnwick, at which Brothers Herod, Clough, W. Garner, J. Parrott, and W. Lister were the speakers. "Next day" (March 2nd, 1830), says Mr. Lister, "I walked, in company with the other four brethren, twenty-five miles to Bedlington, where we held a Missionary Meeting. Next day walked home [to North Shields] twelve miles."*

Still the efforts put forth on the somewhat niggard soil in and around Alnwick were not altogether in vain, as the biographies and journals of some of the workers show. If the societies were numerically feeble, and mostly made up of the poor of this world, there were amongst them some men and women of high principle who did no discredit

* MS. *Journals* of the Rev. W. Lister.

to the Connexion. Such, assuredly, was the aged woman, a member of the Alnwick society, who, too poor to pay her weekly class-pence, still recognised her Christian obligations and, in the spirit of Northumbrian independence, explained to the minister who led the class, "*I clean the chapel for my privileges.*"

The most notable achievement of North Shields Circuit in the early days, was undoubtedly, next after the planting of our Church in Newcastle, the missioning of Berwick-on-Tweed. The first on the ground was William Clough. He began his mission on January 4th, 1829, by preaching on Wallace Green, and also in a large room he had taken on rent. During the three months he spent on the mission, Mr. Clough established preaching-stations on both sides of the border, instituted a Sunday afternoon service at the Town Hall steps, preached to the prisoners in the jail, and laid the foundation of the Berwick society. Mr. Lister, who followed him, is rightly regarded as having been the maker of Berwick Circuit. He it was who,

OLD BRIDGE, BERWICK-ON-TWEED.

building along the lines already laid down, prepared the mission for circuit independence, which was granted in 1831. Himself a fruit of the Northern Mission and called into the ministry by North Shields, his home-circuit (1827), Mr. Lister seems to have understood the Northumbrian and Scottish type of character, with which, indeed, his own had many points of affinity. This sympathetic insight of one who was in the full vigour of early manhood and prodigal of his strength, made his double term of service in Berwick, and his year in Edinburgh (then a branch of Berwick), remarkably successful. During his first term of fifteen months in Berwick, he preached every Sunday afternoon, from April to September, at the Town Hall steps, often to as many as two thousand people. Places as far distant as Kelso, in Scotland, were visited, rooms hired, and services held, with the view, if possible, of establishing new causes. A friendly arrangement was entered into by which Wooler and two other societies

THE PERIOD OF CIRCUIT PREDOMINANCE AND ENTERPRISE. 175

were taken over from the Bible Christians.* A chapel capable of holding six hundred people, also a schoolroom and a manse were built (February, 1830); and, although the debt left on the property afterwards proved burdensome, the acquisition of these buildings so soon after the beginning of the mission, was something of a feat. Converts were made like W. Fulton and Adam Dodds, both of whom afterwards spent two terms of ministerial service in Berwick, to the great advantage of the circuit. Another convert was Dr. W. Landells, the once well-known minister of Regent's Park Chapel, who for some time was a local preacher in the Berwick Circuit. In 1833, Mr. Lister began his second term of three years in the circuit under disheartening conditions. The interests of the station had recently suffered from ministerial bickerings, of which the public were but too fully aware. The circuit had gone backward instead of forward. Retrogression was writ large on its poor manuscript plan showing only six places. The one chapel of the circuit was in difficulties, the mortgagee threatening to foreclose. But the new preacher was known, and received a cordial welcome that was of good omen. The same methods which had proved so successful four years before were again adopted, with the result that a new era of progress set in. Eyemouth, which had been missioned in 1830 and afterwards abandoned, now asked for the resumption of services, and in October, 1835, a new chapel was opened for its twenty members. In June, 1834, Edinburgh Mission was transferred to Glasgow, and at the following Quarter Day Alnwick branch was re-attached to North Shields. When Mr. Lister was leaving Berwick in 1836, he could write: "Through the blessing of heaven, we leave 120 more members than we found, one new chapel, nineteen places missioned, Berwick chapel relieved of its financial difficulties, and all old circuit outstanding bills paid off."

WILLIAM FULTON.

There are one or two peculiarities connected with the planting and subsequent history of our Church in north-east Northumberland that may briefly be pointed out. One thing we cannot find—persecution. More than this: in no other part of England did our missionaries receive such civil treatment from all classes, and in none were they taken more seriously and listened to more attentively. There were many places in England where the missionary no sooner began his service than the bells were set a-ringing to drown his voice; there were still more places where the bells were rung only at the prescribed times—missionary or no missionary; but, as far as we are aware, Berwick was the only place where the bells were stopped ringing, even at the authorised times, so that the open-air service might not be interrupted. Like the Bereans of old, the people of Berwick were "ready to listen, willing to inquire." Probably the attitude of the people to our early missionaries may be explained by the extent to which the seriousness and thoughtfulness native to the Northumbrian character, have, through the long-prevalent influence of Presbyterianism, taken the bent towards a non-priestly religion—a religion which regards the Bible and pulpit with instinctive reverence.

* It was a pious female named Mary Ann Weary, from Cornwall, who was the founder of these societies. She alleged the mission was begun in obedience to a divine impression.

Certainly here, if anywhere, the preacher starts with the great initial advantage that there is a recognised presumption in his favour, and it will be his own fault if he fails to justify that presumption, and does not succeed in turning the sentiment of deference into a reasonable and well-grounded respect.

But our history shows that Presbyterianism can take as well as give, and that she has enjoyed a large reversionary interest in the evangelistic movements our Church has carried on in her midst. From the beginning, Berwick Circuit has given many to other communities. Every revival—and there have been many of them—has enriched the Churches. Such was notably the case after the Eyemouth revival of 1859, in which the Rev. J. Snaith took a leading part at the beginning of his ministry. No doubt the loss was greater in the early days, when chapels were few and accommodation scant; but some fruit was lost even after store-rooms were provided. Of course statistics are not available. If they were, we venture to say the disclosure would be startling as to the number of members and officials of other Churches who received their definite call to the Christian life through the agency of Primitive Methodism. The late Rev. W. Fulton, writing in 1868, says: "There are no Churches in Berwick, the Romanists excepted, which have not benefited by our ministry." What W. Clowes said in 1820 applies with special force to Berwick: "It is true we have received assistance from our friends by a few class leaders, local preachers, and others coming to us . . . but for every old sheep received, we have given in lieu at least two fat lambs."

It would be interesting to know how many ministerial probationers have travelled the Berwick Circuit and its offshoots, and how many ministers Berwick has pledged during the course of its history. In the eighteen years, from 1855 to 1873, the pledges of no less than ten ministers were accepted, amongst them those of John Waite, John Gill, Hugh Gilmore, and R. G. Graham. A large proportion of the ministers of the old Sunderland District had their turn of service in this border region soon after they had put on the harness, so that Berwick has been a veritable training-ground for the ministry. At first sight there would seem to be little connection between these facts and the situation and physical characteristics of the district these young men helped to evangelise. But the connection is not difficult to trace; they are the first and last links in a chain of causation. It is the country, such as we find it, that has limited the expansion of industrialism and checked the natural growth of population. The intermediate links of the chain are obvious enough. Even churches cannot escape the working of the laws of political economy. All that can be done is to recognise their working and to seek to minimise their disadvantages; and this has been the course pursued in relation to Berwick. The industrial revolution which, in other parts of the country, has multiplied mines and manufactories, and doubled or trebled the population, has done little for Berwick except to draw off and provide work and food for its surplus hands and mouths. When we find that Berwick, the chief town of this district, had but 679 more inhabitants in 1891 than it had fifty years before, and that in 1891 the population was actually less by 617 than it was in 1881, we can see what must have been going on all through these years, and form some idea of the difficulties the Churches have had to contend with. We see the youth at the close of his apprenticeship moving off to the busy towns on the Tyne or Wear. We see parents, anxious to put the means of an assured livelihood within the reach of their rising family, migrating to the centres of trade and commerce. It is disheartening to those striving to build up strong societies, to find themselves thus seemingly thwarted by the laws which control the labour-market. Still it is gratifying to know that in this border district the Connexion has held its ground—and something more. In 1842 Berwick had three ministers and 274 members; now Berwick, and its offshoots, Lowick and North Sunderland, together have six ministers and 771 members.

Besides William Fulton and Adam Dodds, the Berwick Circuit has sent out into the ministry others who have long and ably served the Connexion. Among these may be named Michael Clarke, and George Lewins who, after forty-one years of labour in various parts, still holds his place in the ranks. Michael Clarke was born at Ford Moss, and it is interesting to note that John Clarke, one of the Baptist missionaries banished from Fernando Po in 1858, was his uncle. Mr. Clarke was called out by the Berwick Circuit, and in 1853 went out to Melbourne to take the place of John Ride. After an absence of more than a quarter of a century he revisited England, and the

MICHAEL CLARKE.    MR. JOHN BROWN.    MR. GEO. JOBSON.

Conference of 1879, recognising the distinguished service he had rendered Australian Primitive Methodism, elected him as its Vice-President. He was superannuated in 1885 and died 1892.

Of the Berwick laymen who have "obtained a good report," we can but refer to one or two. James Young with a considerable dash of eccentricity, and Michael Clarke of Belfort, were both notable men. John Brown of Ancroft was a fine specimen of a border tenant-farmer—broad-shouldered and broad-minded, to whom the eyes of men turned as one in every way fitted to represent the people at Westminster, though Sir Edward Grey eventually became the accepted candidate. Mr. Brown was, for many years, a conspicuous and devoted worker for our cause. The Allerdean church stands as his memorial. Of Mr. George Jobson, who for forty years was a local preacher and leading official of the Berwick Circuit, the Rev. H. Yooll (2) (who knew him well) says: "He was one of the best fruits of our work in Berwick at a comparatively early day, when loyalty to the cause was often tested severely. His outstanding characteristics were zeal and generosity. The Berwick Circuit covered then what is now the area of three circuits, and Mr. Jobson was one of its tireless workers. In its somewhat varying fortunes he was ever the same devoted son and servant of our Church. His two sons are local preachers with us."

We return to the "old North Shields Circuit" as, in order to distinguish it from the truncated circuit of to-day, it is often familiarly called. The constituent societies of the old circuit were diversified in character. They were not all of the same cast or complexion. The circuit-town—a considerable seaport—and the river-side societies had their distinctive features. Cullercoats, two miles away, was a typical fishing village; while an ever-enlarging proportion of the societies was found in the mining villages to the north of the Tyne.

Amongst the officials of an early date resident in North Shields were Messrs. Stephen Knott, John Foster, and James Hall. Two men who at a later time came to the front and took a prominent part in the management of affairs, were Messrs. John Spence and Thomas Smith. Mr. Spence began life as a working miner at Percy Main, but set up in business for himself and, by dint of push and ability, raised himself to a good social position; in the end becoming an alderman and chief magistrate of the borough. Mr. Spence was full of vitality; without being intellectual or making any pretensions to culture, he had an alert intelligence. He was genial, jocose, ready to show hospitality, and both had it in his power and inclination to be helpful to the society and circuit. As circuit steward and chapel treasurer his capabilities for business found full scope, while he also filled the offices of leader and Sunday School superintendent. Mr. Thomas Smith was a man of a very different type, both in appearance and still more in mental constitution and temperament. With no imagination to speak of, he had an original and vigorous mind that in its workings occasionally threw off sparks of grim humour. Had he but had the advantage of thorough mental discipline in his youth, there is no telling what he might have become or achieved. Even as it was he could not help being a philosopher in his way, a solid preacher, and a man of weight in the counsels of the Church. Moreover, he and his excellent wife having leisure at command, were indefatigable in the more private walks of usefulness. Unfortunately, Mr. Smith had an unyielding and somewhat passional nature. As a retired blacksmith, he might not unfittingly have adopted as his own the family motto: "You may break but cannot bend me." As Mr. Spence, too, had also the defect of his qualities, in a certain over-sensitiveness, it is not to be wondered at that these two estimable men were sometimes in opposition and that the result was friction, from which, now and again during the years, North Shields has unhappily suffered.

JAMES HALL.

J. SPENCE.

The loss of Thomas Nightingale is too recent, and the man himself too widely known, to require much to be said of him here. As one who was frequently elected to attend the Conference assemblies, and who invariably drew large audiences on the Conference Camp-ground; as one too, who ran for the Vice-presidency of the

Conference, and was selected as a morning speaker at the Metropolitan Missionary meeting, he had deservedly achieved a considerable Connexional reputation. In the years to come he will be ranked with the original and popular preachers of his day, and his sayings and doings will enrich the traditions of our Northern churches.

Another valuable official was Mr. Joseph Salkeld, a Cumbrian by birth, who, after some years' residence in Newcastle, settled at Howden-on-Tyne, where he and his worthy wife—strict though kind—dispensed hospitality, and were a stay and help to the church. Mr. Salkeld was a healthy-minded, sunshiny Christian, the influence of whose life "did good like a medicine," purging the mind of black vapours, and causing others to look out on life as smilingly as he looked on it himself. He was a frequent platform speaker as well as preacher and, being full of humour and having a rich repertory of anecdotes, his speeches were lively and entertaining. How often his, "This reminds me of an anecdote," was the introduction to some reminiscence of the past that had its lesson, though no disparagement, for the present.

Many years ago, John Barnard and J. H. Jopling as youths bowed at the penitent-form at Percy Main, along with some ten others. The former was called into the

THOS. NIGHTINGALE.    MR. J. SALKELD.    MRS. E. SALKELD.    RICHARD RAINE.

ministry (1857) by Berwick Circuit. After travelling a few years he settled down in his native circuit, and as a local preacher rendered extensive and valuable service for a long series of years. Benjamin Hall, his early guide and mentor, still survives as the doyen of the North Shields Circuit local preachers. So, happily, does J. H. Jopling who, full of good works, holds a secure and lasting place in the affections of preachers and people. There are many others who in the quieter walks of usefulness have served the interests of these river-side churches—families like the Dodds, the Jewels, the Grants, the Nicholsons, the Rutherfords; and men like J. Spoor, H. B. Thompson, R. Holden, and Richard Raine. Of the last-named two, a further word must be written. Mr. R. Holden decided for Christ at a famous camp-meeting at Dye House, in the Hexham Circuit. In early life he was associated in his employment with Dr. Joseph Parker. He afterwards removed to Chirton, and then to North Shields, where, for thirty years, he pursued the even tenor of his way, filling at one time or another important Church and civic offices, and living a blameless and most useful life. Richard Raine—"the famous Primitive singer and *beau ideal* choir-master"— spent the declining years of his life in North Shields. When in the hey-day of his powers, he was known far and wide as *the* man to head the van of a procession, and he had led the singing at many a historic camp-meeting. To the end, although " the daughters of music were brought" somewhat "low," he retained his enthusiasm for sacred song. Assuredly, with a soul so full of music, he is now right amongst the "harpers harping with their harps."

The society at Cullercoats offered a pleasing variety to the church-life of the circuit. When first missioned, and for some years after, Cullercoats was, as we have said, a typical fishing-village. Its fishermen were hardy, adventurous, and industrious; and their women-folk, clad in the characteristic garb of their class, were as picturesque figures as the Scots' fishwives, whom in many respects they resembled. Like their northern

CULLERCOATS BAY. (Present Day.)

sisters, they toiled hard, taking quite their full share of work as bread-winners for the family. Not only did they look after their households, but they mended the nets, gathered bait, and, above all, they vended the fish. Often might they be seen in North Shields, and even in Newcastle, bending under the weight of three or four stones of fish, carried on their backs in wicker-baskets or "creels," and their cry of "caller herring" was as striking as their appearance. The fishing-people of Cullercoats were clannish, and intermarried so closely that the surnames were few and, for the purpose of identification, nicknames had to be used. In the early 'Sixties, it was said there were six John Taylors in the village, who had severally to be distinguished by a sobriquet. Some of the primitive simplicity and old-world customs which once prevailed may have vanished before the sure oncoming of modern fashions. Cullercoats itself has undergone great changes so as scarcely to know itself. Railway facilities and its nearness to Newcastle have transformed it into a residential neighbourhood, and into a popular sea-side resort. The extent of the change effected may be partly measured by the material advance our Church has made in the village; for Primitive Methodism has done much for the fishermen. From the beginning—probably in the early 'Forties—it got a good hold of them. Its ministrations suited them and helped them, and the experience of Filey was repeated in the moral transformation of the fishermen and their families. At first, services were held in a chapel, jointly used— strange to say—by the Presbyterians and Congregationalists—each of the three

CULLERCOATS NEW CHAPEL.

denominations conducting one Sunday service therein. In the end, the Primitives were left sole occupants of the chapel. The cause prospered. Visitors were attracted to "the Fishermen's Chapel," so much so that the chapel became quite an institution in the village, and it got to be considered quite the correct thing to join in its worship. Visitors admired the heartiness of the services; they liked the look of the fisher-people, who came in numbers, all clad in their Sunday best, and they liked the way in which they threw themselves into the service. It was a new and piquant experience to listen to such preachers as Thomas Wandless and Thomas Nightingale; so that when the visitors went back to the big town, the word was passed round: "When you go to Cullercoats, you must be sure to attend 'the Fishermen's Chapel.'" This is no fancy-sketch, for we write from a four years' experience—1867–71. It was decided the time had come for enlargement; whereupon, ladies of various denominations co-operated with the society in raising £400 by a bazaar, and in 1868 the chapel was rebuilt. That chapel, which may be seen in our picture, is still used as a school and lecture-hall; and, hard by it, there stands a new chapel capable of accommodating five hundred people, which was opened in 1899.

In the march of improvement quite a new village or town has sprung up at the adjoining Whitley Bay, with scarcely any religious provision for the residents. Here, under the superintendency of Rev. G. F. Johnson, a handsome and commodious church was erected in 1904, at a total cost, including land, of £3,200. We leave Cullercoats and its record of progress, just noting the fact that George Dodds, of Newcastle—the trusty comrade of George Charlton in the temperance crusade—in the evening of his life, came to reside amongst the Cullercoats fishermen, and worked for and with them; and here, too, Rev. James Young has chosen to locate, after forty-four years' faithful and fruitful ministerial service; here, too, Alexander Petticrow, who has been called the "Billy Bray of Cullercoats," ended his days. In a recess of these sea-cliffs he found sanctification, and in these streets he witnessed for God.*

Turning now to the colliery societies of the old North Shields Circuit, we find they have all along been a growingly important factor in its life; so much so, that the administrative changes which have taken place in the circuit—its divisions and sub-divisions—have been largely the result of the working of this factor. This is seen in the next important organic change which took place in the circuit after Berwick was parted with. This was the formation of Blyth, first into a branch, and afterwards, under the guidance of Rev. James Jackson—"an able administrator and an excellent preacher" †—into an independent station. Blyth had been remissioned early in the 'Thirties, but had encountered reverses largely due, we are told, to Church dissensions; the chapel became involved, and was ultimately lost to the Connexion. But Blyth was destined to become the head of a vigorous circuit, and, what is more, to become the parent of circuits. The opening of new collieries greatly increased the population of the neighbourhood. Blyth became the centre of a new colliery district, and, more and more, a port of shipment for coals. It is significant that the year when Blyth was made into a station was also the year when Thomas Burt, then a working miner at Choppington, was appointed the Secretary of the Northumberland Miners' Union; nor less significant is it that, largely by the votes of the miners, he was, in 1874, returned to Parliament for the Morpeth Division. These facts point to the growing influence of the miners in the district; and the reference to Thomas Burt is not out of place; for besides his early association with C. C. McKechnie, and others of our ministers in the old North Shields Circuit, he was, during his residence in Blyth, the close friend of

REV. J. YOUNG.

* See Rev. S. Horton's article on him in *Aldersgate*, 1901, p. 219.
† Rev. C. C. McKechnie's MS. Autobiography. For a reference to the troubles in Blyth, see "The Earnest Preacher," p. 125. Joseph Spoor resided at Blyth in 1845.

THE PERIOD OF CIRCUIT PREDOMINANCE AND ENTERPRISE. 183

Hugh Gilmore, and, in association with him and men of kindred spirit, such as Robert Lawther and William Bell, took part in many a local fight for truth and righteousness. In this part of the country, at least, our Church has developed with the development of the coal-trade, and has attended upon its movements. The sinking of a pit has always meant the establishment of a society; for, amongst the sinkers and miners drawn to the spot, were sure to be some Primitive Methodists, who might be counted upon to abide true to their Church, and who, if there were no society already, would see to it that one was founded. So the expansion of the coal-trade, as also its northward drift, go far to explain the history of our Church in South-East Northumberland. Seaton Delaval, which had no existence when Clowes missioned North Shields or Benton Square, becomes,

BENTON SQUARE OLD CHAPEL.

in 1875, the Seaton Delaval Circuit. Ashington, too, made a circuit in 1896 with 405 members, was the creation of the coal trade, and received many colonists from North Shields—men like the Gregorys, the Crawfords, the Mains, and many besides. Amble Circuit, formed in 1897, is the last outcome of this process. Here extension is taking place. A new iron church has been put up at Radcliffe, and Greyton, a new colliery district of 2000 inhabitants, has been missioned with every prospect of success.

There is nothing particularly prepossessing about the pit villages of Northumberland, or any other county. They have features in common familiar to most of us. We can see the rectangular rows of cottages, each one outwardly like its neighbour, the inevitable pit-shaft and engine-house and waggon-way. But nowhere more than amid such depressing surroundings may a man find more use for the second of the two sights God has given him. Here, if anywhere, "among the angular marks of men's handiwork," Sir Arthur Helps' reflection seems very much to the purpose: "The painter hurries by the place; the poet, too, unless he is a very philosophic one, passes shuddering by. But, in reality, what forms of beauty, in conduct, in suffering, in endeavour; what tragedies, what romances; what foot-prints, as it were, angelic and demoniac—now belong to that spot."* Whatever the painter and the poet may do, a Primitive Methodist need not hurry through this district; for human traits, and mementos honourable to his Church, are afforded by every pit-village of old standing hereabout.

OLD CHAPEL, CRAMLINGTON.

Here, for example, is Old Cramlington Colliery. What memories are recalled by the view of its singular old chapel given in the text! It was at an exciting missionary meeting, held here in 1843, the idea of a New Zealand Mission was first broached—the mission to be sustained by the Sunday Schools of the Connexion. The memorial sent from that meeting had its influence. The idea caught on, and, as we shall see, the New Zealand Mission was begun in 1844.

We pass on to Seaton Delaval. Here, in 1859, exasperated by their grievances, the miners struck work without due notice having first been given. In consequence, eight

* "Companions of My Solitude," p. 241.

men were sentenced at North Shields to two months' imprisonment. These were amongst the most intelligent men on the colliery; they were all teetotallers, and they had all been opposed to the strike. Of the eight victims, four at least were Primitive Methodists, viz., Anthony Bolam, Alexander Watson, Henry Bell, and Robert Burt. Henry Bell was a man in many ways remarkable—for his intellectuality, his character, and the physical suffering he was called to endure. Robert Burt, the uncle of Thomas Burt, M.P., was arrested when kneeling by the bedside of his wife, who was sick unto death. When the manager was expostulated with for putting in prison the very men who had opposed the strike, and were the most respectable and law-abiding men they had at the colliery, he replied: "I know that; and that is what I have put them in for. It is of no use putting those in who cannot feel."

As you go eastward from Seaton Delaval, you soon come to New Hartley, a name recalling one of the most appalling colliery disasters of modern times. The sight of the broken beam of the pumping-engine is indeed a grim memento; for, by the breaking of that ponderous shaft, in January, 1862, four hundred and two men and boys lost their lives. We refer to one incident—and to one only—in that long-drawn-out tragedy, because it shows how grace, in the persons of some of our co-religionists, could assert itself as a conquering and sustaining power in a situation dire and desperate. On the body of the back-overman there was afterwards found this memorandum, roughly pencilled on a piece torn from a newspaper:—

"Friday afternoon, at half-past two.
"Edward Armstrong, Thomas Gledston, John Hardy, Thomas Bell, and others, took extremely ill. We also had a prayer-meeting at a quarter to two, when Tibbs, Henry Sharp, J. Campbell, Henry Gibson, and William G. Palmer [exhorted]. Tibbs exhorted us again, and Sharp also."

Four of these who preached "as dying men to dying men" were our brethren; William Tibbs being a class-leader at New Hartley, and Henry Sharp, Chapel Steward at Old Hartley.

The old North Shields Circuit has had its vicissitudes. By the disastrous "long strike" of 1844, which lasted eighteen weeks, the societies were almost wrecked. The miners were ejected from their homes, and had to camp in the lanes, or where they could. But if the societies have at times been "minished and brought low," they have also had their seasons of revival and replenishment, as the following extract from Rev. C. C. McKechnie's MS. autobiography, referring to the great revival of 1867, will show:—

"Contemporaneous with this great and good work in the town [of North Shields], a similar work was going on all over the circuit. I am not aware that a single place in the circuit failed to share in the marvellous visitation. Such places as Seaton Delaval, Cramlington, Dudley, Howden, Cullercoats, where we had a good staff of workers, and a considerable population, reaped the largest harvest. The revival scenes at these places were often glorious. They cannot, indeed, be described without using language that would appear extravagant. Often when I have seen crowds, yea, crowds of men and women flocking to the penitents' form, and with strong crying and tears pleading with God for mercy, I have felt utterly broken down. The whole countryside was moved. It almost seemed as if the Millennium was rushing upon us, and as if the entire population were being enclosed in the gospel-net."

This witness is true, as the present writer can avouch. The numerical returns for the North Shields Circuit for 1868-9 show an increase of six hundred members for the two years.

To give pen-and-ink sketches of the worthies of this part of the old North Shields Circuit is impossible, and we shall not attempt it. The portraits of two or three, out of scores equally worthy, will be found in the text. Fain would we have given one of Thomas Wandless, the eccentric and popular local preacher; but here are Thomas Gleghorn, of whom Rev. S. Horton has written an appreciative sketch;* good John Bell, of Dudley, and his saintly wife, whom the Vice-President of the Conference of 1903 is proud to claim as his parents; and Matthew Lowther, of West Cramlington, afterwards of Chertsey, father of Alderman Lowther, J.P., of Brighton.

THOMAS GLEGHORN.    MR. JOHN BELL, DUDLEY.    MRS. BELL, DUDLEY.    MATTHEW LOWTHER.

PRIMITIVE METHODISM AND THE MINERS OF THE NORTH.

The claim is here made that our Church has materially assisted the miners of Northumberland and Durham in working out their temporal as well as spiritual salvation, and that among them as a class may be found some of the choicest samples of the fruit of our labours. This is the claim made, and it is a large one. But, large though it be, the claim is conceded by those best qualified to pronounce judgment according to the facts with which they are fully conversant. One such expert witness is Principal Fairbairn, who recently wrote:—

"The Primitive Methodist Church has without aid from taxes or rates, achieved for the godly manhood of the miners in Northumberland and Durham more than could be achieved had all the schools been non-provided, all the teachers been appointed by the Church, and all the atmosphere carefully regulated by the local clergy."†

Another witness tells the story of the long, unequal struggle carried on by the miners

* *Aldersgate Magazine*, 1896, p. 616.
† Letter in "The Pilot," January 16th, 1904.

of both counties to free themselves from galling and impoverishing disabilities—from the yearly bond, the truck system, the employment of boys in the pits for as many as seventeen or eighteen hours at a stretch, and other grievances too numerous to be particularised. The struggle, he shows, was often attended with reverses, and the leaders in that struggle not infrequently became marked men and had to suffer the loss of employment, or in other ways were "made an example of." The first attempt to form a union for self-protection, made in 1830 by Thomas Hepburn, a local preacher,* ultimately failed. But still the struggle went on until political emancipation was won, one grievance after another redressed, the Miners' Permanent Relief Fund established, the Mines Regulation Act (1872) passed, and strong unions formed both in Northumberland and Durham, with Thomas Burt and William Crawford—both of Primitive Methodist extraction and training—as their secretaries and paid Parliamentary representatives. As we follow the moving story, it is significant that we are continually meeting with names already familiar to us in our Church-records, showing that those who were prominent workers in the various societies had come to be, by virtue of their character and ability as speakers, the recognised leaders in the struggle for the rights of labour. And they were moderators as well as leaders in the struggle; for there were amongst their followers exasperated men smarting under their wrongs, and there were also no inconsiderable number of young hot-bloods, as well as a sprinkling of men of little principle, to whom Revolution delusively promised quick and large returns, while the methods of Reform seemed tame in comparison and slow in yielding but meagre results. For all this, the leaders, being for the most part Christian men, and shrewd and patient withal, set themselves resolutely to withstand the temptation to resort to violent and illegal methods; and the cause they championed was, in the end, the gainer by their self-restraint and wise leadership, though in many cases the reward came too late to be of any use to them who had earned it. It is a posthumous honour we pay them. All this Mr. Fynes tells us in his book,† and then, in closing his retrospect of the long struggle, he pays a tribute to the work of our Church, only part of which we can quote here:—

"Unsatisfactory though the moral and intellectual condition of the miner to-day is [1873], yet, compared with his condition at the period treated in the opening chapters of this book, there is a miraculous change. Side by side with the Union the earnest men who have been stigmatised 'Ranters'—the Primitive Methodists of the two counties—have been working out the social, intellectual, and moral amelioration of the miners, and in this great reform they have been very materially assisted by the temperance advocates who have from time to time

* " When a mass meeting on Shadin's Hill was threatened by the Marquis of Londonderry and a regiment of soldiers, the miners had already raised their muskets, and in a moment or two a massacre would have begun, but for Thomas Hepburn, a local preacher, who cried out: 'Make way for His Majesty's troops.'"—Hon. E. Richardson, of Australia, in the "Primitive Methodist Quarterly Review." We mistrust the reference to the miners' muskets and the threatened massacre. There is, however, no reason to doubt the substantial accuracy of the story.

† "The Miners of Northumberland and Durham. A History of their Social and Political Struggles. By Richard Fynes." Blyth, 1873.

laboured amongst the miners. . . . Probably no body of men have ever been subjected to so many jibes and jeers from superficial people as those referred to; but without doubt none ever achieved such glorious results as they have done. To many it may be a matter of supreme indifference what is the exact creed professed by Primitive Methodists; but whether they have a creed or none at all, it is impossible for any observing man not to see and admire the bold and ardent manner in which they carry on their labour amongst the miners."—(Pp. 282—3).

It is much to be wished that Mr. John Wilson, M.P., or other competent person, would so set forth the facts known or accessible to them, as once for all to make good Mr. Wilson's own statement: "There has been no more potent factor in the moral uplifting of the population of our pit-villages than Primitive Methodism."* For ourselves, we have said all that space permits us to say on the general question, and cannot, except incidentally, recur to it. Possibly, enough has been written to show that, while our Church has done much for the evangelisation of the mining villages of the North, it has also at the same time been largely helping forward the advance— economic, political, intellectual—of the miners and their families. Even yet much ameliorative work remains to be done, and the fervent evangelic impulse that helped our fathers is still the all-essential qualification for enabling us to repeat the triumphs of the past. That is still primary; the rest is secondary, and will follow. Such is the lesson taught us even by the secular press. When, in 1875, the jubilee of the opening of the Stockton and Darlington Railway was being celebrated, an able writer— probably Mr. W. T. Stead—passed in review the changes effected during the fifty years. In assigning the causes of these gratifying changes he singles out for special mention the labours of the early Primitive Methodist preachers.

"One cause," says he, "of this great change had nothing to do with the railway. To the advent of the Primitive Methodists in the North Country is due much of the transformation undoubtedly effected in the latter part of the first quarter of the century. The 'Ranters,' as they were then universally called, had to bear a good deal of ridicule and opprobrium, but that has long since been forgotten in the good which they effected. The accounts published at the time concerning the results produced by their ministrations among the semi-savage colliers of the North remind us of the glowing narratives of the most successful missionaries, and make us sigh for the dawn of another great religious awakening which would empty the publics of Bishop Auckland, and convert the rowdies of Spennymoor into local preachers."

NEWCASTLE-UPON-TYNE.

Newcastle is a very different town to-day from what it was in 1821, when John Branfoot preached near Sandgate. How different we shall find it hard to conceive. It is only by an effort that we can picture it as a town only one fourth its present size, with no Stephenson's High Level spanning the gorge of the Tyne, and wanting those stately and ornate buildings with which the skill and enterprise of one man enriched it. What Haussmann did for Paris, that Richard Grainger (1798—1861), a man of lowly origin, did for Newcastle. It was old Newcastle he

* *Aldersgate Magazine*, 1896 (p. 690).

found in 1834; he left it modern Newcastle. We have nothing to do with the story of Newcastle's progress from comparative mediævalism to modernism, except in so far as that progress is reflected in the history of our own church-life. It may be a mere coincidence but, nevertheless, it affords a convenient date-mark to note that by taking possession of Nelson Street Chapel in 1838, the first period of old Primitive Methodism in Newcastle came to its end. More than that: Nelson Street was built by Richard Grainger, as was also the chapel we took possession of. It dovetailed into his scheme of architectural reconstruction. Our occupancy of Nelson Street Chapel for some sixty years, was co-eval with a second long and somewhat uneventful period of church-life; but by the acquisition of the Central Church in 1897, a great step

VIEW OF NEWCASTLE AS IT WAS IN 1823.
From an old Engraving.

forward was taken, in which we may, if we choose, fancy a correspondence to the elevation of Newcastle to the rank of a city and bishop's see. True; we have no dioceses, and do not believe in bishops, but these things may afford a shadowy analogue of the fact that the one original Newcastle Circuit has at last become a group of circuits, and that the central city-church stands there in the midst—*primus inter pares*. Unmistakeably, the three periods are there, and these are what we have briefly to consider.

It was only on July 29th, 1822, that Clowes formed the first society of ten members at Ballast Hills. Shortly after, others are "added to the Church," and he records that "some of the worst characters are turning to God here." On October 20th, 1822, the Butcher's Hall, in the Friars, was opened as a preaching-room, and in December, 1823, through the labours, especially of the men already mentioned, this side of the North

Shields Circuit became the Newcastle-upon-Tyne Circuit, with three preachers to work it. On April 4th, 1824, the old Sallyport chapel, previously occupied by the Scotch Church, was opened by J. Gilbert from North Shields, J. Branfoot from South Shields, and N. West from Sunderland. The last-named says: "It was a high day: five souls professed to find the Lord, besides many more who were in distress." Still the cause moved on, surely if steadily. There was not the rush and roar of a great conflagration like that which, in 1854, half devastated Gateshead and Newcastle; yet the anthracite glowed. What J. Spencer wrote in June, 1824, expressed no mere passing phase of the religious life of the circuit but one of its characteristic traits: "There is," says he, "no particular revival, but the work is going pleasingly on." Progress was marked by the securing of a chapel in Silver Street, vacated by the Congregationalists. The street was silvern only in name, as many Silver Streets are; and the chapel itself needed considerable repairs which, it is said, the Rev. S. Tillotson, the superintendent, took off his coat to assist in effecting. Still, the chapel was fairly commodious, and for twelve years—1826-38—Silver Street was the chief centre of our church-life in Newcastle. How much is implied in this bald statement which cannot be drawn out

MR. W. B. LEIGHTON.   MR. PETER KIDMAN.   MRS. R. COOK.

in detail! Some idea of what was accomplished during these formative years may, however, be gained from the plan of the Newcastle Circuit for April to July, 1837, which now lies before us. The ten members of 1822 have now become 1028, of which number 371 are included in the Gateshead Circuit, in this year detached from Newcastle. The plan shows twenty-eight preaching-places, of which Silver Street, Ballast Hills, and three open-air preaching-stands are in the town proper, while three or four others on the outskirts of the town are also supplied with preaching. The Circuit includes Westmoor and Wallsend, and extends to places as far away as Medomsley and Wallbottle, Wylam and Shotley Bridge. The plan shows four travelling-preachers, of whom one is down for the "Scotch Mission," *i.e.*, Dundee— and sixty-two local preachers and exhorters. Besides these, we recall the fact that other labourers have been raised up, and they amongst the most capable and useful, whose names we do not find here because they have gone forth to wider service. Among these we recall John Lightfoot and Mary Porteus; Joseph Spoor and his sister, Jane Spoor, who will afterwards become the wife of Mr. Ralph Cook (himself for many years a prominent layman of the Newcastle Circuit); and the mother-in-law of Dr. Watson; Thomas Jobling, too, was converted in 1828, and has entered the ministry, and will ultimately become General Missionary Secretary; John Matfin, who was converted at Sallyport Chapel in 1824, is now in the ministerial ranks, and also G. S. Butterwick, one of the firstfruits of the Newcastle Mission. Thomas Butterwick will soon follow him, and become one of the best and ablest of our early preachers. These are some of the results of the years which the plan fails to register.

As we glance over the long list of preachers, we notice the names of some who, in 1837, had already "purchased to themselves a good degree"; and we also recognise the names of others who, during the next period, will come to the front and play their part. Here, for example, are the names of W. B. Leighton and Peter Kidman, who had already begun their long and honourable connection with the Newcastle Circuit. Both joined the Ballast Hills Society at or soon after its formation, and did not cease to serve the Church until the year 1884. As they were companions in service, so in their deaths they were not divided.* Every organised form of local Christian philanthropy had Mr. Leighton's countenance and co-operation, so that his life was one of manifold activity. He was not eloquent by nature or a skilful debater, but just a constant, cheerful worker on behalf of deserving causes. The good work, however, for which he merits special remembrance in this connection was the starting, in 1829, of a Sunday School at Ballast Hills. Of this he was the superintendent for the long space of fifty-nine years. After its formation the school grew until it had five hundred scholars and sixty teachers. It had its branches, to one of which the present St. Anthony's Society can trace its origin. Neglected children and youths were gathered in; a library got together, a Mutual Improvement Society established, and Temperance and habits of thrift encouraged. Amid such influences as these many a young man had his intellect quickened and disciplined for service. The Revs. John Davison, the biographer of Clowes, and Thomas Greenfield, were two of many who had a new direction given to their lives by this Sunday School. About the year 1830 Mr. Leighton, then only a young man himself, invited a youth who was playing at pitch-and-toss to go with him to the school hard by. The youth yielded to persuasion kindly given, and from that simple incident Thomas Greenfield was accustomed to date his conversion. Then began, on his part, that course of mental cultivation which in the end qualified him to become a College tutor and Principal, and made him an expository preacher of rare excellence. Thirty years after Mr. Leighton won this youth for his Master, the like process was repeated, and with the same happy results. This time it was William Pears—whose name stands No. 35 on the plan of 1837—who induced his young lodger to accompany him to Ballast Hills Chapel. That youth was Hugh Gilmore, than whom our Church can show no more interesting figure. But at that time the youth, though a lad of parts, was poor, untaught, and undeveloped as a lion's cub. He went, and went again, to Ballast Hills, and soon "experienced a complete awakening."

* Their memoirs, written by Rev. H. Yooll, will be found side by side in the "Supplementary Connexional Biography," issued December, 1885.

Hugh Gilmore never forgot Ballast Hills or its Bible class, of which Rev. T. Greenfield was now the President. Nor did he forget William Pears; for in the last sermon he preached, June 7th, 1891, he thus refers to him: "I lived with a plain, poor man, whose name was perhaps unknown beyond the people in the little row of cottages where we dwelt. I felt that there was something about that man—not from any natural cause—that made him separate from the men with whom I was mixing."

God's promise is "seed for the sower" as well as "bread for the eater"; so it is instructive to note how in Newcastle, as elsewhere, provision was made for our Church's perpetuity and enlargement, as well as for the daily needs of those composing its fellowship.

With the acquisition in 1838 of Nelson Street Chapel, Newcastle Primitive Methodism entered upon the second period of its history, destined to last for forty years. Mr. Clowes had founded the first society in the town, and it was but fitting that he should, on November 21st, 1837, lay the foundation-stone of this

REV. HUGH GILMORE.

historic building. "The chapel was consecrated before it was built"; so spoke the feeling of some who had come under the influence of his address and dedicatory prayer. The chapel was duly opened on the 7th and 12th of October, 1838, by Revs. W. Sanderson, J. Bywater, and H. Hebbron. Its cost was £2,950, and even after the opening services, there remained a debt of £2,000 on the building. It was a bold venture to make. To come out of Silver Street and plant themselves down within the area of the town improvements, as though they were smitten with the architectural fever then raging; and for this to be done, with all the responsibility involved, by men none of whom could give more than a donation of five pounds without a monetary strain—all this was quite enough to give rise to unfavourable comments and head-shakings. So it was; for one whose memory goes back to that time tells us: "The erection of Nelson Street Chapel produced great excitement. . . . Some, of course, thought it very wrong to build such a costly edifice and leave Silver Street Chapel, which was greatly needed in that wicked part of the town."* But the men on the Trust, if not moneyed men, were men of faith and courage, and not wanting either in good-sense and practical discernment. They believed the time had come for a forward movement, and so they acted in accordance with the old "dour" saying inscribed on the walls of Marischal College, Aberdeen: "They say. What say they? Let them say," and they stopped short with no half measures.

When, in 1897, Nelson Street Chapel had been sold and possession was taken of the Central Church, Northumberland Road, not one of the trustees of Nelson Street remained; all had passed away. For once, it will be well to give the names of these

* Dr. Edw. Barrass: "Reminiscences of Primitive Methodism Forty Years Ago," *Aldersgate Magazine*, 1894, p. 527.

fifteen, because among them are the names of many who carried on the work of the church during the years that followed. Speaking generally, their character was marked by stability, which largely contributed to give stability and a certain recognised type and tradition to the church to which they belonged. When death came—as come it did sooner or later—it found most of these men still at their posts. It is not often this can be said of so large a proportion of the signatories of an early trust-deed. The fact, thus lightly glanced at, is an important one for the understanding of the history of Nelson Street in its mid-period. The names of the Trustees were:—John Scott, George Charlton, Joseph Salkeld [afterwards of Howden], David Keell, Robert Barron, Ralph Cooke, John Taylor, Andrew McCree, Thomas McCree, William Armstrong, W. B. Leighton, Edward Holmes, George Dodds, James Thompson, George Moore, Robert Foster, J. Lockey, Joseph Pattinson, R. Robson, James Stewart, and James Gibson. John Scott and John Taylor are names found in this list. The influence their high character and fair social position gave them was profitable for the Church. William Armstrong was a man of meek and gentle spirit, kindly disposed, and a sweet preacher. Edward Holmes was a familiar figure for many years. The writer, who as Newcastle Circuit's "young man," spent three years under his roof, gladly bears witness to his piety and solid qualities. Robert Foster, sen., was quiet, unassuming, intelligent, and an acceptable pulpit man. He and his wife were amongst the first victims of the cholera scourge in 1853; for, just as London had its year of the great plague followed by the great fire of 1666, so, on a smaller scale, had Newcastle in 1853 and 1854; and, in this dread visitation, the angel of death did not pass by our Church. Mr. and Mrs Scott were also amongst the fifteen hundred who were stricken down in that fatal September. For many years Andrew McCree, as Circuit Steward and Sunday School superintendent, was a leading figure at Nelson Street. Though built on hard lines and wanting in flexibility, a stickler for rule and a martinet in discipline, he was an able man and a diligent and conscientious official, and it was wonderful to see how, as the end was approached, his character mellowed and softened.

E. HOLMES.

Undoubtedly, George Charlton's is the best-known name in the list of men of the middle period. C. C. McKechnie, who spent three terms of service in Newcastle, says truly of him:—

"He had altogether a striking presence. Though not a deep thinker, nor given to abstract or speculative inquiries, he had a mind of great activity and force. His mind was eminently practical. He took a deep interest in the social, political, and religious movements of the day. Among temperance advocates he stood in the foremost rank. He was a most effective temperance speaker. Dealing with facts which could not be gainsaid, and putting his arguments and appeals in the plainest and strongest light, and speaking with the fervour of deep conviction. he usually made a powerful impression, and carried his audience with him. He

ANDREW McCREE.

seemed specially fitted and intended for temperance work. Let it also be said, however, that he rendered signal service to the cause of religion. As leader, local preacher, Conference delegate, he made himself felt as a power for good. He was one of the best men I ever met with for open-air services. He never appeared more in his element than when taking part in leading a procession, or in preaching at a camp meeting. He was a leal-hearted, loyal Primitive, proud of his Church, never ashamed to show his colours, and always ready to forward the interests of the Connexion. He might have, as some thought, rather narrow and perhaps unreasonable ideas as to the salaries and accommodation of travelling-preachers; but allowance must be made for the spirit of the times, for the training he had received, and for his extreme democratic views.* With sundry drawbacks, which were greatly modified with advancing years and experience, George Charlton was a splendid character; one of the noblest men raised among the Primitives in the North."—(MS. "Notes of My Life.")

William Stewart and Robert Foster, jun., are names not found in the list of Nelson Street trustees, though their fathers' names are there. Yet the history of

JAMES STEWART.    WILLIAM STEWART.    THOMAS PATTISON.

Nelson Street cannot be written without a reference to them, and both claim their place in the larger history of the Connexion. James Stewart was an early class-leader as well as trustee. He had a kindly, genial disposition and a vein of humour that sometimes ran into fun and banter. In these respects William Stewart showed himself his father's son. But the son was also a keen business man—a man of affairs and, despite a constitution not over robust, he rose to be one of Newcastle's leading tradesmen and Sheriff of the "town and county." Prosperity did not spoil him or wean him from the Connexion. There was no stand-offishness about him or pride of purse, but he was ever affable and accessible. In their well-appointed home, he and his good wife— the daughter of Mr. Thomas Pattison—dispensed a gracious hospitality which, socially, had its value for the Church. He took an interest in the affairs of the circuit (of which he was the efficient Steward), as well as in the wider affairs of the Connexion— in district administration and extension, in Missions, in Elmfield College and Sunderland

* It may not be generally known that the future Mayor of Gateshead was a speaker at two of the immense Chartist gatherings on the Town Moor in 1838-9, at one of which the military appeared; and that George Charlton also identified himself with the miners, and took part in their mass-meetings.

Institute. Meanwhile he had the generous hand, and his family-pew was seldom empty.

Robert Foster, jun., was a young man of promise at the time of his father's death. The pious but heavy duty that now devolved upon him precluded his entering the ministry, in which assuredly he would have taken a high place. But it did not prevent his ultimately attaining to the highest honour the Connexion has to bestow on its laymen. This honour was his when the Conference of 1901 elected him as its Vice-President. Except during the years he resided in London, Mr. Foster has been closely attached to the society that worshipped in Nelson Street, and, under the leadership of Rev. A. T. Guttery, along with Messrs. Hewitson, Stokoe, Morton and others, actively assisted in the transference of the society to what Mr. Foster has himself called "the city church." With no special advantages arising from wealth or position, he has steadily pursued the path of usefulness and the cultivation of mind and spirit. As he took the right road early in life, he has had no need to change his direction. The ideals of youth are not outworn. Hence his life has been a progress, and the influence of that life cumulative. In him we see the harmony of "mind and soul according well." Mental cultivation, though steadily pursued, has not weakened his sense of conduct, of the demand made upon us, amid all the social groupings and combinations of which we form a part, for what is righteous and fitting. Nor is moralist the last word. No fear of "blanched morality" while the life-blood ceases not to course through every duct and vein, suffusing all with the hue of spiritual health, and keeping the heart young and fresh.

ROBERT FOSTER.

Besides those already mentioned, there were others (speaking only of the dead) whose association with Nelson Street was close and long. Such were George Dodds, second only to his friend George Charlton as a temperance advocate, and as a master of incisive Saxon speech; John Ingledew, kind, gentle, unassuming, a man of blameless and attractive character; of quite another stamp was James Bruce, a godly keelman, whose responses and quaint sayings will not readily be forgotten; from the Yorkshire Dales came John Wilson, and from Alston Moor Robert Varty, both of whom were generous supporters of the cause and thoroughly loyal Primitive Methodists. Nor must we forget that

REV. A. T. GUTTERY.

Rev. William Dent, with his alert intelligence and his solicitude for Zion's weal, was for some twenty-three years, as a superannuate, identified with the Nelson Street Society.

As were the men so was the church, in the long middle period of its history. That period we have spoken of as an uneventful one. Such it was in a good sense, and also in a sense not so good. As a rule things moved steadily on. The old hands stood to their posts year in and year out. Now and again, indeed, there might be a breeze stiffening to a gale like that of which the Hymn Book of 1854 was the storm-centre, or like that which in 1855 blew from the high latitudes of Conference.* But by skilful pilotage the storms were weathered, without mutiny of the crew or damage to the ship. Such experiences, however, were exceptional. Novocastrian Primitives were proud of Nelson Street. They regarded it, and rightly, as "by far the most superior place of worship owned by the Primitives in the North." They were proud too of their anniversaries and of their congregational singing, as they had good reason to be; for in the pre-organ days, John Kidd, an enthusiastic musician, led the singing and presided over an instrumental choir. He loved the old hymns, and nowhere were they sung with such verve as at Nelson Street. He set tunes to many of the old hymns; that known as "Happy day," composed for No. 50 in the Small Hymn Book —"I'm glad I ever saw the day," still holding its ground.

JOHN INGLEDEW.

But there is a *per contra* side. Notwithstanding its intelligence, its stability, and other good qualities, it must be admitted Nelson Street lacked aggressiveness. The town grew amain, but the church did not keep pace with its growth. Open-air work indeed was not neglected, and once a year a rousing procession would startle the inhabitants of the lower quarters of the town, and George Charlton and others would deal out straight talk to the people who leaned out of their windows or stood at their doors, and then in the afternoon a capital camp meeting would be held on the Town Moor, and— things moved on in the old regular way. That this was characteristic of that period is admitted by Mr. R. Foster, who says: "As a Christian organisation Primitive Methodism has not been as enterprising and aggressive as it ought; and judged by the census returns it is remarkably behind. But recently a more militant and forward spirit has taken possession of our churches."

JOHN KIDD.

The following notes respecting the later development of Newcastle Circuit may be found useful. They will serve to show how comparatively recent that development has been, and thus confirm the truth of Mr. Foster's words just cited. Dealing first

* With the concurrence of an influential minority, the Conference had appointed as an *additional* preacher to Newcastle one for whom, notwithstanding his acknowledged ability, it could find no place. The circuit stoutly and successfully resisted the impost; and the preacher had a year's rest. See Rev. J. Atkinson's "Life of C. C. McKechnie," pp. 121—6.

with Newcastle: A mission at the west side of the town (Scotswood Road) resulted at length in the building of Brunel Street Chapel. This was in 1870 superseded by Maple Street, which in 1874 became the head of Newcastle II., with the Rev. James Young as its superintendent. Another westward mission, Arthur's Hill, founded in 1842 by Mr. William Armstrong, gave place in 1864 to West Street. This in turn was vacated in 1897 for Kingsley Terrace, now attached to Newcastle II. Eastward, Heaton Road Chapel was built in 1877, and in 1892 was constituted the head of Newcastle III. Another city chapel not shown on our full-page illustration is Derby Street which in 1883 took the place of an upper room where we had long worshipped. Strickland Street is the successor of a joiner's shop in Elswick. Other schemes of local extension are projected. Finally, Newcastle II. was in 1894 again divided by Blaydon and Lemington becoming the heads of circuits. The number of members for the five circuits reported to the Conference of 1904 was 1886, as against 747 when the division of 1874 took place.

Turning now to Gateshead: Its early history was one of toil and disappointment, while its later history has been one of remarkable success. Made a circuit in 1837, it was in 1841 again joined to Newcastle. Its first chapel was lost to the Connexion

JOHN THOMPSON.    E. GOWLAND.    G. E. ALMOND.

through the defalcations of its treasurer. In 1854, Nelson Street Chapel was opened by Rev. Ralph Fenwick. The lineal successor of that chapel, sold in 1886, may be said to be the fine block of buildings in Durham Road, consisting of school and lecture hall erected in 1887, and chapel and manse in 1892-3. Meanwhile, Gateshead was again created a circuit in 1862.

Gateshead II. was formed in 1891. At its head stands Prince Consort Road Chapel, the outcome of a mission begun in 1869. The Teams mission, begun by Messrs. Carr and Scope in 1874, has similarly resulted in Victoria Road Chapel; and the Somerset Street mission, started in 1875, developed nine years later into Sunderland Road Chapel, which has connected with it a Christian Endeavour Hall, said to be the first of its kind in the Connexion. Still another mission resulted in the building of Bank Street School-chapel in 1891. Further extensions are projected.

One cannot but be impressed with the amount of work that has been crowded into a period no longer than is often the term of one man's ministry. How much of this success may have been prepared for by the sorrowful sowing of the previous period—who shall tell? Referring to the progress made by Gateshead since it was made a circuit

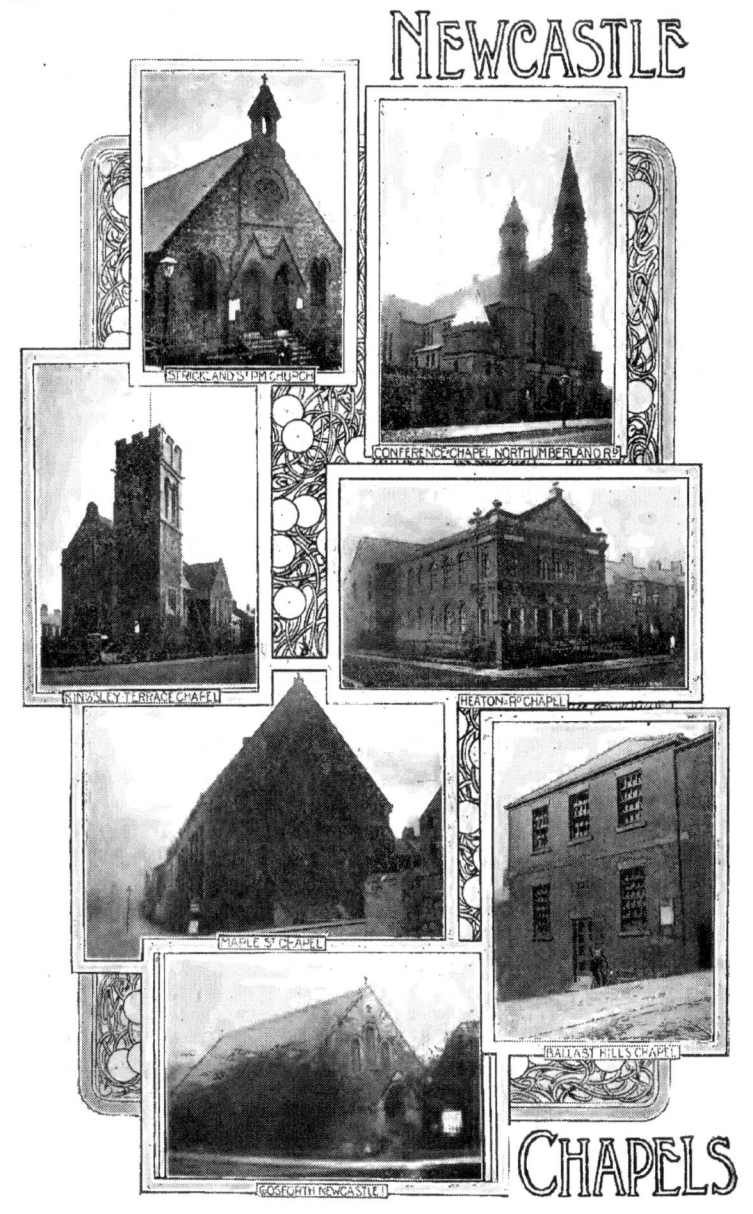

198 PRIMITIVE METHODIST CHURCH.

NEWCASTLE CHAPELS

ST. NICK AND ST. P.M. CHURCH

CONFERENCE CHAPEL, NORTHUMBERLAND RD.

KINGSLEY TERRACE CHAPEL

HEATON RD. CHAPEL

MAPLE ST. CHAPEL

BALLAST HILLS CHAPEL

GOSFORTH (NEWCASTLE.)

in 1862, the Rev. G. Armstrong, to whom we are indebted for many of the facts given, says: "From that time its advance has been rapid and continuous, until to-day its membership slightly exceeds that of Newcastle. Its more prominent leaders included W. Peel, John Thompson, Edward Gowland, John Scope, John Cherry, and G. E. Almond, who is still with us, and is yet a tower of strength. The great feature of Gateshead Primitive Methodism has been its persistent missioning, and its dogged determination to succeed."

Men are of much more value than many chapels, and however beautiful to look at they may be, one would gladly turn to the men who got them built, or, yet more—because they are in greater danger of being forgotten—one would fain recall the men who worshipped in the humbler buildings of the early days. Some of these we have endeavoured to revive the memory of; but, though Nelson Street was the head and centre of the old circuit, there were good men and true connected with its other societies no less worthy of being remembered. From Bessie Newton, of Whickham, the popular preacheress, and Ralph Waller, the Blaydon coke-burner, down to the men of the present, there have never been wanting those who have stood by the cause and furthered its local interests—men like David Wright of Ballast Hills, Thomas Scott of Walker, the Pickerings of Winlaton, and many others who might be named, did space permit. Besides these who have lived and died in the circuit, others have gone forth from it who have done yeoman-service in other parts of the Connexion. In proof of this the names of Benjamin and Ferdinand Spoor, and Thomas Robson may be cited. It was at Walker the brothers Spoor began their course of Christian usefulness which, with concurrent worldly prosperity, was hereafter to make them so influential in the Bishop Auckland Circuit, and far beyond. The father of Thomas Robson was one of the earliest local preachers of the Newcastle Circuit, and it was in the same circuit his son began to exercise those gifts which, after his retirement from the ministry, made him one of the most acceptable local preachers in the Darlington and Stockton District.

BENJAMIN SPOOR.

SUNDERLAND.

John Branfoot was probably our Connexional pioneer in Sunderland. Tradition says he visited the town in 1821 and preached on the pier. Further, that some considerable time after, John Nelson walked over from South Shields to hold a service. A good-hearted woman lent him a chair for pulpit which he placed at the end of the Friends' School—the very building which soon after was obligingly placed at the service of the few who had rallied round the missionary, amongst whom are particularly named— George Peckett, John Tiplady, Benjamin Dodds, and Christopher Fenwick. So far tradition, which agrees with the earliest evidence afforded by printed documents. In the *Journals* of W. Clowes as found in the *Magazine*, he notes being at Sunderland on July 16th, 1822, and adds: "there is likely to be a good work here."

FERDINAND SPOOR.

200 PRIMITIVE METHODIST CHURCH.

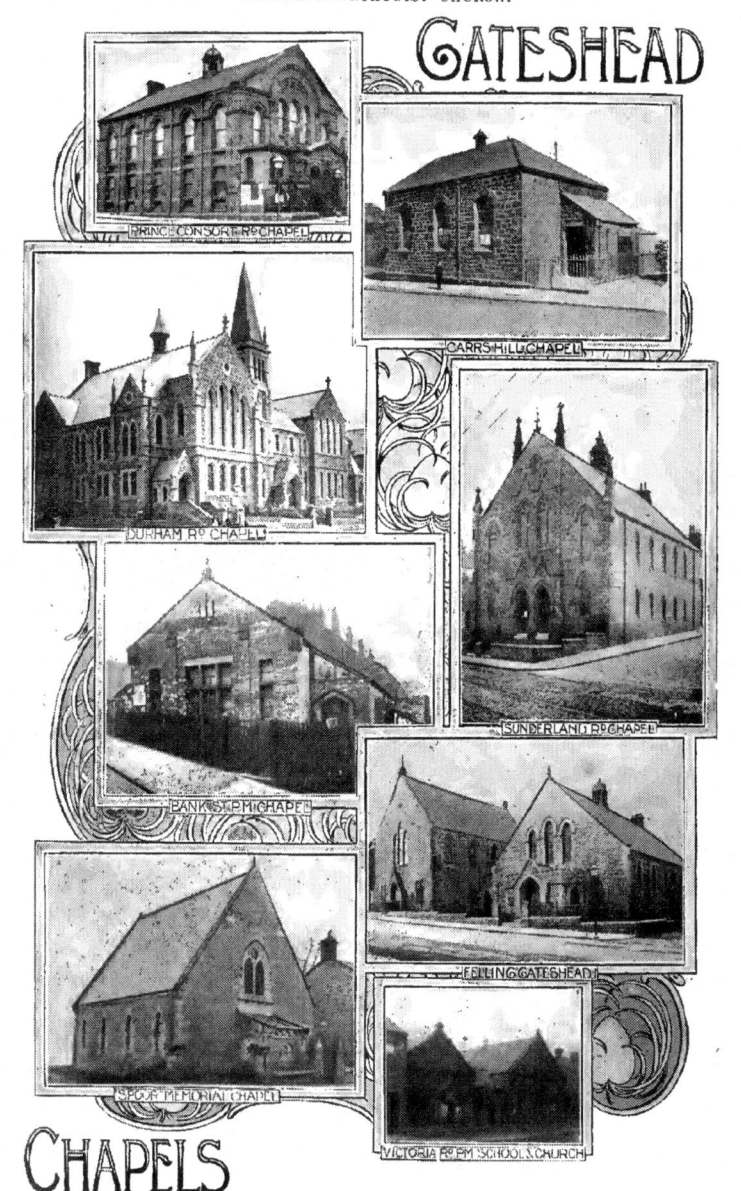

GATESHEAD CHAPELS

THE PERIOD OF CIRCUIT PREDOMINANCE AND ENTERPRISE. 201

On September 1st, he meets the class of six members who then constituted the Society. Under date of October 8th, "I preached," he says, "in a large school-room kindly lent us by the committee of the school. We received it as a very great kindness." This would probably be the service attended by a young man who became a New Connexion minister, and who afterwards recalled his impressions. His ear had been so abused by tales of these new-comers that he went to the room full of prejudice. Mr. Clowes preached from—"We are made partakers of Christ if we hold fast the beginning of our confidence, steadfast unto the end." As he listened his prejudices gradually gave way, and he pushed further into the room. By the time the preacher had finished his sermon, Mr. Lynn's "heart was bound to him in love as a precious man of God. After the singing of the hymn beginning:—

'Come and taste along with me,
Consolation-flowing free,'

VICTORIA HALL, FROM THE PARK, SUNDERLAND.
Scene of the Disaster of June 16th, 1883, in which 182 children lost their lives.

he engaged in prayer, and Divine influence came streaming down in such a way as completely overcame me. I was so affected that I could not stand and sank on my knees. Oh, the unutterable bliss that filled my soul! For many days after, I feasted on the rich supply of grace then given; and ever after I revered the name of William Clowes."[*]

Very soon after this Mr. Clowes went on his Carlisle mission as already described. Not quite a year later the Sunderland and Stockton branches became the Sunderland

[*] "Methodist Records; or, Selections from the Journal of the Rev. Andrew Lynn, 1858."

and Stockton Union Circuit. The Circuit thus formed was of wide area. It embraced the whole of the south-eastern part of the county of Durham, a part which included the towns of Hartlepool, Stockton-on-Tees, Houghton-le-Spring, the ancient city of Durham, and numerous collieries which were springing up and rapidly transforming the character and increasing the population of the district. Such was the old Sunderland Circuit; and as such it remained until 1837 when Stockton Circuit was formed. Two years later the western side was detached to form the Durham Circuit; while Hetton, in the heart of the collieries, continued its connection with Sunderland until 1864. We shall not now interrupt the narrative in order to follow the process of circuit sub-division further, although it has resulted in giving us some twenty circuits instead of the one circuit of 1823.

The growth of the Circuit was rapid. Primitive Methodism quickly rooted itself both in Sunderland and the mining villages. This will appear from two extracts we give from the *Journals* of the time. The writer of the first is Thomas Nelson, whose zeal and unremitting labour had no doubt largely contributed to the success realised.

DURHAM CATHEDRAL.

"*Monday, August 25th, 1823.*—Last year at this time in Sunderland we had six in Society and one leader; but now we have 275 members, eleven leaders, and a very large chapel building. The increase for this quarter is 459. What hath God wrought! Shall I say that this has been one of the best and most wonderful quarters I ever saw before? I have preached nearly every sermon in the open-air, and have seen the good effects of it. I am afraid if our people do not watch, as they get chapels and places of worship, they will cease to preach in the open-air, and, then the glory will depart from us as a people."

Our second extract is from the *Journal* of N. West, and is dated October 15th, 1823. As usual, what he writes is helpful. It gives us a graphic presentation of what was going on amongst the colliers. We see them gladly receiving that form of truth which was to do so much for the moral elevation of their class. Alluding to its being less than a year since our cause was introduced into the northern part of the Circuit, he proceeds :—

"A very blessed and glorious work has gone on for some time in Sunderland and the neighbouring collieries. In Sunderland and Monkwearmouth (which is a village on the opposite side the river from Sunderland) we have nearly four hundred members. In Lord Steward's and Squire Lambton's collieries we have near four hundred more. Some of the most abandoned characters have tasted that the Lord is gracious. Indeed, the Lord and the poor colliers are doing wondrously. Our congregations are immensely large, and well-behaved. It would do any of the lovers of Jesus good to see the dear colliers sometimes under the word. On some occasions (for want of time to wash themselves), they are constrained to come black to the preaching or else miss the sermon. And when the Lord warms their hearts with His dying love, and they feel Him precious in His word, the large and silent tears rolling down their black cheeks, and leaving the white streaks behind, conspicuously portray what their hearts feel. Their hearty and zealous exertions in the cause of God would make almost any one love them. We have five preachers employed in this Circuit, and a blessed prospect."

Thomas Nelson, it will have been noticed, alludes to the building of Flag Lane Chapel as already going on in the autumn of 1823. The date is significant, as is also the fact that the chapel was not opened until September 3rd, 1824. For a society not yet a year old to buy land without money, and to begin to build a chapel to seat a thousand people, was a bold undertaking. Judged by modern methods and requirements it was impolitic and rash to a degree. But it should be remembered that the Society was, thus early, joined by some men of intelligence and character, and that this saved the enterprise from being as Quixotic as at first sight it might appear to be. But even so, Flag Lane was long regarded as a standing monument of the good Providence of God over His people. It was under the influence of this feeling that N. West, after its opening, told the story to the Connexion. To him God's hand was in the building of Flag Lane as surely as it was seen in the rebuilding of the walls of Jerusalem in Nehemiah's days. Difficulties more than enough to daunt any but the most determined were met and overcome. A wall stood on the ground promised them, which wall was claimed by one who refused to sell except at an exorbitant price. Faced with this difficulty, the Society betook itself to prayer. From the prayer-meeting Brothers Peckett and Sharkitt waited upon the owner of the wall who, after some conference, gave permission for its removal. When the work was begun their available capital was but £23, the first shilling of which was given by a coal-porter. This is but a sample of their difficulties and deliverances. More than once or twice the work was brought to a stand for lack of money; but prayer went up continually, and sacrifices were cheerfully made, and all conspired to beg as well as to give and pray. But what is worthy of remark :—we see John Gordon Black and Henry Hesman moving about, interviewing this man and the other, and we are brought back to the conclusion that the character of the men associated with this seemingly rash undertaking was a valuable asset, and this the Church in Sunderland found to its own great advantage in this and subsequent years. It was strong in the moral strength of its earliest and most prominent officials. Of these John Gordon Black was as long as he lived the first and foremost. With his tall, slender, somewhat stooping form, his dark visage, deep-set eyes, Melanchthon-like forehead crowned with steel-grey hair, and his sickly cast of countenance, Mr. Black was a striking if not a prepossessing figure. He gave the impression of strength of character, of knowing his own mind, of the power to lead and command; and fuller knowledge but served to confirm the correctness of such impressions. He had a clear penetrative intellect, and could hold his own in argument even with men who might be more fully informed than himself. By the exercise of qualities such as these Mr. Black prospered in business, and in the end amassed considerable wealth. He was a convinced and loyal Primitive Methodist, whose services in its behalf merited the distinction of his name being included—the only one of the Sunderland District—amongst the original signatories of the Deed Poll. He loved to gather round him ministers of his own and other denominations, so that his home became a rallying-point for evangelical Nonconformity in the borough. The influence

W. HOPPER.    W. B. EARL.    R. HUISON.

of these re-unions, and of Mr. Black's reputation for integrity and public-spirit, were of advantage to the Church to which he belonged. Sunderland Primitive Methodism has always been strong on the social side, and has stood well in public estimation. This is in no inconsiderable measure due to the early example and influence of John Gordon Black. His funeral, in September, 1851, was attended by forty ministers of his own denomination, as well as by many ministers of other Churches.

Next to J. Gordon Black should certainly come a reference to his contemporary, Henry Hesman. As we recall the reminiscences of his physical defects, which after all were but the foil to unusual endowments, we are reminded of Joseph Polwarth, the prophet-dwarf of George Macdonald's story.* As Mr. McKechnie has finely written in his unpublished autobiography: "That dwarfed and deformed figure enshrined a richly dowered soul, clear, piercing, far-reaching in its perception, and with capacities for high and subtle thought." As in addition to all his other qualities, Mr. Hesman had a silvery musical voice, oratorical gestures, and a singular excellence in his style of address, it was but natural that, like the very popular Newrick Featonby, he should be well received as a local preacher by the Societies.

* "Thomas Wingfold, Curate."

Other men, the contemporaries or immediate successors of those just mentioned, were prominent figures in the Sunderland Circuit for many years. Such were Messrs. Whittaker, W. Hopper, W. B. Earl, R. Huison, Thomas Gibson and others we need not name. The fact that Mr. Thomas Gibson finally withdrew from the Connexion does not annul the service he rendered the Sunderland Circuit, and the Connexion generally. In regard to the latter, the practical interest he took in the higher training of the ministry demands special acknowledgment. Men quickly pass, and memory is short. They who can recall Mr. Thomas Gibson as, unimpassionedly, he addressed the Conference, are becoming fewer in number every year. The few, however, who remain will not fail to remember his skill in debate. How clearly he could state a case, marshal his arguments, controvert a position!

The men we have referred to were men of good social position. They were the men who figured on platforms, and had a large determining influence in the councils of the Circuit. They took part in the full-dress debates of the Quarterly Meetings and in the sessions of the District Preachers' Association—large and notable gatherings both. Yet the prominence and usefulness of these men must not be allowed to obscure the fact that the strength of the Circuit, and the secret of its success, were with those more sequestered souls in the various societies who quietly did their duty and gave stability to the cause. This was seen when the troubles arose, ostensibly through the building of Tatham Street Chapel (1875), and the subsequent division of the Sunderland Circuit (1877). We have used the word "ostensibly"; for though these events were the occasion of the divergence, their real cause was something very different from the cause alleged. However the issue may have been confused, the vital question at issue was between the will of the few and the will of the many; whether government by the people for the people was not after all the right kind of government for Primitive Methodism. In the process of getting back on the right democratic lines mistakes may have been committed, but not to have got back would have been the greatest mistake of all.

THOMAS GIBSON.

Sunderland Circuit's Missions.

Sunderland Circuit soon began to carry on missionary operations beyond its own borders. For a number of years it was a Missionary Society in itself, and as such published its own Report. In that for 1835 we read: "Sunderland Circuit's local situation has prevented it from enlarging its own borders much at home, but distant places such as Edinburgh, and other towns in Scotland, have enjoyed the benefit of its surplus moneys; missionaries were sent to these places, and for some time were supported at considerable expense by this circuit; societies were formed through their instrumentality, and they have since either been annexed to northern circuits or formed into new circuits."

Sunderland Circuit led the way in seeking to establish missions in Scotland, and Carlisle Circuit soon followed its lead. Edinburgh was Sunderland's objective, while Carlisle fastened on Glasgow, Scotland's commercial capital. It was in April, 1826, the two chosen missionaries—Thomas Oliver and Jonathan Clewer—set out for the northern metropolis. To save the coach-fare they walked the whole of the distance, billeting and preaching, as they went, at Morpeth, Alnwick, and Belford. Arrived at their destination, they looked round. They first surveyed the city; not as sight-seers, but as prospectors, anxious to find the most suitable spot for the delivery of their message. They were only doing in the Modern Athens what Paul did in the ancient one when, first of all, he "passed through the city," and his "heart was stirred within him." So, as they passed through the Grass Market, the impression they sought was received. Here, where so many of the martyrs had surrendered their lives for the faith, they would open their commission. Accordingly, on April 13th, they took their stand in the middle of the Grass Market, and after singing the hymn "Arise, O Zion," Mr. Oliver preached from, "Is all well? wherefore came this mad fellow to thee?" (2 Kings ix. 11). On the Sunday evening following, a second service was held at the same place, when Mr. Clewer preached. A room, formerly used as a weaving factory, was rented, and a small society formed. At first their efforts were not confined to the city; towns and villages lying within an eight miles' radius were visited. But not meeting with much success in these efforts they resolved to concentrate upon Edinburgh. Much time was devoted to house-to-house visitation in the Grass Market, Canongate, and Westport. In three months 715 families were visited, and the tabulated results of the visitation were published. By this means public attention was drawn to the sad spiritual destitution of the dwellers in these populous Edinburgh slums, and the most effective method of remedially dealing with this destitution was suggested. This method of systematic house-to-house visitation was afterwards adopted by Drs. Chalmers and Guthrie in the parochial and territorial system they introduced.*

REV. THOS. OLIVER.

Unfortunately, the bright prospects of the Edinburgh mission soon suffered disastrous eclipse. Sunderland Circuit had appointed N. West to superintend the mission, and from one with so good a record much was expected. He had already acquired considerable Connexional influence, and was active in originating legislation. His last effort in this direction was to prove his own undoing. At the Conference of 1827 he brought forward a proposal, which became a law, to the effect that any preacher who should refuse to go to his appointed station should, by such refusal, forfeit his position as a minister. What followed furnished a striking instance of the "engineer hoist with his own petard"; for N. West, being now appointed to South Shields, declined the appointment, with the result that the year 1828 saw both the disappearance of

* Nor was the method adopted without acknowledgment. Rev. J. Wenn affirms that, in a private conversation with him, Dr. Guthrie made such acknowledgment.

N. West's name from the list of preachers, and also the first appearance on the statute book of that enactment which led to his passing. But N. West did not leave the Connexion unattended. He took possession of the preaching-room, and drew away the greater portion of the society. Then John Bowes was sent to patch up the rent, but made it worse by going over to the malcontents. Jabez Burns, too, who had given Mr. Petty his first ticket, joined the secessionists. For a time they worked together and established several societies, but ultimately the leaders disagreed amongst themselves, and then parted to go their several ways. N. West went to the United States, where he became a D.D. and chaplain to the Federal forces. Jabez Burns also became a D.D., a Baptist minister, and a publisher of sermons that had some vogue in their day. As for Mr. John Bowes, we are told he became a teetotal lecturer and the advocate of an unpaid ministry. Meanwhile, the Primitive Methodist society was a mere wreck, and W. Clowes might well ask in writing John Flesher: "What shall we do for Edinburgh?" The person thus appealed to was sent to save the situation. Hull Circuit agreed, with certain stipulations, to relieve Sunderland of the charge of Edinburgh; and Mr. Flesher spent some anxious months of 1830-1 in the northern metropolis, away from his wife and family and, vested with plenary powers, did his best to reorganise and strengthen the society. No good purpose would be served by following the earlier history of Edinburgh further in detail. It was transferred to Berwick—to Glasgow. It became an independent station; it came again under Sunderland Circuit's sheltering wing. Good men laboured upon it—men like David Beattie, J. A. Bastow, Hugh Campbell, Christopher Hallam, John Wenn. It gave James Macpherson to our ministry in 1833, which gift compensated for much. Other Churches reaped large benefit from our labours, right along from the time the first sermon in the Grass Market gave Dr. Lindsay Alexander one of his best deacons. In 1838, Edinburgh missioned Alloa and Dunfermline, and two years afterwards Alloa was taken under the care of Sunderland as a separate mission, and such it remained for some years, though a small and feeble cause.

Our remarks on the earlier history of Edinburgh may fittingly end by a glance forward to the next most important event in its history. This was the erection, in 1861, of the Victoria Terrace Chapel, through the energetic efforts of the Rev. J. Vaughan, the superintendent. At his first service in the city he had but eight hearers, and the outlook was anything but promising. But some three weeks after his arrival, great excitement was caused by the fall of a five-storied building, by which several persons were crushed to death and others maimed. It was then the well-known incident occurred: A voice was heard saying, "Heave away, lads, I'm no dead yet." The voice came from a poor fellow buried beneath the débris, who was forthwith extricated. Mr. Vaughan sought to improve the occasion by preaching near the scene of the catastrophe; and from that time a revival began which greatly assisted the forward movement. It might almost seem as if preacher and people had adopted the motto of the brave young Scotsman who was the hero of the hour. A chapel, school, and dwelling-house were built at a cost of £1600, and of this sum considerably more than £1000 was raised. After all the migrations of the years from one rented room to another a home was at last obtained in the chief city of Scotland, within a stone's throw of the old Grass

Market, where the first missionaries had stood. Tranent, too, and Elphinstone were missioned, and a chapel built at the former place. But long before these events occurred Edinburgh had passed from the care of Sunderland Circuit. Its subsequent history, as well as that of Paisley, and Glasgow with its offshoots—Calder Bank, Motherwell, and Wishaw—must be glanced at when we come to consider the work of the General Missionary Committee and the formation of the North British District.

Some time in 1822 a Christian philanthropist in Scotland wrote W. Clowes, pressing him to begin at once an evangelistic mission in that country. Through some mischance the letter was not read by Clowes until a year after it was written. Afterwards, when reflecting upon this incident, Clowes regretted the mischance, and was disposed to blame a malign power for its occurrence. "I thought it was unfortunate that I had not received his letter immediately after its arrival: as I should most likely have missioned Scotland, being at the time at Shields in the North, where the work was going on prosperously. I believe Satan laboured unusually hard to get me out of the North; and I am persuaded that I left it too early." It is not often Clowes criticises events in this way, and acquaints us with his personal predilections. One cannot but think that Primitive Methodism might have got a better start in Scotland if that letter—— but we leave it. Our business is not with the might-have-beens.

FIRST CHAPEL, EDINBURGH.

We have now to chronicle the establishment of a mission in the Channel Islands by the Sunderland Circuit. This was in March, 1832, when the circuit, having been relieved of the Edinburgh mission, was now free to turn elsewhere. Moreover, the circuit was in a very prosperous condition. The tragic death of Messrs. Branfoot and Hewson had been over-ruled for good. The event had left a deep and solemn feeling amongst the societies. The places left vacant were immediately filled, March, 1831, by Messrs J. Petty and W. Lister. It is difficult to realise that at this time Mr. Petty was but four and twenty years of age. He came to the circuit just after he had experienced an extraordinary work of grace in his own soul. He was in a state of spiritual exaltation, and there is ample evidence to show that his preaching of holiness, and the sanctity and sweetness of his own character, had a powerful influence on the societies and especially on his colleagues. "I had not been an hour in his company," says Mr. Lister, "before I was united to him." Almost the first duty of the newcomers was to visit the widows of the deceased ministers. While praying and conversing together, "we had," says Mr. Lister, "a glorious baptism; Mrs. Hewson praised God for a clean heart." Messrs. Lister and Hebbron both became seekers of the blessing of full salvation, and both rejoiced in its realisation. With the preachers thus aglow and the people urged to seek after sanctification of heart and life, a revival broke out, as might have been anticipated. In another way the revival had been prepared for. Towards the close of 1831, Sunderland and the district suffered severely from the ravages of cholera, and the minds of many were seriously turned towards religion, the result being that in 1832 an increase of six hundred members was reported. South Shields Circuit shared in this revival. While it was in progress certain sailors from Guernsey had attended some meetings of extraordinary power, and had expressed a strong desire that a missionary might be sent to their native island. It was therefore resolved that the two circuits, South Shields and Sunderland, should co-operate in sending a missionary. Mr. George Cosens, a native of the West Indies, was the person selected, largely, it would seem, because "his colour would attract in open-air services." Mr. Cosens reached the island in May, 1832, and began his work under promising conditions. Soon another missionary was sent to his support, and then "something happened." At St. Peter's Port, Guernsey, Mr. Cosens, being annoyed at the conduct of some giddy young people who were present at the service, spoke unadvisedly with his lips. The laws of the island are peculiar; Mr. Cosens was summoned and fined, and in April Mr. Petty took his place on the islands, and during his twelve months' stay endeavoured to repair the damage the mission had sustained.

The Norman Isles mission is of some importance historically because it was but part of a much larger scheme which never came into being. The Norman Isles were to be but the stepping-stones to France. Missionaries were to be sent there for a time to acquire the language, and in other ways to prepare themselves for what was to be regarded as their main work—labouring on the soil of France. This purpose is clearly stated in Sunderland's Missionary Report for 1834:—

"We intend, as soon as circumstances will allow, to extend our exertions to the wide continent of France—to a nation proverbial for infidelity and vice—to a people who seldom or never have the opportunity of hearing the Gospel preached in its purity. Our two missionaries, Messrs. Petty and Macpherson, inform us that they have now learned the French language so as to be able to preach in it, and are ready and willing to go to France as soon as the means are provided."

Sunderland's dream of a Primitive Methodist Mission in France has been one of the Connexion's unrealised possibilities. It is a dream which other circuits besides Sunderland have dreamed, even in later years. In 1869, North Shields tried to revive the project of a French mission. A week's Missionary meetings, beginning as was fitting with Old Cramlington, were devoted to the advocacy of such a mission. Much enthusiasm was evoked, and representations were made in the proper quarters; but nothing came of it. As for Sunderland, it is interesting to recall that the town itself has still had its honourable association with the evangelisation of France, since the founder of the Mc All Mission was for some years one of its ministers.

In March, 1834, Sunderland Circuit reported 1400 members, and had a balance at its quarterly board of £50. At the suggestion of the preachers themselves it was resolved to devote this surplus to the establishment of a mission in Dorsetshire. Weymouth, a watering-place beloved of George III., was selected as the headquarters of the mission, and Messrs. John Nelson and Cosens volunteered their services as missionaries. At Weymouth they met with a favourable reception. Their open-air services attracted crowds, and some remarkable conversions took place. The Assembly Room, which had for many years been the scene of dancing and revelry, was turned into a Primitive Methodist chapel, and that too was rightly regarded as a remarkable conversion. Dorchester, the county-town was also visited. A Congregational minister who had known our people in Lincolnshire, welcomed the missionaries. He promised them the use of his chapel when the weather should become too inclement for open-air services. He informed them that though Dorchester had a population of six thousand, no more than about five hundred persons were frequenters of public worship on the Lord's Day; and that, within a radius of ten miles of the town, there were at least fifty villages in most of which there were few Dissenters or persons making a profession of religion. Here, it might have been thought, were so many cogent reasons why the advent of the missionaries to these parts should have been gladly hailed, did not experience show that where the evangel is most needed it is often the least desired. So it was in this case. At Dorchester and in the surrounding villages the missionaries met with a rougher reception than at Weymouth. At first, they experienced considerable annoyance in carrying on their open-air work; guns were let off, bugles were blown, artificial thunder created by a machine brought from the adjoining theatre, and missiles thrown; finally, Mr. Cosens had a bucket of water poured over him while preaching. In the villages persecution took a more subtle but relentless form. Some, whose incognito is preserved by the use of dashes in the Report, resorted to intimidation. To give shelter to the missionary or even to lend him a chair to stand upon, might mean loss of employment or ejectment from house and home. One day, John Nelson walked eight miles to a village during fair-time and, after preaching in the open-air amid interruption from drunken men, he could find no place at which to sleep. Even at the inn where he had previously stayed he was refused a bed. At last a kindly miller took pity on him and allowed him to sleep in the mill, though he intimated that by granting such permission he might jeopardise his tenancy of the mill. Still, despite the boycott, fourteen villages around Weymouth and Dorchester were visited with some degree of success.

On the whole, it must be acknowledged that Sunderland Circuit was unfortunate in its missions. It was so in Edinburgh and in the Norman Isles, and so it was also in Dorsetshire. Here, persecution was not so inimical to the mission as was internal dissension. Paul and Barnabas were not the last yoke-fellows who had so sharp a contention between them that "they departed asunder the one from the other." Mr. Nelson and his dusky-skinned colleague could not agree. The societies took sides with one or the other, and were rent and divided. Mr. Cosens withdrew from the

Connexion and became a Baptist minister. Mr. Nelson, smarting under the judgment which Hugh Bourne and others had taken of this painful episode, also withdrew soon after and entered the ministry of the New Connexion, in which he was spared to labour many years.

"Weymouth Mission," says Mr. Petty, "did not soon recover the shock which the unhappy difference we have just named occasioned, and, perhaps, never presented such a flattering prospect as it did when Messrs. Nelson and Cosens began their missionary labours there. In a subsequent year it was indeed greatly enlarged through the enterprising labours of Mr. Thomas Russell, and in the year 1839 we find no fewer than four travelling-preachers stationed to it, then under the care of Manchester Circuit; but the societies never acquired, unless till recently, the prosperity and strength which most societies in other parts in Dorsetshire have done."—(P. 324).

CHAPTER XVIII.

THE MAKING OF NORWICH DISTRICT.

AT the beginning of 1823, the Nottingham Circuit had six branches—Boston, Spalding, Norwich, Fakenham, Cambridge, and Lynn. Of these, Norwich and Fakenham became circuits in June, 1823, and Cambridge and Lynn in March of the following year. By 1825, Yarmouth and Upwell (afterwards Downham Market) had also become heads of circuits. As these six circuits geographically formed one group, the Conference of 1825 made them into a new District, of which

VIEW OF NORWICH.

Norwich, the capital of the Eastern Counties, was naturally constituted the head. No doubt this step was taken because it was thought it would conduce to the more economical and effective administration of the stations themselves. Such at least is the conclusion to which we must come after reading what Hugh Bourne has bluntly written on the subject: "In 1825, Norwich District was *formed of six shattered circuits* from Nottingham District, with 1546 members. These had been injured by employing

THE PERIOD OF CIRCUIT PREDOMINANCE AND ENTERPRISE.   213

improper characters." After this, we must not picture to ourselves these first East Anglian circuits as starting on their careers with the vigour and freshness of young athletes. There is much that we cannot know, and need not care to know, implied in those words "shattered circuits." All the more remarkable, then, is the progress which the Norwich District made between 1825 and 1842; for by that time the Norwich District had become practically co-extensive with what we know as East Anglia.

We propose, then, in this chapter to show, first, how Primitive Methodism reached and rooted itself in these primary circuits of the old Norwich District, and then, how from these circuits as the nuclei it was carried here and there by missionary efforts, until the greater part of East Anglia was covered with a network of circuits. Unfortunately, there is little information obtainable as to the first planting of our

THE LOLLARDS' PIT.

Church in Fakenham and Upwell Circuits. It was so when Mr. Petty wrote his *History*, and it is now too late to hope that the facts can be recovered. Of our Church-origins in the remaining primary Circuits, especially in Yarmouth, something more is known. We begin with Norwich, and in what follows we shall freely use the information which has been kindly supplied by the Rev. W. A. Hammond, who knows so much of East Anglian Primitive Methodism.

THE PRIMARY CIRCUITS :—I. NORWICH.

The first Primitive Methodist services in Norwich were held on the great open common known as Mousehold Heath, familiar to every student of history as the camping-ground of Ket, the tanner of Wymondham, whose army of 20,000 men gathered in rebellion against Edward VI., and was only defeated by Dudley, Earl of Warwick, after much desperate fighting. Here stands the oak—still known as Ket's Oak—under which the insurgent sat to administer justice. Here, too, is the Lollards' Pit, wherein the early Reformers used to gather for Divine service as in a mighty amphitheatre. Here, as in another Gwennap, they gathered, row upon row, to listen to the Word. To this historic spot the early missionaries wended their way and held services, so that it soon got a new name which needs no guessing. For many years crowds gathered at least once a year for a camp meeting at the old trysting-place.

It was not long before the missionaries found their way into the city. Pockthorpe, its most degraded quarter, was not far from Mousehold, and soon the services were transferred to one of the yards for which Norwich is famous—Rose Yard by name, not, however, so called because it was fragrant with the scent of summer roses, but because a public-house named "The Rose" stood at its entrance. Here the open-air services were continued and at last a chapel secured, and the foundations of Primitive Methodism in the city laid. Encompassed with formidable difficulties the infant cause pressed on its way —sometimes almost crushed with financial difficulties (for some of its early trustees were cast into prison), and sometimes its very existence threatened by dissension; yet, for all that, it had such vitality and vigour that its preachers went through all the country-side preaching the gospel. Not only did they enter the villages contiguous to the city, but, as we shall see, they sent their evangelists to Yarmouth and Wymondham, and even to Colchester, sixty miles away.

OLD ROSE YARD CHAPEL.

Other openings in the city were eagerly tried and cottage-meetings and open-air services held, the most important of which was Lakenham. Here a loft was secured, and services commenced, and, in 1823, a chapel built at a cost of £360—not a large outlay for providing accommodation for five hundred people. Subsequently, however, £900 more were expended upon it, and Lakenham chapel became the headquarters of Primitive Methodism in the city. Out of the way, up a narrow "loak" * called Chapel Loak, that a stranger would have had some difficulty to find, this building yet became the home of a strong church. Crowds gathered to listen to such preachers as John Oscroft, Thomas Charlton, G. W. Bellham, Richard Howchin, Thomas Batty, and Robert Key. Meanwhile, the Rose Yard society emerged from the old yard, purchased an old brewery and, in 1842, built the present Cowgate Street Chapel at a cost of £750,

* "Loak," a lane closed in with gates, or through which there is no thoroughfare.

in which good work has been done in a very needy neighbourhood. In those early days, Norwich Branch with its "appartments" (sic), as the outlying districts were strangely called, carried six preachers, two of whom were stationed at Yarmouth and one at Colchester. In 1825, Norwich had 192 members, Colchester 19, and Yarmouth 112, with seven chapels and twenty-four local preachers all told. The missionary character of the work carried on is evidenced by a resolution of one of the Quarterly Meetings ordering five hundred hymn-books to be bought and one hundred plans printed. Local preachers were to have their licences paid for out of the missionary money, and no person was to be allowed to sing who curled his hair or behaved disorderly during the service.

LAKENHAM OLD CHAPEL AND SCHOOL.

Notwithstanding all difficulties and drawbacks the work grew and prospered. A new cause was commenced in the west end of the city, and, in 1864, a good chapel was erected at a cost of £1300, to which schools have since been added, at a cost of £960, largely through the energy and liberality of Rev. R. Key. In 1872, the old Lakenham Chapel gave place to the present fine suite of buildings in Queen's Road. In 1879, a new mission was opened in Nelson Street, beyond Dereham Road, and a chapel and schools built at a cost of £1200; and, in 1892, a mission was opened in Thorpe, and

216 PRIMITIVE METHODIST CHURCH.

a school-hall built at a cost of £900, which has now given place to the beautiful Scott Memorial Church, erected by Rev. John Smith at a cost of some £6000.

Norwich has had a long succession of devoted, earnest officials. Far away back were William Wilson, William Dawson, John Huggins, and William Elmer. Later on, we have the names of Samuel Jarrold, founder of the well-known publishing house, and Messrs. Reeves, Eggleton, and Spinks. Nor must Elizabeth Bultitude, our last female travelling-preacher, be forgotten. She was converted in 1828 at a camp meeting on Mousehold Heath led by Samuel Atterby, and preached her trial sermon in old Lakenham Chapel. In 1832, she was called to the ministry by Norwich Circuit, and for thirty years discharged

SCOTT MEMORIAL CHURCH, THORPE ROAD, NORWICH.

the full duties of an itinerant, chiefly in the old Norwich District, at a time when the work was arduous, the salary poor, and the difficulties many. At her superannuation in 1862 she settled in Norwich, where she died in 1891, at the ripe age of eighty-one years. The Conference, in its annual address to the stations, noted the disappearance of her name from the list of preachers where it had stood so long, "as though to remind us that the gifts of the Holy Spirit were without distinction of sex."

It is clear even from the brief outline just given that, like many other circuits, Norwich had its intermediate period of reaction and distress. When we find the circuit reduced to one preacher and 109 members, as was the case in 1829, it must, one thinks, have been within measurable distance of extinction. Certain minutes recorded in the books of the Hull Circuit throw unexpected light on this trying period, and when their origin and purport are explained they show that, at the prompting of W. Clowes, Hull was ready to lend a helping hand to a struggling circuit. It could come down from its "high popularity" to act the part of the good Samaritan. W. Clowes visited Norwich in 1830 and again in 1831. In the former year he assisted at a Missionary Meeting in Rose Yard Chapel. He remarks in his *Journal* that the city of Norwich, notwithstanding its thirty-six parish churches and numerous clergy, is fearfully wicked. On his next visit, "after conversing with our friends belonging to Rose Yard Chapel, I saw," says he, "the necessity of a preacher being appointed to officiate therein, and to mission sundry places around the city."

ELIZABETH BULTITUDE.

ELIZABETH BULTITUDE'S HOUSE.

218 PRIMITIVE METHODIST CHURCH.

The outcome of this may be seen in the following enactment of the Conference of 1831 :—

Q.—" How shall Rose Yard be managed ?
A.—" That chapel and its dependencies shall be annexed to Hull Circuit."

And so it was. In June, 1831, David Beattie was sent as a missionary, and in September he was asked if there was room for another. Six months he laboured at Rose Yard, and was succeeded by Thomas Bennett. In 1832, Norwich reported 533 members, and the tide had turned.

II.—KING'S LYNN.

When, in the year 1821, Messrs. Oscroft and Charlton, finding their Lincolnshire Circuits over-manned, skirted the Wash to begin their mission in Norfolk, King's Lynn was naturally, from its position and importance, one of the first places they visited. From the very first they met here with an encouraging measure of success; so much so indeed, that a letter written at the time affirms—"the Primitives are carrying all before them in King's Lynn." The leader of the first class formed is said to have been Mr. Streader, whose son was to share with John Ellerthorpe of Hull, another of our co-religionists, the distinction of having saved so many lives from drowning that the mere recital of their exploits makes up a goodly volume.* But, unfortunately, disaster soon overtook the promising cause; for when Hugh Bourne wrote of "shattered circuits," and of the employment of "improper persons" as the cause of their shattering, he was certainly thinking of Lynn, and of the disloyal and divisive conduct of the preacher once in charge. We have already alluded to these unhappy occurrences, and

BENNET'S YARD.
Where first preaching services were held in King's Lynn.

* See Rev. H. Woodcock's "The Hero of the Humber, or, the Story of John Ellerthorpe," and Rev. S. Horton's "To the Rescue;" being the Life of W. T. Streader.

need not dwell on them further.* The history of Lynn Primitive Methodism began anew in the year 1825, when G. W. Bellham, who had done such good work in the Loughborough Circuit, was appointed to Lynn, his native place, and began his twenty-four years of service in the Norwich District, then in but a rudimentary condition. He had a heavy task before him; but he bravely set himself, in the spirit of Nehemiah, to repair the breach. He brought back concord to the society, built a small chapel, and began a Sabbath school which became, as it still is, one of the most flourishing schools in the District. He also enlarged the bounds of the Circuit by missioning Swaffham,

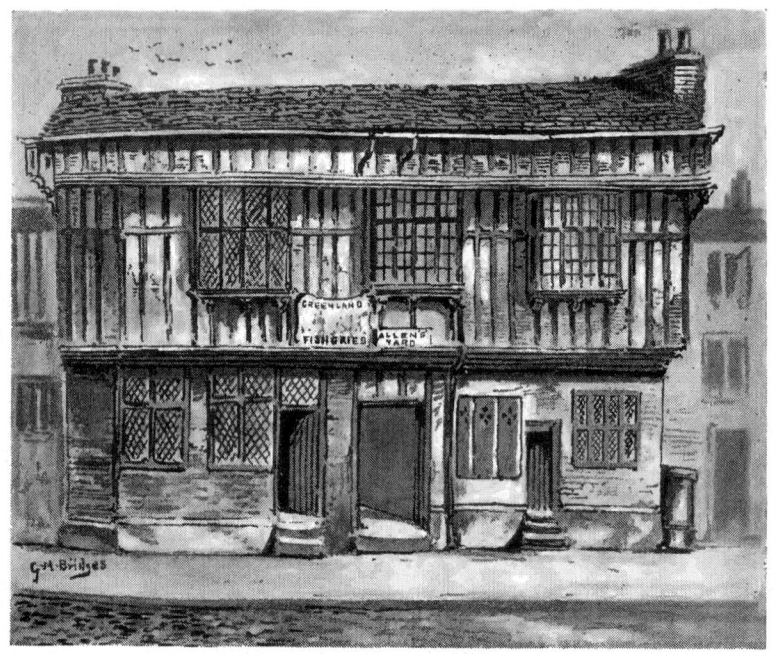

ALLEN'S YARD.
Where the first Primitive Methodist Sunday School was held in King's Lynn.

Litcham, and other places more in the centre of the county. It was at Litcham, while holding a service near the stocks, that the familiar trio of parson, lawyer, and constable came on the scene. In the end, Mr. Bellham was given in charge of the constable, and next day was brought before Col. R——, of Lexham Hall.

"What Act am I taken up under?" asked Mr. Bellham of the Magistrate.
Magistrate.—"The Vagrant Act. You are a common vagrant."
Mr. B.—"I did not do anything to obtain money."

* See vol. i. p. 322.

Magistrate.—"I meant the Riot Act. You collected a great number of persons together, I suppose to make a riot, as it was late in the evening."

Mr. B.—"If I am taken up under the Riot Act, I have no business here. Commit me to prison, and let me take my trial before more than one magistrate."

Magistrate, with an oath.—"Be off out of my sight."

Mr. B.—"It is wrong to swear, sir. Jesus Christ hath said, 'Swear not at all.'"

Magistrate.—"Then don't provoke me." At last the Magistrate, being rather rusty in his law and getting the worst in the encounter, said: "Go about your business."

Mr. B.—"When I am properly discharged, sir."

Magistrate.—"Are you any trade?"

Mr. B.—"I am a shipwright. I served seven years under Mr. B—— of Lynn."

Magistrate.—"You are a fine fellow—a shipwright, a parson, and a lawyer. Well you may go about your business; I have no more to say to you."

Clergyman to the Magistrate.—"Stop, sir, there is something for him to pay. Constable, what is it?"

Constable.—"Eight and ninepence, sir."

Clergyman to Mr. B.—"Eight and ninepence. You will discharge that bill, and then you are at liberty."

Mr. B.—"I am at liberty, sir. The magistrate has set me at liberty."

Magistrate to the Clergyman.—"Let the fellow go."

Clergyman.—"But who is to pay the eight and ninepence?"

Magistrate.—"Pay it yourself; bringing your fellows here."

Mr. B.—"I'll pay it if it is just and right. But I think the debt belongs to Mr. H."

Magistrate.—"Be off."

Mr. B.—"Good morning, gentlemen."

We are told that Mr. Bellham and the clergyman left the room together, Mr. B. saying to him: "God forgive you, sir; I wish you well"; but the clergyman was too chagrined to reply.

The country thus missioned in 1825 by Mr. Bellham became, in 1836, the Swaffham Circuit. From Litcham Messrs. James and Mark Warnes went out into the ministry; while Sporle, near Swaffham, was the native place of Horatio Hall and Robert Ward, the Connexion's pioneer missionary to New Zealand.

Another notable advance was made by the Lynn Circuit in 1831, when John Smith (1) became the superintendent of the station. He had come from his native Tunstall District in exchange for Thomas Batty. His name is carved deep in the history of the Norwich District, not because of any special intellectual powers he possessed, but because of the intensity of his zeal and his single-minded purpose to save men. Well might men, as they reflected on what his advent had meant for the churches of East Anglia, say to themselves: "There was a man sent from God whose name was John." By March, 1832, the membership of the circuit had increased by 234, and the circuit was stimulated to enter once more upon missionary labours. Mr. James Pole was sent to the north-western corner of the county, and missioned Holme, Hunstanton, Ringstead, Docking, Snettisham, and many other places. The mission proved so successful that, in 1836, Snettisham became the head of a new circuit, afterwards to be known as Docking Circuit. The village of Anmer is in the Docking station. From an interesting communication we have received from Rev. F. B. Paston, we learn that the time was when the old squire of the village placed Primitive Methodism under ban. No services were allowed on his estate. At his death the young squire, whose acquaintance Mr. Paston had made, removed the ban and showed himself friendly; but King Edward VII., who acquired the village by purchase and added it to his Norfolk estate, has shown himself a friend indeed to our Church. He has built us a beautiful village sanctuary, which was recently opened by the Rev. Thomas Woodall of Lynn.

In 1833, the membership of Lynn Circuit was reported as 1170, being an increase of 843 for the preceding five years. It should be noted, too, that about the year 1835 Lynn sent W. Kirby to commence a mission at Peterborough which, in 1839, became the Peterborough Circuit.

LONDON ROAD CHAPEL.
The first Primitive Methodist Chapel in King's Lynn.

Returning now to the town of Lynn: the next notable event in its history was the holding of the first of the two Conferences that have met here—that of 1836. The chapel had recently undergone its second enlargement, and amongst the services held therein were preaching services at five o'clock in the morning. At this Conference the Minutes were consolidated by the Conference itself, the onerous duty having apparently been shirked by the General Committee! It had been noised abroad that the authorities would interfere to prevent the processioning of the streets of the royal borough on the Sunday. None the less, the procession moved along, and one of the senior brethren not only preached a short sermon as they went on but also engaged in prayer. The camp meeting, held on Hardwick Green, was said to have been one of the largest ever held. Numberless conveyances of every kind—waggons, carts, gigs, besides single horses—had brought the people from a distance of ten, twenty, thirty, and even forty miles. Lynn's second Conference was held in 1844.

London Road Chapel was opened, March 31st, 1859. The site on which it stands had formerly been occupied by the ancient chapel of St. James. At the Dissolution it became a hospital for "poor and impotent people," and still later a workhouse. The acquisition of such a site for a Primitive Methodist chapel was regarded as little short of a scandal by a certain section of the inhabitants, and every available means was tried to defeat the project—but in vain.

The foundation-stone of this new structure had been laid by Mr. William Lift, of whom a few words must be said. Converted in 1828 when the church was but seven years old, Mr. Lift survived until 1893, thus enjoying sixty-five years' fellowship with the society. For sixty-one years he was a local preacher. "His position in the King's Lynn station was simply unique. He grew up with it, he lived through two generations of members and hearers, he helped to nourish and make it what it is, and in turn he was nourished and sustained by it. In truth we may say that he was in turn both the child and the father of the station. He gave thought and time and strength to promote its spiritual growth, and his wealth to aid its material expansion and financial prosperity. The evidence of this is found in the fact that his name is cut into the foundation-stones of twenty-one chapels or schools, and what is surpassingly better, his name is cut into tables, 'not of stone,' but in tables that are hearts of flesh. Hundreds revere his memory, and hold his name and work in undying remembrance. Having grown up with the station, and become inseparably associated with all its interests and movements, it was but natural for the Quarterly Meeting in 1853 to appoint Mr. Lift as its Steward, and to renew that appointment no less than one hundred and twenty-six times."*

WILLIAM LIFT.

III., IV.:—FAKENHAM; UPWELL.

We regret that so little is known of the earlier history of the Fakenham and Upwell Circuits. These centres, as probably also Wisbech and Cambridge, would be amongst the fifty-seven places found on the plan of the Norfolk Mission, which J. Oscroft says was printed in April, 1821. In 1824, Fakenham Circuit had no fewer than six travelling-preachers appointed to it. In 1826, North Walsham Circuit was formed. This new circuit, as we shall see, subsequently sent Robert Key on a mission which, in 1832, resulted in the formation of the Mattishall—afterwards called East Dereham Circuit. Fakenham also, in 1842, missioned Oundle in Northamptonshire, soon afterwards transferred to the General Missionary Committee.

Upwell's chief claim to notice, in the absence of other information, must rest on the active part it took in early missionary enterprise. In 1828, Brandon, in Suffolk, became a circuit, and it is probable, as Mr. Petty seems to suggest, that it was reached by the first missionaries to Norfolk. At that time, what was known as Marshland Fen, at the western extremity of Norfolk, was a desolate and barren region. Little of it was then under cultivation, and the moral condition of its inhabitants was conformable to their surroundings. They habitually disregarded the Sabbath, and might have said with the navvy, "Sunday has not cropped out here yet"; for there were no ministers or places for public worship. In 1832, Mr. James Garner

JAMES GARNER.

* "William Lift: a Life Nourished by Service," in *Aldersgate*, 1894, pp. 911-13, by Rev. John Smith.

made his way into Marshland, and he was soon followed by other missionaries. For two years services were held in the house of Mr. Collins, then in a lean-to which he erected near his outbuildings. Finally in 1855, largely through the generosity and zeal of Mr. and Mrs. Neep and Messrs. Collins and Taylor, a neat chapel was erected for the society which had done so much for the moral and spiritual enlightenment of that neglected district.

To two missionaries of Upwell Circuit belongs the honour of having materially extended the Connexion in the county of Essex. Messrs. Redhead and J. Jackson were, at the March Quarterly Meeting of 1838, set apart for missionary work; but no precise directions were given them. They went forth almost at a venture, and at the end of a long day's journey, found themselves at Saffron Walden, forty miles away. Here, on the 2nd of May, Mr. Redhead preached in the open-air in Castle Street, and he and his colleague also visited many villages. The entire cost of the mission for two

THE CHURCH AND MANSE, DOWNHAM MARKET.

years was £65, which, we are told, was regarded as unusually heavy! The mission continued to prosper both before and after it was turned over to the General Missionary Committee, and in 1850 Saffron Walden became a circuit with 516 members. Upwell also missioned the city of Ely.

The old Upwell Circuit is now Downham Market, a place first missioned, but afterwards given up, by Lynn. Early in the 'Thirties the Upwell Circuit, under the superintendency of that indefatigable and successful minister, Samuel Atterby, remissioned the place. A cottage was first used for services, and afterwards, in 1834, a barn was fitted up. The first chapel was erected in 1855, largely through the instrumentality of Mr. and Mrs. Kemp, who now resided at Downham Market. We give views of the present Church and Manse, erected in 1871, also of the late Rev. J. Kemish, who spent nine useful years on this station. Downham Market has also been fortunate in having had Mr. W. Sexton Proctor as its Circuit Steward for so many years, a convert of John Smith (1), and a local preacher for fifty-six years. It is singular that this Primitive Methodist official also filled the office of churchwarden for twenty-one years, and was twice elected by the vicar as his warden. The Assistant Circuit Steward, Mr. Rose, has also been, and is, a stay and support to the Circuit.

Nor does this exhaust the missionary enterprises of the Upwell or Downham Circuit. Ely was prepared for self-government by being its Branch, and it began missions at Ramsey (now incorporated with Peterborough) and Buckden.

Wisbech formed part of Upwell Circuit until 1833, when it was granted independence. It was first visited, in 1821, by the Nottingham missionaries, who took their stand in the Horse-Fair. At first they met with considerable opposition, and had to combat strong prejudice, so that slow progress was made. The first preaching-place was the humble cottage of a tinker who was one of the first converts, and this was afterwards exchanged for a barn. Yet Wisbech, from an early date had connected with it some estimable persons who had also, what was very valuable—staying power. Such were Mr. Gubbins,

REV. J. KEMISH.

VIEW FROM THE NORTH BRINK, WISBECH. EARLY 19TH CENTURY.

Mrs. Miller, and especially Mr. M. Taylor and his wife, who were well-known in the district for their hospitality and Christian kindness. A notable acquisition to the society was Edwin Waller, a Wesleyan local preacher, who after mature deliberation, in which he counted all costs, united with the society, and continued to be its staunch friend and supporter until his death, in 1854. We have already met with several bearers of the name of Waller, who have deserved well of the Connexion.

We do not forget the Wallers of the Manchester District, or Thomas Waller, the coke-burner, of Blaydon ; and this Edwin Waller, "earthenware dealer," of Wisbech, was evidently a notable figure in the Norwich District in his day. He was for long the corresponding member of its District Committee; often its chosen representative to the Annual Conference, and in other ways he played an influential part. He was, we are told, and we can well believe it, a man of extensive reading, of close thought, and great originality. Being a man in easy, if not affluent circumstances, he was able to render material help to the struggling societies. He became responsible for the rent of the better preaching-room which was now taken, and he willingly incurred the responsibility of trusteeship for Connexional buildings. In addition to this, by his prudent counsels and his abundant labours as a local preacher, he greatly assisted in the development of the Wisbech Circuit and of Holbeach, which was a branch of Wisbech until 1855. The circuit took its part in missionary efforts in Huntingdonshire and at Ramsey, though the shifting relations of these missions to Wisbech, Upwell, and other circuits is too intricate a matter to be unravelled here.

V.—CAMBRIDGE.

Our two ancient University towns gave our first missionaries a scurvy reception. Oxford well-nigh smothered G. W. Bellham with filth; Cambridge did its best to starve Joseph Reynolds. In August, 1821, he found his way here from distant Tunstall. The letter he wrote giving an account of his experience is, indeed, "a human document"—a transcript from the life, touching in its very simplicity, and revealing a heroism all unconscious of itself, which even hunger could not subdue. As we have said elsewhere, it might have been written by a suffering follower of George Fox long ago. We give an extract :—

"DEAR BRETHREN,—When I left Tunstall, I gave myself up to labour and sufferings, and I have gone through both ; but praise the Lord, it has been for His glory and the good of souls. My sufferings are known only to God and myself. I have many times been knocked down while preaching, and have often had sore bones. Once I was knocked down, and was trampled under the feet of the crowd, and had my clothes torn, and all my money taken from me. In consequence of this I have been obliged to suffer much hunger. One day I travelled nearly thirty miles and had only a penny cake to eat. I preached at night to near two thousand persons. But I was so weak when I had done, that I could scarcely stand. I then made my supper of cold cabbage, and slept under a haystack in a field till about four o'clock in the morning. The singing of the birds then awoke me, and I arose and went into the town, and preached at five to many people. I afterwards came to Cambridge, where I have been a fortnight, and preached to a great congregation, though almost worn out with fatigue and hunger. To-day I was glad to eat the pea-husks as I walked on the road. But I bless God that much good has been done. I believe hundreds will have to bless Him in eternity for leading me hither."

When next the curtain rises on Cambridge, March, 1824, we see it a branch of Nottingham, but about to be made a circuit. Its two preachers are to be lent to it until the District Meeting, and the new circuit is requested not to appoint Delegates to the said District Meeting unless they can pay their own expenses. At Midsummer of the same year, W. Clowes and John Nelson were at Cambridge for the purpose of re-opening the chapel, which had been enlarged by the putting in of a gallery. Clowes, preaching in the evening, had a sprinkling of collegians in his congregation, while the Wesleyan superintendent assisted in taking up the collection.

Again the curtain drops, and Cambridge is lost to view; unless, indeed, the curtain is unexpectedly lifted by the biographer of the Rev. Charles Simeon,* the famous Evangelical leader. There was, he tells us, in Cambridge,

"A certain enthusiastic Nonconformist labourer named 'Johnny Stittle'; a kind of well-meaning, self-constituted city missionary in the viler parts of Cambridge, and called by the undergraduates a 'Ranter.' He used to hold his meetings in a room, and when the attendance grew too large for one room, he threw down the partitions and used the whole floor of the house; and again enlarged his improvised chapel by taking in also the upper story, cutting out the central part of the bedroom floor, but leaving enough to make a wide gallery all round, upheld by pillars. As he was but a day-labourer, it was understood that Mr. Simeon aided him in the expense of these alterations. This man and his services were the butt of many a thoughtless young gownsman, who used to stand outside and look in at his chapel window and listen for amusement's sake, and whose annoyances he yet patiently and kindly bore. On some occasion of bitterness he is said to have invited a railing youth to his house to partake of the 'herby-pie' supper provided for himself and family, and then persuaded him to stay and join in his simple but hearty family worship, which resulted in the young man's beginning to think seriously on religion, and ultimately becoming a valuable clergyman."*

In this extract the "self-constituted city missionary" has given him the same reproachful name our fathers bore; nor, indeed, do we know of any other denomination, besides our own, that, before 1836—the year of Simeon's death—would have made room for John Stittle and his methods. We have not the least objection to acknowledge him as one of ourselves, especially as the sermon given as a specimen of his preaching would do no discredit to any Cambridge pulpit.

In the course of years, circuits, like soldiers on a long march, are apt to drop out of the ranks. So it was with Cambridge, for a short time. In 1842, it ranks as the eighteenth circuit in the Norwich District, whereas it began, in 1825, as the third. The explanation is that for three years—1834 to 1836 inclusive—it disappeared from the list of stations, but came on again in 1837. The plan of 1842 shows six places, which include Waterbeach, St. Ives, and Huntingdon. St. Peter's Street Chapel had recently been acquired, and by 1855 the progress of the circuit was such that a second chapel was secured in Barnwell, the eastern district of the town. This was Fitzroy Street Chapel, the first which the Wesleyans had possessed in Cambridge, and had now vacated. This building was secured on generous terms, and opened by Miss M. C. Buck, the most popular female preacher in this period of our history.

MISS M. C. BUCK.

* "Recollections of the Conversational Parties of the Rev. Charles Simeon, etc.," by A. W. Brown, M.A., pp. 13-15.

Miss Buck was called into the ministry by the Burland Circuit in 1836 and although, unlike Miss Bultitude, she ceased "to travel" in the technical sense, she continued to be in great request for special services. The fact that Cambridge provided for the Conference of 1857 marks the advance which, by this time, it had made.

A word as to the interesting towns of Huntingdon and St. Ives, so full of Cromwellian associations. From the *Journals* of W. Dawson in the *Magazine* for 1822, we learn that as a preacher of the Boston Circuit, he spent a week in missioning this neighbourhood. Under date of September 2nd, 1821, he writes: "I spoke to a large congregation in the market-place at Huntingdon. Some seemed to wonder, some mocked, and some wept. At two, I spoke at Godmanchester: very many attended. At six, T. Steele, from Tunstall, spoke at Huntingdon, together with a blind young man out of Cheshire." He further says he formed a class of seven members at Godmanchester. Whether

THE BRIDGE AND QUAY, ST. IVES, HUNTS.

Wisbech found any vestiges of this visit when it began its missionary labours in Huntingdonshire, we know not. As for St. Ives, tradition, apparently trustworthy, gives 1837 as the year when Primitive Methodism entered the town. It is said to have been brought by one — Bridge and Mrs. Beel. The former is on the Cambridge plan of 1842 and, as a member of the Circuit Committee, was evidently a leading official. The first building occupied is said to have been the old Baptist Chapel in Water Lane, and much later a remove was made to a building on the Quay, said to be the oldest meeting-house in Huntingdonshire, having been used by successive bodies of Nonconformists for two hundred years. This was occupied until the present new and handsome building was erected.* In 1897, the General Missionary Committee made St. Ives a circuit, and it was annexed to the Lynn and Cambridge District.

* See article in *Aldersgate Magazine*, 1896, pp. 282-6.

VI.—YARMOUTH.

Though one of the primary circuits of the original Norwich District, this strong circuit was in its beginning an offshoot of Norwich. Yet persistent tradition points to a man rather than to a circuit, to individual Christian effort rather than to official action, as having paved the way for the establishment of a Primitive Methodist cause in Yarmouth. One Driver, a Primitive Methodist from the Midlands, drawn here by his employment, is said to have preached in the open-air and, if he did not actually organise a society, to have "made ready a people prepared for the Lord." However this may be—and one could wish it might be true—we are on undisputed ground in giving 1822 as the date when the evangelists from Norwich took their stand on the Hog Hill, with their backs to the Fisherman's Hospital wall, and proclaimed the gospel. J. Brame, a travelling preacher, and Mr. J. Turnpenny are said to have been the names of the missionaries. Periodical visits continued to be paid by the preachers from Norwich, and on February 14th, 1823, a preaching licence was obtained for a house in Row 60. In 1824, Yarmouth was made a circuit, and it appears as the fifth station of the newly-formed Norwich District on the stations for 1825.

Just as the magnificent Church of the Nativity, built by Helena, the mother of Constantine, has deep down at its heart the rocky stable where Christ was born, linking together on the same spot the present and the past in striking contrast, so the Temple, the chief edifice of Yarmouth Primitive Methodism, stands on the identical site of the hay-loft which, in 1829, was the society's humble sanctuary. The Temple epitomises the history of our Church in the town, alike in its continuity and the striking contrast it presents to the first and successive buildings it has superseded. First there stood here the hay-loft already mentioned. It was the upper storey of a building which had once done duty as a joiner's shop. Its roof was pantiled, its once unglazed apertures were now filled in with small-paned leaded windows, and it was furnished with stiff rail-backed seats. In front of the loft was an open space, flanked by a saw-pit on one side and by stables on the other. This open space was reached by a path some ten feet wide, having some tumble-down, disreputable town-houses on either hand. For these domiciles the occupants paid no rent: they were mere squatters—unthrifty, idle, depraved; so that intending worshippers had to make their way to the hay-loft through filthy and repulsive surroundings, and run the gauntlet of ribald jests or maledictions. Yet this unsavoury spot had a history going far back; for the hay-loft rested partly on, and partly over, a portion of the old town-wall, and it stood on the Priory Plain, afore-time covered by a religious house. So here, at Yarmouth, as at Lynn and Scarborough, Primitive Methodism put its sanctuary down on the very spot where, in Mediæval times, monks abode, where they paced to and fro in the cloisters and chanted in the choir, until they sank into sloth and vice, and King Henry, as the besom of the Lord, swept them all away.

SAMUEL ATTERBY.

Stage No. 2 was reached when "the diligent and judicious Samuel Atterby" turned the unpolished building into a galleried chapel. It was in 1827 that this first Tabernacle

THE PERIOD OF CIRCUIT PREDOMINANCE AND ENTERPRISE. 229

was reared, and it lasted until 1850. Then, as John Smith, the superintendent, was in declining health and nearing the verge, Thomas Swindell indefatigably laboured at the scheme of enlargement. This was done for both chapel and school at a cost of £750.

In connection with the opening of this second Tabernacle, a truly monster tea-meeting was held that is talked of to this day. Seven marquees were joined to form one tent, pitched in front of the Children's Hospital, and here eleven hundred people sat down at the tables. By the erection of "the Temple" in 1876 the crowning stage was surely reached; but, lest it should be thought that pride had anything to do with the bestowment of the name, its genesis had better be recorded. When it was suggested that the proposed building should be called a "Church," a veteran local preacher exclaimed: "Church? You'd better call it a Temple straight away"; and Temple it *was* called. The only untoward event that marred the success of the Temple, was an accident that

THOMAS SWINDELL.

YARMOUTH FIRST TEMPLE.

occurred while it was in course of erection. By the fall of coping-stones a young workman almost immediately lost his life, and Mr. T. Kirk, a trustee deeply interested in the progress of the building, received such hurt as resulted in his death. Mercifully, Mr. T. W. Swindell, who was with him at the time, escaped without injury. As the Rev. T. Swindell had so much to do with the building of the second Tabernacle, so his son, just named, the Steward of the Circuit, by his zeal, financial skill, and fertility of resource, greatly contributed to bring this larger enterprise to a successful issue.

Yarmouth has a good record for its Sunday School work. Very early a Sunday School was established, at which writing as well as reading was taught. It was located first in the Garden Row, subsequently in the two other rooms shown in our pictures, and then

T. W. SWINDELL.

230 PRIMITIVE METHODIST CHURCH.

it was removed in turn to the old and to the new school-rooms. The weekly marching of the children—at one time numbering five hundred—through the streets to the chapel, stirred up the church people of the town to establish a school for themselves. Messrs. R. Todd, J. F. Neave, Robert Bell, W. Patterson, and W. Buddery have successively laboured through the years as superintendents or Bible-class teachers, in connection with the school. Of these and others, interesting reminiscences are given by Mr. Arthur Patterson in his monograph on Yarmouth Primitive Methodism, to which we express large indebtedness.* Mr. Patterson, as an old scholar and infant class teacher and "lightning sketcher," has found a congenial task; nor would any history of Yarmouth Primitive Methodism be complete which should contain no reference to

PRIMITIVE METHODIST TEMPLE, YARMOUTH.

what Mr. Patterson has achieved in other directions. By his contributions to our Connexional literature, and by his recent works on Natural History, recording the results of years of careful observation, he has obtained a more than local reputation, while the story of his life of self-help and devotion to natural science is worthy to be placed side by side with the lives of Edward, or Dick of Thurso.

Previous to the building of the Temple, extensions in the borough had taken place by the erection, at the South End, of Queen Street Chapel (1867). Mr. George Baker, J.P., materially assisted in this extension, and afterwards received the thanks of Conference for his gift to the chapel of an organ costing £130.

* "From Hayloft to Temple: the Story of Primitive Methodism in Yarmouth." 1903. London, R. Bryant.

THE PERIOD OF CIRCUIT PREDOMINANCE AND ENTERPRISE. 231

ENTRANCE TO SCHOOLROOM, YARMOUTH.
Now a Tramps' Lodging-house.

So far as persecution by the populace is concerned, Yarmouth can show a clean sheet. In the early days, the singing of the old hymns seems to have operated like a charm in mollifying the passions of those whom it drew to the open-air services. Once and again the authorities have backslidden into intolerance, and their attempts to put down preaching in the open spaces of the town have had to be resisted. The worst case occurred in 1854, when several persons were arrested for holding a service at the Hall Quay. At the trial which ensued, the accused were ably defended by Mr. Tillett of Norwich, a staunch Nonconformist. The magistrates found themselves in a cleft stick and, in the end, the case was dismissed. At a later period the authorities had another relapse, but the Rev. John Smith (2) at once took steps to vindicate the right to hold services at the Jetty. It is but due to say that, in 1888, the Salvation Army were much more roughly handled at Yarmouth than our fathers had ever been, and the magistrates incurred considerable odium by instituting proceedings against them—a course which, in the end, produced a strong reaction in their favour.

By successive partitions, Yarmouth has become five circuits at least. As early as 1823, Wangford, twenty miles away, and Beccles fifteen, were within its area, and regularly supplied with preachers. When, in 1833, the Wangford Branch was made a circuit, with Richard Howchin as its superintendent, it reported 233 members. Extensive missionary operations were at once begun in the surrounding villages. More than a score of these were visited, and many of them were morally transformed. The result was seen in the report of 540 members given to the Conference of 1835. Wangford has been, and still is a strong country station, and from the beginning has always had in it a number of loyal adherents of the Connexion.

Lowestoft was an integral part of Yarmouth Circuit until 1870, and Acle and Martham until 1883. Alderman Adam Adams was called

ST. JOHN'S HEAD ROW, YARMOUTH.
Our old Schoolroom on the right.

into the ministry by Yarmouth Circuit, and stationed there 1852-4; but his health failing him he became a successful man of business, and has long been one of Lowestoft's prominent and public-spirited citizens. He has been its Mayor, a candidate for Parliamentary honours, and he is a Justice of the Peace. But, it is safe to say, he attaches more importance to the position he holds as a hard-working local preacher and active official. He has few vacant Sundays; his time being equally divided between his own circuit and lending assistance to neighbouring ones. His Connexional recognition came in 1900 when he was appointed Vice-President of Conference, and as such his portrait will be found hereafter in its due order.

We must refer our readers to Mr. Patterson's book for interesting reminiscences of some of the veteran local preachers of the Yarmouth Circuit—men like John Bitton, who was on the plan of 1824, and preached when he was eighty-four, dying at last, in 1886, at ninety-three years of age; William Perry, forty-six years a local

A. PATTERSON.

YARMOUTH HALL QUAY.

preacher; George Bell, who gave thirty-seven years of his life to the same work, and two sons to the ministry; John Mason, a local preacher for over thirty-six years; and Henry Futter, still spared to the Church he has served so long.

Mr. Patterson also gives the names of some twenty ministers whom the Yarmouth Circuit has sent forth. The list includes the names of J. G. Smith, the son of John Smith (1); of George and Benjamin Bell; G. Rudram and F. B. Paston. But of all who in the early days were closely associated with Yarmouth, none left so deep and lasting an impression on the District, of which they were largely the makers and fashioners, as did John Smith (1) and Robert Key. It was at Yarmouth the former closed at once his ministry of twenty-seven years

RICHARD HOWCHIN.

and his life. It was at Yarmouth, too, Robert Key began his Christian course. The presence at the services of the rough coal-heaver occasioned surprise not unmixed with fear; for it was hard to think anything but a mischievous intent had brought him there. Like Clowes he was a branch, but rougher and more unpromising, of the "olive tree which is wild by nature;" but he was "grafted in"—"brought in" our fathers termed it—and the process was finished on Easter Sunday, 1823, and very soon the new nature began to show itself in the overcoming of the defects of a meagre education and of a strong but undisciplined character. By 1825 or 1826 he had become a local preacher, when local preachers were few and their journeys long and frequent. It is interesting to note that Anthony Race of Weardale, who died at Yarmouth in 1828, was of great assistance to Robert Key by his powerful preaching of the doctrine of entire sanctification, and still more by the exemplification of the doctrine in his own life. The influence exerted upon him by this apostolic man was so great that, we are told, "no wear or tear of years or circumstances was ever able to efface it." In 1828, Robert Key received his call to the ministry.

It is but natural we should desire to know something more than can be derived from

JOHN BITTON.   WILLIAM PERRY.   GEORGE BELL.   JOHN MASON.

tradition, however trustworthy, of these men to whom Primitive Methodism in the Eastern Counties owed so much in the early days. Fortunately, we have a sketch of these two pioneers by a contemporary and competent hand. Mr. G. T. Goodrick, who had himself been a travelling preacher for three years, retired in 1835 to Yarmouth, where he became a leading official. He became well known to the Connexional authorities, and their confidence in him is seen in his appointment as one of the Connexional Auditors. Mr. Goodrick left behind him a "Life" of Robert Key, which has never been published. From this valuable work we take the following discriminating characterisation of John Smith (1) and Robert Key:—

"John Smith—a man of God; of all we have met, we think we never did find a man so much under the influence of 'this travailing for souls.' He was not a great preacher. He had no acquired powers of oratory. His pulpit efforts were generally disjointed in arrangement; and, as a man seeking popularity by such methods, he would certainly have failed. But no hearer could doubt his sincerity, nor fail to perceive, if he had spiritual perception at all, that the preacher felt for souls. Indeed, he was a man of two ideas—personal holiness and the conversion of sinners. These were, one or the other, generally both, the burden of his sermons, and the topics of his conversation. And so constantly and so surely did he think of men as sinners, and the necessity of their salvation, that it sometimes absorbed all other considerations of time and place, and made him silent in the midst of the most congenial society. At other times he would literally groan as if under a burden, and would express himself as if he could not live unless souls were saved. This, to some, seemed to savour of rudeness, indecorum, and even of a pharisaical spirit. But what prayers! what power! what influence attended his words! We have heard him pray until the place was as if shaken. He was as a prince with God, for wrestling he overcame, and streams of mercy flowed among the assembly. We have known him lay his hand upon persons and bring them to their knees without uttering a word; and a whole congregation, as it were, gasp for breath while listening to his impassioned and inspired appeals, in which he was sometimes lost for language, and coming to a sudden stop would electrify his hearers by a single word or shout of 'Glory!'—a shout that was, as a simple countryman expressed it, 'Worth some men's whole sermons.' His soul burned within him to save the souls of others, and, as in other instances, burned too fast for endurance; and after a brilliant career of success in some circuits in the Norwich District, entered into rest, December 7th, 1851, at the early age of fifty-one.

"Between these two men, Brothers Key and Smith, there was a great similarity of feeling, thought, and experience, and if need be, we might almost substitute one mental picture for another; only Mr. Key was of a livelier disposition, a warmer temperament, had greater mental resources, and a greater aptitude for the business and arrangements incident to the establishment of a church or society. He was thus better qualified as a missionary, while his good brother Smith found a field for labour in the already enclosed portions of his Master's vineyard. Both toiled and wept and prayed, 'travailing for souls,' and now both 'rest from their labours and their works do follow them.'"

PRIMITIVE METHODISM AND THE AGRICULTURAL VILLAGES OF EAST ANGLIA.

The work done in East Anglia between 1825 and 1842 was remarkable, even on the imperfect showing of statistics. Here are the figures for the two years set out side by side, making comparison easy and leading to an obvious inference.

	1825.		1842.
Circuits	6	Circuits	19
Ministers	13	Ministers	59
Members	1546	Members	9072

And yet the figures furnish but imperfect evidence. From the very nature of the case a very large percentage of the direct, no less than the indirect, results accomplished, must have fallen to the share of Churches which seemed to have a strong hereditary claim and had more to offer. Often enough they carried off the full stook to their well-filled granary, and left us only the gleanings of our own harvest. The words of Christ were reversed: We laboured, and others entered into our labours. Especially was this the case in Suffolk and Essex, where the Congregational and Baptist Churches have deeply rooted themselves. At Bury St. Edmunds, for example, Mr. Petty tells of a Nonconformist minister who stated that he had admitted eighty persons to church-membership, who attributed their enlightenment to the open-air preaching of the Primitive Methodists. This is not written by way of complaint, but simply to show that, in any estimate of the good effected by our Church in the Eastern Counties during this time, account must also be taken of the extent to which other Churches were augmented and quickened by our labours.

But as to these figures themselves: they represent a most active and persistent village evangelisation. Some idea of the network reticulations of this evangelisation may be gained by an inspection of the circuit plans of the time. Here, for instance, is the plan of North Walsham Circuit, in the north-eastern corner of Norfolk, for the year 1835. And what a plan it is! as large as a page of the *Primitive Methodist World*, having on it the names of sixty-one villages and sixty-nine preachers and exhorters.

And here is the plan of the Mattishall, now East Dereham Circuit and Saham Branch, not much smaller than that of North Walsham, showing fifty-two villages and forty-five preachers. When we get to know how the Mattishall Circuit was carved out of Mid-Norfolk by Robert Key, this plan becomes a most significant broadsheet. The story of the making of this circuit is an interesting chapter in Norfolk village evangelisation—a chapter which rightly begins by showing us the antecedents of these half-hundred villages in the heart of Norfolk; what was their moral and religious condition before Robert Key set foot in them and went on circuit. Had we a map of the England of that time—a map showing, by its gradations of light and shade, how near any district approached to the recognised standard of good morals and religion, or how far it fell short of such standard, then we should find these parts around East Dereham deeply shaded, while some of the villages thereabouts, would stand out on the map like dark islets.

CHURCH OF EAST DEREHAM.
Where Cowper was buried.

In justification of what is here written we would adduce the testimony of Canon Jessopp, the genial archæologist, historian, and broad-minded political economist. No man knows the history of his own county, or the past and present condition of the peasantry of Norfolk, better than he. In 1879, he was instituted to the rectory of Scarning, near East Dereham, and in his "The Arcady of our Grandfathers," he has put down what, by skilful questioning of the oldest inhabitants, he could gather concerning the former manner of life of the labourers and smaller farmers of Scarning and the neighbouring parishes. Arcady, indeed! It is no picture of Arcadian innocence we get from these combined narratives, but rather one of more than Bœotian rudeness. There were, perhaps, fewer public-houses eighty years ago than now, and the drinking of ardent spirits was little known then, though there was much beery drunkenness. There was a strain of cruelty running through social life. Masters beat the boys in their employ, and not infrequently their serving-men; wife-beating was so common as to attract little notice. Cock-fighting was the popular sport; football matches were played on the Sunday. Profanity and dissoluteness were crying evils, while a good part of the little religion there was, ran into superstition or gross formalism. At the annual fair-time men indulged in a surfeit of wickedness and pleasure, as though they would make up by a debauch for the enforced abstinence of the working year. Crime, too, was rife: "During the nine years ending in 1808, there were actually committed to the four prisons at Wymondham, Aylsham, Walsingham, and Norwich Castle, the enormous aggregate of 2336 men and women, to whom we may be sure little mercy was shown."*

Testimony, corroborative of that given by Canon Jessopp, is also furnished by Mr. G. T. Goodrick, already named, who was one of the ministers of Lynn Circuit in 1832, and residing at Swaffham when Robert Key was prosecuting his East Dereham mission. He writes as one who had been on the ground and had an intimate knowledge of the people. The quotation from him here given has a value beyond its special local reference, as it fairly and fully presents the claim of our Church to have fastened on the agricultural villages of our land when others passed them by. He probably had the villages of East Anglia specially in his mind, but his words are equally true of other parts of rural England in the 'Twenties and 'Thirties. After claiming that the Church to which Robert Key was attached had laboured much, and contributed no little, to spread the leaven of righteousness and thereby exalt the nation, he continues:—

"Wesleyanism with its peculiar organisation had won,—and deservedly won, her laurels, and could boast of spoils taken from the hand of the mighty, and these, too, from among the villages and cottages of many a tract of English soil, where the sound of the church-going bell was seldom heard, or if it were heard, it spoke in vain. But it will not be denied that Wesleyanism had not done all that was needed, or all that she could have done; and if the Wesleyans turned their strength to the evangelisation of large towns—so be it; they thought it best, and God is with them. But there was a class to reach, 'a region beyond,' which they had not penetrated; a people to whom religion was unknown except by name, whose morals were loose, and their habits vicious; a class from which the ranks of the poacher, the farm-robber, and the stack-burner were ever and anon recruited. The character of the labouring class in the agricultural counties was fearfully deteriorated; it had become almost brutish. Cock-fighting, dog-fighting, and man-fighting were cruel sports freely indulged in; the cricket club and football had their field-day on the Sabbath, and a drunken orgie at a fair was planned and provided for out of hard-earned wages weeks before its appointed day. Much has been said of the sins of the city, but if we were to care to draw the veil from country-town and village-life of seventy or eighty years ago,† the seeming disparity

---
* "Arcady: For Better or Worse." 6th Edition, p. 50.
† I have altered the figure to allow for the efflux of time since these words were written.

between the moral life of city and country would vanish, or rather the sins of the former would be eclipsed by the deeper darkness of the latter. But God knew it all! and, if we may not claim a plenary inspiration for the earlier missionaries of the Connexion, who will dare deny that the 'Spirit of the Lord God was upon them, anointing them to preach the gospel to the poor'? This was, indeed, mission work—a mission to the heathen in all but in name, and to this work Brother Key addressed himself in all the vigour of manhood, faith in the divinity of his mission, and constrained by the love of Christ to seek the souls of men."—(MS. "Life of Robert Key," pp. 49, 50.)

As the Mid-Norfolk of 1830 may be taken as a typical Norfolk village-mission-field—though it must be confessed the type is very pronounced and at its highest power—so Robert Key may be taken as the type of the East Anglian pioneer missionary. If we had written "the *ideal* East Anglian missionary," we should not have been far wrong. Robert Key began his ministry in North Walsham Circuit in 1828, and thence was sent to open his mission in central Norfolk. The task that lay before him was such as would have tested the physical stamina of the strongest, the courage of the boldest, the resourcefulness of the most experienced. He had no one "to hold the rope."

ROBERT KEY.

He had to make his own way, like a movable column in the enemy's territory, with no base to lean upon. He preached in the open-air or in houses that might be offered him, and suffering as well as labour was his lot. Instead of being welcomed and encouraged as a herald of the gospel, he was by many treated as a pestilent fellow to be got rid of at all costs. Certain places in the district made themselves specially notorious by the bitterness of their opposition. "Shipdham, Watton, and East Dereham," says Mr. Key, "might have been matched against any other three places of similar size for brutal violence and inveterate hatred of the truth. Of the three places I think Shipdham was the worst." At Watton, some years before, a Wesleyan minister had attempted to preach the gospel in the open air, but he was shamefully treated, and barely escaped with his life. Here, on August 16th, 1832, Mr. Key took his stand in the Market-place. It was soon pretty evident that mischief was abroad. A number of men who had been primed with drink by some of the "respectables" of the town, gathered round, and first tried to drown the preacher's voice by clamour and by percussion. Then, a rush was made; the preacher was knocked down, trampled upon and kicked. He struggled to his feet and got on his chair again—still preaching. Another rush—with the result that Key was tossed backward and forward like a football. Then missiles began to fly, and it looked as though the unprovoked riot would end in murder when, suddenly, deliverance came and from an unexpected quarter. Some of the ringleaders, though still under the influence of drink, were seized with compunction, and changed sides. They rallied round the breathless and battered preacher, planted themselves round him as a body-guard, and got him away with difficulty, shouting: "You are right and we are wrong, and no man shall hurt you!" This unlooked-for development was, we are told, a disappointment to the "respectable" men who had instigated the disturbance, one of whom was the person entrusted by a paternal state with the cure of souls.

As for Shipdham, Mr. Goodrick fully bears out what Mr. Key has said of it. "It made itself infamous by its long course of bitterest opposition to the preachers, and no wonder; for, if Satan had a seat upon earth it was there," and more, and stronger words he writes, which we need not give. We will also pass over the details of the annoyances to which the preacher and his little flock were so long exposed, since these had not even the small merit of originality. One little fact, however, we chronicle here, partly to show what spirit the people were of, and partly to embalm the memory of a poor widow, "destitute, afflicted, tormented, of whom the world was not worthy." A poor Frenchwoman of Shipdham became a special object of persecution. Upon her was heaped ridicule, taunts, and blows. She was driven from one lodging to another and, had it been possible, some would have denied her even a pauper's bread; and all because she dared to become, and declared herself to be, "a thorough Primitive."

Though Robert Key had many marvellous escapes from bodily injury, he did not bear a charmed life. Once at Reepham, for example, he was hit with a stone thrown by the hand of the zealous parish clerk, and bled profusely. "But why," it will be asked "were not such miscreants brought to justice?" We answer: once, and once only, was a summons taken out against persecutors, and why the experiment was not repeated the sequel will show. It was at this same Reepham, Key was followed by another preacher who, borrowing a chair, began a service; but he was pulled down, and by clamour and violence compelled to desist. The attack was so outrageous that, in order to avoid worse consequences from the rough and ready action of the justifiably incensed populace, Mr. Key reluctantly consented to seek legal redress. The result shall be stated by Mr. Goodrick:—

"To the everlasting disgrace of the magistrates, the chicanery of the legal adviser, and the subterfuges of the law itself were so well used that, although everybody else saw through the whole thing, justice was blind, and her constituted ministers dismissed the case! and, by way of administering some soothing palliative to the outraged feelings of the influential and respectable blackguards of Reepham, condescended to stoop so low as to pour a tirade of abuse upon Mr. Key, which for virulence of language might have been borrowed from Billingsgate. Such has often been the result of an appeal to the law for protection, especially when the clerical magistrate occupies the bench and derogates from his character as a minister of the gospel by professing to administer criminal law."—(MS. "Life of Robert Key," p. 76).

The language is vigorous, but not one whit more so than that employed by John Foster who, in speaking of these attacks on the inoffensive preachers of the gospel, once so common, says: "These savage tumults were generally instigated or abetted, sometimes under a little concealment, but often avowedly, by persons of higher condition, and even by those consecrated to the office of religious instruction; and this advantage of their station was lent to defend the perpetrators against shame, or remorse, or just punishment, for the outrage."[*] No wonder that, after his first experience of Justices'

---

[*] "Evils of Popular Ignorance," pp. 75-6.

justice, Robert Key should say: "Never more! Come what may I will suffer it, and leave my cause with God."

The outer conflicts Robert Key had to wage during his Mattishall Mission, had their reflection and counterpart in the inner conflicts which formed so remarkable a feature of his experience at this time. As we read of these we are reminded of the views held by J. Crawfoot, H. Bourne, and others of the fathers as to the nature of spiritual conflicts. They would have said, in explanation, that such conflicts were to be expected; that he was taking upon him the burden of souls; that there was "a conflict of atmospheres." Sometimes a darkness which might be felt would come upon him, and a feeling of hardness, and he had to hold on grimly by naked faith, and wrestle until the day broke, and his heart softened again as with the dew of the morning. So it was on his first visit to Saham Toney on June 10th, 1832. While he was preaching in the open-air the heavens became suddenly overcast, and the rain came down in torrents. His appeal for a house or place of shelter in which to finish the service, was met by the offer of a house—formerly a workhouse—capable of holding two hundred people. Many followed him there, but for the first twenty minutes "all appeared hard and dark, and nothing moved." Then the cloud passed, and men and women began to fall to the ground, while others hurried away as if the house were on fire, in impenitent terror and defiance. "Did his spiritual foes," asks Mr. Goodrick, "on leaving Mr. Key, attack his hearers, to drive them from the place?" It was an eventful service. In the fiery trial of that night was forged a link in the providential chain of events which led to the conversion of C. H. Spurgeon; for, amongst those who were won that night, was Mary Eaglen, whose changed and Christly life so impressed her brother that it was one of the main factors in his conversion, which took place soon after. Mr. Eaglen spent two of the thirty-six years of his active ministry in Ipswich Circuit, of which Colchester was then a branch, and it was he who, on a snowy morning in the winter of 1850, directed the youth of God's election to look and be saved. The pulpit in which Mr. Eaglen then stood is preserved in the Stockwell Orphanage. On October 11th, 1864, Mr. Spurgeon preached in the old Colchester Chapel (erected 1839) from the text used in his conversion; and it

REV. ROBERT EAGLEN.

COLCHESTER CHAPEL.
As it was.

was quite fitting that Rev. W. Moore should, in 1897, place a tablet in the chapel commemorative of the event.

Despite the opposition of some unreasonable and evil men in East Anglia (most of whom afterwards got their deserts), "the word of God was not bound," but rather had "free course and was glorified." Some mighty camp meetings gave it impetus and helped it forward. That such numbers of people could be brought together in districts not thickly populated, attested the hold the new religious movement already had got on the rural population. But not as aggregations of people merely, or as imposing demonstrations of growing influence, were these camp meetings mighty. The word belongs to them rather because they were generators and distributors of spiritual force; they were "mighty before God to the casting down of strongholds." Mighty in all these senses was the camp meeting held at East Tuddenham on June 12th, 1831, which may therefore serve as type and representative of many another similar gathering in various parts of East Anglia. "It was thought there were thousands of people present" at this Mid-Norfolk camp meeting. "This," says Mr. Key, "was the most powerful meeting I ever witnessed. It was thought that more than fifty were set at liberty."

We come across traces and echoes of some of these camp meetings in our accepted literature. Readers of *Lavengro* * will recall the fine description of a Norfolk camp meeting in that fascinating book. We challenge that camp meeting for a Primitive Methodist one; for, as surely as it took place as pictured, so surely would no other denomination save our own have owned it at the time, and it is too late now for any other to prefer its claim. Let our readers turn to this passage in *Lavengro*. Our present concern with it is to adduce the testimony of George Borrow—who spent his later years at Oulton, near Lowestoft—as to the ameliorative influences which camp meeting preachers and preaching exerted upon the rural parishes of East Anglia:—

SPURGEON'S TABLET IN COLCHESTER CHAPEL.

"There stood the preacher, one of those men—and, thank God, their number is not few—who, animated by the Spirit of Christ, amidst much poverty, and alas!

* *Lavengro.* Chapter xxv.

much contempt, persist in carrying the light of the gospel amidst the dark parishes of what, but for their instrumentality, would scarcely be Christian England."

Dark parishes they were, indeed, in the 'Thirties, not only in East Anglia, but in many other parts of rural England. While the misguided emissaries of "Capt. Swing" were burning down farmsteads and destroying machinery, Robert Key and his coadjutors were amongst them, practically doing national police-duty, and doing it without pay or recognition, and what is more, they often accomplished by their village evangelism what police patrols and magistrates were unable to effect. The biographies of the time bear witness to the wide-spread alarm which these agrarian disturbances created. Here, for example, is a reminiscence of the childhood days of J. Ewing Ritchie, spent at Wrentham, in Suffolk:—

> "I can never forget the feeling of terror with which, on those dark and dull winter nights, I looked out of my bedroom window to watch the lurid light flaring up into the black clouds around, which told how wicked men were at their mad work, how fiendish passion had triumphed, how some honest farmer was reduced to ruin, as he saw the efforts of a life of industry consumed by the incendiary's fire. It was long before I ceased to shudder at the name of 'Swing.'"[*]

Robert Key, we repeat, was down amongst the rick-burners. In one parish, the miscreants had plotted to burn down all the farm-houses in the district, and had actually succeeded in burning down seventeen, when their incendiarism was stopped by the advent of the Primitive Methodist missionaries, bearing no other weapon than the Gospel. Said a grateful farmer to Robert Key: "It cost me two shillings a night all through the winter to have my house watched, and then we went to bed full of anxiety lest we should be burnt out before morning. But you came here and sang and prayed about the streets—for you can never get these 'varmints' into a church or chapel. But your people brought the red-hot gospel to bear upon them in the street, and it laid hold of their guilty hearts, and now these people are good members of your Church."

Great, indeed, have been the changes for the better brought about in those parts of East Anglia we have glanced at, since Primitive Methodism was introduced into them, and in effecting those changes it has had a chief part. No longer is North-East Norfolk called New Siberia because of the backward condition of its inhabitants, as it was called when R. Key began his labours in the North Walsham Circuit. In this corner of the county is the newly-formed Holt and Sheringham Circuit, carved out of Briston and Aylsham Circuits. The rising watering-place and fishing village of Sheringham is now as bright a spot on our Connexional map as Filey, or Cullercoats, or Staithes, or Banks, of which places it reminds us. In its pretty village-chapel Christians of various communities love to join with the fishermen in their hearty worship, and occasionally, like Dr. Fairbairn, taste a fresh experience in relating their Christian experience at the call of a guernsey-clad leader.

We have glanced at the missioning of North-West Norfolk by Lynn Circuit. The Rev. F. B. Paston tells us that, even in 1862, when he began his labours on the

[*] "East Anglia. Personal Recollections and Historical Associations," p. 31.

Docking Station in this division of the county, the villages of which the circuit is composed, were in a sad condition of ignorance, poverty, and serfdom. The squire and the parson ruled. To eat, to drink, to sleep—this was the routine of the labourers' life. But a few began to think and read and discuss, and got their eyes opened to discern their wants. As formulated, these were—the establishment of a trades union, direct Parliamentary representation, and a living wage. Thirty years after, when Mr. Paston returned to the station, the objects aimed at had been gained. The day of emancipation for the agricultural labourers had come at last. Joseph Arch, the founder of the Labourers' Union and a Primitive Methodist local preacher, was member for North-West Norfolk. The composition of the Parish Council showed that the long sowing and waiting had not been in vain, that the East Anglian peasant had won his freedom and knew how to use it.

We have already quoted Canon Jessopp as to the former condition of the peasantry of Mid-Norfolk. The same high and unexceptionable authority may be quoted as to the influence our Church has exerted and still exerts in East Anglia, where, he tells us, the immense majority of those who attend Nonconformist chapels are Primitive Methodists. This reference to our Church must not suffer curtailment, and it is with a pride, surely pardonable, we give it place here.

"Explain it how we will, and draw our inferences as we choose, there is no denying it that in hundreds of parishes in England the stuffy little chapel by the wayside has been the only place where for many a long day the very existence of religious emotion has been recognised; the only place in which the yearnings of the soul and its strong crying and tears have been allowed to express themselves in the language of the moment unfettered by rigid forms; the only place where the agonised conscience has been encouraged and invited to rid itself of its sore burden by confession, and comforted by at least the semblance of sympathy; the only place where the peasantry have enjoyed the free expression of their opinions, and where, under an organisation elaborated with extraordinary sagacity, they have kept up a school of music, literature, and politics, self-supporting and unaided by dole or subsidy—above all, a school of eloquence, in which the lowliest has become familiarised with the ordinary rules of debate, and has been trained to express himself with directness, vigour, and fluency. What the Society of Jesus was among the more cultured classes in the sixteenth century, what the Friars were to the masses in the towns during the thirteenth, that the Primitive Methodists are in a fair way of becoming among the labouring classes in East Anglia in our own time."*

The Ramifications of Brandon and Wangford Circuits.

Brandon, made a circuit in 1828, demands an additional word. No one, judging by the present shrunken proportions of the "Brandon and Methwold" station, would suspect that its precursor figured so largely in the early history of the Norwich District. James Garner's mission to Marshland has been referred to.† In 1833, Brandon reported 660 members. In 1840, through the labours, in turn, of Messrs. Bellham, Moss, Knock,

---

* "Arcady, for Better for Worse," pp. 77-8.   † See Vol. ii. p. 222.

Winkfield, and their colleagues, the membership had risen to 954. But between these years Rockland Circuit was made with 472 members, so that the actual increase for the seven years was 766. This numerical advance was the more remarkable as, during the earlier part of the septennate, persecution had been bitter and the poverty of the people extreme. At Thelnetham, Rushford, and Bridgham the societies were deprived of their preaching-places. At Tottington, Mr. and Mrs. Cheston (the latter the mother of the Rev. R. Church) were turned out of house and home, and their goods left on the open green for three days and nights because they "harboured the Ranters." Ultimately they found shelter at Thompson, two miles away, and as

ST. NICHOLAS STREET, THETFORD.
Where the First Open-air Service was held, conducted by Mr. J. Kent.

they opened their house for preaching, their settlement there was the means of strengthening the village society.* It was in the face of difficulties such as these that the Brandon Circuit extended itself.

Bury St. Edmund's, Thetford, Watton, and Diss, each now the head of a circuit, are all found on the early plans of Brandon. Bury was successfully missioned in 1829 by G. Appleby and G. Tetley, and formed part of the Brandon Circuit until 1842, when

* See the *Magazine* for 1861, p. 232, which also contains the account of the opening of a chapel at Thompson by Messrs. R. Church, O. Jackson, and W. H. Meadows, very familiar names in East Anglia.

it became a circuit in its own right. Sudbury Circuit has since been formed from Bury. Our Church found it no easy matter to get footing in the ancient town of Thetford, once the capital of East Anglia, a bishop's seat even before Norwich, and boasting of its eight monasteries and twenty churches. The first efforts of our missionaries were unsuccessful but, in 1836, John Kent tried it again, preaching in St. Nicholas Street, and suffered temporary arrest in consequence. After this, a society which proved permanent was established, and a chapel opened in 1839. Under the able superintendency of G. Tetley the Thetford Branch became an independent circuit in 1859, and, to-day, it takes rank as a good country station with some twelve or thirteen separate interests.

Lopham, another old-world place, is on the Brandon Circuit plan of 1834. During the last quarter of the eighteenth century Mr. George Wharton, a good specimen of the old English yeoman, was resident at North Lopham. He accepted Methodism, recently introduced into the village, entertained the preachers, and allowed them the use of his kitchen for their services. His son of the same name succeeded to the paternal estate and, being a lover of old Methodism and camp meetings, he transferred his patronage to the Primitives on their coming into these parts. He granted them the use of a shed roofed with faggots as their preaching-place. This primitive structure had a curious origin. Mr. Wharton was, in his way, a musical amateur, and, on his relinquishing the Grange Farm in favour of his son George, he built the shed to serve the purpose of a music-saloon, to which he might retire at will and play on the bass-viol to his heart's content, without disturbing his wife, who did not appreciate his musical efforts. The old shed, afterwards enlarged and roofed with thatch, became known as the "Old Gospel Shop." Subsequently, we are told, Mr. George Wharton (the third of that name, we take it) built a chapel for the use of the society at Lopham, and also at New Buckenham, Wortham, and East Harling. By his will he devised the chapel to his son John, and, by an arrangement with the devisees, the Lopham chapel and adjoining schoolroom were, in 1861, made over to the Connexion. There is a tablet in the chapel to the memory of "George Wharton, Gent., who died Feb. 4, 1837." "Several members of the Wharton family are buried in and around the chapel, and in a garden adjoining are the graves of Mr. and Mrs. John Rolfe (Lydia Wharton), and Mr. John Bird. The garden is now private property, and owned by a descendant of George Wharton."* The fact that Lopham, beginning as part of Brandon, was afterwards included in Rockland, and is now in Diss Circuit, points to the changes the years have brought.

Rockland was made a circuit from Brandon during 1833, and in 1834 Robert Key,

* See article on "The Lopham People," by Mr. W. H. Berry, in the *Christian Messenger*, 1900, pp. 328-9.

fresh from his triumphs in Mattishall, became its superintendent, and continued such for two years. In 1835 the newly-formed circuit reported 710 members, being an increase of 323. Rockland, in its turn, missioned Stowmarket, which was made a circuit in 1835, with only 95 members.

In 1837 Robert Key began a mission at Hadleigh, in Suffolk, a place famous in ecclesiastical history as the scene of a martyrdom and as the place where the Anglo-Catholic movement had its beginning. On a common near the town Key would read the inscription :—

"Near the spot where this stone stood,
Rowland Taylor shed his blood."

And, only four years before, the meeting had taken place in the rectory parlour of Hugh James Rose from which resulted the "Tracts for the Times." The conditions under which Mr. Key prosecuted his mission in Suffolk were somewhat different from those which had attended his work in Mid-Norfolk. The people seemed more difficult to reach—harder to impress. There was a good deal of Antinomianism about. Many of the people, too, were accustomed to "good" sermonising and plenty of it, and would not be put off with anything else. It is not suggested that Mr. Key had no message for the people; only, that their ecclesiastical predilections or doctrinal errors were such as made his task more difficult, and drove him to study his message, and how he could best urge it home through the resistant coating superinduced by habit or prejudice. Still, Mr. Key met with a measure of success, though not on the scale to which he had been accustomed. Some of the remarkable displays of Divine grace witnessed by him about this time he has duly recorded in his "Gospel among the Masses." One of the places missioned was Polstead—a veritable "Satan's seat," on which a lurid light had recently been cast. A crime perpetrated there was the sensation of the day. For a time everybody was talking of the Red Barn and the murder of Maria Martin. Robert Key tells us that when he visited Polstead it was little better than a den of thieves. "Seventeen houses in the village were unlicensed beer-houses! Barns, malt-houses, shops, and sheep-folds were visited by gangs of armed men for the purpose of plunder, and seldom were the county Assizes held without some criminals from Polstead being indicted." In this notorious place his labours were crowned with marked success. Hadleigh was made a circuit in 1838 with 150 members. In recent years it has been divided up between Ipswich and Colchester Circuits.

We have already seen Wangford, as an offshoot of Yarmouth, attaining circuit independence in 1833. It fell to its lot to work in the easternmost part of England, where the land bulges out like a bellying sail, although the sea has done its best, or its worst, for a thousand years, to throw back the coast-line, so that Dunwich, once a famous city of East Anglia, which fitted out fleets, and through whose brazen gates armies passed, has shrunk to a poor village, the mere wreck of the ancient city, though, until 1832, it returned two members to Parliament. Covehithe, Southwold, and Wrentham, as well as historic Dunwich, are found on the early plans of Wangford Circuit. The making of Beccles and Bungay Circuit is quite recent. Kelsale, near Saxmundham, has had a chequered history. Originally part of Wangford Circuit, it, along with Melton and a few other places, formed a distinct circuit for two years—1837-8. Then it became the Kelsale Mission of Wangford, and so continued until 1862, when it was taken over by the General Missionary Committee, and remained under its care until 1881. The year 1862 was noteworthy for a feat in chapel removing. In 1860, a site of land was purchased at Melton, in the Kelsale Mission, for the erection of a chapel. The site was contiguous to a villa occupied by a barrister. Some few months after the completion of the building, the owner of the villa brought an action against the trustees for an alleged interference with his light. The trial was heard at

THE REMOVAL OF THE CHAPEL AT MELTON, WOODBRIDGE, SUFFOLK.

the Bury Summer Assizes, 1861, and went against the trustees. The animus of the Church party was notorious, and it had won the day. At this juncture Mr. H. Collins suggested that the chapel should be removed bodily. The suggestion that at first seemed so strange was soon taken up seriously. Additional land was bought, and, by an ingenious process we do not stay to describe, Mr. Collins and his brother, as engineers, effected the removal of the chapel. "A Great Moving Day" was announced, and hundreds of people assembled to witness the successful carrying out of the operation. Even then the owner of the villa was not satisfied, but threatened another action because the chapel had not been removed far enough. Counsel's opinion being taken, he advised that as the trustees had yet four feet of land intended for a path, this should be taken advantage of, and the path made to run by the side of the villa for the satisfaction of its occupants. This was done, and the chapel was moved in all some twenty feet eight inches without a window-pane being cracked, or the building suffering the slightest damage. An illustrated account of this triumph of mechanics over bigotry appeared in the "Illustrated London News" of the time. The cost of the transaction was but £31 12s. 6d., though there was a heavy bill of legal expenses which brought the entire cost up to £800.* This, we are told, was paid off, and a few years ago the trustees took over £50 of the debt of a struggling cause at Shottisham.

* "To J. H. Tillett, Esq., solicitor (Melton Chapel case), £280. To W. Harland, to Norwich and Melton, as per order of Conference, £2 3s."—*Minutes of Conference*, 1862. The view given in the text, taken at the time, has been kindly supplied by Mr. Henry Collins, millwright, etc., Melton, through Rev. J. H. Geeson.

CHAPTER XIX.

THE ESTABLISHMENT OF PRIMITIVE METHODISM IN LONDON.

A Retrospect and Forecast.

THE history of Norwich District would be incomplete were we to omit all reference to the fact that for seven years—1828 to 1834—London stood on the stations of that District. During part of this time, Sheerness and other places in Kent were on the plan of London Circuit, so that the Norwich District, before 1842, had stations or missions in Essex, Cambridge, Huntingdon, Lincoln (Holbeach), Northampton, Middlesex, Surrey and Kent, besides Norfolk and Suffolk, in all some ten counties. We see that this connection between London and East Anglian Primitive Methodism was more than a nominal one—that it had practical consequences—when we find John Smith (1) and Robert Key walking all the way from Norfolk to London in order to attend the District Meeting of 1833. That year the District increase was 1638, an evidence of success which no doubt greatly encouraged the delegates. It was during the District Meeting week, while speaking at a missionary meeting in Blue Gate Fields Chapel, that R. Key brought down his fist with such emphasis on the table as to split it in two, while Hugh Bourne picked up the scattered candles. London's connection with Norwich District had some more lasting results; for, while Norwich District gave such preachers as James Garner (1), J. Oscroft, and R. Howchin for the London work, London, in its turn, was the means of strengthening that District by giving it such men as W. Wainwright (1) and G. Tetley. The latter was one of the early fruits of Leeds Primitive Methodism, became a notable figure in the Norwich District, and attained to the Presidency of the Conference of 1855. If for no other reason than the some-time connection of London with Norwich District, we have reached a convenient point for setting forth how Primitive Methodism was introduced into London and how, in spite of great difficulties, it rooted itself there and grew. But there is a further reason. The narrative now called for is historically knitted to what has already been related, and to what yet remains to be told. London has been reached from the north and the east. Leeds and Hull and, after Norwich District, Hull once more, have had a hand in the development of our Church-life in the metropolis. While this has been going on on one side of the island, Tunstall District has been consolidating itself, and preparing for the future Manchester, West Midland, Liverpool, and Shrewsbury Districts. It has also, by its Western and other

W. WAINWRIGHT.

missions, been making its way down the Severn Valley and the Thames Basin. On this side, the outstanding fact is the creation of the Brinkworth District from Tunstall, just as, on the East, the outstanding fact was the creation of Norwich District out of Nottingham. The missionaries of Brinkworth will not be found labouring in London itself, but they will be found labouring very near to it—in Berkshire, Buckinghamshire, and in the home-county of Hertfordshire. Looking forward a few years, we shall see how, when in 1853 the composite London District is to be formed, Brinkworth District becomes one of the largest contributors, surrendering the important circuits of Reading, High Wycombe, and Luton, as well as Maidenhead, towards the formation of the new District. In this transitional chapter we confine ourselves to the beginnings of Primitive Methodism in London.

GEO. TETLEY.

EARLY ABORTIVE MISSIONS IN LONDON.

Hugh Bourne and James Crawfoot spent a fortnight in London in the autumn of 1810. Was this merely a pleasure-excursion, or an evangelistic mission? If only the former, then it belongs to the biography of Hugh Bourne rather than to this History. But it is clear, from the very first mention of the project in his *Journal*, and from subsequent references to the visit, that Hugh Bourne himself regarded it as a "religious excursion," as likely to afford him the opportunity of trying his methods of evangelism in a new and tempting field. While going in and out amongst the Independent Methodists at Stockton Heath, W. Clowes, he says, "Informed me that John Shegog [a Staffordshire man resident in London] wanted me to go to London, and that there seemed to be a call, and that my way was open there. This kept me awake a good while; but I left it to the Lord, and it seemed as if the Lord directed me to go to London. O Lord, Thy will be done." Arrived in London, Hugh Bourne and his companion did not entirely neglect seeing the sights. They saw the king's palace, and climbed nearly to the top of St. Paul's, "and had views of the city. It is wonderful," adds H. B.; "but, O Lord, what shall be done for the multitudes of the inhabitants? O Lord, have pity on them." Lancaster's Free School was visited, and the notorious Joanna Southcote, whom H. B. "thought was in witchcraft." But still their main pre-occupation was evangelism. Each preached in the open-air in Portland Street and Kentish Town. They held various cottage-meetings, at which converts were won. Much space is given in the *Journal* to the astonishing cure, through the prayers and faith of James Crawfoot, of Anne Chapman, a pious young woman and visionist, who, after being seven months in hospital, was dismissed as incurable. What were the results of this short visit? Under date of October 23rd, 1810, Hugh Bourne writes in his *Journal*:—

"Clowes has received a letter from Mr. Shegog, of London, stating that Anne Chapman was at the chapel last Tuesday, and was enabled to stand up and join in the singing, to the astonishment of the congregation; and that her miraculous restoration from what appeared to be the bed of death has raised an inquiry in many as to the deep things of God. He says they greatly desire to see us again ; and that the converts the Lord gave old James and me are going on well, especially sister Chapman and two brethren. He also says that he is endeavouring to fan the flame which the Lord enabled us to kindle in London."

This record explains why, in the autumn of 1811, we find John Benton labouring in London. If he shrank from entering Leicester, we can readily understand why he should feel out of his element in London, and soon return to more congenial spheres of labour. Still, Benton met with considerable success, as Hugh Bourne's *Journal* clearly shows. In proof, we have such entries as these: "Sept. 16th. I received a letter from Mr. Shegog, of London, informing me that John Benton had great and rapid success there." And, a little later: "They have joined about forty-five since John Benton went to London." Then in October, 1811, some four months after the new denomination had been formed by the coming together of the Clowesites and Camp Meeting Methodists, we find Hugh Bourne including High Wycombe and London amongst the societies claimed by the denomination which, in February, 1812, was to take the name of Primitive Methodists. But the society in London was too far away to benefit by efficient oversight. Thus cut off and exposed to all the erosive influences of London life, such an isolated society would be likely soon to fall to pieces and disappear. It is, therefore, all the more surprising to find Hugh Bourne, seven years after, referring to the "London Primitive Methodists," and noting that one of these—W. Jefferson, has been selected to preach the opening sermons at Dead Lane Chapel, Loughborough, and that he is one of the Loughborough Circuit preachers for 1821.* These London Primitive Methodists of 1818 are one of the puzzles of our early history. How shall we account for them? Were they, after all, the representatives of the four classes formed by Benton in 1811, or had a new section of religionists in the meantime sprung into existence and assumed the name Primitive Methodists, while remaining unattached to the Staffordshire movement? No answer to these questions is as yet forthcoming. That there were Primitive Methodists in London in 1818 seems to be indisputable ; that none could be found in December, 1822, is equally indisputable. This will be clear from the subsequent narrative, which also forces on us the reflection that, in the earlier stages of the London Mission, Divine Providence again and again very considerably made up for the deficiencies of human providence.

The Real Beginning of London Primitive Methodism.

Leeds Circuit, finding itself in the possession of a respectable balance, resolved to expend it in starting a distant mission. But where? Sunderland, it is said, was fixed upon as the centre of the intended mission, and Paul Sugden was instructed to make his way there. But Sunderland was now within the area of Hull's new Northern Mission, so the objective of the prospective mission was changed to London. Sugden was accompanied by a zealous unpaid volunteer named W. Watson. When the two alighted (December, 1822)

* See Vol. i. p. 316.

from their coach in the yard of the "Swan with Two Necks," in Lad Lane (now Gresham Street), they were the joint possessors of one shilling, which soon passed into the pocket of the coachman who had touched his hat for the accustomed gratuity. When the guard also approached and touched *his* hat, they told him frankly they were penniless, and what had brought them to the great city. The guard was a kind-hearted Christian man, who knew guilelessness from its subtle counterfeit. He took the missionaries home with him, and not only gave them breakfast, but bought a hymn-book of them so that their next meal might be assured. The lot of the missionaries was no enviable one. They were practically stranded in the biggest city in the world,

THE "SWAN WITH TWO NECKS."

with no supporters, and no material base or supplies for their work. Yet, once more, Providence befriended them. If there were no Primitive Methodists in London there were some Bible Christians who, as usual, showed a kindly spirit. By these the two were engaged as temporary supplies, P. Sugden going into Kent, while W. Watson remained in London. One day the latter, while preaching, let a warm-hearted allusion to the fact that he was a Primitive Methodist escape him. This disclosure led to the discovery of a co-religionist in the congregation. They came together, with the result that next day a small chapel in Cooper's Gardens, near Shoreditch Church, was taken. Cooper's Gardens, euphemistically so called, was a narrow thoroughfare leading off Hackney Road, at a point about a hundred yards from Shoreditch Church, where Hackney Road begins. Access to this thoroughfare was gained through a low, flat archway, or rather, through a door-shaped entry; then, passing some shabby cottages, you had the chapel on your right. In those days the locality did not improve in looks as you went further on, nor was its reputation of the best; for Nova Scotia Gardens, where the notorious murderers Bishop and Williams had lived, were not far away. As for the chapel, well may Mr. Yarrow call it "one of the quaintest of chapels."* Eighty years ago there were hidden away in odd nooks and corners of London many such old conventicles. They recalled the days when Dissenters thought it best to keep their places of worship out of sight as much as possible. Even now, you may occasionally stumble upon a building given up to the most secular uses which yet shows something of the old conventicle look. But

ENTRANCE TO COOPER'S GARDENS.

the number of such buildings is becoming smaller every year. Cooper's Gardens Chapel was a small, almost square building, being about twenty feet each way. Small though it was it boasted three galleries, each reached by a separate flight of stairs. The pulpit was stuck against the left or eastern wall. The chandelier was a hoop suspended by ropes from the ceiling, with tin sconces affixed, and tallow candles were the illuminants. No picture of Cooper's Gardens first chapel is now procurable; hence we have been the more particular to give some idea of its situation and appearance, because this was our first Connexional base and centre in the metropolis. Three generations of chapels stood on this site. Cooper's Gardens first chapel lasted until 1835, then came the second of the name, and in 1852 the third. For fifty-three years—1822 to 1875—

* "The History of Primitive Methodism in London." By William H. Yarrow. 1876.

this spot in Bethnal Green was familiar and dear to Primitive Methodists, the home of a strong and aggressive society, and the birthplace of many souls.

After Cooper's Gardens Chapel was taken, P. Sugden was called in from Kent, and J. Coulson walked from Leeds to supply the place of W. Watson. He walked, because the "cause" could not afford to pay for an inside seat in the coach, and it was too cold to ride on the outside. He entered London late in January, 1823, with three shillings in his pocket, and no very clear idea as to the direction he should take to find chapel or colleague. He had a hazy notion that Cooper's Gardens was somewhere near Shoreditch Church, and so, as he made his way along Old Street, he kept anxiety at bay by lifting up his heart to God and saying, "Lord, it would be a little thing for Thee to let me meet with Paul Sugden." This child-like confidence was not misplaced.

COOPER'S GARDENS THIRD CHAPEL.

The colleagues *did* meet, and that "right early"; for, as Coulson a little later passed along a certain street, he was seen by P. Sugden, who happened to be in a shop at the time. To run out and welcome his colleague was the work of a moment. We may call it a remarkable coincidence, but the men more directly concerned saw the hand of God in the rencontre.

On yet another winter's day, in January, 1824, W. Clowes took charge of the London Mission, and remained in charge until September, 1825. His coming opened a new chapter in the history of London Primitive Methodism, the first chapter having ended disappointingly. During the year 1823, the few and feeble societies had been formed— and prematurely formed, one cannot but think—into a circuit. Local difficulties led to a still further and most unwise division of the circuit into East and West, with the result that might have been anticipated. The societies soon found themselves in difficulties, and an appeal was made to Hull Circuit to save them from utter wreck. The appointment of Clowes at this crisis was a wise step. Never, perhaps, during the course of his active ministry did he give more manifest proofs of the possession of administrative ability, as well as of evangelistic aptitudes, than during his twenty months labours in London. He enforced discipline; curtailed expense wherever possible; reunited the divided East and West, and set himself to restore the societies to solvency. In effecting this last he was greatly indebted to Mrs. Gardiner, one of those "honourable women" of whom there have been "not a few" in the history of our London churches. Mrs. Gardiner is said to have been led to identify herself with our cause in London through the preaching of J. Coulson. She had both the means and the will to further the work of God. The poorly paid, and often insufficiently fed pioneer preachers, were welcomed to her table and followed by her thoughtful kindness. At this juncture, W. Clowes appealed to Mrs. Gardiner, who at once lent him a hundred pounds on his note of hand. With this sum he was enabled to pay off outstanding bills, and relieve the financial pressure on the societies. As for the promissory-note, it was, not long after, taken out of the escritoire and put into the fire as a burnt-offering to the Lord.

Clowes found, as many both before and since his time have found, that London evangelism has its own special difficulties, making heavy demands on faith and patience. Not here, least of all, can the outworks of evil be carried at a rush, but only by the slow process of sapping and mining. Clowes had a sanguine temperament, and had come to London fresh from revivals on a large scale, and so his *Journal* reveals a certain disappointment with what seemed to be, in comparison, the meagre results of his labours. Now he writes: "London is London still, careless, trifling, gay, and hardened through the deceitfulness of sin." And again: "Often have I preached within and without the room [in Snow Fields, in the Borough], and laboured with all the powers of my body and soul; but the pride, levity, and corruption of London appeared to be unassailable; the powers of hell reigned fearfully triumphant, the pall of midnight darkness rested upon thousands of all orders of society. Oh, for God's mighty arm to be outstretched, to shake the mighty Babylon to its centre!"

Any one who reads the accounts Clowes has given in his *Journal* of some of his experiences as an open-air evangelist in London, will cease to wonder that he uses strong language in writing of its moral condition, as he found it in 1824. Let the reader take a brief summary of one or two of the incidents he gives.

As he passes through Clare Market his soul is stirred within him as he sees the awful profanation of the Lord's Day. He takes his stand among the people and beseeches them to turn from their evil ways and seek the Lord. The next Sabbath, true to his promise, he is in Clare Market again. He begins to sing, but is stopped by a policeman and forbidden to disturb the market-people. When asked for his authority, the officer pulls out his truncheon, and says: "This is my authority." An open window is offered him, and from that vantage-ground Clowes "pours the thunders of the law upon the rebels against God and the King." From Clare Market he goes down to Westminster, and stands up again in the open-air. "The Philistines," says he, "were again upon me; the abandoned of God and man, like incarnate devils raged and howled around; however, I cried to the infuriated multitude to repent and believe the Gospel, and, contrary to my expectation, I finished my address, and retired without suffering any injury." We may recall another scene, also enacted in Royal Westminster. While Clowes is leading a camp-meeting, three men, whom a publican had primed with liquor and dressed up with horns and wings and tails, execute a sort of devil's dance on the camp-ground. They yell and rush about amongst the people. The women scream, and for a time the meeting is thrown into confusion. But the preachers do not flinch, and their followers soon rally to their support. Presently, two of the masqueraders slink away, while the third and principal one—a gigantic and fearsome figure to look upon—is surrounded, and sung and prayed over, till he has no spirit left in him. There is something grotesque about this incident, but its sequel was tragic enough; for, in this case, as in a similar one that took place at Walworth, retribution speedily overtook the persecuting buffoons. The ringleader of the Westminster trio was shortly after convicted of pocket-picking and hanged at Newgate, whilst his underlings were transported to Botany Bay for house-breaking.

Clowes now left London for his mission in Cornwall. He had worked hard during his twenty months of service, along with such colleagues as J. Hervey, G. Tetley, and especially John Nelson, who, like himself, had been extraordinarily successful in the North; and yet, in September, 1825, the combined membership of the London societies was but 170. Well might he sorrowfully write: "I have continued to labour in conjunction with my friends in London day and night for the salvation of sinners, but the chariot rolled on slowly and heavily." Still the chariot *did* roll on; London continued to make some little progress, so that in 1826 the societies were formed into an independent circuit which, for that and the next year, stood on the stations of the Hull District. Then, as we have seen, from 1828 to 1834, London formed an integral part of the Norwich District and then disappears, to emerge in 1842 as a branch of Hull. A second crisis had occurred, making the friendly intervention of Hull Circuit indispensable. The crisis was mainly of a financial character, as the following extract from the *Journal* of W. Clowes will show:—

"On February the 27th [1835] I left Hull for London, in order to take the broken-down circuit of the latter place once more under the wing of Hull Circuit. The preachers stationed in London were brothers Oscroft, Coulson, and Bland, and the number of members was 294. On the Sabbath after my arrival I preached at Blue Gate Fields; and on the Monday, I had to advance, on the part of Hull Circuit, £16 to pay the preachers' deficient salaries. The chief of the circuit was in a state of decay, the chapel being involved and most of the places in a shattered condition. After preaching several times, and arranging for the taking of the circuit, I returned to Hull to communicate the result of my mission to our March Quarterly Meeting for 1835."

John Flesher was sent to London in 1835 to save the situation, just as he had been sent to Edinburgh in 1830 for the like purpose. It was a magnanimous act on the part of Hull Circuit to give up its ablest minister at this crisis; nor was this magnanimity a merely transient impulse, but rather a well-defined policy, dictated by a consideration of what was best for the Connexion. For a series of years some of the best preachers on its staff were drafted to the London work. The affairs of Blue Gate Fields Chapel formed the crux of the difficulty Flesher was called at once to face. Its history can soon be told. As early as 1825 we find a society worshipping in New Gravel Lane, in Shadwell. The preaching-room, which was a loft over a stable, was a strange place for one of the best and most well-to-do of the London societies to forgather in; for, over and above the disadvantage of its location, the odour of the stable was often unpleasantly assertive, and the sound of the chaff-cutters at work below jarred on the sensibilities of the worshippers. Yet, for some years, this upper room was the home of a vigorous society, and a Bethel ashore to zealous Primitive Methodists who sailed from North-Eastern ports. In 1829, James Garner (1) began his two years' superintendency, marked by peace and some progress. In 1830, the membership of Cooper's Gardens had risen to 76 and that of Shadwell to 64. When, next year, John Oscroft succeeded to J. Garner, it was felt the time had fully come to give the Shadwell society more eligible headquarters, and, in June, 1832, Blue Gate Fields Chapel was opened. The entire cost of the undertaking was £1300, a sum out of all proportion to the financial strength of the society. What follows is the old familiar story—a crushing, dispiriting debt, accumulating arrears of interest, angry creditors becoming vindictive. From the perusal of private letters of the time and the carefully written minutes of the Trustees' Meetings, we see John Flesher here and there in the Connexion preaching and making collections on behalf of Shadwell Chapel, while, in London, his colleagues were begging almost from door to door for the same object. Thomas Watson, the popular boy-preacher, had worn out three suits of clothes with the severity of this work; and some of Thomas Ratcliffe's begging reminiscences may be read in Mr. Yarrow's book.* But, in spite of all that could be done, Blue Gate Fields Chapel had, in the end, to be sacrificed. All, however, was not lost. Much had been gained. Connexional honour was saved; the just demands of creditors were satisfied; and the society, poor but honest, chastened, and wiser for the experience of the past, could face the future with hope. Mr. Yarrow is careful to inform us that when, in 1837, Blue Gate Fields Chapel was sold for £500, the Connexion did not own a shillingsworth of property in London. True, Cooper's Gardens second chapel had taken the place of the dilapidated structure already described. But this, for the time being, was the private property of John Friskin, one of the most prominent and active officials of the early days. Seeing clearly what was needed, he had bought the old building and some of the adjoining property, and built a chapel which was, in every way, an improvement on the old. This was let to the society at a moderate rental, and subsequently bought on easy terms. From this it will be seen how comparatively recent is the material advance our Church has made in the metropolis, and how considerable and creditable to all concerned that advance has been. In 1837 the membership was 286, and the property owned *nil*. In 1847 the membership was 700, and the value of the three Connexional chapels then owned

* Yarrow's "History," pp. 53—215. Our authority for the wear and tear of the three suits of clothes is the following resolution of the Trustees' Meeting:—"That the £4 entered in the Account Book as a present to Thomas Watson while begging, be granted; as he wore out three suits of clothes while begging."

was £2500. Now, in 1904, there are 9827 members, 115 chapels, and the value of the Church property is £284,308.

After the loss of Blue Gate Fields Chapel the society found a temporary lodgment in Ratcliffe Highway, worshipping in a room that could only be reached by an almost perpendicular ladder. Interesting is this resolution in the old Minute Book, written August 9th, 1838: "That we approve of Brother Flesher's having purchased the lease of a house and ground on which to build a chapel, in Crane Yard, Sutton Street, Commercial Road." Then follow other resolutions which show that much was expected of Brother Flesher. He was to "purchase bricks, timber, and other requisites for the building of the chapel"; to superintend the erection "in all its branches," and borrow the money necessary to complete the building. If tradition be trustworthy, Mr. Flesher did even more than was expected of him, for occasionally he might have been seen dressed as a navvy, wheeling barrows of earth for the foundation. On Tuesday, August 14th, 1838, the sermon in connection with the foundation-stone laying was preached by John Stamp, who, it will be remembered, was at this time on London's Sheerness Mission, which next year obtained circuit independence. 1835-7 was the turning-point of our Connexional fortunes in London. From the time John Flesher took the helm of the labouring ship it righted itself and made headway. The story of the passing of the crisis, as revealed in these old letters and documents, is of more than local interest. It suggests that there was a side to the ministry and character of John Flesher that we have scarcely seen the importance of. We have thought of him as the Chrysostom of the Connexion, "one of England's untitled noblemen," the accomplished editor, the hymnist; but it gives us a sort of shock to see him absorbed in such salvage work as fell to his lot in Edinburgh and London. Could the Connexion find no more fitting work than this for John Flesher to do? It may tend to allay what we regard as our justifiable heat to learn that the real John Flesher was essentially a man of affairs—a man big enough for large affairs, and not too big to find delight in small details. Had he not, unfortunately, destroyed his papers, abundant evidence would have remained to make this fact one of the commonplaces of our history. But it is not too late to form a just estimate of what he did for the Connexion; for, in recent years, from various quarters, letters and documents have come to hand which conclusively prove that, from 1830 to 1850, John Flesher was one of the busiest

MR. AND MRS. FLESHER IN LATER LIFE.

and most influential men in our Church-life. He had an intimate knowledge of connexional affairs, and held the threads of many of them in his hand. He was the confidant of William Clowes, W. Garner, W. Sanderson, T. Holliday, and other men of like age and standing, and he was looked up to by the younger men who were afterwards to have the guidance of affairs. In his person were represented the ideals and strivings of a wider, more liberal connexionalism. In short, we make bold to say, that John Flesher was the man of the transition period which culminated in 1843, but which had begun ten years before. "When any difficulty arose he was sent for. Often John would leave me after the Quarterly Meeting, and I did not see much more

FOREST MOOR HOUSE.

of him until the next." So said his faithful, self-sacrificing wife. On his retirement, he could claim that, "whilst it was never my policy to start divisions and disturbances, it was often my work to have to allay them when raging, and to deprive them, to a certain extent, of the power of a resurrection."* As by common consent, when the denomination or its ministers was defamed in the public press, the task of vindication was left to John Flesher. So, to name but one instance out of many, he had to defend the Connexion against misrepresentation in what it may suffice to call the Stamp Affair, and no little obloquy did he incur by so doing. To him, more than to any other single man, was due the epoch-making events of the transference of the Book-Room from

* Quoted from J. Flesher's Letter of Application for Superannuation, 1852.

Bemersley to London, and the establishment of the General Missionary Committee. To him, also, was owing the improvement of our serials, by giving them a wider outlook and a more literary form. The characteristics of the man—his lawyer-like mind, and his fond, almost finical handling of details, reveal themselves in his very original Consolidation of the Minutes (published 1850). Because he had done many things so well, it was thought he was just the man to prepare the Hymn-Book that was wanted; and here he was misjudged. But one failure leaves untouched the essential greatness of the man and the value of the work he did. The policy John Flesher had worked for, and which he lived to initiate, will come under our notice again, but we may briefly set down here the main facts in his personal history which yet remain to be told. Even when, in 1842, he entered upon his editorial duties, there were already premonitions of a physical breakdown. The throat-trouble had begun to show itself which, with its complications, was to disqualify him for all public work. His affliction deepened so that, in 1852, he sought superannuation. He retired to Scarborough, afterwards to Easingwold, then to Harrogate; and finally, having sequestered himself at Forest Moor House, between Knaresborough and Harrogate, he passed away, beloved and revered, July 16th, 1874, and his remains were laid in the Harrogate Cemetery. It is a coincidence that John Flesher and W. Sanderson should both have been superannuated and have died in the same year; yet more striking, that our two most eloquent preachers of the early period should both have been smitten by disease in such a way as "made their music mute."

MURAL TABLET TO REV. J. FLESHER
IN HARROGATE PRIMITIVE METHODIST CHAPEL.

The plan of the London Mission for 1847 is now before us. When this plan was printed Primitive Methodism had been introduced into the metropolis just a quarter of a century. The plan in question shows some eighteen preaching-stations, including places as far removed from each other as Brentford and Acton on the west, and Woolwich on the south-east. Of the three Connexional chapels on the Mission—Cooper's Gardens, Sutton Street, and Grove Mews, the precursor of Seymour Place, Marylebone—Cooper's Gardens stands first in order, as it was first in numerical strength, having a membership of 260, while Sutton Street comes next with 211. Both before and after 1847, Cooper's Gardens enjoyed considerable prosperity. Joel Hodgson, who laboured in London about this time, speaks of it as a veritable "converting furnace."

The chapel was often too small to hold even the members who sought to attend, so that an overflow congregation was held in the schoolroom. To supply the additional accommodation so urgently needed, the third Cooper's Gardens Chapel was opened in 1852. The same year Parkinson Milson began his two years' memorable ministry in London. At the close of a hard Sunday's labour in connection with a series of Protracted Meetings, when "fourteen persons found salvation," he notes in his diary: "There are some blessed and mighty local brethren here." The "Breakfast Meeting," which stands at the bottom of this plan of 1847, was a notable institution of Cooper's Gardens, and one, so far as our knowledge extends, unique in the Connexion. The local preachers on duty—as most of them usually were on the Sunday—assembled at eight o'clock, and after breakfasting together and discussing some topic or other, separated to go, two and two, to their various and often distant appointments.

Dacre Street, Broadway, Westminster, is the third place on the plan. Ever since the days of Clowes' mission we had been at work somewhere or other in this district, where Wesleyan Methodism has at last got a splendid denominational centre. We say, "somewhere or other in Westminster," for a glance over the plans for successive years will show that this west-end society had flitted from street to street and room to room in an extraordinary manner. For more than half a century we clung tenaciously to Westminster, but were compelled at last to abandon it; and now, alas! the Connexion has no footing in this wide and densely-populated district.

A word must be written of Elim Chapel, Fetter Lane, which stands on the plan after Sophia Street, Poplar. For some time services had been held in various places in the centre of London, viz., Gee Street, Whitecross Street, Onslow Street, then in Castle Street Chapel, Clerkenwell. When, in order to carry out city improvements, the chapel in Castle Street was scheduled for demolition, the society acquired a disused Baptist chapel in Fetter Lane, off Holborn. This was "Elim" Chapel, which in its day had had some notable ministers. At the time of its acquisition— 1845, the idea seems to have been entertained of subsequently making this very centrally-situated building connexional property, but, in the end, this was not deemed advisable, and the chapel was vacated in the 'Seventies, some little time before the expiry of the lease.

In this same year, 1847, George Austin, fresh from his experiences of the Irish Famine, began his first ministerial term of service in London, which extended to six years. His coming was signalised by the formation of some of the western societies—Brentford, Hammersmith, etc.—into a mission, taken charge of by the General Missionary Committee; while the rest of the societies were formed into the London Circuit. When, in 1853, the London District was created, the three chapels we have described—Cooper's Gardens, Elim, and Sutton Street, became the heads of the three London Circuits called, respectively, London First, Second, and Third.

GEORGE AUSTIN.

Further developments of our London Circuits we do not follow at present. It only remains that mention be made of some of those who, for one reason or other, have special claim to remembrance. John Friskin, though not a local preacher, was unquestionably the best-known London layman of the first period. J. Booth, whose name heads the list of local preachers on the plan of 1834, came from Derbyshire in 1826. What kind of man he was may be inferred from a sentence in one of his letters to his mother: "I have worn my coat longer than is respectable, *but I must help the cause.*" It was a loss to London Primitive Methodism when, in 1848, he emigrated to the United States; but he at once joined our Church in Brooklyn, and served its interests many years. Jane Phelps, of Shadwell, whose name stands next to John Booth's, was, from 1839 to 1842, a travelling preacher in the Hull District. Mrs. Maynard and Mrs. Jane Gordon were also notable women of the early days. Ever since the former was converted under the wooden chandelier of Cooper's Gardens in 1827, Maynard has been a name familiar to our London societies. Her eldest son, Thomas Maynard, was a useful local preacher until he, too, in 1849, emigrated to the United States, and united with the Brooklyn church. Mr. C. R. Maynard, of the Stoke Newington Circuit, is the present-day representative of the old name.

JOHN FRISKIN.

When last we saw Mrs. Gordon it was at Filey.* She came to London in 1839, and was closely associated with Sutton Street until her death in 1869. Though a class-leader and an occasional preacher, she is best remembered as the champion Missionary Collector. From the Missionary Reports of a long series of years, any one who cares may ascertain the gross sum she collected for missionary purposes; but who shall tell the miles she walked, or the amount of physical labour she expended? Sometimes the canvasser or collector is the less respected the more he is known; but not so Mrs. Gordon. City magnates did not count her annual visit an unwelcome intrusion. She had none of the ways of the importunate beggar; rather, there was that about her which suggested she was on some high mission it would be an honour to have anything to do with. Attired in old Methodist fashion, and with a Christian calmness and dignity all her own, she was an impressive figure as she went about the disinterested work which more and more became her chief business.

The honour of starting the first Primitive Methodist Sunday School in London belongs to John Heaps—a youth in his teens. The school was begun in Baker's Rents, in Hackney Road, in 1832, and carried on there until accommodation was provided for it in Cooper's Gardens in 1835. When the young man had seen this school established, it is said he set his heart upon doing the same thing for Westminster, and that, to accomplish this, he cheerfully walked Sunday by Sunday from Hackney to Westminster, and back again. The life of this young Christian endeavourer was, alas! very brief, but he did good sowing. John Phillips, a watchman at St. Katharine's Docks, in

MRS. GORDON.

* Vol. ii. p. 106.

conjunction with F. Salter, began a Sunday School in the vestry of Blue Gate Fields Chapel in November, 1832. Phillips was a diligent visitor of the sick, especially of the victims of cholera and fever. He died in 1857.

The portrait of Mr. James Wood, given in the text, links us with the past; for, as a youth, he joined the Cooper's Gardens society as far back as 1839. He was soon put on the plan and was a frequent fellow-labourer in mission-work with John Wilson, who came out of Staffordshire in 1837. Wilson was not easily daunted, or else he would not, after having for two Sundays sought in vain for the Primitive Methodists about *Covent* Gardens (the address his minister had given him), have persevered in his search till he had ferreted them out in *Cooper's* Gardens. No doubt it was the zeal and aptitude displayed by John Wilson during the years he was in London that led to his designation, in the Minutes of 1873, as "Lay Missionary," working under the direction of the General Missionary Committee. James Wood who, as we have said, was requently his comrade, has been equally at home in the pulpit or the business meeting, at the street-corner, or taking part in the discussions of the Sunday morning breakfast meetings. He represents the history of our Church in the metropolis for the last sixty years; for he still survives, and although he has lost his sight and his old-time vigour, he has not lost his interest in all that pertains to the Church of his early choice.

JAMES WOOD.

The claims of Thomas Church and W. H. Yarrow to special recognition chiefly rest on what they did in the way of authorship. Edward Church, the father of the first-named, was one of the fruits of London street-missioning. A back-slidden Methodist official, he was reclaimed as the result of an open-air service, held near Whitecross Street prison, by John Oscroft in 1831. He at once joined the Cooper's Gardens society, though he afterwards identified himself with Elim. His son, Thomas, received his first ticket of membership in 1841, and though, in his later years, he was unknown to our churches, yet for a quarter of a century he was a prominent figure, and both by voice and pen did his best to further the interests of Primitive Methodism. He wielded a "versatile and subtle pen," and as he took part in most of the denominational movements and controversies of his time, he came in for a full share of the hard knocks that paper controversialists usually get.* When the much needed Primitive Methodist Bibliography comes to be prepared, it will be seen that

---

* "Versatile and subtle pen," are T. Bateman's words, occurring in a caustic letter which appeared in the *Wesleyan Times* of August 29th, 1866. On the publication of the Conference Minutes, a lively discussion arose on the Conference Address, prepared by Rev. W. (afterwards Dr.) Antliff. In this discussion Messrs. Bateman and Church were on opposite sides. T. Church had signed himself "A General Committeeman," whereupon he is exhorted "to calmness and propriety of speech and writing, and a manifestation of all the qualifications, mental and spiritual, which are expected to adorn the character and conduct of every member of the Primitive Methodist General Committee." Seven distinct publications of Thomas Church are known to us, the most important of which bear the titles, "Popular Sketches of Primitive Methodism: being a Link in the Chain of Ecclesiastical History" (1850), 351 pp.; and "A History of the Primitive Methodists."

LONDON CHAPELS — Caledonian Rd, London Fields, Stepney, Hammersmith, Camden Town, Canning Town, Stoke Newington, Kentish Town.

Thomas Church was about the first, and certainly the most prolific, of our lay authors, and he must have an early place amongst those who have attempted to write the general History of our Church. Nor should it be forgotten that he was the projector of the first newspaper that has borne the denominational name—"The Primitive Methodist Advocate."

Mr. Yarrow was a man of more sober and more reliable type—an excellent preacher, and one of the founders in 1850 of Philip Street, Hoxton. The esteem in which he was held, and his repute as a preacher, led to his being invited to become the minister of the Primitive Methodist Church of Shenandoah, U.S.A. The invitation was accepted, and he sailed in 1876, but not before he had prepared for the press his well-known and valuable "History of Primitive Methodism in London"—a book which it would be well if some competent hand would bring down to the present time and re-issue.

No pretence is here made that we have mentioned *all* those to whom it was chiefly owing that the London Mission had, by 1853, become three circuits. By no means. Other names of early workers might easily be recalled who each contributed his quota towards the common result—such names as Hawksworth, Chapman, Beswick, Garrud, Hensey, Hurcomb, Martin, Kemp, Cranson, and Wesson. But what has been said must suffice for the present; only, as showing that 1853 was but the starting-point of fresh developments, we give the portrait of Peter Thompson, a Primitive Methodist navvy from Witney, who that year missioned Canning Town. It is interesting to note that C. G. Honor, who entered the ministry in 1854, was one of the small band of missioners, and that, after experiencing some rough handling by the mob, Peter and he were marched off to Poplar Police Station. John Rackham, converted at Cooper's Gardens in 1842, had then already entered the ministry; and John Wenn, a local preacher on the station, began his honourable course by becoming, in 1853, the additional preacher on the newly-formed London Third station.

PETER THOMPSON.

We shall have to return to glance at the later and, it may be added, the creditable advance of our Church in London, especially as regards the multiplication of chapels. In the meantime, the page of views here given as an instalment will, in part, prepare us to recognise how great has been the material advance made in recent years.

CHAPTER XX.

LIVERPOOL CIRCUIT,

AND THE BEGINNINGS OF SOME CIRCUITS OF THE LIVERPOOL DISTRICT.

WE have already glanced at the "origins" and subsequent development (as far as 1842) of the circuits comprised in the Manchester District that was formed in 1827. One circuit only, then standing on the stations of that District, has been reserved for notice at this point—Liverpool. It is due to a city which by its geographical situation and national importance was, we may say, predestined to become, and actually has become, the head of a District, that we should present what little can be gleaned respecting the beginnings of our Church within its wide area—beginnings small and feeble at first, but which have now happily attained goodly dimensions. We have just told the story of the early struggles of Primitive Methodism to gain a footing in London—the most populous city of the world: it does not seem unfitting now, therefore, that we should do the same for the second largest city of England, more especially as the history of our Church in both cities presents certain points of analogy. Each was visited by a founder and leading missionary, before a cause was permanently established. In both, the cause was introduced about the same time, and, still more noteworthy, both have made up by their later development for the comparative slowness of their growth in the early period. We have already tracked the course of our Connexional aggressive movement from Yorkshire and the Humber till, by way of the Eastern Counties, it converged on the metropolis. It now remains, in some succeeding chapters, to show how a similar process went on in the West; how from the Mersey and Dee and Severn our missionaries at last reached what we know as the home-counties, and the very suburbs of London. As John Smith (1), a Burland man, became, in Thomas Bateman's phrase, the "bishop of Norfolk," and found his way to Blue Gate Fields, in attending a Norwich District Meeting; so John Ride, whom Burland sent to mission Liverpool, became the Apostle of Wiltshire, and lived to become the successful superintendent of Cooper's Gardens. The movement rounds itself off to completeness.

Besides Liverpool, other contiguous places, which were early reached by our Church, and have had some interesting passages in their history, may be shortly glanced at. As circuits attached to Liverpool District they may be of late origin, but their beginnings carry us back almost to the beginnings of the Connexion. Of these Ellesmere Port and Buckley may be taken as examples.

LIVERPOOL.

Clowes' clear ringing voice was heard preaching the Gospel in the streets of Liverpool as early as 1812. He was on a visit at the time, just as he was on a visit to Newcastle when he preached there, and also in North Shields, in the autumn of 1821. The

Liverpool visit was paid to Charles Mathers, a Burslem potter, who had been Clowes fellow-workman in Hull and his pal in wickedness. Mathers had afterwards removed to Liverpool and, while working at the Herculaneum Pottery, had come under powerful religious impressions that were deepened by the tragically sudden death by drowning, in 1811, of T. Spencer, the gifted young Independent minister. He united with the Wesleyan Methodists, but rather as a seeker than as one who had found salvation. Sick of soul, he bethought him of his old companion who had experienced the great change. He said within himself: "If only I can see Clowes, he will tell me how he found peace, and how I too may find it." Thus motived he set out to walk to Staffordshire, and the first day got as far as Knutsford, where he stopped at an inn for the night. While at prayer in his bedroom "the Lord appeared in power, loosed him from his guilty chains, and set him free. He then was convinced that the Lord could convert souls without William Clowes." Mathers now travelled on to Staffordshire with a buoyant heart, telling people on the road what the Lord had done for him. "When we met together," says Clowes, "we were glad, and, some time after, I spent a week with him and his wife"; and it was during this visit that Clowes preached at Liverpool, "near the theatre," and also at Runcorn. From the fact that Mather's memoir was written by Clowes, we may fairly infer that he died in 1819 a Primitive Methodist; but as the memoir is silent as to *where* he died, we cannot be sure that he died a *Liverpool* Primitive Methodist.

The next event connected with Liverpool's origin known to us, is John Ride's arrest for street-preaching, and his speedy release through the alleged intervention of Dr. A. Clarke. The date of this incident may approximately be fixed as March or April, 1821; for, Thomas Bateman tells us, it was the March quarterly meeting of Burland Branch which sent John Ride on his mission, which embraced "the city of Chester, the town of Wrexham, several growing places in Wirral, and the great town of Liverpool at the end of them."

Next, we have the published recollections of Mr. Henry Howard—one of the original members of the first society-class formed in Liverpool—by the help of which the story is carried a stage further.[*] According to Mr. Howard, on a certain day—probably May 31st, 1821, a young man, plainly attired, might have been seen trying to escape from a number of persons who were following him and pelting him with mud. He and his assailants had just landed from the packet plying between Runcorn and Liverpool. The young man was James Roles, the Preston Brook preacher, and this was how he came to the Liverpool mission. He had been redeeming the time by preaching to his fellow-passengers, and some of them were now in this fashion requiting him for his well-meant efforts. The young man's plight was observed by the proprietor of an hotel which stood near the landing-stage. The preacher was invited to enter; his clothes were cleaned, and he was urged to remain until he could leave with safety. Mr. Roles stayed three days with his hospitable entertainers, who afterwards declined all remuneration, and then found lodgings with Mrs. Bentley in Westmoreland Street, where the first class was afterwards formed. Mr. Howard further states that on Sunday, June 3rd, he heard James Roles preach at the top

[*] "Primitive Methodist Jubilee Report, January 29th, 1872." Drawn up by Rev. W. Wilkinson.

of Gascoyne Street, Vauxhall Road, in the morning, and at six p.m. in Galton Street, Great Howard Street; and that he heard him again on the Sunday following. Then J. Platt, a native of Faddiley in Burland Branch, took the place of J. Roles, and, on June 17th, a class of seven members was formed. The small society took and fitted up a room in Upper Dawson Street, behind St. John's Market, which was opened by one Jane Gordon.* So far Mr. Howard, whose statements must be harmonised—and probably are harmonisable—with a couple of entries found in Thomas Bateman's *Journal* of a little later date. On October 2nd, 1821, he writes: "We have opened Liverpool, but it is too far away; we cannot work it as we ought. So we are taking steps to get the Preston Brook Circuit to join us—for them to take it one fortnight and we another." The arrangement thus foreshadowed did, in fact, obtain between Michaelmas and Christmas, and so on January 27th of the following year, Thomas Bateman writes again: "We have given up Liverpool to Preston Brook, our hands being too full, and so many more wanting us. But, alas! for Liverpool. I fear it won't be worked very well." He intimates that Burland was the more reconciled to surrender Liverpool because James Bonsor, "that successful missionary," was at Christmas appointed to Liverpool. He arrived on January 12th, but, if we may judge by his *Journal* in the *Magazine*, he remained there only three weeks, then moving on to Chester. Still, while he was in Liverpool he worked hard, as he had done in Manchester and, indeed, as he invariably did. His Sundays especially were crowded with services of one kind or another—indoors and out-of-doors. He speaks of having joined six members at one service, and of having witnessed many conversions. In March, John Abey and Sarah Spittle were appointed, and between the Conferences of 1823 and 1824, Liverpool was made a circuit, and its name duly appears on the stations for the latter year, with Paul Sugden and S. Spittle as its preachers.

The chapel which James Bonsor more than once refers to was possibly old Maguire Street, since Mr. Howard tells us that this was occupied, conjointly with the Swedenborgians, at the close of 1821 or beginning of 1822. The Primitives had the use of it at 9 a.m. and 6 p.m., and the Swedenborgians took their turn at 10.30 and in the afternoon. This singular arrangement, though the result of a friendly agreement, ended as it might be expected to end. The sequel of the joint occupancy reminds us of the cuckoo in the hedge-sparrow's nest. The Primitives grew and the Swedenborgians did not; and in 1823 they vacated the building, and left the more vigorous section in sole possession. It was held on rent until 1828, and then purchased for £600 and retained until 1864. Thus Maguire Street must be added to the long list of plain old-fashioned chapels, of which Cooper's Gardens was the latest example, which, during the early years, played so large a part in the life of our churches in the large towns. We have no picture of Maguire Street to present to our readers, but in lieu of it we have a description given by one who knew it well:—

"Externally there was nothing but a dark gable-end, with a dwelling-house on each side, which formed part of the front, and not in the least detached. A door, level with the street, led into a passage between the houses, and running their

---

* It is hardly necessary to say that this person was not Mrs. Jane Gordon, of Filey, who was not converted until 1823.

depth ; at the end of which, on the ground-floor, was a large room used for Sunday School and other purposes. On each side, at the end of the passage, was a flight of stone steps leading to the chapel. Internally there was nothing to alter my estimate of our position in this large and wealthy community. A few rows of pews and forms in the centre of the floor, and a single row of three pews fixed lengthwise to the wall on either side, made up the accommodation below ; while a gallery crossing the end of the chapel, and reached by a flight of stairs, to be seen when you had ascended from the passage on the right-hand side, afforded all the accommodation above. A large dome-like window in the roof, and two large circular-headed windows, looking into some crowded courts behind, afforded all the light admitted into the place. The pulpit, fixed against the wall between the long windows, faced you as you entered. The singers occupied the space on the left of the preacher, the pulpit-stairs that on his right."*

The situation of the chapel had little to commend it, nor were its approaches at all prepossessing. The opening of the new docks had changed the character of Vauxhall Road and the streets branching from it, much for the worse. There was a large Irish element in the population of the district, and legalised drunkeries abounded, so that those who would worship in Maguire Street had often to run the gauntlet of unseemly sights and brawls. But, despite these drawbacks, there is evidence to show that the old building could inspire warm affection in those whose "due feet" did not fail to attend its ordinances. "Friends," said Samuel Atterby (who travelled here in 1841-3), "if it should please God to end my period of work while in this circuit, let me be buried in this 'Glory hole.' I can ask nothing better." There would be many who could appreciate this enthusiastic outburst, for many a stirring meeting was held in the schoolroom to which he referred and in the chapel above. W. Clowes was at Maguire Street, June, 1829, when several persons "were in distress for their souls, and cried to God for mercy." It was the Sunday after he had assisted at the embarkation of the first missionaries to the United States. William Knowles, who was Liverpool's only minister when the Conference of 1829 met, was one of these pioneer missionaries. Thus early did Liverpool's sympathetic connection with the wider missionary movements of the Connexion begin to show itself. All down the years we meet with other indications of this connection. Thomas Lowe, an early enthusiast of African missions, went out into the ministry from Liverpool in 1836. Captain Robinson, of the "Elgiva," and ship-carpenter Hands, who prepared the way for our mission to Fernando Po, were both members of Liverpool Second Circuit ; and W. Holland, who succeeded Messrs. Burnett and Roe, the pioneer missionaries on that island, was also another of Liverpool's gifts to Primitive Methodism. The Liverpool societies have not been slow to speed the parting and to welcome the returning missionary, or to remember him practically while absent on the field—as the provision of a boat for the use of the Fernandian mission showed. In rendering such service, Ex-Vice-President Caton has been conspicuous.

Thomas Bateman spoke truly of Liverpool when he said : "It did not improve as

* "Gatherings from Memory," a series of interesting articles on the early history of Liverpool Primitive Methodism, said to have been written by Mr. H. Simpson, which ran through the *Christian Messenger* of 1875.

THE PERIOD OF CIRCUIT PREDOMINANCE AND ENTERPRISE. 269

LIVERPOOL CHAPELS

PRINCES AVENUE. YATES ST. TUE BROOK. BOUNDARY ST. JUBILEE DRIVE. EVERTON RD. BOOTLE. AINTREE.

fast as was desired or expected." In 1829, when the numerical returns of the stations are first given, it reported but 143 members, and the second hundred was not turned until 1832, in which year it had but one preacher. It was not until 1860 that Birkenhead, which had been made a branch in 1857 under W. Wilkinson, became an independent station with 260 members, and with J. Macpherson as superintendent, leaving Liverpool with 500 members and three preachers—J. Garner, J. Travis, and E. A. Davies. From these facts it will be seen how comparatively recent has been the development of our Church in the city by the Mersey, which now has, including Birkenhead, seven stations and an aggregate membership of 1536. We reach the same conclusion if, turning from the numerical returns of then and now, a comparison be instituted on the material side. It is not so much a development we see as a revolution. Since 1849 the old chapels have gone as though they belonged to another dispensation. In the early part of 1834, Maguire Street was the only chapel possessed by the Primitives in Liverpool, though services were held in rooms and houses at various points; but towards the end of the year a chapel was opened at Mount Pleasant, afterwards superseded by Walnut Street Chapel; another chapel in Prince William Street, which had belonged to the New Connexion Methodists, was acquired, and a chapel was also opened at Bebington, on the Cheshire side. Save that Walnut Street has taken the place of Mount Pleasant, the plan for the first quarter of 1849 shows no alteration. Liscard, Birkenhead, Prescot, Lime Kiln Lane, Bootle, Garston, and Wallasey are names of places found on this plan. Afterwards the Seaman's Chapel in Rathbone Street was obtained, and in 1860, under the superintendency of James Garner, "Pentecost" and the "Jubilee" chapels were opened.

REV. W. WILKINSON.

Who and what sort of men were they who preached in these old chapels and rooms that, like themselves, have long since passed away? Here, on an old plan of 1834, we have their names. Thanks to documents and reminiscences penned long ago, some of these names stand out in momentary distinctness, so that they become something more than names to us, and we can recognise their individual traits. Here, for instance, as the file-leader of the locals is J. Cribbin, a Manxman, but long resident in Liverpool, a notable figure in his day, who, in the decline of life, will die in distant New Orleans. No. 6 is J. Murray, "a Christian lawyer," whose face, meant for smiles, cannot disguise the marks of care and sorrow. Next to him stands the name of G. Horbury, the circuit-steward, a Yorkshireman, who had been associated with the founders; a stickler for rule; a plain-haired Primitive himself, and who expected all his brethren to "wear their hair in its natural form." No. 13 is Hannah Ashton, who was skilled in helping the penitent out of the Slough of Despond, and often held the hand of those who went down into the dark river. Then comes W. Gibson, once a prosperous merchant, but whose ships foundered one after another, so that at last a tablet placed over the door of his residence at Everton had inscribed on it the words: "I was brought low, but the Lord raised me up." No. 17 marks the name of F. Hunt, who died in 1849, on his way into the interior of South America. Lastly, at the bottom of the list of locals on "full" plan is the name, written with his own hand, of Richard Corfield, who in 1834 had just come

HOUSE OF MR. JOHN WYNNE AT POOLTOWN, ELLESMERE PORT.

from the Oswestry Circuit, and who was to do yeoman service for Liverpool Primitive Methodism until his death in 1900. He came a country-bred youth into the great

BUCKLEY TABERNACLE.

town. For a time he was almost stunned by the tide of life surging around him. It was some time before he could find his feet or adapt himself to his environment;

everything was so strange and new. He had his struggles with the seductions and distractions continually presented. But he was a strong man and won, anchoring himself among his own people. But as we read in the autobiographic memoranda he has left, of his self-chidings and struggles, we think we can the better understand

MRS. STOCKTON.    MR. J. STOCKTON.    MRS. D. LEWIS.

the greatness, and the inevitability, too, of the leakage that must have gone on in the early days of our Church, consequent on the migration of our adherents from the villages into the big towns. Many of the best men in the Liverpool societies, like Richard Corfield, were from the country, but these, it is to be feared, were but the salvage of those who had drifted. They were the stalwarts—men like John Gledsdale, S. Wallington, H. Simpson, James Kennaugh, and others who might be named.

Some of the societies no longer forming part of the original Preston Brook, Chester, or Liverpool Circuits were missioned quite early. For example, the societies of Frodsham and Kingsley, now giving their joint names to a circuit in the Liverpool District, were visited by H. Bourne as early as 1819. Parr, now part of the Earlstown Circuit, in 1836 had been recently missioned by Liverpool, and had a society of twenty-six members. As late as 1839 no permanent footing had been got in Birkenhead, but, two or three years after, the opening of new docks and streets brought an influx of population to the district, amongst which were found some zealous adherents of the Connexion, one of whom opened his house for services, and a cause was established which continued to grow.

Ellesmere Port, at the mouth of the canal which connects the Mersey and the Severn, has an interesting history which links us with the past. In this comparatively modern village our Church holds a commanding, it might even be said a unique, position. It possesses property to the value of about £9000, including a splendid chapel with an average congregation of six hundred, large

T. HALES.   R. WOODWARD.

Day Schools, Public Hall and Institute, the latter comprising Café, Recreation Rooms, etc. The foundation of this success was prepared for in the old cottage at Pooltown (shown in our illustration), where Mr. John Wynne and his twin-daughters resided. For more than eighty years services were held in this cottage, and only ceased to be held there some few years ago, on the erection of a neat chapel at Pooltown. Mrs. Lewis, one of the daughters, still resides in the cottage; the other daughter was married to Mr. John Stockton, who not only opened his house for the first services held at Ellesmere Port, but in other ways greatly assisted in the establishment of the society which has attained such proportions. He is worthily represented by his grandson—Mr. W. Stockton. Others who by their character and long service contributed to mould and strengthen the cause at Ellesmere Port, were Mr. Richard Woodward and Mr. Thomas Hales. The latter, who came from Shropshire in 1840 to take up the position of canal manager, retired to Ellesmere on vacating his post, and died in 1892. As superintendent of the Ellesmere Port Sunday School, it was, for a number of years, Mr. Hales' custom to write a hymn for the recurring anniversary. Several popular hymns, of which probably the authorship has hitherto been unknown or wrongly attributed, came from his pen in this unobtrusive way—hymns such as "Sabbath Schools are England's glory"; "When mothers of Salem"; "I'll away to the Sabbath School"; "When the morning light"; and "Till Jesus calls us home."

EDWARD BELLIS.

Buckley Circuit, formed from Chester in 1871, as was also Wrexham, is entirely within the Welsh county of Flint. Alltami, missioned more than seventy years ago, may be regarded as the mother-society of the circuit, since in 1838 it built its first chapel and missioned Buckley. The "Tabernacle," which in 1875 took the place of the chapel built in 1841 and enlarged in 1863, is the largest building in Buckley, and shares with the City Temple the distinction of being one of the very few Nonconformist places of worship in which Mr. Gladstone delivered a public address.* "Among the many names cherished in the station," says one who has written of it, "are those of such men as Charles Price, clear-minded, methodical and faithful; Edward Davies, the father of Rev. E. A. Davies; John Roberts, the quaint, emotional Welsh preacher; Peter Kendrick, kindly, loyal to his Church, mighty in deed and word; Edward Davies, of 'The Mount,' who, though not a local preacher, was a devoted member and official of our Church for more than fifty years."† To these names may be added those of Mr. E. Bellis, a tried and trusty friend of the Buckley Circuit, and W. Wilcock, of Penyffordd, who as a leader in the last tithe-war in North Wales had his goods distrained. His cause was ably championed through the press and on the platform by Rev. J. Crompton, who was minister of the Buckley Circuit at the time, and had a long and useful term of service there.

* The address was given at Buckley on Monday evening, November 1st, 1885.
† Rev. J. Phillipson in *Christian Messenger*, 1900, pp. 215—17.

CHAPTER XXI.

THE EXTENSION OF TUNSTALL DISTRICT IN SHROPSHIRE AND ADJOINING COUNTIES.

THE appearance on the stations of Oakengates in 1823, of Shrewsbury and Hopton Bank (afterward Ludlow) in 1824, and of Prees Green in 1826, registered the geographical advance the Tunstall District by this time had made, chiefly in Shropshire, but with extensions into other counties. By this enlargement the foundations were laid of the whole of the modern Shrewsbury, and of a goodly portion of the West Midland District. Moreover, some of these new circuits, almost from the time of their formation, threw out missions into more distant counties, the fruit of which was seen after many days. Indeed it would be a fairly accurate generalisation to say that we owe the beginnings of our present Brinkworth District to Shrewsbury; of South Wales District to Oakengates; of Bristol District to Tunstall and Scotter's "Western Mission"; and of Devon and Cornwall District to Hull and the General Missionary Committee. Besides being fairly accurate, the generalisation also furnishes a useful clue to guide us through the maze-like complexities of our Connexional development in the South-Western counties. Following, then, the actual sequence of events, we now proceed to glance at the making of the four Shropshire Circuits already named, beginning with the earliest—Oakengates.

OAKENGATES.

Hugh Bourne had frequently visited Shropshire on his missionary excursions; but if any fruit remained of these early labours it had been gathered by other communities. To the missionaries sent out by Tunstall in the autumn of 1821 Shropshire was new ground. They felt their way by Newport and other places, meeting on the whole with no great success, until they came into the neighbourhood of Oakengates and Wellington, lying almost under the shadow of the Wrekin. Here, in the populous coal and iron district of the county, James Bonsor, as leading missionary, and his colleagues at once met with much success. Hugh Bourne came to assist at the first camp meeting ever held in this part of the country, on May 19th, 1822—the great camp meeting day. Even at this date "the Shropshire Mission" had so far prospered that it had already become "the Oakengates branch" of Tunstall Circuit; and in December, 1822, it became the Oakengates Circuit, and in 1827 had seven preachers put down to it. In 1828 the name of the station was changed from Oakengates to Wrockwardine Wood, probably because a chapel was built at the latter place at an early date, while, for a long time, all efforts to secure a suitable place of worship at Oakengates proved unavailing. Subsequently, however, a site was obtained near the Bull Ring, where the first

THE PERIOD OF CIRCUIT PREDOMINANCE AND ENTERPRISE. 275

missionaries had taken their stand, and when this building was sold to the Birmingham and Shrewsbury Railway Company, the considerable sum realised by the sale enabled the trustees to erect a much larger one in a prominent situation, and place it in easy circumstances. In 1834 Richard Davies, himself a fruit of the Shropshire Mission, was, through the influence of James Bourne, appointed to Wrockwardine Wood. The circuit had declined, and there were special difficulties, both legal and financial, pressing upon the trust of Wrockwardine Wood Chapel. Thus early the remarkable business abilities of Mr. Davies, from which the Connexion was afterwards to reap such advantage, were recognised by the discerning. During his four years' term of service the station experienced renewed prosperity. Wrockwardine Wood Chapel was freed from its difficulties, and additional land bought on which a preacher's house was built. Chapels were also opened in the summer of 1835 at Wellington and Edgmond. There is a story relating to Edgmond Chapel worth telling, since it shows how formidable were the difficulties that had to be overcome by many a village society before it could secure its own little freehold and all that it insured—independence of outside interference and a reasonable guarantee for the future.

At the time the story opens, Edgmond, now on the Newport station, was a village in which there was no religious competition. The State-Church had it all its own way and, whether coincidence or consequence, the village was in a bad way. The clergyman was one of the old type, now almost obsolete. He kept his pack of hounds, and was not more eager to chase the fox than to drive Dissenters from his parish. True to the adage, "Like priest, like people," many of his parishioners were not only benighted themselves, but stoutly resisted the introduction of the light. Several attempts had been made by zealous members of other Churches to preach the Gospel in the village—notably by a Methodist and a Congregational minister, but they had been driven away, bemired with the filth of the kennel through which they had been dragged. Now Mrs. Jones, a Primitive Methodist local preacher and leader of Newport, who brought the letters to Edgmond every morning, was deeply concerned at the moral condition of the place. At her request preachers were sent from Wrockwardine Wood to mission the village, and preaching was established at its outskirts. But the distance of the preaching-house from the village and the bad state of the roads, coupled with the persecution to which both preachers and congregation were subjected, militated against success, so that at the September Quarterly Meeting of 1834 the question of the abandonment of the place was seriously discussed. However, it was finally decided to try what effect would follow from holding a camp meeting before relinquishing it altogether. The meeting was duly held in a field lent by a farmer, who had opportunely quarrelled with the rector, and it was in every way a great success. In response to an appeal Mr. Minshall offered his house, which stood near the Church, for the holding of services, and a small society was formed, of which Mrs. Jones, the letter-carrier, became the leader; while Mr. Vigars, as the result of the camp meeting, became a staunch adherent of the society. The ire of the clergyman was great. Unmoved alike by the clergyman's persuasions and threats, Mr. Minshall was summoned to appear before the Petty Sessions at Newport for permitting an unlicensed conventicle to be held in his house, the clergyman publicly boasting that the fine about to be

s 2

inflicted should be distributed among the poor of the village. Mr. Davies took care to appear at the Justices' Meeting, and as the clergyman sitting with the magistrates was allowed to pour forth a tirade of abuse against the Church of which Mr. Davies was the recognised minister, Mr. Davies also claimed and secured the right to speak in vindication alike of the Church and of the accused. What followed shall be given in Mr. Davies' own words :—

"Here one of the magistrates looked at the clergyman, and asked : 'Who is the owner of the house in which the meetings are held?' I knew what that meant, and said : 'Please, your worship, it is now of little moment who his landlord is, because *land is purchased on which to erect a chapel in the centre of the village.* The deeds are executed and the works are let to undertakers, and long before a legal notice to quit can expire, the man's house will not be needed for our services.' 'I never heard a word of that,' said the parson, looking at the magistrates. 'They must have been quick in accomplishing the thing, and very sly about it.' 'Yes,' said I, 'both rapidity and secrecy were needed, when we considered the gentleman we had to deal with.' The magistrates then retired for consultation, and on their return into court the chairman said to the poor man : 'Your house is properly licensed, and you have a perfect right to worship God in your own way. The case is dismissed.' We bowed, and were about to leave the court when the parson asked the magistrate in a loud voice : 'Who is to pay the expenses?' The chairman looked at him, and sternly said : 'Pay them yourself.' On leaving the court a gentleman desired me and the poor man to dine with him, declaring, although a Churchman, that he was highly pleased with the result of the trial. The chapel was completed in a few months, and the two ministers [Messrs. T. Palmer and J. Whittenbury] who had been so cruelly treated in the village by the persecutors some time previously, were honoured by an invitation to preach the opening sermons, which was cheerfully accepted . . . . Henceforth the little chapel at Edgmond had rest, and the hand of the Lord was upon it for good."[*]

DARK LANE CHAPEL.

THOMAS TART.

WM. WITHINGTON.

[*] Rev. R. Davies' signed contribution to "A Book of Marvels or Incidents of Primitive Methodism," by Rev. W. Antliff, assisted by numerous contributors. An account of the opening of Edgmond Chapel is given in the *Magazine* for 1836. The names of the actors in this episode have been kindly supplied from local sources by Rev. W. Forth.

Another chapel in this same coal and iron district which also has its history may be briefly referred to. Dark Lane is the somewhat significant name given to a mass of dwelling-houses in the postal district of Shifnal, in the present Oakengates and Wellington Circuit. The chapel, which has been erected on one side of this populous neighbourhood perpetuates, by means of marble tablets, the memory of two men who were devoted workers of the society for upwards of fifty years, and through whose prayers and labours the erection of this building was largely due. Thomas Tart (died 1892) and William Withington (1902) were, it is said, accustomed to kneel on a certain piece of land to pray that the way might be opened for the erection of a much-needed chapel in the place. In 1863 permission was given to stake out a site,

THE MARDOL, SHREWSBURY.

but before building operations could begin there was a change in the ownership of the land, with the result that the chapel had to be built on the very spot on which they had offered so many prayers. The land is spacious, and the saintly William Withington, during his latter years, took an interest in neatly keeping its flower-beds.

Some of the changes the years have brought to what we may call the home-part of the old Wrockwardine Wood Circuit may be briefly noted. Dawley Green and other places in the neighbourhood were successfully missioned in 1839-40, with the result that Dawley became an independent station in 1854. Madeley, that will ever be sacred as the place where the sainted Fletcher laboured and which holds his ashes, formed a part of Dawley Circuit until 1881, when it also came on the list of stations.

Here, too, the venerable Joseph Preston died in 1896 in the 94th year of his age and the 73rd of his ministry. Stafford also was for some time a branch of Wrockwardine Wood, and Oakengates and Wellington, and Newport Circuits were made from it in 1865 and 1893 respectively.

SHREWSBURY.

The first missionary to Shrewsbury whose name is given was Sarah Spittle. On Sunday, June 30th, she preached thrice in the streets of the picturesque old city, led the class, and "joined" nine new members. She remarks that there are now forty-four in society, and "a good prospect." From this it is clear that Sarah Spittle must have been preceded to Shrewsbury by some other missionary. James Bonsor followed on August 4th, by which time the society numbered sixty. It was harvest-time; and it was then, and long continued the custom at that season, for the Mardol, one of the principal streets of the city, to be thronged by men waiting to be hired for the harvest. James Bonsor was moved by this strange profanation of the Lord's Day, to try to engage some of these for his Master's service. He took his stand in the crowded street and began to preach; but before he had got through the service he was marched off by the constable to the Court House; and then, as he would not promise "never to preach there more," he was led off to prison, singing all the way, and followed by an immense crowd. Prayer was made for the missionary at the different chapels, and as a practical proof of good-will on the part of some of the citizens, they provided him with no less than eight breakfasts! His detention was but short; at noon, he was taken before another magistrate who set him at liberty, and at night he was preaching again with "not quite all the people of Shrewsbury" to hear him.

James Bonsor's arrest and what followed was the talk of the city. It resulted in calling attention to the missionaries and securing for them a large measure of public sympathy. Shrewsbury did not forget, and is not likely to forget, the hero of the Mardol hirings and the eight breakfasts. When, in 1828, he died at Preston-on-the-Weald Moors, prematurely broken and worn-out with his excessive labours, the Circuit Committee decided "that the Shrewsbury Chapel be in mourning for James Bonsor for six weeks," and, as a token of respect to his memory, his funeral sermon was preached. But while James Bonsor is remembered, Sarah Spittle must not be forgotten. Both before, and for some weeks immediately after the Sunday of the imprisonment, she laboured in and around the city—sometimes preaching at a camp meeting, at other times in the street, or at the Cross—so that she is entitled to rank as one of the planters of our Church in Shrewsbury. One of the earliest converts in the city was a girl—Elizabeth Johnson. She soon began to exhort, and when but sixteen years of age went out, in 1824, as a travelling preacher, labouring first in South Wales, and afterwards in Wrockwardine Wood, Preston, Ramsor, Darlaston, and Burton-on-Trent Circuits. Elizabeth Johnson is better known as Mrs. Brownhill; for, in 1828, she was married to Mr. W. Brownhill of Birchills, Walsall. Almost until her death,

MRS. ELIZ. BROWNHILL, née JOHNSON.

in 1860, she preached in the pulpits of what are now circuits in the West Midland District. Three of the sons of this girl-preacher of the early days have been Primitive Methodist Mayors of the borough of Walsall and, in the language of one of them, Mr. W. Brownhill, J.P.: "The greatest honour in the family is the life of the mother; and they are following her in trying to make the world better than they found it." Sarah Spittle, the Shrewsbury pioneer, and Elizabeth Johnson, one of its proto-converts, show us once more, how largely in the early days our Church availed itself of female agency, and with what far-reaching and satisfactory results. Shrewsbury, which from 1823 had been a branch of Oakengates, was in 1824 made a circuit. "Castle Court Chapel was purchased at a cost of £850, and was opened in June, 1826. It was an old ecclesiastical building under which, at the time of purchase, were two vaults. Originally it was a portion of the old Town Prison or House of Correction. It stood within the ancient walls of the town, and overlooked the beautiful vale of the Severn."*

MR. W. BROWNHILL, J.P.

In this old-time chapel the brethren met to discuss the affairs of their wide circuit, with its branches and distant North Wales and Belfast missions; for Shrewsbury has been a prolific mother-circuit from which, during the course of the years, the following circuits have been formed, viz.: Brinkworth, 1826; Bishops Castle, 1832; Newtown (Montgomery), 1836; Hadnall, 1838; Minsterley, 1856; Church Stretton, 1872, and Clun, 1884, from Bishops Castle; Welshpool, 1877, from Minsterley.

Though it is impossible to follow in detail the history of each of these derivative circuits, reference must be made to the missioning of Bishops Castle in August, 1828, by Richard Ward and Thomas Evans, a local preacher. The full and interesting *Journals* of Richard Ward, who came from Farndale near Kirby Moorside, reveal a cheery and intrepid spirit which, with Divine assistance, was his best qualification for what seemed a forlorn hope; for Bishops Castle had a bad name that found expression in more than one reproachful proverbial saying. It was called "the Devil's Mansion," and other uncomplimentary names. Dissent was represented by one small Independent chapel with an almost extinct church. Other denominations had tried to gain a footing —and tried in vain; the Primitives being amongst the baffled ones. Only the previous year, W. Parkinson, one of the Shrewsbury preachers who had been a missionary in Jamaica, made the attempt. He ought to have succeeded; for he had as his ally the clergyman of a neighbouring parish, who sometimes preached for the Primitives and let them preach in his kitchen. But the two were stoned out of the place. When, on the 10th August, Mr. Ward and his companion saw Bishops Castle in the distance and "heard the bells giving notice for steeple-worship," they found it needful to encourage each other in the Lord, and succeeded, Mr. Ward's faith mounting clear above all discouragements, so that he had even a foresight of the day when Bishops Castle should be a circuit. Their reception was rough, and it would have been rougher still, had not a noted fighter who stood wishful to hear, sworn to defend the missionaries against

* Communicated by Rev. A. A. Birchenough.

the violence which threatened. The pugilist was one of the first to enroll himself a member of the society afterwards formed. A woman, "with tears in her eyes," offered her cottage for the evening service, but as the mob threatened to burn it down or unroof it in case the offer was accepted, they preferred to take their stand again in front of the Castle green. Here they managed to deliver their message, though under strange conditions; for, while some wept under the influence of the truth, others mocked and swore and threw stones. No sooner was the service ended than the preacher and his friends were chased by the stone-throwers, and had to take to the pastures in order to escape the hail of missiles. Mr. Ward, however, seems to have thought that on the whole his mission had opened promisingly, and the next two Sundays found him again at Bishops Castle. Tact and courage won the day. When Sunday, August 24th, closed rowdy opposition had died down. A society was established and friends raised up— notably Mr. Pugh, a respectable tradesman of the town, who became a local preacher, as did also his two sons. The Pugh family were of great service to the new cause, and in one of their houses services were held. In 1832, Richard Ward's prophecy had its fulfilment, for in that year Bishops Castle began its influential career as a circuit. The circuit early gave some useful men to the ministry of our Church, such as Thomas Morgan, John Pugh (son of Mr. Pugh already named), Richard Owen; also Robert Bowen, of Asterton, who, in 1851, began to travel in his native circuit, and died at Bishops Castle in 1896. A sister of his (who afterwards became the wife of Rev. Philip Pugh) was instrumental in the conversion of the revered James Huff, whose long ministry of forty-six years was one of remarkable spiritual power and fruitfulness. In the official memoir of Mr. Huff, written by the late Dr. Ferguson, we are told: "In 1887, at the time of his superannuation, it was said that out of sixty ministers given to our ministry out of the county of Shropshire, forty had been led to Christ by our sainted friend." If this statement be even approximately true, James Huff has indeed carved his name deep in the history of Shropshire Primitive Methodism. He was appointed a permanent member of Conference in 1886, and in 1903 died at Bishops Castle where, in 1842, he had begun his ministry.

REV. JAMES HUFF.

It was at a camp-meeting lovefeast, conducted by James Huff, that a youth named Richard Jones made the great decision. The youth developed a character marked by a fine combination of strength and tenderness. As leader, local preacher, circuit steward, district official, Mr. Richard Jones, of Clun, was widely known, trusted, and respected. At Clun especially he was the stay and guide of the society; and it was chiefly through his liberality and guidance that the present church, school, and manse were erected, forming, as they do, a block of property which is an ornament to the

RICHARD JONES.

town, a credit to the Connexion, and a tangible memorial of the faith, tact, and sacrifice of Mr. Jones, who died January 20th, 1900.*

To the list of ministers raised up by the original Shrewsbury Circuit must be added the eminent names of Philip Pugh and Richard Davies. The former entered the ministry in 1836, and died in 1871. As early as 1839 T. Bateman notes in his *Journal:* "We have got a new staff of preachers. Pugh is a young man from Shrewsbury. *I think there is something in him*—studious, obliging, and a tolerable preacher." The judgment shows the discernment of the writer, but even he when he wrote it, could not have divined what possibilities of solid, continuous growth were latent in this studious youth from Shrewsbury, whom he lived to see worthily filling the office of Editor and President of Conference (1867). Richard Davies was one of a number of youths who, in 1823, invited the Primitives to Minsterley, promising to find the preacher a room for the services and to provide him with board and lodging. Entering the ministry in 1825, he was sent to the Wiltshire Mission, but returned to Shrewsbury the next year. For six months he was wholly engaged in missioning neglected villages, in five or six of which he succeeded in forming societies that were incorporated with the Shrewsbury Circuit. This young miner of Minsterley was to become General Book Steward and the first Secretary of the Primitive Methodist Insurance Company.

RICHARD DAVIES.

Probably stimulated by the success of its Wiltshire Mission, Shrewsbury Circuit in 1832 led the way in establishing a mission in the North of Ireland. Here are one or two items from the old minute-books which, doubtless, got written down only after much discussion of "pros and cons": "March 18th, 1832: That Brother Haslam go into Ireland as soon as he can after next Monday." "September 5th, 1832: That Brother Haslam beg at every house in Shrewsbury for Ireland." Unfortunately, T. Haslam soon withdrew from the Connexion, and his place on the Mission was taken, December, 1834, by W. Bickerdike. On entering upon his duties Mr. Bickerdike had his modest presentation, as the following entry shows: "December, 1836.—That Brother Bickerdike have one volume of our *Large Magazine* given him as a token of respect." The good opinion evidently already formed of W. Bickerdike was abundantly justified by his after career. He applied himself vigorously to repair the mischief caused by the withdrawal of his predecessor, and succeeded (1836) in building a chapel in Belfast to take the place of the room in Reas Court. In 1839 the powerful Dudley Circuit relieved Shrewsbury of the charge of the Belfast Mission. When, in 1843-4, the three Irish missions were taken over by the General Missionary Committee, it cannot be said that they had hitherto proved particularly successful, or answered the expectations of their promoters.

HOPTON BANK, OR LUDLOW.

Hopton Bank, afterwards called Ludlow, represents the south-western extension of the young and vigorous Darlaston Circuit. Hopton Bank must not be thought of as

* Rev. W. Jones Davies, a spiritual son of Mr. Jones, has published an "Appreciation" of Mr. Jones, in which are to be found interesting notices of Bishops Castle and Clun Circuits.

a comparatively compact circuit of the modern type, but rather as a tract of country extending from Kidderminster to Presteign. About midway between these two extreme points is Hopton Bank which, probably for that very reason, was made the titular head of the circuit; but as the ancient town of Ludlow was the more convenient town for the preachers' residence, the name was changed. We are not able, any more than was Mr. Petty, to furnish interesting particulars as to the first missioning of this wide district. From the memoir of Mrs. Grace Newell, who is stated to have provided a home for the first missionaries that reached Presteign, that town and other places in Radnorshire, were visited as early as the autumn of 1821. Again, in the memoir of Samuel Morris, who was born at Fordham near Clee Hills in 1815, we are told that the Darlaston Circuit missioned Fordham and the district around while he was but a small boy, and that the Morris family opened their house for preaching, and were among the chief supporters of the Hopton Bank Circuit. Samuel Morris began his ministry in his native circuit in 1836 and, what was very unusual at that time, spent the whole of his probation upon it. Once more: we find that Thomas Norman was one of the preachers of Darlaston Circuit in 1823 and stationed in Ludlow when seized with mortal sickness in the spring of that year. These small pieces of evidence justify the conclusion that, from 1821 onwards to 1824, when Hopton Bank was made a circuit, extensive evangelisation in this wide district was being carried on under the direction of Darlaston.

We get an interesting side-light on the missionary activity of the Ludlow Circuit (as we will call it) from the life-story of Elizabeth Smith, afterwards Mrs. Russell. We see the geographical direction that missionary activity took, how far it reached, and, above all, how simply and trustfully it was undertaken and carried on. Elizabeth Smith is one of the most picturesque figures in our early history. She deservedly takes a high place among the many female-workers of the early decades, and the reference to her here is the more in place as we shall soon meet with her hard at work in Wiltshire. She was converted at the Christmas of 1825, while on a visit to Ludlow, her native place. She soon began to exercise in prayer and to exhort, and when, in the September of 1826, a request came out of Radnorshire that a missionary might be sent to a part of the county as yet unvisited, Elizabeth Smith was urged to undertake the mission, and, despite the opposition of her friends, gladly consented. Her going forth was apostolically simple. The superintendent put a map of the road into her hand, and supplemented it with verbal directions. Said he: "You will have to raise your own salary—two guineas a quarter." "Oh, I did not know I was to have anything," was the answer. She travelled the whole of the first day, and night found her on a lonely common—or rather "moss," for it was partly covered with water, and there were deep treacherous peat-holes, like miniature tarns, all around. Fully alive to the danger, she mounted a ridge and began to sing, "Jesu, Lover of my soul." While still singing she saw a light gradually coming towards her. Her singing had been heard by the residents of a cottage that stood on the edge of the common, and one of them bearing a lantern had come out to learn what was the meaning of this unusual nocturnal hymn. Guided by her voice, he made his way to where she was standing. She found shelter in the cottage which, indeed, proved to be the very house to which she had been directed. "Of course," says the narrative, "they all believed the hand of the Lord was in it."

Elizabeth Smith met with another similar experience while pioneering in "wild Wales." When crossing the Llandeilo rocks overlooking the valley of the upper Wye, the mist came on, and she got off the track. In a few moments she would have fallen over the precipice, had she not given heed to a premonition so real to her that it sounded like a voice crying: "Stop! come back!"

We are not surprised to learn that Elizabeth Smith "practised great frugality so as not to be burdensome to the friends, that she won the affections of the people, and that the Welsh mission as carried on by her cost nothing to the Ludlow Circuit."

Richard Jukes, the poet-preacher, has been more than once referred to in these pages. In him we have another link connecting Ludlow with the general history of our Church; for he was a native of Ludlow Circuit, joined the society in 1825—the same year as Elizabeth Smith—and in 1827 began his ministry of thirty-two years by being appointed one of the six preachers of Ludlow Circuit. When, in January, 1900, Mr. James Tristram died at the patriarchal age of 91, there passed away one who had been connected with Ludlow Primitive Methodism ever since the day when the missioners from Darlaston held their first service in Old Street. He was seventy-three years a local preacher, and when a young man was engaged by his circuit to mission Much Wenlock, Madeley, Iron Bridge, and other places. From 1886 to 1896 James Tristram was a permanent member of Conference, and his descendants of two generations are in the ranks of the ministry. With but a reasonable degree of prosperity premised, it was inevitable that Ludlow Circuit should be divided, comprising, as it did, portions of four counties—Shropshire, Worcestershire, Hereford, and Radnorshire. It was natural, too, that when the division was made it should take effect at the extremities. This is indeed what happened, and the statement of the fact summarizes the external history of the circuit for a period extending beyond 1843. First, Presteign was detached in 1828, and Kidderminster followed in 1832. Even then the process of division was only begun, for Presteign still included Knighton, which has since been made a circuit; and for some years after 1851 Ludlow had no less than five branches, viz., Leominster, Leintwardine, Weobley, Bromyard, and Worcester—all of which are now circuits of the West Midland District.

"The Shropshire Station," and Prees Green Circuit with its Offshoots.

Things which happened together must needs be told one after the other; so, at the very time Oakengates, Shrewsbury, and Ludlow were at work in the central and Southern parts of Shropshire, Burland was at work in the Northern part of the county. Thanks to the carefully-kept *Journal* of Thomas Bateman, we can follow the progress of the mission from October, 1820, when "the work was opening out in Wirral and Shropshire," to 1826, when the Prees Green Circuit was made. Here also, just as had been the case at Oakengates and Shrewsbury, a camp meeting and an imprisonment were outstanding events having important consequences.

At the Whitsuntide of 1822, news reached Burland that some new converts were arranging to hold a camp meeting at Waterloo, between Wem and Whitchurch. Dubious as to the young people's ability for the work in hand, and having a wholesome dread of possible irregularities, the Circuit Committee deputed G. Taylor, J. Smith, and T. Bateman to take charge of the camp meeting. They rose early, for they had a long walk before them. An unexpected rain-storm, for which they were unprepared, led them to turn into the preaching-house at Welsh End, to dry their clothes by the peat-fire. But the drying process was slow, and time pressed, and they resumed their journey. When they reached Waterloo the camp meeting was already in progress.

BAILEY HEAD, OSWESTRY.

They found a Mr. Humpage in charge, who gladly resigned its management into their hands.* All went well until about the middle of the afternoon service, when a number of young sparks rode up and formed in line on the outskirts of the crowd, and seemed disposed to mock; while others, who had behaved decorously enough up to that time, gave signs of following their lead. The conduct of the disturbers was felt to demand a public reproof, and Thomas Bateman was chosen to administer it. Taking as his text the words: "Suffer me that I may speak; and after that I have spoken mock on," he gave a pointed exhortation, every word of which seemed to find its mark. It was

* We conjecture this Mr. Humpage to be the person already mentioned in Vol. i. p. 520, in connection with Darlaston.

noticed that the heads of the youths soon drooped; they listened to the end, and then rode quietly away.

This originally unauthorised camp meeting had on it the seal of the divine approval; for its results, immediate and remote, were remarkable. Thirty years after, Thomas Bateman was riding through Whitchurch on his way to open a chapel in the neighbourhood of Wem, when he met with another horseman who also was going to the chapel-opening. From him he learned that the faithful words spoken so long ago had borne almost immediate fruit in contrition and amendment of life; that the young men (of whom the horseman was one), as they rode away from the camp-ground, had made vows—vows that time, and the efforts some of them had afterwards made to help on the evangelisation of the country-side, had proved the sincerity of.

Waterloo, like the battle of that name, was one of the "decisive" camp meetings of our early history. It wonderfully opened up the way into this part of Cheshire and the borders of Wales. Many requests for the establishment of services at places around Ellesmere, Wem, and even Oswestry were urged, and, from this 26th May, 1822, increasing headway was made in the district. In June there had been but four local preachers in this part of the Burland Circuit, whereas in September there were thirteen, besides some prayer-leaders. It was now determined that this side of the circuit should be constituted a branch, under the name of "the Shropshire Station." This somewhat unusual designation was chosen for reasons similar to those which often decide the election of a pope. Strong rival claimants, who will not give way for each other, will sometimes combine to elect some cardinal whom no one had thought of as a possible competitor. Market Drayton was the more important place, and it had memories. But Market Drayton was at the extremity of the branch. Prees Green was central, but——in short, they shrank from calling it as yet "Prees Green Branch," and fell back upon the neutral "Shropshire Mission." Three preachers were put down to the mission, and one of them—W. Doughty—was appointed to break up new ground.

WILLIAM DOUGHTY.

W. Doughty found his way to Oswestry, and on his third visit, there occurred his arrest and imprisonment which, next to the camp meeting already referred to, turned out to the furtherance of the cause. On June 8th, he took his stand at the Bailey Head, opposite the Red Lion, and because he saw neither law nor reason why he should desist from preaching when Brynner, the constable, and his assistant told him to do so, they carried him off, and eventually put him in a grated cell under the council chamber. A good woman named Douglas brought him food, and though the place in which he was confined was, to use his own words, "too dark to write clear," he did indite "a letter from prison" to his benefactor which after being revised by Mr. Whitridge, the kindly Independent minister, was printed, and may still be read. The Independents, both minister and people, showed W. Doughty much kindness. Acting on the advice of one of them—Mr. Minshall, a solicitor—he refused to walk to Shrewsbury to serve his sentence of a month's imprisonment, so a tax-cart was provided to carry him there. He told the crowd, gathered in Salop Road to see him off, that in a month's time they would see him coming down this road, and, said he, "I shall sing this hymn"—giving out a line of it; and he kept his word. From this time Primitive Methodism gained a footing in Oswestry. Even the magistrate who had committed him to prison granted him his licence, and granted it with kindly words. W. Doughty is said to have sought the protection of a licence, warned by the recent experience of Mr. Whittaker of Knolton Bryn, who had been fined by the magistrates of Overton twenty pounds for preaching in an unlicensed house.* In those days licences, whether for places or persons were useful, even indispensable documents. But, though Mr. Doughty might now enjoy immunity from persecution in Oswestry, he occasionally met with it elsewhere. For example, it is stated that when he and J. Mullock were at Tetchill, two men on horseback charged them, and that Mr. Doughty was ridden over, and his head so cut that the blood ran through his hat. One is glad to learn that a gentleman of public spirit—Mr. Hughes of Ellesmere—took up the case, and brought the miscreants to justice.†

For a time the services in Oswestry were held in the house of Mrs. Elliot, who also extended hospitality to the preachers. She stood by W. Doughty at the Bailey Head on the 8th June, as also did her daughter, who had a sweet, well-trained voice and greatly helped in the singing. Elizabeth Elliot deserves to be remembered alike for her graces and her fate. She should be placed side by side with Thomas Watson, and John Heaps of Cooper's Gardens, as an example of the amount of work that was done—and well done, in the early days by those who were still in their teens. Doughty's imprisonment affected her more than his sermon. She joined the church and began to preach. "She was," we are told, "an excellent speaker; generally short, but very powerful." She was in great request, very useful, much beloved. But her promising

TABLET IN OSWESTRY CHAPEL BURIAL GROUND.
Removed from old Chapel.

* "Early Recollections of Mr. William Doughty, and of Primitive Methodism in Oswestry." By Mr. Thomas Minshall. 1873.

† "Career of William Doughty: his Preaching, Punishment, and Prison Thoughts." Reprinted with additions from the "Oswestry Advertiser," April 8th, 1863.

life had an early and tragic close. On Saturday, April 23rd, 1825, she started for her Sunday appointments at Llandreino, in Montgomeryshire. As she stepped into the ferry-boat at Pant (Llanymynech) she said, in parting with a friend whose hospitality she had shared: "Pray for me." Now, the river Virniew, swollen by the rains from the Welsh mountains, was in angry flood. There was a chain across the river to keep the cattle from straying. Instead of crossing below the chain, the boatman fatuously attempted to cross above stream, and the boat, being violently thrown against the chain, capsized, and Elizabeth Elliot and the boatman's wife were drowned.

At the June Quarterly Meeting of 1825 the Shropshire Station got itself made into the Prees Green Circuit. We say "got itself made," because the making was done

PREES CHURCH.

against the wishes of the parent circuit, and "rather prematurely," Hugh Bourne thought. Thus a mere hamlet came to give its name to a historic circuit which embraced more than north Shropshire, and is now represented by at least seven circuits. Hard by is the village of Prees, with its "weather-beaten church on the hill." Of this church Archdeacon Allen, the friend of Edward Fitzgerald and Thackeray, was vicar from 1846 to 1883. The vicar was on good terms with his Primitive Methodist parishioners. He took the chair at the lectures Robert Key delivered on his periodical visits to the village. He co-operated with them in Temperance work. When some one asked him to preach in the Primitive Methodist chapel he, in 1874, wrote to Dean Stanley inviting his views on the general question whether there is any law to prohibit a clergyman of the Established Church from officiating in any meeting-house in his parish; Archdeacon Allen evidently believing there was no such prohibitive law. In this letter to the Dean he says: "The Primitive Methodists have done a great work at Prees in encouraging sobriety and thrift. Thirty years ago there were ten houses in Prees where intoxicating liquor was sold; now there are only two, and in only one of these can drink be consumed on the premises. This happy change is not due solely to the Primitive Methodists, but they have been special labourers on the side of sobriety." Who were these "special labourers" who commanded the Archdeacon's respect and willing co-operation? Materials for an answer are supplied by Rev. S. Horton, himself a native of Prees:—

"Two brothers of the name of Powell got converted at a camp meeting. From being the ringleaders in wickedness they became the ringleaders in righteousness. They were men of marked ability and force of character. William Powell prospered greatly, and became the head of a large firm, employing some hundreds of men. He could neither read nor write when he was converted and, when he commenced work as a local preacher, used to recite his hymns and passages of Scripture from memory. But he was a force in the neighbourhood that made for righteousness, and everybody respected his sterling integrity and uprightness of character. Another village-reformer of a different type was Samuel Adams, a well-read, thoughtful man, with deep spiritual insight, and a lover of everything beautiful and true—the leading temperance reformer of the place. Then there was also Joseph Ikin, one that feared God and eschewed evil, whose descendants are among the prominent supporters of Methodism in the neighbourhood to-day. These and others, less prominent but like-minded, were the leaders of the Primitive Methodist Church, and were by training and conviction Nonconformists of the old sturdy type, that resisted church-rates, and would to-day undoubtedly, if alive, have led a campaign for 'passive resistance' against the Education Bill."*

To these names must be added that of Thomas Rogers, whose long and honourable connection with our Church was recognised by his election as a permanent member of Conference. He was house-carpenter at Hawkstone Park—the seat of the family to which belonged Lord Hill, Wellington's second in command, and the eccentric Rowland Hill, of old Surrey Chapel. Lord Hill of Hawkstone both gave and sold several sites for the building of chapels in this neighbourhood, and it was through Thomas Rogers' influence, it is said, that the first of such sales was brought about.

Much was said in a preceding part of this History of the "vision-work" which marked the formative period of the Connexion. Hugh Bourne came across it again when on a visit to Prees Green Circuit in October, 1828. Two young women went into trance while he was there; and, though he was struck with "the dignity with which the two young persons conducted their cause," and thought their singing when in the trance was "beyond anything he remembered to have heard," yet the counsel he gave the society indicates a more critical attitude towards these doubtful phenomena than he had taken twenty years before. "I gave them," says he, "the general advices usually given in our Connexion, and which are: (1) None to go in vision if they can avoid it. (2) Not to lay too much stress upon it. (3) That faith, plain faith,

---

* Article on "Archdeacon Allen" in *Primitive Methodist Quarterly Review*, July, 1903.

which worketh by love, is greater than these things; but that if any one's faith was strengthened by them, so far it was well."

When in 1833 Oswestry was formed into a circuit, a huge cantle of territory lying to the west was cut off from Prees Green. Still, Market Drayton remained to it as a branch and, more singular still, Longton in the Potteries was also a branch until 1836, when it appeared on the stations for a time as a separate circuit, with Thomas Russell as superintendent. Market Drayton continued connected with Prees Green until 1869, and Wem until 1878.

Oswestry and its Offshoots.

Oswestry Circuit had a good start. It had a membership of 697, and a good staff of workers and capable officials. Its "lot"—no narrow one to begin with, was capable of indefinite enlargement in certain directions; for its way lay open into the Welsh counties of Flint, Denbigh, and Montgomery. Its history shows that it can fairly claim to have been a missionary circuit. It *did* cross the English border. Three other circuits have been formed from it and, in addition, it undertook for some years the responsibility of the Lisburn Mission. Moreover, it was long known for the liberal support it gave to the general missionary fund.

In Oswestry itself, a building called the Cold Bath had been transformed into a chapel, which was opened by Thomas Bateman on December 12th, 1824. Soon after this, W. Doughty retired from the ministry and began business in one of the houses attached to the chapel; but he still continued a most active official, as the plans and documents of the times clearly show. In, or about, 1840, a new chapel was built in Oswestry, and by this time chapels in other parts of the wide circuit had been acquired. Trouble, however, arose in Oswestry, which led to a serious secession and to chapel embarrassments. The primary cause of the trouble seems to have been disagreement on a point of doctrine. Some young men adopted and publicly advanced views on infant purity which we take to have been practically identical with the published views of Rev. Nathan Rouse, which brought him under the discipline of the Wesleyan Methodist Conference. It was maintained as a direct corollary of John Wesley's doctrine of Christian Perfection that, in the case of children born to parents who are themselves entirely sanctified, the entail of original sin is broken. Senior officials, if they did not understand or share the views of their juniors, were dissatisfied with the treatment meted out to these by the local and District courts, and W. Fitzgerald and R. Thomas, who had been zealous co-workers with W. Doughty from the beginning seceded, and many others with them.[*] W. Doughty himself followed in 1846 (though his family did not), and the secessionists built a chapel for themselves as an "Independent Methodist" society. We shall not seek to follow the secession through its subsequent vicissitudes. Our only reason for referring to it at all is, that the crisis it created served to bring out the high qualities of Mr. Edward Parry and other of the Oswestry Circuit officials; and, secondly, because the secession itself is one of the very few in our history which are distinctly traceable to doctrinal differences.

[*] J. Whittaker, W. Fitzgerald, and R. Thomas are the first three names on the plan of 1843 after the travelling preachers.

Our fathers were too busy pressing home vital doctrines to have time or disposition to dispute about minor ones.

In writing of Mr. Edward Parry and the special service he rendered at this critical time, we will borrow the words of Mr. T. Ward Green, the present owner of "The Wood" estate, Maesbrook, and a leading official of the Llanymynech Circuit:—

MR. EDWARD PARRY.

MRS. PARRY.

"The Oswestry Circuit of that time was an immense affair, more resembling in its area and agencies an ecclesiastical diocese than a Methodist station. Of this important and influential circuit Mr. Parry was for thirty-seven years the steward, and on his retirement from office, his co-officials presented him with an illuminated address. It is not too much to say that Primitive Methodism in North-west Shropshire owes much of its present position, and possibly its very existence, to Mr. Parry's continued devotion and sagacity. A few years after he joined the community a disruption of a most threatening character took place in the Oswestry society; nearly all the original members left us, and the heavily burdened chapel was being offered for sale. At this supreme crisis in our local history, Mr. Parry came forward, consulted solicitors, undertook responsibilities, obtained new trustees, raised fresh loans; in short, saved the property to the Connexion, and the young cause from ruin. As far back as 1832 he missioned Maesbrook; Morton and West Felton were also opened by him, and at each of these places we have still progressive societies. He six times represented the Tunstall District in Conference, and was delegate from the Oswestry Circuit to District meeting the same number of times."*

ORIGINAL MEETING-HOUSE AT MAESBROOK, LLANYMYNECH.

Mr. Parry died in 1894 in the eighty-seventh year of his age, and was interred in the graveyard attached to the Knockin Heath Chapel, which represents the oldest interest in the present Llanymynech Circuit. His eldest son is an official of long standing and the present Steward of Ellesmere Circuit.

Reference is made in the above quotation to the missioning of Maesbrook in 1832. Services were at first held in an old farmhouse in the hamlet of Llwynygo, i.e., the Cuckoo's Grove, which forms part of the Maesbrook Wood estate. One of the earliest converts

* Memoir in the *Aldersgate*, 1895.

was Mrs. Ward, the widow of the late owner of the estate, who was married to Mr. Edward Parry. Her only son, Samuel, attended the services in the farmhouse and in 1841, when only eighteen years of age, became an exhorter. He celebrated the attainment of his majority by giving a site for the building of a Primitive Methodist chapel fronting the avenue to his own house. Mr. Ward was a well-read man and became a popular local preacher, and also took an active interest in connexional movements. His patrimonial home, known as "The Wood"—comfortable, old-fashioned, picturesque—came to be as well known to the Primitive Methodists in the West, as Bavington Hall had been known to Primitive Methodists of the North. Leading ministers and laymen constantly found their way to this hospitable homestead. In the days of the undivided Oswestry Circuit, it was the custom for one Quarterly Meeting of the year to be held at Maesbrook, in an upper room of one of the farm-buildings; and when we are told that the 'squire and his lady cheerfully dispensed hospitality to some two hundred circuit officials at these times, we get a striking illustration of that period in our

MR. S. WARD.

THE WOOD HOUSE, MAESBROOK.

history which we have called the period of circuit predominance and enterprise. The Oswestry Circuit Quarterly Meeting was a more important gathering, so far as numbers went, than the Conferences of the same period. The fact, true of that day but true no longer, sharply contrasts the past with the present. Mr. Ward's useful life came to

292　PRIMITIVE METHODIST CHURCH.

PRESIDENTS OF CONFERENCE FROM 1860 TO 1874.

a close in 1896, and he, too, lies in Knockin Heath Chapel graveyard. It is pleasing to know that the interest Primitive Methodists feel in regard to The Wood does not all belong to the past as in the case of Bavington Hall, but that its present owner, Mr. T. Ward Green, is carrying forward the old traditions, and is his uncle's successor in the stewardship of the Llanymynech Circuit.*

Besides Mr. E. Parry and S. Ward, J. Grindley of Knockin Heath, and Stephen Batho and R. Mansell were faithful adherents of the cause in the time of crisis in the Oswestry Circuit already referred to. Stephen Batho, who died in 1879, was a local preacher forty-five years. Richard Mansell was converted at Haughton in the Ellesmere Circuit in 1834, was a most acceptable local preacher for sixty years, and for a considerable time the Steward of the Oswestry Circuit.

STEPHEN BATHO.

RICHARD MANSELL.

It is noticeable that women were as actively associated with the beginnings of our Church in North-west Shropshire as they were elsewhere. Thus it was in the 'Twenties at Knockin Heath, where the three daughters of a large farmer in the neighbourhood of Ellesmere, named Bickley, greatly stimulated the cause. So also at Rhosymedre and the district around. Mary Owens—said to have belonged to the family of Admiral Rodney—was for many years an active worker and altogether a remarkable woman. Married to Richard Williams, himself a local preacher, she and her husband were associated in usefulness. In 1827 they took a house and introduced Primitive Methodism into Rhosymedre, and subsequently assisted to do the same at Black Park. R. Williams was also leader of a class at Ruabon for sixteen years. During the forty years Mary Williams was a local preacher she missioned much in Shropshire and the bordering counties, and even found her way to London in 1847 to assist John Ride in his evangelistic work.

In the *Magazine* we have an account of the opening of the first chapel at Rhosymedre in 1833; a larger one was built in 1842. When the latter, through depression of trade and removals, was brought into financial straits, Mary Williams got leave to beg through the then extensive circuit in order to raise the sum required for arrears of interest and save the chapel— and she succeeded in her object. The late John Evans did much to consolidate the cause at Rhosymedre, and Henry Lloyd that of Black Park.

MARY WILLIAMS.

In its Jubilee year—1873, Oswestry Circuit was still undivided, having 900 members and 121 local preachers. Soon after, its partition began by the making of Rhosymedre, 1877; Llanymynech, 1878; and Ellesmere Circuit, 1895.

* For Mr. S. Ward, see an interesting article in the *Aldersgate Magazine* for 1897—" A Shropshire Village Yeoman," by Rev. A. A. Birchenough.

CHAPTER XXII.

The Formation of the Brinkworth District.

88. BRINKWORTH, 1825. S. West W. Strongman J. Baker S. Turner A. Sly J. Blackmore W. Wigley 89. BLAENAVON, 1826. J. Hibbs H. Higginson 90. WITNEY, 1826. G. Appleby E. Lowe 91. FROME, 1827. J. Prince W. Turner J. Guy S. Price 92. PILLAWELL, 1827. J. Morton F. R. Broom	93. HAVERFORDWEST, 1828. J. Gregory 94. MOTCOMB, 1828. R. Davies W. Langley W. Yapp 95. REDRUTH, 1828. W. Driffield J. Richards S. Wilshaw 96. ST. AUSTELL, 1829. T. Ford R. Tuffin B. Tripp J. Clark J. Noot One to be obtained 97. BATH, 1829. E. Foizey	98. STROUD, 1830. J. Horsman M. Bugden 99. SALISBURY, 1831. J. Preston A. Woodward 100. SHEFFORD, 1832. J. Ride H. Hayes G. Wallis E. Bishop G. Price J. Coxhead W. Wiltshire J. Rumming T. Jackson E. Wheeldon M. Moor A. Goodwin S. Wheeler 101. MORETON, 1833. J. Morish 102. ST. IVES, 1833. H. Pope T. Meredith

BRINKWORTH DISTRICT AS IT FIRST APPEARED ON THE STATIONS OF 1833, WITH THE YEAR OF EACH CIRCUIT'S FORMATION.

IT will conduce to clearness if, in this chapter, we confine ourselves to giving in outline a sketch of those evangelistic efforts of certain circuits, the combined result of which is seen in the Brinkworth District formed in 1833. That result is set forth above in the transcript of the stations of the Brinkworth District as they first appeared in the Conference Minutes; the only alteration made being the insertion of the year when each circuit was formed, in place of the letters L.D. or T.P.D. of the original draft—letters which have now lost their interest for us. Several distinct lines of agency converged in the making of Brinkworth District. First, in order of time, came Tunstall and Scotter's joint "Western Mission" which, from Stroud in Gloucestershire, reached Frome and Bath in Somerset, Motcombe in Dorset, and Salisbury in South Wilts. Second, Oakengates' missions to the Forest of Dean and Hereford, and to Blaenavon in South Wales. Third, Shrewsbury's mission to Brinkworth in Wilts, and thence to Shefford or Newbury in Berks. Fourth, Hull's mission in Cornwall represented by St. Austell and St. Ives. Lastly, we have Haverfordwest in the Welsh Peninsula, as the solitary outcome of the agency of the abortive Missionary Committee of 1825. Brinkworth District's fifteen stations of 1833 had, by 1842, become thirty, with fifteen branches and missions. Taking these lines of agency in their order, we have first, then :

I.—THE WESTERN MISSION.

In 1823 Tunstall and Scotter jointly undertook a mission to the West of England. It almost looks as though this enterprise was regarded at the time as one of the weightiest the Connexion had as yet entered upon. Tunstall appointed its own special committee of management, and hoped that Scotter would do the same : other circuits were also asked to co-operate. If we may regard this as an early attempt to establish a General Missionary Committee, it was destined to be unsuccessful. The circuits did co-operate, but each co-operated in its own way. James Bonsor was chosen to be the leading missionary. When last we saw him he was at Oakengates and Shrewsbury. After his imprisonment at Shrewsbury he fell again into the hands of the police at Bridgnorth, and spent a night in prison. Next morning three proposals were made to him from which to choose : to promise that neither he nor his colleagues would preach any more in the streets of Bridgnorth ; to find bail for his appearance at the Sessions ; or to be sent to Shrewsbury jail. "Then," said Bonsor, "I will go to Shrewsbury ; for I was there a few months ago and they used me extremely well. They brought me eight breakfasts to prison one morning, and promised that they would use me well if I came again." Plainly, nothing could be made of such a man, so, after straitly charging him not to preach in the streets again, the bailiffs dismissed him in a friendly way, shaking him by the hand, and promising to protect him against persecution when preaching in licensed houses. And, when, soon after, three of the worst persecutors were brought before them, they made good their promise.

THE CROSS, STROUD.

This was in November, 1822, just before Oakengates was made a circuit. In 1823 Bonsor is Tunstall's leading preacher, and on June 7th he set out on his mission, calling at Worcester and Tewkesbury on his way. At the latter place he was once more arrested for preaching in the open air. He was asked to find bail but refused, and as the

Dissenting ministers of Tewkesbury very handsomely spoke up in the court on his behalf, and public opinion was on his side, Bonsor was, after much discussion, liberated. He visited also some of the villages round Gloucester, but no permanent societies were formed either at Tewkesbury or Gloucester at this time. His objective was the cloth-manufacturing district of the county, and here he met with an encouraging degree of success. At Stroud, tradition says, he preached at The Cross, and at the close asked the crowd if he should come again, to which the response was a hearty "Yes." At many villages in the Stroud-water valley and among the pleasant Cotswold Hills societies were established. A chapel was built at Chalford, in the Golden Valley, as early as 1823, and the theatre at Stroud was fitted up as a place of worship—a conversion which led

CHALFORD CHAPEL, BUILT 1823.

the people jubilantly to sing: "Praise the Lord! the case is altered, now this house belongs to the Lord."

In 1824 there were five preachers on the Western Mission; three years later the direction of that Mission had passed from Staffordshire to Somerset. We can see what happened when we turn to the Conference stations for those years. In 1825, Tunstall has eleven preachers; in 1826, seven; in 1827, but two. First, Stroud Branch was detached from Tunstall and joined to the adjoining Brinkworth Circuit, on its formation in 1826. Owing to slackness of trade and the poverty of the people, Stroud still needed financial support and oversight, which Brinkworth was ready to supply. In 1826, James Bonsor's name disappears from the roll of preachers. There is reason to believe that he had been closely connected with Stroud and district to the last, and hence his retirement from the Connexion would tend to accentuate the temporary difficulties of the Stroud Branch. In 1830, Stroud became an independent but numerically feeble circuit, with 101 members, thirteen local preachers, and one chapel. It was never to be its lot to become a great missionary circuit like its powerful neighbour, Brinkworth. In fact, the Stroud-water valley was an eddy of the particular stream of evangelization which the Western Mission originated. The main volume of the stream rolled on. FROME Circuit, formed in 1827, with J. Ride, T. Haslam, and S. Spittle as its preachers, shows the course taken, and the point reached, up to that time. We find W. Paddison, in 1826, holding camp meetings at Clandown and Nunney, and missioning various places between Frome and Bristol in the vicinity of Wells. Bristol itself was visited, and a small society formed which, however, soon became extinct, so that a more vigorous and sustained attack had to be made on Bristol a few years later. In Bath, the famous city of pleasure, greater success was gained; in 1828, W. Towler was appointed to labour in the city and its immediate neighbourhood. Frome's mission to Glastonbury in 1843, which afterwards extended to Bridgewater, belongs to a much later period. Frome's main missionary efforts lay in another direction at the time of which we write. The line of advance went obliquely forward into Dorset, and on to the sea-coast. Trowbridge, in Wilts, was visited, and Enmore Green and Motcombe, and other places round Shaftesbury, in Dorset, were successfully missioned. MOTCOMBE, made a circuit in 1828, played an important rôle in the evangelization of large portions of some of the Southern counties. One of its missionaries seems to have been the first Primitive Methodist to preach in Hampshire—this was under a tree at Breamore in 1830—and also first in the city of Winchester. But the circuit was not strong enough to sustain the required mission, and the duty was afterwards undertaken by Shefford Circuit. Salisbury, and some of the villages around, were visited by Motcombe preachers as early as 1827. Regular preaching services were established in the city, and since 1831, when SALISBURY was made a circuit, it has had a progressive history, which may be said to have culminated in 1893 (when Salisbury shared with Southampton the distinction of giving its name to the Salisbury and Southampton District); and the neighbouring circuits of Wilton and Woodfalls are its offshoots. But Motcombe's most distinctive work has been done in Dorset; in the towns and villages of that Wessex whose physical features and people have been illuminated by the genius of Thomas Hardy. In 1833, Motcombe penetrated deeper into this interesting district—reaching Blandford on the Stour—Thomas Hardy's "Shottsford Forum." How this was done Richard Davies tells us. In 1831 he says—

"From Frome we removed to the Motcombe station, and resided at Enmore Green, Shaftesbury. Two rooms were rented for our accommodation, very scantily furnished, owing to the poverty of the station. Its funds were insufficient for the salaries of a married man and a single one, and to remedy this state of things the Quarterly Meeting resolved to employ a third preacher and to set me at liberty to mission some villages and towns which lay round about us, some near and some a long way off. Several new societies were formed and added to the circuit, and worked afterwards by the three preachers alternately; and by this means the funds were augmented and the station relieved of debt."— (*MS. Autobiography.*)

Blandford Branch, comprising such villages as Durweston, Stickland, etc., was the outcome of this mission. Soon the old seaport town of Poole, situated on its spacious harbour, was reached, and adjoining villages evangelized ; and when, in 1838, POOLE became a circuit, it joined hands with the Weymouth and Dorchester Mission, already referred to. As for fashionable, far-stretching Bournemouth, it was not yet thought of. Where it now stands was then but a heath, scored with chines running down to the sea, and covered with odorous pines. Its astonishing development belongs to a later period. We have only to add that, in 1842, Motcombe had the Sherborne Branch and Stoke Mission under its charge, and that Blandford was made a circuit in 1880.

From this sketch of the Western Mission it will be seen that, from start to finish, that Mission gave some six circuits to the Bristol, and seven to the Salisbury and Southampton Districts. There is not one of these circuits which may not feel itself to be historically linked to the powerful but distant Tunstall and Scotter Circuits, inasmuch as it has been directly or indirectly the beneficiary of the Western Mission.

II.—OAKENGATES' MISSIONS.

Blaenavon, Cwm, and Pillawell, which came on the stations severally in 1825, '26, and '27, form a group of circuits that were the direct or indirect outcome of Oakengates Circuit's early missionary labours. The facts as to the origin of these three circuits show that the tracts of country they named, though each had its distinctive physical and industrial features, were so geographically contiguous as to be within the walking powers of the missionary. They were visited in succession by the same pioneer, and came on the stations one after the other, in the same order in which they were visited. Ever since their formation these three circuits have had a continuous history, and that history, important as it is, may be compressed into the statement of the capital fact that from them the whole of the present South Wales District, including also the missions within its area, has sprung. When, in 1888, the South Wales District was formed, it might almost seem as though the principle determining the grouping had been, to include in the new District none but those stations which derived from Oakengates through Blaenavon, Cwm, or Pillawell. Of course, no such idea would influence the minds of those who were responsible for the division made, yet the coincidence of the arrangement with the actual course of development is striking.

BLAENAVON.

The Black Mountains that rise frowningly from the valley of the Usk in Brecknock, and southward sink down slopingly through West Monmouth, Glamorgan, and part of Carmarthen, form the great South Wales coal-field, covering the hill-sides for a distance of 900 square miles—rich, too, in iron and copper. All this mineral wealth has not only made the hill-country a populous hive of industry, but accounts for the remarkable development of the Bristol Channel ports of Newport, Cardiff, and Swansea. Blaenavon is on the north-eastern edge of this district, where the hill-country of Monmouth rises from the valley of the Usk, which river has bent round to pass through Monmouthshire to find its debouchure in the estuary of the Severn. It was this district which was the scene of the Chartist rising of 1839 when, on a stormy November night, the miners and iron-workers poured down from the hills into Newport and came in conflict with the military. Some twenty persons lost their lives, and Frost, and two other leaders of the abortive rising, were sentenced to be "hanged, drawn, and quartered," though the sentence was afterwards commuted to fourteen years' penal servitude.

When Oakengates sent a missionary to Blaenavon it was like succouring like—one coal and iron district lending a helping hand to another. The missionary selected was James Roles, whom we saw making his entry into Liverpool pelted with mud. He found his way to Blaenavon just about the time James Bonsor was beginning the Western Mission. Writing on August 10th, 1823, he reports that he has already preached at seven distinct places, and gathered seventy in church fellowship, of whom forty were in Blaenavon. Another missionary has been sent to assist him, and applications for their services are constantly being received from various quarters. The first chapel in South Wales is said to have been built at Beaufort about this time.

Cwm.

The reader should be advertised that he will not find Cwm in any gazetteer or on any ordinary map. It is not even a hamlet, much less a considerable village or town. It is only the name of a small estate with its farmhouse and flour-mill attached, situate in the parish of Cloddock, in the south-west corner of Herefordshire. The Cwm * lies under the mountains which rise just within the Welsh border and are called the Black Mountains, from the dark heath with which they are covered. To get here from Blaenavon was no difficult matter. No mountainous barrier intervenes between Herefordshire and central Monmouthshire, as a glance at the map will show. But what the particular reasons were which brought James Roles, or other missionary, into this secluded corner are not stated and, however easy, it is useless to conjecture what those reasons were. What is clear is that the missionary from Blaenavon found his way here in the early part of 1824, and met with hospitable entertainment at the Cwm, where Mrs. Phillips resided on her own property with her sons and daughters. Henry, one of the sons, entered the ministry in 1846, and rose to be President of the Conference of 1878. One of the daughters, too, joined the society established at the Cwm in 1824, and in 1830 was married to W. Towler, one of the earliest missionaries in these parts, and who attained to a position of considerable influence in the Connexion. There were other families of good standing in the neighbourhood who identified themselves with the cause, such as Messrs. J. and W. Gilbert. At the adjoining village of Longtown there had been a Methodist cause, but it had become extinct, so that the advent of Primitive Methodism to the neighbourhood was opportune and welcome. In 1825, Thomas Proctor entered upon his all too brief but successful ministry by being appointed to the newly-formed Blaenavon Circuit, and was at once sent to extend that circuit's mission in Herefordshire.

* *Cwm* pronounced *Coom*, is a Welsh word signifying a dingle or small valley in a range of hills. The word occurs frequently in the Saxonised form of *Combe*.

It may be questioned whether in the long roll of the worthies of our Church we have met or shall meet with a name that should more absolutely command our respect and reverence than should the name of Thomas Proctor. He was dominated by one supreme passion—to be entirely consecrated to God in the work of the ministry. As far as we can see that passion was without any taint of fanaticism. We can observe no trace of self-seeking or self-glorification; no eccentricities even in speech or conduct which jar and offend, while we readily excuse. And yet, although there was a "sanity in his faith and a sweetness in his disposition" which told powerfully upon some of the families of the district, like that of the Llanwarnes of The Park, who were brought to God under his ministry, and did much in their turn to support and extend the cause; yet these were exceptions. They were outnumbered by the ignorant, the prejudiced, and the persecuting. Thomas Proctor had often to endure privations—hunger and cold, and the brutal assaults of men who pelted him with rotten eggs and sludge and stones. All this he bore uncomplainingly. "When he could obtain no house for shelter, and no food for money, he frequently retired to the shade of some bush or tree for study and prayer, got what sustenance he could from the hedges, and in the evening went into some neighbouring village to preach in the open-air, often to endure insult and persecution in various forms." No wonder that Thomas Proctor succeeded; that he laid the foundations of the Cwm Circuit deep and firm, or that success was won at the cost of health and life. For some months in 1826 W. Towler was associated with him in labour, and that year Cwm was made a Circuit. He laboured on until October, 1827, when he went to his home in Yorkshire for a short rest and change; but it was to die. Mr. Petty who laboured in the Cwm Circuit in 1835, and had abundant opportunities to learn the character of his predecessor and the effect of his ministry, has penned a noble tribute to Thomas Proctor, of which we cannot forbear quoting a portion.

"His ministerial course was short, but it was a glorious one. His talents were respectable, his piety profound, his conduct in all things exemplary. For deep humility, quenchless love for the souls of men, and intimate communion with God, he may be fairly classed with Brainerd, Fletcher, and Bramwell. It is affecting to think that a young man of his character, and of his physical strength, should have been brought to the grave in a little more than two years, through the hardships, privations, and excessive toils he endured in Herefordshire He fell a martyr to his work; but he accomplished a wondrous amount of good in a little time, and left a name fragrant as ointment poured forth. The remembrance of his excellencies will long continue in the families by whom he was entertained, and the report of his exalted piety will descend to their posterity."

In 1828 a little white chapel was built at the Cwm on a site given by Mrs. Phillips. The modest building might almost be regarded as an annexe of the adjoining farmhouse, where the early preachers found shelter and the comforts of a home.* Chapel

* The farm was also the manse, as the following extract from the MS. journal of Richard Davies shows: "In 1828 I removed to the Cwm Circuit, in which I had no home in one sense, but two good ones in another. I was all welcome to the comforts and care of two families, in particular. The one with Mrs. Phillips of Cwm and her two sons and three daughters, one of the happiest families I ever met with; the other with Mr. Llanwarne of the Park, a very kind and hospitable family. Hence I had much to be thankful for."

and farm—nothing more, gave the name to, and formed the centre of, one of the most important circuits of Primitive Methodism in the early days. This is the outstanding fact challenging attention in relation to the early history of the Cwm Circuit. In 1835, when John Petty was on the circuit, it had its home-branch, with fifty-four distinct preaching-places; its Bromyard Branch in East Herefordshire, and its Monmouthshire Mission; these together employing eight travelling preachers and having an aggregate membership of 796. Nor does this fully represent the missionary activity of Cwm Circuit at this time; for the Circuit Report of 1836 says: "We have taken up Tewkesbury and its neighbourhood as a mission"; and we learn from Mr. Petty's *Journal* that at the June Quarterly Meeting of 1836, "an order was made out for employing a hired local as an additional missionary on the Monmouthshire mission, and to extend that mission into Brecknockshire, and as far as Brecon, the county town."* Primitive Methodism does not seem, however, to have struck root either in Gloucestershire or Brecknockshire through Cwm's efforts at this time. Bromyard Branch, as we have seen, was afterwards taken charge of by Ludlow; but Cwm's hold on Monmouthshire was more lasting. Joseph Grieves and Thomas Llanwarne carried on a vigorous mission in the hilly and thinly populated district to the east of Abergavenny. When, as the outcome of this mission, the Rose Cottage Branch of Cwm Circuit was formed, we get still another example of a single house becoming the titular head of a station. Rose Cottage is now included in the Abergavenny mission. The Thomas Llanwarne just mentioned was a man remarkably successful as an evangelist. He belonged to a family that has done much for the extension and strengthening of the Cwm Circuit and its offshoot—Kingstone, made a circuit in 1892. Indeed, one cannot but feel that, next to the devoted labours of its pioneer preachers, the healthy development of this rural circuit is largely attributable to the unusual number of families of standing and high character that from the beginning have been identified with its societies. Besides the Gilberts and the Llanwarnes, yet another such family was that of which Mr. John Gwillim was the head. In 1830 he took up his residence at the Wayne, and soon after he and his wife joined the society. Mrs. Gwillim was the daughter of Mr. Rogers, the vicar of Cloddock—a man so liberal and evangelical in sentiment that, when he had concluded the services in the parish-church, he would frequently be found worshipping with the Primitives in their humble sanctuary or in the open-air. John Gwillim, jun., entered our ministry in 1843; in 1856-9 he was superintendent of Cwm Circuit, and he died when stationed at Presteign in 1867. He was, we are told, "noted for hospitality and benevolence." William Gwillim was a well-read, intelligent, public-spirited yeoman. He began to preach in 1832 and to the end of his life, which extended to 1896, he rendered exceptional service to the Primitive Methodism of this part of Herefordshire. Mention should be made, too, of the Hancorns of Ploughfield, and of Mrs. Lea and her daughters of Yew Cottage near Madeley, who joined the Church about 1830. At her own expense Mrs. Lea fitted up the "Cottage Chapel" near her own residence, as also a chapel at Shenmore. Of this lady (who died in 1855) and her family Mr. Petty writes: "This highly respectable and pious family rendered eminent service to the community in various

* "Life and Labours of Rev. J. Petty," by Rev. James Macpherson, p. 287.

ways, and greatly contributed to the establishment and increase of the societies. They patiently bore the sneers amd contempt of many in their own rank, cheerfully encountered persecution in different forms, and zealously endeavoured to spread evangelical truth and Christianity in many of the surrounding villages and hamlets."

PILLAWELL AND ITS OFFSHOOTS.

The Forest of Dean is "an island of the coal measures," lying between the Severn and the Wye. Still mindful of its fellow colliers, Oakengates sent James Roles to this secluded corner of Gloucestershire to seek them out, just as before it had sent him to Blaenavon. We find him at Pillawell in the autumn of 1824, and we may reasonably conjecture that he reached it from Cwm, where he had been doing pioneer work. We are furnished with no particulars of his experiences in opening the mission, but it is evident he met with a fair measure of success before moving off to Pembroke Dock; for in December, 1826, Pillawell was made a circuit. A "circuit" indeed it was, being forty miles in length and extending some miles beyond the city of Hereford, which was visited in August, 1826, if not before.

From the *Journals* of some of the earliest preachers who travelled this circuit some idea may be gained of the moral condition of the people of the Forest at the time, and of the difficulties and privations that attended the work of the missionaries amongst them. For example: Richard Davies, who was here in 1827, tells us that there was then not a single Connexional chapel in the circuit, but that the first was soon afterwards built at Lydbrook. Pillawell got its chapel in 1835, at a cost of £70! He notes the long and toilsome journeys and "the lack of suitable and seasonable refreshments." From what befell Edward Beard of Oakengates, we can see that pioneering under such conditions exacted its penalties. He was one of the first missionaries to this district, and preached at Ross and other places in Herefordshire; but, like Thomas Proctor, he was soon forced to relinquish his work and to return to his native circuit broken in health.

On a certain day in 1829, Joseph Middleton, now the Pillawell preacher, walked fourteen miles with the snow reaching to his knees; and yet, though the weather was so wintry, it was spring by the calendar, being April 3rd. "Plainly a portent!" said "a certain individual near Broad Oak." "God is angry with the Ranters for using His name so frequently in their prayers, and so has sent this unseasonable weather as a punishment!" The diarist's blunt comment is: "What ignorant stuff!" But probably this man, with his warped and ill-furnished mind, thought he was drawing a pious and legitimate inference from the facts of the universe. His sapient conclusion was of a piece with the reasoning of those dwellers under the Black Mountain who counted Thomas Proctor and his followers as the false prophets who were to rise in the latter days, with whom therefore it was a self-denying virtue to have no manner of dealings, not even monetary ones. From boycotting the "false prophets" to stoning them was but a short step.

If this was how the Revival and its agents were conceived of by some in 1829, there were others who, with or without theorising, set their faces against it. It was so at Newnham on Severn—a town which for many years had been as notorious as

Bishops Castle for the bitterness of its opposition to religion as evangelically presented. Nevertheless, Samuel Morgan and Richard Morris, two local preachers, had the temerity to attempt a service in the streets of Newnham on August 2nd, 1829. "They had not unfurled the banner of the Cross more than a quarter of an hour when two constables came up, and without any authority from a magistrate put the hand-cuffs on Mr. Morgan and led him, with Mr. Morris, to the stocks, in which they confined them three hours and a quarter." But though their feet were fast in the stocks, their tongues were free: "they faithfully warned the people standing round, and like the Apostles they prayed and sang praises unto God."*

On another day, we see William Leaker, the superintendent, spending the whole of the day on his knees in the Forest of Dean, wrestling with God on behalf of the distressed condition of the Pillawell society. It was March 21st, 1832, the day appointed by authority as a day of humiliation, fasting, and prayer on account of the ravages of the cholera in the land. As Mr. Leaker rose from his knees to go to his evening's appointment he rejoiced in the assurance of victory. The national fast-day was the day-dawn to the Pillawell Circuit which, "from that time, became an important and interesting field for Primitive Methodist enterprise and toil."†

OLD PRIMITIVE METHODIST CHAPEL, HEREFORD.

These excerpts from the old *Journals* throw their flash-lights on the early history of what has now come to be the Pillawell, Hereford, Monmouth, Lydbrook, and Lydney Circuits of the South Wales District. Primitive Methodism did not win a place and position in Hereford without a struggle. Indeed, for a number of years, it would be truer to say that it had to fight for its existence, rather than that it flourished. It was eighteen

---

* Rev. Joseph Middleton's MS. *Journal*.

† "Life and Labours of Rev. Wm. Leaker," p. 33. We have also in this connection quoted from the MS. Autobiographic Memoranda of Rev. R. Davies.

years before Hereford became the head of a circuit. The society, numerically feeble, had to do its best to grow in a niggardly soil and in the cold shade of opposition, such as often rests on Dissent in cathedral cities. During this time there was much adverse sentiment to face, and frequently the roughs took advantage of it to annoy the worshippers at their camp meetings, and even in their own rented room in Union Street. But, at last, persecution was undone by its own act, and better times came. On August 26th, 1833, when Mr. J. Morton, the superintendent, was holding an open-air service at the Friars', in the neighbourhood of Quaker Lane, he was arrested by the direct orders of an irascible magistrate. Mr. E. Pritchard, attorney and Congregationalist, generously undertook to plead Mr. Morgan's cause before the mayor and magistrates on the following day; while Mr. Morgan, by his firm though respectful attitude made a powerful impression on the crowded court. Messrs. Pritchard and Yapp stood bail, but when the Sessions came no "true bill" was found against the street-preacher; and, after this, street preachings were unmolested, and public sentiment became much more favourable. The Circuit Report of 1836 speaks of the prosperity of Hereford. "The room is now generally crowded; there are now eighty members, whereas in 1829 there had been but twenty-two." Persecution is spoken of in the past tense: "At Hereford our people have been persecuted, and on various occasions life has been in danger. Several attempts have been made to obtain redress but we could not succeed, because many of the higher powers were utterly opposed to our cause. But now some of the respectable inhabitants are favourable towards us, and use their authority for our benefit, and some of our most violent persecutors are gone the way of all flesh, some are transported, and some converted to God." In June, 1838, a chapel was opened in the city, and in 1840 Hereford became the head of a new circuit with two travelling preachers and 220 members. The present beautiful church in St. Owen's Street was erected in 1880 at a cost of £3561, and yet within twelve months after its opening the building was out of debt. It has seatage for six hundred people, and the schoolroom behind has accommodation for three hundred scholars.

PRIMITIVE METHODIST CHURCH, HEREFORD.

The name of Mr. T. Davies, J.P., will always be associated with the building of St. Owen Street church, as well as with the early struggles of Primitive Methodism to secure a position in the city of Hereford. Converted about 1830 he removed to Hereford, and from that time to his death in 1893 he stood by the cause. In his case physical strength was mated with a resolute will. These qualities had their use in the early days of persecution. The sight of his stalwart figure among the little company acted as a wholesome restraint on the roughest of the crowd, some of whom knew the power of his grip. Mr. Davies was a builder, and prospered in business. That, too, was of advantage to the Church. To the building fund of St. Owen's he gave £200 and Mrs. Davies £25. By acting as architect and superintending the erection, and in various other ways, he is said to have saved the trustees quite another £200. The confidence of the Connexion in him was expressed by his being appointed the first Treasurer of the African Missionary Fund. He was a local preacher of considerable ability, and was the first Circuit Steward elected in the Hereford Circuit, and he held that office until his death. He was highly esteemed by his fellow-citizens, and for many years held the position of town councillor and justice of the peace. His good wife was "a help meet for him." Her sympathies were with the poor and suffering. These were her clients, for whose sake she gave gifts and made personal sacrifices.

MR. T. DAVIES, J.P.

MRS. DAVIES.

The present Steward of the Hereford Circuit is Mr. T. A. King, whose career offers another example of the success which so often crowns persistent effort. By success we do not mean that which is measured by mere material wealth: that is common and cheap. By success we mean the fruition—the return into the man's own personality—of his endeavours after self-improvement; the development of special gifts and faculties, or the acquisition of knowledge. In Mr. King's case irrepressible instinct has made him become a craftsman of so superior a kind that his work need not fear comparison with that of the acknowledged artist. This instinct for giving expression to what the eye saw or the mind conceived awoke early, and not amid circumstances that might seem likely to foster it. As a lad of seventeen he worked for some months in the yard of a monumental mason, his employment being to clean and prepare the surface of the gravestones. But he rose step by step. He sought to supply the defects of a somewhat meagre education, and to become more deft of hand in carving, modelling, etc., until he has made for himself a name and a position as a sculptor. Those who have seen the busts of Revs. C. T. Harris and J. Odell done by his chisel, will hardly have been able to stifle the wish that he may yet live to give us the "counterfeit presentments" in marble of the founders of that Church to which Mr. King by birth and life-long attachment belongs.

MR. T. A. KING.

Monmouth, another county-town, was missioned in the early part of 1835, under favourable conditions. Mr. Bell, supervisor, who had been a local preacher at Louth, gave a hearty welcome to his co-religionists, and by his zealous labours and liberality greatly assisted in establishing and strengthening the Monmouth society which, by March, 1836, numbered forty members. After the separation of Hereford from Pillawell, Monmouth became the residence of the superintendent. In 1869 we find "Monmouth and Lydbrook Circuit," and in 1891 each of these towns became the head of a station, as in 1880 Lydney already had become.

THE PEMBROKESHIRE MISSION.

Once more, and finally, we follow the stirring James Roles—this time to Pembrokeshire, where he had gone, probably at the beginning of 1825, to establish a mission as the agent of Oakengates Circuit. Becoming somewhat embarrassed, Oakengates offered its mission in the Finisterre of Wales to the General Missionary Committee which had been appointed by the Conference of 1825. The offer was accepted, and in November of the same year, James Roles sent a roseate report of the prospects of the mission to the Committee. Twelve places had been opened, and ten or a dozen other places wished to have preaching established at them, etc. The same sanguine note is clearly perceptible in the Secretary's endorsement of the report: "This letter," writes Hugh Bourne, "contains an account of the first-fruits of the labours of the General Missionary Committee of the Primitive Methodist Connexion. The opening of their missionary labours the Lord has thus crowned with success." At the bottom of the stations of 1826 we still have, "Pembroke Mission: J. Roles"; but, even before the words were printed, the fair prospects had been dashed and the mission become like a wilted flower. It was even in contemplation to withdraw the preachers and relinquish the mission but, ultimately, it was decided to continue one man on the ground and see what could be done. A youth between eighteen and nineteen years of age was selected to go to a station which was "in a manner a complete wreck." When John Petty, for it was he, appeared before the Committee composed of men with whom we are already familiar—Hugh and James Bourne, James and Thomas Steele, James Nixon, John Hancock, C. J. Abraham, John Andrew (sen. and jun.), W. Barker, and Joseph Bourne—his youthful appearance excited grave misgivings. But James Bourne had full confidence in the young man, and he was sent to Haverfordwest, arriving on July 26th, 1826. He found two local preachers, eleven members, and one on trial!

The moving story of John Petty's two years' labours in Pembrokeshire deserves to be placed side by side with that of Thomas Proctor in Herefordshire. He, too, had his full share of long journeys, toils, and privations; and, though he did not suffer so much direct persecution, yet, when we remember his youth and the comparative isolation and loneliness of his lot, from which he would not escape even when the chance was afforded him, we are presented with an example of moral heroism which cannot fail to be inspiring to those, especially, whose situation at all resembles his in that they are striplings called to "endure hardness" that might tax seasoned veterans, and yet who have to endure it alone. It is this aspect of the young missionary's Pembrokeshire labours which is new to us and which we would fasten upon. We have had, and shall have again in plenty, instances of missionaries "roughing it" and, so to speak, "fighting with beasts at Ephesus"; but the sight of a mere youth in his teens treading his own special winepress alone, and coming out at the end of the ordeal, chastened, strengthened, and victorious, is a picture of our own early times that has its own distinctive quality and value. In Pembrokeshire John Petty had no colleague, few fellow-labourers, and not many congenial friends. The moral ground was sterile, and the progress made for a time almost inappreciably slow; yet, when in January, 1827, the General Missionary Committee declared it had no funds, that the mission must no longer look to it for support, and had better give up its preacher, use the mission's money to pay the rents of the rooms, and hope ere long to be received as a branch by Cwm or Blaenavon Circuit, the youth who was more than three hundred miles from home and friends, instead of welcoming the prospect of gaining a more congenial sphere, pleaded to be allowed to remain on the mission at his own risk until Conference: nay, to be permitted to remain a year beyond that Conference if there were no guarantee that in 1827 a preacher should step into his place. His plea was heard. He was allowed to stay with his own poor people; to sink or swim, as the case might be. And he did stay until 1828, and did not sink, or the mission either. Credit must be given to the impecunious Committee that it let John Petty have his way, and afterwards handsomely acknowledged that "he had fully brought up the work," and "that his being appointed to Haverfordwest had made him expert in the office of superintendent."* The truth is, the time to establish a central or general Missionary Committee had not come, and the attempt made, being premature, was comparatively fruitless. What the "first-fruits" were we have seen; and, though certain circuits might be subsidised, yet the first General Missionary Committee has left no distinctive mark on our history. In 1828 John Petty left for Brinkworth—where we shall soon follow him—and Haverfordwest was declared a circuit.

This narrative will have shown that Haverfordwest (now Pembroke Dock) can claim to be the Connexion's premier mission station. It has passed through many vicissitudes but it is a mission station still. It was a circuit until 1836 when, presumably, it was taken under the wing of Blaenavon or Swansea. Some few years after, it took circuit-rank again, but only to be received in 1851 by the General Missionary Committee. It must be admitted that in the county of Pembroke the Connexion has lost ground; that fewer places are preached at in 1905 than in 1828; that chapels have been lost, and Haverfordwest itself has been abandoned. Our business is to record facts rather than to express opinions; but it does seem that, so far as the Peninsula of Wales is concerned, the Connexion ought either to have attempted less than it has attempted or, what would have been better still, that it should have attempted much more. Either it should have relinquished the Peninsula altogether, or have made a vigorous effort to establish a chain of missions from Swansea to Milford, including Carmarthen, Llanelly, and Tenby.

The Development of South Wales District.

For some years Blaenavon was the only circuit in the Southern part of the Principality, and it may fairly be regarded as the "procreant cradle" of the South

* The Committee's Letter is given in Vol. i. p. 344.

Wales District. When Cwm was parted with, its work lay chiefly among the hills and valleys of Monmouthshire. With the possible exception of Newport, it had not yet found its way to the sea-coast,—to the growing towns at the mouths of the rivers that were the ports of shipment for the vast mineral wealth of the mountainous hinterland. But in 1834 it turned its attention to Swansea. At the beginning of that year, in response to an application for a missionary, Joseph Hibbs, the superintendent, went down to Swansea to prospect, and found "a great part of the town much neglected for want of open-air preaching and family visiting." Reporting to his Committee on his return, Henry Higginson was instructed to open a mission at Swansea. He had entered the ministry in 1833, just after having given proof of his fitness for the work by his remarkable labours in Darlaston Circuit during the visitation of cholera, so that Blaenavon was his first station. He walked all the way to Swansea, arriving there on the third day, and was kindly received by Captain Alder, whose wife had been a member of the South Shields society. He began his labours on March 16th, 1834, by preaching on the Pier Head where, as he reports, "the nobility and gentry are often seen promenading." Some had told him "they thought the back streets would be best. I said, I had been *there* long enough. I would try what the *front* would do." Henry Higginson was not the man to take a back street or seat if a front one was accessible. He was but two months in Swansea and its neighbourhood, but in that time he seems to have made a considerable impression by dint of hard work and a striking personality. He was tall; of commanding appearance; with a good address. He had received an education above the average, and yet that educational superiority formed no barrier to his mingling freely and unaffectedly with the people. Moreover, there was a dash of originality and even eccentricity about him which in itself was taking; and as this became even more strongly marked as he grew older, it is no wonder that tradition—to which a striking personality dashed with eccentricity always appeals—still loves to talk of his doings and sayings. The young missionary seems to have been treated with respect and kindness by all and sundry. He had sometimes a thousand people at his services on the Pier. "All denominations flocked to hear him." During his two months' mission he visited the Mumbles, Merton, Llanmaddock, and other places, and left 44 members, thirty of them being at Swansea and ten at the Mumbles. The superintendent, Joseph Hibbs, now took his colleague's place and carried on the work, spending much labour upon family visitation, which, he observes, was something new in Swansea. He, too, was generally cordially received, though he met with a cold reception at Neath and found it "a hard place." On July 6th, a room, capable of seating 300 people, was opened by E. Foizey of Bath, and J. Prosser of Presteign. Swansea soon became a Circuit (1835), and Joseph Hibbs was its first superintendent. In 1836 chapels were erected at Swansea and Llanmaddock, the one at Swansea serving

REV. JOSEPH HIBBS.

until 1860, by which time it had evidently come to be considered as behind the times ; for in the *Magazine* report of the chapel opening, George Dobson quaintly remarks of the old chapel : " The up-tendencies of the times and the lowering sanitary changes occurring in and around its immediate locality, will not admit the application of the Scripture precedent and commendation—'Beautiful for situation,' etc."

Progress in this rapidly developing district was marked by the formation in 1841 of the Tredegar Circuit from Blaenavon—or rather from Pontypool Circuit, as it now came to be called. This arrangement was tantamount to a partition of the hilly hinterland already referred to. In 1851 we find Tredegar Circuit still including, amongst other places, Merthyr and Dowlais in Glamorgan, Brynmawr on the borders of Breckon, as well as Rhymney, Ebbw Vale and Blackwood in Monmouth. Some of these places are now themselves the heads of circuits.

ALD. J. RAMSDALE. J.P.

It seems singular that Cardiff—whose progress in recent years is said to have been the most remarkable of any town in the kingdom—was not seriously attempted by the Connexion until 1857, when it was missioned by Pontypool Circuit again under the superintendency of Joseph Hibbs. Afterwards Cardiff came under the care of the General Missionary Committee and, in 1879, it was made a circuit. Newport with Caerleon and Risca had already, in 1872, been detached from Pontypool to form a new circuit. During the superintendency of P. Maddocks, Canton and Mount Tabor chapels were erected, now the heads, respectively, of Cardiff First and Second. Alderman Joseph Ramsdale, J.P., the Steward of Cardiff Second has, ever since he came to the town in 1870, rendered eminent service to Primitive Methodism in the town and district. Here also resides Rev. J. P. Bellingham, who entered the ministry in 1852 and retired in 1904. Mr. Bellingham merits record here, not merely because of his long and fruitful ministry, but also because of the interest he has taken in scientific questions in their bearing on Christianity, and because his pen has been freely used in the service of our Connexional literature. In 1904 Mr. Bellingham was appointed a permanent member of Conference.

In 1885 Aberavon and Briton Ferry were taken from Swansea and formed into a mission-station. Abergavenny, too, formerly a branch of Pontypool, has also become a mission station. But there has been loss as well as gain in South Wales. Carmarthen was made a circuit, with Joseph Hibbs as its superintendent, in 1839, and in 1842 we had a chapel there and 143 members. In 1851 we had connexionally ceased to be, and now we have no foothold whatever in the county of Carmarthen, and Pembroke Dock Mission is our solitary outpost in the peninsula of West Wales.

It will have been noticed how frequently the name of Joseph Hibbs has recurred in writing of South Wales. His ministry was largely bound up with South Wales, and the course of that ministry singularly followed the lines of its connexional development. Appropriately enough,

REV. J. P. BELLINGHAM

he began his labours in Oakengates (Wrockwardine Wood) Circuit. The next four years he spent in Blaenavon; the following four in Swansea; and then three more were spent in Carmarthen. After this he had two other terms of service in Pontypool and one in Tredegar. As we have seen, he had much to do with the missioning of Swansea, of Carmarthen, and Cardiff. With the exception of a term in Truro and another in Bristol, the whole of his forty years' ministry was spent in Blaenavon, or in circuits that grew out of it, largely under his direction. No wonder that Joseph Hibbs was spoken of as "The Bishop of South Wales."

In turning from Blaenavon or Pontypool we give portraits of Isaac Prosser and Alderman Henry Parfitt, J.P. The former joined the society at Blaenavon about 1857, and as Class-leader, Circuit Steward, Trust Treasurer, etc., rendered inestimable service to the society especially in its time of trial and adversity. He was an overman in the mine, and met his death by the fall of a mass of rock, September 27th, 1898. Alderman Henry Parfitt, J.P., was a good friend and adherent of our Church in Pontypool—a staunch Nonconformist, a keen politician, and a devoted worker for the public good. He also died in 1898.

III.—Shrewsbury's Wiltshire Mission.
Brinkworth.

In the autumn of 1824 Samuel Heath, one of the five preachers stationed to Shrewsbury by the preceding Conference, took his way South in order to open a new mission. He had volunteered for this work because the circuit, having relinquished a mission in Wales, had now a preacher to spare. At Cirencester he was stoned and otherwise ill-treated, although several persons are said to have received good under his preaching who afterwards joined other Churches. Some years had to elapse before the Connexion got a permanent footing in Cirencester, and when at last this was done, it was through the agency of the very circuit whose founder was Samuel Heath, the rejected of Cirencester. So the missionary passed over from Gloucestershire into the adjoining county of Wilts. Now, whether S. Heath had received general instructions to seek to establish a mission that would be in alignment with the one already recently established, we cannot be sure; but this, as things turned out, was what really took place, so that Shrewsbury's Mission is quite properly spoken of in the *Magazine* as having been "into the parts bordering on the Tunstall Circuit's Western Mission." Instructions or no instructions, Samuel Heath felt it was plainly the will of heaven he should open his commission here. It did not take long to convince him that he might travel far before he found any piece of English soil that stood more urgently in need of the preaching of the Gospel in all plainness and directness than did the northern part of Wilts in which he now found himself. And yet we are told that, some seventy-five years before, John Cennick, the hymn-writer and former friend of Charles Wesley and Whitefield, had not only preached in a chapel in the parish of Brinkworth, but had extensively evangelised the surrounding district, so as even to acquire the name of the "Apostle of North Wilts." But three quarters of a century afterwards there was very little to show for all this evangelistic effort. "The spiritual results of Cennick's teaching had, to human observation, almost wholly disappeared. No doubt the moral atmosphere retained some of the evangelical sentiment with which it was once so strongly charged, but the power and spirit and activities of his propaganda had passed away." His hold upon Brinkworth may at one time have been influential, but "the nature of his church organisation failed to invest it with permanence."*

OLD PRIMITIVE METHODIST CHAPEL AND MINISTER'S HOUSE, SHEFFORD, BERKS.

A little later on we shall have to consider more fully the social and moral condition of the people of the Southern counties, especially in its bearing on the severe and widespread persecution to which the pioneers and makers of the Brinkworth District were exposed. But there is one incident in which Samuel Heath figures we will refer to, because it took place at Wootton Bassett (now in the Brinkworth Circuit) and brings before us the contest called back-swording—once a favourite diversion at the revels held on feast and fair-days in Wilts and Berks. Thomas Hughes shall tell us how the "noble old game of back-swording," as he calls it, is played. Despite the name, no sword is used by the contestants: "The weapon is a good stout ash-stick with a large basket handle, heavier and somewhat shorter than a common single-stick. The players are called 'old gamesters,'—why, I cannot tell you,—and their object is simply to break one another's heads: for the moment that blood runs an inch anywhere above the eyebrow, the old gamester to whom it belongs is beaten, and has to

* The quotations are from "Pioneer Work in the Old Brinkworth District, being Memorials of Samuel and Ann Turner." a series of valuable articles which ran through the *Aldersgate Magazine* for 1900, from the pen of Mr. Turner of Newbury.

stop."* Though the genial author of "Tom Brown's School Days" laments that "the noble old game is sadly gone out of late," and has done his best to glorify and rehabilitate it—for all that, the sport was quite as brutal in its way as the football match played at Preston on Maudlin Sunday, and quite as significant of the rough manners of the people. S. Heath chose to take his stand and preach in the main street of Wootton Bassett just at the time when the crowd were gathered to witness a back-swording contest. He went up and down the country preaching from one favourite text which spoke of judgment to come; nor did he think it needful, for prudential reasons, to change this text for a more conciliatory one, now that he was going into the midst of Vanity Fair at an hour when the people were excited by witnessing a gladiatorial combat on a small scale. The missionary began his service, but before long he was haled before the local authority (Mr. Petty says it was the mayor) for unwarrantably interfering with the due order and observances of the Fair. After some altercation he was let go, and promptly returned to the same place to finish his sermon. Nor did he preach in vain. Many returned to their homes in the surrounding villages under conviction of sin, and some of the inhabitants of Wootton Bassett never forgot that day's service. Soon afterwards a long room, which had been used as a ball-room in connection with a public-house, was taken on rent, and for some time used as a place of worship. Of course the worshippers for a time suffered from the usual annoyances; but the society continued to prosper, and it is recorded that "the cruel and barbarous practice of back-swording was entirely abolished in the town." At Brinkworth, a village midway between Wootton Bassett and Malmesbury, a strong society was established, and a great moral change wrought in the face of considerable persecution, which the clergyman-magistrate was averse from punishing as it deserved. Malmesbury, however, was easily first in the bitterness, and we might add—the nastiness of its opposition to the new movement. Not only were the windows of the preaching-room continually being broken, but "intestines of beasts and all manner of filth were thrown in upon the people. On one occasion during service, an impious man got the Bible out of the preacher's hand and put it into a pot then boiling on the fire! He was brought up before the civil authorities, and fined *one shilling and fourpence* for his impious deed!" These facts were told Mr. Petty in the neighbourhood not long after they occurred.

Samuel Heath had found a fine field of usefulness, such as the prophet found in the Valley of Vision. He asked for additional labourers, and two Shropshire preachers were sent him in succession, each of whom began his ministry on the Wiltshire Mission. The first to come was Edward Vaughan, a man of whom the Connexion knows but little, since he died as early as 1828. But, in his brief ministry he did good service, not only in Wiltshire but in Blaenavon, the Isle of Man, Tunstall and Boston, in whose churchyard his remains are buried. In his own quaint way Hugh Bourne

* The following is taken from the *Reading Mercury* of May 24th, 1819:—"Peffard Revel will be held on Whit-Monday, May 31, and for the encouragement of young and old gamesters, there will be a good hat to be played for at cudgels; for the first seven couples that play, the man that breaks most heads to win the prize; and one shilling and sixpence will be given to each man that breaks a head, and one shilling to the man that has his head broke."

has summed him up in the words, "Edward Vaughan was of slender abilities in regard to management; but in the converting line the Lord put great honour upon him. His faith in the Lord was great, an extraordinary power attended his word, and many souls were converted to God through his ministry."—(*Magazine*, 1836, p. 437.) Vaughan was followed in March, 1825, by Richard Davies, from whose MS. Autobiographic Memoranda we can gain an authentic and helpful glimpse of Brinkworth Circuit in the making.

"In due course I reached Seagry, then the centre or head-place in the Mission and was kindly received by my senior brethren in the work and others. We all went to work in good earnest and many and striking conversions occurred at many places. Several powerful societies were formed. We were bitterly opposed in our work by parsons, magistrates, and roughs, as vile as the beasts at Ephesus, but we, trusting in God, defied them all, rejoicing in these tribulations. For a long time we preached twice a day on week-days, at noon in towns, and in villages in the evening, walking many miles daily. Our greatest want was suitable places to worship in, and we were often led to be thankful for cart-sheds, barns, workshops, cottages, and good village-greens as our sanctuaries. The first chapel built was at Seagry, and others followed in due time, which led the people to believe that the Primitive Methodists meant to remain and labour amongst them, although some ill-disposed persons had said they would not do so. Amid our heavy persecutions and trials we were blessed with many friends who liberally supported the cause of God according to their ability. There were now five missionaries on the Mission, which extended over many miles of country, and such was the liberality of the societies and congregations, and the profits arising from the amazing sale of Hymn-books, Magazines, Nelson's "Journal," etc., that no demand was made on the funds of the Shrewsbury Circuit. On the contrary, that circuit received considerable pecuniary aid from the Mission."

Brinkworth became a circuit between the Conferences of 1826-7, and at the same time it took over the Stroud Branch of the Western Mission. Mr. R. Davies intimates that his own unexpected recall to the home-branch in May, 1826, was the circumstance that incidentally brought about the severance of the connection between Shrewsbury and its powerful Mission. It was felt that his removal was likely to be detrimental to the interests of the Mission, and that it was time to protect itself against the risks of similar "untimely and uncalled for removals of preachers" in the future by applying to be made into an independent station. The General Committee of the time gave its sanction, and the Shrewsbury Circuit acquiesced, as the following laconic minute in the Circuit books shows:—"That the Wiltshire Mission become from this day a circuit by itself."

Brinkworth began its career as a circuit, having five preachers appointed to it by the Conference of 1827, of whom S. Heath was still the superintendent. Unfortunately, his name must be added to the list of pioneers, who, like J. Benton, J. Nelson, W. Doughty, J. Bonsor and J. Roles, soon dropped out of the ranks. Ideally one could wish it had been otherwise, but historical fidelity demands that the fact be duly noted. After what has been written of Hutton Rudby, Scotter, Ramsor, Prees, and especially of Cwm, the reader will feel little surprise that a village of scarcely more than a thousand inhabitants should have become not only the head of a powerful and aggressive circuit, but also the head of a District which at one time extended into some ten counties. What *may* awaken surprise is the fact that this village of the Wiltshire Uplands should through all the changing years have maintained its District primacy, and has not yet lost it, though Swindon has been admitted to be its consort, so that the style now runs, " Brinkworth and Swindon District." Our surprise will diminish in proportion as we come to know the history of Brinkworth, especially the history of its achievements as a missionary circuit, and it is these achievements we have now to chronicle. Nowhere is our Connexional history more complex and difficult to follow than in this section. The figures called up before us are so many and always in motion; names of towns and villages occur with bewildering frequency; persecution seems everywhere, so as almost to defy record. For result we feel like an uninstructed civilian who is watching from a church tower the progress of a big battle to which he has not the key. Can this complexity be simplified? Having regard to where the events happened, as well as to the events themselves and the order of their happening, can any guiding lines be traced which will save us from losing the sense of direction and progress in the midst of this mass of detail? We think so—that the task of simplification is not so hopeless as at first sight it looks to be. For example, if we keep an eye on the whereabouts and the movements of John Ride from 1828, when he was appointed to Brinkworth, to 1844, when he went to Cooper's Gardens, we shall see how the battle is going, or, to speak without figure, we shall be able to follow the main lines of advance which first took their direction from Brinkworth.

Brinkworth (1828-31), Shefford (1832-6), Reading (1837-43), London (1844-7)—these were the successive stations of John Ride for a period of nineteen years. As the superintendent of Brinkworth he directed the missionary efforts of that circuit chiefly in Berks, and Shefford Circuit was formed in 1832, of which he became superintendent. Agents were multiplied, and a vigorous evangelisation was carried on in Hants of which Mitcheldever (1835) and Andover (1837) Circuits were the outcome, as also in Berks represented by Faringdon (1837) and Wallingford (1837) Circuits. The magnitude of Shefford Circuit's operations may be judged from the fact, that in 1835 it had no fewer than eighteen preachers labouring under the direction of its Quarterly Meeting. But John Ride kept to Shefford's *main line* of advance which was to Reading (1837). Thence, still under his direction the work branched out in various directions. Aylesbury in Bucks was reached and became a Circuit in 1840, and from Aylesbury, Luton in Bedfordshire was made a Circuit in 1843. In this same year—1843— Wallingford had its two branches of Oxford and Witney, and its two missions—Thame and Camden. Andover had its Romsey Branch and Lymington Mission in the New Forest. Reading had High Wycombe and Windsor Branches, both of which were made Circuits in 1848, the latter taking the name of Maidenhead Circuit. Besides these it had no less than five missions, viz.: St. Albans, Hertford, Henley, Brentford, and Essex. These were during the year transferred to the care of the G.M. Committee. In the meantime, the prolific mother-circuits of Brinkworth and Shefford had not been inactive. After parting with Shefford, Brinkworth successfully missioned both Chippenham and Bristol (made circuits in 1835 and 1837 respectively), and in 1843 it had its Cirencester, Cheltenham, and Worcester Branches, and its Filkins and Tormorton Missions, and as late as 1854, Malmesbury at last yielded to the vigorous assaults of George Warner, and in 1858 was made a circuit. Finally, Shefford in 1843 had its Marlborough Branch and its Petersfield and Aldermiston Missions. It is better to give these dry but necessary details once for all. But to revert to our clue, which is as we have seen, the movements of John Ride; Brinkworth, Shefford, Reading, mark the main lines of Connexional advance on this side, though what we may call the branch extensions are scarcely of less importance. For fifteen years John Ride is the superintendent of these three historic Circuits, which were the successive centres of that semi-circular sweeping movement by which our Church reached the home-counties. After his three years term at Cooper's Gardens, John Ride was in 1848 put down for Hammersmith with the words:— "To evangelise or open a fresh mission." As though his work in England was finished and he desired more worlds to conquer, he in 1849 went as a missionary to Australia: but excessive labour had debilitated his frame, and he was compelled to superannuate in 1853 and died 15th January, 1862.

REV. GEO. WARNER.

Some elementary knowledge of the physical geography of the counties of Wilts, Berks, and Hants makes the outline facts just given still more significant. Some one has called Wiltshire "a mere watershed—a central boss of chalk, forming the great upland mass of Salisbury Plain and dipping down on every side into the richer basins

NEWBURY: THE TOWN BRIDGE OVER THE KENNET.

of the two Avons on the West and South, the Kennet on the East, and the Thames on the North." The elevated table-land of Salisbury Plain which is a continuation of the Hampshire Downs divides Wilts into two parts. It fell to Motcombe and Salisbury as representing the Western Mission to evangelise the Southern part of

Wilts and a large tract of Dorset. To Brinkworth fell the northern division of the county. Here the escarpment of the table-land overlooks to the North the Vale of Pewsey, a tract of country which runs across the county from West to East in which is situated Devizes. The northern side of the Vale of Pewsey is bounded by the upland plain of the Marlborough Downs with their continuations in Berks—White Horse Hill and Ilsley Downs overlooking to the North the Upper Valley of the Thames, called the Vale of the White Horse and the Valley of the Ock in which are Wantage, Alfred's birthplace, and Faringdon. Southward, the hills fall in gentle slopes to the Valley of the Kennet in which are Hungerford, Newbury and, at its junction with the Thames, Reading. Then come the Hampshire Downs, and at their foot the river-valleys of the Test and Itchen wherein lie Winchester and Southampton. Evangelisation went on in the country now under consideration conformably with that country's physical features. First of all, as Nature had divided Wiltshire into two parts, the Western Mission had to do with the one, and the Wiltshire Mission with the other—the northern part of the county. Starting from Brinkworth as a centre, it soon reached Shefford and the Valley of the Kennet, where are the towns of Hungerford and Newbury, now the heirs and representatives of the old Shefford Circuit. It descended into the Vale of the White Horse in the Upper Thames Valley, and thence crossed over into Oxfordshire and the Vale of the Thame. From the Valley of the Kennet it ascended the northern slopes of the Hampshire Downs, and then following the downward course of the rivers reached Winchester, and finally the New Forest and the low-lying country by Southampton Water. Soon also it reached Reading and the Lower Thames Valley, and thence spread out into Buckinghamshire—the Vale of Aylesbury—on the one hand, and into Surrey on the other. Then, while the country watered by the Southern Avon was left to Motcombe and Salisbury, Brinkworth turned its attention to the Vale of Pewsey, and followed the course of the Bristol Avon by Calne and Chippenham and on to Bristol itself; it even extended into Gloucestershire to the North. Chronology and geography are the two eyes with which even the humble history of the making of the Brinkworth District can easily be followed.

But what was the social and moral condition of this particular District in 1830, when Brinkworth Circuit was about to enter upon its missionary labours? This was just what John Ride and the Brinkworth Circuit authorities wanted to know, and so, in their own primitive fashion, they sent a walking commission of inquiry into the north-eastern corner of Wilts, and into the Vale of the White Horse—so dear to Thomas Hughes, in order that they might see and learn for themselves the real state of things, and ascertain whether these villages did or did not need the simple gospel carrying to them. As the Israelites sent forth spies into Canaan before attempting to take possession of the land, so in a sense did Brinkworth Circuit send forth *its* spies, who indeed saw the "nakedness of the land." The Berkshire Mission was inaugurated at a famous Missionary Meeting held after the Quarterly Meeting on Good Friday, 1829. At this meeting there was much earnest prayer on behalf of the proposed mission, and faith rose so high that many gained the assurance that, for every penny given that day, a soul would be won. John Ride and John Petty (who, in 1828, had come from Pembroke Dock to Brinkworth Circuit) were deputed to go into the parts already mentioned and survey the land. It was on April 27th, 1829 they set out on their mission, which it would be incorrect to regard as merely a reconnaissance, inasmuch as they preached at cross or on village-green wherever opportunity offered. These two Johns—Ride and the still youthful Petty—he was only twenty—were in order of time the foremost pioneers of the Berkshire Mission. The first Primitive Methodist sermon in Berkshire was preached at Bourton. They found this fair and goodly land, so rich in historic memories going back to the days of good King Alfred, a moral wilderness indeed. Dissent was practically unknown, and there was throughout a sad dearth of evangelical preaching. At Ashbury a sermon had not been preached by a Dissenter for forty years, although here, mercifully, there was a good evangelical clergyman, the same who afterwards hailed the advent of the Primitives' missionary, by exclaiming, "Now my curate has come!" They preached at Ramsbury, where years before Dr. Coke had attempted to preach, but "was attacked by a turbulent mob headed by the vicar of the parish." Stones and sticks were plentifully used. Dr. Coke was violently pushed from his stand, and his gown torn into shreds. Nothing daunted, he continued the service. The vicar then thought of another expedient, and gave the order, "Bring out the fire-engine." The mandate was obeyed, and both preacher and congregation were compelled to retire before the well-directed volleys of this liquid artillery.* Here, strange to say, their service was unmolested, but that cannot be said of the one held on May-day at Aldbourne. Never, surely, was a religious service "begun, continued and ended" under conditions more extraordinary and embarrassing. A troupe of merry-andrews were on the ground in front of the cross, with the double purpose in view of interrupting the preacher and of competing with him for the attention of the vast audience. There was hand-bell ringing, and the concerted shouting of children, to say nothing of a prancing steed bestridden by a man bent on mischief. Yet John Petty—saint and scholar to be—went on steadily and solemnly with his discourse on the Second Coming of Christ, not even turning his head to see what was the danger threatening from behind, although that there *was* danger he could see from the tell-tale faces of those in front. At the very hour this strange May-day service was being held, the friends near Wootton Bassett were praying hard and long for the missionaries.

But lest it should be thought that our picture of the bygone Wiltshire and Berkshire wilderness is overdone, we would like, as we have done in the case of other districts of England, to adduce corroborative evidence drawn from an unbiassed and unimpeachable source. For our present purpose, therefore, we will call as witness Mr. Richard Heath, author of "The English Peasant," admittedly an authority, and who himself states that "so far as he has personal tastes and sympathies they are with the liturgy of the Church of England." In the book just named he refers to the agrarian disturbances which, as we have seen, were rife in various parts of England in 1830-3—in the Southern counties amongst the rest. In December, 1830, three hundred persons were tried at the special assize at Winchester. The Duke of Wellington was sent down to support the judges. "They were brought up in batches of twenty

* "Life of the Rev. Thos. Coke, D.C.L.," p. 62.

at a time, and all had sentence of death recorded against them, Six were actually sentenced to suffer on the gallows; twenty were transported for life, the remainder for periods varying according to judicial discretion. The *Times* newspaper for December 27th, 1830, commenting upon the Winchester trials, did not mince matters.

"We do affirm that the actions of this pitiable class of men [the labourers], as a commentary on the treatment experienced by them at the hands of the upper and middling classes; the gentlemen, clergy (who ought to teach and instruct them), and the farmers who ought to pay and feed them, are disgraceful to the British name. The present population *must* be provided for in body and spirit on more liberal and Christian principles, or the whole mass of labourers will start into legions of a banditti—banditti less criminal than those who have made them so—than those who by a just but fearful retribution will soon become their victims."

But what has all this to do with Brinkworth's Berkshire Mission? Much every way. It shows that that mission was begun and carried on at an unprecedentedly critical time in the national life. It may also go some little way to explain why the "peasant preachers" of our Church had not only to suffer from mobs—ignorant, brutalised by neglect, and driven by poverty almost to desperation; but also why their betters, including the large farmers, the clergy, and even the magistrates, were too often not merely suspicious but bitterly hostile. We were between two fires. The labourers— poor souls—did not know their true friends; and those of a higher social grade so far misconceived our character and aims as to suspect us of designs intended to be subversive of the existing order.

Referring to the formation of the Labourers' Union in 1872, through the instrumentality of Joseph Arch, Mr. Heath asks: "What had given the labourer courage to claim his rights? I will answer that question by giving the following narrative." The story of "Old Ben Roper," the Primitive Methodist local preacher—which we found in the *Magazine* for 1858, is the narrative he proceeds to give in full. This story, touching as it is and well worth reprinting, we omit. What follows this narrative, however, we venture to quote, as it is germane to the matter in hand.

"Many respectable people would have called old Ben a 'Ranter.' I should call him a primitive Christian, for though I do not believe the poor in Judæa had fallen so low as the English poor have done, some of the apostles were not in a much more exalted station than old Ben. Poor and ignorant as he was, it was men like him who woke in the dull, sad minds of his fellow-sufferers a new hope, a belief that there was indeed a Kingdom of Heaven worth struggling to obtain. The very ignorance and poverty of the labourers cut them off from knowing anything of the Gospel, even in its narrow English form. They were too ignorant to understand any one who did not speak their language and think their thoughts, too poor to support any kind of ministry.

"In the source from whence the foregoing narrative has been taken [*The P. M. Magazines*] will be found, through a long course of years, the obituaries of Christian apostles, some of whom laboured all the week for a wage of a few shillings, and then on Sunday walked twenty or thirty miles to preach the Gospel. One such, having six children, for weeks ate nothing but bread, although he had five miles to walk daily to a barn where he was employed as a thresher. 'Yet,' we are told, 'he sometimes so felt the presence of God that he seemed to have strength enough to cut the straw through with his flail.' Believing literally in our Lord's promises, he realised their fulfilment, and in moments of dire necessity received help apparently as miraculous as that given to Elijah. Nobody, of course, will believe this who supposes that there is no other kingdom but that of Nature. However, these things are realised by the poor who have the least faith, 'for *theirs* is the Kingdom of Heaven.'

"These were the kind of men who prophesied in 'the valley of the dry bones'; but, of course, Resurrection is no agreeable task to unhealthy souls. Like the sickly sleeper, who has passed a night full of horrible dreams, and has just fallen into a heavy slumber before dawn, the benighted villagers cursed the heralds of the coming day, and bid them begone. They pelted them with mud, stones, and rotten eggs; sometimes threw ropes over them to drag them to the river; often sought to drown their praying and preaching with fire-shovels and tin-kettles. In these persecutions they were sometimes led on by the authorities; and constables wishing to ingratiate themselves with the upper classes laid information against these poor preachers as disturbers of the peace."*

We do not follow Mr. Heath in his further reference to the gross malversation of justice by which John Ride and Edward Bishop were imprisoned at Winchester in 1834, as that will shortly come before us. The long citation from Mr. Heath's book we have given—creditable alike to his discernment and his heart—amply sustains our contention that, in the early 'thirties our land, and not least in its southern counties, was indeed in a parlous state, and that, under God, its rescue from that state was largely due to the earnest and often ill-requited efforts of Primitive Methodist missionaries. And yet, there are journalists and publicists amongst us who, posing as experts, and professing to give a list of the great historic revivals which have swept healingly over our land, will leap at once from John Wesley and Whitefield to General Booth, as though there had been nothing but stagnancy lying between! So little do they know of the history of their own land, or so much have they forgotten.

The dark shadow which rested on our land in 1830 cast its gloom over the Marlborough Downs, and was felt by Brinkworth's missionaries. They had enough to do to keep it from getting into their souls and, as with mephitic vapour, stifling their faith and paralysing their efforts. John Petty had been replaced on the Berkshire Mission by Richard Jukes, to whom was soon added John Moore. In September, 1829, Thomas Russell took the place of the latter. The work was toilsome and the prospect gloomy. The nights were getting cold, making open-air services a risk to health. At Church Lambourne, over-exertion in order to make himself heard above the din, caused him to rupture one of the smaller blood-vessels. Houses in which to hold services were difficult to get; for even though the "common-people" might be favourably disposed, they went in fear of their masters or landlords who threatened

REV. THOMAS RUSSELL.

* "The English Peasant. Studies: Historical, Local and Biographic. By R. Heath," 1893, pp. 54-5.

them with loss of work or roof-tree if they harboured the missionaries, or in any way encouraged them. When in pity a house at Lambourne was offered Mr. Russell, he was obliged to walk at once to Salisbury in order to procure a licence. It was a dreary journey of thirty miles, a large portion of which was over Salisbury Plain, which he travelled on foot, with snow on the ground. Still a beginning was made.

The first society on the Mission was formed at Upper Lambourne, and in December, 1829, there were forty-eight members on the Misssion. John Ride himself became Mr. Russell's colleague in labour. And now we come to an incident, which, though it may be deemed small in the eyes of the world was yet fruitful of results and has withal a grandeur and pathos all its own. The scene of the incident is Ashdown on the Berkshire Downs, where nearly a thousand years before, King Alfred and his brother gained a victory over the Danes. As for the time it is a dull, cheerless day in the month of February, 1830. We give the incident, we cannot do better, in the words of a writer in the large *Magazine* for November, 1886, who has drawn out the significance of the event under the strikingly appropriate title of "A Parallel and a Contrast"*: "Two men of solemn mien, and dressed in the garb of peasant preachers, are to be seen approaching Ashdown Park Corner, where the treeless, rolling downs are varied by a coppice or small wood. The younger man had already that morning walked ten miles across the downs to meet his companion for prayer and counsel, and they were now returning together. Reaching the wood they had to part, as their destinations lay in different directions. They had already shaken hands. But no; they must not, should not part until it had been fought out on their knees whether their mission was to prosper. 'Let us turn in here and have another round of prayer before we part,' was the remark of one of them, and turning aside into the coppice and screened by the underwood, and being far away from any habitation, no more secluded spot for communion with God could be found. Oblivious of the snow, and of personal considerations, they throw themselves upon their knees, and in an agony they pour out their souls to God. The success of their mission, which is for God's honour, and the salvation of souls, is summed up in the burden of their prayer, 'Lord, give us Berkshire! Lord, give us Berkshire!' The pleading continued for hours. At last the younger one receives the assurance, and rising to his feet, exclaims with an outburst that betokens a new-found possession, 'Yonder country's ours, yonder country's ours! And we will have it,' as he points across the country, the prospect of which is bounded by the Hampshire Hills some thirty miles distant. 'Hold fast! I like thy confidence of faith!' is the reply of the more sober pleader. They now part with the assurance that 'yonder country is ours.'"

Such was the conflict in which were arrayed on one side, the powers of darkness, and on the other the two men sent forth to establish the Primitive Methodist Mission in Berkshire. Up to this point the opposition had been so violent as sorely to try the faith of the missionaries. On leaving the wood, John Ride and Thomas Russell, for these were the men whose names will be imperishable as the pioneers of Primitive Methodism in Berkshire, went to their respective appointments. On the following night Thomas Russell was at Shefford; the word touched the hearts of Mr. and

* The writer is Mr. Turner of Newbury.

Mrs. Wells, who built a house which served as the missionaries' home and the place for worship. This, indeed, has been the roof-tree of Berkshire Primitive Methodism, the original home of its early preachers, as well as its first meeting-house. Few incidents in the religious history of the county are of greater significance than this afternoon prayer in the wood at Ashdown. Had the pleaders lost faith in their cause the religious aspect of the county would have been different. Remarkable revivals of religion followed this time of wrestling prayer, the habits and practices of the people became changed, scores of sanctuaries were erected, until now there are more Primitive Methodist congregations in Berkshire than of any other Nonconformist body, and probably more Primitive Methodist Chapels. It is surely a noteworthy coincidence that almost on the spot where the struggle for Saxon and Christian supremacy in England was decided, there also took place a struggle which decided whether Primitive Methodism was to be a power in the county. It is also illustrative of the way in which God honours prayer, for while Messrs. Ride and Russell pleaded for Berkshire, He gave also territory beyond.*

IV.—HULL'S MISSION IN CORNWALL.

As the present chapter is already sufficiently long, we will glance at the "origins" of the three Cornish Circuits that were included in the newly-formed Brinkworth District of 1833, reserving for a final chapter a glance at some of the lights and shadows of Brinkworth District when it was in the making. We got to Cornwall just as we got to Hull and Leeds—by invitation. The invitation was addressed to William Clowes while labouring on the London Mission, and it came from Mr. W. Turner, of Redruth. He had formerly been for a few months a preacher among the Bible Christians, but had withdrawn, and for two years he and his wife had been working as unattached evangelists in and around Redruth. They had succeeded in gathering some one hundred persons into their societies. These societies Mr. Turner was now anxious to hand over to the Primitive Methodist Connexion in the hope that the flock hitherto his care would be duly shepherded, and the work of evangelisation be vigorously pushed forward. Hull Circuit's Quarterly Meeting acceded to the request, having first received the required assurance that Mr. Turner and his followers would in all things submit to the discipline of the Primitive Methodist Connexion.

Mr. Clowes arrived at Redruth on October 5th, 1825, on what proved to be his last general mission. Though exhausted with his all-night coach journey from Exeter, he yielded to the importunity of the friends to preach to them the same night. "While waiting on the Lord in the meeting I felt," he writes, "a girding on of the Divine power; the *mission baptism* began to flow upon me"—which surely was of good omen for the success of the mission. As the people retired from the service they were overheard saying—"He'll do; he'll do." His next duty was to hear Mr. Turner preach his trial sermon as a candidate for the "full plan." The sermon was indifferently good, but at one point in his discourse the preacher went off into a fit of holy laughter, which many in the congregation seemed to find infectious. Clowes met with this

* It may be as well to state that the account of this incident is taken from the writer's smaller History of the Primitive Methodist Connexion.

laughing, dancing and shouting several times during his Cornish mission, and he did not approve of it, but expostulated with those who indulged in these histrionic manifestations. If they felt happy, let them bless the Lord as the Psalmist did, when he called upon his "soul and all that was within him to bless and praise His holy name." As to Mr. Turner, it may be said parenthetically, he seems to have honoured the terms of his agreement. He remained loyal to the Connexion to the end of his long life. For ten years he was a travelling preacher in the Connexion, and then located at Frome, where he had previously travelled. As a local preacher, class leader, and diligent family visitor he made himself useful and respected. He passed away as recently as 1880.*

Our interest in all that relates to William Clowes must not induce us to follow him in his itinerations from place to place, or to note every incident which occurred. Enough to say that his labours were chiefly confined to Redruth and its vicinity, varied by occasional visits to St. Austell and the Downs, where Mr. Turner's people had chapels—one the walls of which was of mud, and the other of mud and stone. He also found his way once, at least, to St. Day, where on a subsequent visit in 1833 he had one of those experiences of a ghostly kind, such as John Wesley loved to take note of, and such as now find their way into the Transactions of the Psychical Research Society.† The impression one gets from the careful reading of the *Journal* so far as it relates to this time is that, while in Cornwall, Clowes was not equal to his former self; that his excessive labours and, we may add, the sins of his youth, were beginning to tell upon him, and that there were already premonitory signs of that somewhat serious breakdown which occurred in February, 1827, and which led to his ceasing to have charge of a station from December of the same year. His experience was marked by swift and sharply contrasted alternations of mood. Now he was in a state of exaltation, with all the old sense of freedom and power. "He felt the priestly vestments cover his soul as the glory covered the mercy seat." Then he was down in the trough of depression, fighting for his life: he felt as if he were near the gates of hell. These varying subjective states were the spiritual counterpart and reflection of the vicissitudes of his lot and circumstances from day to day. Toil and exhaustion, mental tension and reaction swiftly succeeded one another. Like Paul he knew what it was "both to be filled and to be hungry, both to abound and to be in want." Now he was well and comfortably lodged, with a good table spread before him ; the next day might find him at a loss for a meal or a bed. One day, when no hospitable door stood open, he went on the top of Charn Bray Rock. He bethought him there of what Wesley and Nelson had done in the same county and under the like circumstances, and looked round, if haply he might find some blackberries with which to appease his hunger. One blackberry, and that an unripe one was all he could find—and he dined off that. At another time he wandered pensively on the cliffs. He lay down on a rock and watched the waves as they dashed against the reefs. He peopled the solitude with the forms of friends whose love he cherished. Then the thought of the London

* See his memoir in the *Magazine* for 1881, written by Rev. J. H. Best.

† Clowes' *Journal*, p. 338. See also article by Rev. E. Bocock on "William Clowes and the Ghost," *Aldersgate Magazine*, 1900, p. 530.

Mission and the urgency of its affairs pressed in upon him. "Oh, that £100 that was owing to Mrs. Gardiner! What was to be done about that?" He prayed, and tried to believe that God would give them a happy issue out of all these troubles. Soon after, G. Tetley sent the happy news, that Mrs. Gardiner had consigned the promissory note to the flames.

Though Mr. Clowes was not privileged to see such remarkable results follow his labours in Cornwall as he had witnessed in the North, yet his labours met with a considerable measure of success. When, just before his removal, the Quarterly Meeting of the Mission was held February 26th, 1826, it was found there were 225 members in church-fellowship and that the financial affairs of the Mission were in a satisfactory state. Mr. Petty thought it unfortunate that Mr. Clowes was removed just at the turn of the tide; for soon after his removal one of the most remarkable revivals for which even Cornwall has been distinguished broke out; and there can be no question that this revival was largely due to the sound preparatory work done by Mr. Clowes during the four months he was on the Mission. John Garner succeeded Mr. Clowes as superintendent in September, 1826, and he had as his colleagues Messrs. Driffield, Abey, and Hewson, all of whom we have met before. W. Driffield was a Cleethorpes man. He was taken out to travel by Hull Circuit, and while in the town he lived under Mr. Clowes' roof. He laboured on the Bridlington and Scarborough branches, was arrested for preaching in the open-air at Beverley, laid the foundation-stone of its first chapel, became responsible for a hundred pounds of its cost, and along with John Verity begged a considerable sum of money on its behalf. Fourteen consecutive years of his ministry were spent at Redruth, St. Austell, and St. Ives, and being a man of some means, as he evidently was, he cheerfully undertook monetary responsibilities in connection with buildings erected or rented by the denomination. At Redruth he is said to have found an unfinished chapel, which he got completed at a loss to himself of nearly £300. It need scarcely be said that the chapel thus referred to was not the one shown in our illustration,

PRIMITIVE METHODIST CHAPEL, REDRUTH.

which was built in 1884. He paid the first rent of the room at Penzance, Newlyn, Falmouth, and Truro. He introduced Primitive Methodism into various places both in the western part of Cornwall and in some parts of Devonshire. "I missioned," he says, "Devonport, Exeter, Bridgerule, and Barnstaple, and my responsibilities at one time must have amounted to nearly £2000." He subsequently travelled in Brinkworth, Salisbury, Motcombe, and Banbury Circuits, and at his death in 1855, his body was carried to Wootton Bassett for burial. It is due to such a man, who was also "a most powerful and zealous revivalist," that his name and work should be remembered, especially by the circuits he helped to found and establish. With such fellow-labourers as these, we are not surprised to find John Garner reporting that in ten months six hundred persons had united with the Church. In 1828 Redruth became a circuit with twelve preachers.

One of the most notable gains of the great Cornish revival of the 'Twenties was the acquisition of Adolphus Frederick Beckerlegge to the Church and the ministry. Were it not that the memory of men is so short, Mr. Beckerlegge would rank in the general regard of the Connexion as one of the most remarkable men it has produced. And yet he is chiefly remembered on the strength of one or two extraordinary sayings which have stuck like burrs and been carried along by the years, while his more solid qualities and extensive services have been almost forgotten. There is no memoir of him in the *Magazine* of the time, and the regulation record of his death, in the Conference Minutes of 1867, is scarcely longer than an ordinary tombstone inscription. Happily, Dr. Joseph Wood did much to recall to the attention of a later generation of Primitive Methodists one who would have a strong claim to remembrance, were it for no other reason than that, but for his influence, Dr. Wood might never have entered our ministry. But apart from this, Mr. Beckerlegge was in every sense an uncommon man. From his name to his calligraphy everything about him seemed exceptional. He had a commanding presence, a fine voice, a refined pronunciation, and as a preacher he was far beyond the average. He was born at St. Ives in 1798, and after receiving a Grammar School education, settled in business as a watchmaker and jeweller at Penzance. Any worldly ambition he might reasonably have cherished was set aside when the call of the Church came. He carried out the injunction he himself afterwards laid on young Joseph Wood when he found it difficult to choose his path: "There is not the money in the ministry, but there is the glory; *and you must go for the glory.*" Mr. Beckerlegge was stationed in 1828 as one of the preachers of Redruth, and after subsequently travelling in some of the leading circuits of the Hull and Nottingham Districts he returned to St. Ives, where he was under the superintendency of that apostolic man—C. T. Harris. Superannuated in 1862, Mr. Beckerlegge died at Flushing in 1868.

Before leaving Redruth to glance at some other places that formed part of the mission, we would refer to two captains of industry who have lately passed away who were rightly regarded as the two pillars of the Redruth Church, and whose names will serve to link together for us its past and its present. Captain John Hosking, who died June 21st, 1901, was for many years probably the best-known and most highly respected layman of the Cornwall and Devon District. His biographer, the Rev. J. H. Best, says: "When comparatively young he qualified himself for and attained the position of mine captain, and after being thus employed for many years he was appointed mineral agent, and had the direction of the mining department of Tehidy estate. He was calm, genial, kind in bearing, wise in counsel, and of a truly catholic spirit." For forty-seven years he was a local preacher, and at the time of his death he had two classes under his care. For many years he was also Circuit Steward and school superintendent. He loved good, sound literature, and even during his last affliction this love showed itself. Books were strewn round his pillow, and when free from the paroxysms of pain he found solace in turning to the words of some master of thought.

CAPT. J. HOSKING.

Captain C. F. Bishop was the manager of two important tin-mines employing more than a thousand men, and he had come to be regarded as one of the leading authorities on mining in the country. Beginning life as a working miner, he had by dint of perseverance worked his way to this honourable position. He efficiently discharged the duties of a local preacher for forty years, and was also a class-leader and active worker in the Sunday school. Together with Captain Hosking he was very helpful in the building of the Redruth chapel. Nor should his systematic liberality to the poor go without mention. Captain Bishop died November, 1902.

CAPT. C. F. BISHOP.

ST. AUSTELL.

The great revival already spoken of was not confined to Redruth, but was mightily felt in the St. Austell part of the station, where John Hewson was stationed. In July, 1827, Joseph Grieves, whom we saw last in Weardale, was sent to assist him. Shortly after his arrival a notable camp meeting was held on the "Wrestling Downs," so called because the annual wrestlings which took place at the parish wakes were held there. These were due to come off on the Sunday after the camp meeting, which was one of great power. One of the umpires was arrested by the Spirit of God, abandoned the sport to which he had been addicted, and united himself with the Church. The wrestlers left the camp-meetingers in possession of the field, and retired to a spot on the other side of the town. A chapel was afterwards erected on the "Wrestling

Downs." How powerfully the revival had affected the district will be made evident from Mr. Grieves' statement that in September, 1828, there were 457 members on the mission (St. Austell) and 282 on the home branch (Redruth). In 1829 St. Austell was made a circuit. It afterwards became a station under the care of the General Missionary Committee and so far prospered, especially under the superintendency of Mr. E. Powell, that it was again made an independent circuit.

St. Ives and Penzance.

Penzance, the last town in the South-west of England, was visited by John Garner while he was at Redruth. He walked there, preached in the Green Market to an attentive congregation, then made his way to Newlyn where he also preached, after which he returned to Redruth, having preached twice and walked thirty-seven miles.

PENZANCE FROM THE HARBOUR.

Shortly after, Mr. Teal was appointed as a missionary to Penzance. He was successful in raising a society of twenty members at Penzance and one of about thirty at Newlyn. But this devoted young man caught cold at a camp meeting, and consumption soon claimed him for its victim. His place on the mission was taken by Joseph Grieves. From an interesting article which appeared in the *Magazine* for 1857, we are told that the first place occupied in the town was a low dilapidated schoolroom in Market Jew Street. Thence a removal was made to a schoolroom in South Parade. Queen Street Chapel and a schoolroom in North Street were successively occupied until 1839, when a new chapel was opened in Mount Street by Messrs. Cummin, Driffield, and Wigley. This building was enlarged in 1848, 1851, 1853, and 1857 under the care severally of Joseph Best, Robert Tuffin, John Sharpe, and Robert Hartley.

St. Ives was "opened" by Joseph Grieves on July 15th, 1829. "When he arrived at the river Hayle to cross from Penzance to St. Ives the tide was up; under these circumstances passengers had to wait the reflux of the waters before they could proceed. He went into an old church, nearly buried in the sand, where he spent about three hours in prayer, beseeching God to go with him. A few apples made the missionary's dinner. The tide having now ebbed he prepared to cross. While taking off his stockings for this purpose, a strong man offered to carry him over on his back, and after a little difficulty Mr. Grieves reached his destination. He went to a "decked boat" on the Quay, and stood upon it, and there alone and a stranger began to sing "Come, oh come, thou vilest sinner," etc. The people were struck with astonishment, and a crowd, chiefly made up of sailors and fishermen with their wives, soon gathered round. With great liberty the preacher offered gospel terms to the worst of sinners. Many wept and earnestly entreated another visit, promising a place to preach in. When he returned the following week he had nearly two thousand persons to preach to. "The hearts of many were smitten; numbers dated their first religious impressions from this night." As the result of this and subsequent visits a remarkable revival of religion broke out which extended to the other Churches of the town, and a striking reformation took place in the manners of the people. We read of no persecution being encountered by the missionaries; on the contrary, they were welcomed and treated with kindness and respect by all classes. In June, 1830, there were 136 members in society. The Penzance mission became first the St. Ives' Branch of Redruth Circuit, and then in 1833 St. Ives became the head of an independent station. A large chapel was built in St. Ives which Mr. Grieves had the gratification of opening. An interesting incident occurred at St. Ives in 1839, while Mr. Driffield was on the station—made such in 1833 with Penzance as its second place. The Rev. Mr. Malkin, clergyman of the Established Church in that town, became converted to God during a powerful revival of religion. "Attracted by a spirit of curiosity, he entered the chapel at a late hour one evening, when the Spirit of God instantly arrested him. In a few days he obtained pardon, left the Church, and preached his first evangelical sermon in our (the Primitive Methodist) Chapel from 'Come, and hear, all ye that fear God, and I will declare what He hath done for my soul': Psa. lxvi. 16."[*]

No good purpose would be served by occupying space in showing what was done by the Connexion in the county of Devon during the first period of its history since, unfortunately, the efforts put forth, however successful they might seem to be at the time, were destined to end in failure and withdrawal. The story of the renewal of missionary effort in this charming county—this time happily successful—belongs to a later period of our history. Mr. Petty lived nearer the time when these [events happened, and presumably was conversant with all the facts; hence, we shall content ourselves with reprinting and handing on his well-weighed words on this sombre episode in our history.

"It is painful to add that, notwithstanding the labour and toil which several of the first and succeeding missionaries spent on the mission stations in this fine county, and the cheering prospects which for a time presented themselves in

[*] "Memoir of Rev. W. Driffield." *Magazine*, 1855, p. 259.

some of them, a succession of calamities befell them all; and through the improper conduct of one of the preachers, the inefficiency of two or three more, the lack of sufficient connexional support, and of courage and perseverance under difficulties, the whole county was abandoned by the Primitive Methodist Connexion! It is humiliating to record these facts, but truth and fidelity demand their insertion in these pages. It was certainly not honourable to the community, nor in harmony with the spirit of enterprise and perseverance which it has generally displayed, to relinquish all the mission stations which it had in the county, though several disasters had occurred on them. However, the labour, toil, and expense spent thereon were not altogether in vain. A few souls were brought to the Lord under the ministry of the missionaries, who died happy in communion with them; several acceptable and useful travelling preachers were raised up, who have rendered good service to the Connexion, namely, Messrs. Chubb, Rooke, Grigg, Mules, etc., and the Wesleyan and Bible Christian communities largely shared in the fruits of the missionaries' labours on the before-named stations. It was well that these two denominations were able to collect into church-fellowship the scattered remains of the societies unwisely relinquished by the Primitive Methodists."—*History*, p. 292.

Mr. Petty's closing reference to the Bible Christian Church challenges an observation or two on the early relations of that community with our own. The experiences of the two denominations at the opposite extremities of England were curiously parallel. In Northumberland societies that had belonged to the Bible Christians fell to our lot, and their minister withdrew. In Devon much the same thing happened, only in this case it was we who withdrew and left our sheep to be gathered into the Bible Christian or Wesleyan Methodist fold. But the parallel is not merely an incidental or superficial one: it goes much deeper than this. The two denominations were alike in the time and circumstances of their origin, the class of people they worked amongst, the agents they employed, the spirit that animated them, the methods of evangelisation they employed. Each was so like the other that they might have been called the Methodist twins. Even in later years, when each denomination has developed its specific differences, the curious resemblance between them has struck the attention of observers.*
To any one who knows the early history of both communities it will be matter for wonder why they that were so much alike and so near together did not come nearer still, and it will be cause for regret that alliance or union was not something more than one of the might-have-beens of history; for union was never, perhaps, so near as it was a few years after the origin of both denominations. Even as early as 1820 our fathers were no strangers to the idea of amalgamation with another religious body. In that year, as the old Minute-book of the Hull Circuit shows, overtures were made for union with the Primitive Wesleyans of Ireland. Of course the overtures came to nothing, as they were bound to do. The two denominations had very little in common. Each attached quite a different meaning to the word "Primitive." To the Primitive Wesleyans it meant holding tight to John Wesley's High-Church notions—

* "The Bible Christians closely resemble the Primitive Methodists in character and spirit."— Rev. J. Telford: "Popular History of Methodism." "There is a striking resemblance between this body and the Primitives."—" The Revised Compendium of Methodism," by James Porter, D.D.

no service in church-hours, no sacrament except at the hands of the Church clergyman—notions that the Wesleyan Methodists had quite properly discarded. What *we* meant by "Primitive" need not again be stated. The Primitive Wesleyans ran off with John Wesley's antique garments and having arrayed themselves in them, said: "We are the true followers of John Wesley—the primitive Wesleyans." The Primitive Methodists cared not one jot for the out-of-date clothes. What they were anxious about was to catch his spirit and to follow his methods of evangelisation. A year after Hull Circuit had ineffectually flirted with the Primitive Wesleyans, Conference by resolution opened the pages of the *Magazine* to Mr. O'Bryan, the originator of the Bible Christian community, and articles from his pen appeared there dealing with passages in his own life and with the question of female preaching. The observations which these articles drew forth from Hugh Bourne on "the remarkable similarity between the two bodies as regards their practical recognition of the ministry of females" have already been given (vol. ii. p. 3). This interchange of courtesies might easily, one thinks, have led on to a union of the forces and fortunes of the two denominations. But neither was this to be. Each denomination took its own course, like the rivers Severn and Wye which rise near together and then diverge, but only to approximate again and to mingle their waters at last in the same broad estuary. It may be this last feature is a parable of the future, as the other features are a parable of the past, and that it is to a broad United Methodism we are tending.

CHAPTER XXIII.

BRINKWORTH DISTRICT, 1833-43.

LIGHTS AND SHADOWS.

PERSECUTION—but persecution not without its alleviations and compensations is what we wish to write of in this chapter. If the question were simply this:—"How does this particular southern district of England compare with other districts you have passed through, in regard to the amount of persecution the Connexion's missionaries met with in doing their work?" there could only be one answer. "It compares unfavourably with other districts, and for the reasons already stated. You must take your Persecution Map and with your brush put dabs of colour on the counties of Wilts, Dorset, Berks, Oxon, Surrey; and on Hants it must be darker than anywhere else in England." We will suppose the brush has done its work. But in reality the sombreness of the story is relieved by many touches of brightness, and our Persecution Map gives only half the truth. There is the courage and cheery hopefulness with which the missionaries met their persecutions. There is the success that at last came to them as a reward. If they had persecutors they also had an ever-increasing band of faithful men and women who "through good report and evil," clung to them and the cause. If there were raging mobs and hostile squires and parsons and magistrates, there were here and there humble cottages and farm-houses where they found sympathy and shelter. So the missionary's experience, as he toiled on, was chequered with light and shade like a moonlit path through the trees. This is the impression we ought to gain. Emphasis must of course be laid on the fact that this was connexionally our Persecution Area. Yet we must not forget to put the lights in. To leave *them* out would be like stopping short with Christ's words: "In the world ye shall have tribulation." We must go on and hear the finish: "But be of good cheer; I have overcome the world," and then we have the darkness shot through with light. Somehow, this passage haunts the mind as we write of Brinkworth District's formation and extension; and it does so because men endured and overcame in cheerful mood as their Master had done.

In the parts already named, persecution was so common as to be the rule rather than the exception. This being so, it follows that all the pioneers of the old Brinkworth District came in for their share of it when labouring hereabout. Some might be more daring, or less prudent and tactful in their handling of the mob; more aggressive in manner and more provocative of speech, being less able to withhold the retort, and given to speaking their mind. No doubt this was so, and perhaps explains a good deal. But even the meekest and most self-restrained evangelist did not always escape; nor did the gentle women whose sex should have been their protection. Several pious females were employed on the mission, and broke down in health. "S. Wheeler was taken out, but could not bear up under the toils. Then Miss Evans, but she found the journeys too severe, and persecution too violent." Ann Godwin, afterwards the wife of H. Green, the Australian missionary, was brought to death's door as the result of her trying experiences. At Childrey "it was grievous to see the young women with their plain neat bonnets crushed down on their heads and their frocks torn." At Foot Baldon, in Oxfordshire, a female preacher was knocked down with a stone. As for Elizabeth Smith (afterwards Mrs. Russell), during the two years—1830-2—she was on the mission, she moved about amongst the rough crowds as though she had a charmed life. At notorious Ramsbury she walked up the avenue to the barn where she was to conduct the service, singing with great sweetness and pathos. The path was lined with men provided with stones, eggs, and other missiles ready to fling; but as their ringleader saw and heard the preacheress, "dressed in the characteristic garb of a Friend," he was overawed, and turning to his followers, he said with authority: "None of you shall touch that woman." And this disarming of opposition as by the mere efflux of her own personality was an incident often repeated. In referring to Miss Smith as associated with Thomas Russell while pioneering in Hampshire, Mr. Petty writes: "It may be questioned, however, whether his excellent and devoted female colleague, who laboured with him in the gospel, was not still more successful than he. The novelty of female preaching attracted crowds to hear her; and her modesty and good sense, her clear views of evangelical truth, her lucid statements, and her solemn and pathetic appeals to the heart and conscience, under the Divine blessing, made deep impressions, and rendered her very useful among the peasantry in Hampshire." With this well-deserved tribute we take leave of one of the most attractive figures in our history. Elizabeth Smith's all-too brief life ended February 21st, 1836.

We have spoken much of John Ride, and Mr. Petty in his history devotes very considerable space to the doings and sufferings of Thomas Russell, as we too have done or shall have to do. But the portrait-group of some of the Brinkworth District pioneers—all of whom we believe ended their days at Newbury in the very heart of the country they helped to evangelise—should serve to remind us that neither John Ride nor Thomas Russell had a monopoly of toil and persecution. They were but the first among many brethren. For besides the veterans of the group referred to, there were others, their compeers, who also did their part in the same work and bore the brunt of opposition in doing it. The names of some of these will come before us. With all this mass of material to choose from, all that we can hope to do is to single out what may rightly be regarded as typical examples of persecution. As these examples are to stand as representative ones in our annals, they may be considered almost in the light of documents which must be handed down in the very form in which they were received. First then, in the order of time, we give what should be known in our annals as "The Chaddleworth Case, 1830." The persecution which clothes itself under legal forms is more hateful than mob violence and it is harder to bear. It admits of less excuse, and is felt by the sufferer to

SOME PIONEERS OF BRINKWORTH DISTRICT.

be a deeper outrage. Chaddleworth, in Berkshire, affords a glaring and typical example of this kind of persecution of which Thomas Russell was the victim. He was sentenced to three months' hard labour, ostensibly, for selling without a licence, but, really, because he would persist in preaching the gospel in the streets of Chaddleworth—that is the fact as it stands forth in its shameful nakedness. It was a "put-up job" on the part of the clergyman and a magistrate. The phrase used has vile associations and may look objectionable in print, but the writer knows no other phrase that will quite so well convey the meaning intended. It was known that Mr. Russell occasionally sold denominational magazines and hymn-books to his people. Here was material to hand for the making of a cunning trap. But the official representatives of Law and Religion would not themselves set the trap. That work was assigned to the parish constable, who was a tenant of the magistrate. Unsuspectingly, Mr. Russell walked into the trap. He was, as we have said, sentenced to three months' imprisonment *with hard labour* in Abingdon jail. But even then he might have been let go, had he but consented to give an undertaking not to preach any more in the neighbourhood. But that undertaking he would not give; so he was stripped, made to put on a felon's garb, and sent to work the tread-mill. When appetite and health both failed, the prison doctor said: "He came here to be punished, and punished he must be"; and he was ordered back to the wheel.

But this prison episode is not without its touches of brightness. It called forth sympathisers and protectors, and was overruled for final if not immediate good to the cause which was sought to be crushed. The Nonconformist ministers of Abingdon—

Mr. Wilkins (Congregationalist), Mr. Kershaw (Baptist), and Mr. Loutit (Wesleyan), made themselves fully conversant with the facts. They were deeply concerned as well as interested, and at once brought the case under the notice of the Religious Protection Society of London. Mr. John Wilks, the secretary, energetically bestirred himself in the matter, with the result that Mr. Russell was liberated from prison on June 5th, 1830, when he had served but one month of his sentence. Some little time after his release Mr. Wilks sent to request his presence in London, and remitted him money, through Mr. Kershaw of Abingdon, to bear his expenses thither. Mr. Russell accordingly repaired to the metropolis, and had several interviews with Mr. Wilks. At last, Mr. Wilks asked Mr. Russell what he wished to be done. Mr. Russell replied: "All I wish is to go on preaching unmolested by the magistrate." Mr. Wilks rejoined: "Mr. Russell, your spirit is that of a Christian, and your wish shall be granted. Go on, sir, in your work, and we will protect you." At parting, Mr. Wilks kindly gave Mr. Russell three pounds to meet his expenses, and Mr. Russell bade him adieu with a grateful heart, and returned with fresh courage to prosecute his missionary work in Berkshire. The good work had progressed during his imprisonment, and a powerful camp meeting, the first held in the county of Berks, was held on Bishopstone Down, near Ashdown Park, on Sunday, May 30th, 1830. Some thousands attended in the afternoon; much divine power attended the word preached, and great good was effected. At night, an excellent lovefeast was held at Bishopstone, and several persons labouring under a burden of sin, found peace in believing.

Let us note that what we see at Abingdon—the sympathy of the Free Church leaders taking a practical form—was repeated again and again in other parts of the Persecution Area. So it was, as we shall see, at Faringdon, at Shaftesbury, and notably at Winchester. More, perhaps, in the Southern counties than in other parts of England, prominent leaders of the Free Churches made it quite clear on which side their sympathies lay. They came forward as vindicators and protectors, moved to action not merely by a feeling of common humanity but by enlightened self-interest and the elementary instinct of self-preservation. They had the discernment to see what were the issues involved; what were the aims, the tendencies, the possibilities of the new movement. They were not slow to recognise in it a new, and what in the end might prove to be a valuable ally. It therefore behoved them not to allow a movement of so much promise to be crushed before it could acquire strength and show its power.

The story of Thomas Russell's savage handling by the mob in King Alfred's native Vale of the White Horse may stand as a typical case of its kind.

"Mr. Russell entered upon the Faringdon mission in full expectation of severe persecution, in which he was not deceived. Before four o'clock in the morning of the third Sunday in April, 1832, he prepared for his journey to the scene of his intended missionary operations. His mind was oppressed with the burden of the work before him, and the dread of persecution and suffering; but he was supported with a sense of the Divine approval and the hope of success. When he arrived at the summit of a hill about ten miles from Wantage, he saw the town lying before him, and instantly a dread of what awaited him well-nigh overcame him. He met two men who knew him, and they advised him to return on account of the severe persecution which they expected he would have to encounter. He thanked them for their sympathy but went forward on his journey. At nine o'clock he stood up in the market-place and began to sing a hymn. He next knelt down and prayed, and concluded without molestation. But ere he commenced preaching a number of ruffians surrounded him, and he had not spoken long when a more violent company arrived and pushed him from his standing-place, driving him before them like a beast. He heard some of them cry, 'Have him down Mill Street!' and suspecting, perhaps properly, that they intended to throw him into the river which flows at the bottom of that street, he determined if possible to prevent being driven down it, and managed to keep in the market-place. After being driven to and fro an hour or more, his inhuman persecutors paused, when Mr. Russell threw open his waistcoat, and in the true spirit of a martyr cried : 'Lads ! if the shedding of my heart's blood will contribute to your salvation, I am willing for it to be shed on these stones.' At this moving statement those who were nearest him drew back a little, and seemed to relent; but a violent gang outside the throng pushed forward and urged the rest to reaction (*sic*). A respectable looking person, who Mr. R. afterwards learned was the chief constable, came to him and said : ' If you will leave, all will then be quiet.' Mr. R. replied : ' If I have broken the law, punish me according to the law, and not in this manner.' The constable then withdrew without ever attempting to quell the lawless mob, who again assailed the solitary missionary with ruthless violence. At length the beadle came and seized Mr. Russell by the collar, and led him to the end of the town, and there left him. Mr. Russell's strength was almost exhausted with the violent usage he had suffered in the market-place; but determining if possible to address those who had followed him thither, he stood upon the side of a hedge and preached as well as he was able. But his persecutors were not yet satisfied; they pelted him with stones, eggs, mud, and everything they could render available for the purpose. Even women, unmindful of the tenderness of their sex, joined in this cruel treatment; some of them took the dirt out of their patten-rings to cast at the preacher ! When Mr. Russell concluded the service he was covered from head to foot with slime, mud, rotten eggs, and other kinds of filth ; and his clothes were torn, and his flesh bruised. As soon as he got alone by the side of a canal, he took off his clothes and washed them. Then putting them on wet, 'enduring hardness as a good soldier of Jesus Christ,' he proceeded to Faringdon, where similar treatment befell him. When he came to a pool of water outside the town, he washed his clothes a second time, and then went five miles further to Shrivenham, where he was met with another violent reception. At a brook he cleaned himself a third time, and then proceeded to another village, where he preached in peace, except that a person threw a stone or other hard material at him, which cut his lip. After this he walked six miles to Lambourn to rest for the night. He had been on foot eighteen hours, had walked thirty-five miles, had preached four times, and had gone through an amount of suffering such as none but a strong, healthy man could have endured. Next day, however, he walked twenty miles to the other side of his mission, and during the week preached at several fresh places."

The story does not end here, for on the following Sunday Mr. Russell again visited Wantage and Faringdon, only to experience similar treatment. At Faringdon, especially, he was so savagely baited that a respectable inhabitant of the place could not help exclaiming: "If I had a dog which had to suffer what that man endures, I would cut off his head to put him out of his misery." Yet when Mr. Fox, a member of the Society of Friends, deeply stirred by the inhuman treatment Mr. Russell was subjected to, wrote to a clerical magistrate on his behalf the only answer he got was : "The people have as much right to take the course they do as the preacher has to preach in the streets." This magisterial dictum deserves to be placed on record; as a specimen of callous feeling and perverse thinking it would be hard to beat. If these were the sentiments of the magistracy no wonder the mob waxed bold and wantoned in their excess. Still, in spite of mob and magistrates, Thomas Russell held on to Faringdon, and his tenacity had its reward. In June, 1832, Mr. Wiltshire was added to the staff of the mission and its borders were enlarged. Under the labours of Messrs. G. Price, W. Hervey, and W. Peacefull so much success was realised as to justify the mission's being formed into an independent circuit, and as such it stands on the Minutes for 1837, with H. Heys, Thomas Cummin, and M. Bugden as its preachers.

It is time to put the lights into our picture of the conditions under which Shefford Circuit was formed and extended, lest a wrong impression be left on the mind of the reader by its unrelieved sombreness. Over against the fact of the prevalence of persecution must be set the compensating fact that a constantly increasing number of adherents were won for the cause whose sympathy and co-operation augured well for still greater success to come. It would be a mistake to suppose the missionaries to have been men of a sad heart and rueful countenance, having no helpers, and conscious of fighting a losing battle. So far from that being so, they knew they were on the winning side, and were persuaded that opposition would gradually die down, and in the end die out altogether. They were men of faith; so in Thomas Russell's phrase they "tugged at it," and bore persecution and privation in good spirits as being part of the day's work. Even the "Vale," as they called it—the Vale of the White Horse—was for them something more than a metaphorical vale of tears. How often at the close of a powerful service the doxology was sung for those who, in the expressive phrase of the time, had been "brought in!" Nothing cheers like companionship and belief in ultimate success; and Shefford Circuit was succeeding and, consequently, the company of the faithful was being steadily enlarged. In this country, which John Ride and John Petty had surveyed, and Ride and Russell had prayed for at Ashdown, there were now, at the end of 1832, eleven missionaries at work and some eight hundred members in church-fellowship. As yet sparsely dotted in this tract of country, were cottages and farm-houses which were veritable houses of refuge and pilgrim-inns, where the weary and often buffeted missionary was sure of a hearty welcome and of the best the house could afford. These Gaiuses of the pioneer times who ministered out of their poverty and, in some cases, out of their comparative abundance, have almost as strong a claim on our remembrance as have the men to whom they ministered, since without them it is difficult to see how the bounds of the Connexion could have been widely extended in the Southern counties, or Primitive Methodism have rooted itself amongst the villages as it has done. We can only make brief mention of a few of these successors of "the well-beloved Gaius." There were such in Wiltshire—at the generating-point of this wide-spreading evangelistic movement. For example, under the powerful ministry of Samuel Turner, Miss Asenah Ferris was converted. She discarded her fashionable attire and cast in her lot with the contemned Primitives. Subsequently she became the wife of Mr. Smith of Wootton Bassett. She and her husband became local preachers; their house was always open for God's servants; they did much in helping to build the chapel and to found and maintain the Day Schools afterwards established. After Mr. Smith's death in 1845 the widow continued her good works, and, in 1849 was married to Mr. Abraham Woodward of Broad Town, member of a family to whom the Primitive Methodism of Brinkworth Circuit owed much.

Another Wiltshire guest-house was the home of Mr. John Davies, on the Marlborough Downs, where the little flocks often met for shelter and for worship in the time of persecution at Ramsbury and neighbouring places. It was at Ewin's Hill Harriet Maslin of Ramsbury gave her first public exhortation. She was, we are told, diligent in attending the five o'clock services, which were held all the year round, and took her turn in speaking with the rest of the new converts. In 1834 she came on the plan, and in 1837 became the devoted partner of Mr. George Wallis.

A simple incident in the life of George Wallis, who was one of the gains of the Wootton Bassett revival, and, as a young man of twenty-one, became one of Shefford's first staff of preachers, brings us into Berkshire, and at once illustrates the scarcity and the value of these hospitable homesteads of those early days. Sometimes an incident like this illumines past conditions as no number of generalised statements could do. Like a snap-shot, true to the actuality of things, it has a vivid suggestiveness as to the past out of all proportion to the apparent unimportance of the incident itself at the time it occurred. "A few miles from Newbury there stands an old farm-house, then occupied by Mr. Simon Goddard, who espoused the cause of the missionaries and threw open his home to them. One evening Mr. George Wallis, who had been preaching at a distant village, made for this hospitable house, but reached it to find the inmates had all retired to rest. Not caring to disturb them he crept into a heap of straw for the purpose of passing the night. Later on came along Mr. Thomas Russell *who had been unable to find shelter elsewhere.* The family were soon roused by the new-comer, and the youthful missionary, like John following the bolder Peter, left the straw for more comfortable quarters." We have no report of the table-talk that took place on the morrow when the family and guests assembled at meal-time. Such a report is wanting to complete the picture; but we may be sure the talk would turn on the progress of the work of God; on the latest additions to the roll of converts; incidents of the campaign would be related, and the latest novelty in persecution described. We can imagine how Thomas Russell would tell how some one at Faringdon, with a turn for calculation, had estimated that no less than two sacks of potatoes had been flung at the preacher and his congregation in the streets of that place, and we can picture the zest with which he would round off the story by the

THE PERIOD OF CIRCUIT PREDOMINANCE AND ENTERPRISE. 337

statement that some of the thrifty people of Faringdon had picked up and planted these tubers and were calling their produce "Faringdon-Russells." Our pioneers were not altogether devoid of the sense of humour, and many incidents happened in the 'Thirties in the persecution-area, which would appeal to that wholesome sense, like the incident just given.

In this connection respectful mention should be made of Mr. G. T. Phelps of Hungerford, who is one of the very small number still surviving who have sustained an active connection with the Church in this part of the country since the early days of struggle. Much might be said of the character and work of Mr. Phelps and his excellent partner. What is emphasised here however is the fact that for forty-eight years Mrs. Phelps was the light of a home whose hospitality was unceasingly and ungrudgingly

NANCY STREET'S HOUSE (WITH NANCY IN FRONT), QUICKS GREEN, BRADFIELD CIRCUIT, BERKS.

dispensed. No wonder that, under the influence of her saintly and beneficent life, her children should turn out well. When she died in 1898 three of her sons were ministers of the gospel—one of them being Rev. T. Phelps, a well-known minister of the Salisbury and Southampton District—while her three daughters were the wives of Primitive Methodist preachers. One of her last utterances, disclosing what had been the bent of her life, was: "Always make room for the preachers"!

We get glimpses of other early befrienders of the cause : of the Alexanders of Ramsbury, one of whom offered his joiner's shop for the first meeting-place, which offer necessitated another journey to Salisbury to get it licensed ; of William Hawkin, who, when he was an agricultural labourer earning but six or seven shillings a week, lost his

Y

employment for entertaining the preachers, but he took care to keep his integrity and his religion, and lived to become a prosperous farmer ; of George and Thomas Waite and Isaac Hedges who, with several others, started for Heaven at a service in a gravel-pit at Hoe Benham in 1830, and became "eminent in the good cause"; of Mr. Kirby who invited the Primitives to Bradfield, and of Mr. Nullis of Ashmanstead who "became a great helper in our chapel-building at Burnt Hill, and whose son, Isaac, became mighty in the ministry with us." The reference to Bradfield is interesting because, as Thomas Russell asserts, from Bradfield the work opened out to Reading.

The name of Isaac S. Nullis brings before us a remarkable personality. His life was an intense one though, measured by years, it was not long. It was his companion, George Smith, who induced him to attend a prayer meeting in Mrs. Ann Street's cottage, Quicks Green ; and here the great "turn" in his life was experienced. This humble cottage is connexionally historic and as such we have pleasure in giving a view of it, especially as it also shows us " Nancy" Street herself—a notable figure of those days. Isaac Nullis and George Smith both became local preachers in the Reading Circuit. The latter was a useful travelling preacher for thirty-nine years (ob. 1897), while Isaac Nullis also toiled successfully as a home-missionary for a few years. He died in 1868, leaving testamentary gifts to his Church, and his remains lie in the graveyard opposite the cottage where he found the Saviour. There too is buried the mortal part of Ann Street. The "Life" of Isaac Nullis has been written by Mr. Jesse Herbert. It shows us a man whose course was marked by consuming zeal in seeking the souls of men : it also contains many instances of remarkable answers to prayer. Those amongst us—and surely they are an increasing number—to whom prayer is a subject of absorbing interest, who seek to investigate its achievements, its laws, its possibilities—should keep Isaac Nullis in remembrance. His life has instruction for us and, it is to be feared, admonishment as well.

In turning to Hampshire, we cannot do better than preface our account of the fierce persecutions our pioneers underwent in this county, by describing a journey which Hugh Bourne took along with Thomas Russell in September, 1832, from Shefford across the North Western borders of Hampshire on to Salisbury. To us the story of the advance of Primitive Methodism from county to county has all the interest of a moving drama, and so the description of this journey comes in at this point with all the appropriateness of an Interact, equally related as it is to what has gone before and to what it foreshadows as about to happen. But let us give Thomas Russell's narrative :—

"Mr. Hugh Bourne was frequently requested to pay us a visit; but from the press of business and calls elsewhere he did not visit us till Monday, September 10th, 1832. However, his coming then was very opportune, for surely no men needed fatherly counsel and comfort more than we did ; persecution raged on every side, and our lives were often in danger. Nor can I forget his arrival at Shefford the morning after our quarterly meeting. Brother Samuel West, who had come to see his friend [John Ride] and assist us at the quarter-day, was praying at full stretch and in the full glory. Faringdon and Wantage mission was then the burden of our cry, and many a hearty "amen" ran through the house, when suddenly, at a quick pace, in walked a man with a broad-brimmed hat, all covered with dust, a brown top-coat that had weathered many a blast, an umbrella which had been stretched against many a storm, and a well-known carpet-bag. No sooner was he in than he was on his knees, and with loud responses he joined in our devotions. The voice was familiar to myself and Messrs. Ride and West; and when we rose from our knees we gave him a hearty welcome, and announced him to the rest of the brethren, and most tenderly and affectionately did he listen to our tales of success, and those of woe about the persecutions then raging, particularly in the vale of Wantage. He gave us good counsel, and most earnestly prayed for us, and the preachers then separated for their appointments. On Friday, September 14th, I drove Mr. Bourne into Hampshire to Hartbourne [Hurstbourne?], to Squire Blunt's. I was delighted with the ease and freedom as well as ability with which Mr. B. conversed with the good gentleman on Cobbett and other authors, as he had a large and valuable library. In the evening, at my request, Mr. Bourne preached [in Mr. Farr's house at Bindly] from 'the Great White Throne,' and many felt the force of truth. The next morning I accompanied him fourteen miles towards Salisbury. In all the journey I found him very conversable, and as we crossed the Hampshire hills, where the boundary-line parts it from Berkshire, he said: 'That might form the boundary of two circuits, and you might take Hampshire.' But I said, 'No, sir'; and I went on to explain that I was very much attached to Mr. Ride and that we wrought well together. Besides this, I wanted Shefford Circuit made stronger before a separation; Mrs. Ride, too, was a great counsellor. We prayed by the wayside at parting when within seven miles of Salisbury, and I returned with redoubled resolution to my station, and was glad that in some measure persecution had begun to abate, and the way to open in new places."*

This record gives us an authentic glimpse of the past. We see Hugh Bourne, as he crossed the Illsley Downs, manifesting the same habit of close observation of the natural features which met his view as he had shown when he strode over the twenty miles of wild country between Penrith and Alston Moor. No fox-hunter or general had a keener eye for the salient features of a landscape than he; but to him, as he jogged along in his chaise, these hills did not suggest sport or strategy, or even picturesqueness—they presented themselves to him as the natural boundaries of circuits. We see, too, that at the time to which this incident belongs, as the result of Thomas Russell's and Elizabeth Smith's short tentative missions within the borders of the northern division of Hants in 1831-2, some useful adherents had already been won, that houses were available for preaching, and that guest-houses stood open— in short, we see that a base for future labours on a larger scale had already been secured. As early as 1831, when Thomas Russell made his excursion into Hampshire, two families were won whose adhesion was of the greatest value to our Church in the trying days that were to come. For if persecution had by this time somewhat abated in the Vale of the White Horse, it was yet to gather and break in Hampshire. On his first visit to Linkenholt Mr. Michael Osmond showed himself very friendly, and united with the society that was formed, as did also his brothers Richard and Stephen,

* Combined quotation from T. Russell's "Primitive Methodism in Berkshire," 1885, and a letter by him included in Walford's "Life of Hugh Bourne," vol. ii. pp. 403-5.

and his sister—afterwards Mrs. Tasker. Messrs. Richard and Michael, we are told, at one time rented the whole of the parish of Linkenholt, and were able to retire with a competence when none of the subsequent occupiers succeeded. Stephen Osmond entered the ministry and travelled for some years; while Richard, after having been an active and efficient local preacher in the Andover Circuit, on his retirement from business removed with his family to Bath, and interested himself in mission work in a neglected part of the city. A building was secured, and a congregation and Sunday school formed. After her husband's death in 1865, Mrs. Jane Grundy Osmond felt it a sacred duty to carry on the work initiated by her husband. She and her family liberally aided in the erection, in 1881, of Claremont Church and school buildings, which became Bath Second Circuit. Mrs. Osmond died December, 1892.

MR. R. OSMOND.

MRS. OSMOND.

Among other of the earliest converts of Thomas Russell were Mr. and Mrs. Farr of Bindly, in whose house Hugh Bourne preached his famous sermon on "the Great White Throne." No less than two hundred persons are stated to have been converted in that farm-kitchen. Miss Farr, who had strong mental powers and had received a superior education, became a local preacher, and in 1837 was married to George Price, one of the makers of the Brinkworth District. He it was who, in 1838, took charge of Shefford Circuit when John Ride moved on to Reading; he purchased the Union Chapel, Newbury, which for thirty-eight years served the uses of the denomination until superseded by the present handsome Gothic church during the superintendency of Mr. Edward Alford. Mr. Price died suddenly in full harness in 1869, while his widow survived until 1895, dying at the residence of her eldest son, who was at the time the Steward of the Croydon Circuit.

For Hamphire the curtain rises in the spring of 1833 on scenes of mob-violence and legal oppression that throw a lurid light on the social and moral condition of that part of England in the 'thirties. Already, since 1832, Shefford had had its branch in Hampshire of which Mitcheldever was the centre: now, at its March quarter day, 1833, it was resolved to send George Wallis and W. Wiltshire to begin a mission at Andover. Nothing will be gained for our

PRIMITIVE METHODIST MANSE AND CHAPEL, NEWBURY.

purpose by keeping these two missions rigidly distinct, since they were contiguous to each other and were being pushed forward at the same time. All we can hope or shall attempt to do is, by samples, to convey a sufficient impression both of the amount and virulence of the persecution, in its two forms, with which Shefford's devoted missionaries had to contend on both branches before they became circuits— Mitcheldever in 1835, and Andover in 1837. On three successive Sundays Mr. Wallis visited Andover. His first service, on May 5th, was held amid a scene of great disturbance. On the second Sunday a godless gang broke up the service and knocked the preacher down. On the third he was pulled down while preaching in the market-place and he and his colleague were dragged through the streets by the beadle and the constable, while the mob, with discordant cries, struck them with besoms, sticks, and whatever came handy. The skirts of their coats were torn off, and there is a record, in the circuit books, of a grant of money for making good their sartorial loss. Years after, Mr. Wallis pointed out to his son the place in Old Basing where he had taken his stand and was thrice knocked down by a mob who trampled upon his body till they thought life was gone, and then ran away. Once it was his lot, with others, to be drenched with bullock's blood! At Alresford, some seven miles from Winchester, certain of the inhabitants had in readiness against the coming of Mr. Watts, six dozen of rotten eggs, a tub of coal-tar, and two bundles of rods. "On his approaching the place where he intended to preach, they hailed him with shouts of rage and madness. He called at a friend's house, which was instantly beset by the mob, and to escape their violence. he was obliged to conceal himself; they broke the windows, and covered one of the room floors with eggs." Fortunately some of the persecutors left their devil's work to go to church; then Mr. Watts made his escape, but was followed by numbers who stoned him more than a mile. Primitive Methodism has had its revenge on Alresford: it has planted there its first Orphanage. At another village in this same county the clergyman threatened to prosecute the preachers should they dare to preach in his parish. When, undeterred by his threats, Mr. Watts duly made his appearance, the haughty priest went round ordering his parishioners "to go into their houses and shut their doors and windows:" and they did as they were told. Further south, at Stockbridge, persecution was no less virulent. Here, William Fowler, a young preacher, who soon after finished his course with joy, was violently assailed. He and his friends were enmeshed in a rope flung round them and were being dragged towards the river. When some of those enclosed drew their clasp-knives and cut the rope, they were beaten with the pieces, and then pelted out of the place. At St. Mary Bourne, in order to escape further ill-usage, Mr. Fowler and his followers deemed it advisable to put on the smocks of some labouring men, and thus get away from their persecutors.

But enough, and more than enough of such incidents as these, which, though they are but a few out of the many that might be given, yet revolt us by their brutality and weary us with their monotony, since they lack even the poor merit of the inquisitors' torments—ingenuity. The facts are set forth, not to raise pity, except for the poor neglected misguided men who, by a strange perversity, abused their best friends. Rather are they given to show that Hampshire sorely needed the Gospel at this time, and that our missionaries willingly braved much, and counted not their lives dear unto them in the attempt to supply that need.

But a few words must be said of the much more reprehensible attempt to set the law in motion against the missionaries—to compromise them and their work by confounding them and it with the machinations of revolutionaries, at that time a quite legitimate reason for alarm. Perhaps the worst case of the kind that occurred in Hampshire—at any rate the one of most notoriety—was that in which Messrs. John Ride and Edward Bishop were the sufferers. On Tuesday, June 8th, 1834, the quarterly meeting was held at Mitcheldever and it was arranged to hold a missionary meeting at its close. As the cottages available for services would not accommodate the congregation expected, it was arranged that the meeting should be held on a piece of waste ground on which services were accustomed to be held. Despite the notice affixed to a neighbouring cottage prohibiting the meeting under legal penalties, it was agreed, after serious deliberation, to hold the meeting as arranged. The speakers confined themselves strictly to the subject of missions and the meeting closed in an orderly and peaceable manner. For all this, shortly afterwards, "says Mr. Bishop," a summons reached us, under the hand of Sir Thomas Baring, Bart., of Stratton Park. This legal instrument charged John Ride and Edward Bishop, *on the oath of Thomas Ellery, with leading and heading a riotous mob at Mitcheldever—with being armed with bludgeons, and that they did, by force and arms, put His Majesty's peaceful subjects in fear—that they obstructed the thoroughfare—and that they were a nuisance.*

EDWARD BISHOP.

The sequel of the story shall be told in the words of Mr. Richard Heath, from whose work we have already quoted.*

"On such a charge John Ride and Edward Bishop were cited before the magistrates of Winchester on July 19th, 1834. No breach of the law being proved against them the magistrates offered to let them go, if they would promise not to preach again at Mitcheldever. Refusing to do this, they were bound over to be tried at the Quarter Sessions, and during the twelve days they were finding bail, they were kept in the same prison in which the victims of 1830 had been confined.† I do not suppose they had any idea of the dignity of their martyrdom, or how really they were being associated with the sufferings of Christ. For we must not expect the thoughts of even the poorest among English evangelists to rise above the level of nineteenth century Christianity. However, no one can preach the Gospel of the Kingdom or sincerely pray that that Kingdom may come without helping to bring about a revolution of the most radical description."

We may smile at, while we forgive the implied assumption that John Ride and E. Bishop were simple-minded evangelists who were incapable of understanding the relations and issues of the events in which they were leading actors. Never was there a greater mistake. We doubt whether even my Lord Bishop of Winchester himself was as wide awake to the "condition of the people question" in his diocese as was Edward Bishop.

* "The English Peasant." Quoted *ante* vol. ii p. 55.
† "The fortnight we spent in that county jail was the best portion of college life with which we had ever been favoured."—*E. Bishop.*

THE PERIOD OF CIRCUIT PREDOMINANCE AND ENTERPRISE. 343

This is clear from his published views and from what we know of the man; and in far-sightedness, "in understanding of the times to know what Israel ought to do," in mental vigour, E. Bishop was but one of a number of men who in the wide old Brinkworth District laid the foundations of the Connexion deep and strong—men like S. Turner, C. T. Harris, and many others who might be named.

Connexionally as well as nationally better times came to Hampshire. Andover, with its missions extending to the New Forest and the Solent, became one of the widest circuits in the Connexion and did good work. As for Winchester, it was long a struggle to gain a Connexional foothold in the ancient city, but in 1852 Mitcheldever made another vigorous attempt to mission it, which proved successful. Through all these years of persecution and struggle the Rev. W. Thorn, Congregational minister of Winchester, had shown himself our vindicator and friend. His church having built a new sanctuary on a portion of the site of the old prison where Messrs. Ride and Bishop were incarcerated, their vacated chapel was secured on most favourable terms, and Mr. Thorn, Dr. Beaumont, and E. Bishop were among those who took part in the opening services. The occasion naturally lent itself to retrospect and to comparison.

SAMUEL TURNER.

"Let any Christian man," says Mr. Bishop (and we must remember the words were written in 1853), "calmly contrast the religious state of this country now with what it was nearly thirty years ago, and he will find facts which must cause his heart to rejoice. The religious and educational efforts which have been employed for the benefit of the people have produced great results. Religious services and Sabbath schools have been greatly increased. There are villages in which we found, in 1832, only *one* religious service on the Sabbath day, and *no* week-evening lecture, and *no* Sabbath school; in which there may now be found *four* or more religious services on the Sabbath, *two* or more on week-evenings, and *two* Sabbath schools; and he must be under the influence of strong prejudice who will not admit that the labours and sufferings of Primitive Methodist preachers have, under God, had much to do in producing this happily altered state of things. Let this be admitted or denied by erring men, the record of these brethren is on high, and their work with their God."

C. T. HARRIS.

The Windsor Mission of Reading Circuit will furnish our next sample of persecution. April 12th, 1835, is given as the date when the first effective move was made on Reading. On that Sunday a full day's services were held on Forbury Hill, the preachers being Messrs. Ride, Bishop, Kirby (of Bradfield), and, in the evening, Mrs. Ride. From this day began Mr. Jesse Herbert's life-long connection with the Reading Circuit. For some time he was engaged in home-mission work like his friend Isaac Nullis, but, his health breaking under the strain that work imposed he returned to Reading in 1841, and henceforward, until his death in 1896, did much to extend and consolidate Primitive Methodism in the town and neighbourhood. He was a local preacher for fifty-nine years, and the founder, in 1858, of the Young Men's Bible Class—the greatest work of his life—of which he had charge for thirty years. As an active and public-spirited citizen of the

MR. JESSE HERBERT.

A VIEW OF THE FORBURY, IN READING.

biscuit-town he was respected and trusted, serving as a member of the School Board for fifteen years, and being rate-collector for twenty-three years. Mr. Edward Long, the father-in-law of the late Rev. R. W. Burnett, and Miss Mary Bovaston (Mrs. Joseph Coling) were also amongst the earliest members and local preachers of the Reading Society. Mr. Long was for many years the Steward of the Circuit, and died in 1897.

MARY BOVASTON.

MR. E. LONG.

THE PERIOD OF CIRCUIT PREDOMINANCE AND ENTERPRISE. 345

In October, 1835, St. Giles' Hall, in London Street, was taken on rent for religious services and served until 1839, when a building in Minster Street, formerly a Baptist chapel, was secured. This more commodious building formed the chief centre of the society until 1866, when a hall was purchased and converted into the present chapel in London Street. Meanwhile, Shefford had made Reading a circuit. This was done in March, 1837, just two years from its opening. The circuit began its career with 450 members and four preachers, John Ride being the superintendent. His transference from Shefford to Reading was not effected until Shefford's other missions—Mitcheldever, Faringdon, Andover, and Wallingford—had all likewise been constituted circuits. His transference to Reading, therefore, showed that another stage in the advance of the Connexion on London and the home-counties, from this side, had been reached, and that Reading was regarded as a convenient base for pushing the advance still further. Hence it is to be noted that it was in 1836, just before these changes were made, that Shefford Circuit reached its acme. On the stations for that year it has twenty-three preachers and 2031 members, thus ranking next to Hull, which the same year had twenty-five preachers and 4438 members.

During its first year an outrageous case of persecution (of which we can give no particulars) cost the Reading Circuit the sum of £150. Despite this untoward event, a mission in the county of Surrey was resolved upon. On April 17th, 1838, Messrs. Ride and Aaron Bell* set out on their pioneer journey, walking thirty miles as far as Guildford. On their way, John Ride accosted an old lady, a native of those parts, and a dialogue took place, of which the following is a specimen:—

Mr. Ride.—"Do you know anything of Jesus Christ?"
Aged Woman.—"There is no man of that name living anywhere about here."
Mr. R.—"Do you know the way of salvation?"
Aged Woman.—"I have lived here many years, but I have never heard of such a way yet. But there are some men making a new road down yonder; you had better ask them if that is the way of salvation."

After this, one can well believe the statement of Mr. John Guy, who in June succeeded Mr. Ride on this mission: "The people were the darkest I had ever met with." Reading Circuit continued to prosper. In 1839 it employed eight preachers and reported 600 members. In 1840 the number of its preachers had risen to twelve and its membership to 871. The circuit was enabled to enter more extensively upon missionary work through the liberality of Mr. Thomas Baker who, though a member of another community, contributed the sum of £100 towards the employment of five missionaries in the neighbouring counties. Messrs. Guy, Hedges, and Grigg were appointed to the Windsor Mission in 1839. "Their labours were hard, their privations many, and their persecutions neither few nor small." As a concrete illustration of this statement of Mr. Petty's, let us give a leaf from the experience of Mr. Grigg, one of the pioneers of this mission. In his experience we have the same combination of light and shadow which we have met with elsewhere.

On the 24th of September, Mr. Grigg went to preach at Winkfield-row. He had

* This devoted young minister lost his life in August, 1838. In passing through Eton he turned aside to bathe in a back stream of the Thames, and was drowned.

previously heard of the moral degradation of many of the inhabitants, and they had been informed of his coming to preach to them. He selected the Green in the centre of the village for the purpose—but ere he began the service, he sat down on some logs of wood to rest a little and to read a portion of the Bible. Mrs. Searle, a woman of great physical strength and of a generous disposition, but not then renewed by Divine grace, came to ask him whether he were the gentleman that was going to preach. Being answered in the affirmative, she strongly advised him not to make the attempt, assuring him that he would be "roughly handled." Mr. Grigg replied that he was often cruelly treated, and that he could not conscientiously leave the place without attempting to preach. "Then," said his generous adviser, " I will lend you a chair to stand upon, and you had better stand near my garden gate." Mr. Grigg did so, and began to sing a hymn. He had sung one verse in quietness, when a number of young men came out of a public-house opposite, and one of them overturned the chair upon which Mr. Grigg was

MRS. OSMAN'S RESIDENCE.

standing, by which he was thrown upon the ground. His kind female friend, not having yet learned that the weapons of the Christian warfare are not carnal but spiritual, struck the disturber on the back of his head, and knocked him down. Then seizing the chair with one hand, and Mr. Grigg with the other, she pulled him within her garden gate, and said, " Stand and preach there." Mr. Grigg proceeded with singing, and the persecutors began to pelt him with flint stones and other missiles, and to besmear him with the sediment of a horse-pond close by. When he had finished singing he knelt down to pray ; and while in this solemn act of devotion, his godless persecutors rushed through the gate, seized him, tore his coat, and dragged him out of the garden, and along a flint road about fifty yards. Turning to the ringleader, the suffering missionary inquired what he had done to be served in that manner. The persecutor candidly replied that he could assign no reason for the ill-treatment,—and apparently conscious that he was liable to be prosecuted, and fearing the result, he expressed a hope that

Mr. Grigg would not "do anything in the affair." The latter replied that if he and his companions would promise never to molest him or any other preacher any more, he would freely forgive them. They promised that they would never interfere again, and he shook hands with them, and returned to his former standing-place, where, though his coat was torn to rags, his person besmeared with filth, and blood was flowing from his wounded face, he preached to those who were willing to hear. After the service, his kind friend took him into her house, procured him water to wash himself, cleaned his clothes as well as she was able, whilst her husband prepared some tea for his refreshment. They expressed their deep sympathy with him in his sufferings, and regretted that they could not accommodate him with lodgings. He thanked them for their kindness, prayed with them, bade them good night, and then tried all the public-houses, and several of the farmers and cottagers in vain to obtain a night's lodging. Being at length told that no one dare entertain him, through fear of the most influential persons in the parish, he ceased to inquire further, and being too remote from the residence of any friend, he walked on the road till midnight, and then went into a field, where he slept till five o'clock in the morning. But his patient endurance of the inhuman treatment he received was not in vain. He shortly afterwards received a written invitation from Mrs. Henry Osman and her mother-in-law, Mrs. R. Osman, to visit Winkfield-row again, engaging, if he did so, that bed and board should be found and a room provided for the services. These two good women were true to their promise: they took a house and furnished it with forms and candlesticks and everything that was necessary, and became responsible for the rent. When the room became too small, Mrs. R. Osman gave the use of her dining-room till the present chapel was built. From that time, until her death at the great age of 89, Mrs. H. Osman continued to take the deepest interest in the cause. For years she provided the school-treat, and at the time of her death she had money put aside for that purpose. Her eldest son, Mr. H. M. Osman, became a local preacher in 1858, and has been the mainstay of the cause for many years. The farm is still in the family, and "the prophet's chamber" has been kept for the use of the preacher from that day to this. It is pleasing to know, too, that the Amazonian, Mrs. Searle, afterwards became a convert, and that her two sons are, or till recently were, local preachers with us. So trial and suffering pass while the good they yield are abiding.

By its Thame mission, Wallingford, made a circuit in 1837, carried Brinkworth District into the southern projection of Oxfordshire and into Bucks. This geographical extension enlarged the persecution area; progress had its attendant shadow. Bicester and Ambrosden, in Oxon., should be marked on our connexional map with crossed swords as though they were battle sites, for at these places two of the very worst cases of persecution recorded in our annals took place. For the credit of our countrymen, and also for the sake of our readers, we are glad to say they are also the last cases we shall need to refer to in this chapter. Not that it is affirmed there was no persecution after 1843, but only that the cases that did occur after that date were isolated ones, all taken together not being numerous enough to compromise a county, or characterise a period. With the close of the first period, persecution, as quite an ordinary thing to be expected and reckoned with, went out—and went out flagrantly and stormily.

The date of the Bicester man-baiting was July 31st, 1843. Already, in the March of the same year, Mr. George Stansfield had served seven days in Dover jail for having sung and prayed in the streets of Margate—the happy hunting-ground of nigger-minstrels. Let it be noted that it was the rector of St. Peter's who, as the spokesman of the Bench, announced its decision.

GEORGE STANSFIELD.

So little did Mr. Stansfield look like a misdemeanant that the prisoners took him, from his dignified and gentlemanly bearing, to be some one who had come to inspect the prison. The chief victim of the savage attack at Bicester was S. West, the joint re-opener of Bristol, the remissioner of Oxford, and the man, who, of all who preached at the Conference camp meeting at York in 1853, made the profoundest impression on C. C. McKechnie.* This was the man who bore the brunt of the Bicester baiting, his colleague, C. Elford, having succeeded in escaping into a friendly house. As for S. West, he was treated in much the same way as Thomas Russell was treated at Wantage, but with aggravations. He was made a spectacle to scoffing ladies and gentlemen (?) who saw him driven from one side of the market-place to another—soused with water, and buffeted. In their small way, they behaved as heartlessly as the spectators in the amphitheatre, whose upturned thumbs gave the signal for the dispatch of the gladiator, "butchered to make a Roman holiday." "It is as much fun as a bull-bait," was their delighted comment, as they saw Mr. West driven from under their window where he had vainly thought he would find protection. Though the chief actors in this disgraceful scene escaped all legal pains and penalties, men noticed with awe how soon, by the act of God, retribution came upon some of the ringleaders.

The sufferer in the Ambrosden case was Isaac Hedges. In the early days Brinkworth District grew its own preachers. It was argely self-sufficing and was extended by those who were the first-fruits of its own missionary labours. Men like James Hurd, George Wallis, W. Brewer, E. Rawlings, J. Guy, G. Obern, T. Cummin, J. Best, the brothers Harding, and many others, became the successors

SAMUEL WEST.

* "Of all the preachers Samuel West produced the mightiest impression. He attracted an immense concourse and preached with extraordinary unction."—*MS. Autobiography*. By a slip Mr. McKechnie has written "Nathaniel West," but he disappeared years before. S. West was a delegate to the York Conference.

of the pioneers by whose instrumentality they were won. Such was Isaac Hedges, a plain, fear-nought, laborious preacher, who never forgot the gravel-pit where he was converted, and who did his best to bring men and women out of Nature's quarry. For standing in front of a wheelwright's shop at Ambrosden in Oxfordshire and preaching to five persons, on July 16th, 1843, Isaac Hedges was sentenced to twenty-one days imprisonment, with hard labour, by the Rev. A. B. Matthews and Mr. W. Davis, surgeon. We give the names, and not dashes, and let the record stand without comment.

As a sort of appendix to this chapter, a few words must be written concerning Brinkworth's resumption of missionary labours, which resulted in the enlargement of the District in another direction. The reference to these productive labours has been deferred until this point in order that we might uninterruptedly follow the development of Shefford Circuit. After parting with Shefford, Brinkworth Circuit seemed to be suffering from a temporary reaction, and missionary labours were suspended. But it was soon borne in upon the minds of its leading officials that a circuit only "gains strength as it goes." In June, 1832, Messrs. S. Turner and J. Baker were sent to open Chippenham. Though, at this time, Mr. Turner had but just entered the ministry, he soon gave proof of possessing, in happy combination, qualities which afterwards made him one of the most successful superintendents of the Brinkworth District. With the zeal and courage of the evangelist he united the prudence and discernment of the man of affairs. The missioning of Chippenham was successful despite the ill-concealed opposition of the magistrates. A collision with the authorities was, however, avoided, without any sacrifice of principle. A society was formed at Chippenham on October 2nd, 1832, and the way soon opened for the purchase of the Friends' meeting-house which, with the enlarged accommodation supplied by the putting in of galleries, served the uses of the society until 1896, when a handsome church was erected. Marshfield and Calne were also successfully visited; and five months after entering upon the mission, Mr. Turner was able to write: "We now preach at thirteen places, three of which are market-towns; the work of conversion is going on, and we have one hundred members." In 1835 Chippenham became a circuit with 350 members and employing three travelling preachers.

A famous union camp meeting of the Brinkworth and Shefford Circuits, held on Bishopstone Downs—one of many such historic gatherings—coincided with and inaugurated a yet bolder enterprise, the missioning of Bristol. The two Samuels, West and Turner, whom Mr. Petty describes as "zealous, laborious brethren," were designated for this important work, which, under the Divine blessing, proved successful. On Sunday, July 14th, 1832, the mission was opened in Poyntzpool (one of the lowest parts of the city). Here Mr. West preached. In the afternoon Mr. Turner preached in Queen Square, and in the evening his colleague stood up at the Drawbridge. From the first the services were fruitful in conversions, nor do we read of any special persecution being encountered. The first Bristol society was formed on August 4th, and on the 25th, an old building called Dolman's Chapel was opened by E. Foizey. This building, dating back to the middle of the eighteenth century, had formerly been used by John Wesley, and also, it would seem, by Dr. Ryland, and was more or less in use by our people until 1849, when Ebenezer Chapel was opened, under the superintendency of C. T. Harris. No one has left a deeper impress of himself on Bristol Primitive Methodism than C. T. Harris, eleven years of whose remarkable ministry were spent in the city.

PRESENT VIEW OF BUILDING KNOWN AS DOLMAN'S CHAPEL, BRISTOL.

The first chapel in this neighbourhood was built in 1841, at Kingswood, which, along with Bedminster and Fishponds, shared in the labours of the pioneers. In 1835, Bristol was made a circuit, but its progress was comparatively slow. In 1843, it had but two preachers and 284 members, and though, for convenience, we give here the views of its chapels, they belong to a much later stage of its connexional development. It was not until the last year of the nineteenth century was reached that Bristol became a Conference town, while Reading had its first Conference as early as 1841.

The Reading Conference of 1841 is noteworthy. It was held at the time when, and in that part of the country where, the evangelistic movement we have been following

THE PERIOD OF CIRCUIT PREDOMINANCE AND ENTERPRISE. 351

Bristol Chapels

was nearing its completion. We do not know much about the Reading Conference, There were troubles, we are told; and as the thorny Stamp Case had to be dealt with, it is likely enough some minds were lacerated. But the most significant thing about the Conference is, that it was held at Reading. No Conference had ever been held so far South before—a plain proof that the Connexion had made notable advance in this part of the country, and had effectively occupied the county town of Berks, though that town had been the head of a circuit only four years. The time and place of this Conference are significant, too, when we notice how the district, for which Reading was one of the chief generating stations, was the focus on which various lines of evangelisation were evidently converging. Some of these lines, extending far from their base, had been interrupted, and in some cases even broken off, but the vigorous Brinkworth District had resumed them and carried them forward. The statement of a few facts will make this plain.

Burland still held on to its Northampton mission, and Hull to Bedford; but Hull and Driffield's mission to Hertford was, in 1840, taken over by Reading and greatly extended, so as to include Rickmansworth, Watford, St. Albans, and other places. Academic Oxford, which was "stormed" by W. Bellham in 1825, was remissioned from Witney in 1835, by Joseph Preston, who bluntly calls it "a sink of iniquity." The society he then formed had, in 1838, become extinct, though three local preachers resided in the town. S. West, the superintendent of Wallingford Circuit, visited it that same year and re-formed the society. Mr. Dingle—one of the local preachers already referred to— erected a small chapel for the use of the society, which was taken on rent, and in 1845, Oxford attained circuit independence. As for Witney itself—it formed part of the Brinkworth District at its formation in 1833. In 1836, Joseph Preston, its superintendent, successfully missioned Chacombe, and other places, in north Oxfordshire, which, in 1840, were constituted Banbury Circuit. In 1841, Witney became a branch of Wallingford and remained such till 1844. We turn to Buckinghamshire and Bedfordshire. On April 21st, 1839, while still a branch of Shefford, Aylesbury began its mission in the straw-plaiting towns of Luton and Dunstable. S. Turner and H. Higginson were our connexional pioneers in these towns, and were favourably received by the inhabitants. In Luton especially, rapid progress was made. Seven months after the first sermon had been preached in the town, a flourishing society had been raised, and a chapel built. Aylesbury became a circuit in December, 1839, and about the same time took over the derelict mission of Buckingham belonging to distant Congleton. At one time Aylesbury was an immense circuit extending over a large part of two counties. In such a circuit there was room and need for the display of Mr. Turner's qualities as an evangelist and administrator. When, after a four years' term, he removed from the circuit in 1842, he left 435 members more than he had found, and ten chapels where there had been none. High Wycombe affords yet another instance of the complementary and terminal character of Brinkworth District's work at this time. As early as 1811, Hugh Bourne refers to Wycombe as the location of a society. We hear nothing more of the town until April 8th, 1835, when we find James Pole, one of the preachers of Hounslow Circuit, then belonging to Norwich District, after a walk of twenty miles, preaching in Queen's Square. This extension into Bucks was the salvation

THE PERIOD OF CIRCUIT PREDOMINANCE AND ENTERPRISE. 353

Luton Chapels

HIGHTOWN LECTURE HALL

CHURCH ST

GEORGE ST

CARDIGAN ST

PARK TOWN

HIGHTOWN

H. MOODY PHOTOGRAPHER

MOUNT TABOR

z

of the Hounslow Circuit, which now took the name of High Wycombe, and continued to form part of the Norwich District until 1840. Then as a branch it too came under the protection and governance of Reading until 1848, when it resumed its status as a circuit.

These facts will suffice to show what was the part taken by Brinkworth District in the geographical extension of the Connexion. It fell to its lot to cover the last lap of the course; to round off and wind up a movement which had been going on for just a generation. When, in 1843, we see Hull and Reading—two great missionary circuits—handing over their missions to the newly established Missionary Committee, and when we see John Ride removing from Reading to Cooper's Gardens, we feel we have seen the end of the Period of Circuit Predominance and Enterprise, and that the Period of Consolidation is about to begin.

BOOK III.

THE PERIOD OF CONSOLIDATION AND CHURCH DEVELOPMENT.

INTRODUCTORY.

THOUGH we speak of *the* Period of Consolidation, a more thorough analysis of the facts of our History will show that, since 1843, in reality there have been *two* well-defined periods in that History—one of which closed in the memory of many yet living. Indeed, the very description of the period we have given, like a binary star, is clearly resolvable into two; for Church development implies something more than Consolidation. The establishment of Foreign Missions, of a Connexional Orphanage, the entrance upon Social work in London and other large cities—these, to name only a few of the new departures of the later years, are signs, not so much of consolidation, as they are signs of a functional equipment for those higher duties which have come into view along with the attained consciousness of true Church life. There may be a "Society"—there may even be a large "Connexion"—with no Foreign Missions, and without any provision for higher ministerial education, and the advancement of Christ's Kingdom in social forms of service. But there cannot be a true Church without these things. Hence, the History of Primitive Methodism, from first to last, is viewed by us as the setting forth of the process by which what began as a purely evangelistic movement gradually evolved and organized itself into a Church. The movement, in its first form, had been animated with a spirit of evangelism so aggressive that it could not rest until it had practically overrun this country from Berwick to Penzance, and from Kings Lynn to Monmouth, with extensions into Wales, Scotland, Ireland, and the great continent of America. When this movement closed in 1843, it did not at once attain to the full consciousness of Church-life. It entered upon its second phase, one intermediate and largely preparative and transitional. It had taken just one generation to secure the area for future working and more thorough cultivation; to get together the material which was to be fashioned and wrought into another wing of the building of God. It was to take yet another generation of strenuous endeavour to conserve the gains of the past, to acquire the needful "plant" for future work, to get rid of particularism, whether in the form of circuit or district prejudices and partialities, and to become possessed with the "Connexional spirit," as we term it—the sense of our participation in a corporate life with all its enjoyments and responsibilities. Then, and not till then, did we come to feel that the union of heart and purpose we had arrived at in our Church relations, was too real and spiritual a thing to be fittingly described by a word so suggestive of material and artificial attachments as the word "Connexion." If we be asked: "And when, pray, did your denomination arrive at this consciousness of Church-life?" it may be difficult, or even impossible, to answer the question, just as we may be unable to tell the precise day or hour when the consciousness of our own individuality first dawned upon us. It is certain the consciousness of Church-life is enjoyed and claimed now. It is printed on every quarterly ticket of membership. There stands the claim—"Primitive Methodist Church."* More significant still: while every digest of the laws of the denomination, up to and including 1892, had been content to use the word "Connexion," the latest Consolidated Minutes—those of 1902—ousted that word wherever possible in favour of the word Church. Now, official endorsement almost invariably lags behind the communal consciousness; it follows rather than leads public opinion. It is a fair inference therefore that there must have been a strong church-sentiment at work for some years before its emphatic official endorsement.

We have already written: "In the century's evolution of our Church we have had in turn the flourishing and energising of the Circuit, the District, the Church; just as in the order of Nature, we have first the blade, then the ear, then the full corn in the ear" (vol. i. p. 159). We can be in no doubt as to when the second period began, nor shall we be far wrong if we make its close approximately coincide with the passing of another generation—1876. The relaxation of the stringent rules relative to the stationing of preachers, which began in 1872, by the concession of invitations to preachers within their own districts and ended by the levelling of district "barriers," as they were significantly called—these successive enactments marked the opening of the era of Connexionalism, as we have already defined that term.

There is no need to delay the narrative by seeking to point out the various characteristics—the drawbacks or the advantages—of Districtism: some of these will meet us as we proceed. One feature of the period however should be pointed out, as it has an interesting bearing on the sequence of events. The very segregation of the Connexion into Districts, for a generation, was an ultimate advantage. Each District being more or less like a garden enclosed, naturally tended, within limits, to develop itself in its own way under the influence of its dominant minds—the typical "District-men of the 'fifties and 'sixties." It is no mere fancy that would find in each of the leading Districts of that time, a physiognomy and tone of its own; it had its ideal, to be kept ever in view and striven for. It might be better chapels, as in the case of Hull District; or African Missions, or ministerial education, as in the case of Norwich and Sunderland and Manchester Districts. Though this District individuality might sometimes have its inconveniences, and even dangers, in the end it served to enrich the Church as a whole. Thus we shall see how almost every District became a contributor to the general good, and how the District Period naturally merges into the Church Period.

* The ticket is shown vol. i. p. 112.

CHAPTER I.

THE PASSING OF THE PIONEERS.

THE Conference of 1842 deemed it prudent to superannuate both Hugh Bourne and William Clowes. The event was significant of the changes the years had brought and prelusive of the still greater changes that were to follow.

To Mr. Clowes superannuation would come as no shock, since he had virtually been superannuated as long ago as 1827. The Hull Circuit's Quarterly Meeting of that year, perceiving plain signs of failing strength in Mr. Clowes, had decided that "he should be without ministerial charge, and receive his usual salary; but if his health permitted him to labour in other stations, at special services, then the remuneration received for his services should be paid into the Hull Quarter Day." The arrangement then made had continued until 1842, so that to Mr. Clowes superannuation meant little more than that he must now look to Connexional Funds rather than to the Hull Circuit for the very modest provision needful for his support.

But to Mr. Bourne, superannuation came as a painful surprise; as a strong man armed. "It was contrary to his wishes and repugnant to his feelings." He had not sought it, nor, when it came did he like it, though he submitted to it. Mr. Walford is of opinion that the superannuation was premature, and that though Mr. Bourne was now seventy years of age, there were no signs observable of failure of power, either physical or mental, sufficient to justify the step taken by the Conference.* But Mr. Walford is scarcely an impartial witness. The presumption is in favour of the Conference's having tried to do the right and just thing; and if it be suggested that even the Conference is not always infallible, then we must add, that acquaintance with all the facts of this particular case will not dispose us to challenge either the sincerity or the wisdom of the Conference's action. Even in 1838 the course now taken had been foreshadowed; for, in recording the appointment of Hugh Bourne as Editor, it was added: "But if Hugh Bourne, through indisposition, be unable to fill the office of Editor, that John Flesher be called in to assist." This same Conference of 1838 took another significant step in the same direction. Up to that time the appointments of the General Committee Delegates to the various District Meetings had invariably been made by the General Committee itself. These appointments had almost invariably been given to Messrs. H. and J. Bourne and W. Clowes; but by far the largest number of District Meetings were attended by Hugh Bourne. Now, however, the Conference of 1838 took the appointment of General Committee Delegates into its own hands. H. Bourne was deputed to attend the Tunstall and Brinkworth District Meetings of 1839; W. Clowes the Hull,

---

* Memoirs of the Life and Labours of the Venerable Hugh Bourne (vol. ii. pp. 292-3).

W. Garner the Sunderland, James Garner (1) the Norwich, and John Hallam the Manchester District. Thus a partial devolution and distribution of official authority took place which distribution became the usage.

"But," it will be said, "Hugh Bourne lived ten years after 1842, and during that decade he performed an amount of labour truly astonishing. He was always on the move; travelling from circuit to circuit. That did not content him; he even crossed the Atlantic to visit the mission stations in Canada and the United States; he threw himself with enthusiasm into the struggling cause of Christian Temperance. Does not all this look as though Mr. Walford was right and that the Conference was wrong in superannuating Hugh Bourne in 1842?"

All this is true, and the question is a perfectly natural one. No one can look with any other feeling than admiration on the sight of the brave septuagenarian toiling to the very end on behalf of the cause he loved so well. But the history of this period will remain something of a puzzle unless we recognise that the declining age of our founders, with its limitations and infirmities, created difficulties which the men of the transition period had to face and deal with as wisely and as considerately as they knew how.

Old age may bring with it other infirmities besides dimness of vision or stiffness of limbs. It may bring with it infirmity of temper or of judgment; and surely these infirmities are just as valid disqualifications for holding a position where self-control and sober judgment are essential as colour-blindness would disqualify a man for being a signal-man. In order to convey the meaning intended, it will be sufficient to give one illustration of the friction and embarrassments caused by this personal factor, which those who had the guidance of affairs at this time had to reckon with. The incident is not the only one that might be given, nor is it by any means the most painful. Indeed, it has its humorous side, and it may also have the further use of suggesting the dangers that might be lurking in the District system—the danger of "Particularism" as we have called it. In passing, we need not do more than allude to the Newcastle Conference of 1833, when Hugh Bourne made a three hours' vehement attack on Clowes and his policy.* Mr. Walford does not make the slightest reference to this Conference, nor, as far as we can find, do any of the later biographers of Hugh Bourne, who have largely followed Walford. The incident has little interest for us now,—since Christian forbearance prevented any serious consequences resulting therefrom; its main value

---

* The evidence for the statements made in the text, and the evidence for much more than is there stated, is supplied by various letters and documents of the time now in our possession. Chief amongst these are a number of memorandum books, in which, with his own hand, W. Clowes narrates the facts, and replies, one by one, to the charges made against him and the Hull Circuit. W. Clowes writes in an admirable spirit. He indulges sparingly in invective and confines himself mainly to a defence. These valuable documents, which include letters of Clowes, Flesher, and others, were long in the possession of J. Bywater. At his death they came into the hands of the late Rev. G. Shaw, who, in the presence of the late Dr. J. Wood, handed them to the writer on the understanding that they should ultimately become the property of the Connexion. The importance of these documents cannot well be exaggerated, and, in view of their disclosures, less could not well have been said than is said above.

consists in its showing how, in Hugh Bourne's case, the stress of the years had disturbed the fine balance of imagination and judgment, imparting to his anxiety for the welfare of the Connexion an element of morbidity, and making him look at men and things through an atmosphere of illusion, especially at all that related to W. Clowes and the Hull District. There was nothing in the affair that need disquiet the reader. The incident has now sunk to the dimensions of a storm in a tea-cup, although at the time it might look portentous enough.

Soon after this Conference a circular bearing the imprint of the Bemersley Book-Room appeared with the strange title :—

A FEW PLAIN FACTS.

FAITH AND INDUSTRY SUPERIOR TO HIGH POPULARITY,

As manifested in the Primitive Methodist Connexion between the Conference of the year 1824, and that of 1833—nine years.

Tunstall, Norwich, and Manchester Districts were the Low Popularity Districts, and Nottingham, Hull, and Sunderland, the "High." Nevertheless it was sought to be shown, that, despite their elevation and prestige, the Districts of "high degree" had in nine years only added some 276 members to the Connexion, while in the Districts of "low degree" there had been an increase in the same period of 14,814 members. "If any error be discovered, please to make it known," said the circular. Copies were disseminated, and in due time, found their way to Hull. W. Garner was one of the ministers in the town at the time. Speaking of the circular, he says :—

"This eccentric missal answered its purpose for a moment. It was no doubt aimed at William Clowes, and it hit the mark. It wounded his spirit . . . . He keenly felt the stroke, and expressed his astonishment at the unprovoked and needless attack. But he did not allow it to do him much harm. We nevertheless thought it best not to allow the document to be circulated and remain silent; and therefore decided to put in a rejoinder. The circuit records were accordingly examined with a view to ascertain the numerical result of Hull Circuit's labours, apart from those of the entire District."

CLOWES' CHAIR.

Mr. Garner goes on to say, that the result of his examination showed that from the day Mr. Clowes entered Hull, in 1819, to 1835, that circuit had raised 14,116 members, or about one-fourth part of the entire Connexion. These findings were published on the Hull Circuit plan.

From this it will be seen that Primitive Methodism has had its "fly-sheets." Mr. W. Lister gives us a glimpse of the Sunderland District Meeting which, in 1835, was held at Northallerton. Hugh Bourne was G. C. D. of that assembly, and here the fly-sheet made its appearance, and was duly dealt with, as the following extract from Mr. Lister's *Journal* will show.

"It was the first time I had met with Hugh Bourne in a business meeting. He was firm but I thought a little captious, and at times his movements were not likely to promote brotherly-kindness. He had a paper which he had got printed—[Here follows a description of the circular.] In the midst of a discussion on decreases of members he introduced the paper for the Secretary to read to the meeting. This led to some angry remarks. Mr. Dawson took up the subject by asking—Who the author was? What was the design for wishing it to be read? etc. Mr. B., finding himself taken to task and pressed with questions, begged to have the paper handed back and the matter to drop. To me there appeared a lack of judgment, whatever might be said in favour of an anxious wish for the prosperity of the cause. The whole thing was calculated to provoke disaffection and I fear would do no good."

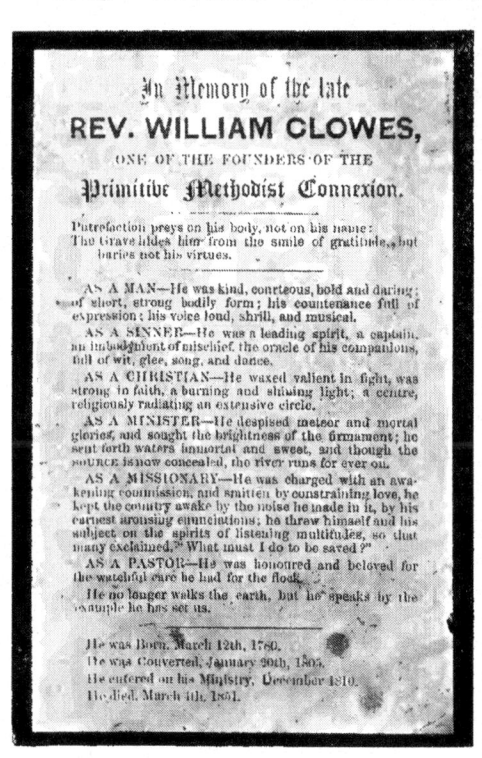

The Conference of 1842, as we have said, "deemed it prudent to superannuate both Hugh Bourne and W. Clowes." After superannuation—death. There may be a considerable interspace between the two events, as there was in the cases of our founders; but the interval, though of interest to the biographer, may be passed over by the historian, as it has no direct bearing on events. It is significant that Clowes' *Journal* ends with his superannuation, though he continued to visit the Churches as much and as long as health and strength would permit. He resided in Hull, where he led his class, and went in and out amongst the people by whom he was affectionately known as "Father Clowes." How great was the value of his prayers and holy life to Hull Primitive Methodism who shall estimate? The last meeting he attended was one in Mason Street Chapel to make arrangements for the erection of a new chapel in Jarratt Street, better known as Clowes' Chapel. In February, 1851, he was stricken with paralysis and died March 2nd, 1851, sixty years to the month and day after John Wesley.* As Parkinson Milson stood in the death-chamber he noticed upon his coffin-lid, representations of quivers filled with arrows. "I was much affected," says he, and thought: "How he hurled the arrows of Divine truth." Of him it might have been said: "Thine arrows are sharp in the heart of the King's enemies; whereby the people fall under thee." His remains were followed by a large concourse of people and, amidst tokens of the deepest respect and reverence, were laid to rest in the Hull General Cemetery. Messrs. Harland, Bywater, and Lamb took part in the service at the grave.

W. CLOWES' TOMB.

The old table-tomb, which was erected by subscription, has given place to a worthier memorial. At the initiative, and mainly through the exertions of Rev. W. Smith, a lofty obelisk of granite (unveiled September 29th, 1898) now marks the spot where W. Clowes lies; and clustered round it are the resting-places of many noted adherents of our Church—so many indeed, that the sacred spot is known as "Primitive Corner."

Hugh Bourne did not long survive his old friend, but he was full of work almost to the last. There is something pathetic in the circumstances of his death. He suffered excruciating pain in his foot. Nature was at last exacting a full penalty. Yet, as we look upon the scene, we do not think so much of Nemesis as of vicarious suffering. We are reminded of the words of the dying De Quincey who, as the attendants were moving him in bed and lifting his feet, said:

HUGH BOURNE'S TOMB.

* By a strange blunder March 4th is given as the date of Clowes' death on the Funeral Card printed at the time, shown on the other page.

"Be gentle; be tender. Remember that those are the feet that Christ washed." So those poor much abused feet remind us of the Christly service they did all through the years—running to and fro doing the Master's will. Unlike W. Clowes, speech was not denied him in the extreme hour, and his last words show how the mind harked back to the scenes and figures of the past. He was heard to murmur—"Old companions! Old companions! My mother!" He died October 11th, 1852. His body was taken to Englesea Brook for burial. The whole country through which the cortege passed from Bemersley was moved. It was computed that in Tunstall market-place 16,000 persons were present as Mr. Leech gave the address. At Englesea Brook hundreds filed past the open coffin; and the great number of Sunday school children present was a most appropriate feature of the occasion. Messrs. Sanders, T. Russell, and Higgins committed the body to its rest in the graveyard of the Englesea Brook Chapel; and a subscription tomb was afterwards, largely through the exertions of Mr. Flesher, placed over the grave.

We shall not attempt here an estimate of our two chief founders or draw out the contrast between them—striking as that contrast was. This has already been done by Mr. Petty in his History. He had personal knowledge of both Hugh Bourne and W. Clowes, and it is right that his summing up of their characters and work should be handed on to another generation of readers than that for which he wrote.

"His own denomination owes him a great debt of gratitude for the sacrifices he made for its welfare and the energetic and efficient manner in which he promoted its interests. He was not indifferent to the prosperity of other communities, in whose well-being he sincerely rejoiced; but believing that the Providence of God had called him to labour among the community in whose formation he had taken so prominent a part, he consecrated all his powers both of body and mind to promote its weal. His life was bound up in its prosperity; his constant study, his unvaried aim was to minister to its usefulness; his toilsome and zealous labours were all intended to enhance its well-being. And it is difficult to calculate aright the amount of good which he accomplished by his caution, his forethought, his energy of purpose, and his determined perseverance. The regulations he successfully sought to carry into effect for the benefit of the community, in some cases, bore hardly upon the regular ministers, and it cannot be denied that a few of them presented an aspect of severity which it would be difficult, if not impossible, to justify; for instance, one which provided that if unpleasantness should arise in any society which should call for investigation, and a travelling preacher should be found faulty in the least, he should pay all the expenses attendant on the inquiry, though other parties might be far more blameable than he: an example of partial legislation which a later Conference saw proper to abolish; but, notwithstanding imperfections of this character, which Mr. Bourne's measures occasionally displayed, his influence in the management of connexional affairs was, on the whole, salutary, and even eminently beneficial. For many years he was the leading spirit in the denomination, and took an active part in its most important transactions. In pulpit and platform efforts Mr. Clowes was incomparably superior to Mr. Bourne; in legislative or administrative ability he was immeasurably inferior. Both exerted a powerful and beneficial influence in the Connexion, but it was in some respects different. Both commanded veneration and esteem by their years, their manly piety, their eminent usefulness, and their high position in the Body; but Mr. Bourne's influence was exercised with more apparent authority, and with occasional harshness and severity; Mr. Clowes' with more paternal kindness and with a winning sweetness of disposition and manner. Mr. Bourne sometimes erred on the side of severity; Mr. Clowes occasionally on the side of leniency. The former had much of Luther in his temperament; the latter, more of Melanchthon. Their difference of views in certain cases, and the different course they pursued in some matters of discipline, unhappily caused a measure of estrangement between them for some years; and in moments of severe trial, Mr. Bourne sometimes spoke of Mr. Clowes in unwarrantable terms, for which, on more than one occasion, he had the manliness and grace to express his deep regret,—and in his calm moments he frequently spoke and wrote of his early friend in the highest strains of eulogy. In many respects, however, these distinguished men greatly resembled each other. Both were actuated by a pure and ardent desire to promote the extension of the Redeemer's kingdom. Both were zealous in an extraordinary degree in their efforts to snatch perishing men as brands from the burning. Both looked for *present* effects, through the blessing of God on their labours. Both used great plainness of speech in their public addresses. Both enforced with uncommon clearness and power, the doctrine of a *present salvation* through faith in our Lord Jesus Christ. Both were firm believers in the theology of Wesley, and great admirers of his character and labours. Both were mighty in prayer, and strong in faith. Both were eminently prudent in the management of societies and the erection of chapels. Both were men of strong determination and of fixedness of purpose. And well was it for the body of which they were the principal founders, that both of them were permitted to live to a good old age, and to promote its well-being by their sanctified wisdom and growing piety.

"Who, of the two, was the more useful we presume not to determine. Their talents and acquirements materially differed, and so did the sphere of their labours. Mr. Bourne had more strength of mind; Mr. Clowes more fire of imagination. The former had more learning; the latter had a richer command of language, and a more fluent utterance. Mr. Bourne took a much larger share in the management of the Connexion than Mr. Clowes; the latter did incomparably more than he in active labours to extend its borders. While Mr. Bourne was efficiently serving the denomination as the editor of its magazine, and as the ruling mind in its General Committee and annual assemblies, Mr. Clowes was pursuing evangelical labours, or Home Missionary operations, with apostolical ardour and success. Both excelled in their spheres of operation; both were eminently adapted to the work respectively allotted to them. Mr. Bourne could not have accomplished what Mr. Clowes effected; Mr. Clowes could not have performed what Mr. Bourne achieved. The Connexion has abundant cause to "glorify God in" both of them, and to render Him unfeigned thanks for the incalculable benefit derived from their judicious counsels, their extraordinary labours, their earnest prayers, and their fervent piety. They were holy and useful in their lives, and in their death they were not long divided. Their mortal remains do not indeed rest in the same sepulchre; but their immortal spirits have met in the regions of the blessed. They mingle, we doubt not, in the blood-washed throng before the throne of God, and unite in the loud hosannahs chanted to the Saviour's name."

CHAPTER II.

MEN AND CONFERENCES OF THE TRANSITION—1843-60.

ON the retirement of Hugh Bourne and W. Clowes the direction of affairs naturally devolved on those who were themselves no longer young; who indeed were veterans of such long standing that, if they were not the actual founders of the Connexion as a distinct community they had, nevertheless, worked side by side with the founders; men who had been the makers of the Connexion and the pioneers of its geographical progress during the period of circuit predominance and enterprise we have been following. We may call these men the Men of the Transition, since the terminal points of their activity fell on either side of 1842, overlapping and bridging the two periods. As a matter of course some of these men became holders of connexional offices, and so they head the succession of Editors, Book Stewards, and Missionary Secretaries, whose grouped portraits are given in this chapter with the double purpose of being convenient for present and future reference. Still, it is not the offices these men filled we are now considering, but rather their fitness and inevitability for office, as being the chief representatives of the Men of the Transition to whose lot it fell to be the shapers and directors of the Connexion until the early 'sixties.

All through this period the governing power, so far as the Conference was its depositary and organ, was exclusively in the hands of the Men of the Transition—ministers and laymen. In this respect the Conference presented a marked contrast to the District Meetings, which were elected on a much broader suffrage and which, consequently, grew in popularity and influence, while the Conference was little known, jealously guarded its deliberations from publicity, and did its best to wrap itself in obscurity and mystery. It is in the contrast between the District Meetings and the Conference, in the explanation of this contrast, and in the consequences practical and sentimental that resulted from this difference, that we shall find the key to the history of the time—a time less familiar to our people than any other in our annals, since it is out of the range of the personal experience of all, except a very limited number, and lies under the still further disadvantage that the material for rightly judging of it is scanty in the extreme.

In 1845 the rules regulating the appointment of District representatives to Conference were revised in the direction of stringency. Hitherto superintendents of three years' standing, and lay officials who had been such for the year immediately preceding, had been eligible. But, in 1845, the time-qualification was greatly lengthened both in the case of minister and layman. It was enacted that no preacher must be sent to Conference unless he had travelled eighteen years and been a superintendent twelve. The layman, too, must have been a member twelve years and an official ten. Such was the law

CONNEXIONAL EDITORS FROM THE BEGINNING TO THE PRESENT.

determining District representation to Conference until 1865, when it underwent some relaxation. From this it will follow that no one entering the ministry in 1841 or '2 could, or as a matter of fact did, take part in the deliberations of our chief assembly before 1859 or '60. Before they had become eligible on the old and more liberal qualification, the stringent provisions of 1845 came in to bar their entry. When we look down the list of men who were pledged in 1841 we find such names as C. Smallman, S. Antliff, T. Southern, P. Clarke, R. Bootland, W. Yeadon, and D. Ingham. The list for 1842, includes such men as J. Huff, E. Morton, T. Whitehead, J. Holroyd, J. T. Shepherd, R. Church, and J. Mules. All these were prominent District men and some of them attained to connexional eminence, yet it is safe to say of one and all of them : it took twenty years for time to mature their qualifications for Conference. Their qualifications blossomed with the coming of the first grey hairs or of baldness. Samuel Antliff was fortunate in making his début in Conference in the nineteenth year of his ministry, while C. C. McKechnie was not eligible—because of the twelve years' superintendency requirement—until he had actually travelled twenty-seven years.

The value of a knowledge of these facts consists in their enabling us to picture the composition and almost the personnel of the Conferences of the 'fifties. We see that the asembly has on it the aspect of maturity and even of age. It is a *Gerousia*— a senate ; made up of old officials, of men whose connexional record goes back into the preceding period. It is an assembly with conservative tendencies, having in it many who think the old times were better than the present. The younger rising men are not here. Their time is not yet come. As yet they are finding an outlet for their energy in Circuit and District administration, with the result that Districtism is being fostered at some expense to Connexionalism. Some day the rôles of District Meeting and Conference will be inverted ; but that as yet is in the future.

If we pass from the constitution and composition of the Conference to look at the way it hedged itself about with restrictions so as to secure the minimum of publicity, we shall better understand why we know so little of these early Conferences and their doings. The endeavour seems to have been to make them as much like meetings with closed doors as possible. Certainly Conference hearers were not encouraged. How far they were to be allowed was regulated by the same Conference of 1845, which decided that the first and second oldest local preachers residing at a town within fifty-one miles of a Conference-town might be admitted as hearers on showing a certificate properly signed. These certificates were closely scanned, for the post of door-keeper was a responsible one, and any laxity in the discharge of his duties rendered him liable to censure and even fine.*

To all this must be added that the published records of the transactions of the Conferences of this transition time seem to have been prepared on the principle of giving the minimum amount of information such as contemporaries find most interesting and the historian most helpful. We look in vain in the Minutes of 1841 for any

* It is fair to say that the stringency of the rule was somewhat relaxed in 1850 ; but only in favour of *Male* travelling preachers, and other leading officials of the male sex.

reference to the "Stamp Case"; or in the Minutes of the early Fifties for information as to the genesis of the Hymn Book of 1853 and the controversy which grew out of its publication.

To get to Conference has always been a legitimate and laudable ambition. Men were moved by this ambition even in the early Middle period of our history when, in comparison with the Conferences of these later days, our chief assembly was but a numerically small, less popular, and—having regard to the qualification for election— a more exclusive body. Men were not disposed to sit down quietly under their exclusion. "District Meetings were all very well, but, after all, Conference was Conference, and——," in short, they would like to form some of its constituent atoms. Those who were debarred by the existing years-of-travelling rule, and those who *were* qualified but who, in the number of competitors, felt that their chance of often getting to Conference was but slender, put forth efforts to secure such changes in the law as would obviate for them its exclusive effects. They were not conspicuously successful. An early and interesting example of such infructuous efforts is supplied by the minutes of an "Association of Travelling Preachers formed at Pontefract in 1845."* Its declared object was to enable preachers who had travelled fifteen years and been superintendents ten years successively, to have a seat and a voice in Conference on condition that they bore their own expenses to the Conference town and supported themselves while there. The Association sought to gain its end by legislation, petition, etc., and there is evidence that in these respects it was not inactive. We have not a list of the members of the Association, but J. Bywater was the Secretary and W. Taylor the Treasurer; and these, together with W. Sanderson and G. Lamb, formed the Committee. It transpires, too, that J. Flesher was an honorary member of the Association, and had given one pound to its "campaign fund"; so that it is evident even some leading men of the transition were in sympathy with the endeavour to enlarge and popularise the Conference, and could have had no part in framing or passing the reactionary rules of 1845. The proposals of the Association were a plagiarism; evidently they were suggested by the Wesleyan Conference, of which the legal hundred is the core. Had the legislation promoted by the Pontefract Association met with favour instead of repeated rejection, then the Primitive Methodist legal Conference must still have remained that part of the composite body which consisted of the permanent members, "the four" elected by the previous Conference, and those duly sent up by the District Meetings. But Conference reform was not destined to come on these lines, but rather by the removal of restrictions and by the method of expansion and evolution.

We have alluded to the Hymn Book of 1853 and to the controversy which followed on its publication. Each of the three chief periods of our History has had its Hymn Book, and each was a characteristic product of its time. The first period had its "Small" and "Large" Hymn Book, not inappropriately bound together like the Old and New Testaments; for the Small Hymn Book went back to the time of our

* The Minute Book of the Association, as also the copies of many letters written to ministers on the aims and progress of the Association by the Secretary, are in our possession.

GENERAL BOOK STEWARDS TO 1885.

"origins." It was reminiscent of Lorenzo Dow and camp meetings, and was essentially a revival Hymn Book; while the "Large," as it was called, provided a greater variety of hymns for the uses of public worship. The Middle Period gave us Mr. Flesher's compilation, while the "Hymnal" is the worthy exemplar of the Church Period of our history. It is with the Hymn Book of 1853 and the controversy it roused that we have now to do.

The early portion of the Middle Period was a trying and somewhat uneasy one as most transition periods are. The cars rocked as they got on the new rails. Controversies, big and little, there were in plenty; but most of them involved no great issues and have no lessons for us of the present. Such was that which arose in 1847 respecting the founding of a Local Preachers' Provident Institution, which, therefore, it is not worth while dwelling upon. Of a somewhat different kind, however, was the Hymn Book controversy. It did raise an issue of some importance. Altogether apart from the question as to the merits or demerits of the book itself, it was alleged that the Hymn Book had been sprung on the Connexion. It was in the North and especially in Sunderland and Newcastle where dissatisfaction with the book was most deeply felt, and where it took its most active form. C. C. McKechnie—afterwards Editor and President— became the Secretary of an association pledged to secure, if possible, the withdrawal of the book. Trenchant reviews of it were written and the Connexion was "circularised." The circular was signed by Messrs. Thos. Gibson and Joseph Fawcett of Sunderland, and A. McCree and George Charlton of Newcastle. In this circular the third and last reason for the action taken is stated to be :—

"The indifference manifested to Connexional Opinion in that the new Book was authorised, *stereotyped*, and issued without an opportunity being given for the Connexion to judge of its suitability."

To this the General Committee in its counter-circular to the stations replies :—

"That the statement about the issue of the New Hymn Book manifesting 'indifference to connexional opinion' is not in harmony with the facts of the case, both the *preparation* and *publication* of the book having been directed by duly elected delegates or representatives of the Connexion in Conference assembled, comprising a considerable number of intelligent connexional office-bearers capable of expressing their views and those of the brethren whom they represented, and who were not *distinct* from the Connexion, but forming an important and influential part thereof."

From the strictly legal side the circular of the General Committee was a complete answer and put the agitators in the wrong. Undoubtedly the Conference had authorised the preparation of the Hymn Book, and had entrusted the work to Mr. Flesher, though when, and under what circumstances this was done, does not appear. It may be a search through the Conference Journals would show, but the published Conference Minutes and our Histories are silent. Formal authorisation was probably given in 1851, and by the close of 1853 the book was printed and stereotyped and twenty thousand copies sold. But the Hymn Book controversy naturally grew out of the working theory of the Conference in use and favour at the time, and this incident came to reveal its drawbacks and possible dangers. To us the chief value of the incident lies in its bearing on the history of the evolution of the Conference. The questions as to whether or no Mr. Flesher was the best man who could have been selected for the work of compiling a new Hymn Book; whether he were a poet as well as a great preacher and rhetorician; whether his hymns, and those of his wife, possessed or were destitute of poetic merit; whether, above all, he was or was not justified in mutilating and amending the hymns of others—all such questions have undoubtedly their interest, but just now we are more interested in the aforesaid question of the evolution of Conference. For that there has been evolution here is plain. In the early 'Fifties the ideal Conference would seem to have been a select assembly in which men should deliberate and decide *in camera*, uninfluenced by the outside non-conferential world, which must be told hereafter as little as possible. How far we have got from such ideas! Instead of seclusion and reticence, the ideal of Conference has become publicity and frankness. We smile at the old restrictions on hearers as we see our people flocking to the Conference town like the tribes going up to the sacred feasts. Representatives of the press are welcomed and even thanked for the fulness and accuracy of their reports.

There can be no question that the Hymn Book controversy and other incidents of the kind have helped to bring about this change of view and sentiment. The controversy had no serious results but closed amicably. The case was taken to the Conference of 1854, where G. Charlton represented the Northern dissentients. But mutual concessions were made. On the one side the withdrawal of the Hymn Book was not pressed, withdrawal being manifestly impossible. On the other side an undertaking was given that some of the most objectionable features of the book should be removed. We agree with the late John Atkinson that it was fortunate for the Connexion at this juncture that the opposition

"Was calmly and fairly met by those who were in official position at the time . . . The Rev. John Petty, with his colleagues in London, Revs. T. King and J. Bywater, and the Rev. W. Garner, who was then in Hull, by the Christian spirit they manifested, and the concessions they made, earned the gratitude of the Connexion, for they did much to save it from a disastrous agitation. Their efforts were appreciated by the brethren who had taken an active part in the agitation, and a working settlement was reached which restored harmony and peace . . . And in justice to Mr. Flesher and his work, it must be acknowledged that the book possessed qualities that at first were not recognised, as is evident from the fact that for over thirty years it met the growing needs of our Church life, a very sufficient testimony that it was not devoid of excellence. Another very good effect came out of this controversy. When another hymnal was necessary the Connexion was taken into confidence." [*]

Perhaps these Conferences of the 'Fifties may be made something more real to us if we give the plan of the Conference held at Sheffield in 1852. The reader, if he has good eye-sight or artificial aids thereto, will not fail to make out many names with which he has by this time become very familiar. There is no breach of continuity; for it must be

---

[*] "Life of the Rev. C. C. McKechnie," by J. Atkinson. The best, and in fact, the only published account of the Hymn Book controversy is Mr. Atkinson's chapter on the subject, based on Mr. McKechnie's MS. Autobiography.

THE PERIOD OF CONSOLIDATION AND CHURCH DEVELOPMENT. 373

GENERAL MISSIONARY SECRETARIES.

remembered we are dealing with a Conference composed of men elected on the eighteen years' qualification for preachers, and twelve years' for laymen, so that they are Men of the Transition whose names are found here. Forming our opinion of the Conference by these names, we see at once that, in its personnel, it was a strong Conference. It was the first from which both our founders were absent. Hugh Bourne's name heads the list; but, though he had signified his intention to attend, when the time came he was too ill to do so. From other sources than the Minutes—which as usual are silent about such matters—we learn that the intelligence of his critical condition was the occasion of an impressive scene in the Conference. Mr. John Reynard of Leeds was present as a delegate, and writing to Mr. James Bourne, he says: "This morning a letter was read from you in Conference, giving an account of the affliction and present state of your

brother, which was received with deep sympathy by the Conference, and a motion was made that we had a few moments' prayer on his behalf, when Bro. Harland offered up a very powerful appeal to the Throne of Grace, followed up by prayers and tears which I doubt not had audience with Heaven, and prevailed."

An increase of 1,203 was reported for the year 1852, but there was to be no increase again until 1856, so that for a triennium the course of the Connexion lay through a valley of Humiliation. The Conference of 1855 reported 4,126 members less than in '52—2,055 being the loss for the single year '54-5—the heaviest decrease recorded in our annals. The explanation of these facts is in great part to be found in the condition of our land at the time, socially and ecclesiastically. The gold-fields were spreading their lure and attracting thousands to California and Australia. In one year 672 members were lost to the Connexion from this single cause alone. The Norwich and Brinkworth Districts, in especial, were drained and enfeebled by this exodus, some of the societies being brought nearly, if not quite, to extinction. In the Eastern Counties a series of disastrous storms and floods added to the difficulties of the time. Strikes, abnormal dearness of provisions, must be mentioned as contributory factors to this complication of adverse causes. Ecclesiastically, too, we must remember that this was the period when Ritualism began to exert its baneful influence, and that for Methodism it was the period of strife and disintegration. The Parent Body was disrupted. In one year—1849-50— it lost nearly 57,000 members, and in the five years ending in '55, it was depleted to the extent of 100,469 members. All this was not to the advantage of our Church but very much the reverse. Ecclesiastical strife is a fire which scorches the finer feelings. You cannot come near it without getting the wings of your soul singed. We are glad to record that our Church preserved her neutrality and did not seek to profit by plunder or by others' misfortune. We may be mixing our metaphors but we will write it—All honour to our pilots who skilfully and resolutely kept the vessel's course midway between the rocks and the whirlpool, though it was not done without scathe and strain.

That it was indeed a trying time will appear from a part of the Conference Address to the Churches for the year 1854:—

"If we have not entered into the arena of religious strife, we have unavoidably occupied its immediate vicinity; and many a missile which has been aimed at other objects has fallen among our tents and created some alarm and misapprehension in timorous and unstable minds. Names have been confounded with *things*. In the midst of this confusion it has been found impossible, in numerous instances, to correct the errors of good but misguided men. An unskilful captain may navigate a ship in favourable seas and with a fair breeze; but a dangerous ocean and foul winds may baffle the most experienced commander. Nor is it less difficult for organised Churches to make headway in a troubled state of religious society. If progress is not impossible, it is nevertheless unusually difficult."

Among the names of the delegates to this Sheffield Conference we note the names of several who were destined to attain to note and exalted Connexional position. Such were Moses Lupton and Thomas Smith, who began their ministry in 1822 and 1834 respectively. There is another name which calls for special remark—that of William Antliff —who was rising, nay, had already risen into prominence, and was to be, probably, the best known and most influential figure in the middle period of our history. William Antliff came of a godly Methodist ancestry, whose home was at the village of Caunton in Nottinghamshire. William Antliff, the elder, joined the Primitives on their first coming into these parts, but was suddenly removed in the midst of his usefulness. A sentiment graven on his tombstone was objectionable to the High Church rector, who had it

REV. W. ANTLIFF.

chiselled out, and there the defaced stone stands. Perhaps it was the assurance the erased line gave of William Antliff's eternal safety that gave the offence. Be this as it may, its erasure did not put the good man's safety in question, and was a petty thing to be done by one who afterwards became a famous rose-grower and Cathedral dignitary. The son and bearer of the dead man's name joined our Church when a boy, and "made his first out-and-out attempt at preaching" at Eakring. In 1830, when little more than sixteen years of age, he entered the ministry, his first station being Balderton. We have already seen him winning his youthful spurs at Nottingham in the troublous times of 1834.* W. Antliff was more fortunate than his brother in getting to Conference when young in the ministry. He got there under the old qualification as early as 1838, and it may be questioned whether any other preacher—even Hugh Bourne himself—was officially present at a greater number of Conferences than he. His commanding appearance, his pleasing elocution, his skill in debate, his remarkable knowledge of the Connexion and its laws and usages, all combined to make him a great figure in Conference, and other Connexional Courts. Such was W. Antliff, who was present at this Conference of 1852, and was there appointed "vice" to Mr. Petty, who now, as Connexional Editor, took the place of Mr. Flesher, this year superannuated.

W. Antliff was also at the next Conference—that held at York in 1853. Here C. C. McKechnie, who was present at this Conference as a hearer, along with his friend George Race, had his first opportunity of seeing and hearing the future President, Editor, and College Principal. It was an interesting meeting of two notable men, who, while in many respects they represented different types, and were often found on different sides, were yet both to hold the same high offices, to become leaders of Connexional thought, and the shapers of its polity and policy in the later Middle period of our history. The relations of the two to the existing régime were somewhat different. In his autobiography, Mr. McKechnie notes that Mr. Antliff was "a coming Conference man;" but, while the latter was among the Men of the Transition, he could scarcely be said to be one of them. He was rather the harbinger of the new period already preparing, and was so regarded by the then occupants of the Government benches. As for Mr. McKechnie his development was slower. He had not yet come to the front, except in his own district, and was unknown by face to such men as John Garner and Thomas Holliday, to whom the young Scotsman was now introduced by Henry Hebbron. So, men come and go, and the strangest thing about this wave-like succession is, that those who go may little suspect who will afterwards fill their places.

At this Conference there was a big debate on the Teetotal question, to which Mr. McKechnie listened with interest. "The preponderance of opinion, and of oratorical power, were in its favour. Mr. Antliff led the Temperance party and he did his duty well. He spoke with fluency and fervour and commanded a good hearing."

Returning to our Plan of the Sheffield Conference of 1852: as we again glance down the names of the delegates, we are struck with the fact that the plan might serve as a biographical epitome of our history up to this time. There is scarcely an unknown name in the list, or one that fails to call up reminiscences or provoke remark. John

Ante Vol. i. p. 241.

THE PERIOD OF CONSOLIDATION AND CHURCH DEVELOPMENT.   377

Wood of Nantwich, James Broad of Congleton, William Mason of Leicester, Samuel Raines of Winster, David Hodgson of Croydon, William Byron of Louth, George T. Goodrich of Yarmouth, George Wakefield of Scotter, Richard Mason of Edenfield, George Race, John Reynard, George Charlton, Joshua Rouse, Charles Bowman, W. T. Lumley —all these names of notable laymen—and many more besides these, are to be found here. With interest we notice the name of Charles Morse of Stratten St. Margaret's, in the list of the representatives of the Brinkworth District. For fifty years Mr. Morse was a member and local preacher in Wiltshire, where his son, Mr. L. L. Morse, has more than filled his place as a devoted adherent of our Church and the liberal supporter of its institutions and movements. Thus C. Morse's name links together the past and the present—1852 with 1896—when his son was elected Vice-President of Conference.

REV. W. LEA.

MR. J. SPENCER.

As the plan shows, Mr. W. Lea was the superintendent of the Sheffield Circuit at the time the Conference of 1852 was held. He did good work during his term in the circuit, especially by the erection of new schools for Bethel Chapel (opened October, 1852). We give also the portrait of Mr. J. Spencer, a leading Sheffield official of the time. There are many references to him, and to his hospitable home, in the memoirs and letters of contemporaries. He was a friend of Hugh Bourne, and was present at his funeral. Mr. Spencer was an active and capable circuit official, a member of the Nottingham District Committee, and frequently represented that district in Conference.

1860 was the Jubilee Year of our Church. It had been long looked forward to and was prepared for. The preceding Conference, held at Newcastle, asked the question: "What are the arrangements for the approaching Jubilee?" and framed the answer in some fifteen resolutions, which, for convenience of reference, we will set out in a paragraph, though in a condensed form.

(1) March 11th, 1860, to be set apart as a day for thanksgiving and prayer. (2) One public meeting at least to be held in each station, and attended by an efficient deputation. (4) Sermon or lecture, and collection at each society, if possible. (5) The Fund to be kept

H. HODGE.

over for four years. (6) A camp meeting to be held in every station on the last Sabbath in May. (7) Stations to be willing to allow their preachers to serve as deputations. (8) (9) Provide for the appointment of Local and District Treasurers and Secretaries. (11) H. Hodge to be the General Treasurer and John Bywater, General Secretary. (12) The objects to which the Fund are to be applied are : (*a*) The General Missionary Fund. (*b*) General Chapel Fund for grants and loans. (*c*) A school for preachers' children and children of members. (*d*) The education of acceptable candidates for the ministry and itinerant preachers on probation. (13) A Large Committee appointed. (14) The executive to consist of the Hull members and the District Committee. (15) Contributors free to choose the object for which their contribution shall be applied.

It should be added, that a medal to commemorate the Jubilee was struck, both sides of which are shown in the accompanying illustrations.

OBVERSE OF JUBILEE MEDAL.   REVERSE OF JUBILEE MEDAL.

From all this it will appear that the arrangements for the appropriate and profitable keeping of the Jubilee of the Connexion were not wanting in elaborateness. It was inevitable that the Conference of this notable year should be held on the soil whence our Connexional fathers sprang, and where, through them, our Church had its beginnings. This forty-first Conference had its sessions in the Jubilee Chapel, Tunstall, which had been enlarged and beautified during the year. The Conference camp meeting was held on the historic ground of Mow Cop, on Sunday, June 10th, and on the following morning the Jubilee sermon was preached by Thomas King, the oldest travelling preacher in active work.

By the time the Jubilee Conference of 1860 had come and gone, many of the Men of the Transition had themselves passed off the stage. This was the fact that was present to the minds of the men who assembled at the Tunstall Conference of 1860. The Jubilee celebrations had many aspects, some of them practical enough. There were questions the Jubilee would assist in answering—such questions as: To what extent will this appeal to Connexional loyalty and sentiment be successful? What disclosures will it yield as to the financial resources of our people, or their sympathy with education and the higher training of the ministry? How will the index-finger point? These were some of the questions which awaited their answer then, and some of the points raised by these questions we ourselves may have to look at in another connection. But somehow, that morning, when the delegates had taken their places and looked round, and were made to realise, by the epochal character of the gathering, how many once familiar faces and figures had gone, their dominant feeling was the feeling of the transitoriness of human life—the life of the generation as well as of the individual. Unbidden, the sacred words came to remembrance—"Your fathers, where are they, and the prophets, do they live for ever?" This feeling found its expression in the Conference Minutes of the year.

"The Conference is impressed with the fact, that not one of the brethren who were life-members of the Conferences, as per provisions of the Deed Poll, has lived to see the Conference of our Connexional Jubilee year, although Mr. James Bourne was spared until the beginning of the present year. The aged pilgrim arrived at the threshold of our jubilant season, but ere we commenced our songs in the militant Church, he joined the Church triumphant in Heaven."

So also Mr. Petty, who brings down his valuable History of the Connexion to the Jubilee Conference of 1860, closes his survey of the course of events by giving brief sketches of several prominent men of long Connexional standing who had passed away during the last decade. These are J. G. Black, J. Reynard, John Garner, Thomas Dawson, James Nixon, Robert Atkinson, James Bourne, and John Day. All these, with the exception of the last-named, were, at the time of their decease, permanent members of Conference, though R. Atkinson was privileged to attend only one Conference in that capacity. He died at Thirsk, August 12th, 1858, in the thirty-ninth year of his ministry.

Mr. John Day entered the ministry in 1821. He was, says Mr. Petty "a man of sound judgment and respectable abilities, and travelled in many of the most important circuits with acceptability and success." In January, 1859, he entered upon the office of Book Steward, at the advanced age of sixty-three years, but died suddenly at Luton, while attending the District Meeting of the London District, after delivering an appropriate address to the young ministers finishing their probation, and assisting in the administration of the Lord's Supper.

CHAPTER III.

REMOVAL OF THE BOOK-ROOM TO LONDON.

From Sutton Street to Aldersgate Street.

THE changes that took place after, and largely in consequence of, the retirement of Hugh Bourne, were epochal. Probably the supersession, though gradually accomplished, of circuit missions by a General Missionary Committee was the more radical and far-reaching change, but the changes which took place in Book-Room affairs were scarcely less important.

Chronologically, and for other reasons, these new departures call for notice here, and must not be held over until we come to deal with the later institutions of our Church properly so-called. For the functions discharged in our Body by the Book-Room and the General Missionary Committee, and the relation of the one to the other, would be much better denoted by some analogy borrowed from the human organism than by the word Institutions. If we were to call one the brain and the other the motor nerves of our denomination we should not be far wrong. From the very beginning of our history the relation between the two has been exceedingly close and sympathetic. The Book-Room has helped on the Missionary work. With his usual sagacity Hugh Bourne soon saw that this might be, and so he was resolved it should be. Hence he lost no time in bringing about the establishment of a Book-Room, so that, if Institution it be, the Book-Room was our first institution—almost coeval with our first efforts in Church organisation. Events proved Hugh Bourne was right. It is difficult to see how the missions of the Connexion could have spread from county to county without the aid of the Bemersley Book-Room. Many a mission, on new ground, was soon more than able to pay its way because of the astonishing number of hymn books and other publications that were sold. In some cases the mission became richer than the parent circuit, and for a time, their natural relations were inverted; we see the mission subsidizing the circuit instead of the circuit subsidizing the mission. And in more recent years: it is difficult to see how our Church could have done what it has done, or been what it has been, had it not been for Book-Room allocations. If it had not been for the grist the Book-Room brought to the mill there must have been much less grinding done. But returning to the earlier days: not only did the Book-Room help on mission-work by supplying the sinews of war, but it gave it moral support. The Magazines fanned the missionary spirit, spread intelligence of Connexional progress, and brought widely separated labourers into touch with one another. The close connection between the Book-Room and Missions continued even after 1843. They migrated to the Metropolis together. The Book-Room and the Mission House were practically under the same roof in old Sutton Street, and, as we shall see, it was some time before the offices were entirely separated—the Assistant Book Steward being also the Treasurer of the Missionary Fund.

We trust we have given sufficient reasons why we do not relegate the Book-Room and the establishment of the General Missionary Committee to the later section dealing with Institutions; also reasons why they should be treated sequently, the Book-Room coming first.

The Conference of 1842 appointed J. Flesher Editor, and re-appointed John Hallam Book Steward, and James Bourne Connexional Treasurer. The Book Committee for the year was composed of H. Bourne, J. Bourne, J. Flesher, J. Hallam, and R. Jukes, the superintendent of Tunstall Circuit. The new Editor proceeded to Bemersley to take up the duties of his office. Now the troubles of editors are proverbial, and Mr. Flesher had his full share of them. From a MS. book now before us entitled—"Memoranda of certain things which transpired at Bemersley and the neighbourhood, beginning from September, 1842,"—we can learn what was the nature of these troubles. He was hampered by his committee, and by the opposite views held by himself and one member of the committee especially (not Hugh Bourne), as to the style in which it was expedient the articles appearing in the Magazines should be written. What were the committee-man's views on style would have mattered little had the Editor but had a free hand. But he had not. The old rules regulating the mode of preparing the Magazines had been solemnly re-enacted on Mr. Flesher's appointment to the office. Strictly enforced, these rules made the question of an article's fitness or unfitness for publication in the Magazine turn, not on the judgment of the Editor, but on a show of hands of the Book Committee.* Mr. Flesher was counselled and warned that there must not be too great a departure from the old style, etc., lest old friends should be alienated. Now Mr. Flesher was severely conscientious and took a serious view of his editorial duties and responsibilities. He could not listen and smile and say nothing, and allow things to settle themselves, which they often do without our interference. This was not his habit or temper of mind: hence, in committee he did not flinch but stood on his rights as understood by the Conference, and as interpreted by common sense; and as he was loyally supported on this, as on other occasions, by Mr. Hallam, he was not overborne. Yet, if Mr. Flesher was conscientious and determined, he was also keenly sensitive, hence we find him almost plaintively recording:—"My situation as Editor is difficult, not from this source alone, but also from the awfully imperfect style in which most of the original articles are written. I have already repented often that I accepted the Editor's Office."

But bigger troubles were looming, compared with which clashing views on editing and literary style were light as air. Mr. James Bourne's temporal affairs were becoming embarrassed. Once he had the reputation of being a comparatively rich man, and had he but remained content with the safe returns of his printing and farming all might have been well. But he became "entangled with the potters," and there were already ominous signs of the impending crash which, when it came, entailed so much suffering upon Hugh Bourne, although he had neither seen it coming nor was he in any way involved, except as a sufferer. Mr. Flesher observed these signs and notes them in

* This curious regulation remained some time on the Statute Book. In 1849 a parenthetic clause appears—("unless there be an understanding between him and the Committee.") In 1860 this has become incorporated with the Rule. In 1870 the Rule itself has disappeared.

OLD BOOK DEPÔT, SUTTON STREET.

his "Memoranda." There was danger lest Book-Room affairs and Friendly Society affairs should be complicated with the concerns and shaky fortunes of private persons. It was highly expedient that the Book-Room should be extricated from the danger of local entanglements.

The inconvenience of Bemersley as the Seat of the Book-Room was more and more making itself felt at the stage the Connexion had now reached in its history. Allied to this question of locality—of fitness and relative convenience—was that of economy. The "Memoranda" recall a session of the General Committee (December 9, '42) at which Mr. Flesher fully delivered his sentiments on this subject. There was a discussion on a matter of finance, affecting the Conference Fund, in which Mr. H. Bourne defended his views on the ground of economy. Thereupon, writes Mr. Flesher,

"I replied, and in the course of my remarks said: Economy was a good thing; that the argument had opened upon me a flood of light which, by God's help, I would improve; and that, as a servant of the Connexion, I would press economy, not only on the Conference Fund, but also on the affairs of the Book-Room, and

OFFICE, SUTTON STREET.

also on those of the *Printing*. Having given firm, free, and full utterance to these views, I felt delivered from heavy mental darkness under which I have struggled for some time. I took this deliverance as a signal that God approved of my conduct in notifying my purpose; and I now pray that I may not sin against God and the Connexion by allowing the latter to lose hundreds a year through having its printing executed dearer than the printing of any other Connexion in the Kingdom, while all its other establishments are wrought on the severest economy. . . . I am happy that J. Hallam takes the same views as myself, and is maturing plans to effect an alteration. God, being my helper, I will support him in carrying them out."

After this, and more than this, written in the same tone of high seriousness, we shall probably be right in concluding that the chief factor in the removal of the Book-Room to London was economy. In the extract given, Mr. Flesher writes as though the thought of economy had come to him as a revelation in the meeting of the General Committee; but, doubtless what is meant is, that then and there the thought first found expression, and crystallised into a resolve by which his mind was relieved from darkness. But there is evidence to show that, for some time before this meeting, Mr. Flesher had been revolving the subject and making inquiries, and that the thoughts of others were turned in the same direction. Mr. W. Harland tells us that young Thomas Church of London, meditating a modest publishing venture, had obtained specimens of various styles of printing, with quotations of prices. These he showed to Mr. Harland, who thought them worth sending to Messrs. Flesher & Hallam. Some time after, he was requested by them to call on some respectable city firms for the purpose of making inquiries. Thus, by the interaction of causes and the co-operation of various persons, the materials were ready at the Conference of 1843 for discussing the question of the removal of the Book-Room to London, and for coming to an intelligent decision. That decision was that the removal of the Book establishment to London should take place as early as possible. The imprint of the Minutes of this Conference is. "Tyler and Reed, Bolt-Court, London," and the address of the Conference Offices is "Sutton Street."

It will be remembered that when John Flesher built Sutton Street Chapel in 1838,

PACKING AND FORWARDING DEPARTMENT, SUTTON STREET.

our Church secured its first Connexional Chapel in London. It was to Sutton Street inquiring and discerning eyes were turned at this juncture. "Can you by any means find room for us, so that we may set up our staff by your side?" the look said. We have the answer in certain resolutions passed by the trustees of Sutton Street at their meeting held on July 6th, 1842, the gist of which was, that two cottages and the preacher's house in Chapel Place, of which the trustees were the lessees, should be let to the Connexion for Book-Room and other purposes. The offer was accepted; forty-one pounds eight shillings was paid as rent the first year, as the accounts show. Thus the "central wheel of management" that directed the administrative and disciplinary affairs of the Connexion, its missionary operations, and the preparation and dissemination of its publications, was set up in the vicinage and on the very premises of Sutton Street. For many years to come notable men in the Connexion would live and labour here, pass in and out of that gateway, preach and worship in that Chapel, and, from their modest Offices and Committee Room, keep in touch with the most distant parts of the Connexion. For years to come, too, country Primitives on their occasional visits to London would, as in bounden duty, bend their steps to Commercial Road, E., in order to see the great wheel in motion, and those who directed its revolutions. Nor was Sutton Street, apart from its temporary convenience, so unsuitable a location for a Connexional centre at that time as might be thought, or as it afterwards came to be. The East and North-East of London had long been a stronghold of Nonconformity, and the tradition and sentiment of Nonconformity were still a power, though a diminishing one. The Colleges of Hackney and Stepney had been famous in their day, and it would be some time yet before Congregationalism moved citywards and acquired its Bicentenary Memorial Hall and City Temple. Then, after a time, Primitive Methodism will follow in its track and hold its Connexional Committees in New Surrey Chapel—a name redolent of Nonconformist traditions—and then in Aldersgate, close to where Milton once lived and where he lies buried, and hard by Smithfield where the martyrs suffered. A word or two respecting the external history of the Sutton Street Book-Room may be given—the tenure on which it was held and the term of its occupancy. In July, 1850, a lease of the property for twenty-one years was obtained from the Trustees. In 1876 all interest in the property for the remaining term of the lease which would expire in 1897 was purchased, the actual owners of the property being the Mercers Company. But before 1897 came Sutton Street knew us no more. On October 25th, 1894, one of the largest and most influential Committees ever held in the Connexion's history assembled in the Library of the Memorial Hall, to consider the report presented by the Sites Committee. After a prolonged discussion of the comparative merits of various sites and buildings referred to in the Committee's report, the choice fell on a noble block standing at the junction of Jewin and Aldersgate Streets, the property of the Hon. Company of Goldsmiths, from whom the property was acquired for a period of sixty-five years, for the sum of £7850. After structural alterations, electrical installation, etc., the new premises were formally opened on June 6th, 1895, in the presence of a large and representative gathering. The doors were opened by the retiring Book Steward, Mr. J. B. Knapp; the incoming Steward, T. Mitchell, also took part, and the Editor, H. B. Kendall, B.A., gave an address, in which the significance of the event in its historic aspects was sketched. But it was only by gradual steps this comparative climax was reached. The two converted cottages with their five small rooms—some of which are shown in our illustrations—grew like a tree, thrusting out extensions here and there, regardless of beauty but with much regard to utility and convenience, until at last both school and chapel of Sutton Street were annexed. In 1861 R. Davies added a large wing with a gallery at a cost of £418. G. Lamb built a further extension of one floor. J. Dickenson annexed the school and J. Toulson the chapel. Finally the Book-Room spread its branches beyond Sutton Street, and a house in Johnson Street was acquired. Until 1857 oil and candles were the illuminants; then for something more than a generation gas reigned; last of all came the era of the electric light. The three successive stages not inaptly symbolise the progress made.

We have the same growth and development in the staff of the Book-Room. At first, probably there was but one assistant, in addition to the two conferentially appointed

PRIMITIVE METHODIST BOOK-ROOM, ALDERSGATE STREET, E.C.

1843-75. BOOK-ROOM MANAGERS. 1875-1903.

Book Stewards. This assistant was Mr. Brown, who was the permanent manager of the Book-Room, until his death at the Christmas of 1875. In the memoir of Mr. George Baron it is stated that so much of the Bemersley stock as it was thought necessary to remove to London was placed in his charge, by him conveyed to London and housed in the new Book-Room; that Mr. Baron paid repeated visits to London, as he had done to Bemersley, to help in the management; and that when unable any longer to do this he recommended Mr. Philip Brown for the office. In 1873 there were the manager and five assistants. In 1875 Mr. T. C. Eamer, who had entered the establishment in 1865, succeeded Mr. Brown. For twenty-eight years, under the direction of successive General Book Stewards, he continued to discharge the duties of Manager with much energy and ability. His appointment as Manager of the Wesleyan Book-Room, which took place in 1903, may justly be regarded as a recognition of his business qualifications and as a compliment to the Institution in which those qualifications were acquired and exercised. On Mr. Eamer's translation to City Road, Mr. A. E. Spratt, who also had risen step by step to the position of chief clerk, was appointed to succeed him. All this time, as the business of the Book-Room flowed with constantly increasing volume, additions continued to be made to the staff, until at the present time it consists of the Manager and twenty-eight assistants, while at the monthly packings some twelve others are temporarily engaged.

It now remains to indicate the succession of Book Stewards and Editors from 1843. That succession will most conveniently be set forth in tabular form. But the somewhat complex arrangements that obtained from 1843 to 1848 need a word of explanation. During these five years the duties attached to the various Connexional offices were discharged by four persons. Two of these create no difficulty as, during the whole of the time, John Garner was the Secretary of the Missionary Committee and John Flesher the Editor. There remained four offices for two men. Two of these offices were held

REV. EDWIN DALTON.
GENERAL BOOK STEWARDS, 1885—1905.

jointly, viz., the Book Stewardship and the Missionary Treasurership, while two offices were held separately—the Secretaryships of the General Committee and of the Book Committee. It is as though Messrs. Bryant and Welford should be joint Book Stewards and joint Missionary Treasurers, while Mr. Welford should retain the Secretaryship of the General Committee in his own hands, and Mr. Bryant should act alone as Secretary of the Book Committee. In 1848 the Book Steward ceased to have a divided responsibility or to be called to perform other functions than those which concerned the Book-

THE PERIOD OF CONSOLIDATION AND CHURCH DEVELOPMENT. 389

THE GENERAL OFFICE AND PART OF THE OFFICE STAFF

A CORNER OF THE ORDER DEPT.

THE GENERAL BOOK STEWARD AND HIS OFFICE

THE MANAGER'S OFFICE

A SECTION OF THE COMMITTEE ROOM

THE RETAIL DEPT.

THE FORWARDING DEPT.

Room. He became its exclusive officer. In other departments, however, co-ordination continued for some time to prevail: one man continued to fulfil diverse offices. On the retirement of John Garner in 1848, William Garner became Missionary Secretary, General Committee Secretary, and Treasurer for the Missions. In further elucidation of the Table it may also be stated there is evidence to show that Thomas Holliday declined to act in Book-Room affairs until 1845; that in 1850, the five years' rule relating to the holding of Connexional office became absolute; that the official year then closed on December 31st, and that the incoming Book Steward was "assistant" for the six months immediately preceding his formal entry on office in January. Finally, it may be mentioned that John Petty's appointment as Assistant Editor was occasioned by the declining health of John Flesher, and that from the time of his taking up his duties Mr. Petty was virtually the Editor.

Book Stewards.		Editors.	
1843-5.	{ John Hallam. / Thomas Holliday.	1843.	John Flesher. / John Petty, Assist. 1851.
1846-7.	{ Thomas Holliday. / William Garner.	1852.	John Petty.
		1857.	W. Harland.
1848.	Thomas Holliday.	1862.	W. Antliff, D.D.
1854.	Thomas King.	1867.	P. Pugh.
1859.	John Day.	1871.	J. Macpherson.
1859.	Richard Davies.	1876.	C. C. McKechnie.
1865.	William Lister.	1887.	Thomas Newell.
1870.	George Lamb.	1892.	H. B. Kendall, B.A.
1875.	J. Dickenson.	1901.	Henry Yooll.
1880.	R. Fenwick.		(Present holder of the Office).
1885.	Joseph Toulson.		
1890	J. B. Knapp.		
1895.	Thomas Mitchell.		
1900.	Robert Bryant.		
1905.	Edwin Dalton.		

TABLE SHOWING THE SUCCESSION OF BOOK STEWARDS AND EDITORS FROM 1843 TO THE PRESENT TIME.

Mr. John Hallam, the first Book Steward under the new régime, died September 8th, 1845. His last days were clouded by anxieties and troubles associated with his office. We have already narrated the circumstances which led to his introduction to participation in Book-Room Management (Vol. ii. p 7), and his appointment by the Conference of 1838 to be General Book Steward has also been referred to. Hence arose one of those minor tragedies of life in which we see a man taken from a post for which he is eminently fitted, and set to fill another for which he is unfitted. Let any one read Mr. Hallam's papers and journals as found in the Magazine for 1835, and he will find reason to conclude that Mr. Hallam had a genius for family visitation. In his practice it became a fine art. He was an ideal pastor and circuit superintendent. He knew the deep things of experience, and how to handle the human heart, but the intricacies of a big business were a confusing mystery to him. Hence, while he was an excellent man against whose moral character there rests no imputation, in the absence of a capable business manager, he was overweighted by some of the duties of his office.

The method of book-keeping and stock-taking in use from 1838 was defective; so much so that when Thomas Holliday was appointed Joint Book Steward, he declined responsibility until the method in practice had been revised. Mr. Holliday was instructed to point out to Mr. Hallam the defects of the system in use, and to explain the features and advantages of the better system proposed to be adopted. The accounts from January to December, 1844, were kept on this system, and in 1845 Mr. Holliday took joint office. Meanwhile, the accounts from 1838 to 1844 were submitted to careful scrutiny by duly appointed auditors. Mr. Hallam willingly agreed to such a course, and, notwithstanding his declining health, rendered all the aid he could to the investigation. The results showed that an error of judgment had been committed. Mr. Hallam accepted the findings, and in his will made provision for the complete rectification of the error. This is the sum of what can be said against Mr Hallam, and it is better the real facts should be given rather than that wrong impressions should be made by the use of vague general terms. Besides, the episode has its lesson, which should not be passed over. We would vindicate the memory of John Hallam. Here to explain is largely to exculpate. What was the impression the good man had left on the mind of such an acute observer as Thomas Bateman will be clear from the following entry taken from his *Journal*:—

"*October 12th, 1845.*—Chorley, at two, I preached a funeral sermon to a host of people for my old friend John Hallam. I believe he was a good man, and very useful in the Circuits where he travelled. He always had increases. He was one of the best family visitors I have known, hence his constant success. Quite true his sun has set under a cloud. For some time he has been Book Steward, and it is said there are some errors in his accounts. I don't understand it exactly, but, although I much regret it, yet my confidence in his integrity is unshaken."

It must not be thought that we are going to pass from portrait to portrait in the succession of Book Stewards and Editors and appraise the merits or demerits of each. We shall attempt no such invidious task. Of course, as we—reader and writer alike— look at the portraits, it is almost unavoidable but that we should say of this or that one: Here is a man who was a born Book Steward or Editor; and here is one who was made such by the suffrages of his brethren. But both he that was born to the office and he that was made for it did their best, "and both will get their penny at last." Such thoughts as these, we say, will come to the reader as well as the writer; and to the reader we leave them. But, indeed, the history of the Book-Room with its associated office, is largely an impersonal history; it is the growth and development of an Institution—if we must use the word. The history offers little in the way of piquant personalia or of "secret history." With Canning's Knife Grinder we may say—"Story, sir! There is none to tell." There are no secrets to drag to the light, or many interesting incidents to impart. If we cannot speak of the "fierce" light that beats upon the Steward's Desk or the Editor's Chair, we can say that all has been open to the light of day. And as to the interesting details: We have been struck in consulting our own nine years' experience, and in reading the experience of Editors Petty

* See Dr. W. Antliff's clearly-expressed views as given in a Note to Walford's Life of Hugh Bourne, vol. ii. p. 290.

PRESIDENTS OF CONFERENCE FROM 1875 TO 1886.

and McKechnie in their recorded lives, how little there is in an Editor's life to tell. Not that there is not toil, and that in plenty. But the work is monotonous and devoid of incident. The most precious and volatile part of it is diffused, and is now, one may hope, circulating and working in men's lives; and as for the heavier, palpable, and tangible part of the work, is it not entombed or enshrined in that goodly row of volumes? So also is it largely with the Book Steward and his work. The men and their work are lost and absorbed in the Institution they help to direct and extend; and the capital gratifying fact remains that the history of the Book-Room from 1843 has been one of steady and almost amazing progress. It was already a success in 1844 when Thomas Bateman attended the Lynn Regis Conference. One might perhaps reasonably have expected him to be in sympathy with the old régime, and to have looked doubtfully on the new departure. But no! Here is his judgment.

"*June 13th.*—Some very important steps had been taken by direction of last Conference which were now found to promise much . . . The Book-Room was

ORDER DEPARTMENT, SUTTON STREET.

moved from Bemersley to London. This had been long desired, but there were obstacles in the way. Now, Mr. J. B.'s affairs having taken a strange and unexpected turn to the surprise of everybody, the way was open, and although it had only been moved a few months, *it promises well*, [Italics our own] the Stewards having sent between One and Two Hundred Pounds for the Mission Fund."

We shall not burden our pages with tables showing the turn-over and the profit of each year's working—even if all the materials for setting forth such a table were available. Nor shall we give a table showing the comparative circulation of our serials at different epochs. We do not do this here because the inferences sometimes sought to be drawn from such figures as these are not to be trusted. The broad fact remains that the volume of Book-Room business has gone on increasing, is pointed to as an example, and that, despite the fact that now and again there may have been a slight retrogression. But, unless this retrogression cannot be accounted for by temporary and contingent causes, it does not afford a safe basis for inference, and it is dangerous and wrong to begin to locate blame. The tide may still be rising though now and again a wave may

VICE-PRESIDENTS OF CONFERENCE FROM 1884 TO 1893.

fall short of the point reached by its predecessor. There is one fact, very soon stated, but yet which means so much that it deserves to be printed in big letters and to be worn as frontlets before the eyes of the Connexion. The gross amount of Book-Room allocations to various Connexional Institutions and objects since 1843, is £167,647 9s. 10d.

And as for Magazine circulation: Figures here too may be deceptive, unless it be incontestably certain that extent of circulation is *per se*, the unfailing criterion of quality. But our history traverses this canon. There may be a *succès d' estime*—a general and well-nigh universal acknowledgment of the intrinsic literary quality of serials, while a success of circulation that ought to follow is denied. Why this should be so even experts may find it difficult to say. The causes are complex and are to be found in such considerations as the condition of the Book Market, the competing claims of other printed matter—the degree of Connexional interest in Connexional literature or Connexional prosperity.

Briefly, it may be chronicled that in 1865, during the Editorial term of W. Antliff, the "Christian Messenger" and the "Child's Friend" were originated, making the

PRIZE DEPARTMENT, SUTTON STREET.

magazines issued from the Book-Room four in number. The new ventures met with immediate success, the circulation of the "Messenger" reaching 30,000, and the "Child's Friend" 21,500. In 1873, during J. Macpherson's editorship, the "Teachers' Journal" began its useful course. During what must be called the brilliant period of C. C. McKechnie's editorship, which extended to eleven years, the Large Magazine was greatly improved both in character and appearance. Now, writers were first paid for their contributions to our serials. The "Christian Ambassador" was transformed from a shilling tri-monthly magazine into the "Primitive Methodist Quarterly Review," selling at two shillings, and soon took high rank amongst publications of its class. "Springtime," the literary child of Mr. McKechnie's affection, designed specially for the "young men and maidens" of our Church, began in 1886, and at once became a favourite. To Mr. McKechnie also fell the onerous duty of seeing through the press the new Hymnal, to which we shall have to refer in another connection. Since 1892 all the Magazines issuing from the Book-Room have been enlarged and remodelled. The "Large" or the "Sixpenny" Magazine, as it had been called, now became the "Aldersgate," enriched by serial stories by such writers as Joseph Hocking and original articles by writers of good repute. The "Juvenile Magazine" became "Morning"; "Springtime" was adapted so as to become the recognised organ of our Societies of Christian Endeavour, while the "Christian Messenger" has been and is doing a useful work in helping forward the culture and training of our local preachers. Lastly, it may be added that 1905 has witnessed the effecting of still further improvements in the "Primitive Methodist Quarterly Review," which have been received with much favour.

The "Christian Ambassador."

This would seem to be a convenient time for placing on permanent record the facts, so far as they can be recovered, concerning the origin and development of the "Christian Ambassador," with which Mr. McKechnie was associated until his death in September, 1896, though it should be said that from 1894 Dr. John Watson, while nominally only Assistant Editor, discharged the full duties of the office, and continued to do so until his own impaired health necessitated his retirement. He was succeeded in the Editorship in 1903 by H. B. Kendall, B.A.

The Preface to the first volume of the "Christian Ambassador" is worth giving for the light it throws on the circumstances of its origin and the aims and motives of its promoters.

"In the autumn of 1849 several Primitive Methodist ministers happening to meet on a missionary occasion at Sunderland, the conversation turned on various topics relative to the ministry of the Connexion; and, in particular, many remarks transpired on the necessity of something being done to associate the preachers more closely for purposes of mutual improvement, with a view especially to aid and encourage probationers in qualifying themselves for their important work. After this conversation steps were immediately taken to form a Preachers Association in the Sunderland District; and the promptness with which the brethren in the various circuits responded to the appeal, the heartiness with which they have co-operated during the seven years of the Association's existence, together with the beneficent influence exerted upon the minds of the brethren generally at the yearly gatherings and by means of epistolary correspondence;— these considerations lead us to hope and believe that the movement was of God.

"To this Association the present volume owes its existence. The various papers of which it is composed were mostly read at the yearly meetings of the Association. It was judged desirable, however, that they should be circulated in a permanent form, as the younger brethren among us required something of the sort to guide them in their work; and as it was also hoped that a somewhat higher tone migh be imparted to the character of our people generally.

"Of these Essays different opinions will be formed. In judging of their merits, however, it ought to be considered that the writers are for the most part unpractised in the art of literary composition; and also, that the audience they specially address is composed of persons who, like themselves, have not been favoured with regular scholastic training."

"If this small work afford direction or encouragement to any young brother in the pursuit of his studies; if it contribute, in however small a degree, towards the development of a higher type of character in the Primitive Methodist churches; if in any way which God may please, it subserve the interest of truth and righteousness—the Editors will be amply rewarded."

Mr. W. Lister was appointed the business manager, and Messrs. Thomas Smith and C. C. McKechnie joint editors. But this arrangement lasted only a short time, Mr. McKechnie becoming sole Editor in May, 1855. As the first volume of the "Christian Ambassador" is now exceedingly scarce, it may be interesting to refer briefly to its contents and writers. The Editor himself has two articles—"The Lamb in the midst of the Throne," and "Religion's Ultimate Design," besides a trenchant review (far too trenchant, one cannot but feel) on Walford's recently published "Life of Hugh Bourne." Messrs. R. Fenwick, J. A. Bastow, T. Greenfield, J. Lightfoot, W. Dent, T. Butterwick, W. Antliff, and P. Clarke, have signed contributions. Of the laymen who contribute to this volume two are yet with us—Robert Foster and John Coward; while George Race has three articles and J. Fawsit one. As might be expected, many of the articles bear on the office and work of the Christian ministry; no less than ten out of the number being of this character.

The first number of the "Ambassador" was published in October, 1854. It was designed to be a bi-monthly publication, and it was expected that two years would see the completion of the volume; but this was not to be. As we have seen, it took two years for the first volume of the Magazine to struggle into existence, and, singularly enough, it took three years for the "Ambassador" to be born. How was this? The answer throws some light on the Transition Period. It shows us that conservative and progressive forces were at work and did not fully understand each other. We see how some of those who had the guidance of affairs, regarded movements, which we can now see had in them the germs of much promise, with jealousy and even alarm, and how they lost their composure as they read the expression of opinions which, to us, appear comparatively mild and harmless. The establishment of a Preachers' Association in the Sunderland District was eyed askance. It was thought the Association "might become a hot-bed of revolutionary ideas and disturb Connexional peace."* Several papers which had been read before the Association were, for some reason or other, declined insertion in the Magazine, and this fact no doubt had something to do with the inception of the "Christian Ambassador." But it was an article by one who afterwards became President of Conference that gave the greatest alarm. Yet really in Mr. H. Phillips' article on "The Present as contrasted with the Past condition of the Connexion" there would seem to be little to alarm anybody. In these days it would be deemed quite tame and innocuous. However, the publication of this article led to correspondence and to the temporary stoppage of the "Ambassador" by the General Committee. After an interchange of views a satisfactory working understanding was arrived at, and being let go, the first volume got itself completed in July, 1857.

In October, 1857, the "Christian Ambassador" began to be published as a quarterly

* Rev. J. Atkinson, "Life of C. C. McKechnie," p. 214.

and, with the exception of one year, when there was a reversion to the old bi-monthly form of publication, it has continued a quarterly ever since. It entered on a further stage of development in January, 1863, as thus described by Mr. McKechnie in his Autobiographic Memoranda:—

"In the year 1863, the 'Ambassador' underwent a great change. Previously, though serving a good purpose among many of our preachers and people, it bore a sort of nondescript and ephemeral character. Its general contents and get-up seemed to indicate that it was nothing more than a temporary makeshift. And indeed, this was very near the idea formed of it for the first few years of its existence by its principal supporters. Now, however, in 1863 it, as it were, dropped its temporary features and assumed a permanent form, or at least, a form which promised permanence. While enlarged from sixty-four to ninety-six pages, and bearing the usual marks of regular periodicals, the quality of its literary papers was improved, and the price raised from eight-pence to a shilling. It had now become recognised indirectly as a semi-connexional organ, and though not patronised so generally as we thought its merits deserved, it nevertheless received considerable support. An important circumstance to be noted is, that at this time the Sunderland Preachers' Association, to which the "Ambassador" belonged, surrendered its copyright to the Preachers' Friendly Society, and thenceforth it became the property of that Society, yielding it its profits and subject to its control. Though having more than sufficient to do in managing the North Shields Circuit, I continued to edit the 'Ambassador,' and had every reason to believe that it exerted an influence for good among our preachers and people."

It is hard to repress a feeling of envy when we learn that the Primitive Methodist Quarterly Review started on its career with a circulation of 2,368 and yielded a first-year's profit of £207 to the Preachers' Friendly Society.

BOOK COMMITTEE AND AUDITORS.

The Book Committee, of which the General Book Steward has always been the Secretary, has differed in its constitution at various times and has fluctuated in its numbers. We have seen who composed it in 1843. From 1844 to 1847, inclusive, it was the same in its personnel as the General Committee. In 1848, however, there was a reversion to the old type of Book Committee. All through the 'Fifties the committee was a small special one composed of persons resident in or near the metropolis. For the three years ending in 1850 it consisted of but three persons—T. Holliday, J. Flesher,

GEORGE BARON.
(Connexional Auditor.)

THE PERIOD OF CONSOLIDATION AND CHURCH DEVELOPMENT.   399

and W. Garner. For a few years after this it was a mixed committee of ministers and laymen, but it still continued a small committee, the persons composing it never exceeding ten in number. Then in 1863 the Book Committee once more lost its separateness and was but the General Committee discharging special functions under the direction of the General Book Steward. This obtained until the formation of the special and influential Book Committee that dates from 1895 and that may be said to be a feature of the latest phase and period of Book-Room administration. This would seem to be the time also to refer to the Connexional Auditors who, as Conferentially appointed officers, have since 1843 been annually closely associated with the Book-Room, in order to examine the year's accounts, setting forth the year's working of the department. The accounts of the Missionary Society have also come under their inspection; but it is with the relations in which they have stood to the Book-Room that we have now specially to do. At the very beginning of this period the auditors had an onerous piece of work to do, and the manner they discharged their duty tended to inspire that confidence which was the best foundation for progressive development. It may serve a useful purpose to give here in tabular form the names of these men of Connexional standing, approved business ability, and high character, who, in succession, have cheerfully rendered this particular form of service to the Connexion though at an expenditure of considerable time and toil to themselves.

J. HUNT.
Connexional Auditor.

It will be noticed how many of these men we have already met with—men like S. Longdin, J. Sissons, J. Rouse, G. Baron, T. Dawson, G. T. Goodrich. We have seen them rendering distinguished Connexional service in their several localities. The portraits of many of these men have already been given; those of Messrs. J. Jones and J. Coward will be found among the Vice-Presidents, while that of Mr. Joseph Hunt, an influential layman of High Wycombe and former Missionary treasurer, and the portraits of Messrs. Amos Chippindale of Harrogate, and J. Brearley of Halifax, are inserted in the text. Our three present auditors —Messrs. Chippindale, Brearley, and Greenhalgh—have a long and honourable record of service rendered in their own Districts, and in the general administration of Connexional affairs, and that record does not need to be set out here at large. In fine, the list we give

MR. AMOS CHIPPINDALE.
Connexional Auditor.

MR. J. BREARLEY.
Connexional Auditor.

not only shows who have acted as auditors since 1843, but gives us the names of some men of Connexional mark in the period of consolidation and organisation.

1843	S. Longdin, J. Sissons.
1845	S. Longdin, T. Dawson, J. Sissons.
	"The auditors have great satisfaction, in examining the accounts, to find them clear, distinct and correct."
1846	S. Longdin, J. Sissons.
1847	Emerson Muschamp, W. Garner, T. Dawson.
1848	S. Longdin, T. Dawson.
1849—50	J. Sissons, T. Bateman.
1851	T. Bateman, J. Reynard.
1852	Joshua Rouse, T. Bateman.
1853	T. Bateman, T. Dawson.
1854	T. Bateman, W. M. Salt.
1855—8	T. Bateman, Joshua Rouse.
1859—60	Joshua Rouse, G. T. Goodrich.
1861—2	Joshua Rouse, J. Sissons.
1863—5	T. Bateman, J. Hunt.
	(A Report of the Book Committee begins in 1865 to be attached to the Balance Sheet).
1866	T. Bateman, J. Hunt.
	(The monthly circulation of the Magazines now first given).
1867	T. Bateman, J. North.
1868—9	T. Bateman, J. Hunt.
1870	T. Bateman, Joshua Rouse.
	(Up to this point the Financial year ended December 31st, and the audited accounts are given in the Conference Minutes of the year following Now the Financial year is made to end March 31st, so that 1871 is from January, 1871, to April, 1872).
1871	T. Bateman, Joshua Rouse.
1872—8	T. Bateman, G. Baron.
1879—82	T. Bateman, G. Baron, John Lowe.
1883—4	T. Bateman, James Greenhalgh.
1885—6	G. Baron, J. Greenhalgh.
1887	J. S. Parkman, John Jones, J. Greenhalgh.
1888	J. Jones, James Richards, J. Greenhalgh.
1889—94	J. Jones, John Coward, J. Greenhalgh.
1895	J. Jones, J. Greenhalgh.
1896	J. Jones, Amos Chippindale, J. Greenhalgh.
1897—1905	A. Chippindale, J. Brearley, J. Greenhalgh.

TABLE SHOWING THE SUCCESSION OF AUDITORS FROM 1843 TO THE PRESENT.

CHAPTER IV.

THE RE-ORGANIZATION OF THE MISSIONARY COMMITTEE.

THE Conference of 1843, which removed the Book-Room to London, also re-organized the Missionary Committee and located its executive in the metropolis. We say the Conference "re-organized" the Committee rather than that it established it; for a Missionary Committee had been established as far back as 1825, but its income had been small and its operations had been conducted on a very limited scale. Its income for the year 1826 had been £49 8s. 1¼d., and in 1843, after seventeen years, it was but £125 14s. 2¼d. making, with the balance of the preceding year and the balance of the Charitable Fund, a total sum of £311 3s. 10½d. Its expenditure for the year was but £17, consisting of grants to Lancaster Mission, to Tunstall on behalf of its Irish Mission, and to Reading Circuit's Missions. Still, the idea of a centralised Committee directing the missionary operations of the whole Connexion by means of contributions from all the Circuits was *there*, waiting its time to become effective. Like a rudimentary organ, the day would come when it would be called upon to perform its functions for the general good of the body to which it belonged. By 1843 this time seemed to have come. No doubt the missionary policy pursued during the first period had justified itself. Circuit missions, as the usual and favourite aggressive agency, were well adapted to a period marked by general enthusiasm; just as the revolutionary ardour of France made its citizen army for a time carry all before it. But by 1843 something of the old ardour had died down. The disadvantages of the old system were beginning to show themselves.* Circuits were pre-occupied with efforts to conserve their gains and consolidate themselves. Hence, many of the leading minds in the Connexion were of opinion that the time had fully come for a change of policy. Says Mr. Flesher: "Hitherto the Connexion has been isolated in its missionary operations. Each circuit which has been able has employed a missionary, and with few exceptions has had to support him with its own resources. In the youth of the Connexion this plan appears to have been best adapted for the diffusion of its energies through the land; but growing events seem to demand a different state of things, and hence arrangements were made at the Conference to concentrate our missionary energies, in part, that we may try on a partial scale whether the plan is not better suited to the altered state of the Connexion."

The administrative changes effected in 1843 were regarded very differently by our

---

* "But the system was clogged with numerous difficulties. The *managing* committees were too many. In action some of them were too slow; others were too precipitate. Some had large funds at their disposal; others were compelled to alter their course for the want of a little money."— W. *Garner*, "Life of Rev. John Garner."

chief founders. The mind and will which re-organized the old Missionary Committee and breathed new life into it, came from Hull rather than from Tunstall, as also did the movement which resulted in remodelling the Book-Room and changing its location from Bemersley to London. Here we have the first and palmary example of the way in which Districtism, by encouraging the growth of variations, has in the end modified and enriched our Connexional life. Other examples of the working of this same principle—so active in the middle and later periods of our history—will meet us as we go along. Tunstall had had a long and, on the whole, a successful innings: it was now Hull's turn to contribute to the general good by carrying through its legislative proposals. What Hugh Bourne was likely to think of these may be gathered from a remark of his which Thomas Russell has preserved for us. "I took the liberty of questioning him as to the General Committee's not continuing an efficient minister under its direction. He replied: 'I do not believe the Lord designs the General Committee to have such a care on their hands; as *I believe it would cramp individual and circuit effort.*'" Though this remark was made in 1832 there is no evidence to show that Hugh Bourne was of a different opinion in 1843. As to Clowes' feelings and attitude towards the new departure, we have positive evidence. According to the testimony of W. Garner, not only did he approve of the changes effected in 1842-3, but he largely contributed to bring these changes about. Mr. Garner's precise words are: "Through the influence of W. Clowes, chiefly, the missions belonging to Hull Circuit were given up to the Conference of 1843 as a nucleus for a new missionary organization." Other facts confirm this explicit statement. The "nucleus of the new missionary organization" was, with the exception of Oswestry's Lisburn Mission, composed exclusively of the missions of Hull Circuit, viz., London, Newport (I.W.), Portsmouth, Southampton, Brighton, Bedford, Sheerness, Ramsgate, Maidstone, and Canterbury. These missions were to be taken over by the Committee as soon as possible and, in the meantime, were to be under the management of Hull and Oswestry Circuits. Further, the Missions were to belong to Hull District; their chief officer, together with the Book Steward, was to have a seat in the Hull District Meeting; and this arrangement held good until the formation of the London District in 1853.[*] Lastly, Hull District was to be exempt from the levy made on the other circuits, but was "affectionately desired to continue its powerful missionary services and operations, and to afford the Missionary Committee pecuniary aid equal, at least, to that which it has had to allow in support of these missions" (*Minutes*, 1843).

Constitution and Officers of the General Missionary Committee.

For many years the General Missionary Committee was composed of the same persons as the General Committee. It was one body discharging different functions. But in 1888 the Quarterly Committee was created and, in the end, this strong and thoroughly representative body, like Moses' rod, swallowed up the Fortnightly Committee, thus effectually cutting off all occasions of conflict as to respective rights and powers. The Quarterly Committee is a circulatory one, while its executive, composed of fifteen

---

[*] Still later—1871—the Missions were formed into a separate District.

persons, holds its monthly meetings in London. We should bear in mind what has already been stated, that, until 1864, the Secretary of the General Missionary Committee was the same person as the Secretary of the General Committee. Little change has taken place during the years either in the name or functions of the Missionary Committee's chief officer. He is still modestly called its "Secretary," and as such, through his Committee he still has the oversight of both the Home and Foreign Missions, no division of these two departments having as yet taken place. And yet when, as early as 1845, we find John Ride set apart as visitor of the Home Missions and as such invested with rather large powers, we can easily see how development might have proceeded on somewhat different lines from the lines actually followed. In the *Minutes* there are no less than a dozen regulations relating to his visitorial functions, one of which suggests the tireless energy of the man:—

> "John Ride shall be seriously and importunately desired not to arrange work that cannot be executed regularly by himself in his sundry visits, or by any man of ordinary mental and physical energy; for while the Conference is desirous on one hand, not to countenance an *effeminate*, indolent ministry, it is wishful on the other, that such a system of labour shall be adopted as will not hastily ruin the health of the labourers."

After 1845 we hear no more of the visitorial powers of John Ride. The episode suggests the passing reflection—how close Primitive Methodism has kept to strict Presbyterial lines. It has not even succeeded in developing a "District Superintendent" or "Chairman of the District," although it has had nearly a century in which to make the experiment. Indeed, in some respects, our Church is more rigidly Presbyterian than it was in the days when Nottingham urged the appointment of Thomas King as District Superintendent,* and when, for a time, Hugh Bourne was really such, and, year after year, he sat as General Committee Delegate in some of the District Meetings.

It was not until 1851 that the Treasurership of the Mission Fund was made a distinct office. On January 1st of that year Joseph Hunt of High Wycombe took up its duties, and thus was the first of a line of distinguished laymen who for more than half a century have gratuitously discharged responsible duties. We will now give—as we have done in the case of the General Book Stewards, Connexional Editors, and Auditors—a table showing the chronological succession of the Secretaries of the General Missionary Committee and of the Treasurers of its funds. The portraits of all of these have already been given in other connections.

A supplementary remark or two may be made on the following table. It is to be noted that, although by the rule of 1850 the term of connexional office was limited to five years, four Missionary Secretaries have not served the allotted term, while only in one instance has that term been exceeded.† The rule of 1850 laid great stress on seniority as a condition for office. Other things being equal, seniority was to decide

---
* See *ante* vol. i. p. 448.

† In 1888, the rule of 1850 was brought up again and re-affirmed, but it was added—"This legislation shall not apply this year to the General Committee Secretary and the General Missionary Secretary."

404 PRIMITIVE METHODIST CHURCH.

GENERAL COMMITTEE SECRETARIES FROM 1865, WHEN THE OFFICE WAS SEPARATED FROM THAT OF GENERAL MISSIONARY SECRETARY.

the appointment. This naturally resulted in veterans being designated to the office. Though they might not be old as counted by years, they had seen much service. The excessive labours of their youth and prime had left their mark. The old wounds they got when in the "active work" sometimes smarted and even crippled them as they sat at the departmental desk or visited the outposts. So John Garner was but forty-three years of age when he entered upon office, but the toil, persecution and exposure he underwent in the pioneering days had planted the seeds of disease in his otherwise strong constitution, and he became the victim of recurring attacks of asthma. His experience of London winters was a veritable martyrdom. "The Missionary Committee indulged him with an easy-chair in which he might recline when he dare not venture to lay his weary head upon his pillow." When he left the Mission House his active labours for the Connexion were done, and at quiet Burnham, near Epworth, he patiently awaited his release from cruel suffering, which release came February 12th, 1868. His body was interred near the pulpit of the old sanctuary.

JOHN WELFORD,
Present General Committee Secretary.

SECRETARIES OF THE GENERAL MISSIONARY COMMITTEE.	TREASURERS OF THE GENERAL MISSIONARY FUND.
1843. John Garner.	1843. Thomas Holliday.
1848. William Garner.	1844-5. { Thomas Holliday. / John Hallam.
1854. John Bywater.	1846-7. { Thomas Holliday. / William Garner.
1859. Moses Lupton.	1848-50. William Garner.
In 1864 the office was dissociated from that of Secretary of General Committee, and the Missionary Secretary is now also styled "Superintendent of the Home Missions."	The Treasurership becomes a separate office.
	1851 (Jan.) Joseph Hunt.
1865. Thomas Jobling.	1856 „ Wm. Byron & J. Maltby.
1869. Samuel Antliff.	1863 „ John Maltby.
1874. William Rowe (1).	1864. James Meek.
1878. William Cutts.	1869. Thomas Gibson.
1883. John Atkinson.	1871. Henry Hodge.
1889. James Travis.	S. Antliff filled the new office of Deputy Treasurer and Financial Secretary from '77 to '81. In the latter year the Secretary of the General Committee was appointed Deputy Treasurer. This arrangement continued until 1902, when Thomas Mitchell, the Secretary of the Chapel Extension Fund, was appointed Deputy Treasurer.
1894. John Smith.	
1899. R. W. Burnett.	
1902. John Slater.	
1903. James Pickett.	
(Present holder of office).	
	1890. W. P. Hartley.
	(Present holder of office).
	TREASURERS OF AFRICAN FUND.
	1871. William Beckworth.
	1875. Thomas Davies.
	1878. Thomas Lawrence.
	(Present holder of office).

TABLE SHOWING THE SUCCESSION OF SECRETARIES OF THE MISSIONARY COMMITTEE AND THE TREASURERS OF ITS FUNDS FROM 1843 TO THE PRESENT TIME.

So it was, too, with John Bywater. His strong frame had become broken and disabled by rheumatism, and a year after vacating his office, finding himself unequal to the duties of a station, he sought superannuation.

Next, we have the case of John Jobling, the Tyneside youth, and early companion of Joseph Spoor. He had already laboured as a minister thirty-two years in the Manchester District when he became Missionary Secretary. He had proved himself "a thoroughly upright, industrious and hard-working labourer in the Lord's vineyard." and withal a man of remarkable prayerful spirit. He had seen a net increase of 1619 on his stations, and had superintended the erection of thirteen chapels. He gave himself to his new duties with anxious assiduity, but, as his friend Dr. W. Antliff testified, "the pressure on his nervous system seemed more than he could well sustain," and,

THE OLD AND NEW CHAPEL, EPWORTH.
Old Chapel, date 1821, built on Piece of Ground John Oxtoby prayed for. Rev. John Garner is buried in the Chapel.

after four years at the Mission House, his superannuation was swiftly followed by death, July 22nd, 1869.

William Rowe (1) was no novice when he took up the direction of Missionary affairs. During his thirty-four years' ministry in the Manchester District he had become known as a popular pulpit and platform speaker, as well as a capable superintendent. "Connexional honours are onerous," as quaint Thomas Greenfield was wont to say. So William Rowe was to find. "His pulpit and platform labours, and the responsibilities of the mission-office were too much for his strength"*

* Official Memoir by Rev. J. Travis, *Conference Minutes*, 1888.

and he was superannuated in 1878, with one year of his allotted term still to run.

The cold print of the last lines of the first column of our table brings the truth home to us that the office of Missionary Secretary—never a light one—has become heavier still with the passage of the years. So much is this the case that only the most vigorous, and those who are happily constituted as to temperament and nerve, may hope to bear up under the strain of its heavy and constant demands. By a touching coincidence the same Conference Minutes of 1903 contains the memoirs of two Missionary Secretaries who fell at their post. That amiable man and veteran missionary, R. W. Burnett, died June 21st, 1902, of a disease contracted in Africa's malarial climate; while John Slater, genial, hearty, strenuous, passed away March 17th, 1903, not unfittingly, while on a preaching visit to Manchester Fourth Circuit, on which he had spent eleven years of laborious and fruitful service, and where the noble church which overlooks Ardwick Green will long perpetuate his name.

METHODS OF HOME MISSIONARY ADMINISTRATION.

Evidence is not wanting to show that the new system was regarded in the light of an "experiment"—this is the very word used by W. Garner to describe it. The efforts were tentative; the Connexion was somewhat timidly feeling its way towards the effective control of the Home Missions by a central authority. In proof of this, it is only necessary to adduce the fact that Circuit Missions were not superseded at one stroke, but only gradually, and by steps and stages. Indeed, in 1844, the Circuit Missions outnumbered those under the immediate control of the Missionary Committee, the actual numbers being:—

Circuit Missions 35	Preachers ... 39	Members ... 2684
General Missionary Committee's Missions ... ... } 27	,, ... 36	,, ... 2521

Thus the two systems worked, and continued for some years to work, side by side. Gradually the number of Circuit Missions decreased, but the system was in vogue for some twenty years longer, and, we believe we are right in saying that the last Circuit Missions (old style) were the Bromyard Mission of Ludlow, and the Falmouth Mission of Truro Circuit, which stood on the list of stations in 1861, and were taken over in 1862.

The existence of so many Circuit Missions had an important bearing on the amount of revenue available for missionary purposes; for the circuits which still held to their missions needed their revenue to maintain these missions, and were allowed to retain and use it for that purpose. So that the Missionary Committee had to look for its supplies to those circuits which had no missions of their own. The financial arrangements made show that the Connexion was still mainly composed of what were really missions; or, to put the fact in another way, that there was little to choose between the so-called circuits and missions.* Circuits, themselves poor and weak, were yet expected to lend a helping hand to those stations that were still poorer and weaker than themselves. Those which had no Circuit Missions were required to send the whole of the missionary money contributed for special purposes, i.e., for the Australian and New Zealand Missions, but were allowed to retain a fixed proportion of the general income raised at not less than half the places on their plan. The proportion of money to be sent to head-quarters varied in successive periods, though the variation was steadily in the direction of increase. In 1842, the proportion to be sent was one-eighth; in 1843, one-sixth; in 1849, one-fifth; in 1861, one-third, and in 1870, one half. Finally, in 1876, in view of the increased demands likely to be made on the Mission Fund, it was enacted that the whole of the missionary money raised, both general and special, should be remitted to the respective treasurers. So we may say that for some thirty-three years the Connexion was in missionary matters resolutely trying to get from fractions to whole numbers. There was neither stop nor stay till that was accomplished. Everything was provisional and temporary; nor could it fail to be otherwise, until not merely one central missionary executive had taken the place of many local ones, but had also got the power to handle and dispose of *all* the money raised for avowedly missionary purposes on *all* the circuits and missions. In the meantime, until this desirable goal was reached, the Connexion got a good drilling in fractions.

But it might, and often did, happen in this fractional period, that the minimum proportion of missionary money could not be sent as a first charge without reducing the preachers below the level of what was then considered a living wage. Recourse was therefore had to a Fund which was the outcome of the troubles of the period ending in 1828. As we have seen, owing to the drastic measures then taken, a considerable number of "runners out" left the ministry, and some of the worthy men who took their places found the circuits so impoverished that even the moderate salary then allowed was not forthcoming. The Charitable Fund was established to aid these worthy embarrassed men to tide over their difficulties. The first report of this Fund is given in 1830, when the income is set down as £27 13s. 5¼d., and that amount is shown as having been expended in paying half the deficiency in the salaries of the preachers in Retford, Norwich, Cambridge, and Whitby Circuits. In 1842, the sum of £216 odd was paid in this way, and it was ordered that each circuit should contribute at least twelve shillings a year towards this Fund, but that travelling preachers should not be *obliged* to contribute anything as hitherto they had been required to do. The Charitable Fund was essentially a branch of Home Mission finance. As its design was

* "Very many of our stations were made into circuits, or continued in the list of circuits when the missionary institution was formed, and subsequently organized, with the understanding that they should be entitled to a stipulated amount of assistance from the missionary revenue, and without such an arrangement it would have been impossible to sustain such stations in an efficient condition. *The mere circumstance of changing the name or title of a station did not, and could not, change their real missionary condition,* and consequently as a mere matter of simple justice did not require such stations on their becoming or remaining circuits to forego their claim to aid from the Missionary Committee." *W. Garner in the "Primitive Methodist" September 3rd,* 1868. Mr. Garner it must be remembered was Missionary Secretary from 1848 to '54, and also Missionary Treasurer for some years, so that he writes with authority.

to assist poor but improving Circuits, it answered the purpose of a sustentation or auxiliary fund; indeed, this latter name was in 1865 given to it, as being "more agreeable and appropriate." During this fractional period, as we have termed it, repeated enactments on salaries were made with the view of adjusting the rate of salaries paid to the proportion of missionary money sent. This sliding-scale arrangement, which was an attempt to strike an equitable balance between the competing claims of the local and central authorities, was in force until 1876. In that year—so notable in various regards*—the tangle of fractions, of checks and counter-checks and compromises was nearly threaded, and the firm ground of a clear common-sense principle set foot on at last. "See to it," said the authorities, "that you send the whole of the net proceeds of your missionary meetings to us. That done, you can pay your preachers what you please; only take care not to pay them less than what we regard as the 'irreducible minimum.'" The Auxiliary Fund was now abolished, and the Missionary Fund became available for the helping of needy circuits. Then another step in advance was taken in 1888 by the establishment of the Missions Quarterly Committee. But here a slight and temporary deviation into fractions was made. The "seventy-five per cent. arrangement," as it was called, provided that any District whose annual missionary revenue should be in excess of the sum sent by that District to the Deputy Treasurer for the Audit of 1888, should be allowed to retain three-fourths of that excess sum for the purpose of extending and strengthening connexional interests within the District. Here we have an evident attempt to encourage Districts to do what had been done with such conspicuous success by many *Circuits* in the first period. The method has in it great possibilities, as some recent examples show. The seventy-five per cent. arrangement lapsed in 1898, which year is memorable for the establishment of the Connexional Sustentation Fund. Now it was required that missionary meetings should be held at all the places in a Circuit at which there were regular preaching services. Further, the Missions Quarterly Committee was constituted the allocating authority for making grants to needy stations.

Thus, then, next to 1843, '76, '88, and '98 are notable dates for Home Missionary administration. Of these, '98 was as the goal to which things had been tending ever since the re-organization of the General Missionary Committee, while '76 and '88 were waymarks on the road. These modifications of administration were not made without much anxious deliberation. Many were the Connexional Committees that sat to consider questions of finance and administration, as the records show. There were long and lively discussions in the newspaper press on Home Missionary and other Connexional affairs. The Westgate proposals for a fixed salary, as against the Equalization Fund,†

---

* 1876 was also the year in which the representation to Conference was placed on a numerical basis.

† EQUALIZATION FUND.—The roots of this Fund go a good way back in our history. There were legislative proposals from seven Circuits on the question at the Conference of 1851, and John Flesher was desired to draw up a report on the subject. This report, which was issued in 1852, consists of eight pages of small type, and is of an elaborate character. Mr. Flesher was in favour of District Funds rather than of one Connexional Fund, which he deemed unworkable. On this permissive line Districts wanting an Equalization Fund have been allowed to establish one. Hull District was the first to avail itself of the privilege, in 1870. Now every District has such a Fund except Sunderland, Darlington and Stockton, Carlisle and Whitehaven, North British, and the Missions Districts. The "North" has stoutly resisted the Equalization Fund from the beginning.

were as the flag round which the tide of battle surged. Much dust was stirred while the controversy was going on. No doubt mistakes were made, and needless delays took place. All who had the direction of affairs were not equally far-sighted. Some could not see a long way before them, while others had a clearer prevision and a more statesmanlike grasp of affairs. But still, the main thing to notice is that, with all abatements, and on the whole, progress was being made towards greater simplicity and efficiency of administration. It is but fair to our predecessors to recognise the difficulties under which they had to carry on their work, not the least embarrassing of these being of a financial character. They would have gone faster and done much more had larger resources been at command. As it was, we venture to say few Societies have carried on so large a business with so small a capital.

Other recent Connexional developments closely related to Home Mission work may be noted here in order to get a connected view, though their more detailed consideration will be necessary when, in closing, we have to look at some of the present features of our Church-life, of which the quickened interest in social work, and improved methods of finance are amongst the most striking. Amongst these may be mentioned, Large Town Missions, social and Philanthropic Agencies (especially in London), the Van Missions, Evangelists in the Rural Districts, the Missionary Jubilee Fund, and the Church Extension Fund.

Some Results.

For our own instruction and use we have drawn up a table showing the circuits made from the Missions by the General Missionary Committee from 1843 to the present, with the number of ministers and members in them at the time of their transference to the Home Districts. Though the preparation of this table entailed a considerable amount of research we are still doubtful as to its absolute correctness in every particular, owing to the difficulty of procuring precise information on some points. Still, we have reason for believing it to be approximately correct, and although we shall not take up our space by giving this table in full, we can by its help do something towards answering the question : What has the General Missionary Committee been doing in the Home-field through all these years? First, then, our table shows that in the sixty-two years from 1843 to 1905, some ninety-four Missions that had been under the care of the General Missionary Committee were formed into independent circuits, having on them at the time of their formation 142 preachers and an aggregate membership of 18,133. Since they achieved their independence some of these circuits have been divided again and again; while, on the other hand, there have been one or two cases in which a circuit on being let go was found on trial unable to walk alone, and so was taken back on the Missions until it should be qualified for self-government. So Dover stands twice on our table. It was made a circuit in 1882, as also were Deal and Folkestone. In 1885 it reverted to the Missions; but in 1904, under hopeful conditions, Dover and Deal took its place amongst the circuits of the London District.

REV. I. DORRICOTT.

No doubt this promising state of things is largely due to the fact that, for the space of ten years during its second probation, the Dover Mission was under the judicious superintendency of Isaac Dorricott. With the co-operation of such officials as Messrs. S. Lewis and G. Brisley, and the liberality of Mrs. Russell—the widow of the late Thomas Russell—steady advance was made. Old Peter Street (1860) was replaced by the church and schools in London Road (1902), one of the neatest and completest blocks of property the Connexion possesses in the south of England. Thus the old mission and young circuit enters upon its career under favourable auspices, just at the time when the ancient Cinque Port seems destined to play even a more important rôle in the future than it has done in the past. This reference to Dover points the moral that, after seeming failure and trying delay, success may come at last. The husbandman has to exercise "long patience"; so has the General Missionary Committee; and sometimes the long patience has its abundant reward.

PRIMITIVE METHODIST CHURCH, LONDON ROAD, DOVER.

To the figures already given as to the work of the General Missionary Committee, there should be added some dozen Missions which, after a time, were either joined to neighbouring circuits as branches or were incorporated with circuits. A typical example is afforded by the case of Southampton which, after being for five years a mission station became, in 1848, a branch of Andover. Then, in 1904, we have the Eastleigh Mission taken over and becoming part of Southampton First. So also Diss Mission in 1871 became a branch of Rockland, and in 1885 Longton a branch of Hanley; while Marlborough, Richmond, Haywards Heath, etc., have undergone absorption. Geographically the chief work of the General Missionary Committee has been carried on in the South Midlands, the South and West of England, and in parts of Scotland and Wales. This is only what we might have looked for. When the Committee was re-organized the geographical extension of the Connexion was not complete, nor can we say that it is even now complete. There are still spatial gaps to be filled up, tracts of country and good-sized towns and villages where the denomination has not got a footing. The General Missionary Committee took up the unfinished work of such missionary circuits as Hull, Scotter, Burland, Reading, and Manchester. Circuits, the outgrowth of the Committee's labours, have been formed in Cornwall and along the sea-coast to the mouth of the Thames, including the Isle of Wight and the Channel Isles. London, too, and the Home-counties, parts of Essex and Kent, and the tract of country extending from Gloucester to Peterborough have been the field of its operations. The circuit gains resulting from these operations are registered on the District stations; so that, tracing the circuits to the Districts to which they have been attached, we find that the two London Districts have profited the most by this accretive process, and next to

STROUD ROAD PRIMITIVE METHODIST CHAPEL, GLOUCESTER.

them, the Salisbury and Southampton, the North British, and the Devon and Cornwall Districts. In 1851, London was a single circuit made from the Missions; in 1881, London XIV. is on the stations. Next year, the cumbrous method of distinguishing the stations by ordinal numbers was discarded in favour of local designations, London I. giving place to Hackney Road, London VI. to Croydon, etc. While here, as elsewhere, the division and sub-division of circuits has gone on apace, the outstanding fact remains that the General Missionary Committee has handed over to the two London Districts eight metropolitan and twenty-seven provincial stations, while it has contributed seven each to the Districts already named. There is no need to go into details as to the gains of the other Districts since, so far from modifying, they would but confirm the

THE PERIOD OF CONSOLIDATION AND CHURCH DEVELOPMENT. 413

FIRST PREACHING ROOM OVER BAKER'S SHOP IN GROVE STREET, GLOUCESTER.

conclusion already reached as to where the General Missionary Committee has been doing its chief work during the last sixty years.

To give the history of every mission the General Missionary Committee has undertaken, or even to sketch the history of those which have attained circuit rank is plainly impossible. If it *were* possible it would still be unnecessary. It will be enough to single out from the rest one or two examples of successful missions, and, for a combination of reasons, Gloucester, Northampton, Bedford, and Peterborough shall be taken as our samples. There are points of similarity recognisable in all of these as well as some points of difference. They are all important towns or cities, three of them being county capitals famous in the annals of Nonconformity, while the fourth is the seat of a bishopric which has been filled by such eminent ecclesiastics as Archbishop Magee and Mandell Creighton. From the present position of Primitive Methodism in these places, no one, unacquainted with the early history of our Church, would suspect that they had ever been Mission stations, much less would he suspect that they were once feeble and struggling mission stations. Yet such they were. The cause of this is perhaps not far to seek. They all may be said to have been situated in the Primitive Methodist Mercia, just as some of them are within what was the old Mercia of the Heptarchy. The name is strictly appropriate because these towns lie on the *marches* or outskirts of the old Districts of Tunstall, Nottingham, Norwich, and Brinkworth; hence they lay remote from the circuits responsible for their care and were difficult to work. In this frontier country we have had some losses. Once we had circuits and

SECOND PREACHING PLACE, RYECROFT STREET, GLOUCESTER.

missions bearing names now unfamiliar to our people. Welton, Daventry, Chacombe, Moreton-in-the-Marsh, Filkins, no longer figure on the list of stations. It is well we can also point to some substantial gains in this same Mercian land. That under the management of the General Missionary Committee the four places already named qualified themselves for circuit independence; that on the foundations then laid they have risen course by course; that Kettering, the scene of past failures, is now one of the Committee's most promising missions—these are facts justificatory of the policy of 1843, and suggesting the hope that still more old ground may be recovered and new ground won.

Gloucester, the birthplace of Whitefield and the home of Robert Raikes, is said to have been missioned by J. Richards, the superintendent of Pillawell, as early as 1837. Though the difficulty and expense of working the mission so far from the centre led to its practical abandonment, occasional open-air services were still held in the city down to 1854. Late in '54, on the invitation of a worthy man—W. J. Wellington—the Committee sent J. Howard as a missionary to Gloucester. The first meeting-place was an upper room behind a baker's shop in Grove Street; then the ground-floor of

REV. J. RICHARDS.　　MR. W. J. WELLINGTON.　　REV. LEVI NORRIS.

a house in Ryecroft Street was taken, the rooms of which could be thrown together by folding-doors. The Committee was happy in its next appointment. In '56 John Wenn found a small church of twenty-one reported members, and at once set himself to encourage self-reliance and vigorous methods of evangelisation. Out-door services were begun. Some notable conversions took place—especially that of an avowed atheist—which had for result the bringing of the work of the society into public notice. In 1858, the first Barton Street Chapel (now used for business purposes) was opened by Robert Hartley, one of our chief pioneers in Queensland, who was then stationed at Bristol. As a pendant and contrast to the views of our first preaching-places in Gloucester, we give a view of the Stroud Road new church, erected in 1901 under the superintendency of Levi Norris, at a cost of £2680. The present Barton Street Chapel was opened in 1882 at a cost of £3786, and Milburn Street in 1880.

Cheltenham's early history resembles that of Gloucester. It, too, was a derelict mission. For two or three years it stood upon the stations as one of the branches of Brinkworth; then, in 1845, it disappears; but while Mr. Wenn was on the Gloucester station it was re-missioned. He himself thus describes the circumstances in notes taken from his *Journal* of the time.

"In August of this year 1856, Mr. Joseph Wellington accompanied me to Cheltenham, where we had no interest except in the prayers and expectations of Miss Mary Ducker, a Primitive Methodist from Wiltshire. This good sister had for years been waiting for a door to be opened 'of the Lord' in this town. After some conversation we informed her that we had come not merely to see the beautiful, and at that time especially, the renowned town of Cheltenham, but to preach the Gospel in its streets and 'gather a people for the Lord.' Thereupon Miss D. said she thought she knew of five or six persons who had been Primitives elsewhere, but had joined other Churches, who would help to sustain the service. She volunteered to look them up, but returned saying that 'they all with one consent began to make excuse.' Consequently, the three of us held a service at the top of Winchcombe Street, after which I asked the loan of a cottage in which to hold a class meeting. One was offered and we entered it, the children gathering about the windows to see what was going on. After singing and prayer and 'the relation of our experiences,' I asked Miss D. if she would be our first member in the church at Cheltenham. 'We have no church,' was her reply. 'No; but we shall have,' I remarked. 'In that case,' she went on, 'I shall be delighted to have my name down as the first member.' Accordingly, having brought a class-book with me, I produced it and wrote her name in it. She paid her contribution, and the cause was started.

"How often since have I wished that I had that class-book! I should value it almost beyond any other book in my possession; for it contained not only the honoured name of Miss Ducker, but also a record of progress in the number and liberality of members such as I have rarely witnessed elsewhere. And that progress and liberality were, I am bound in honesty to say, largely the result of the modest, brave, self-denying, unresting labours of the lady who was not only the first member but, until the church became too large for her to take oversight of all,—the 'Leader' of the rest. Her whole soul was bound up with the prosperity of the cause. She never rested until she had obtained respectable lodgings for me when I was at work in the town, nor until—when we came to have local preachers—their needs were provided for at her expense in the house of a poor member.

"In all weathers during the winter of 1856-7 we were out-of-doors, usually returning to the cottage of a chimney-sweep—whose wife was a member—for prayer and class-meetings, and for an occasional preaching-service when the rain pelted us in . . . As the winter waned, an empty chapel, situated in a slum off Winchcombe Street, facetiously called 'Mount Pleasant,' was offered us on rent and accepted. But ineligible as was its situation and unpretentious as were its architectural features, it was a great and joyful day for us when we took possession of it; and that joy was enhanced when whole families were swept to the Cross and into the Church by the high tides of grace that were flowing.

"Just prior to my leaving the station in 1859, a lady hearing of the nature and success of our work, sent for me and offered to sell us King Street Chapel. 'At what price?' I queried. '£450.' 'Too much,' I replied. 'Well, how much can you give?' 'Subject to the approval of our General Missionary Committee, £300.' 'Well, you are doing good work and you shall have it.' The bargain was struck but not completed until the arrival of my successor" [W. Mottram, own cousin to the famous George Eliot].

In closing his interesting narrative of the re-introduction of Primitive Methodism into this part of Gloucestershire, Mr. Wenn adds: "On the whole I have never left a station on which I was permitted to witness such signal displays of Gospel power as on what are now the Gloucester Circuit and the Cheltenham Mission." Gloucester was made a circuit in 1897 with Thomas Randall as its superintendent, who is now spending the days of his retirement in the city with which he has been so closely associated.

NORTHAMPTON.

The beginnings of the Northampton Mission are fully described by Thomas Bateman.

"*June 30th, 1834.*—Having begun to hold missionary meetings and collect money by boxes and books, and having already £20 in hand, as we still retained the missionary spirit and could see no chance of extension about this part of the country, we obtained the services of James Hurd as a missionary, and we sent him away with directions to go into the regions beyond, not only where we as a circuit had not yet gone, but to where none of the Primitive Methodist missionaries had as yet found their way. So he set out, scarcely knowing whither he went. He journeyed as far as Northampton, where he pitched his tent and commenced his labours."

Burland's Northampton Mission was for a long time hard and unproductive soil, and sorely tried the patience and taxed the resources of the distant parent circuit. One would like to know the reason for this. It could not be that Northampton or Kettering was averse from religion and unfriendly to Dissent. In past years Northampton had been favoured with the ministry of such men as Philip Doddridge and Dr. Ryland. It was at Paulerspury, a few miles off, that William Carey was born, and in the river Nen, just beyond Doddridge's chapel, he was publicly baptized. At Kettering, sturdy Andrew Fuller exercised his ministry, and there the Baptist Missionary Society was formed. Perhaps these very facts put us on the track of the explanation sought. Northampton was a stronghold of Dissent, but of a Dissent of a respectable and self-sufficing kind, not likely to take kindly to our modes of evangelism. The ground was pre-occupied and, it may be, impregnated with Calvinism. Whether this was so or not, one thing is clear—our missionaries found the people unimpressionable. Their ministry was not followed by such crowds as had gathered to hear the first missionaries in the neighbouring county of Leicestershire. It was not persecution they had to complain of; but rather of indifference. The people were difficult to get at; hard to move. One special reason for this unpropitious state of things is alleged to have been the doings and disappearance from these parts, of the Revivalists, founded by Richard Winfield. These people once had a strong footing in Northamptonshire, but had died out. Ordinary persons found it difficult to distinguish between the Revivalists and Primitive Methodists. They sang the same hymns, and were much alike in other respects; so the public looked mistrustfully on a body of religionists that might be here to-day and gone to-morrow, and turned aside to communities which could, as they thought, offer them better sureties as to their permanence. All this had to be lived down; and that took time.

The Memoir of John Petty affords ample evidence of the fact that the two years—1842–4—spent by that devoted man on the Northampton Mission were the most distressful period of his life. Though now in the prime of manhood as years go, his health was indifferent, and his strength severely taxed by the long, trying journeys and exposure. Besides this there was a burdened chapel to give him anxiety. This would be Horsemarket Chapel, built in 1840, and rebuilt in 1872. What troubled him most—he was denied his wonted success. Men's hearts seemed cased in mail. The work of conversion flagged. "Never," says he, "did I labour in soil so unfruitful, or see such little good resulting from my labours." He goes to Kettering and buys a penny roll, and walks about till the time of service. He has an uncomfortable night, and next day spends the dinner-hour in the fields. His luncheon is some bread and cheese a kind body had given him; but he comforts himself with the reflection that "the God of Home as well as Foreign Missions is his support and strength." Then he arises and walks forward to Pytchley and visits thirty or forty families. He attends a round of missionary meetings in another circuit. At Daventry the collection is put off to another meeting; while the proceeds of the other three meetings totalled eight

HORSEMARKET CHAPEL (OLD).

shillings and sixpence. However, he philosophically adds: "The company of Brother Wiltshire and the other preachers was profitable and agreeable, and in some measure compensated for the bareness of the places."

In 1852 things had not grown much more promising, as we find J. Barnes writing: "It is well known that Northamptonshire has been and still is, to a great extent, a barren soil for Christianity in the form of Methodism. Primitive Methodism has had to struggle with formidable and various difficulties for many years. . . . Our chapels have been a source of great grief and toil to many of our friends, particularly in Northampton." He reports that "they had just raised their banner in the streets of Towcester" (where we are afraid it has ceased to wave), "that the mission is thirty-two miles from end to end, that they suffer from the lack of local preachers, especially on the Brigstock and Kettering side of the station." In 1866 the General Missionary Committee was asked to take over the Brigstock side. This does not appear to have been done; but, in 1868, the Raunds Branch was taken over as a separate mission, and, in 1875, this became the Wellingborough Circuit. At the long last our Church seems to have got a firm hold of Kettering, and the omens are favourable that this shoe-town will become the head of a sound and progressive station. No sooner had Northampton been granted independence in 1856 than disaster came upon it, caused by the misconduct of a junior travelling preacher who shall be nameless. Much against their will those good men and true, Dennis Kendall and Reuben Barron, had to appeal for assistance—December, 1857,—to the Auxiliary Fund, the appeal stating that two places, 132 members and many hearers had been lost to the station, while many who remained had become unsettled.

Thanks to a succession of faithful and hard-working ministers, and the co-operation of the societies and officials, the breach was in time repaired, and now our Church in Northampton holds a position in striking contrast with that it presented in the first half of its history. 1876 saw the building of Kettering Road Church, which ten years after became the head of Northampton Second. Theophilus Wallis, its first superintendent, was succeeded by George Parkin, B.D., and he, after eleven years of efficient service, by H. J. Pickett, who is still on the ground; thus, for twenty years, Northampton Second has had but three ministers. From feeble beginnings Kettering Road Society has grown into a strong, progressive church, with a large Sabbath School, and one of the best Sunday morning congregations in the Connexion. This church, and Northampton and the district generally, owes much to the Gibbs family. Mr. Gibbs, sen., was among the first-fruits of Primitive Methodism in Northampton. On the testimony of Jesse Ashworth (who was superintendent from 1873 to '78), we learn that not only was Mr. Gibbs a useful class leader but also one of those local preachers who would walk twenty-two miles out, conduct several services, and then walk back, getting home at two or three o'clock on Monday morning. Joseph, his son, prospered in business, joined the Church, and became useful in various departments of denominational service. He was Circuit Steward, Joint Treasurer of the Chapel Aid Fund, Treasurer of the District Orphanage Fund, and one of the Connexional representatives to the Methodist Œcumenical Conference at Washington in 1891. Reverence, love of the beautiful both in nature and art, and beneficence were leading traits in his character. He died March 19th, 1893.

KETTERING ROAD PRIMITIVE METHODIST CHAPEL. (NORTHAMPTON II.)

We give the portrait also of William Gent, a local celebrity of his time. His had been a wonderful conversion; and when made a local preacher in the late 'forties, his force of character, powerful voice, and ready utterance drew crowds to hear him in the open-air. He passed away February 8th, 1882.

MR. G. GIBBS.    MR. J. GIBBS.    MR. WILLIAM GENT.

Besides the two chapels already named we may chronicle the facts that in 1892 St. James' Hall was bought, afterwards the scene of a stiff and memorable education fight; and that in 1899, Harlestone Road Chapel was built under the superintendence of Jabez Bell who, as we shall see, had made his mark on the mission-field.

HARLESTONE ROAD PRIMITIVE METHODIST CHAPEL (NORTHAMPTON I.).

BEDFORD.

The cradle of Primitive Methodism in Bedford was rocked in storm and was all but swamped. It was March, 1834, when Nottingham Circuit Quarterly Meeting resolved to send T. Clements to open a mission in Bedford. He was to go in a month's time, and to be pledged in 1835 "if his way opened." His way did *not* open; for the General Committee deeming him unsuitable, declined to sanction his continuance. Instead of returning to his station as instructed, he remained as the head of a society of "Independent Primitive Methodists." As such he struggled on for a time, and then besought Hull Circuit to receive him and his societies. That circuit, rather imprudently one cannot but think, acceded to the request, and Clements dropped the "Independent" and again became a Primitive Methodist. But he and the colleague assigned him could not agree, and were both removed, and in 1841 Clements' name disappears from the

HASSETT STREET CHAPEL, BEDFORD FIRST CIRCUIT.

stations. That same year Jeremiah Dodsworth was made superintendent of the Bedford Mission, and threw himself into his work with both zeal and prudence. He had need of both, for Clements returned to the scene of his past mischief, drew away a number

BUNYAN'S COTTAGE, ELSTOW.

of his former friends, and did his best to prejudice the minds of the public against our Church and its representatives in Bedford. The Hull Circuit Missionary Report for 1841 has this reference to the troubles of the time: "Bedford Mission continues its onward, its upward course—a subject this that demands our most sincere and fervent thanks to God. In this mission a base and strenuous effort has been made to malign the Connexion, and to ruin the interests of Zion ; but God, even our God, has been at the right hand of our esteemed friends, and hence they have not been greatly moved."

Elstow and Bedford will always be linked in thought with John Bunyan. It is therefore of interest to note that among the places missioned by Mr. Dodsworth was Elstow, and that, for a time, religious services were held in the very cottage where Bunyan first saw the light. In 1844, Bedford had 176 members and Northampton 174 ; in 1853 the figures were—Bedford 217, and Northampton 220 ; so that the curious parallelism between the two towns extends even to the number of their members. In this same year of '53 the Committee reports the station to be gradually acquiring strength and importance ; that, under the successive labours of Messrs. Parrott, Cooper, and their colleagues, it had greatly improved ; that in Bedford there was an excellent chapel with a preacher's house attached, and five chapels in the surrounding villages, all Connexional property; and that eight or ten other places were served with preaching. The mission was made into an independent station in 1857 with 248 members, and in 1897 the circuit was divided, Hassett Street remaining the head of Bedford I., while Cauldwell Street became the head of the Second Circuit with R. N. Wycherley as its superintendent.

PETERBOROUGH.

Peterborough is another of these District borderland towns which had their early Connexional vicissitudes. Its missioning by Lynn, and its formation into a circuit in 1839, have already been mentioned (vol. ii. p. 221). We have the plan of the Circuit for 1847 now before us, which shows thirteen preaching places. One is rather surprised to find Brigstock, first missioned by Northampton in 1842, on this plan as a mission of Peterborough, with Grafton, Sudborough, and Geddington as associated places. Yet this is not so surprising as that Brigstock should, in 1846, be found attached to Fakenham as a mission ; for, after all, Peterborough is partly in Northamptonshire, while Fakenham is in the heart of Norfolk. Such chopping and changing as we have here shows how difficult it was found to work some of the outlying places of this geographical district. We notice among the three-and-twenty locals, all told, having their figures on this plan, that W. Edis is No. 7 and Isaac Edis No. 12. When the latter died in May, 1902, there passed away the representative layman of Peterborough Primitive Methodism, whose life had more than spanned its history in the city and district, and who had largely contributed to make it what it had become. At the time of his death he had been Circuit Steward fifty years, while his first wife was the daughter of Robert Lee, the Circuit Steward of 1847. He had attended seventeen Conferences, filled the offices of Sunday School superintendent, leader, local preacher, and Society Steward. Throughout he had been a lover of Connexional literature and a liberal contributor to its institutions. For a time he was on the Board of Guardians, and a member of the County Council.

MR. ISAAC EDIS.

No wonder his funeral was one of the largest that had taken place for some time in the city, or that the London District should mark its sense of the loss it had sustained, by deputing Henry Carden to attend the funeral as its representative—a minister who, as a former superintendent of both Peterborough and Northampton, could with full knowledge testify to the worth and work of the deceased.

At the Conference of 1853 the Ramsey part of the Peterborough Circuit, with a mere handful of members, was taken over by the General Missionary Committee, and next year Peterborough itself was attached to the mission. So Peterborough temporarily fell out of the list of circuits and parted company with Norwich District. If we inquire into the causes of this decline, we must remember that 1853-4-5 were

PETERBOROUGH NEW ROAD PRIMITIVE METHODIST CHAPEL.

the three lean years of Norwich District's history, as also of the Connexion, judging by the heavy successive decreases of the time. Norwich District's net decrease for the triennium was 1665. The action of the political, economic, and ecclesiastical causes which left their mark on the general numerical returns had full play in the Eastern Counties.* Emigration alone was accountable for the loss of 160 members of the 410 reported as the decrease of the Norwich District for 1853. Disastrous floods were another adverse item not to be left out of the account. "In some parts of the [Norwich] District," says W. Garner, "the long-continued and heavy rains which fell during the winter, produced alarming floods, laid thousands of acres under water, involved the destruction of property to a vast extent, compelled the inhabitants

* For these causes, see *ante* vol. ii. pp. 374-5.

to escape for their lives, broke up preaching-stations, scattered societies, and seriously interrupted the wonted labours of the preachers; heavy losses were the unhappy result."* In the light of these facts it is probably more than a coincidence that by 1854 the membership of Peterborough had been reduced to one hundred, and that it passed into the hands of the General Missionary Committee.

From 1855, under the three years' superintendency of William Freear, the mission began steadily to revive. During the eight years' term of his successor—Jesse Ashworth (1858-66)—much was accomplished for the numerical and material progress of what, in 1862, became again the Peterborough Circuit, standing next to Northampton and Bedford on the stations of London First District. The New Road Church was built in the city, and many country chapels erected. It would be difficult to say how much Peterborough Circuit owes to Jesse Ashworth; for, after his superannuation in 1879, he ultimately settled down at Etton, near the city, and continued to take a deep interest in all that concerned the station. He watched, and assisted in, its development. He also to the very close of his long life of eighty-four years preached and lectured throughout the Connexion, and was welcomed wherever he went. On the day of his interment in the quiet churchyard of Glinton (February 19th, 1904), it was noticed that three local rectors were present, and two of them subsequently in their parish churches drew the attention of their congregations to his life and example. It remains finally to be noted that, like Northampton and Bedford, Peterborough Circuit has been divided. This was done in 1898 when Cobden Street Chapel, built on a site presented by Mr. I. Edis, became the head of the Second Circuit.

* "Address of the Primitive Methodist British Conference to the Societies in Foreign Missions."— *Minutes*, 1853.

CHAPTER V.

THE COLONIAL EXPANSION OF PRIMITIVE METHODISM.

SINCE Professor Seeley wrote his famous book on "The Expansion of England" we have gained a new conception of the course and meaning of English history. He showed that the development of constitutional liberty, culminating in 1688, was followed by a still more remarkable development—the Expansion of England into Greater Britain. The significance of this latter development is lost upon the historians of the old school, so that when they have described the successful struggle for liberty they sink the historian in the mere annalist or chronicler. What they have written of the later stage of our history seems, by contrast, tame and uninteresting. As one reads of the conflicts between King and Parliament, of the rise and downfall of ministries and the rest, one might fancy oneself looking upon the mimetic play of feeble shadows trying to do over again what had already been done long since by the stalwart figures of the past. What is set before us somehow lacks vraisemblance. What is wrong? The historian, Professor Seeley tells us, needs vastly to enlarge his stage, to open a new scene, and bring into the foreground new actors; then there will be no reason to complain that the dramatic movement is lacking in interest.

Now, though we have to work on a much smaller canvas than Professor Seeley, we may take warning and gather some useful hints from his imperial presentation of facts. If there be any danger of our interest flagging as we follow the later history of our Church, that interest should be stimulated anew by seeing that, from 1843 and onwards for sixty years, we were taking our part in that great movement which Professor Seeley felicitously calls the Expansion of England. If one kind of development had ceased, another development on a much wider scale then began. It is only in a general sense that 1843 marked the termination of the Home-missionary period of our Church. But, even admitting that the most romantic and heroic period of our history coincided with the beginnings of the Industrial revolution in England, we have only to lift our eyes to see this period beginning again—in 1843—in the new lands under the Southern Cross or in the vast stretches of Canada, whither our missionaries had followed the tide of emigration. In Great Britain a good work had been done under the peculiar conditions of a very old civilisation: in Canada and Australasia our fathers succeeded in laying the foundations of churches in lands raw in their newness; and they did so under conditions so strange and difficult as to test their physical stamina, their resourcefulness, and their faith. No wonder that many failed; the still greater wonder is that so many remained firm, and did work that abides—work of such a quality as justifies us in regarding them as pioneer missionaries of the first order. It is a thousand pities that the projected History of our Foreign and Colonial Missions has not been written,* for it would certainly have contained chapters quite as romantic as any found in the life of "Peter Cartwright, the Backwoods Preacher," while it would have done justice to such outstanding men as R. Ward, J. Long, J. Sharpe, R. Hartley, M. Clarke, and others whose names will come before us—men who gave proof of higher qualities than those of endurance and courage. The remembrance of these men and their doings is our permanent possession.

True, our Canadian and Australasian churches, with the exception of those of New Zealand, have left us, and some may think the knowledge of this fact enough to discount any interest which might be felt in their founding and development. But this would be to take a very insular and short-sighted view of the matter. The history of our Colonial Missions is no mere parenthesis having no close organic connection with the rest of the narrative. The enthusiasm of the 'forties and 'fifties for Colonial missions was the old missionary passion finding a new outlet and, as we have said, it providentially fitted into that great movement still going on—the expansion of England into Greater Britain. On the forefront then of this chapter, we record the facts that our contribution to the Methodist Church of Canada was 8223 members, and to the Methodist Church of Australasia, 11,683. The Primitive Methodists of the U.S.A. number 6834; while there still remain in New Zealand 2536 members who are in communion with the parent Church, making in the aggregate 29,276, a number of adherents quite sufficient to constitute a respectable denomination, and a number actually in excess of those found combined in the two denominations of the Independent Methodists and Wesleyan Reform Union.

In 1835 the European settlers of Australia, including Tasmania, amounted to 80,000. By 1851 the population had risen to 350,000. The discovery in that year of the gold-fields caused a sudden and enormous rush of immigration from all parts of the world. We have not the emigration statistics for 1851-2; but the returns issued by the Board of Trade show that during the thirty-six years—1853-88—1,324,018 emigrants left British ports for Australasia. Amongst these were many who had been members and adherents of our Church—how many we shall never know. It could not have been otherwise. Our work has largely been amongst the class which is as sensitive to economic and social conditions as the barometer is sensitive to atmospheric changes. Our adherents have been migratory—not from choice but often from grim necessity. The closing of mines and factories, the fluctuations of trade, the decay of home-industries and of the villages—these, and the play of a hundred similar causes, have often made havoc of our societies. Relatively, no denomination has suffered more from "removals" than ours. But it is well to remember that, while emigration (limiting ourselves to that for the present) has often weakened, and sometimes even depleted our societies, and been responsible for much Connexional leakage, it has yet worked out a counterbalancing advantage. "They that were scattered abroad" became

* The reference is to the Resolution of the Conference of 1892. "That as it will be the Jubilee of the formation of our Missionary Society next year, we deem it desirable that a history of our missionary work be written, and we request the Revs. John Atkinson and James Travis to undertake the work."

the cause and occasion of our Colonial Missions. It was by a process of natural expansion our Colonial Missions were established. It was so in the United States of America, and in Canada. It was so also in Australia, as we must now briefly try to show.

Among the early settlers in South Australia (Adelaide) were several who had been adherents of Primitive Methodist societies in various parts of the fatherland. These drew together and, on July 26th, 1840, they held an open-air service in the streets of Adelaide, and the same evening met for worship in the house of Mr. Wiltshire, and organized themselves into a society. From this time church-life proceeded on the lines they had been accustomed to in the old country. Mr. Bullock "from Yorkshire" gave them a site of land for a small chapel, which was opened October, 1840. The society held a Quarterly Meeting in March, 1841, when it was found there were 16 members, 7 local preachers, and 22 Sunday School scholars. Thus there was a Primitive Methodist church "in being" at the Antipodes as early as 1840, though it was some years before it found official recognition in the *Minutes* of Conference. The home-circuits of Darlaston and Oswestry, to which two of the leading-spirits of the Adelaide society had belonged, were urgently requested to send out a missionary. But the responsibility was too heavy for even these enterprising circuits to undertake. Rather did it seem that so weighty a business should be carried through by the Connexion as a whole; and the matter came under consideration at the Conference of 1842. During the delay, and while discussion as to ways and means was going on, the Bottesford Circuit threw out the happy suggestion that the mission should be sustained by the Sunday School children of the societies throughout the Connexion. But though the suggestion was enthusiastically taken up and the required means soon forthcoming, there was still further delay, this time caused by the difficulty of securing right men for the work. During this pause the famous missionary meeting was held at Old Cramlington, which enlarged the scope and field of the contemplated mission by the inclusion of New Zealand. It is evident that Robert Ward had originally been designated for Australia, but now his destination was changed for New Zealand; while Joseph Long of Darlington Circuit and John Wilson of Ipswich Circuit were designated for Australia. After unaccountable delay, Mr. Long and his colleague sailed June 12th, 1844, six weeks after Mr. Ward, and after four months' voyage arrived safely at Port Adelaide. So there quietly slipped on to the stations of 1845, the lines:—

New Plymouth,
New Zealand.
R. WARD.
South Australia.
J. LONG.
J. WILSON.

There the lines stand at the end of the Home Missions, undistinguished by any prominence or peculiarity of type or display, as though nobody was aware of their significance. What concerns us now to note, however, is the fact that when the two missionaries landed at Port Adelaide it was as the ministers of a church which had been in existence and at work four years and three months!

THE PERIOD OF CONSOLIDATION AND CHURCH DEVELOPMENT. 427

What was primarily and markedly true of South Australia was also true without exception of all the Australian colonies. Adelaide may stand as the type of the way in which Primitive Methodist societies were first established and extended in the Colonies. So it was in New South Wales, the premier colony of Australia. Certain persons resident in Sydney forwarded to Adelaide, 1200 miles off, an urgent request for a missionary. In response to this request, J. Wilson went to Sydney in the spring of 1847. In this one case, however, the principle of a church before a minister did not work well. A false start was made with consequences that a little preliminary sifting and disciplining might have obviated. "The men who had taken the lead in sending for a missionary proved to be of questionable character, and their reputation reflected no credit upon the infant cause."* The bright prospects at Sydney, and at Morpeth, a hundred miles away, were soon obscured. Mr. Wilson succumbed to the difficulties he met with at Morpeth and withdrew; while E. Tear, who had been sent out from England, struggled along with a faithful remnant to build a small chapel at Sydney, opened in 1849. In 1854, when J. Sharpe arrived from England, there was but one mission in New South Wales with 116 members.

JOSEPH LONG.

PRIMITIVE METHODIST CHAPEL, HOBART TOWN, (1861).

The founding of our Church in Victoria was in its circumstances almost a replica of that of Adelaide. A group of recently-arrived immigrants formed themselves into a class on January 21st, 1849, and held an open-air service on Flag-staff Hill. Already an urgent request had been sent to England for a missionary; the foundation-stone of a small chapel in La Trobe Street had been laid, and a Quarterly Meeting, held December, 1849, had drawn up a statement of the society's position and prospects for transmission to London. But even while they were doing it, John Ride, the veteran missionary, was far on his outward voyage, arriving at Port Philip, January 17th, 1850. The wisdom of this appointment may well be questioned. Primitive Methodism never had a more laborious or capable missionary than John Ride, but he was now fifty-five years of age. Failing health soon necessitated his superannuation, and Michael Clarke stepped into the place he vacated. At this time there were in the Colony of Victoria two stations—Melbourne and Geelong with 133 members.

Turning now to Tasmania we meet with the same interesting

E. C. PRITCHARD.

* Petty's *History*, p. 484.

class of facts. In the 'fifties, among the immigrants who settled in the north and north-east of the island, were many hailing from East Anglia, including as a matter of course some who had been members and local preachers. These held a camp meeting on a hill now forming part of Launceston, November 28th, 1858, at which the Rev. J. Lindsay, a Presbyterian minister, took a prominent part. The little band—twelve in number—formed themselves into a class, and sent £60 as their contribution towards meeting the expense of sending a missionary. In 1858, J. Langham arrived as the first missionary, and he was soon followed by J. A. Foggon and E. C. Pritchard. The latter—still happily surviving in the home-land—was the pioneer of our Church to Hobart Town, the capital of the island. Its first chapel, still in use, was bought from a branch of the Presbyterians in 1861. It was in this chapel Dr. Paton and his companions were first welcomed in the Southern world as missionaries, Mr. Pritchard being present and taking part in that service.

Lastly, we have Queensland, the youngest Australian Colony, which affords another instance of a people "prepared of the Lord" asking and waiting for a missionary, but not waiting with folded arms. W. Colley, a native of Strensall near York, was in 1860, our pioneer missionary in Queensland. The first chapel in the colony was that of Fortitude Valley, a suburb of Brisbane, built on a site of land given by James Graham who, years before, had proposed in his heart that if ever a preacher should come to this part of the country this spot should be given to the people of his early choice.* In 1863, J. Buckle was appointed to Brisbane and Robert Hartley to Rockhampton, and each did splendid work in establishing and extending our denominational interests in their respective centres. It shows that big maps are indispensable where Australian matters are in question when we find Mr. Buckle telling us that, when in Brisbane in 1866, his nearest colleague in Rockhampton was separated from him a distance of 441 miles by the overland route, or 550 by sea—a distance as great as that between London and Edinburgh.†

COLONIAL MISSIONS IN THE PROVIDENTIAL ORDER.

We have preferred a high claim for Primitive Methodism in its first period—that it did much to prevent a national revolution and greatly helped to pave the way for peaceful reform. Now the claim is made that by its Colonial Missions, which were a marked feature of its second period, our Church, along with others, rendered a national service. By its pioneer work amongst the pioneers of the new lands it helped to "prepare the way of the Lord," and assisted in laying the foundations of our Colonial Empire in righteousness. It is not claimed that our Church did all that it might have done in this behalf, but it was early in the field, toiled hard in its preventive and constructive work; nor, as the facts already given show, did it toil in vain.

One has only to ask: "What would have been the result for Greater Britain and the world if, when the tide of immigration was rolling in on the new lands with such volume in the 'forties and 'fifties, all the Churches at home had with one consent taken

* *Primitive Methodist Magazine*, 1861, p. 119.
† *New South Wales Primitive Methodist Messenger*, April, 1862.

up a waiting attitude and said, 'Let us go on for a time as we have been going on, and look after our home-population. When the rush is over, and the gold-fever has abated, and the settlements and the cities have got a little age upon them,—*then* we will send missionaries with the Gospel, and take possession of these new lands in the name of Christ.'" Why *then* it would have been too late. The tares the devil had industriously sown while the Churches were sleeping would have been coming up vigorously. The mischief would have been done. It would have been like applying salt to flesh too long exposed to the sun. It is a truism that when men lose touch with Christian civilisation—take a plunge into an unaccustomed medium—they are in danger of throwing off much that Christian civilisation has given them. Whether it be at Californian diggings or Australian gold-fields, at "Roaring Camp" or Burra Burra or Ballarat, in the backwoods of Canada or the Bush of Australia, it is the easiest thing in the world for character to deteriorate. There is a tendency to revert to primitive rudeness. Religion with its sweet and regular observances is never more needed than it is under such conditions of life. As well might the dweller amid malarial swamps forget to bring, or throw away, his Peruvian bark. Human nature being what it is, the pressing duty of the Home Churches at the time we have reached was to prevent the deterioration and lapse of Englishmen who had gone beyond the seas. Beyond that, it was to insure that religion should be incorporate with the embryonic life of states and nations yet to be, so that religion might grow with their growth and become strong in their strength.

The Colonial Missions were much in the thought of Primitive Methodists forty and fifty years ago. The *Magazine* and Missionary Notices of the time give much space to intelligence from the various fields as to the arrival of missionaries, the establishment of societies, the building of chapels, etc. It is not necessary for us even to epitomise all this. These items were the chronicles of a day. But in these communications we occasionally meet with matter of deeper import. Some of the more thoughtful of the missionaries write as though they would fain supply those "bigger maps" we have spoken of, and help their readers to study them through colonial eyes. They set themselves to remove misconceptions and prejudices, and to make it clear how great are the differences between evangelistic work in Canada, Australia, and New Zealand, and the same work as carried on in the old country. They emphasise the special difficulties the colonial evangelist is everywhere confronted with. Thus, level-headed Michael Clarke once and again reminds his compatriots in the old land of these difficulties, and makes them the basis of a claim upon their sympathy and patience.

"Here we are, in a foreign land, with its often debilitating climate, interminable forests, scattered and migratory population, partly indicated and half-formed roads, pursuing our work isolated, and frequently discouraged by the delirious excitement of gold-getting, the inordinate habits of speculation, enterprise, and extortion, drunkenness, the hydra-headed monster-crime of this country, antagonistic to the spread of the Gospel."—(*Magazine*, 1859, p. 567).

At times the missionary speaks out still more plainly concerning the rapid deterioration of character which sets in—for which the "fell lust of gold" is mainly responsible.

As one reads it becomes clear that the good men who founded the societies in Adelaide, Melbourne, and the other chief cities of Australia were after all but a faithful "remnant," the mere salvage from the crowd of professedly Christian emigrants.

"There are many, we fear, who forget to bring their religion on board with them; many more who throw it overboard before they reach the shores of Australia; and more still who on reaching these shores, become swamped in the morass of its engrossing worldliness."—(W. Calvert in *Magazine*, 1855, p. 369).

"Many of our members of course are noble exceptions to this worldliness; but some (I speak it with the deepest sorrow) prefer going into neighbourhoods where the means of grace can never reach them; far away into the bush, and all for the sake of a little gain which often turns out to be no gain at all, but a serious temporal loss, and of course invariably a spiritual one."*

One concrete case is better than any number of generalised statements. One out of many such we give, from the experience of a missionary who rode out from Bathurst to see for himself what the moral and spiritual condition of the people was like. "I stopped," he writes, "another down-the-river man. 'It's no use,' said he, 'for you to take any trouble with us old hands; we're hardened. It's three-and-twenty years since I spoke to one of your sort, and it's no use deceiving you—I don't believe I have a soul; *it's dead and done with.*'"—(*Magazine*, 1858, p. 291).

No more witnesses need be cited to prove how urgent was the need fifty years ago for pushing forward the Australian Missions. The more far-seeing were chiefly moved by the reflection that men "whose souls were precious in Christ's sight" were in danger of losing the very faculty for religion, as though their souls were "dead and done with." Men whose souls were dead within them would have made but sorry empire-builders. The appeal was taken up and pressed home by the authorities—notably by the Editor. A stirring article from his pen appeared in the *Magazine* for 1855 under the title,—"Great Want of more Missionaries for our Canadian and Australian Missions; an Appeal to Preachers, Missionary Collectors, and the Friends of our Missions." To Mr. Petty, next to the demands of the work at home, the duty of the hour was to strengthen and extend the Missions in the Colonies. "Shall we," he asked, "as a section of the Church neglect our duty to our blessed Saviour, and to our brethren and countrymen who have emigrated to Canada and Australia, and who loudly call for sympathy and assistance?" He speaks of the Connexion's "manifest duties to our Colonies abroad." "We have not at present," he goes on to say, "the means of engaging in a mission to the heathen, but we have abundant means of engaging largely in Colonial as well as in Home and City and Town Missions. . . . Oh, that we may *know our mission*, listen devoutly to the calls of Providence, and enter fully those fields of usefulness to which we are invited."

The facts and appeals published in our denominational serials were not without effect. A group of Newcastle officials, whose names have come before us, jointly contributed £25. That may now appear a trifling sum but, in forwarding the amount to the Treasurer, George Charlton wrote words which showed that he and his friends

* "Thoughts on the Difficulties of the Missionary Work in Australia," by an Australian Missionary.—(*Magazine*, 1862, p. 569).

had got the true perspective: "The importance of the Australian Colonies at this crisis cannot be over-rated. The future stability, progress, and religious character of that important country depend to a great extent on the efforts of this generation." These are weighty words, and doubtless they were needed at the time; for, in the 'fifties and early 'sixties, there were those who almost resented the fact that we had no "Foreign" Missions in the true acceptation of that term. They chafed under the postponement of missions to the heathen while attending to the wants of the colonists who, it was hinted, ought by this time to be well able to look after themselves. These opponents or lukewarm supporters of the current Missionary policy needed to have brought home to them the significance—in view of the future—of the work that was being done. We, too, as we look at the matter historically, may well ponder George Charlton's words. The "this generation" he spoke of has passed; but its "efforts" were not in vain. Those efforts were timed by Providence and fitted into the providential order. To us who occupy the vantage-ground of a new century the marvellous advance of our Colonies is a most impressive fact. In view of that advance, which is bound to go on beyond any limit we can set, who can fail to see that what was done for the Colonies in the middle period of our history was wise husbandry? If that were a waste of time and effort, then is the sower who goes forth to sow foolishly spendthrift of both. What was done was done for God and for God's redeemed world, and whether the results be surnamed after us or not is a matter of infinitely small moment.

PROGRESS OF THE AUSTRALIAN DISTRICTS UNTIL THEIR SEPARATION.

We will briefly glance at the progress of the Australian Missions, taking them in the order of their formation. Joseph Long, our pioneer missionary in South Australia, remained at Adelaide until the early part of 1850, when he removed to New Zealand, in which new colony we shall soon see him also doing excellent pioneer service. At this time there were two mission stations in South Australia—Adelaide and Mount Barker, with 143 and 90 members respectively. W. Whitefield arrived from England in December, 1851, for the purpose of superintending the new mission at Kooringa, about one hundred miles from Adelaide, where were the famous Burra Burra copper-mines. He had no sooner begun his labours in this apparently promising district than the gold-fever broke out; and when gold holds out its lure it is not copper that is going to keep men back. So the Burra was forsaken and the mines closed for want of men to work them. Even Adelaide was "almost deserted by its able-bodied male population, and its recently flourishing settlements were reduced to a comparative wilderness."* The missionary in charge thought it his duty to follow the greater part of his flock to the diggings, and Mr. Whitefield repaired to Adelaide to look after the enfeebled societies left without a pastor. For this service he received the thanks of the Home Committee.

A good deal of wastage went on amongst the pioneer preachers of all the Colonies—of Adelaide amongst the rest. There were occasional withdrawals, early superannuations through physical breakdown, invalidings home, etc. Nor is this at all

* Conference Address, 1853.

to be wondered at. For one thing, the untamed wildness of the country and the material conditions under which the preacher had to pursue his labours made heavy demands upon his strength and endurance. The journeys were often long and arduous and, leaving bushrangers out of the reckoning—not unfrequently attended by mischances more or less serious. Of E. Tear, who came to New South Wales in 1847 and was transferred to Mount Barker in 1852, we are told that in riding through the bush from an appointment he struck against a tree and was thrown to the ground, where he lay stunned for a time. Some while later, a damp bed in which he passed the night did him still greater physical mischief, and in 1858 he was compelled to seek superannuation. William Whitefield has been already named. His health failed, and he too retired from the active ministry in 1861. His death was hastened (1871) by falling into a deep "creek" in returning from fulfilling an appointment in the Willunga Circuit. Such incidents were by no means uncommon in the early days, and must not be left out of the picture of pioneering in the Colonies.

During the 'fifties the slender staff of missionaries in South Australia was reinforced by various brethren sent out from England, who had done good service there previous to their selection. J. D. Whittaker and H. Cole arrived in '54; J. G. Wright in '55; John Standrin in '57, and Joseph Warner and Thomas Braithwaite in '59. The first-named laboured in South Australia until 1861 when, on account of his health, he removed to Wellington, New Zealand, dying there in 1862. H. Cole laboured in South Australia until 1874, in which year he was transferred to Victoria. On his death in 1890 it was said: "Our present standing at North Adelaide is very much due to the zeal and faithful labours of H. Cole." J. G. Wright's active ministry lasted forty-seven years, and it is said he had an increase on every station he travelled. John Standrin we have met with before—as a convert at Ashton-under-Lyne and the leader in a great revival at Knowlwood.* Thomas Braithwaite affords another example of the wear and tear of a colonial missionary's life. After eleven years he was invalided home and died at Richmond (Yorks) in 1872. Of all the names we have mentioned that of Joseph Warner will be most familiar to British Primitive Methodists, and it is a name deservedly held in high esteem by all who were privileged to know the sterling qualities of the man. For nearly sixteen years Mr. Warner did yeoman service in South Australia, and then returned to this country, where his wide experience and sober judgment of Colonial affairs were ever at the service of the Home authorities. Mr. Warner finished, as he had begun, his ministry at St. Austell in 1893, and died in 1900. One who knew him well wrote: "Had he been favoured with more robust health, a touch of brilliance and a dash of pushfulness, he would easily have reached a position in the front rank of our Connexional life."† Even as it was, despite these minus quantities, the more discerning could easily recognise in Joseph Warner "a still, strong man, . . . who could rule and dare not lie."

From 1857 the mission stations in South Australia made steady advance. In that year the three missions already named were constituted circuits and formed into the

---

* See vol. ii, p. 46.
† Rev. W. Sawyer, quoted in *Aldersgate Magazine*, 1901.

Adelaide District. New men came to the front—capable men like J. Stuart Wayland, James H. Williams, John Goodwin, Henry J. Pope, W. Diment,* and others of whose character and work we might speak more fully did space permit. But to us in this hemisphere Adelaide has a special interest as having been the scene of the labours of a succession of gifted ministers. John Watson (afterwards Dr. Watson) left Aliwal North for Adelaide in 1884, and returned to England in 1889. Hugh Gilmore took charge of Wellington Square Church in 1889, until his lamented death in October, 1891. He was succeeded by John Day Thompson in 1892-7. Thus, for thirteen years, a trio of ministers of marked individuality fulfilled their ministry in the progressive city of Adelaide. They were very variously gifted. Dr. Watson was pre-eminently a theologian rather than an ecclesiastic; broad-minded, but thoroughly evangelical in sentiment. Hugh Gilmore was no trained theologian, still less a scholastic or typical Churchman, but he was, above all, a convinced Christian democrat with the gifts, fervour, and calling of a poet-prophet. J. Day Thompson—the bold thinker, the sworn foe of traditionalism, possessed to the finger-tips with the scientific spirit, and yet, with all this, as in the case of Dr. R. F. Horton—whom in many respects he so closely resembles—the spiritual, mystic side of his nature will not be repressed but successfully asserts its rights. It was a rare succession of men, and when, after J. D. Thompson's return to England, Brian Wibberley entered upon it, the succession becomes yet more striking.† We do not say a deliberate attempt was made to found "a select preachership" beyond the seas; to try the experiment whether the Primitive Methodism of the old land would not be found even better adapted to the progressive lands under the Southern Cross. All the same, we see now an experiment *was* being made. Now, for the success of an experiment, much will depend upon the conditions under which it is tried. In England, under the shadow of the dominant Church, a thinker or leader of the people is heavily handicapped. By the spirit of caste society is sectionalized as though divided into water-tight compartments. We can only reach our own little world. Time is consumed and temper ruffled in fighting for the veriest elementary principles. In Australia they *have* religious liberty, and a Christian leader has no need to have his credentials *visé* by Society or the Church before men will listen and follow. Two of the "select preachers" we have referred to are with us to-day. But Hugh Gilmore is gone; and we may very properly ask— What was the result of the experiment in his case? We have called him a Christian Democrat. Is such a title incongruous as applied to a Primitive Methodist minister? By no means. We firmly believe that Primitive Methodism is much more democratic than its polity. At its core—in its true inwardness—it is in deepest sympathy with Christian Democracy, and what is now largely implicit will, by a process of immanent

MR. J. DAY THOMPSON.

---

* "The large and beautiful church in Tynte Street, which is the pride of our people, was built under his superintendence [in North Adelaide]."—Official Memoir of W. Diment, *Conference Minutes*, 1892.

† Brian Wibberley was a pupil of the writer, and went out to Australia in 1886. Besides his ministerial gifts he has won for himself considerable reputation as a musical composer.

logic, show itself explicitly, as it is increasingly showing itself, in movements and institutions. If any man we have had may be regarded as the representative and exponent of Christian Democracy, it is Hugh Gilmore. In that remarkable and intensely interesting series of papers published in the 'eighties, entitled "Spiritual Revealings,"* he wrote: "Now I began to question with myself whether this [the ecstatic mind, and consequent indifference to the common concerns of the daily life] was being religious, and I was compelled to acknowledge that the teaching of our Lord and his apostles clearly show that not in isolation and meditation do we serve God, *but in the service of man*. This was the ground to which I attained years ago, and where I must stand; which I still believe to be the ground of spiritual and rational

WELLINGTON SQUARE CHURCH, NORTH ADELAIDE.

Christianity." Such being Gilmore's convictions, what was the influence of his ministry in Adelaide during the brief period allowed him by Providence in which to work? For the answer we fall back upon the testimony of others competent to give an opinion. Dr. Watson in his funeral sermon for H. Gilmore refers to the features of his ministry in Wellington Square; and his biographer and old friend, Ebenezer Hall, speaks of the larger ministry which made him a power in Adelaide and far beyond:—

"The North Adelaide Church, now that a gallery has been put into it [by Gilmore] is commodious and splendidly situated, and the people were prepared to give their

* These ought, by all means, to be republished along with a new edition of the Twenty-two Sermons stenographically reported, and published after his death.

confidence to a true man. His congregations were overflowing from the first. Artisans, professional men, statesmen, crowded his ministry; Agnostics and Socialists, who had not darkened a church-door for years, sat alongside of men of different creeds. Each man felt that there was a preacher who had a message for them. The pulpit was the great power he wielded, but, as in England, his energies ran out in various directions. All the Churches laid his services under contribution for special occasions, and crowds came whatever church he was in. He was literally always at work. He was an enthusiast in the advocacy of Land Nationalisation; then he became an ardent worker in the Single Tax Crusade. Not only did he preside at Mr. Henry George's own meetings; he strove with all his might to spread his economic doctrine by personal persuasion and by lectures, speeches, and classes. For a time he edited the *Pioneer*, the Single Tax organ, and wrote much for its columns, he was also President of the League. The celebrated Sir George Grey presided at one of his lectures, and was so much impressed that at the close he paid the highest tribute that one man can pay another. He said: 'I have never heard an address so eloquent, arguments so cogent, or seen an audience so moved.' Another chairman said he was the 'finest speaker in Australia.' In a strike of dockmen and sailors, Gilmore stood out boldly for the men. So popular was he that if he stole into a meeting to enjoy it unobserved, some one was sure to recognise him, and then clamorous shouts would be raised of 'Gilmore! Gilmore!' till he was obliged to come to the front. The Irish, who were delighted with his advocacy of their cause, reverenced him, and doffed their bonnets as he passed. Once a week he conducted a class of young men for the study of Christian Sociology, and on another evening he had a class for business men. One of the chief, and certainly one of the most practical of all his schemes was the organisation and working out of 'The Commonwealth.' The city was mapped out into districts, and bands of men and women (not concerning himself as to who or what they were, only they must be followers of Christ, and willing to serve men), went from house to house to seek and save the lost. The struggling poor were assisted, waifs and strays were picked up, the drunkard reclaimed, new arrivals in the colony looked after, men and women out of employment assisted to get work. Bands of Hope and Temperance propaganda were carried on vigorously, Free Libraries established to bring healthy literature to the people, and bands of ladies, or rather, sisters of the people, were to minister to the sick in their homes. Reports were to be brought in regularly and discussed. This Christ-like programme was a sign and proof of the one consuming passion of his life—to save men; becoming 'all things to all men that he might save some.' If he was first to organise, he was also first to work."

The "experiment" must be pronounced to have been a success, and an object-lesson as to the possibilities of Primitive Methodism in the direction of social service; an object-lesson similar in character to those supplied in the Home-land at Clapton, Whitechapel, Southwark, and elsewhere, which also owed their origin to personal initiative—to the Christ-enkindled enthusiasm of humanity. But all this time Gilmore's work was nearing its completion. Insidious disease was undermining the citadel of life. We draw the veil over the last pathetic scene, only lifting it a moment to see how the whole city was moved by his loss. When the day came for his remains to be interred in the cemetery at Payneham, where so many of his co-religionists lie, a vast crowd assembled to pay the tribute of respect to his memory. It was felt that Adelaide and the colony had lost one of its best and greatest men.

The progress made by New South Wales was less rapid and at first more interrupted than in the other Colonies. One proof of this we have in the various administrative changes made by the Home authorities. In 1857 Sydney was made a circuit and, being the only one in the Colony, it was attached to the Melbourne District. One thinks bigger maps were wanting when this arrangement was made, as the Sydney delegate would have to travel 1200 miles to attend his District Meeting. In 1859 the two New South Wales circuits were constituted the Sydney District, while the Missions in the Colony continued to be managed by the Home executive. In 1865 *all* the stations of the Colony reverted to the old footing of Missions, and such was their status until 1870, when important changes were made. As these changes affected all the Australasian stations they had better be summarised here once for all. The Conference of 1870, then, resolved: "That the Australasian Circuits and Missions shall be united and formed into three Districts.

THEOPHILUS PARR, M.A. The Victorian District shall consist of the circuits and missions in that Colony and Tasmania. The South Australian District shall consist of the stations in South Australia and Queensland. And the New South Wales District shall consist of the stations in that Colony and in New Zealand." At the very next Conference, however, it was found necessary very considerably to modify these arrangements. New Zealand appealed against being administratively joined to New South Wales. Nor can we wonder at this unwillingness when we remember that Sydney is some 1130 miles distant from Auckland. Hence it was decided that after the Conference of 1872 the New Zealand stations should be constituted a separate District; also that those in Queensland should at once be attached to New South Wales. But this union lasted only until 1873, when Brisbane became the head of a new District. The partition of Brisbane in 1889 gave Queensland a second district in Rockhampton. The same year Sydney District was divided, and for some years Newcastle stood as the head of a District. Theophilus Parr, M.A., who like Dr. Watson had done good service in the African mission-field, went out in 1890 to take charge of Newcastle, and after spending some ten years in New South Wales resumed his place in the Home ministry. Matthew Reavley and William Atkinson were also amongst those who about this time reinforced the ministerial staff in New South Wales. A few words may be added as to the numerical progress of the denomination in New South Wales. In 1871 the Sydney District had 815 members; whereas, in 1901, when it last stood on the stations, the number reported was 2036. In 1897, when the Brisbane and Rockhampton Districts parted company with the British Conference, the reported membership was 2120. From this it will be seen that Primitive Methodism had made encouraging progress in Queensland, the youngest of the Colonies.

The coming of John Sharpe to New South Wales in 1854 has already been mentioned. He spent twenty years of the best part of his life in the Colonies, returning to England in 1874. Fifteen out of this score of years were spent in Sydney and its immediate neighbourhood. John Sharpe is a figure that ought to receive more than casual mention in any History of Primitive Methodism. He was no ordinary man in whatever light we view him. This impression is strongly confirmed by a close inspection of the neatly-arranged documents and letters he has left, setting forth his relations to New South Wales Primitive Methodism and the Home authorities. Thoroughly conscientious, his course was always straightforward, like a Roman road. "Upright and Forthright" might have been his chosen motto. He had a vigorous mind and strong will; yet, though firm, he was unassuming and courteous. He was a great reader, and well versed in Ecclesiastical History, especially in all the points at issue between Romanism and Protestantism—a very serviceable mental equipment for a Christian teacher set down in Sydney forty years ago. Nor was he indisposed to enter the controversial lists, seeking truth rather than victory. Under the *nom-de-guerre* of John Search—a name that Thomas Binney had already made famous—he wrote several series of articles in the *Protestant Standard* on such subjects as "Mariolatry," "Readings in Romanism," "Popery in Ritualism," etc. In these articles we do not find much of that rhetorical invective so frequently indulged in by some controversialists. The writer goes to the original authorities for his facts, and finds in them the material for his arguments which he knows how to drive home with force. If these articles were collected and published even after this long lapse of time they would still have their distinctive value, and would make a volume of fair size. For some years Mr. Sharpe edited the "New South Wales Primitive Methodist Messenger," and some of the characteristic qualities of the man are revealed in the sermons, selections from books, comments on current topics, and reviews contributed by him to that periodical. Amongst the last-named, the notice he wrote in 1866 of Bastow's "Biblical Dictionary" may be singled out as a good specimen of his acumen and fair-mindedness. In these respects it compares very favourably with the official review of five closely-printed pages which appeared in the denominational *Magazine* for 1862. In the preparation of this notice the Editor had been assisted by several brethren whose names are not given. The task of examining the Dictionary had been put in commission. The standard to which the critics appeal and by which Mr. Bastow was found wanting was Adam Clarke's "Commentary" and Watson's "Institutes." Referring to this, Mr. Sharpe says: "We thought then and we think still, that this was rich—rich indeed. And we were led to wonder if Mr. B.'s critics had never heard that both Drs. Clarke and Watson had themselves been charged with heresy." All this may appear very trivial now, for there is nothing staler than the controversies of bygone years. It is referred to here because John Sharpe's review is an Antipodean side-light on a little-known episode in the literary history of the denomination. Bastow's "Biblical Dictionary" was the most considerable and scholarly contribution as yet given to the world by the denomination, and ought not to be forgotten. As to John Sharpe, though he was not "tainted with German Neology," as the phrase went, he was clear-sighted and broad-minded, as the following additional extract from his review will show :—

JOHN SHARPE.

"We are free to admit that Mr. Bastow advances some few things which do not square with our views; but what then? Does it necessarily follow that, fully as

438   PRIMITIVE METHODIST CHURCH.

we may be persuaded of the correctness of our opinions, and firmly as we may hold them, that we are infallible—and the error is wholly on Mr. Bastow's side, and that therefore we must brand him as heretic and his book as dangerous? Let us rather hope that additional reading and meditation may bring fuller and clearer light to all concerned, modifying their views and drawing them closer to the one grand centre of all truth. We have very little faith in those who appear

SOME PORTRAITS OF DECEASED AUSTRALIAN MINISTERS.

(1) Rev. W. Gould, died 1902; (2) Rev. H. Cole, died 1891; (3) Rev. G. Grey, died 1902; (4) Rev. J. Langham, died 1883; (5) Rev. R. Allen, died 1899; (6) Rev. G. Watts, died 1899; (7) Mrs. Watts, a devoted minister's wife and lady preacher, died 1899; (8) Rev. M. Clarke, died 1892; (9) Rev. J. Smith, died 1901; (10) Rev. G. Hall, died 1871; (11) Rev. F. Sinden, died 1897; (12) Rev. W. J. Bray, died 1897.

to think that to them is given a full and unlimited commission to hunt out and to hound down what they consider heresy. We have no sympathy with them; we feel no interest in their work. If the class may be judged of from the few we have known, it surely does contain some strange and some very unlovely specimens of human nature."*

Like Mr. Flesher in Hull, John Sharpe in Sydney was called upon to vindicate Primitive Methodism through the press. A minister who had once done good work in England was now pursuing a divisive policy; and the public mind had to be disabused. So his pen was kept busy. Finally, we may say of John Sharpe that there was scarcely any official position he was not qualified to fill; but the position of Editor was that for which his bookishness, his practised pen, and his mental tastes peculiarly fitted him. Yet on his return home, save that he made a distinct impression on the Conference of 1876, no special Connexional recognition awaited him. The prime of his life had been given to Australia, and his strength was not now what it had been. He travelled a few years longer, and then came superannuation (1890), and death (1895), quickly following on that of his faithful wife. That fine poem, "Under one Roof," is the poignant expression of this double loss.†

REV. H. HEATHERSHAW.

We can only mention and must not linger over the names of other men who gave lengthened service to New South Wales and Queensland—names such as J. F. Foggon; Bernard Kenny, the fervid Irishman, who wherever he happened to be—in Scotland, Ireland, or Australia, was always the inveterate foe of Popery; George James, one of the prime movers in the movement which resulted in Methodist Union; W. Sparling, the first Primitive Methodist minister who died in New South Wales;

BOOK-ROOM, LYGON STREET, MELBOURNE.

and W. Kingdon. For Queensland, J. Buckle, who prior to his sailing for Australia did good work in Scotland, and Robert Hartley must not be forgotten. The influence of the latter, especially in Rockhampton, was profound and has been lasting. Among the papers of John Sharpe are preserved many intimate letters of Mr. Hartley, which show the transparency of his character, the close friendship existing between the two men, and their anxious toil for the churches under their care.

In Victoria and Tasmania Primitive Methodism was more prosperous than in some of the other Colonies. From the statistics of the Melbourne District, given for the last time in

REV. W. HUNT.

* Mr. Bastow was our Erasmus, and Erasmus was no martyr but died in his bed. The critique in the *Magazine* of '62 closed with the statement: "We have received from the author of the Bible Dictionary the most frank assurance that 'anything unsound, or against the vital doctrines of John Wesley and the Church of England, I shall be happy to alter, nay I shall think it a duty and privilege to do so.'"

† *Aldersgate*, 1900, p. 859. In any Primitive Methodist Anthology this poem would deservedly take a foremost place.

the *Conference Minutes* of 1901, we find it then reported 27 Ministers and 10 Home Missionaries, 125 chapels and 1306 members. We give the portraits of some of the deceased ministers of the Melbourne District, and would also make mention of Henry Heathershaw and Thomas Copeland, who have filled the office of Book Steward (Lygon Street, Melbourne), and other positions of trust. Our historic survey of Primitive Methodism in Australia may very fittingly close with a reference to William Hunt, who attended the British Conference of 1899 as the representative of the Australian Districts in the settlement of the financial questions connected with the proposed Union of the Methodist Churches. The ability and courtesy shown by Mr. Hunt in the conduct of these delicate negotiations were recognised by a special resolution of the Conference.

New Zealand.

The history of Primitive Methodism in New Zealand readily lends itself to summarisation. In 1870, after a quarter of a century's labours, there were but three stations in the Colony, all of them in the North Island, though situated at widely separated points and in different Provinces. The earliest of these was at New Plymouth, in the South-west of the Island, in the provincial district of Taranaka; the second at Wellington, in the district of the same name; and the third in the North, at Auckland, which, until 1864, was the seat of government. With the early history of these three stations the name of Robert Ward is closely linked, and next to his the names of Joseph Long and Henry Green. The apparently slow progress made in the Colony by the denomination during the first twenty-five years (in 1870 there were 396 members all told) was but the reflex of the state of the Colony during the same period arising out of the gold-discoveries and their resultant fluctuations of population and trade, and the unsettledness and disorganization caused by the Maori wars. These events reacted on the policy of the Missionary executive at Home, which, so far as New Zealand was concerned, was timid and unaggressive. But when in 1873 the first District Meeting was held in New Zealand as already mentioned, a more prosperous era had begun as well for Primitive Methodism as the Colony. No doubt Mr. Ward's visit to England in 1871 largely contributed to the inauguration of that more forward policy on the part of the executive which may be dated from this time. The fruit of this was seen at the first District Meeting, when three new stations in the South Island were represented, as well as the three old ones in the North Island. These were Christchurch, in the province of Canterbury, and Invercargill and Dunedin, in Otago—all chief towns admirably situated, in view of the prospective development of the Colony, and likely to afford good strategical bases for Connexional extension. Mr. Ward was the first minister stationed at Christchurch, and he was the president of the first New Zealand District Meeting; so that his pioneer efforts did not stop short with the North Island or with the old era. Since then, there has been development. The six stations of 1873 have grown into the 15 Circuits and 15 Missions of 1905. But New Zealand is the country for making experiments, and there has been development of another kind; the District Meeting has become the New Zealand Conference. This title was first assumed by permission of the

THE PERIOD OF CONSOLIDATION AND CHURCH DEVELOPMENT. 441

Home authorities in 1893, and it is to be noted that two ladies took their seats in that assembly as duly elected representatives, six years before a lady was elected to sit in the British Conference. Should the proposed legislation to divide the New Zealand stations into Districts become law and the missing link be supplied, it is more than probable that five of the towns already named will become the heads of the administrative units.

The history immediately before us will be best approached by our following the movements of Robert Ward. He was in the strictest sense a prospector, a pioneer and planter of churches. Such was his relation to New Plymouth, Wellington, Auckland, and largely also to Christchurch.

A valedictory service was held at old Sutton Street Chapel on April 30th, 1844, when Messrs. Ward, Long, and Wilson related their experience and call to the mission-field. The sermon was preached by Joseph Preston, who next day went on board the "Raymond" "to see and pray with Mrs. Ward and the children." He was much impressed with the missionary's wife, whom he pronounces a "noble woman," and he records in his *Journal* that "so great had been her desire to be employed in mission-work that she had often wished she had been a man; and that when the letter of invitation to the mission-field came she had sung and danced for very joy." Emily Brundell, like her husband, was born and bred in Norfolk, and it certainly was not unfitting that the first to cross the line as a Primitive Methodist missionary should have hailed from a district which has always taken a peculiar interest in missions.

ROBERT WARD.

The "Raymond" landed on August 29th. Only three years before, the first batch of settlers had arrived in the "William Bryan." As most of them had come from Devon and Cornwall, they gave the name of the chief town they had been familiar with in the old country to the new settlement. So New Plymouth naturally recalls the famous New England Plymouth Rock of the Pilgrim Fathers. Robert Ward landed, a stranger amongst strangers. There was nothing to distinguish him from the immigrants he had voyaged with. He was unknown; his coming unprepared for and unexpected. There was no nucleus of a church, however small, awaiting his fostering care, as was the case in the Australian Colonies. Single-handed he had to begin from the bottom, and he lost no time in beginning. On Sunday, September 1st, he opened his mission by preaching in the open-air, taking as his text, "This is a faithful saying," etc. He toiled on amid manifold discouragements, rendered all the greater by the depression which rested on the infant settlement. Still he gathered a few into church membership, and in November his hands were strengthened by a small society of Bible Christians coming over to him. These good people had formed themselves into a society on landing, and had even built themselves a small chapel. They had no minister over them, nor any prospect of obtaining one. On the other hand,

Mr. Ward had no chapel and was short of helpers. So it seemed to be for the interest of both societies—so alike in doctrine and discipline—to join their forces. The union thus effected worked well and was never regretted. The five local preachers gained by the union were a welcome reinforcement, and enabled Mr. Ward to extend the mission.

When just two years had passed Robert Ward had the joy of welcoming a colleague. It was on September 1st, 1846, that H. Green and his wife—whom we knew in the Brinkworth District as Ann Goodwin—landed from England. Now, at last, Mr. Ward found himself in circumstances to carry the Gospel to the natives of the settlement. He had applied himself to the study of the Maori tongue and, if we may judge by an incident he tells, he had attained to tolerable proficiency in its use. Coming one day upon a group of natives who were reading the New Testament in turn, Mr. Ward took his place at the bottom of the class; but he gradually worked his way up until he became head-scholar, and was rewarded by being made monitor, which enabled him to assume the functions of catechist. At another time he had received a rebuff at a *pah* or native village, and was returning home weary and dispirited, when he saw a light and heard voices in the bush. It proved to be a party of natives, who permitted him to preach to them. He chose for his subject the Lord's conversation with Nicodemus and, surely, never was the great truth of the New Birth enforced under more picturesque conditions: "Stars gleamed through the foliage of the trees, the fire lighted up the swarthy countenances of the hearers, and at a few yards distance the darkness wrapped us round." During this time he endeavoured to systematize his labours amongst the natives by drawing up a plan and time-table for his own guidance. His "Circuit" comprised eleven *pahs*, all situated within ten miles of his home, which he made it his business to visit in turn. In carrying out his self-imposed duties he was often weary and hungry, and occasionally he was fain to sleep on the ground wrapped in his cloak. These facts are of peculiar interest. They show that during the last four months of 1846 Primitive Methodism had, in Robert Ward, one who was to all intents and purposes doing the work of a foreign missionary. It is difficult to see what definition of a foreign missionary can be framed which will exclude him. He was devoted to the work of teaching and preaching to men on their own ground who were of another hue, and spoke another language which he himself had laboriously mastered: a missionary in Bengal or Madras could do no more. After some months of labour of this kind Mr. Ward was reluctantly driven to the conclusion that, with the staff available, a simultaneous mission to the colonists and natives was impracticable. Yet limitation in one direction led to extension in another. In January, 1847, Mr. Ward paid a pioneer visit to the rising settlement of Port Nicholson where, for several weeks, he did as he had done in New Plymouth after his landing there—he visited and preached in-doors and out to the settlers and soldiers, and thus paved the way for the arrival of H. Green as the first appointed missionary to Wellington, May, 1847. Thirty-four members were reported at the first Quarterly Meeting, held in September. Mrs. Green established and taught a day-school; a mud chapel was built, and when this was destroyed by the terrible earthquake of 1848 it was replaced in three weeks by a plain weather-board building. In 1857 Mr. Green removed to New South Wales,

THE PERIOD OF CONSOLIDATION AND CHURCH DEVELOPMENT.   443

and he was succeeded in turn by Joshua Smith from England, J. D. Whittaker (who died in 1862), Charles Waters (1864), and R. Ward, who came from New Plymouth in 1868. During his term several chapels were built, including Sydney Street, "which was soon filled with attentive worshippers, among the most constant of whom were the then Premier of the Colony, the Hon. (afterwards Sir) William Fox and his wife." In 1870 Wellington became a self-supporting station, and at the close of that year Mr. Ward returned to England on furlough.

We have now to see how Primitive Methodism got to Auckland, the third station in the North Island. James Harris, a former member of Cooper's Gardens Society, London, had emigrated to New Zealand in 1838 and was now residing at Auckland. As early as 1846 he had urged, and he continued to urge, that a missionary should be sent there, he promising to lend him all the assistance in his power. Until a third man was on the ground it was difficult to see how this was to be done; and there was considerable delay in supplying the third man. In these circumstances Mr. Ward paid two separate visits to Auckland in 1849, for the purpose of establishing and organizing a society. It was on his return from Auckland the first time that Mr. Ward made a journey that probably holds the record among the pedestrianising experiences of Primitive Methodist preachers. Even the journey of Clowes and Wedgwood over Morridge was as nothing—a mere holiday jaunt—compared with Robert Ward's journey from Kawhia mission-house to his home in New Plymouth. The full description of that journey is too long to be given here, but something of its unique character may be gathered from the fact that, when he bade adieu to Rev. John Whitely and his hospitable wife, he had before him a walk of a hundred miles over rough and dangerous country. He had to cross swamps, climb mountains, creep along narrow and precipitous ledges, make his way over rock-strewn beaches, sleep in native *pahs*, and, once at least, his Maori guide and himself had to make their bed on the sand. Such was missionary pioneering in the early colonial days.*

When at last, in accordance with instructions received from England, Joseph Long reached New Plymouth from Australia, Robert Ward was at liberty to proceed to Auckland, where the society he founded stood much in need of his oversight. Here he continued from May 1850, to 1858, and then changed stations with Joseph Long. The latter was at Auckland until his removal to Tasmania in 1864, while R. Ward's second term at New Plymouth extended to 1868. It will thus be seen how closely the early history of these two stations was identified with the two pioneers of our denomination in the Southern hemisphere. Within this period fell the excitement of the gold-fever—1851. R. Ward felt the full force of this in Auckland. The necessaries of life rose almost to famine prices. His quarter's salary did not meet his quarter's flour-bill. By reason of the fluctuations of population, the chapel he had built in Edwardes Street on land given through the Government by Sir George Grey, was alternately filled and emptied. Worse than this, he keenly felt his isolation by

* For a full description of this journey see "Jubilee Memorial Volume, or Fifty Years of Primitive Methodism in New Zealand," 1893—a very useful book, to which we acknowledge our indebtedness. The Rev. J. Whitely referred to above was murdered in 1869. His death marked the close of the Maori war.

the Home authorities and the lack of Connexional information.* Then the beginning of Mr. Ward's second term in New Plymouth coincided with the breaking out of the Taranaki war, which greatly disorganized the work of the church. Two of his sons bore arms as volunteers, and one was wounded. Often had he to minister consolation to the dying and the bereft. Later, Mr. Long and the society in Auckland had similar experiences to pass through during the nine months the Waikato war was raging—1863-4. It is necessary these facts should be written in order that we may learn through what difficulties Primitive Methodism in New Zealand had to struggle in its earlier years, and also that we may duly appreciate the courage, staying-power, and unshakable loyalty of our pioneers.

Wellington and Auckland hold the dust of R. Ward and Joseph Long. The former died in harness at Wellington in 1876; the latter ended his days in retirement at Auckland in 1892. At Wellington, too, the only superannuates in the New Zealand Conference—W. J. Dean and Joseph Dumbell—are spending their declining days. To Wellington and Auckland, also, A. J. Smith devoted ten years of fruitful service. He arrived in New Zealand in 1879, and in 1891 returned to England to take an honoured place in the ranks of the British Conference.

MR. D. GOLDIE.

We must refer our readers to the official history of New Zealand Primitive Methodism for notices and portraits of many devoted men and women who have served the Connexion during the first fifty years of its history in the Colony. We are, however, able to give the portraits of two prominent laymen out of the many equally worthy of recognition. Mr. David Goldie, M.H.R., of Auckland, has for many years taken a leading part in the administrative life of the Colony, in Temperance and Sunday School work, as well as in the progress of his own Church. He was president of the District Meeting of 1885. Mr. Charles Manly Luke, J.P., of Wellington, is, perhaps, even still better known to Primitive Methodists in this country, as he represented the New Zealand churches at the Scarborough Conference of 1905. He, too, is deservedly popular in the Colony, and was president of the District Meeting of 1890.

Pleasing evidence of the loyalty and perseverance of Primitive Methodist settlers in New Zealand is furnished by the early history of the Christchurch, Invercargill, and Dunedin stations—the three stations represented at the first District Meeting of 1873 still undescribed. The colony established on the east coast of the South Island under High Church auspices is commemorated in Canterbury, the name of the province, and Christchurch, its chief city. How our Church got a footing amongst the "Canterbury Pilgrims" is succinctly told by Rev. J. Cocker.† "In 1860 a few

MR. C. M. LUKE.

* Quite sufficient evidence for this statement will be found in the "Jubilee Memorial Volume" already referred to (see especially p. 145). After 1859 a very different policy was inaugurated (p. 153).

† *Aldersgate Magazine*, June, 1905.

Primitive Methodists met in the city and formed themselves into a society. For a time they carried on a mission, but ultimately the services fell through, several of the leading workers having moved to other parts of the Colony. Eight years later services were again commenced and, in 1871, Robert Ward was appointed first minister of the Christchurch Mission. The work prospered, and the surrounding districts were missioned by labourers sent out by the Christchurch Mission. To-day there are in the Province of Canterbury six Circuits and one Branch with eight ministers labouring upon them."

There is something in the very remoteness of Invercargill, and especially of its offshoot—Bluff, which strikes the imagination. There they stand on the confines of Southland, as the southern outpost of the empire, looking out towards the mysterious Antarctic Sea. Mr. C. Froggatt, from the Ludlow station in Shropshire, was the chief means of planting our Church in this southern Finisterre in 1872, and now the bells of Primitive Methodist churches call our people to their Sabbath worship.*

It was in January, 1875, during his official visit to the Australasian Churches, that Dr. S. Antliff, accompanied by W. J. Dean, organized the first Primitive Methodist society in Dunedin. The society of fifteen members then constituted kept together until the settlement of the first minister in 1876.

We cannot follow the process by which the circuits whose origin has been described have branched out and multiplied. Some idea of the way in which this extension has been brought about may be gained from the subjoined quotation, which for several reasons is worth giving. It relates to Greendale, one of the six circuits deriving from Christchurch, "the City of the Plains." The picture the quotation calls up has about it the colour, the spaciousness, the fresh breeziness of the new world. It shows us the original settler at work; and in this case the settler bears a familiar name which recalls Yorkshire Primitive Methodism, and we see how the piety of many of the emigrants from the old country was hardy enough to bear transplanting to a land on which other constellations look down.

"A short time previously [to R. Ward's taking charge of Christchurch], Mr. George Rudd had taken up his residence at Greendale, about thirty miles distant from Christchurch on the plains. In those early days there were no well-kept fences and fruitful cornfields, no comfortable homesteads; but as far as the eye could reach on every side, one wide expanse of brown tussocks, which swayed in the wind like the billows of the ocean. They had a monotony of their own, those extensive plains, before the settler cultivated them—a monotony which reminded one of the ocean—of its boundless expanse and freedom. Overhead arched the sky, deep blue in summer; and away from your feet the brown flat stretched, on the one hand to the distant horizon, where, from the roundness of the earth, it left a golden line against the blue; and on the other to the mountains, whose rugged crests for nine months in the year were white with snow. The story of Mr. Rudd's settlement on the plains reads almost like one of the pastoral scenes in the Old Testament.

* "A fine bell was also purchased and hung in the belfry [of Don Street Church, Invercargill] which on Sabbath days since then [1880] has called the people to the house of prayer." "At the Bluff there hangs in the belfry a small bell which once belonged to the 'Ann Gambles,' a ship which was wrecked on the rocks near by."—" Jubilee Memorial Volume," pp. 263-4.

"In the year 1867, in the month of October, Mr. Rudd and his youngest son James set out from their cottage on Shand's Tract, to the land which he had selected on the banks of the Hawkins, with horses, plough, dray, dog, etc., not forgetting, too, some loaves of bread which Mrs. Rudd had baked for their use. Remembering that their loaves were to last them a fortnight at least, they kept them in a basket which was placed in a hole dug out of the tussocks. 'Well do I remember (we quote from Mr. James Rudd) the first time we got the horses into the plough. I was very anxious to steam ahead, but father, not forgetting that the blessing of the Lord resteth upon those who acknowledge Him in all their ways, said, "Now, Jim, my lad, we must ask the blessing of God on our labours." The horses were started a few yards, the sod was turned up, and then we knelt down by the plough, and father told the Lord how we had come to this new country, and invoked His blessing upon our labours. And who shall say that God was not present? We were a lonely pair upon that lonely plain, yet God was surely there and heard our petition. Our first crop was put in, and proved the goodness of our Father in heaven in giving us a plenteous harvest.'

"There can be little wonder that prosperity crowned the labours of the pioneer settlers. God has said: 'Them that honour Me I will honour.' In due course a sod house was erected, with a roof of thatch, and there Mrs. Rudd and the other members of the family took up their residence. The farm flourished, and from time to time other settlers arrived in the district. That sod cottage, the first house of the Rudds at Greendale, was a hallowed spot. There the family altar was erected, and morning, noon, and night that gracious God whose blessings were so richly bestowed was acknowledged and devoutly worshipped. Mrs. Rudd was a true mother in Israel. Her cheerful spirit, her strong common sense, and her true piety, made a deep and lasting impression upon her sons and daughters, each of whom, in early life, professed conversion and in later years rendered valuable service to the Church."

It adds interest to the foregoing narrative to know that Mrs. Rudd was the sister of Jeremiah Dodsworth, author of "The Better Land." Before her marriage she was nurse in an English family in Paris, at whose house Louis Phillipe, king of the French, used to visit *incog.* One night, when seeing him to the door, he said: "I wish I were half as happy as you seem to be."*

The United States.

How Primitive Methodism was carried to the U.SA. has already been described (vol. i. p. 438), and it has also been stated that the Conference of 1843 had before it what were considered as *bonâ fide* overtures from the "American Primitive Methodist Church" for re-incorporation with the parent body. Still, ever since 1843, the relations between the two Churches have been anything but close; for the most part sentimental rather than real. What intermittent bond of connection there may have been has been the personal one supplied by the men whom the mother-Church has occasionally given or lent to its daughter Church in the States. Very soon after the Conference of 1844 Hugh Bourne crossed the Atlantic to visit the churches of Canada and the United States, returning in time for the Conference of 1846. He went out invested with the title of "Adviser from the English Conference." It would

---

* Rev. H. Woodcock's "Primitive Methodism on the Yorkshire Wolds," p. 163. See also *ante* vol. ii. p. 61.

be easy to attach too much significance to this visit, and to credit it with results it was never expected to yield. Our venerable founder volunteered for this work and, although many thought it unwise for one who was more than seventy years of age to undertake such a task, yet out of respect for the man they yielded to his urgently expressed desire. The expedition, from first to last, was a remarkable feat of zeal and endurance, very characteristic of the brave old man. More cannot well be said of it than this. Mr. Petty's statement that "his visit was not the most happy, either for himself or the leading brethren there," is amply borne out by the documentary evidence. The adviser and the advised did not always see eye to eye; for their standards of measurement were not the same.

For three months Hugh Bourne did duty as emergency minister in New York city, and before he embarked for home met with William Towler who, in January, 1846, had arrived to take over "the general superintendency of the United States Missions until the General Missionary Committee should direct otherwise." W. Towler was a man of fine presence and of equally fine character, a minister of experience, and an eloquent preacher. His appointment involved a double sacrifice; the Connexion parted with a minister doing good work at home in order that he might go on what was little better than a forlorn hope; while Mr. Towler himself left an assured position for one full of uncertainty and trial. We have now before us in MS. his "Notes, Correspondence with the General Missionary Committee," etc., which gives the history of his appointment, and his experience in fulfilling it until August, '46. The reading of this book heightens our estimate of Mr. Towler's character and ability; but it also leaves us with the decided impression that the United States Mission before 1843 makes the least brilliant page of our history, and that the less said about some who tarnished it the better. Not only is it true, as the first Missionary Report says, that "These Missions have suffered more from defections in their missionaries than any belonging to the Connexion;" but the conduct of some who were for a time the early agents of the Society was such as to invite failure and bring reproach on the denomination. Yet had Mr. Towler only been spared a few years he might have rallied the faithful remnant, and given character and strength to the churches. But, alas! he was struck with mortal illness soon after his return from Toronto, where his public efforts had made a great impression, and, to the grief of all who knew him, he died December 4th, 1846, in the fortieth year of his age. With his premature decease the bond of connection—apparently dependent on the slender thread of a human life—snapped, and the American Primitive Methodist Church resumed its independent course.

We anticipate a little in saying that in 1875 Joseph Odell went out to the U.S.A. to take charge of the church at Brooklyn, and remained there until 1880. In what follows we give the substance of a communication, kindly supplied by him, in which he not only refers to his own experience at Brooklyn, but touches on the difficulties Primitive Methodism has had to contend with in the U.S.A., and the causes of its comparative failure.

The great Methodist Episcopal Church of the U.S.A. is distinctively and aggressively Evangelistic. It is also most patriotic and American in its relations; while our little churches appeared to be "very small English colonies," living within themselves, and not appealing to the young life of America. The "old country stamp" of our services appeared as recently as 1878-9; for all the Primitive Methodist churches on the stations were using the old Hymn Book, published from Sutton Street, containing the national anthem—"God save the Queen"—while no opportunity was given for the national airs of America to be sung at the services. Then the opportunities, both of social position and increasing salary, proved inducements to many of the missionaries, and they left us and joined the larger forces found everywhere around them. But there were some loyal men who continued their labours and retained their interest in the denomination. Where these laboured, as in Pennsylvania, the churches kept together in a little Conference, and found in Charles Spurr a faithful representative of our Connexion. In the West, chiefly in Wisconsin, there continued a small Conference of varying fortunes. The earliest centres were at New Diggings and Mineral Point. At the latter place the church continues, and has an influential position and a creditable structure of its own. For this position the Connexion is indebted in large measure to Mr. Philip Allen, sen.; and his son, P. Allen, the chief banker of the town, is to-day the honoured lay-leader of the church, and nobly supported the Rev. R. Chubb in the erection of the present church-buildings. The minister now there is Rev. T. W. Walker, one of the earliest representatives of the Evangelist's Home.

In New York city and Brooklyn little has really been done, although Brooklyn has always had a centre of Connexional life since the first missionaries arrived, and several of these made "Little Jacob," the first church in that city, a kind of head-quarters. It was not until 1875 that a suitable church-building was secured in that delightful city, and, unfortunately, the opening services had scarcely closed, and no proper adjustment of any of the funds had been possible, nor any mortgage secured, when a gross scandal occurred. At two weeks' call, in the month of March, 1876, Joseph Odell, with his wife and young children, arrived there to enter the breach and to stand for the virtue of clean life and the vindication of Primitive Methodism. Mr. Odell was lent for the emergency. It was a severe ordeal. Circumstances invested the already grave position with prejudice. The city sided with the violators of morality and left the mere handful of heroic Primitive Methodists to their fate. For many months the new minister received not a visit of welcome or recognition, save from English ministers, and these came rather out of sympathy than from admiration of the position. But faith in God and fidelity to truth won. Converts were made each Sabbath; vast and far-reaching improvements commenced; new missions were opened, and new institutions sprang up which greatly stirred the city. A Temperance organization called after the pastor, "The Odell Temperance League," achieved marvellous reforms; four drinking-saloons around the church were closed. This, of course, led to retaliation by the liquor-interest; the parsonage front was twice smashed in, and the pastor needed the special care of the police authorities. Such victories largely augmented the church and congregation and restored the confidence of the city. There were noble men associated with this church. Mr. Howard Darsley has for many years been its chief pillar. As a loyal Primitive Methodist he has been a tower of strength to every connexional cause, and a most hospitable friend to many ministers and their families. During the period of Mr. Odell's ministry Mr. John Thatcher and his excellent wife became active members of the Brooklyn church, and ever since those days have never ceased to love its services and to look after its needs and expenses. To this day this family make Brooklyn Primitive Methodism a first call upon their estate, time, and service.

The Brooklyn church shares with mother Tunstall the honour of having received into its fold—the former in 1875—that remarkable and much-mistaken man—Joseph Barker. The life-history of Joseph Barker is full of thrilling interest—of adventure and change; and his lapse into infidelity was most painful and pathetic. It was, when on a visit to England and amongst old friends in the Potteries, that he was restored to the fellowship of Jesus Christ. Love conquered where argument would have been useless. On Mr. Barker's conversion the Press of the time made its comments; but its reality became evident. He sought everywhere the company of simple believers. He gave his library to the Primitive Methodist College, Sunderland, and on his return to U.S.A., joined the Brooklyn church, and spent a lengthened period in residence there. He also made a will giving to the Primitive Methodist Connexion vast tracts of land in Nebraska. Mr. Odell, on going to U.S.A., carried this document with him and verified its value, and interviewed the son and heir of Mr. Barker. Direct information was given to the General Committee, and a sum of money was accepted by the Connexion in settlement.*

The Brooklyn church still continues, but finds itself a down-town problem. In later years, and during Mr. Odell's stay in Brooklyn, a new movement was inaugurated in the New England States. Mr. N. W. Matthews left Mr. Odell's roof, and went first to Trenton and then to Lowell, Mass. He has proved most efficient and successful, and now the best Primitive Methodist Churches and Conference can be found in the region nearer Plymouth Rock and in the old Colony.

CANADA.

The planting of Primitive Methodism in Canada has already been described (vol. i. p. 438). The first chapel built at Toronto in 1832 is shown in our picture. The plainness and simplicity of the building itself, the planked side-walk, the domestic fowls quietly pecking on the roadway—all these are quite in keeping with early colonial days, when what is now one of the most advanced cities in the British Empire was vulgarly known as "Muddy Little York." This somewhat primitive yet commodious structure served its day, and was superseded by Alice Street in 1854—the very year

---

* "The Primitive Methodists at Tunstall invited me to join their community, and as soon as I consistently could, I did so. I was afterwards accepted as a local preacher. My labours as a preacher and lecturer have been mostly in connection with that community. I was specially struck with the zeal, the labours, and the usefulness of the Primitive Methodists while on my way from the wilds of error; and my intercourse with its ministers and members since I became a Christian, has proved to me an unspeakable comfort and blessing. I have received from them the greatest kindness: and I pray God that I may prove a comfort and a blessing to them in return."—Joseph Barker's "Teachings of Experience," p. 170. In the preface to this remarkable book Mr. Barker names J. A. Bastow as one who helped to lead him back to Christ.

in which the Canadian churches were empowered to hold their first Conference and were free to enter upon *their* period of Church organization and development. Then, in 1874, the society that had successively worshipped in Bay Street and Alice Street (burnt down in '73) took possession of the noble pile of buildings in Carlton Street, which cost 50,000 dollars. At this time all the signs were prelusive of change. Primitive Methodism was being drawn into the current which ten years later was to merge it in the great Methodist Church of the Dominion. So it will be seen that the three buildings of our picture not inaptly symbolize the successive stages through which Canadian Primitive Methodism has passed; and it will be well to keep these stages in view as we proceed.

Everything goes to show that the missions in British North America were the most popular, and were regarded as being on the whole the most successful of our Colonial Missions. For one thing they had the advantage of being in closer touch with England, and though they had difficulties of their own to face, they were free from some of the special difficulties which militated against success in Australasia. Had

ALICE STREET CHURCH, 1854.   BAY STREET CHURCH, 1832.   CARLTON STREET CHURCH, 1874.

the Missionary Committee only been able to send out more men of the right stamp when emigration was at its height, the success realized would have been vastly greater than it was. The bulk of the Canadian immigrants did not remain stationary. Population did not agglomerate in one or two centres merely, but spread out like a fan, or like projectiles from a machine-gun. Clearly, therefore, the policy needed was to have a sufficient number of missionaries to follow in the wake of those going to take up land in the back settlements. Even as it was, with the limited means and few men at command, this kind of work was not neglected.

It was well for Primitive Methodism that it had, from the first, some families of standing and character connected with it who stood by the cause and rendered it increasing help as their own temporal circumstances improved. Chief among these were Messrs. W. Lawson, R. Walker, and J. Elliott formerly of Carlisle Circuit, and T. Thompson formerly of Driffield. Than R. Walker it would be difficult to point to a layman of finer type. He was no seeker of office, yet there were few positions of trust he did not fill. He was a generous giver to good causes, and he gave from principle and by rule. Mr. Walker was not unknown by face to Primitive Methodists in this country: he was chairman of the great public meeting at the Grimsby Conference of 1869, and with J. C. Antliff, B.D., represented Canadian Primitive Methodism at the Methodist Œcumenical Conference of 1881. He survived his friend and fellow-worker, W. Lawson, ten years, dying in 1885.*

Among the pioneer ministers of Canada, or among those who immediately succeeded the pioneers, were N. Watkins, W. Summersides, W. Lyle (1833–57); J. Lacey ('36–65), "a walking cyclopœdia of divinity, a man whom men crowded to hear"; W. Jolley ('38–44); M. Nichols ('41–54); John Towler, brother of W. Towler ('43–51); Thomas Adams ('44–65); Robert Boyle, D.D. ('46–80), an Irishman, "sensitive, clever, popular, much in demand among the churches"; James Edgar, D.D. ('46–80), "a man nearly all soul and sympathy"; John Davison ('47–61); John Garner ('48–81), the son of the John Garner we know so well, and son-in-law of John Flesher; W. Gledhill, an eccentric but saintly man, who returned to England in 1861.†

Matthew Nichols will be an unknown name to Primitive Methodists on this side the Atlantic; but it ought not to be unknown. In his ardent piety, consuming labours, and early death he reminds us of Thomas Proctor and Atkinson Smith and with such men as these he should ever be bracketed. He was a Norfolk lad who emigrated to Canada, and was carried off by cholera in the very midst of his successful toil. That he was a man of grit as well as grace may be inferred from his experience in opening the Guelph mission: "On this mission he was an entire stranger, and had to practise self-denial, suffer privations, endure fatigue, and perform labours sufficient to wreck a Herculean constitution." Yet go where he might, "he rode on the crest of a wave of perpetual revival enthusiasm." He would overwhelm a whole congregation with emotion while preaching from the text, "What mean ye to weep and break mine heart." His memory was revered by the many steadfast converts he had won.

John Davison was a man of very different type who demands an additional word. He was a convert of William Morris, the potter-friend of William Clowes, and joined the first society formed in Newcastle-on-Tyne. He entered the ministry in 1823, and soon gave evidence of the possession of those solid qualities which marked his after career. He was the step-son of William Clowes, and we are indebted to him for the publication of the *Journals* of William Clowes (1844) and also for the "Life" published in 1854. In 1847 he yielded to the request of the General Missionary Committee to go out to Canada, and for some years acted as a kind of Colonial Bishop, being vested

REV. JOHN DAVISON.

* See *ante* vol. i. p. 438 for his portrait. There is a good sketch of Mr. Walker in "A Memorial of the Centenary of the Venerable Hugh Bourne," 1872. See also "Old-Time Primitive Methodism in Canada," by Mrs. Hopper, 1904.

† The dates cover the years of active ministry in Canada. The brief characterizations are quoted from R. Cade, D.D., in "Old-Time Primitive Methodism in Canada."

by the Conference with authority "to visit the stations, counsel the missionaries, preachers and societies, and to open new missions." He started the *Evangelist* on his own responsibility, and when in 1858 that journal was merged in the *Christian Journal*, he became its editor, and also Book Steward until his superannuation in 1866. He also compiled the first *Book of Discipline*, and for nine years— '57–66—was Missionary Secretary. He was present as a delegate at the Grimsby Conference of 1869, and died in 1884 with the words upon his lips: "I believe in the communion of saints, the forgiveness of sins, the resurrection of the body, and the life everlasting."

It was fitting that such a man should be the General Committee Secretary of the first Canadian Conference which was held at Brampton, named after Brampton in Cumberland by Mr. John Elliott, one of the first settlers, and a devoted Primitive Methodist. At this time, April, 1854, there were two Districts, 15 stations, 23 ministers, and 2326 members.

REV. W. ROWE.

For the sake of convenience and more efficient working the Canadian "appointments" were, in '60, re-arranged in six Districts. The establishment of a Book-Room, the publication of a denominational organ, and the appointment of a General Missionary Secretary, were all movements in the same direction. The question of the better education of the ministry also forced itself to the front, and in '66, T. Crompton stands on the stations as Theological Tutor. Next year G. Lewis, B.A., is, in addition, named as English and Classical Tutor. We judge Mr. Lewis would be the first minister in the denomination who obtained a diploma by residence at a University, as J. C. Antliff, B.D., was the first minister of the British Conference to do so. In 1870, however, the Institute was discontinued, and it was decided that young men who took the two years' course at Toronto University should have one year deducted from their probationary term. It should also be stated that Dr. S. Antliff visited the Canadian churches in '71, and G. Lamb in '76, when his presence at a critical time was of great value.

During this period several ministers went out from England who took an active part in the expansion and internal development of Canadian Primitive Methodism. Messrs. T. Crompton and W. Rowe arrived in '54, W. Bee in '56. Still later, J. F. Porter and G. P. Clark went out in '71 and '72 respectively, and after some years' labours returned to do good work under the British Conference. By special request Thomas Guttery went out in '76 and J. C. Antliff, B.D., in '80.

Mr. Rowe rendered efficient service in Canada. For five years he was General Missionary Secretary and Book Steward, and from '71 to '73 was in the Editorial chair. Not only did he fill these positions of trust. In Toronto the Church never prospered more than during Mr. Rowe's superintendency. Churches were erected in Parliament Street, Queen Street, a new church built at Yorkville, and the

REV. T. GUTTERY.

ministerial staff increased. The stations constituting the London District were, with the exception of two, created and formed by Mr. Rowe, who spent several years in following the settlers into new townships and organizing them into Primitive Methodist churches.* Through failure of health Mr. Rowe superannuated in 1873 and returned to this country, and was cordially received by the Conference. He afterwards filled the position of Principal of the Ladies' College, Clapham Common, and is now enjoying a hale and vigorous old age, still often filling the pulpits of the churches near his residence at Kew.

Thomas Guttery went out to Toronto in 1871, and returned to England with impaired health in 1879. He was pastor of the Alice Street (afterwards Carlton Street) Church for five years, and then of the Yorkville Church. He was known as the foremost representative of his Church and as an eloquent preacher. He edited the *Christian Journal* with an ability which amply justified his appointment in '92 as vice to the Connexional Editor. As we all know, he did not live to reach the position for which he was so eminently fitted. Though he bravely battled with disease, it was in vain. During the sittings of the Edinburgh Conference of '95 the end came, and the lips of one of the most eloquent ministers Primitive Methodism has produced were closed in death.

The last, like the first Primitive Methodist Conference in Canada, was held at Brampton, in 1884.

* "Old-Time Primitive Methodism in Canada."

454 PRIMITIVE METHODIST CHURCH.

PRESIDENTS OF CONFERENCE, 1887—1897.

CHAPTER VI.

THE MATERIAL EXPANSION OF PRIMITIVE METHODISM.

THE material expansion of the Connexion since 1843 has been a noteworthy feature of its history. The multiplication of chapels and schools, and the improvement in the architectural character and adaptability for worship and work of the buildings owned by the denomination are facts which, from the very nature of the case, catch the eye and impress the mind. Wherever you may go—alike in town and country—you come across fabrics which bear on their front the denominational name. Those who are old enough to remember how the Connexion was off for chapels forty or fifty years ago, and how it is provided for now, will best be able to appreciate the contrast that memory calls up before them. When we see that the present value of our Connexional property is estimated at more than four millions and a half sterling, we do not need to be told that this sum represents in the aggregate an amount of enterprise, thought, and activity on the part of ministers and people truly astonishing. That activity has been pretty general throughout the Connexion, and has been constantly going on, though, naturally, it has had its varying degrees of intensity at different periods.

This marked activity of our Church on the material side has not escaped the notice of critical observers. Sometimes, indeed, there has been the hinted reproach that ministers and people were too much absorbed in bricks-and-mortar and money-raising, as though this were the be-all and end-all of a Church's existence. The danger may readily be admitted, as also the easy possibility of succumbing to it. At the same time, it needs to be pointed out that, though the danger might be avoidable, the necessity that created and involved the danger was not. The chapel-building era was bound to come, and to come with the insistency of "the strong man armed." So much ground had been quickly covered during the specially missionary period, that the housing of the new converts, the making provision for their needs, and the creation of the plant needful for future working, were practical matters admitting of little delay. So our fathers thought,—and hence we find Robert Smith and John Jobling writing in 1853: "The most casual observer of the Connexion's interests must have remarked that suitable chapels, on good sites, and in workable circumstances, are among the most effective secondary agencies for promoting the welfare of old societies and congregations, and for giving permanency and extension to new ones. Hence the importance of both building such places and of attending wisely and diligently to their affairs when erected."*

The chapel-building era developed here and there a minister of a special type. These men of the time became known as "chapel-builders" and "debt-reducers." The biographies and obituary notices of the time witness to the current belief that

---

* General Chapel Fund Report, 1853.

some degree of such work as this would come in the way of a minister's regular duty, and must not be shirked; hence, next to his having had no decrease on his stations, it is counted to him as a distinction that he has built or enlarged so many chapels.

We would assign 1847 as about the year when the Chapel Building Era began. In 1843 the reported number of chapels is 1278; the number of rented chapels and rooms is not given. If the figures for 1845-6 are correct, then there was an actual decrease of chapels for those years on the number reported in 1843. The increase began with 1847, when the numbers stood—Chapels, 1421; Rented Chapels and Rooms, 3340; and ever since that date any decrease in the number has been apparent rather than real, to be accounted for by the loss of the Australian or Canadian churches. The annual statistics also disclose the interesting fact that while, in 1847, the rented rooms outnumbered the Connexional chapels by more than two to one; in twenty-one years the ratio was reversed. By 1868 the Chapels outnumbered the Rented Rooms, the precise figures being 3235 chapels and 3034 rented places. All this not only points to the inference that the Connexion has sustained its chief losses in those localities where we had but the precarious tenancy of a rented building; but still more unmistakeably it shows that very much of the activity displayed in chapel-building, especially in the early years, consisted in substituting for a building held on rent, and probably ill-adapted to its purpose, one held in trust for the Connexion, and built expressly for worship and Christian service. But still another inference is suggested, and one of more sinister import. If there had not been a decline of home-missionary enterprise on the part of the Circuits during this period, would there have been this steady diminution in the number of Rented Rooms?

The statistics of the number of chapels built in successive years confirm the view that the period of greatest activity in chapel-building falls within the triennium—1850-79; and that this activity reached its height during the decade 1863-72 when no less than 1191 chapels are reported to have been built, giving an average of two chapels for every week of the decade. Of course there are chapels *and* chapels, and the mere number of chapels built gives us no clue to their actual cost and value. Unfortunately, it was not till 1871 that the cost and value of newly acquired Connexional property began to be published in the yearly *Minutes* of Conference. Any estimate, therefore, relating to the comparative value of property in the earlier and later periods is precluded. We can, however, ascertain the value of the property acquired in 1870-9. The value of the 897 chapels built in these ten years was £1,057,511, which figures give an average per chapel of £1179.

Chapel-Building under Regulations.

The "boom" in chapel-building, as we might well call it, was not allowed to go on without surveillance or without an attempt being made to regulate it. The need for this must have been brought home to the minds of the fathers by the disasters in Kent and Louth Circuit still fresh in their memory—disasters which had been largely brought about by John Stamp's reckless chapel-building and chapel-buying. It was high time a stop was put to the building of chapels without leave asked, without trustees, without any reasonable prospect of paying for them. Hence the prudential

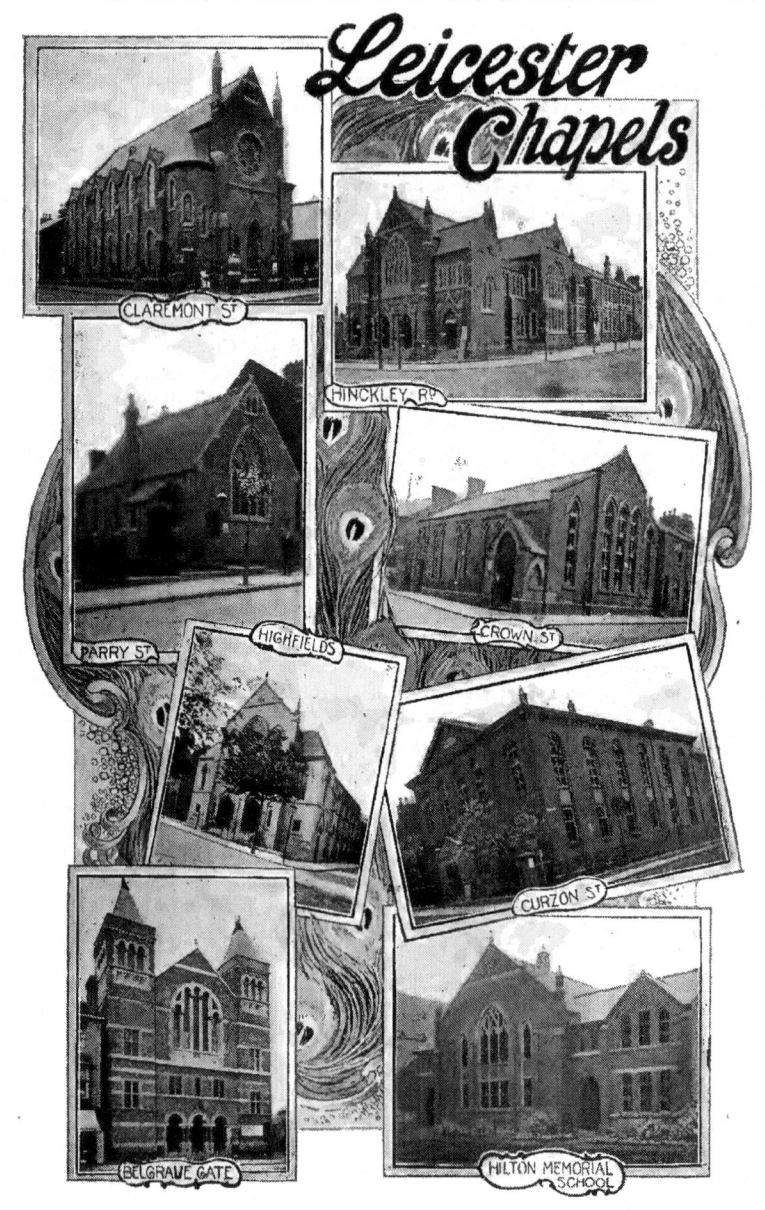

THE PERIOD OF CONSOLIDATION AND CHURCH DEVELOPMENT. 457

Leicester Chapels

CLAREMONT ST.
HINCKLEY RD.
PARRY ST.
HIGHFIELDS
CROWN ST.
CURZON ST.
BELGRAVE GATE
HILTON MEMORIAL SCHOOL

enactments of 1843 which, amongst others, contained a regulation requiring one-third of the money the chapel would cost to be raised.

By 1882 the recommendation had stiffened into a statutory requirement, and the "one year after opening" had contracted into "six months." Moreover, the application for leave to build was to show that one-fourth of the estimated cost had already been raised. These more stringent regulations were passed not a day too soon, and the effects of their working were all to the good. They might to some extent react upon building projects—nipping some of them in the bud,—but they also did something to check the accumulation of debt on connexional property, which had long been out of proportion to the money raised, and a source of growing anxiety and weakness to the churches.

The requisite machinery for the carrying out of these regulations had long been available. District Building Committees had been established in 1835, and District Chapel Committees in 1847. In the same year—'47—the General Chapel Fund was created for the purpose of rendering financial assistance to distressed chapels. Though much crippled in its praiseworthy endeavours by limited resources this fund saved many chapels to the Connexion, and, as the aid it rendered was conditional upon local effort, the fund materially helped to reduce chapel debts. The Loan Fund, which is now a section of the General Chapel Fund, though with a separate Treasurer, was launched as a centenary commemoration of the birth of Hugh Bourne. For many years the Leeds District was the managing committee of the General Chapel Fund. At present it is constituted on a much wider basis, having on it not only persons elected by the Districts and Conference, but also the Secretary and Treasurer of the Connexional Fund, the General Missionary Fund, and two members elected by the Chapel Aid Association, and two by the Directors of the Insurance Company. In fact the General Chapel Fund is thoroughly representative of the improved and Scientific Finance which we take to be a striking feature of the latest period of our history. This will appear all the clearer after we shall have made brief reference to the origin of the Insurance Company and the Chapel Aid Association just mentioned, and what they have done and are doing to help to place our Connexional property in a sounder financial position.

Hull Leads the Way.

From facts and figures and regulations relating to chapels let us turn to some typical examples of chapel building. We cannot do better than begin with Hull, since, as the late Dr. Wood contended, it was there the chapel-building era of the Connexion commenced. Dr. Wood furthermore claims that to John Bywater belongs the honour of inaugurating this era. Other men of mark might be chapel-fillers; John Bywater was pre-eminently the chapel-builder. Such honoured men as Flesher, Sanderson, and Lamb might build chapels occasionally, but they did not take to the business as though "to the manner born," as did Mr. Bywater. Such are the views of Dr. Wood who, we must remember, had been the colleague and intimate friend of Mr. Bywater in Hull, and who writes as one thoroughly conversant with the facts of the case.[*]

[*] See a series of valuable articles on—"Recollections of Rev. John Bywater and early chapel-building in the town of Hull."—*Aldersgate Magazine*, 1898.

THE PERIOD OF CONSOLIDATION AND CHURCH DEVELOPMENT. 459

When Mr. Bywater went to Hull West Branch in 1847, there were three chapels in the town—West Street, Mason Street, and Nile Street—and all of them were crowded.* He soon saw what was needed, and he had the requisite courage and ability to push forward and carry through a new chapel project. Thornton Street Chapel, situated not far from the Pottery at which William Clowes had worked, was opened in 1849—that year of ill omen, when no less than two thousand persons were swept off by the cholera in Hull in the short space of three months. Thornton Street proved a great success but, unfortunately, after a fire which broke out on Easter Sunday, 1856, all that was left of the Chapel was bare blackened walls. The congregation found shelter in a vacant Episcopal Chapel hard by, which was lent gratuitously, and the new Thornton Street Chapel, improved and somewhat enlarged, was opened in September of the same year.

Meanwhile—in 1850—John Bywater had removed to Hull East Branch where a still weightier task awaited him, and a still stronger title to grateful remembrance was to be won. All were agreed that increased chapel accommodation was urgently needed, but opinion was divided as to the particular policy to be pursued in supplying that need. Some were of opinion that a Chapel should be built beyond the bridge in the Holderness Road direction, while others advocated the replacing of Mason Street by a large central Chapel. Mr. Bywater was strongly in favour of the latter policy, and by his tact he so far disarmed opposition as to be able peaceably and strenuously to proceed. A splendid site was obtained in Kingston Square in the centre of the town; Mr. William Sissons was called in as architect, Mr. Musgrove was the bricklayer, and Mr. Margison, a trustee and official, undertook the joiner-work. It is interesting to note that Messrs. Sissons and Margison were respectively the architect and contractor for the Thornton Street Chapel of 1856 just mentioned. Mr. Clowes was fully in sympathy with the views of Mr. Bywater, and some of the last meetings he attended were in connection with the Jarratt Street project. The foundation-stone of "Clowes' Chapel," as after the death of Mr. Clowes it was decided to call it, was laid on the Good Friday of 1851. There were troubles and accidents as the big building (it was to seat 1400 people) went up. The far-end gable gave way, killing two workmen and injuring others. The arch that supported the massive stone-steps subsided under the superincumbent weight. There began to be pessimistic whisperings and head-shakings. When a heavy thunderstorm passed over the town, and the rumour spread that the unfortunate gable had been struck by lightning, some said it was plain to see God was against the project. Amid all this the calmest and most cheerful man was John Bywater, although he had been struck down by illness. When the news was brought him that the gable had fallen—"Then," said he, "they must build it up again, and do it better next time." July, 1852, saw the opening of Jarratt Street, when sermons were preached by Mr. Bywater and Dr. Beaumont, whose impressive death took place (1855) in the pulpit of Waltham Street Chapel, not far away. It is but natural that something like a halo of sentiment should invest Jarratt Street Chapel, as though it were a personal entity. At its inception Clowes assisted. He bore the undertaking up before God in prayer. His shadow seemed to rest on its

* For previous references to these chapels see *ante* vol. i. pp. 373, 386, 457.

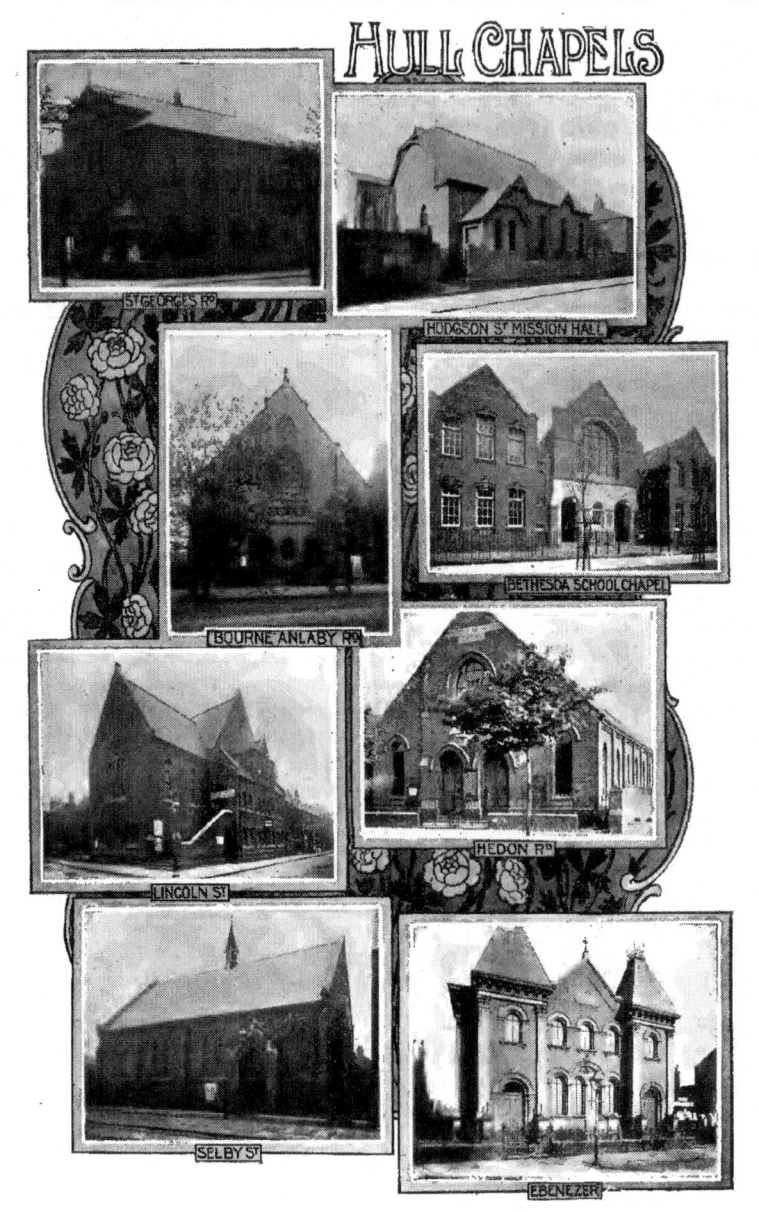

THE PERIOD OF CONSOLIDATION AND CHURCH DEVELOPMENT. 461

Hull Chapels

St Georges Rd

Hodgson St Mission Hall

Bourne Anlaby Rd

Bethesda School Chapel

Lincoln St

Hedon Rd

Selby St

Ebenezer

foundation and opening services. It bears his name and stands as his memorial. Ministers of power have preached from its pulpit. Three Conferences have held their sittings within its walls. It is right we should speak of it here; and although it has now stood more than half a century, and many sanctuaries fair to look upon have sprung from it, yet, to our partial eyes, this mother-chapel in its goodly proportions recalls Milton's words concerning our first mother Eve—"fairest among her daughters."

Since the erection of Jarratt Street the multiplication of chapels and the division of circuits have gone on apace in the town of Hull. As long as Mr. Clowes lived there seemed to be an indisposition, even on the part of some of the stronger Branches, to part company with Hull Circuit which, one may say, was at that time a congeries of Branches. But, in 1853, the two Town-Branches of West and East became respectively Hull First and Second Circuits, while Scarborough and Brigg Branches were formed into separate stations. The only Branches still retained were Barton and Patrington which were attached, the one to Hull First, and the other to Hull Second. By successive divisions and sub-divisions the two Hull Circuits of 1853 have become the eleven of 1905, employing eighteen ministers, who minister to some twenty congregations within the borough, as well as to a number of country congregations.

MR. SAMUEL HODGE.

We will borrow from Dr. Wood's informing articles a brief account of the course chapel enterprise took in Hull after the erection of Jarratt Street:—

"The two chapels next in time to Clowes' Chapel were Holderness Road and Jubilee, Spring Bank. The one was undertaken by Rev. William Garner, and the other by Rev. John Petty. Each seats more than a thousand persons, and is a noble and commanding structure; and each since its erection has had considerable additions made to its schoolroom accommodation. The Rev. Thomas Whitehead had the honour of building our largest chapel in Hull, the fine Gothic building in Anlaby Road, which seats 1420. The year after, Henry Hodge's Memorial Chapel, Williamson Street, with seating accommodation for 1400 persons and a splendid suite of school-rooms and class-rooms, was built under the superintendency of Rev. Parkinson Milson, to provide for the overflow from Holderness Road, and this has now become the head of Hull Sixth Circuit. About the same time, the writer was busy in getting a better home for old Church Street society by the erection of Lincoln Street Chapel—the Samuel Hodge Memorial—to seat 950 people, with commodious school and class-rooms. Rev. R. Cheeseman commenced and Rev. F. Rudd completed the Fountain Road premises which provide for 800 worshippers, and a large Sabbath School, and are situated in the midst of a rapidly-growing population. This was the second great offshoot from Clowes' Chapel, and it very much weakened for a time the old congregation there. In 1878 our early companion and intimate friend, Rev. Thomas Whittaker, had to provide for the overflow of Jubilee Chapel, and courageously did he undertake the erection of Ebenezer on Spring Bank, one of the finest Methodist structures in the town, seating about 1200, and having first-class accommodation for all departments of Sunday School work. In 1881, a second offshoot from Great Thornton Street, under the vigorous superintendency of Rev. W. Robinson, undertook the erection of Hessle Road Chapel and Schools, another magnificent pile of buildings of which any Church might be proud, and where there are seats of the most approved style for 1000 worshippers. Lastly, St. George's Road in the Fifth Circuit, and Lambert Street, seating 850, another branch from Clowes' Chapel, are noble monuments of the skill and enterprise of Rev. Thomas Mitchell. All these were large and expensive erections, involving an outlay of from £3000 to £8000 or £9000; yet they are all plain Methodist chapels, without spires and costly ornamentation. We could go on when Mr. Bywater had set the example and made a beginning; but we claim him as the leader of the forward chapel movement in the town of Hull."

It must be admitted that for one city this is a goodly record, amply justifying reference being made to it here. And yet, since Dr. Wood wrote, the work of material extension has gone on, as the reader who inspects the views of Hull chapels inserted in the text will discover; and we may add further—the work is still going on; for some of the most recent acquisitions to our chapel property in Hull are not shown in our illustrations. As supplementary to these we give the portrait of Mr. J. Wright, formerly the well-known architect of some of the principal Hull chapels of the 'sixties and 'seventies. Towards the erection of Williamson Street Mr. Henry Hodge gave no less a sum than £600 and, quite properly, that chapel stands as his abiding memorial. His grandson, Mr. Edward Robson, worthily maintains the honourable traditions of the family for liberality, and activity in various forms of service.

MR. J. WRIGHT,
Architect of the principal Chapels in Hull and District.

There can be little doubt that Hull, by the number and still more by the position and character of its chapels, provided an object-lesson for the Connexion at a time when it was needed much more than it is to-day. Hull in these respects set a high standard and an inspiring example which must often have had its influence. That it had in one case is clear, from the following little anecdote, with which we may appropriately end the present section:—

"In the year 1874 Mr. T. W. Swindell and the late Mr. Robert Bell visited Hull during the sittings of the Conference, the latter in the capacity of delegate, the former merely as a visitor. They were impressed with the proportions and imposing exteriors of the chapels, more especially with the Jarratt Street edifice, as they sauntered up and down outside it.

"'We're not up-to-date at Yarmouth!' remarked Mr. Swindell, in which opinion Mr. Bell concurred. Whereupon the former, waxing eloquent and enthusiastic on the subject, made up his mind, on returning, to lay before the Yarmouth trustees the startling proposition to pull down the old barns and build greater."*

The outcome of this resolve was the transformation of the Yarmouth "Tabernacle" into the "Temple," as already told (vol. ii. pp. 223-9).

* "From Hayloft to Temple," by Arthur H. Patterson," p. 88.

MATERIAL EXTENSION IN SOME OF THE LARGE TOWNS.

We have said (vol. i. p. 293) that at first Primitive Methodism put its main strength into village evangelisation; that it was in fact and by preference a village rather than an urban movement; and that it was only tardily and by degrees that its reluctance to attack the rapidly growing cities was overcome. But, true though these statements may be of the first period they no longer hold good if applied to the middle and later periods of our history. Indeed, to say this does not fairly represent the full extent of the change which has taken place. Perhaps it might be too much to say that town and village have exchanged their rôle; but it would be quite correct to say that the tendency is in another direction than formerly. The swinging pendulum is not where it was sixty years ago. The time came when not only was there no reluctance to lay, as it were, sap and mine to large towns, but when the doing so satisfied a preference and became the recognised policy. Now the big towns and cities of England bulk largely before the eyes of the Connexion as they do in the general affairs of the country. We find many of these places in the list of Conference Towns, simply because the Connexion has won for itself a position in these towns and can rely upon meeting with hospitality and have the use of buildings (usually its own) capable of accommodating the crowds that come together at such high times.

The evidence goes to show that by 1870 the Connexion had become much more alive to the needs and possibilities of large towns—to the need of their evangelisation, of the living voice of the preacher, of sanctuaries easily accessible and inviting, and to the possibilities they offered for Connexional extension. The writer of the Conference Address of that year seems naturally to slide into the use of military figures when referring to the condition of the large towns and the manifest and urgent duty of the Church in relation thereto. Says he: "Our large towns and growing colonies claim our best attention and *must be cared for*. The time has come when bolder aggressions must be made on the strongholds of the enemy. We, as a contingent of the army of Immanuel, must be prepared to take part in the conflict that is assuredly thickening around us. We ask for an increased liberality from our friends to enable us to extend our conquests still further and to secure the spoil already taken." The action of the General Missionary Committee in establishing some large town-missions and special missions in London is approved by a subsequent Conference, and the Committee is encouraged to go further in the same direction. In this newly-awakened solicitude to do something more considerable for the large towns and cities, our Church has shared in a feeling very general at the time in the religious world, and that has gone on growing in intensity. Dr. Guthrie's "The City, its Sins and Sorrows," "The Bitter Cry of Outcast London," and General Booth's "Darkest England" were successive publications which made this feeling vocal and reacted upon it.

No doubt there has been considerable numerical increase in favour of our Church in the large towns. Roughly speaking, some 38,584 adherents out of a total of 201,333 are to be found in the eighteen most populous towns of Great Britain and Ireland. Poor as such returns may be they give a hint of the position of our Church in relation to large urban centres. Whether the increase that has taken place has been at all proportionate to the growth of the towns themselves during the same period is another matter; and it would probably be found that in the case of towns of abnormal growth the increase has not kept pace with the growth by a long way.

But when, still having the large towns in view, we turn from numerical increase to material extension, there can be no question that there has been a notable advance. The reader has only to look at the views inserted in the text of chapels owned by the Connexion in Hull, Leicester, Sheffield, Nottingham, and other large towns to be convinced of this. To give the history and description of every one of the buildings represented might be interesting to those locally concerned. But to do so in the space at command is quite impossible, nor is it necessary. The views might be allowed to stand as they are. Even without a word written, they afford a striking illustration of the remarkable advance the Connexion has made on the material side in the large towns. Any observations we may make as we go along must be regarded as supplementary, intended to point out certain facts or features of more than local interest.

MANCHESTER.

Some—and only some—of the Manchester Chapels have been shown (vol. ii. p. 27), and amongst these is Upper Moss Lane, which merits a word. Chronologically, Moss Lane comes between Great Thornton Street and Jarratt Street Chapels in Hull. It was opened in November, 1850, the first sermon in connection with the series of opening services being preached on a week-day by Dr. Beaumont in Cavendish Street Congregational Church. Moss Lane has been enlarged from time to time, and now affords sitting accommodation for 850 persons. Including the cost of these successive alterations and enlargements, the sum of £7,562 has been spent on the building. In 1900, when the jubilee of the Church was celebrated, through the efforts of the church and congregation the building was entirely freed from debt. Since then a long-cherished desire of the Church has been gratified by the erection, during the superintendency of Rev. A. Beavan, of Sunday-school buildings admirably adapted for their purpose. The cost of this undertaking was about £4,000, more than half of which has been raised.

About the same time that Moss Lane Chapel was built the Manchester Second Circuit was formed with Charles Jackson as its first Superintendent, and the late Joseph Graham as his colleague. Mr. Jackson has long since passed to his eternal rest, but his name is still cherished by many who knew him, and very highly esteemed him as a faithful and able minister of Jesus Christ.

REV. C. JACKSON.

MR. JOHN WAINWRIGHT.

When John Wainwright died in 1903, at the patriarchal aged of 96, there passed away a Primitive Methodist of probably the longest standing in the country. He had been a member of our Church in Manchester for about seventy-five years. At the time of his death he was the oldest trustee of Moss Lane, had held the offices of class-leader and society-steward for more than half a century, and had been a member of the order of Rechabites for more than sixty years. His life affords another example of self-help. Left an orphan at three years of age, and having to make his way in the world by his steady industry and thrift, he rose to a good social position. Primitive Methodism in Manchester owes much to John Wainwright. He was given

SUNDERLAND CHAPELS.
CLEVELAND RD.
WILLIAMSON TERRACE.
TATHAM ST.
MAINSFORTH TERRACE.

to hospitality, and his home was ever open to the ministers of our Church; the venerable Hugh Bourne himself had several times been his guest. He was a loyal and devoted Primitive Methodist, and laboured hard and contributed generously to promote its interests.

More than one reference has been made to Higher Ardwick Church, the head of

Manchester Fourth Circuit, one of the most costly, imposing and beautiful structures possessed by the Connexion. Two out of the five Manchester Conferences have held their sittings within this commodious building. Mr. W. E. Parker, Vice-President of the Conference of 1895, is associated with the Higher Ardwick Society and Circuit. His attachment to our Church is hereditary, and he is widely known as a veteran official and a local preacher of proved efficiency and great acceptability.

Four years after Mr. William Windsor of the Manchester Third (Broughton) Circuit was by the suffrages of his brethren elected Vice-President of the Conference held at Grimsby. The honour was amply deserved, and the mark of confidence well bestowed; for, notwithstanding the exacting claims of professional life, Mr. Windsor has for years devoted much of his time and his business ability and gifts as a speaker to the internal and administrative work of the Church of his youth.

A view of Great Western Street will likewise be found on our full-page group of Manchester Chapels. It was built in 1878, the school in '81, and the Lecture Hall in '97—the entire cost of these erections being £8,000, notwithstanding which, the church is now out of debt. That Great Western Street is a commodious and well-equipped building, is evident from the fact that the important Conference of 1906 is to hold its sittings within its walls.

NOTTINGHAM AND SHEFFIELD.

The later history of Primitive Methodism in such towns as Derby, Nottingham, Leicester, Sheffield, Leeds, Sunderland, and Newcastle, brings out in bold relief the same truth which is illustrated by our denominational history in Hull and Manchester, viz., that the obtaining at an early period of a Connexional freehold in a growing town is an unspeakable advantage. Given also a number of families and officials of proved loyalty such a material centre serves as a rallying point, and tends to give continuity to the Church's history and solidity and effectiveness to its operations.

In the case of Nottingham and Sheffield the lesson stands out with special prominence, for, in both these towns, the mother-chapel is not only still in being but, by reason of modern improvements and adaptation to present-day requirements, both Canaan Street in Nottingham and Bethel in Sheffield are entering upon a new lease of life, and a new chapter of their history is opening. We have already told of the origin of Canaan Street and the acquisition of Hockley Chapels. Now, even as we write, pleasing intelligence comes to hand from Rev. J. T. Gooderidge, the indefatigable superintendent of Nottingham First Circuit, which we cannot do better than give in his own words : " You know that our work began in the old Factory in 1816 (within twenty yards of the present building), and from that very year, continuing through '23 and '28 when old Canaan Chapel was built and enlarged, down to the present, we have been nearly hidden by old dilapidated houses and other unsightly property. I know of no other Church that has been so exceedingly fruitful in best work, yet so buried out of sight. Well, all this is now being altered, and for the first time in our history our beautiful church and schools will have a frontage to, and be entered from, Broad Marsh, thus bringing us right out of a hidden corner into one of the busiest thoroughfares of the city." The good work thus outlined, of which Mr. Gooderidge

468 PRIMITIVE METHODIST CHURCH.

Nottingham Chapels

CANAAN. HOCKLEY. FOREST RD. HARTLEY RD. BLUE BELL HILL. MAYFIELD GROVE.

writes with an enthusiasm so justifiable is a matter of more than local interest, and will be accomplished at a cost of £600, the greater part of which is already assured. We cannot pass from Canaan Street without mention of Mr. J. W. Allcock, who by long service, tried loyalty and liberality, has proved himself the worthy successor of the officials of the past, such as Messrs. Barker and Spencer.

Sheffield has been conspicuously enterprising and successful in chapel enterprise and, largely no doubt in consequence of this, it stands next to Hull among the large towns of the land for the number of its members. Bethel Chapel has been the root of this material extension and vital growth. From it the ten existing Sheffield Circuits have directly or indirectly been made, and now in its old age, like Canaan Street, it is renewing its youth by becoming a Central Mission, which is now being vigorously prosecuted by Rev. Sydney A. Barron and his staff of workers.

The first Circuits to be formed from Bethel were Stanley Street (1857), whose present chapel was built in 1855. From this vigorous Circuit Sheffield Third (Petre Street) and Sixth (Attercliffe) were formed in 1872 and 1887 respectively. From the ranks of the local preachers of this offshoot of Bethel the Revs. N. Haigh, G. Cooke, R. Bryant, I. Hadfield, and B. Senior have entered the ministry.

The story of the building of Petre Street, the largest chapel owned by the denomination in Sheffield, is one of peculiar interest owing to the mingled disaster and success which attended it :—

"When the building was approaching completion the roof was blown down during a winter storm, causing some hundreds of pounds damage, the cost of which, however, the contractor bore. Scarcely had the injury been repaired, when, on the 31st January, '68, a terrific storm broke and raged for two days and nights, to the full violence of which the chapel was exposed by its lofty, and at that time, isolated position. For forty-eight hours the building stood, but the hurricane so increased in fury that at last it gave way, and the roof fell in, bringing the walls down to the floor. It is impossible to describe the anguish and despair which fell upon the little band of members and trustees, who had spent hours in anxious watching, when the building collapsed, and their holy and beautiful house, in one tremendous crash, became a heap of ruins. This disaster involved the trustees in financial difficulty, as the second loss, about £1,200, fell on them. However, they bravely faced the situation, and six brethren from Stanley Street, whose names are worthy of honourable record—R. W. Holden, J. B. Brailsford, H. Morten, T. Crookes, G. Smith, and C. Easby—voluntarily offered to become trustees and share the burden. This practical sympathy infused new life into the dispirited church. The public generously responded to the appeal for help. Mr. Holden alone collected £200. The members contributed weekly to the restoration fund, and the difficulty was overcome.*

"Mr. Robert Moss, who since 1863 has been General School Secretary of Bethel, has interested himself in writing in MS. a History of Bethel, which we trust will one day see the light. Mr. Moss tells us that the formation of Sheffield Fifth (John Street) told rather heavily upon the mother-church. The circumstances which ultimately led to the creation of this new Circuit are of sufficient interest to be summarised here.

* See a clear and informing article on "Primitive Methodism in Sheffield," by Rev. T. Campey. *Aldersgate Magazine*, 1901, pp. 413-24.

"In the year 1863 two zealous Scripture-readers, belonging to St. Mary's Church, were wishful to establish an open-air mission in a populous district belonging to the parish. It was finally arranged that the services should be held in front of the house of a Mrs. Wright, who was an attendant upon the Church services; but on beginning their work, these good men discovered that the service was likely to prove a failure from their inability to sing. Mrs. Wright, noticing they were at a loss, suggested that Mr. John Nutton, a member at Bethel, should be brought in to assist. He readily complied, and also sent a messenger to the house of Mr. Henry Adams, then living in FitzMaurice Street, asking him to lend his aid. The two,' says Mr. Moss, 'did their utmost to assist these gentlemen of the Established Church, but a strong opposition to the mission sprang up from the landlord of the "Sportsman Inn," close by. While the service was proceeding, drink was handed round, then followed fiddling and dancing as an accompaniment. This systematic opposition raged so strongly that after two attempts the Scripture-readers were driven off the field. But Messrs. Adams and Nutton continued the work with such vigour and persistence, in defiance of persecution, that the *habitués* of the tavern were won over, and refused any longer to do the landlord's bidding—threatening indeed to drop their custom if he did not cease his opposition.

"'The end was accomplished. The devil had overshot his mark, and the mission got a footing. Mr. Nutton then opened his house for services, and the mission was placed upon the plan. In a short time its success necessitated the procuring of larger premises. An old paint-shop in Mary Lane was rented, known on the plan as New Hereford Street.' The cause continued to grow until, during the ministry of Rev. J. Dickenson and his colleagues, the site in John Street was procured, and in '63 the chapel was erected, and in '77 became the head of Sheffield Fifth, which for rapid and vigorous development has had few equals in the Connexion. From this station were formed, in '99, Sheffield Eighth (Heeley) and Ninth (South View Road, Abbeydale)."

With Sheffield are linked the names of the foremost ministers of the old Nottingham District; for Sheffield was not constituted a separate District until 1885. Besides those previously mentioned, such outstanding figures as John Dickenson, J. T. Neale, Charles Lace (the blind preacher), W. Cutts, C. H. Boden (author of "Lowly Heroes and Heroines of Primitive Methodism"), J. Hirst, J. Gair, and Robert Robinson. The last-named, who died in 1899 in the eighty-sixth year of his age, spent no less than fourteen years in Sheffield. For eight years he was employed as Town missionary and was eminently successful. It was whilst he was labouring in this capacity, and during the superintendency of R. Parks, that James Caughey visited Sheffield. From November 25th, '57 to January 26th, '58, Mr. Caughey conducted services in Bethel Chapel, when 1380 persons professed to have received the assurance of pardon or of sanctification.

CHAS. H. BODEN.

Mr. Henry Adams of Sheffield is a pronounced progressive in regard to chapel extension, and his influence and liberality have been a very considerable factor in the development of Primitive Methodism in Sheffield and the district. Mr. Adams was born at Hollinsend in '36, and went to Sheffield in '63, some two years

THE PERIOD OF CONSOLIDATION AND CHURCH DEVELOPMENT. 471

DERBY CHAPELS

KEDLESTON ST.
CAMPION ST.
DALE RD.
TRAFFIC S.
MOUNT ST.
CENTRAL.

after his conversion. In this same year he became an agent for the Refuge Assurance Company, and began what was destined to be one of the most successful careers known to the Assurance world. In this work he discovered and developed his genius for business. For many years now he has been a Director of the Company, for which he was once only an agent. Mr. Adams has been the Steward of Sheffield Fifth since its formation, and for many years he has been recognised as one of the leaders of our Church, in both its District and Connexional Courts, and he was elected Vice-President of the Conference of 1883. Mr. Adams has taken a remarkable interest in chapel-building affairs. In Sheffield Fifth, Eighth and Ninth Circuits, and in Hoyland Circuit particularly, our places of worship are memorials of his enterprise and liberality. Mr. Adams' private beneficence is well known, his beneficence is not confined to his own Communion, nor does Mr. Adams' Christian life exhaust itself in officialism. He is exemplary in his attendance at the means of grace—even on the week-night—and he loves an old-fashioned Methodist prayer-meeting. In all his life-work Mr. Adams has had a willing helper in his devoted wife.

BIRMINGHAM.

Since this section deals with the subject of Connexionally-owned property in large towns, it would seem that Birmingham has no part or lot in this section before the year 1851, when the first small Connexional Chapel was built. This was New John Street, built in the last year of Henry Leech's useful term in the Birmingham Circuit. This rather singular fact sets us on the inquiry for an explanation; for Birmingham had been missioned under hopeful conditions as far back as 1824 by James Moss. But the roseate prospect he saw around and before him was soon beclouded; and though diligent and capable ministers like Thomas Nelson, Thomas Russell, and many others laboured in the Circuit there was, even after many years, little to show as the net result: in 1840 the total membership was only 340.

The history of Primitive Methodism in Birmingham then, begins after the turn of the half-century, and the history of the material extension of our denomination in this big city—the capital of the Midlands—is a much later story still. Prior to 1853 there were happenings in plenty—a succession of events: but these do not make history. For *that* there must be continuity and progress. What happens must not be fortuitous, but foreseen, prepared for, and related both to what goes before and follows after. The lack of a true Connexional centre in Birmingham was an evidence, and largely the cause of that lack of continuity and progress which marked the earlier history of our denomination there. Its experience emphasises and underscores the lesson: that a good chapel in a large town tells heavily in favour of the denomination to which it belongs and that knows how to use it. It is like an investment which, prudently handled, will yield a good return. Birmingham had no Canaan Street or Bethel or Mill Street as Nottingham and Sheffield and Hull had, and hence its early history compares unfavourably with theirs. Its societies flitted here and there from rented room to rented room, until we get bewildered with the very names of the various localities. But this after all is only half the truth. Chapels may be one cause contributing to success, but they themselves are an effect.

Birmingham lacked chapels because it sorely lacked in the early days capable and reliable officials. So much was this the case, and so well was the fact known, that when in 1834 Richard Ward was stationed by the District Meeting to that town, John Hallam said to him: "You will have need to say your prayers very much"; and when he began his labours in the station he found it was even so. There had recently been in the Church dissension so violent that it had resulted in a split, and those who still remained were at variance among themselves. In his own quaint and vigorous way Richard Ward notes in his *Journal*, "I think it would have taken the twelve apostles with spectacles on to have found Bible religion amongst the officials." But there must have been Bible religion somewhere or the Church would have died out? There was; but it was found in the private membership. So he goes on to add : "But some of the members were of another spirit, and evinced by their works that they loved the Lord, His house, His people, and His cause."

But we must make a distinction between Birmingham—the town, and Birmingham —the Circuit. The former may have little history before 1853 worth the telling, but

HOME OF MR. JOSEPH ARCH.

the latter has more history than can well be told. The Birmingham Circuit was an immense field, and into its wide area men went forth from Birmingham as a centre, diligently to break up the ground and scatter the seed, which was to bear fruit in the after days. We cannot forbear taking a brief backward glance, to remind ourselves that it was so. When, then, Richard Ward was stationed for Birmingham Circuit in 1834, he not only preached in some of those many rooms—now forgotten—we have referred to, but he went out for three months to the Worcester Branch and visited Malvern and Pershore. Then he proceeded to Stratford-on-Avon and Warwick Branch, and he puts down in his *Journal* the observation that "In these places the work is low. There is too much talk and stir about Shakespeare, that bad man! for them to make much out in religion." Then he moves on to Coventry Branch, and anon we find him on the Redditch and Bromsgrove side of the Circuit, where "there are some very powerful, active, lively and zealous workers, and large congregations amongst the nailers and needle-makers." Lastly, he is sent as Birmingham's leading missionary to the city of Lichfield, where we have already seen him toiling and suffering, and succeeding (vol. i. p. 523).

Such was the Birmingham Circuit of old time. Within that wide area of the Midlands, there is much biography that might even yet be profitably gleaned. We do not forget that Joseph Arch, the agricultural labourer of Barford, in Warwick, was converted through the agency of our Church, became a local preacher, and a rustic Moses, to lead his down-trodden class from serfdom to something that, in comparison, was liberty. At King's Norton, in old Moundsley Hall, lived the family of the Wheildons, one of the daughters of which amiable and hospitable family became the devoted wife of Samuel Turner, who had received his first call from Birmingham. There is another name we would mention with pardonable pride—that of George Russell of Warwick, one of the most eloquent local preachers and temperance advocates Primitive Methodism has produced. We meet with his name continually on the plans of this wide district, beginning in the 'forties, and it is clear that his services were in very great and constant request, and were ungrudgingly rendered.

One who knew him well says:—

"Men who had heard John Bright often said that George Russell was the most eloquent and rousing speaker they had ever listened to, John Bright only excepted. He could hold large audiences in the open-air spell-bound for an hour at a time, and in Warwickshire, Northamptonshire, and Leicestershire no preacher was more acceptable in the 'fifties and 'sixties at the chapels of the Free Churches than George Russell. His social and political sympathies with the masses were very strong. As a Chartist, a Radical, a Temperance man, and preacher, he voiced their aspirations, and fearlessly championed their cause. He had a considerable gift of rhyming, and wrote hymns which were sometimes printed on the Circuit plans."

To this testimony it may further be added that George Russell had signed the pledge as early as 1837, and was associated with many of the early advocates of the cause. He addressed meetings with John Hockings, W. Bearn, and several of the "men of Preston." He had the honour of being chairman of the meeting at which Thomas Cooper, the Chartist, signed the pledge, Mr. Russell himself handing him the pen.

But to return, after this seeming digression, to the city of Birmingham. The view we give of the Chapels built or acquired for the Connexion in quite recent years, shows that a forward movement on the material side has begun, and that already very encouraging advance has been made. The Conference Hall Birmingham Fourth Circuit, an entirely new interest, was built in 1895. Sparkhill Church (Stratford Road), in the Fifth Circuit, a very fine block of property, was built in 1895, under the superintendency of George Edwards, at a cost of £6,500. This enterprise was materially assisted by Mr. William Adams, son of Mr. Henry Adams of Sheffield. Bristol Hall, in Birmingham First Circuit, built in 1900, at a cost of £7,000, took the place of Old Gooch Street built in 1852. Lastly, the Church of the Saviour, where the once popular George Dawson carried on his ministry, was purchased in 1896 by the General Missionary Committee, and here after initial discouragements William Sawyer is bravely and vigorously working.

THE PERIOD OF CONSOLIDATION AND CHURCH DEVELOPMENT. 475

BIRMINGHAM CHAPELS

LORD ST.
CHURCH OF THE SAVIOUR
REGENT ST.
SPARKHILL
CONFERENCE HALL
HOCKLEY
MORVILLE ST.
BRISTOL HALL

More extended reference must be made to the Conference Hall. That a new Circuit should be created, and such a building as this be erected, without assistance from any Connexional Fund, was so remarkable an achievement that the Conference of 1899 passed a resolution of recognition and appreciation of Mr. Odell's work. With this high endorsement we will let Mr. Odell outline the course of his long and strenuous ministry in Birmingham, of which the Conference Hall may be regarded as the crown.

"In view of the advances in other parts of England, Birmingham Primitive Methodism has a poor record. At Inge Street, near the Bristol Road, the Society established itself and continued until Gooch Street Chapel was erected in 1852. There was toil and disaster in the building of that place: but it became a centre of service and extension. It is evident, however, that the drifting kind of life which formed its official *personnel*, constant additions and then withdrawals of those coming from the 'Black Country,' or the Potteries, affected the work injuriously. It is a long story of re-missioning and retiring from places. There is little of settled character or sustained continuity in these records. At the time of the Reading Conference of 1885 there were three stations, and two of them were subsidized by the General Missionary Committee. At this date, and forward to the present, Joseph Odell's name appears on the stations. It marks the new period of substantial extension. The site of Sparkhill Church, now the head of the Fifth Circuit, was secured during Mr. Odell's earliest superintendency, and, characteristic of the old spirit of evangelism, the first service on the site was held by the pioneer staff of 'The Evangelist's Home.' Greet was missioned and held against continual difficulties. King's Norton was restored to the Plan, and a bright opening, followed by fruitful service, appears. At King's Heath Mr. Odell placed a tent, and a staff of young men, frequently joined by Mrs. Odell, sustained the work until a permanent provision was made for the little Church.

"But the chief mission of this eventful period, covering twenty years, was the establishment and progress of the cause at Small Heath. The Conference Hall is the present material expression of the work of those years. The enrolment of thirteen members in the house of Mr. Thomas Strange is the concrete fact from which have grown the varied agencies of a permanent and self-sustained work. Neither the buildings, nor the minister's stipend, nor the multiplied forms of effort—including most of the social agencies of other somewhat imposing 'Central Missions'—having ever received financial aid from Connexional Funds. This evidence of entirely self-sustained work is the more remarkable because it relates to, and is supplied by, an artisan and poor neighbourhood. During nineteen years, approximately, more than £30,000 must have been raised and expended on buildings, school rents, furnishing, salary of minister, while the voluntary labours of a most heroic and noble staff of helpers (whose names are in the Book of Life) represent a sum in value inestimable. With hosts of children, and frequently immense congregations, and a new and permanent average membership of nearly 300 members, the Conference Hall became the active and live centre of Mr. Odell's riper ministry in Birmingham, and continued so until the exhaustive labours of these strenuous years rendered it imperative that he and his wife should be released for both change and rest. But this release did not come until further properties had been secured, and the Conference Hall work made the base of other valuable centres. Yardley Road property, with a corner site, large iron church, and manse, together with considerable furniture being given as an

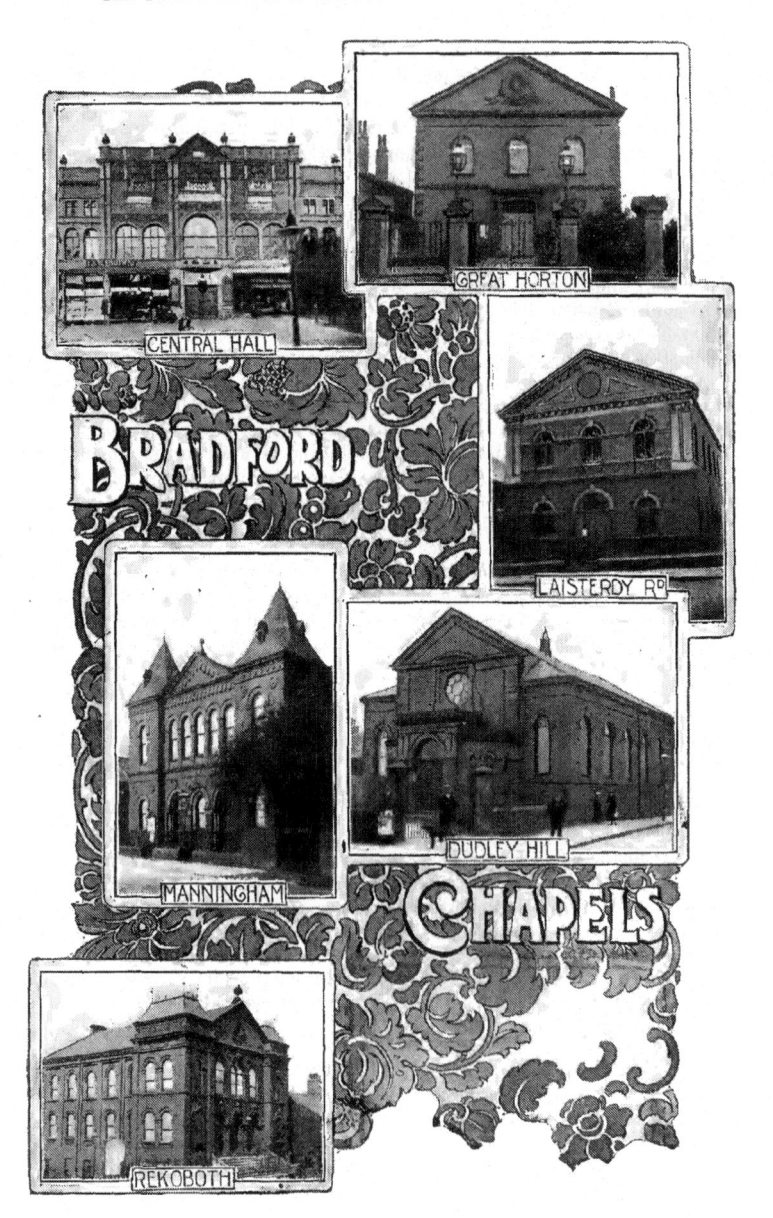

THE PERIOD OF CONSOLIDATION AND CHURCH DEVELOPMENT. 477

BRADFORD CHAPELS

CENTRAL HALL
GREAT HORTON
LAISTERDY RD
MANNINGHAM
DUDLEY HILL
REKOBOTH

absolute freehold to the Connexion, and held properly in trust for circuit work—the donors being excellent ladies whose father had felt the joy of simple and sustained evangelism. The 'Romance of Evangelism,' and the conflicts inevitable, where work is promptly done and property wisely and legally secured, form chapters that may yet appear in the enlarged notes of Mr. Odell's very busy life. Later still, Olton property—freehold site and chapel valued at £1,000, on account of unique position, was obtained by Mr. Odell. And here the heroic comrade of Mr. Odell, and the undaunted chieftain of Temperance Reform, Joshua Mosley, was class-leader and local preacher, and in this 'snug little chapel by the wayside,' as he called it, he spent his last Sabbath on earth, and shortly went in triumph to God. While on this, the south side of Birmingham, extension everywhere marked the possibilities of Mr. Odell, another side of the Worcestershire border was reached by the judicious and enterprising labours of Rev. Jas. M. Brown, who knew Birmingham life more intimately by an earlier residence in the Evangelist's Home, and new buildings were erected at points for larger and more permanent structures. And at length the old Gooch Street Chapel was disposed of, and the Bristol Hall erected—an achievement due to the remarkable patience and industry of Rev. W. S. Spencer, who has laid the Connexion under obligation by an enterprise carried through amidst apparently insuperable difficulties."

NEW TOWNS AND THEIR DEMANDS:—MIDDLESBROUGH.

There are some towns which have sprung into existence during the very period we are now dealing with. They have been created by the Industrial Revolution. Though as yet not populous enough to warrant their inclusion amongst the big cities of the Empire, they are on the way soon to become such. Crewe, Barrow-in-Furness, and Middlesbrough are towns of this type. Of these we may take Middlesbrough as the representative. It has no long past history to look back upon but it makes ample amends by taking a far look ahead, and its proud motto is "Erimus." As a town it is not so old as Primitive Methodism, for it celebrated its Jubilee only in 1881. In 1829 the site was occupied by a solitary farmhouse surrounded by marshy land; to-day it is a busy, well-equipped town of near 100,000 inhabitants.

Towns of phenomenal growth like these lay a heavy burden of responsibility on the Free Churches. It is so easy to refuse the burden; and yet not to take the burden up would prove a disaster. We have almost the colonial problem of the 'fifties meeting us here on our own English soil. To make religious provision for the people at all commensurate with the demand created by a population ever increasing at an abnormal rate, leaves to the Churches planted in such a town, no time or room for indulgence in a "rest and be thankful" spirit. No sooner is one new chapel fairly opened than lo! as if by a magician's wand, the fields are covered with houses, and the Church must bestir itself if it would not be beaten in the unsanctified rivalry of the gin-palace and the music-hall.

Both Crewe and Middlesbrough have shown a praiseworthy degree of enterprise in facing their responsibilities. They are both amongst the best Circuits in their respective Districts, and their faces are still set towards the future, and their hearts are full of hope. As to Middlesbrough, the writer of these lines may for once indulge

THE PERIOD OF CONSOLIDATION AND CHURCH DEVELOPMENT. 479

in a personal reference. Five years of hard work and happiness were spent by him in "Ironopolis," along with W. A. French and Frederick Ash, who were successively his trusty colleagues; and sweet are the memories of toil sweetened by sympathy and success. Since then, under the ministry of the late R. G. Graham, R. Hind, and W. G. Bowran,—whom we all know and are proud of as "Ramsay Guthrie"—under

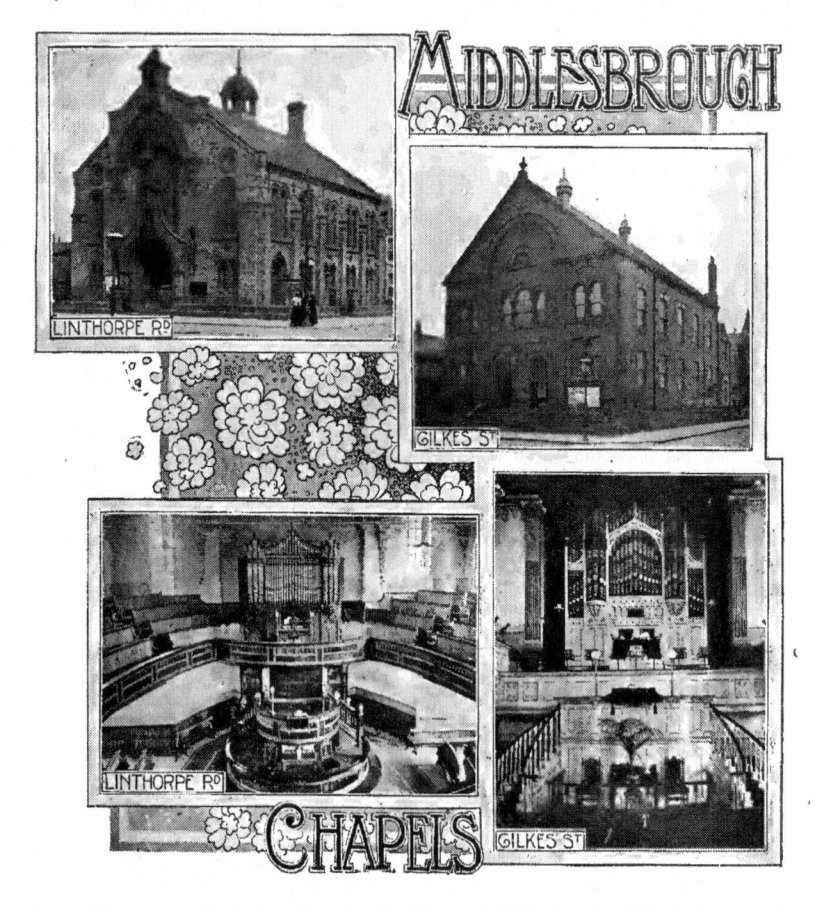

these able men and their colleagues in labour, Middlesbrough Circuit has greatly progressed. Eston, once a part of it, has become a circuit, and the beautiful Church on Linthorpe Road, shown in our illustration, has taken the place of old Richmond Street Chapel with its memories. Middlesbrough Primitive Methodism is doing, and will do its best to make the town motto true of itself.

T. ROBINSON. W. E. PARKER. L. L. MORSE.
W. McNEILL. W. GLASS.
W. WINDSOR. A. ADAMS.
R. FOSTER. F. C. LINFIELD. J. BELL.

CHAPTER VII.

FOREIGN MISSIONS: THEIR ESTABLISHMENT AND PROGRESS.

WE now begin what might very properly be called the *second* part of Book III. of this History, which will briefly have to follow the most striking developments of our Church-life in recent years. These we take to be the establishment of Foreign Missions; the provision for Education—ministerial, secondary, Sunday school, and local preachers'; improved methods of Finance; and Philanthropic and Social Agencies. Two of these—Education and Finance—manifestly relate to methods; they have to do with efficiency rather than with what are ends in themselves. But a Christian community which at last establishes Foreign Missions, and takes its part in the work of social amelioration, has attained to a worthier and more adequate conception of the privilege and duty belonging to those who "are being saved." The universal aspects of Christianity in their relation both to the race and the individual are recognised, and the challenge they present accepted. It is seen that the Church's concern is equally with *all men* and with the *whole man;* that it is no mere family, sectional or even national affair, but "Catholic" in the truest sense of that much-abused term, and that it is as Catholic for the individual as it is for the race. "All men" means Foreign Missions; the "whole man" means the obligation to do good to and redeem from evil the body, mind, and soul of the man. If, then, our reading of the later history of our Church be the right one, Foreign Missions and Institutional Churches mark the latest advance, while Education and Finance, as indispensable to efficiency, are helpful auxiliaries.

Home Missions, Home and Colonial Missions; Home, Colonial and Foreign Missions—these are the three stages of our history regarded in one aspect; and these three stages very fairly coincide with the periods when, from another point of view—that of form—the denomination was successively a group of missionary circuits, a group of associated Districts, and lastly a homogeneous Body—a true Connexion—or as we prefer to call it—a Church.

We have to show in the next section how strikingly the history of the growing sentiment in favour of Foreign Missions illustrates the advantages for the general good finally accruing from the working of Districtism. If Hull District was mainly responsible for the important changes effected in 1842-3 and if it inaugurated the Chapel-building era, it is quite as true that Norwich District's contribution to our Connexional life has been that it kept to the fore, canvassed and urged in season and out of season, the desirability and necessity of entering upon the Foreign Mission field. In the end its persistency was rewarded. It got its way, and its way was right, and the denomination was the better for it. So, if it be asked—"How got you to Africa?" the answer is—*via* Norwich District.

THE TIME OF PREPARATION: NORWICH DISTRICT'S SUCCESSFUL EFFORTS.

At the Sheffield Conference of 1837 one of the Norwich District's representatives was a local preacher from Yarmouth. Joseph Diboll was a shoemaker by trade, but he had thoughts far beyond his last. His strong and cherished desire was that the denomination to which he belonged should send its missionaries to Africa, and he was ready with his "Here am I, send me." As the result of his pleadings this early Conference passed the following resolution:—

REV. J. DIBOLL.

"(7) The Brethren of Yarmouth Circuit being of opinion that the Primitive Methodist Connexion ought to prepare to mission in AFRICA, what is the opinion of the Conference on this subject?

"*A.*—The opinion of Conference is, that so soon as Yarmouth Circuit by itself, or jointly with any other circuit or circuits shall have a clear providential opening to mission in Africa, that the other circuits will yield them what assistance they providentially can.

"*∗*∗*∗* It will be well to make this a constant subject of earnest prayer throughout the Connexion. And who knows what the Lord may do!"

There was not much encouragement to be got from such a resolution as this with its final fatalistic note—its *kismet*. We are still in the circuit-dispensation; the time for combined Connexional action was not yet. Whether Yarmouth Circuit had received any other damper between '37 and '40 we cannot tell, but in the latter year the Circuit book shows this churchyard record:—

"(3) Resolved: That Africa be buried; no more to be raised from the dead by us alone; but should there be a combination of effort, we pledge ourselves to be foremost to effect its resurrection from the dead.

"O Lord, hasten the day when 100,000,000 of human beings who have only 111 ministers besides teachers shall be converted to the Gospel. Amen."

Finding no door of access to Africa through his own Church, Joseph Diboll sought another door elsewhere. By a singular coincidence he was destined not only to see Fernando Po, but to have the door of its evangelisation shut against him. He offered himself to the Baptist Missionary Society, and after a short term of service at Hemsby in Norfolk was appointed to Sierra Leone. He was at Clarence (afterwards called by the Spaniards Santa Isabel) when the man-of-war arrived bringing the Jesuits with their intolerant edict which proved fatal to the Baptist Mission on the Island of Fernando Po.

Joseph Diboll's dropped mantle was soon taken up. Without prejudice to others it may be affirmed that Thomas Lowe and Mr. James Fuller of Swaffham parted it between them. Thomas Lowe in several

REV. THOMAS LOWE.

THE PERIOD OF CONSOLIDATION AND CHURCH DEVELOPMENT. 483

regards deserves a word or two of recognition and remembrance here. His active ministry extended to the unprecedented length of fifty-eight years. He had a fervent, optimistic temperament and a highly rhetorical style. He was something of a poet too, and an occasional author, "The Pilot of the Galilean Lake" being perhaps his best known and most useful book. His enthusiastic, untiring advocacy of the African mission, however, is that feature in his character and ministry with which we are now most concerned. "He was," says Mr. A. Patterson, "'gone' on Africa. A large map of the continent hung on the walls of his study. The shelves of his library bristled with books on Africa. In whatever company he found himself the con-

PRESIDENTS OF CONFERENCE FROM 1898 TO 1903.

versation was sure to turn on Africa." It is claimed for Thomas Lowe, in the official memoir, that no man had done more than he to rouse the missionary spirit lying dormant in the Connexion; that his speech on Africa at the Metropolitan Tabernacle produced a powerful effect; that it was through reading his poem on "Africa's Wrongs" W. B. Luddington first became possessed with the desire to carry the evangel to Africa; and that Rev. Thomas Stones, our present trusted African missionary, was one of the fruits of his Wolverhampton ministry. Mr. James Fuller was, in his own way, quite as great an enthusiast for missions in general, and for

H H 2

African missions in particular, as the more eloquent minister. He had the liberal hand, and gave much and systematically to the cause so near his heart.

Under the influence of these and such as these it was soon seen that, so far from being dead and buried, the proposed mission to Africa was very much alive in East Anglia. Evidence of this was unexpectedly supplied at the District Meeting of 1852, held at Swaffham when, without pre-arrangement, the missionary meeting was turned into an African one, and no less a sum than £40 was then and there assured. Rev. John Smith, our great authority on missions,—himself a Norfolk man and veteran African missionary—believes that this was the first African missionary meeting in Primitive Methodism, and that as such it claims the notice of the historian. We agree with him, and hence make no excuse for placing on record the few words which introduce the Report :—

"At a MISSIONARY MEETING which was held at Swaffham, Norfolk, May 3rd, 1852, in connection with the twenty-seventh annual meeting of the Norwich District, 'the place was shaken where they assembled,'—the Holy Ghost fell upon them, and without premeditation or design on the part of the assembled brethren, the claims of Africa, with its vast population of seventy millions, were so forcibly impressed upon the hearts of the people that, immediately, the munificent sum of £40 5s. was subscribed in furtherance of the above object.

"At the same time, the following ministers, Thomas Lowe, William Wood, and John G. Wright presented themselves as 'the messengers of the Churches' to the dark-browed tribes of Africa. Hallelujah! 'Ethiopia shall soon stretch out her hands unto God.'"*

ROBERT KEY, *Treasurer, pro. tem.*
GEO. T. GOODRICK, *Secretary, pro. tem.*

But the atmosphere of the quickly ensuing Conference at York was very different from that of the District Meeting at Swaffham. It was as the difference between a refrigerating chamber and a greenhouse. "That the opening of a mission at Port Natal, Africa, is considered premature." Such is the brief curt record that alone remains to tell that the subject of the African mission came under discussion. Five years later the Conference thermometer registered a few degrees higher—only a few. "That while the Conference wishes to cherish a spirit of missionary enterprise, yet, on account of the embarrassed state of the Mission Funds, the Conference cannot at present commence a mission at Port Natal." The late Dr. S. Antliff was present as a hearer at this Cambridge Conference, and sat in the gallery by the side of Mr. Fuller. He tells how Thomas Lowe came in laden with books and papers, and how he waxed warm in his pleadings. So did Mr. Fuller. "I have no doubt there are persons who would give £10," said the pleader. Mr. Fuller leaning over the gallery responded heartily, "I will." But as we have said the vote recorded was adverse, and Mr. Fuller had an explanation to offer. "It was," said he, "because the proposition came from the little Norfolk District that it was not carried. Had it come from Nottingham or Manchester or some large District it would have been adopted."

* The whole of this interesting document, with the names and contributions of the donors, is given as an appendix to Rev. J. Smith's Hartley Lecture on "Christ and Missions." J. G. Wright afterwards went to Australia. See *ante*, p. 432.

THE PERIOD OF CONSOLIDATION AND CHURCH DEVELOPMENT. 485

Some advance was made at the Conference of 1858 held at Doncaster, at which Robert Key and Messrs. G. T. Goodrick and W. Lift were the representatives of the Norwich District. This Conference decided that as soon as the friends of the Norwich District should raise £500 over and above their ordinary missionary revenue one

THE BANNI MISSION

THE MISSION HOUSE

MISSION CHAPEL BUILT 1900

THE COCOA FARM PREMISES

A ROAD THROUGH THE COCOA FARM TO THE BEACH

missionary should be sent to Port Natal: if they succeeded in raising £1000 then two missionaries should be sent. Upon this, Thomas Lowe issued a circular in which he not only made a strong appeal for subscriptions, but gave information—geographical, statistical, etc., about Africa. The circular, it should be said, bears the names of many of the leading preachers and laymen of the District.

We hasten to chronicle what was done at the Jubilee Conference of 1860—one of the greatest Conferences in our history. At this memorable Conference the definitive step was taken. No longer was it to be a question of Norwich District, or of what Norwich District might or might not do. The Connexion as a whole became committed to the African mission. The General Committee was authorised " to send two men to this interesting part of the field of missionary labour as soon as suitable men could be found." After this, postponement there might be and was, but there could be no going back. As soon as the decision was announced, "such a manifestation of divine influence was felt as led to a loud burst of praise to God." No fault can be found with the temperature of *this* Conference. Even the scanty records yet remaining of its doings glow with feeling. Amongst the delegates sat Thomas Lowe, W. Lift, and James Fuller. It was a proud high moment for them and the District they represented. After the vote was taken, Mr. Fuller rose and with full heart and faltering voice said, " Here's my £20 to begin with." As for Thomas Lowe he was exultant: the letter he wrote home that day (which we have read) is punctuated with Hallelujahs!

FERNANDO PO.

R. W. Burnett and Henry Roe, our pioneer missionaries to Africa, set sail on January 25th, 1870, and landed at Santa Isabel, Fernando Po, on February 21st.

The date of this event and its *locale* alike challenge a word of explanation. Between the authorisation of the African mission and its establishment there was an interval of nine years and eight months. Like the abeyant period of camp-meetings it was one of those times of retardment and tarrying which lead men to say regretfully with Paul, " I purposed . . . but was let hitherto." The only explanation forthcoming of the delay is the difficulty experienced in securing suitable men. But surely the explanation itself needs explaining; and the explanation if sought for would probably be found to run down deep into the particular condition of the Churches at the time. Those who remember the period in question, or who have made a study of its characteristics, will know that it was not a period marked by fervency of zeal or hopeful aggressiveness, nor will they be in any danger of regarding those days as better than these we are living in. Speaking generally, the Free Churches of the land, ours amongst the number, have a much firmer grip of the essential truths of the evangelical faith now than was the case in the 'sixties—those days of blatant agnosticism and negative theology. There is evidence—and the evidence may be taken for a symptom—that men otherwise qualified than by mere enthusiasm were backward in offering themselves for the mission-field. Here, probably, we have our hand on the indicator. The unwillingness or readiness of men to offer themselves for service in the parts beyond is a sure gauge of the amount of virile force and motive power possessed by a Church. The missionary spirit which constrains men to offer themselves, and makes willing hands hold the ropes, is but the outworking of the "vivid evangelic feeling," and this spirit, thank God! is much more in evidence in these latter days than it was forty years ago. All this, of course, is written without prejudice to those who *did* offer themselves. Because we cannot help thinking of the number who hung back and declined the call, we honour all the more the small band of volunteers who stepped to the front.

Then again the *locale* of the African mission was quite other than it was expected to be. Port Natal had been ear-marked as the Connexion's intended sphere of missionary operations. The platform and printing-press had familiarised our people with the name, the physical features, and many advantages of the Colony. Yet, by one of those strange turns of events which sometimes occur, the unexpected happened. The first foreign mission was not planted on the Continent of Africa, but on a small island off its West coast—an island whose very name probably, not even Thomas Lowe had mentioned in his many African speeches and writings. More than this: when the next mission in the order of time was begun in Africa, it was not established in Port Natal but in Cape Colony and the borders of the Orange Free State.

It ought to be unnecessary at this time of day to locate and describe Fernando Po; but it is safer not to assume too much exact knowledge on such subjects. Let us therefore put down—encyclopædia fashion—a few particulars respecting the island which for more than thirty years has seen the coming and going of our missionaries.

> Fernando Po is an island in the Bight of Biafra (itself a part of the Gulf of Guinea), with an area of 671 square miles. It is forty-five miles in length and twenty-five in breadth, but the nature of its surface—heaved up in mountainous masses and scored with deep ravines, and its dense vegetation make these figures misleading; to traverse or even to explore it throughout its whole extent is difficult if not impossible. The island, oblong in shape, with steep rocky coasts, and disposed in a NNE. direction, is bisected by 2° 39″ N. latitude. Its northern half is almost entirely occupied by the volcanic peak (10,000 feet), known to the English as Mount Clarence, to the Spaniards as Pico Santa Isabel; and its southern half contains a short range lying East and West. The island is covered with luxuriant vegetation. The average annual temperature at Santa Isabel, the capital (population 1500), is 78° Fahrenheit. The island is inhabited by the Bubis, a Bantu tribe, who number 20,000 to 25,000, and by some negroes from the mainland who are found chiefly at the capital. Maize and yams, cocoa, coffee, palm oil, and palm wine are the principal products. Discovered by the Portuguese Fernão de Pao in 1472, the island has belonged successively to Spain (1777—1827), England, and Spain (since 1841). Here ships call to replenish their wood, water, and provisions.

This last reference to Fernando Po as a convenient port of call explains why on a certain day in August, 1869, the ship "Elgiva" dropped her anchor and remained some days off Santa Isabel. The master of this ship, Capt. W. Robinson, and ship-carpenter James Hands were both members in the Liverpool Second Circuit, the latter being society-steward, assistant class-leader, and a zealous labourer.[*] Being good Primitives they carried their religion with them on ship-board and on the outward voyage, nor did they throw it off when they landed amongst the Fernandians and Krumen. Finding that though the Baptist missionaries had quitted the island the year before, the little flock left behind had not lost its relish for divine things, they tried to break to it the word of life. They sang and prayed, and ship-carpenter Hands preached to the people and won their hearts. They would have made him their

---

[*] Ship-carpenter Hands died at Bonny soon after—October 1st, 1869, and Captain Robinson died August 10th, 1872.

minister then and there ; but, of course, that could not be. Yet the outcome of this unofficial evangelising—which reminds us how many such incidents must have occurred amongst the isles of the Ægean Sea and along the Mediterranean sea-board in Apostolic times—was that a requisition was dispatched to Mr. Crooks of Liverpool, James Hands' leader, asking that a Primitive Methodist missionary might be sent. This requisition was handed to Mr. Wilkinson, the superintendent, and by him forthwith forwarded to the General Missionary Committee.

As the petition bore the date August 28th, '69, the answer to its prayer was not long delayed, for, as we have said, it was on February 21st, '70, our first missionaries arrived. When the "Mandingo" cast anchor in the bay, two men with dusky faces habited as Englishmen sprang lightly on deck to welcome the missionaries. They announced themselves as T. R. Prince and J. B. Davies, two of those who had attached their names to the requisition. Of these signatories Mr. Prince is the only one who survives. For this reason, and because he has ever been a good friend to the mission and is a good specimen of the Fernandians of Santa Isabel, we give his portrait and an authentic note or two respecting his life, supplied by Rev. G. E. Wiles, returned missionary.

Born at Sierra Leone about 1834 of heathen parents, T. R. Prince was when quite a child taken to Lagos, and there educated in the Church Missionary Society's Institute. On leaving the Institute he became for a time Government clerk at Cape Coast, but soon left the service and returned to Lagos. In '54 his uncle sent him to Fernando Po, where he became clerk to the English Consul. Finding his duties uncongenial he would have returned to Lagos had not the Consul—Mr. Beecroft—urged him to join the staff of the Baptist Mission. He did so, and as schoolmaster he had among his earliest pupils Rev. W. N. Barleycorn, his brother and sister, and many of those who are now the oldest members of our Church. The Baptist missionary urged him to give himself to the ministry, and suggested his going to England to the Baptist College, of which Dr. Angus was then the Principal. But Mr. Prince resolutely refused baptism, having been baptised in infancy; consequently he left the mission staff and re-entered business. As a trader and cocoa farmer he was industrious and prosperous. All through the years he has been loyal to our Church, has stood by it through all its chequered experiences, and freely given to it his presence, prayers, labour, and substance. He is with us still, and at seventy-one years of age is present at the services, twice every Sunday, often facing elementary conditions which keep away younger and stronger but less earnest men. He is a fine specimen of a simple-hearted, humble, but really intelligent Christian African.

MR. T. R. PRINCE.

The 21st February, 1870, was, then, a memorable day for Fernando Po. On the early morning of that day as the "Mandingo" drew near the island, it was observed— "Midnight is passed; the [Southern] Cross begins to bend." The familiar stellar phenomenon may be construed as a symbol of good omen. For Fernando Po the longing for the breaking of the day was at last to be gratified, and the religion of the cross, as contrasted with that of the crucifix, was bending benignly over the island. On the evening of this same day, which began so auspiciously, the first Primitive Methodist service was held in the house of "Mamma" Job. At this significant service the cross was pre-eminent. The first hymn sung was "There is a fountain filled with blood," the text of the sermon and the key-note of all that followed was, "God so loved the world, that He gave His only begotten Son, that whosoever believeth in Him should not perish, but have everlasting life." "Tank God! tank de Missionaries! and tank de good people of England!" expressed the gladsome feelings of the people when, as the service ended and lantern-in-hand and carrying their seats on their heads, they made their way home along varied paths. One can readily understand why the late Rev. T. Guttery, in speaking of this service at the Metropolitan Tabernacle, should say :—

REV. HENRY ROE.    PETER BULL.    REV. R. S. BLACKBURN.

"Next to that undying camp-meeting on Mow Hill, we will tell our children of that first service at Mamma Job's house. The facts of 1870 begin a new chapter in the Connexion's life."

On the 28th February, the first class was formed consisting of eleven persons, all of whom, though they bore English names, were Africans, representing various and distant tribes. Some of them, like Mamma Job, were redeemed slaves, while others were the free children of such. One of the eleven was Peter Bull, a native of the Island, who afterwards did good service as an interpreter for the missionaries when preaching to the Bubis. Some of the first members were the fruit of the Baptist Mission, while others gave their names as anxious "to flee from the wrath to come." Rev. Henry Roe had the joy of witnessing the first conversion on March 6th, when a young Fernandian woman named Jane Scholar yielded to the Saviour. She afterwards died in the faith. The pioneers met with much success. At the first Quarter Day, held on April 21st, there were reported forty-five African members and an income of £4 5s. 4d. Several visits were paid to the natives of the interior; a Sunday and Day School were commenced, and W. N. Barleycorn joined the Church, and, under the guidance of the missionaries, began to acquire knowledge, and already gave proof of that capacity, steadiness, and usefulness so conspicuous in his subsequent career, amply justifying the statement of the Rev. D. T. Maylott that "if the Fernando Po Mission had done nothing more than effect the conversion and training of W. N. Barleycorn, it would still be a glorious success."*

The story of those early days of the mission as told by the Rev. Henry Roe in his little books†—to which the reader is referred for details—has in it many idyllic touches. You cannot fail to catch the notes of gladness and hope. But still, even in those first days, the influences which have made the Fernando Po mission a difficult one and costly, in another than a monetary sense, were not absent or irrecognizable. There might be sunlight in plenty and luxuriant vegetation, but, occasionally, the tornado wrought fearful havoc, and always the climate was treacherous and secretly sapped the strength of the willing workers. Both missionaries lost an infant child, and they and their noble wives were prostrated by sickness, and it soon became clear that no

REV. M. H. BARRON.    REV. W. B. LUDDINGTON.    REV. W. HOLLAND.

lengthened term of continuous service was possible in such a land, even for those who in England were strong to labour; that only by frequent reliefs and relays of workers could the mission be sustained. One of the panels in our combination picture shows the sacred corner in Santa Isabel, where lies the dust of some of those who have sacrificed their lives at the post of duty. R. S. Blackburn after eight months of devoted service died April 22nd, 1892. In the obituary notice of him it is said that "his career furnishes a specimen of consecration to God worthy to rank with that of Henry Martyn and others of kindred reputation. Thus has fallen our *first* standard-bearer, whose remains await, on a heathen soil, the resurrection of the just." By his side lies M. H. Barron who was inspired to give himself to the African work by listening to missionary addresses by Messrs. R. W. Burnett and R. Fairley. He threw

* The statement was made at the Conference of 1872. So also the Rev. N. Boocock says: "The best thing the Fernandians ever did was to give the Rev. W. N. Barleycorn to the work of the ministry. Mr. Barleycorn is a fine Christian gentleman, and a faithful minister of the Lord Jesus Christ."—*Aldersgate Magazine*, May, 1905.

† "Mission to Africa," "West African Scenes," and "Fernando Po Mission."

himself with much zeal into every department of the work, but was suddenly called home on January 22nd, 1901. Here, too, in the cemetery at Santa Isabel lie the remains of Mrs. Maylott and Mrs. Boocock. To this roll of the honoured dead must be added the names of W. B. Luddington and his wife, who after three terms of service in the Island died soon after their return to England, and of Mrs. Buckenham who in 1886 succumbed to a last attack of fever while on board a steamer for a few hours' voyage. "Within twenty hours Mr. Buckenham returned to the island sad and lonely, his wife in her grave on the mainland."

From the very beginning the work of evangelisation in Fernando Po has been retarded by maleficent influences other than those due to climate. It is significant—and one may even say portentous—that the "Mandingo" which brought our first missionaries to the Island also brought nine hundred gallons of rum. Time has wrought no mitigation of the evil. Now, thirty-five years after the landing of our first missionaries, Mr. Boocock has to write:—"I am extremely sorry to learn that there is a growing tendency among the Fernandians to trade with these solutions (rum and gin) on the assumption that they are a necessity, being as much a common currency as pounds, shillings, and pence are to us in England. Personally, I look upon trade-rum and gin as unmitigated curses." So serious is the evil that the Missionary Report for 1904 is constrained to say:—"The white man's drink is working deadly and increasing havoc and making our labour doubly difficult, and in some instances terribly threatening it. Our representatives, however, are bravely battling against its destructive operations."

Fernando Po belongs to Spain: the Jesuits have a mission on the Island; and it is a far cry from Fernando Po to Madrid. The inference is obvious; for the Society of Jesus is in its essence always the same, however much it may choose to vary its methods. That we have still a footing on the Island is not due to the goodwill of the Jesuit Padres. But for the courage and tact of our representatives, and the might of England in the background, we must have been driven from the Island years ago. Still, the opposition of the Jesuits has shown itself fitfully. It has not been a constant steady pressure, but has been felt more or less acutely according to the character and personal qualities of the Governor for the time being. If he has been a man of liberal mind and independent spirit our work—evangelistic and educational—has been allowed to proceed in quietness. But if, on the other hand, the Governor has been a bigoted Spaniard, or, worse still, a bigoted Roman Catholic, and as such subservient to the Padres, then all kinds of vexatious restrictions have been placed on that work. Some of the Governors have been not only models of courtesy, but personal friends of our missionaries and in sympathy with their work, while others have been the reverse.

As early as 1872 the educational work was interfered with. Messrs. Burnett, Roe, and Maylott were each threatened with a fine of £20 16s. 8d. for having, as was alleged, objected to a list of their scholars being taken. Refusing to pay the fine, Messrs. Roe and Maylott were threatened with summary banishment; but on an appeal to the Consul the matter was not pressed. Thus the storm blew over; but twice in the history of the mission the storm has not blown over, but has burst with full fury. The Rev. W. Holland thus tells the story of his banishment.

"When we went out in 1877, Captain Salgado had already begun his repressive measures by closing the Sunday School. Then, in succession, there followed the closing of the Day School, the two weekly (from house to house) cottage prayer-meetings, Mrs. Holland's girls' sewing class, our weekly singing practice, all services after sunset. The bell—a large one I got out from England, and by tremendous human labour had fixed some twenty feet high in the yard behind the Church—had to 'hold its tongue.' The name 'Zion Primitive Methodist Church' was an 'outward manifestation' and must be effaced. Singing at funeral processions, and then the processions themselves, were disallowed. I think the last of the repressive measures was, the sound of singing must not be heard outside the Church. For some twelve months or so, almost each day found me wondering what new trouble the next day would bring What a number of letters passed between us, and what hours and hours were wasted either at the Government House or the Mission House—he at times violently excited, quite menacing in words and tone and manner, and I, to a Spaniard I dare say, provokingly cool. The end of the matter was he sent me a 'writ of banishment' in forty-eight hours, with, I think, some thirty shillings to pay my fare to the nearest port. I returned the money, endorsing the envelope 'Declined with thanks' and, on the advice of H. B. M. Consul—Captain Hopkins—a true friend of the mission, who once took the Sunday services for me when I was ill—I hurried home. A deputation, introduced by the late Mr. S. Morley, waited on the Under Secretary for Foreign Affairs. I read and then handed to him a complete statement of my case. In a few months information came from the Foreign Office that the Spanish Government 'disavowed' the Governor's action in reference to my banishment; and a few weeks later came another dispatch saying they 'disapproved' of his action, and I was at liberty to return to the Island, which I did at once, bearing, I think, letters of authority from both the Spanish and British Governments. On reaching the Island, I found Captain Salgado had gone back to Spain, whether recalled or not I never knew. Consul Hopkins said, 'Now we'll go in for compensation," but his sudden death soon after cut short his good purpose, or probably something would have been done for me and the Society.

"My banishment, with that which led up to and followed it—all the worry and strain—told upon me so much that, after being out there again for some eighteen months, I had a most dangerous illness. My life was almost despaired of, and I was carried on board in an utterly helpless condition, but, thanks to my good wife and the Divine Helper, I recovered."

The Report of the General Missionary Committee to the Conference of 1886 has an extended reference to the scandalous treatment of Rev. W. Welford. This reference, because of its intimate bearing on the conditions under which our work in Fernando Po has been carried on, must be given here. Needless to say such incidents as these, with all that they involve, must have been detrimental to the mission, exceedingly trying to the missionaries and their families, and a source of anxiety to the Executive at home. These incidents have been costly ones too, such as, one thinks, would justify the suing of some one for "material damages." Two of our Missionary Secretaries—Revs. J. Atkinson and J. Travis—have been necessitated to journey all the way to Madrid in order to straighten out matters and secure more satisfactory relations between the Spanish Authorities and the Mission. The reference in the Report runs:—

"The work in Fernando Po has been seriously interrupted during the year by the action of the Spanish Authorities. The schools have been closed, and every indication that the mission premises are used as a place of worship has been removed by order of the Governor. Singing in the chapel has been prohibited, and all service in the cemetery at the burial of the dead. The missionary was subject to interference and annoyance of the most vexatious kind, and was at last imprisoned on board the pontoon, where he was kept for a month subject to insult and indignity from day to day, and was only released on the interference of the Commanders of Her Majesty's gun-boats who fortunately visited Santa Isabel. The people were watched as they went to and from the meetings, they were insulted by the Romish priests in the streets, summarily fined, dragged to prison, and persecuted in a great variety of ways; still they remained steadfast in the faith. The missionary and his wife were ultimately banished. The case has been placed in the hands of Her Majesty's Government, and the Governor of the island, having been recalled to Spain, the whole matter is undergoing investigation. The Committee desire to place upon record their unqualified approval of the course pursued by the missionary, the Rev. W. Welford, and his devoted wife, in the remarkably trying circumstances in which they were placed during their stay in Fernando Po; and they desire also to express their admiration of the manner in which the Rev. W. N. Barleycorn, the native minister at George's Bay, and the members of the church generally, acted during the painful ordeal they have been called to endure. Since Mr. Welford left the island there has been no further molestation of the Church, though the restrictions as to work and worship have not been removed. The Rev. R. W. Burnett, his wife, and son have been sent out to take charge of the mission till the case is settled."

At this point we set out in tabular form the names of the band of deserving men who have gone as our missionaries to Fernando Po. Let the reader scan it closely and take notice of the figures which follow the names; for these will show that some whose names are on the list have had two, three, four, and in the case of Rev. R. Fairley, no less than five terms of service on the Island, while others have done good service in other parts of the Foreign field.

1870.	R. W. Burnett	...	4	1888.	S. Blenkin	...	1
	Henry Roe	...	1	1890.	J. Burkitt	...	1
1871.	D. T. Maylott	...	2	1892.	F. Pickering	...	1
1872.	W. Holland	...	4	1894.	N. Boocock	...	1
1873.	W. B. Luddington	...	3	1895.	T. C. Showell	...	2
1874.	S. Griffith	...	1	1898.	R. W. Burnett (2)	...	1
1875.	Theo. Parr	...	1	1899.	M. H. Barron	...	1
1878.	R. S. Blackburn	...	1	,,	G. E. Wiles	...	2
1883.	H. Buckenham	...	1	1900.	T. Stones	...	1
,,	R. Fairley	...	5	1901.	J. Nichols	...	1
1885.	W. Welford	...	1	,,	Moses Holmes	...	1
,,	Harvey Roe	...	—	1904.	H. M. Cook	...	1
1888.	Jabez Bell	...	3				

LIST OF MISSIONARIES TO FERNANDO PO: THE YEAR OF THEIR FIRST APPOINTMENT, AND THE NUMBER OF TERMS THEY HAVE SERVED.

During his term of office as General Missionary Secretary, Dr. S. Antliff publicly stated that Dr. Underhill had recently written to inquire if the Primitive Methodists intended to carry their mission to the Bubis, or to confine it to the English-speaking people of Santa Isabel. The reply was, "We have bought property, intend to remain, and cover the whole Island with Primitive Methodism." On the strength of this assurance the Baptist Missionary Society has honourably refrained from attempting to re-establish its mission on the Island, and other Missionary Societies have in like manner respected our declaration of policy, and have come to look upon Fernando Po as lying entirely within the sphere of our influence. Such an understanding and virtual compact creates responsibility. It can hold good and be respected only so long as we seek to honour its engagement by endeavouring to evangelise the Island. As the sole representative of Protestantism on the Island, we are bound to spread its principles amongst the people, or else allow other Churches to lend a hand in doing a work for which we are unwilling or unequal.

How far then has the promise held out by Dr. S. Antliff been made good? The island has *not* been covered; but, in addition to Santa Isabel, three other mission-stations have been planted in the most accessible and best-known part of the Island, at points strategically situated for keeping in touch with our base at Santa Isabel, and for getting into touch with the native Bubis, and carrying on amongst them evangelistic, educational, and industrial work. These stations are at the rising towns of San Carlos on the South-west, Bottle Nose on the North-west, and Banni on the North-east, while Santa Isabel is on the North of the Island. As early as 1871 the Rev. D. T. Maylott was appointed to begin a mission in St. George's Bay, as it was then called—a beautiful bay nine miles across from point to point. His serious break-down in health retarded the opening of the mission, but W. N. Barleycorn as native teacher did useful pioneer work, and in 1873 Mr. and Mrs. Luddington began to build on the foundation already in some measure laid. Messrs. Luddington and Barleycorn laboured zealously, and their zeal had its reward. During the first six months Mr. Luddington made no less than twenty-five visits to the bush in the interior in order to induce the native boys and girls and adults to attend the Sunday School and services. A house and church were built on the beach, and, though a comparatively rude structure, Mr. Luddington was rightly proud of it; and it may be added, this first piece of Connexional property on the Island was paid for by the islanders themselves. Mr. Parr removed the mission some four or five miles up the mountain-side to Rajah, in order to be nearer the Bubi town, and, when, some years later, it was deemed desirable to add the industrial to the educational and spiritual work of the mission, its location was again changed. Rajah being situated too high for cocoa to do well, the mission was placed half-way down to the beach. There it is to-day—a cocoa-farm covering some thirty acres or more in the midst of dense primeval forest.

We ought to chronicle here an early and interesting attempt to transliterate the language of the Bubis—to analyse its grammatical forms and give its vocabulary— a task admittedly difficult of accomplishment. Through the courtesy of the Rev. T. Parr, M.A., we have had the opportunity of inspecting a small, thin, quarto volume, which should have its place in the bibliography of Primitive Methodism whenever that very desirable work shall be executed. The volume in question bears the title:— "Parr's Bubi na English Dictionary, with Notes on Grammar, George's Bay District, Primitive Methodist Mission Press, George's Bay, Fernando Po, 1881." The preface to this little volume gives a sufficiently full account of its genesis and of the difficulties surmounted in its preparation.

"When appointed to George's Bay in the early part of 1873," says Rev. W. B. Luddington, "we found the mission in its infancy, and the language entirely unwritten. Steps were immediately taken for securing a vocabulary; but, for various reasons, the work proceeded slowly. In March, 1873, about a fourth of what constitutes the present dictionary was put into the hands of the Rev. T. Parr, prior to his taking charge. Being well-adapted to the task, he already having made some proficiency in philological studies, his acquisition of the language was surprisingly rapid, and ere the completion of his term of service, he preached (of course imperfectly) in the native tongue. Notes on Grammar and an extended vocabulary were prepared by Mr. Parr, and these were kindly passed over to me when leaving England two years ago. . . . The typographical part of the work is only that of an amateur, with a small press and limited materials, which must account for its defectiveness. To Mr. W. N. Barleycorn, Peter Bull, and several of our young native converts, both Mr. Parr and myself are greatly indebted."

For some little time longing eyes had been turned to the South-east of the Island—forty miles from Santa Isabel, to a place called Biappa. Mr. Holland devoted a week to prospecting in that part of the Island and drew up a lengthy Report, which was adverse to any attempt at settlement there. Moreover, it was suggested that Banni on the North-east coast, twelve miles from Santa Isabel, would form a much more eligible location. Both Messrs. Holland and Luddington satisfied themselves by a personal visit as to the eligibility of the proposed mission, and, during Mr. Buckenham's term, the mission was tentatively begun. But to Rev. Jabez Bell belong the honours of Banni. "Bell of Banni" might well be his honorific title. He bore with wonderful patience the early hostility of the natives, and the frustration of cherished hopes, and at last, by the sheer force of his example and personal influence, he won over the natives. His long and efficient service amid most trying conditions, and the signal success of this Industrial Mission are highly appreciated by our Church. It is pleasing to be able to give the unsolicited private endorsement of this judgment by one of our veteran missionaries who says:—"Mr. Bell's self-denial in the initial stages of the Mission no one has any idea of. I said when out there spending some time on the Mission—'Not one in a thousand would practise such noble self-abandonment in the interest of missions as he did.'"

Bottle Nose made its first appearance on the stations in the Conference Minutes of 1896. This place of strange name is a kind of half-way house between Santa Isabel and San Carlos. Our early missionaries knew its sheltered cove well; for often, in boating between the two places mentioned, they would land on its little beach, so that their Krumen might prepare their "chop," while they themselves welcomed a short respite from sea-sickness, and drank their refreshing cup of tea.

Two outstanding features of our Fernando Po Mission have been and still are—the spirit of self-help and liberality shown by our adherents, and the remarkable success of our Industrial Missions. In regard to the former that acute observer, the Rev. N. Boocock, points out that during the last twelve years the Church at Santa Isabel has raised more money for the African Fund than any Church in Primitive Methodism, averaging as it has done more than £150 per year, and with a membership numbering less than 130. Nor, as he also points out, has this been done without an immense struggle and many instances of real self-sacrifice.

ALIWAL NORTH.

Where is Aliwal North, and how came we to plant ourselves there? As to the latter, largely, it would seem, as the result of unforeseen events and circumstances. A Mr. Lindsay, we are told, a gentleman formerly in communion with the Primitive Wesleyans, had settled in what was then the Orange Free State. Mr. Lindsay was anxious to secure the appointment of a Primitive Methodist missionary, and with that end in view, entered into communication with our General Missionary Committee, guaranteeing the salary of a young man for the first year. The appeal was considered and responded to, and Rev. Henry Buckenham, formerly a devoted local preacher in the East Dereham Circuit, and at that time on the Burton-on-Trent Circuit, consented to become the Connexion's pioneer missionary in South Africa. He sailed in the "Marsden," October 5th, 1870, and after touching at Cape Town, landed at Port Elizabeth on November 20th. Thence he travelled up the country, 300 miles, arriving, *en route*, at Aliwal North, on the Orange River, which divides Cape Colony from the Orange River Colony. Here he found Mr. Lindsay, who had settled in the town, and here, accordingly, Mr. Buckenham elected to pitch his tent. Meanwhile, it is said, instructions came to hand from the General Missionary Committee, to the effect that their missionary should make his way to the newly-discovered Diamond Fields. But this was not done; and the situation as it then presented itself was accepted, with all that has followed. This explains why, without pre-announcement, or even prevision, "Aliwal North, Henry Buckenham" unobtrusively appears on the stations in the Conference Minutes of 1871.

For a Sunday or two, while a room was being fitted up, services were held in a Dutch Church. A Sunday School was opened January 15th; an evening school for coloured people on July 18th; and in the following month Mr. Buckenham, in conjunction with Mr. Lindsay, opened a day school. Ten pounds was all Mr. Lindsay had to lay down to make up the deficiency on the year's working, so liberally did the congregation that had been gathered contribute to the support of the missionary. During Mr. Buckenham's term, a church, vestry, and house were built at Aliwal, and land secured at Jamestown, on which our second chapel in South Africa was afterwards erected. Mr. Buckenham returned to England in August, 1875, his place having previously been taken by Rev. John Smith, another Norfolk District man. As showing that Yarmouth Circuit still retained its practical interest in African missions, let it be noted that that Circuit contributed £200 towards defraying the cost of conveying Mr. Smith and family to their destination. At this time the membership at Aliwal was reported at 15; in 1879 when Mr. Smith was relieved by Rev. J. Watson it stood at 130. In 1881 the ministerial staff was strengthened by the addition of J. Bradley and J. Msikinya. W. N. Barleycorn in Fernando Po and J. Msikinya were *our first coloured ministers;* they began their honourable ministry together, their names appearing on the same Conference Minutes of 1881. In 1883 Dr. Watson removed to

Adelaide, South Australia, and Rev. J. Smith returned to the scene of his former labours. After a second term of five years, in which the mission underwent development and made gratifying progress, Mr. Smith was succeeded by Rev. G. E. Butt. The General Missionary Committee had looked out with some considerable degree of anxiety for a successor to Mr. Smith; the more so, as it was in contemplation to establish a Technical School. The Committee were wisely guided in their selection of a man, since Mr. Butt not only possessed the necessary ministerial qualifications, but the secular training he had received eminently fitted him to take charge of the proposed institution. In 1888, therefore, Mr. Butt entered upon what proved to be his seventeen years' superintendency of the mission. His son, Rev. G. H. Butt, was already on the staff as minister and schoolmaster.

REV. G. E. BUTT.
(President of Conference, 1905.)

By common consent Aliwal North is regarded as our widest and most prosperous mission station. We should, however, think of Aliwal as the centre of a diocese rather than as a circuit of the normal type; since the so-called circuit is some 150 miles long by 50 miles wide, contains eight sub-centres, each in charge of a trained agent, and each having grouped around it several preaching-stations. The superintendent of such a wide, polyglot station as this—for the Gospel is preached in three languages—who has to keep his hands on the various strands of the work—spiritual, educational, technical—must needs be a man of affairs, with a wide outlook, and possessing considerable organising power, and such the successive superintendents of Aliwal have been. Despite the periods of unsettledness which have recurred, the shifting of the population both native and European, and the temporary upsettal and ravages of the late war, the progress of the mission has been remarkably steady and gratifying. Thirty-four years ago we began with one member—the missionary himself; in 1905, the total membership is reported as 1608. Commensurate with the numerical advance recorded by these figures there has also been an augmentation of the teaching staff, and an increase in the number of buildings belonging to the Mission. As completing the outline of the Aliwal North Mission's history, it must be added that on Mr. Butt's return to this country, where the deserved honour of being elected President of the Conference of 1905 awaited him, the Rev. F. Pickering took charge of the Aliwal Mission.

The educational work carried on at Aliwal North has long been an outstanding feature of the mission; and, in its bearing on the future of the natives themselves receiving instruction, as well as in its bearing on the future development of our missions in South Central Africa, it is a feature deserving all the prominence given to it. It was in 1889 Mr. Butt started the Training School. Before starting it he visited all the kindred schools of other Churches that were within his reach. He was especially attracted towards the French Mission in Basutoland. Here he found three schools at work for the higher education of the natives; the normal school, to train teachers; the Bible school, to train evangelists; and the industrial school, to teach trades. It occurred to Mr. Butt that it would be well to unite these three sections of the same

THE PERIOD OF CONSOLIDATION AND CHURCH DEVELOPMENT. 499

ALIWAL MISSION

ALIWAL NATIVE CHURCH

LAYING FOUNDATION STONE OF NEW NATIVE CHURCH

GROUP OF NATIVE TEACHERS

THE LOCATION CHURCH NATIVE

HALF CASTE CHURCH

THE SEWING CLASS

SOME OF THE MISSION SCHOLARS

work in one school. The Aliwal School, therefore, is founded on that broad basis. It was an experiment, but it is proving a successful experiment. The school was started sixteen years ago with four pupils. Writing in 1903 Mr. Butt says: "Before the war we had twenty-seven pupils; but the school was broken up by the Boers. Many of the students joined the British forces, and we had virtually to begin our work again. We have now fifteen."

The Training College, then, has the threefold aim before it of making Scholars so far proficient in the elements of ordinary education as to pass the standards; to make evangelists, and to qualify "the boys" for industrial life. A gratifying measure of success has been realised in each of these departments of endeavour. "All our male teachers on the station, excepting one," says Mr. Butt, "have been trained in our own schools, and we have sent five to the Zambesi." In regard to the industrial department he further says:—

"The first care is to teach them self-help. They prepare their own food, mend and wash their clothes, clean their rooms, and do all that is necessary to enable them to live as good Christians. All this, as a source of education, is more important than it seems. In their heathen state the women have to do all the work, excepting look after the cattle, and it is only as they are brought to understand the dignity of all useful labour that they are prepared to treat their women with proper respect. They are also taught gardening, including grafting, planting and pruning of fruit-trees, the cultivation of all the various kinds of vegetables which can be grown in the country, and in a small way they are taught to grow corn also.

"The chief feature, however, of the Industrial section is the Carpenters' Shop. Here the first thing the boys learn is to break, or spoil the tools. But while there is a great difference in the degree of aptitude shown by the boys, many of them take quickly to the mechanical part of the work. The great difficulty is to get them to understand the principles of design. To see a piece of work set out on a board, and then see the various parts at which they have been working, when put together, answer to the design, is a source of great wonder to them, and they often express their surprise by saying, 'The English are very clever people.'"

If the reader will turn to the illustrations of our Aliwal North Mission, which have been taken expressly for this History, they will find further light cast on the Training School as a useful and money-saving institution. Referring to the view of the Head Master's House (p. 501), Mr. Butt says:—

"I am very proud of this house. It is my own design, and *the whole of the work was done by the students under my direction.* They quarried the stones and put in the foundations; made the bricks and burnt them; put the roof on; did all the carpentry and painting; and also made much of the furniture. For the house and furniture the General Missionary Committee made us a grant of £350. The dining-room has a panelled ceiling, and also a dado. The best bed-room is fitted with wardrobes; and, as you can see in the picture, it has a beautiful verandah on two sides. Had it been built by contract it would have cost from £1,000 to £1,200. The difference between that amount and £350 is what was saved by our labour. We had to pay for nothing but the timber, iron, paint, and paper. It is an object-lesson in what the natives can be got to do when carefully instructed and directed. All this industrial work is done out of school-hours.

THE PERIOD OF CONSOLIDATION AND CHURCH DEVELOPMENT. 501

ALIWAL MISSION

EUROPEAN CHURCH AND TRAINING SCHOOL

EUROPEAN CHURCH JAMESTOWN

STUDENTS IN TRAINING SCHOOL

TRAINING SCHOOL WORK SHOP

THE PARSONAGE

HEAD MASTERS HOUSE

"The students also built the workshop, and they did the carpentry of the Training School, making even the seats and the desks. They did the carpentry of the Half-caste Church and of the Location Church [since successfully opened]; with the result that the door and window-frames you see in the walls have been made; the windows, doors, and pews are ready, and we are now preparing for the roof. We have also done all the carpentry work for six new churches in the Orange River Colony; and we have just made many doors and windows to replace those destroyed by the Boers in the war. I have dwelt at large on this part of our work, because it supplies the secret of much of our extension. Six of our churches have been built without any cost to the General Missionary Committee, and this could not have been done but for the Training School. As far as their scholastic work is concerned, we put them through the teacher's course under Government—the same course that is taken by the Europeans. This of course is the work of my son. But I train them as evangelists, giving them a Bible-lesson every evening, and they visit the out-stations to preach."

We are not now writing a full history of our African Missions. That, we trust, will before long be done by some one qualified for the task by intimate knowledge and long experience. But sufficient has been written to fit Aliwal North into its place in this general History, and sufficient to convince our readers that the Connexion has abundant reason to be satisfied with the founders and developers of that mission, and with the visible fruitage of their conscientious labour.

South-Central Africa.

There can be no question that the policy which resulted in the planting of our mission in Central Africa was largely shaped by the Rev. John Smith. Mr. Smith is a man of ideas, enlarged by study and practical experience on the mission-field. His study of the missionary problem as it presented itself to him,—not merely in books, but on the banks of the Orange River, made him dissatisfied with the position and prospects of our Church in Africa. He saw no hope of any great enlargement of the sphere of operations in South Africa. His reflections crystallised in the conviction that "if we mean to do any real lasting work we must go out into the clear open field of untouched heathenism." He soon reached another conclusion: that the evangelisation of Africa could best and most quickly be accomplished by the Africans themselves, who must therefore be trained and qualified for the purpose.[*] What Mr. Smith believes he believes firmly, and defends and presses strongly; and so the ideas he explained and advocated so persistently and strenuously, gained acceptance, and are already bearing fruit.

At the Conference of 1886 the question of opening a Mission in Central Africa was introduced by a letter from Rev. J. Smith, and was referred to the Missionary Committee. That Committee sought further information regarding climate, &c., from Mr. Smith, who pressed the Conference of 1887 to attempt the Mission; and the whole question was relegated to a large Conferential Committee, which met in Leicester, in October of that year, and decided to send a missionary expedition to seek a sphere of labour North of the Zambesi. Mr. Smith urged the Conference at Liverpool in the

[*] See Rev. J. Smith's printed Report on Missionary Policy and Extension considered at Leicester, October, 1887.

THE PERIOD OF CONSOLIDATION AND CHURCH DEVELOPMENT. 503

NKALA MISSION

NATIVE EVANGELISTS HOUSE

MISSION HOUSE LOOKING EAST

MASHUKULUMBWE WITH CONES

MISSION STATION LOOKING WEST

NATIVE MUSICAL INSTRUMENTS

THE MISSION CHURCH

FIRST RELIGIOUS SERVICE AT NATIVE FUNERAL

THE CEMETERY. THE WHITE CROSSES SHOW THE GRAVES OF THE MISSIONARYS & FAMILIES following June to carry out the decision of the Leicester Committee. The General Missionary Committee communicated with certain brethren, whose names were submitted to the Quarterly Meeting of the Missionary Committee, held at Peterborough in October, 1888, and the issue was that two ministers—Rev. Henry Buckenham and Arthur Baldwin—and F. Ward as artisan missionary were appointed to the work, who sailed from Dartmouth on April 26th, 1889.

The step thus taken by the Connexion marked an important advance. It was indeed a new departure. Quite truly the General Missionary Committee, in its Report to the Conference of 1890, affirms:—" This is the greatest and most important enterprise which our Church has ever undertaken. We are entering upon pioneer missionary work, and, at the command of the Master, going to convert people who know nothing of His love and power." Hitherto, even in Africa, we had gone where we had been desired and invited; now we were going where our presence was not asked for, but where, for that very reason, our presence was the more urgently needed. Let this fact with its implications be duly pondered.

The Zambesi Mission Party reached Mashukulumbweland in December [1893] and are now engaged in erecting Mission premises and in ministering to the people." (G. M. C. Report, 1894.) The words are soon written and read; but though the words are true enough, yet to leave them just as they stand, would be to offend against the truth and to do a wrong to the living and the dead. In fact, those years of wandering, of weary waiting and frequent mischance, of heroic endeavour often frustrated, make a story which " when written will not only tend to popularise our African missions, but cannot fail to be an inspiration to us all" (Conference Address, 1897). But who can write this story except one—Rev. A. Baldwin—the sole ministerial survivor of the pioneer mission party, and the brave and trusty colleague of Mr. Buckenham, until the lamented death of the latter, July 11th, 1896? This so obvious consideration determines us to let Mr. Baldwin speak for himself of those trying initial days, so that the reader may gain something like an adequate impression of what was then done and suffered. Did we write, " speak for himself"? That is what Mr. Baldwin does not do. He speaks of Mr. Buckenham, but says little of his own share in the experiences, and nothing of his chivalrous conduct to Mr. Buckenham and his sorely stricken widow.

Our delays are well known to the friends at home. I mean the fact that we were nearly five years from leaving England to reaching Mashukulumbweland: but all the trials, disappointments, persecutions, anxieties, and worries of those years can never be known, nor yet fully imagined. We have helplessly watched our oxen die until not one has remained. We have been again and again ordered to leave the country; have had our boys taken from us, and all our food-supplies stopped so that we should be starved out, in fact, have had all the vial of King Lewanika's wrath, brewed by the machinations of a wicked trader, envious of the Chartered Company and the influence the missionaries had over the king, poured on our heads; still, Mr. Buckenham never lost heart. Others, whilst sorry for our position, were sure that the king would never relent, and that we should have either to return home or go and seek a field elsewhere : but his faith never wavered, his hope never died. He always seemed to see the silver lining to the cloud, to peer through the darkness to the morning that would assuredly break: and that faith, after being severely tried, God honoured by giving us an open door and every facility for entering it.

No man could have worked harder or thrown more heartiness into his work than our brother did. In training oxen and driving wagons, in performing long tedious journeys, both in the height of the rainy season, and when the summer's sun was blazing, in executing the many repairs needed to the wagons, gear, and other utensils, and in building-work on our new stations, he was always engaged. From "dawn to dewy eve" Mr. Buckenham toiled incessantly through all these years without ever taking a rest. He never spared himself, but even when suffering great pain, has, in his desire to push on the mission, continued at his post. Many, many times he has been compelled to put down his tools and go to his bed, but the moment he was a little better he would be back again.

The magnanimity of his nature was shown in his conduct *re* the question of his return. His engagement with the General Missionary Committee was simply to locate the Mission, and having successfully done this he might have returned home in 1894; but, so much as he longed to return for his daughters' sakes, he forewent his privilege, and in the spirit of Mackay of Uganda declared that it was no time to thin the ranks, but rather to reinforce them. Again last year, after being so ill, and the Committee invited him to return home, he gave his personal interests but secondary consideration. He longed to see a network of stations speedily established across the country, and so decided to stay two or three years longer. He had already formed a plan which was to first see me housed at Nkala, and then go further inland, pitch afresh his tent, and there break up the ground for founding a third station. But his work was finished.

In November he was stricken down again, and although occasionally he seemed better, and we grew at these times hopeful of his recovery, it became evident that only a return home, and the best medical treatment, would suffice to restore him : so, reluctantly, he decided to leave his much beloved work. It was then at the height of our rainy season, when travelling, in his condition, was impossible, and they had to wait, wait, wait until the roads became passable. Meanwhile their dear little girl, Elsie, the child of the Mission, the sunshine of our life, the beloved of everybody, of even the poor, naked, savage Mashukulumbwe—she was taken by the angels on February 3rd, 1896, adding a load of sorrow to the already heavy burden of sufferings being borne by our brother. These were dark days in the history of our Mission. At length the rains passed, and on April 29th, after much worry and delay through the conduct of the porters, Mr. and Mrs. Buckenham turned their faces homeward. There were no oxen to draw a wagon, and they had to be carried in hammocks. It was a cruel journey, for the carriers, seeing Mr. Buckenham's helplessness, took base advantage to travel only when and as far as they liked. Some days they would not stir, but spent the time in trying to extort promises of exorbitant pay on reaching Kazungula. Consequently the journey was greatly prolonged, and his sufferings intensified. On reaching Kazungula, he had to take to his bed, and for seven weeks bravely bore acute affliction ; then, on the morning of July 11th, at 8.30, without a struggle, he quietly fell asleep, and was borne to his eternal home and rest. A mound, under a great mosinzela tree, enclosed with a stout fence of mopani poles to preserve it from the wild beasts, marks his resting-place. A rustic cross has been erected at the head, with a board affixed, on which is painted "Rev. H. Buckenham, Born May 7th, 1844. Died July 11th, 1896."

Our mission in North Western Rhodesia, as this region of South Central Africa is termed, is still in its formative stage. The country is being prospected, and central mission-stations with their outposts planted at the most promising points. There have been losses and disappointments. We have regretfully to record the death of Mr. Walter Hogg, artisan missionary at Sagolas, and Mrs. Pickering and Baldwin have been removed by death, but still the work goes on, and the future is full of promise.

The Report presented to the Conference of 1905 states:—

"At Nkala, the congregations are good, and 83 children have their names on the school register. At Nanzela, at the best season of the year, the congregations sometimes number 200, while there are 73 children in the school. Rev. E. W. Smith has given much attention to the arrangement of the language, the compilation of a grammar, and of a book of Scripture stories and other linguistic work, all of which must be of great value in the years to come. At Sajobas, the work is exceedingly full of promise. A good native teacher has been secured during the year, and most gratifying reports reach us of the labour amongst young people. Opportunities for extension appeal to us on every side. As to Livingstone, our establishment is too recent to afford much data for report. Undoubtedly in that region great possibilities are opening to us."

Southern Nigeria.

For some years the General Missionary Committee desired to establish a Mission on the river Opobo in the Oil River Protectorate. Acting on instructions, Rev. W. Holland crossed over from Fernando Po and spent three weeks prospecting in this district, and reported favourably upon it. But, doubtless for sufficient reasons, the Committee turned its attention to another district on the mainland of the West Coast of Africa; and in 1894 "James M. Brown, Acqua River," appears on the stations. The mission then begun, and subsequently carried on by Messrs. T. Stones, W. J. Ward, C. F. Gill, N. Boocock, R. Banham, G. H. Hanney, W. Glover, and W. Christie, is now known as our mission in Southern Nigeria and is one of our most promising fields of labour. It is in British territory; conveniently situated with regard to Fernando Po, and contains a large population eager to have missionaries labouring amongst them. We have now three centres in this district—Oron, Jamestown, and Urea Eye, and almost any number of possible sub-stations. A new Training Institute has been opened at Oron particularly for the equipment of native teachers, and the societies of Christian Endeavour throughout the Connexion have nobly responded to the appeal made and have raised £1000 to defray the cost of the Institute.

Lastly, we must note that Rev. J. Pickett (General Missionary Secretary), and Alderman F. C. Linfield, as a Conferentially appointed deputation, have just set sail (December, 1905) to visit the West African mission stations. They will closely scan our work—old and new—and form their judgment on the evidence. Important developments and, possibly, some modification of policy and changes in method, may be looked for. Africa looms large before the Connexion, but there is a growing conviction that, while our mission on this vast continent must be vigorously pursued, it is high time we turned our attention to India or China.

CHAPTER VIII.

DEVELOPMENTS IN SOCIAL SERVICE.

PIONEER EFFORTS.

WHAT is the estimate we would place on the social agencies of the Church will be clear from what has been said: they are the legitimate fruit of the Church's activity. Holding such views, we have always regarded January 18th, 1895, as an important date in the history of our Church, for, on that date, Social Work received formal and official recognition. The longstanding, the magnitude and success of Rev. Thomas Jackson's efforts in this direction, had led to the appointment of a strong sub-committee to consider the whole question of the relation of Social Work to the missionary labour of the Church. The findings and recommendations of this sub-committee were adopted by the Quarterly Missionary Committee held at Nottingham. The first and most important recommendation that received the confirmation of the Committee was that: "*We recognise Social Work as a part of Christian endeavour and service.*" Then were specified certain conditions needing to be fulfilled in order that Social Work should secure official recognition and assistance, and it was affirmed "that in our opinion the Social Work done by the Rev. Thomas Jackson of the Clapham Mission fulfils the conditions laid down in the foregoing resolutions and deserves distinct recognition"; and, in a final resolution, the Committee declared "that in our judgment the work carried on by Mr. Jackson is worthy of the support of our people, and we authorise the adoption of such means for its support as Mr. Jackson and the General Missionary Committee may deem desirable."

How Mr. Jackson was led to devote himself so largely to this form of Christian service is a story which links on to and continues that of London extension, and takes us back to the year 1876, when Mr. Jackson was just beginning his ministry. As a successful town-missionary he had been recommended by the Sheffield Third Circuit as a suitable candidate for the ministry and, after passing a creditable examination, his name had been placed on the reserve list. The call came in September, 1876, when Mr. Jackson was selected by the General Missionary Committee to open a new mission at Walthamstow. From this point the story may be told in Mr. Jackson's own words:—

"My instructions were to open a new mission at Walthamstow and superintend, *pro tem.*, the Bethnal Green Mission, which at that time was without a minister. The enterprise of Rev. R. S. Blair had secured at a nominal rent for three years a disused Independent Chapel (with sitting accommodation for 600 persons) in Marsh Street (now High Street), Walthamstow, and services had been held in it for nine months by the Poplar Circuit and good work done in the open air. But the conditions were unfavourable to progress, and Mr. Blair, with the circuit's approval offered the chapel to the General Missionary Committee. The two small mission-rooms that comprised the Bethnal Green station—West Street and Squirries Street—were in squalid neighbourhoods. One was a rented room, and in an unfit condition for services; the other was Connexional property and seated sixty persons. It had cost £250, and had that amount of debt upon it. The former was given up at once, and the other subsequently sold to the London City Mission.

"I entered upon my new duties on October 12th. The first Sunday I preached in London I preached at West Street in the morning, and had three persons as congregation. In the evening I preached at Squirries Street when, during the earlier portion of the service, I had only the chapel-keeper as my congregation. In the afternoon I visited the notorious Mile End Waste, and was shocked by the profanity and Sabbath desecration that I witnessed. I took my stand amidst the hubbub and alone commenced to sing a hymn, and then exhorted the unsaved to turn from their sins and serve God. The experience of that first Sunday greatly distressed me; but it so profoundly stirred my soul that I resolved with the help of God, I would devote myself unreservedly to the work of serving and saving the poor in the East End. A mission in notorious, defiled and squalid Whitechapel from that day was the goal of my missionary ambition; but for twenty years the way did not open. It did come at last with the acquisition of the Working Lads' Institute.

"The second Sunday in London was spent at Walthamstow, where my congregation numbered three persons in the morning and five in the evening. For a time my wife and I had to act as chapel-keepers. I resolved to devote my attention to the poorest districts, and systematically visited from room to room and house to house. The sights of suffering and privation I met with powerfully affected me. My rule was to pray with every person or family I visited whenever possible. But to pray with starving persons and not do something to relieve their suffering I felt to be impossible. As we had no funds, and my salary was only one pound per week, my wife and I resolved to consecrate to our mission-work the few hundred pounds we had saved and the proceeds of the sale of our Sheffield house and furniture. On Lord Mayor's Day, November 9th, 1876, we held our first gathering of destitute men and women from the slums. A meat-tea was provided, followed by an evangelistic service. During the subsequent winter months when distress was acute, fifty families were provided with a breakfast each Sunday morning in our schoolroom, the proceedings being closed with a short gospel address and prayer. The late Marquis Townshend, hearing of my efforts for the destitute poor of Bethnal Green and Walthamstow, sent me several liberal donations. The idea of appealing to the public for funds to carry on this benevolent ministry did not occur to me until all our private means had been expended and we had experienced considerable domestic impoverishment. The effect of this personal contact with the poor in their homes and of the manifestation of interest in their struggles, was to induce many to attend the services, and scores were converted. Being pitchforked into the superintendency, the arduous duties of a new station, the demands of probationary studies, the erection of two new school chapels during probation, and details associated with the social ministries to the needy, rendered the demands upon health and strength at times very exacting.

The Clapton-Park Mission.

"Early in the year 1884 the late Mr. J. S. Parkman, one of the most generous of our London laymen, offered to contribute £100 per annum for the purpose of opening a

THE PERIOD OF CONSOLIDATION AND CHURCH DEVELOPMENT.   509

new mission in a crowded and poor district of London. The General Missionary Committee accepted the offer, appointed a sub-committee to select the locality for the new enterprise, and appointed me to take charge of the new mission. A disused and dilapidated building, previously used as a theatre, was taken on rent for twelve months. The building situate in Clapton Park was known as 'The Dust Hole,' and had had a most disreputable record. The late Rev. J. Atkinson, then General Missionary Secretary, and the late C. C. McKechnie, then Editor, invited me to spend an evening with them at the house of the latter to talk over the project, and both assured me that the plans I had sketched for future work along evangelistic and social lines, not only commended themselves to their judgment and sympathy, but excited their admiration. The General Missionary Committee voted £40 to furnish an eight-roomed house for me, and on July 27th, 1884, the first services were held. The theatre had seatage for one thousand persons, and about twenty attended the first service. The Connexion had previously no congregation or property in that neighbourhood, and my wife and I were the only members. I directed my chief attention to the poorest and non-Church-going section of the population, and so came in contact with many needy and destitute families and persons. During the first winter I was at Clapton, I had occasion to call at a School-board School in the poorest district, and was informed by the head teacher that a considerable number of the children attending his school were totally unfitted for their school duties through lack of food, and he deplored having to teach children who had not broken their fast. I engaged

PRIMITIVE METHODIST HOME OF REST, SOUTHEND.

there and then to supply a breakfast the next morning to 300 of these starving children; and so the next morning saw our first children's free breakfast at Clapton. The same winter, in order to relieve the great distress among the families of men out of work, we started a soup-kitchen, and supplied 10,000 soup-dinners to the poor of the district. A Labour Bureau was opened, and the names of the unemployed registered with a view to assist them to procure employment.

"After twelve months' work at the Theatre, a Church of ninety members, and a Sunday School of 150 scholars, and twelve teachers were reported. In the autumn of 1885 a site was purchased on Blurton Road, and the Clapton Park Tabernacle erected and opened with a debt of £2,260 upon it. The total cost was £3,200; and the property is now debtless. The neighbourhood of Southwold Road was missioned, a site secured, and a temporary mission-room erected at a cost of £700, this, too, is now debtless.

"The wish to help the respectable poor who had been ordered rest and change of air at the sea-side with a view to their regaining health and resuming employment, led me to open a temporary Home of Rest at Southend-on-Sea in 1894. There being no Primitive Methodist cause there I also opened a mission. In due course the present church and school-rooms costing £2,900 were erected, Shoeburyness and Southchurch were missioned and societies formed, and a splendid freehold site was purchased by a personal friend, and conveyed to the Connexion. There have since been school-chapels erected at Shoeburyness, Southchurch, and Leigh, and at the Conference of 1904 Southend was made into an independent circuit. The present Home of Rest is connexional and freehold, and was opened in 1902. It cost £3,800, and is now debtless.

"The sight of poor persons suffering through not being able to pay for a doctor, yet shrinking from the idea of having the parish doctor, led me to commence a Medical Mission to assist such cases—twopence to be paid for medicine and advice whenever possible. Finally, in each instance when the urgent need for some additional agency was made clear to me, I took the responsibility for commencing such agency and for raising the necessary funds. I have never asked sanction from either the General Missionary Committee or any local committee for the social ministries I have engaged in; and as I have not involved others in any financial obligation, I have not been interfered with or censured."

The Working Lads' Institute.

A statement casually read in the columns of the *Christian* for October 16th, 1896, had important consequences. The statement was to the effect that the Working Lads' Institute situate in the Whitechapel Road had been entirely closed for want of funds, and would shortly be sold, and probably used as a Music Hall or Theatre, if some person or Institution did not come forward to the rescue. As Mr. Jackson read the statement and pondered all it meant, the resolve was formed to step into the breach—to prevent such a gross prostitution of a noble building with all the loss and discredit it would involve. Accordingly, he made an earnest appeal to the General Missionary Committee that it should purchase the property and let it become part of his mission. A sub-committee was appointed to inspect the property and report. A special meeting of the General Missionary Quarterly Committee was held at Nottingham, November 18th, 1896, to consider the proposal to purchase the Institute, and to hear Mr. Jackson's prospective plans for work in Whitechapel should the property be acquired. After prolonged and full discussion the vote was taken, when it was found that thirteen members had voted for, and ten against the proposal, others remaining neutral. The project was the boldest and weightiest that hitherto had engaged the attention of the General Missionary Committee. What wonder that to some members the step proposed should appear a reckless one, likely to result in disaster, or at the least to gift the General Missionary Committee with a white elephant of enormous size. Others, however, while they felt the seriousness of the undertaking, yet had such confidence in

THE PERIOD OF CONSOLIDATION AND CHURCH DEVELOPMENT. 511

Mr. Jackson's judgment, and his capability to meet the demands of the situation, as to induce them to vote in favour of purchase. A deposit was paid, and on December 7th Mr Jackson took possession. The price paid for the freehold premises was £8,000; a further sum of £1,200 was spent on repairs, renovation, furnishing, etc., and on April 22nd, 1897, the Institute was formally re-opened during the sittings of the General Missionary Committee at the Institute. With a debt of £9,200 and no society or congregation, operations began. The General Missionary Committee paid the interest on the debt, but all other working expenses had to be raised. As head of the re-constituted Working Lads' Institute, Mr. Jackson re-furnished and re-opened the Home for orphan and friendless lads, re-commenced the meetings and clubs for such, set on foot the usual order of services held by Primitive Methodists, also a Sunday School, Band of Hope, and Christian Endeavour Society, inaugurated a service for poor women on Monday afternoons, which has grown to be one of the largest of its kind in East London, besides other social agencies.

After the work had been in progress some three years and had attained considerable success, the rear portion of the premises was required for a new Railway, and the sum of £20,500 in cash had to be paid by the said Railway Company; valuable fittings also in addition had to be allowed, and all damage made good to that portion of the building affected by the demolition. The debt of £9,200 was paid off, and all money advanced by the General Missionary Committee returned, so that instead of the possible burden and disaster which some had foreshadowed there was presented a record-achievement in the history of Primitive Methodism. We have now freehold premises second to none the Connexion possesses in London which, with the Home of Rest at Southend, represents in value upwards of £30,000, and debtless.

The Mission has now—1905—165 members, 250 Sunday School scholars, and 18 teachers. The Women's Meeting has 400 members; the Home has admitted, sheltered, fed, clothed and found employment for upwards of 500 orphan and destitute lads; the Medical Mission has assisted 60,000 needy cases; 50,000 free breakfasts have been supplied to necessitous children; 10,000 homeless men have attended a weekly service and been provided with a supper; 5000 needy persons have been assisted to a holiday in the country; 60,000 articles of clothing have been distributed to the poor, and in various other ways the spiritual ministrations of the Mission have been accompanied with such temporal assistance to the indigent and suffering as to render the influence for good of the Whitechapel Mission an extensive and uplifting force in the East End.

Successive Lord Mayors and Sheriffs of the City of London have testified to their appreciation of the work of the Institute by their presence at its annual meetings. Apart from the cash received from the Railway Company, Mr. Jackson has raised for all purposes since the Whitechapel Mission was opened upwards of £10,000.

Such is a plain, unvarnished story of the developments from small beginnings of a work whose magnitude and meaning will, we are persuaded, be more fully understood and appreciated years hence than it is to-day. That work is the outcome of the devotion, persistency, and organizing power of Mr. Jackson supported by his noble wife, whose name must ever be linked with his.

South-East London Mission.

It was early in the year 1872 when the South-east London Mission, or, as it was originally designated, Southwark Mission, had its birth. Like many another enterprise which is transforming human lives and homes and localities, it was humble and unpretentious in its origin. A small band of sincere and enthusiastic Christian men held open-air services in the Old Kent Street in the morning, and in "The Mint" in the evening, and sang and prayed and preached until they gathered around them a few saved souls who formed the nucleus of a church. For a time the newly-formed society rented a room in Cole Street, Borough, and eventually removed to a building in Trinity Street, which had previously been occupied by the Catholic Apostolic Church, and the lease of which for the remaining thirty years was acquired on behalf of the Connexion.

For nearly twenty years the Southwark Mission struggled bravely and, in spite of its crushing debt and the surroundings of poverty and squalor, did heroic and self-sacrificing work for the social and spiritual redemption of the neighbourhood. Among the ministers of marked ability who superintended and co-operated in the development of this mission may be mentioned such honoured men as Dr. Samuel Antliff, William Wardle, James Pickett, Joseph Aston, George Bell, and George Doe. These brethren with great devotion sought to develop the work of this mission, and not without some success.

But the surrounding neighbourhood was so poor and degenerating every year, and Trinity Street Chapel was so gloomy and depressing in appearance, that the mission never achieved the success that was expected and desired by the authorities of the Connexion.

At the Conference of 1891 an unusual event occurred. The attention of the Missionary Secretary, Rev. James Travis, had been called to Mr. James Flanagan, who was engaged as Mission Preacher at the Albert Hall, Nottingham, and who was considered a most fitting man to secure

REV. JAMES FLANAGAN.

for the Primitive Methodist ministry, and having in mind the desirability of a forward movement for South-east London, with Trinity Street Chapel as the centre, he interviewed Mr. Flanagan, and, impressed with his pre-eminent fitness, urged him to make formal application to enter the ministry. His case was considered at the suggestion of Mr. Travis, on the motion of Dr. Antliff, who characteristically said—"The course I propose is without precedent. *We* have all had to *apply* for admission; but if God goes out of His way to make an extraordinary man, ought not the Connexion to go out of its way to find a place for him?" The Conference enthusiastically and unanimously received him and gave him the full status of an approved minister, and appointed him to lead the forward movement in connection with the Southwark Mission. Immediately after his arrival in London and his taking up the work at Trinity Street Chapel Mr. Flanagan explored the locality in which God had called him to labour, and he was amazed at the poverty and degradation that met him on every hand; while the sense of his own helplessness, with meagre resources at command and an uninviting building, nearly overwhelmed him.

For several years he laboured by night and by day in conjunction with his small band of workers, and was often ready to abandon the work in despair because he felt so powerless to grapple with the problems that faced him on every side. One urgent need was, what Mr. Flanagan suggestively designated—" a better workshop," and one of two courses only seemed possible. One was structurally to alter and adapt Trinity Street Chapel to its new requirements, and the other was to seek a new site and build a large Mission Hall with a suite of rooms elsewhere. After lengthy and repeated consideration and efforts, the former was found to be not only impracticable but impossible.

In 1897 an admirable site in Old Kent Road—on which stood a disreputable drink-shop known as "The Old Kent Tap"—offered itself. With a frontage of 63 feet and a depth of 175 feet, it appeared to all concerned a suitable spot on which to erect the new quarters of the South-east London Mission.

Negotiations were therefore entered into with the Corporation of London, and it was ultimately agreed to acquire it on an eighty years' lease at an annual rental of £122 10s., with the option of purchase for the sum of £3,500 at any time within seven years. Plans of St. George's Hall were then prepared by Messrs. Banister, Fletcher and Sons, and after various alterations and additions were approved, the whole structure involving an outlay of upwards of £12,000, toward which the Missionary Committee contributed £3,000 providing the whole was raised.

During the next three years Mr. Flanagan was engaged mainly itinerating the country in search of funds, and with marvellous success—unparalleled in the annals of Primitive Methodism—raised upwards of £8,000, so that when the late Rev. Hugh Price Hughes preached the Dedicatory Sermon of the new premises on January 4th, 1900, only £1000 remained to be obtained to defray the cost of the structure, and this was forthcoming within a month, leaving only the organ and furniture to be paid for, to provide which a loan of £1000 was secured, which sum is being liquidated by annual repayments.

During the nine years which had preceded the opening of St. George's Hall—years of keen struggle and exacting toil—Mr. Flanagan had not overlooked the social require-ments of the neighbourhood, and had established a variety of institutions which met a real need, many of which have been continued with increasing success up to the present. One of the first of these to be mentioned is the Waifs' Festival, to which were gathered the poorest children—many of them ragged, barefooted, and pinchfaced. At first, only a few hundreds could possibly be invited to share this festivity, but year by year the number increased, until now, as many thousands of poor children as hundreds in the early days of Mr. Flanagan's ministry participate in this annual festival.

The ministry of old clothes was instituted by Mr. Flanagan at an early period of his London experience of missionary life, and this, too, as a social agency has been greatly owned of God in influencing the poor of London's slums to believe that some one cared for them. The Brass Band, the members of which are all converted, total abstainers, and in active fellowship with the Mission; the Gymnasium, Girls' Institute, Young Women's Parlour, Lodging-house Services, and other institutions of a more or less kindred nature, were each a potent force in developing the strength and expansion of this Mission; but after the headquarters were transferred from Trinity Street Chapel to St. George's Hall, these institutions not only developed, but others were added, some of which have become very far-reaching in their work and influence.

The Women's Settlement—another outcome of Mr. Flanagan's brain and heart—was established by him soon after the erection of St. George's Hall, and though the idea was unfavourably received in some quarters of the Connexion, it nevertheless caught on, and early in 1901 became an established fact, and each year the roots of this institution have struck deeper. Without a penny grant from any Connexional fund, the Women's Settlement has not only met a conscious need in providing training for good and intelligent young women who desire to devote their lives to the work of Sisters of the People in one of the best spheres that could be found for such training, but it has inspired and maintained the confidence of sympathetic friends all over the land, and its revenue increases year by year. After nine months' training, including instruction in anatomy, medicine, and nursing, the Sisters, unless permanently retained for the work of the Mission, take appointments in churches or circuits as Sisters of the People, and in this way are supplying a felt need throughout the Connexion.

In 1902 a serious question arose concerning the purchase of the freehold upon which St. George's Hall stands. It had to be bought before March 25th, 1905, or the opportunity would be for ever lost. The work of the Mission having grown it was obvious that Mr. Flanagan could not itinerate the country and collect money as

REV. J. JOHNSON.

before, and at the same time efficiently supervise and properly administer the affairs of the Mission.

In order to relieve Mr. Flanagan of responsibility as superintendent, and to liberate him for another tour in search of funds, the Conference of 1902 was asked to appoint a new Superintendent to the Mission, and to give Mr. Flanagan the commission he desired.

After lengthily deliberating on the situation the Conference by a decisive vote requested the Rev. Joseph Johnson, who for fourteen years had been the superintendent of Stoke Newington Circuit, and who by his special gifts under God's blessing had more than quadrupled the membership of Stoke Newington Society, and for one purpose and another had raised upwards of £18,000, to undertake the superintendency of this Mission. Though reluctant at first to remove from Stoke Newington, where he had so many happy and tender associations, and where he had endeared himself to thousands outside his church by his services to the people as a Guardian of the Hackney Union, also where he had engaged to remain for a further term, he eventually acquiesced in the will of the Conference, whereupon he was appointed to be superintendent of the Mission. Subsequent events have shown the wisdom of the Conference in making this appointment, for during the three years and upwards which have since elapsed, the Mission has grown immensely, and now has a position among the social and regenerating agencies of London it never enjoyed before.

One of the first movements of Mr. Johnson was to get the name of the Mission altered from "Southwark" to that of the South-east London Mission. Additional institutions were established for dealing with some of the social problems of the neighbourhood in a more definite manner, and these, together with the Home for Cripples and Poor Children established at Walton-on-the-Naze in the spring of 1905, all of which are supported by voluntary subscriptions, have created a network of Primitive Methodist Agencies on an extensive scale, for reaching the poor and afflicted. East Street Chapel, Walworth, the deed of which is the model chapel deed of the Connexion, was affiliated with this Mission, and under the labours of the Mission staff, and especially those of Mr. John Moseley, has entered on a new lease of life, and is now a flourishing Mission centre.

In June, 1905, Rev. James Flanagan completed his task of raising £3,500 for the purchase of the freehold of St. George's Hall, and this was paid to the City Corporation, and the land on which these famous premises stand became the property of the Connexion. On the completion of this, a determined effort was made to retain the services of Mr. Flanagan as yoke-fellow with Mr. Johnson in the work of the mission, but the Conference, meeting at Scarborough that month, felt that the time had come when Mr. Flanagan should be appropriated for other work, and accordingly he was appointed Home Missionary Advocate and Connexional Evangelist, and Rev. John Clennell was appointed colleague to Mr. Johnson in place of Rev. W. T. Hosier, who had ably served the whole of his probation on this mission, and who was removing to Chorley Circuit.

Whitechapel and Southwark are our two most conspicuous centres of Social Work in London, but they do not exhaust the list. We do not forget—nor does the Connexion forget—the good work of this character that has long been carried on at Surrey Chapel, and that is now being carried on by Rev. James Watkin—one of the busiest men in London. Nor must we forget that at Clapton the Rev. W. Watson is energetically pursuing the social ministries established by Rev. Thomas Jackson.

LIVINGSTONE HALL, EDINBURGH.

In consequence of the continual decline in our Church at Edinburgh the North British District appealed to the Conference held at Grimsby in 1899 to take special measures in order to save it from utter extinction. The Conference requested the Rev. S. Horton, then stationed at Hull, to undertake this difficult task, and he consented to go. After two years' uphill work in the Church in Victoria Terrace, the Edinburgh Literary Institute—a magnificent pile of buildings in South Clerk Street—came into the market. A Committee was appointed to inspect, and if convinced that the buildings were suitable, to purchase. This splendid block was bought for £10,500, and about £2000 were spent on alterations and furnishing. By the consent of the family of David Livingstone, it was named the Livingstone Hall. A very fine statue of the great missionary, by Mrs. D. O. Hills (the only one for which he ever sat) stands in the lobby. The work was transferred from Victoria Terrace—the old Church passing into the possession of the managers of St. Giles' Cathedral—to be used as a Mission Hall—the opening ceremony being attended by nearly all the leading ministers and City Council. Here a vigorous policy on Forward Movement lines has been pursued.

Livingstone Hall Edinborough

Considerable success attended the services, and in four years the membership increased from 65 to 150. Social Agencies were set in operation especially amongst slum children and young girls. A Police Court Mission was commenced, and the magistrates have repeatedly called public attention to the splendid work done amongst young women who for one reason or another find their way to the police cell. In October, 1903, a Home for Friendless Girls was opened by the wife of General Wauchope—the whole of the furnishing having been paid for by W. P. Hartley, Esq., J.P., and George Green, Esq., J.P., Vice-President of the Conference of 1904. During the year 1903-4 no less than 380 girls were dealt with by the matron and sisters, and seventy-eight were provided for in the Home. A small Hall has been rented in the Canongate for work amongst the mothers and children of that slum district, and a vigorous Sunday School established. The other agencies include popular concerts, men's meetings, temperance work, mothers' meetings, etc. After six strenuous years the Rev. S. Horton resigned the Superintendency, and the Rev. S. Palmer took his place.

THE CONNEXIONAL ORPHANAGE.

The work carried on at Alresford (Hants) under the Master and Matron—Mr. and Mrs. Turner—is too well known to need description here. The Orphanage has a sure hold on the sympathies of Primitive Methodists, and though its proposed extension at Harrogate will mean an increased call on the liberality of our people, its future is none the less assured.

MR. GEORGE GREEN, J.P.
Vice-President of Conf., 1904.

All honour to the unpretentious but devoted man whose memory is preserved by the inscribed plate shown in our illustration. Joseph Peck was the real founder of the Orphanage. A Connexional Orphanage was his dream by night and the burden of his prayers by day. He talked of it with all and sundry, and one such talk with a benevolent lady—Miss Onslow—opened the door for the accomplishment of his desires. Sympathising with his purpose, she offered him a suitable building on advantageous terms—£500, with all the furniture, etc. He closed with the offer, and liberally seconded by Mr. B. Walmsley of Leeds, a small trust was formed and the project brought before the Connexion. The six Circuits of Leeds united to give the enterprise a good send-off—just on the eve of Conference. Mr. W. Beckworth presided at this meeting, and Rev. R. Harrison and Mr. T. Lawrence moved the committal resolutions, with the result that the "Orphanage received the *imprimatur* of the Conference." It is matter for regret that Mr. Peck did not remain in closest association with the Orphanage, though he never lost his interest in it; and his death took place with extreme suddenness when returning from the Orphanage Committee of

THE PERIOD OF CONSOLIDATION AND CHURCH DEVELOPMENT. 519

the Bristol Conference of 1900. Rev. W. R. Crombie, the second Secretary, and Alderman Smith, the Treasurer, have both passed away, but their places are worthily filled by Rev. J. F. Porter and Mr. J. Hewitson.

REV. J. F PORTER.
Secretary of Orphanage.

MRS. HIRST.

REV. J. HIRST.
(Aged 92.)

Brief mention must be made of another praiseworthy organisation for social service— the *Local Preachers' Aid Fund*, Rev. T. J. Gladwin, Secretary, which in December, 1904, had 115 local preachers on its books, all of whom were over seventy-five years of age. These had been assisted monthly from the Fund, while many others not so far advanced in years received help in time of their acute distress.

Nor should we forget that other Fund, rightly termed the *Beneficent Fund*, which was established to supplement the inadequate sums due to the annuitants of the Preachers' Friendly Society. And who shall estimate the help and added comfort this Fund, sustained by the free-will offerings of our people, has brought to "aged and worn-out preachers"? Some of these have had a unique record and retrospect. Of one such we must make mention. The Rev. John Hirst stood on our ministerial roll for the long space of 72 years—1826 to 1898. His career spanned very much of the history we have been writing. He knew the founders, and was the friend and helper of Dr. S. Antliff, W. R. Widdowson, and many others. He did hard pioneer work for many years, and on his retirement in 1861, he settled in Sheffield, and continued to preach and lead two classes until 84 years of age. His noble wife belonged to the Society of Friends; was delicately nurtured and educated at Adworth School with the Brights, but was expelled from the Society because she had married outside its pale. She too was on the plan and preached from 1835 to 1891; so that their united service for the Connexion extended to 128 years! Surely a notable if not a unique record. All of their many children followed in their steps, and, with one exception, all were connected with our Church, and some of their children's children are to-day in our ministerial ranks.

MR. J. HEWITSON.
Treasurer of Orphanage.

CHAPTER IX.

EDUCATIONAL INSTITUTIONS.

THE roots of our Educational Institutions go farther back in time than might be thought. When it was proposed to appropriate a part of the proceeds of the Jubilee Fund for the purpose of establishing a Middle-Class School, and making some provision for the education of candidates for the ministry and preachers on probation, there were many who regarded the proposal as new as it was objectionable. Writing—November, 1859—on the Jubilee Fund, Robert Key says:—

> "The objects for which the money is to be applied are not exactly to my taste. I wish the Conference could have seen its way to have applied at least a part of it to some foreign field—say Port Natal—or any other part of the world where we have no mission station. Most of the Connexional chapels are, or ought to be, getting into better circumstances, so as to need but little aid, and that aid could be provided by the present income of the funds. 'The School for Preachers' Children' will, I think, not meet with much sympathy in this part of the Connexion, and as for the last object named [ministerial education], it is so vague that I do not understand it."

This time-faded script is suggestive. Once more it shows that we must allow for the play and clash of District sentiment and ideals. Norwich District had long been ardent in its advocacy of Foreign Missions, but lukewarm as to the necessity for making educational provision; while some other Districts were ardent where Norwich District was cool. No: the proposals of the Jubilee Fund referred to were not new, whatever else they might be. Far back in the Connexion's past there had been an educational question. In the remarkable "Consolidated Minutes" of 1849, codified by John Flesher, under the heading of "Schools" he says:—"We have three kinds of Connexional Schools, *and one kind in prospect:* namely, Sabbath, day, and night schools: the one in prospect is designed for the education of preachers' children," and then he calmly proceeds to give nine rules as to the maintenance and conducting of the school which was still some fifteen years from its birth! And as to the cognate question of ministerial education: Dr. S. Antliff tells us that, as far back as the Lynn Conference of 1844, John Gordon Black brought forward a proposal for a Ministerial Training College, but it met with an overwhelming defeat.

An educated ministry was the ideal which T. Southron and many of the leading men of the Sunderland District—both ministers and laymen—set before them and steadily worked for. This ideal called into existence the Preachers' Association with the "Christian Ambassador" as its organ. The same ideal was cherished in the old Manchester District and there took a still more practical shape. Under the direction of James Macpherson, assisted by James Garner and Thomas Hindley, the probationers of the District who cared for it received stated instruction. At first Mr. Macpherson met them monthly, then fortnightly, and at last weekly, at different parts of the District to suit their convenience, and raised by subscriptions what sufficed to pay their travelling expenses and their meals for the day. This mode of tuition obtained from 1860 to 1870, when Mr. Macpherson removed to London, so that some of the Manchester probationers who afterwards attained eminence, though they never went to College, still had enjoyed all the advantage of qualified tutors. Not a few convinced educationalists—amongst whom was Mr. Petty himself—were disposed to see in the system of ministerial training pursued in Manchester District the model to be followed throughout the Connexion. As yet the establishment of one central Institution did not commend itself to them; and when, in the early 'sixties, the examination of probationers was instituted, the young men had tutors assigned them—in the Minutes of Conference. But the office was in most cases a sinecure, and the young men made no complaint. Opinion, as represented by the two strong Districts of Sunderland and Manchester, shared by the enlightened men of other Districts, gradually grew in strength until, at last, it became powerful enough to triumph over the defenders of a more timid or obscurantist policy. Yet the prejudice against a college-trained ministry was still strong enough to render it expedient to move cautiously. This fact should be borne in mind when we institute comparisons between the advanced college-course of to-day and the very modest curriculum of thirty years ago; or as we note the evident anxiety of the College authorities to allay all suspicion that the training given will make the students less fitted for the plain duties of the Primitive Methodist ministry. Without in the least calling these declarations in question, one can see now that these declarations were partly called forth by the knowledge of the prejudice still existing in certain quarters against Colleges and all their works.

ELMFIELD COLLEGE, YORK.

The Conference of 1863 held at York, authorised the establishment of a Connexional School to be called the Primitive Methodist *Jubilee* School on premises to be engaged on rent or lease, situate on the Malton Road, in the city of York. The Rev. J. Macpherson notes, with evident regret, the narrowing of the foundation settlement: in 1859 the contemplated school was to be "for preachers' children and the children of members," whereas in 1863 the third regulation ran: "*boys only* shall be admitted into the school at present."

Evidently these arrangements met with complete success. A larger number of boys than the rented house could accommodate were immediately available; and as the

Minutes of Conference of the following year show, steps were forthwith taken to purchase the property which had been rented for a sum not exceeding £1350, vest it in Trustees on behalf of the Connexion, arrange for its enlargement so as to adapt it for the purpose of a great middle-class school, and appoint a representative Committee of Management.*

The trustees appointed were twenty-seven in number—eighteen laymen and nine ministers. As an abiding interest attaches to the list of trustees, it will be well to record here the names of these representative men who cheerfully undertook responsibilities for an undertaking which they rightly believed would strengthen and conserve the best interests of the Connexion:—James Meek, Henry J. McCulloch, Thomas Bateman, Thomas Gibson, William Hopper, William Stewart, James Whittaker, Henry Hodge, William Hodge, Ralph Cook, Joseph Fawcett, William Briggs, William Newton, Jonathan Gaukrodger, Thomas Large, Joseph Wrigley,

THE GOVERNORS OF ELMFIELD COLLEGE.

* See an interesting series of Articles on Elmfield College, by Rev. T. Mitchell, *Aldersgate Magazine*, 1898, pp. 64, 142, 613.

James Nott, Thomas Warburton, William Antliff, Samuel Antliff, John Petty, James Garner, Moses Lupton, George Lamb, Richard Davies, William Lister, and Henry Phillips. Alderman, afterwards Sir James Meek, was appointed the Treasurer, and Rev. S. Antliff, the Secretary of the Managing Committee, while to the important office of first Governor of the College, the Rev. John Petty had already been appointed, and took up his residence at Elmfield House in the first month of 1864. This was an eminently judicious appointment, in itself going far to ensure the success of the school; for Mr. Petty had the entire confidence of the Connexion. Nor was the appointment of Dr. S. Antliff as Secretary less happy. As a leading figure in the Nottingham District, and of constantly enlarging influence in the Connexion, he was from the inception of the enterprise to his death the fast friend of the College, and laboured assiduously to promote its interests. This must be reckoned to him as not the least of the services he rendered to our Church. So Elmfield began its long career of usefulness which would take a book fully to set forth. All we may do is to give the portraits of its successive Governors who, with their wives as the Matrons, have had the direction of the Institution; also to record the names of the men, eminent in the scholastic world, who have succeeded in placing Elmfield in a high position amongst the middle-class Schools of the country.

REV. R. HARRISON.
President of the Conf. of 1904.

GOVERNORS.	HEAD-MASTERS.
1864. John Petty, obit. April 22nd, '68.	1864. J. K. Dall, Esq., B.A.
1868. Thomas Smith, obit. November, '79.	1871. W. J. Russell, Esq., B.A.
1880. Robert Smith.	1878. Dr. J. M. Raby, B.A., B.Sc.
1889. Robert Harrison.*	1880. T. Gough, Esq., B.A., B.Sc., F.C.S.
1891. George Seaman.	1886. W. Johnson, Esq., B.A.
1896. John Gair.	1892. R. G. Heys, Esq., B.A.
1901. W. R. Crombie, obit. April 20th, '04.	(Present Master).
1904. George F. Fawcett.	
(Present Governor.)	

TABLE SHOWING THE SUCCESSION OF GOVERNORS AND HEAD-MASTERS OF ELMFIELD TO THE PRESENT.

Of the past Governors of Elmfield only two survive—Revs. R. Harrison, President of the Conference of 1904; and G. Seaman. No less than three have fallen at their post—the last to fall being our cheery, indefatigable and much-lamented brother, W. R. Crombie.

Of the past Head-masters—of their scholastic attainments, the efficiency to which they raised the school, the high positions which some of them at present fill—much might be written. We must, however, confine ourselves to the present respected occupant of the post. He is not only an efficient head-master but is linked by many ties

* To the great regret of the Committee, Mr. Harrison retired at the close of 1890 on account of the serious illness of Mrs. Harrison, the matron.

of memory and association with the denomination he so ably serves. He is a child of the manse, being the son of Rev. Henry Heys, who did good work in the pioneer days and died at the patriarchal age of eighty-five. The present Head-master was one of the first boys entered at Elmfield; in due time he married a daughter of its first Governor, and he was secured by the governing body of Bourne College as the first Head-master of that Institution. Here he remained six years, and then became proprietor and principal of a private school, which prospered greatly under his care. In Hull, where he was then located, Mr. Heys was widely known and respected. For six years he was a member of the Hull School Board, and no doubt he looked forward to striking his roots yet more deeply in this progressive city. But, being a Primitive Methodist of approved fidelity, he yielded to the solicitation of the Elmfield Committee of Management that he would fill the vacancy created in 1892 by the resignation of Mr. Johnson.

Possibly there may have been a time in the history of Elmfield when quite enough attention was devoted to the scoring of scholastic successes; when effort was concentrated on the clever boy. That is all very well; but all boys are not clever, and there is something quite as difficult to get, and more valuable when it is got, than the honours of the schools. Whatever may have been the case formerly, we are persuaded that parents may now send their sons to Elmfield—be those sons clever or ordinary—with the assurance that they will not only receive as good an education there as is provided at any institution of a similar kind but that, in addition, influences will be brought to bear on them that will help them to become healthy, manly, self-reliant young fellows, braced for life's tussle, and who will never be ashamed of the form of religion professed by their parents. The Rev. A. T. Guttery has very rightly spoken of the "Elmfield type." There is such a type. We know it well, and like it. We ourselves have invested in the type, and know the truth of what we aver. It is pleasing to recall how many who are doing good service in the ministry and amongst our Churches owe much of what they have become to the "fortifying curriculum" and discipline of Elmfield and Bourne Colleges.

R. G. HEYS, ESQ., B.A.,
Present Head-master of Elmfield.

BOURNE COLLEGE, QUINTON.

Elmfield and Bourne Colleges are sister Institutions, and closely "feature" each other. They had a similar origin, their objects are identical, and the course of both has been marked by progress and success. Bourne is a younger Elmfield planted in the busy Midlands. The desire for such an Institution, centrally and conveniently situated, was long felt by some of the leading ministers and laymen in this, the oldest part of the Connexion. The desire at last took shape in the purchase of a building in Birmingham, originally called St. Chad's Grammar School. Originally it belonged to

THE PERIOD OF CONSOLIDATION AND CHURCH DEVELOPMENT. 525

the Roman Catholics, but it had passed into the hands of the Birmingham Corporation, from whom it was bought for £525 on a lease of seventy-eight years, and subject to an annual ground-rent of £60. Soon the premises were felt to be inadequate, and, at the suggestion of the Conference, the Trustees agreed to the formation of a Limited Liability Company with a view to securing a more eligible situation for the College and buildings better adapted for its growing needs. A site, consisting of some nineteen acres, was purchased at Quinton, five miles to the south-west of Birmingham, and the new building—which has since been very considerably enlarged and improved—was opened in 1882. The Company is not run with a view to large dividends, but in the interests of Primitive Methodism. The College has won for itself a high position amongst the secondary schools of the country, while, in a denominational point of view, it enjoys the confidence of the Connexion. The Reports presented to the Conference year by year have recorded

REV. G. MIDDLETON, F.G.S.
Governor of Bourne College.

J. S. HOOSON, ESQ., B.A.

a gratifying number of scholastic successes, and the "old boys" of Bourne are giving a good account of themselves. The Rev. George Middleton, F.G.S., the present Governor and Secretary, has been associated with the Institution from the beginning. As already stated, the first Head-master was R. G. Heys, B.A., who was succeeded by J. S. Hooson, B.A., the present occupant of the post. Mr. Hooson, too, is a "child of the Manse," and that the head-masters of both our Collegiate Schools, and Professor Peake of Manchester College, are alike the sons of ministers who toiled hard on a meagre allowance in the early days of the Connexion, is a fact to be dwelt on with satisfaction.

MINISTERIAL TRAINING INSTITUTION.

For a time Elmfield House did double duty. It was both a superior school and a seminary for the training of a limited number of young men for the ministry. The Connexion approached the question of a separate college warily. This will be evident from the following resolution passed by the Conference of 1865 :—" Arrangements shall be made by the Jubilee School Committee to provide accommodation in Elmfield House for twenty students intended for the ministry, and John Petty shall be their tutor." A committee was appointed to provide means to sustain the Institution and to arrange with the General Committee to have one student at least sent from each District to the Institute, which, if practicable, was to be opened on July 25th, 1865. The Committee appointed consisted of nearly one hundred persons—which looks as though it were deemed desirable to stir and quicken interest, as well as to enlist it in the service of the new movement.

To Mr. Petty, therefore, was assigned the work of directing the studies of twenty young men and of superintending a large school of 120 scholars. The conscientious discharge of this double duty was enough to break down the strongest man though he were in the prime of his strength, and Mr. Petty *was* conscientious, but he was neither young nor strong. On April 22nd, 1868, to the universal regret of the Connexion, he "ceased at once to work and live." But, before this sad event occurred, the Conference had decided that a new Institute should be opened at Sunderland, and that Dr. W. Antliff should be its Principal. Meanwhile, until the old Sunderland Infirmary should be adapted for the purpose of a Primitive Methodist Theological Institute, the Rev. Thomas Smith, in addition to taking over the Governorship of Elmfield, also took charge of the students for the remainder of the college-year. In 1868 Dr. Antliff entered on his thirteen years' tenure of the office of Principal, retiring in 1881, mellowed in character and rich in experience. His place was taken by Thomas Greenfield, who, since 1877, had acted as Assistant Theological Tutor. Mr. Greenfield was a unique personality—a man whose diction was steeped in Scripture, of which he was an unrivalled expositor. Humble-minded as a child, he was also shrewd, and a sayer of quaint and unexpected things. Of him it could truly be said, "Gladly would he learn and gladly teach," for he was a born teacher, and would rather sit at the feet of a child and learn something than go to Conference. Mr. Greenfield was within his own range one of the most considerable Biblical scholars our Church has produced —whose character and works we should not willingly let die. Many are the fine expositions of Scripture lying half-forgotten in old volumes of the Magazines, etc., which ought to be reprinted in a volume that should stand on a handy shelf by the side of his "Expository Discourses." Mr. Greenfield remained at the Institute until it was finally closed; and the building was afterwards sold and the proceeds given to the new College which had been opened at Manchester.

We shall not dwell on the discussions and troubles of those times, when, for a brief while, the Connexion had two Colleges, and neither of them full. It was a passing period of depression; the times were hard, and few additional men were wanted for the circuits. It passed; and then the decision was arrived at that Manchester College

REV. THOS. GREENFIELD.

THE PERIOD OF CONSOLIDATION AND CHURCH DEVELOPMENT. 527

would best serve the interests of the Connexion, and must be re-opened under its Principal, James Macpherson.

To confine ourselves at present to the building: the College as it now stands is a composite structure, having been erected sectionally at three separate periods. It is situate on the south side of Manchester, with Lancashire Independent College a half-mile to the north-west, and Didsbury Wesleyan College three miles to the south-east.

The foundation stones of the original erection were laid on June 24th, 1878, by James Smith Sutcliffe, Esq., of Bacup, Henry Lee, Esq., J.P., of Sedgeley Park, and W. Beckworth, Esq., of Leeds. The last of these survives, and to the present his interest in the College remains undiminished. The building was opened for use on August 22nd, 1881, at a cost, including furnishing, of about £8,200. It provided accommodation for the Principal and thirty students. It consisted of sixty students' rooms,—a study and bedroom for each; library, lecture and dining rooms, with

MANCHESTER COLLEGE BEFORE ENLARGEMENT.

Principal's house. The original Theological Institute now makes up one wing of the present premises, and is well represented in the accompanying illustration.

Merely one year's training in the Theological Institute was never satisfactory. Its greatest advantage was its revelation to everybody of the necessity for a longer period. Fifteen years after the opening of the College the Committee asked the Conference of 1895 to sanction the enlargement of the Institution, that students might have a longer training. Through the genuine interest and generosity of Mr. W. P. Hartley, J.P., of Aintree, the College underwent an important extension between the Conferences of 1895 and 1897, when a new wing was built parallel with the original, comprising sixty new studies; while the front was extended by the addition of entrance-hall, new dining hall, library and lecture-hall. This extension was made at a cost of £12,000, the whole of which Mr. Hartley generously defrayed.

528 PRIMITIVE METHODIST CHURCH.

In order to accommodate students for a three years' course of training, Mr. Hartley again offered the Conference at Newcastle-on-Tyne, 1903, further to enlarge the College so as to provide for the residence at once of 105 students. This was on the basis of estimating an average requirement by the Connexion of thirty-five students as probationers annually. These extensions have been carried out in a most munificent and complete manner. Mr. Hartley desired and readily accepted any suggestion which meant efficiency and usefulness in this large and final extension. This last enlargement comprises 105 new studies built in the form of a quadrangle; new lecture-hall, library, dining-hall, tutors' rooms, sick-rooms with baths, etc.; also a handsome College-chapel. The previous dining-hall and library are used as class-rooms or for other purposes. The

PRINCIPALS OF THE MANCHESTER COLLEGE FROM THE BEGINNING TO THE PRESENT.

electric light is installed in the whole of the new premises, and also in part of the old. The College-chapel occupies the north corner of the wide frontage; a short corner connecting it with the main buildings. It contains 160 sittings, with organ. The whole of the cost of this last enlargement is borne by Mr. Hartley. It is his gift— one of his gifts—to his Church.

The site of the College, of course, has had to be extended, till what was under two acres now comprises an area of over six acres. The grounds form nearly a square, and the chief-rents of the last two extensions have been bought out according to the requirement of the vendors.

In 1886 Mr. Henry Hodge gave £1000 to found a scholarship in memory of his departed friend—Rev. George Lamb. The following year—the Queen's Jubilee year—the College was declared free from debt. Still, the question of the maintenance of the College pressed heavily, and the term of residence was felt to be almost ludicrously inadequate. Dr. Joseph Wood, who succeeded to the Principalship in 1889 on the retirement of Rev. James Macpherson after thirteen years of service, claimed that the maintenance of the College should be considered a first charge upon the Church. In his frank and fearless way he wrote in the Report to the Conference of 1890: "We hope the Conference will make better provision for the maintenance of the Institution or else relieve us." The two defects referred to were remedied. In 1891 Mr. W. P. Hartley offered the Conference £200 per annum for five years on condition that the students' term of residence should be lengthened to two years, and the services of a University Graduate secured. The Conference of the following year gave effect to these suggestions by confirming the appointment of Mr. Arthur S. Peake, M.A.,

PROF. A. S. PEAKE, M.A., B.D.    REV. A. L. HUMPHRIES, M.A.    REV. W. L. WARDLE, M.A., B.D.

Fellow of Merton College, Oxford, and Lecturer at Mansfield College, to be the tutor in Biblical Introduction, Exegesis, Theology, and the History of Doctrine. It was a notable departure which must have gladdened the heart of Dr. Wood, who at that Conference felt compelled to retire after occupying the post of Principal four years.

"The raising up of Professor Peake among us is nothing else than providential." The words which were true in 1892 have acquired an added truth by the passing of the years. It is indeed a matter for justifiable pride that one of our own "bairns," in whom scholarship, aptitude to teach, the power to inspire affection, deep religiousness of spirit, and modesty are found in happy combination, and who is admittedly one of the foremost Biblical scholars of the day—should have so much to do with the shaping of our future ministry.

We give portraits of those who have filled the important office of Principal of the Manchester College, also of Professor Peake and Revs. A. L. Humphries, M.A., and W. L. Wardle, B.D., the present tutors.

The Sunday School Union.

Though for the sake of convenience and chronological sequence the establishment of the Sunday School Union is noted here, and its work since 1874 briefly outlined, it must be affirmed with emphasis that the objects aimed at by the Union are much more than Educational. CONSERVATION rather than Education is the proper word here. In harmony with the new and truer conception of the relation of child-life to the Church,

SUNDAY SCHOOL UNION SECRETARIES.

which so strikingly marked the advance of the nineteenth century, the Church and the School are regarded as essentially one, and Sunday Schools are no longer looked upon as " Merely Seminaries for teaching, but saving agencies" (*Sunday School Report*, 1893).

Leeds District had much to do with the inauguration of the new movement. In 1869, we are told by Rev. J. Macpherson, the Schools in the four Manchester Circuits were formed into a Union which gradually assumed considerable importance; but even before this a Circuit Sunday School Union had been formed in Leeds with which, it is interesting to notice, Mr. W. Beckworth, the first treasurer of the Connexional Union, was associated. After long and mature deliberation the proposed scheme, the principle of which had been approved in 1871, was adopted by the Conference of 1874. The Rev. Joseph Wood was appointed the first Secretary of the Union, and in 1875 set apart to the work. The objects of the new department were stated to be:—To benefit the schools in every possible way in their equipment and management, and their work and productiveness; to incorporate them more fully with our various Connexional institutions, and *weld them into vital union with the Church, sharing in her life, and affording a principal field for her activity."*

The first Secretaries had uphill work to do in the early stages of the Union, and right along the duties devolving upon them have been arduous; but no department of our Church-life has yielded better results, and its history has been one of steady expansion and ever-growing usefulness. The organisation of the Union has been gradually perfected. In 1877 Catechumen classes were established, and in 1879 District Sunday School Committees. Still later Examinations for Teachers and Scholars were originated, and a Triennial Teachers' Conference. In process of time differentiation took place. In 1896 *The Young People's Society of Christian Endeavour* was formed, and the following year the Rev. G. Bennett was appointed its Secretary. The Society has now 3030 branches, with a membership of 106,130. It has its organ in "Spring Time," its Reading Union conducted by Rev. P. McPhail, and its Holiday Tour Department. What it has just done for our African Missions has already been noted. The *Temperance Society and Band of Hope* was also, in 1897, made a separate department of the Union with the Rev. T. H. Hunt as its Secretary. The valuable annual Reports furnished by him show that he is fully conversant with all the phases of the Temperance movement, and that he is zealously striving to deepen Temperance sentiment amongst us, and organise it for more effective service. Lastly, the *Bible Reading and Prayer Union*, of which we believe the Rev. Luke Stafford was the originator, had, in 1889, 374 branches and 15,826 members. Now the Report of its Secretary, Rev. J. Johnson, shows that in 1905 it has 2,061 branches, and a membership of 92,000.

Let the pleasing facts be noted that on the Home stations we have 4,127 schools, 60,073 teachers, and 466,154 scholars, 76,427 of whom are members of the Church. A recent interesting announcement is to the effect that Mr. L. L. Morse, J.P., has undertaken to found a Lectureship in connection with the Sunday School Union. The first lecture will be delivered at the Triennial Sunday School Conference of 1907 by the Rev. T. H. Hunt.

Full of hope and promise is the legislation (1904) for the *Training and Equipment of Local Preachers*, which owes so much to the initiative and energy of Rev. H. Yooll and Mr. H. Jeffs.

CHAPTER X.

IMPROVED METHODS OF FINANCE.

THIS Church-era of our History is marked by improved methods of Finance. Let any one take up an attitude of detachment both to the past and present, and seriously set himself to study their resemblances and their differences, and the fact named must strike him forcibly. It is like the difference between the primitive financial methods of the small inexperienced retail dealer, and the extensive operations of a large business-firm. But finance is not everything! No : but it is very much. And there is this peculiarity about it that, like the atmosphere, it is felt everywhere, though itself escapes observation. It penetrates to, and pervades each department, and tends to increase the efficiency and extend the range of each department's operations.

It is but just to say that this improved state of things is largely due to the zeal and ability of a few men—both ministers and laymen—who, during the past two or three decades, have largely had the direction of affairs. Notably among such ministers must be named John Atkinson, James Travis, and Thomas Mitchell. We may not always be mentioning their names, or tracing movements back to them as their originators, but there the fact remains, that the improvements effected, and the new methods adopted, are the outcome of the secret cogitations and plannings of these and such as these. And who shall estimate the influence which Mr. W. P. Hartley has exerted during the last few years? It is not simply the amount of money he has given to the various Institutions and movements of the Connexion—great though that amount has been. While his liberality has been an ensample and stimulus, his remarkable business ability, which has raised him to a conspicuous position in the world of commerce, has also been freely consecrated to the service of the Church. His resourceful brain has teemed with plans for its advantage, and he has always been ready to adopt and materialise the suggestions of others, as in the founding of "The Hartley Lectureship," on the suggestion of Dr. J. Ferguson, the distribution of standard books to ministers, local preachers, etc. In short, we are persuaded that when the future historian of our Church comes to write once more of the period beginning, say, with 1885, when Mr. Hartley came forward with his offer of £1000 towards the extinction of the troublesome missionary debt, he will distinctly have to recognise what a powerful factor systematic beneficence guided by business methods increasingly became in our denominational life ; that the new finance and new liberality somehow transfused a new energising spirit into almost every department of Church-work.

Before giving one or two specific illustrations of successful finance, brief reference must be made to the Missionary Jubilee effort of 1892 and onwards, which itself offers one of the most striking illustrations of the views here advanced. The Rev. J. Travis, Missionary Secretary, was the President of the Norwich Conference of 1892, and he suggested that the time was eminently favourable for making an effort to raise £5,000 for missionary purposes during the year. Subsequent discussion in Committee resulted in a much more ambitious effort being made. Mr. W. P. Hartley promised that if the Connexion would make a bold attempt to raise £50,000 in five years, he would give £1000 a year. It was also suggested that the money raised should be equally divided among these four funds, viz., the Missionary, the College, the Superannuated Ministers' Widows and Orphans, and the Chapel Loan Funds. When these proposals were presented to the Conference, the effect was almost electric. The proposals were adopted with enthusiasm, and before the Conference closed the sum of £16,000 was guaranteed.

MR. W. P. HARTLEY, J.P.

The President, with Mr. W. P. Hartley and Rev. T. Mitchell, who was the Secretary of the movement, as he is now the Secretary of the Church Extension Fund begun in 1900, were deputed to visit the Churches. They travelled far and wide, and with the assistance of local deputations sought to impart information and awaken interest in the movement, and with the happiest results. The three colleagues in service were doing something more than raise money: they were really and truly Connexional Evangelists.

The Jubilee effort of 1860 realised £4,728. What the outcome of the Missionary Jubilee effort of 1892 the figures following, with the explanatory remarks of Mr. Mitchell, will show. The three "Jubilee Campaigners," as they had been facetiously called, very properly received the thanks of the Conference of 1900 for their services.

	£	s.	d.		£	s.	d.
By cash from subscribers	38,447	18	11	To amount distributed to the various funds concerned	38,600	0	0
,, ,, Sunday Schools	1,365	1	8	,, College Fund, special	7,000	0	0
,, ,, Interest	2,735	7	5	,, Working Expenses	1,373	8	1
By special gifts (W. P. Hartley, Esq.)	7,500	0	0	,, Cash with C.A.A.	2,374	19	11
				,, ,, Treasurer	500	0	0
				,, ,, Sunday School Union	200	0	0
	£50,048	8	0		£50,048	8	0

"As the movement extended over a number of years, the payments as they came to hand were invested with the Chapel Aid Association, and the interest accruing devoted to the payment of the working expenses. At first this investment was comparatively small, but as additions were annually made it soon reached considerable proportions; and at the close it was found that the interest alone reached the handsome sum of £2,735 7s. 5d., and as the total working expenses of the whole term were only £1,373 8s. 1d., not only was *every* donation applied, without deduction for expenses, to the fund, but the considerable sum of £1,361 19s. 4d., as excess of interest over working expenses, helped to swell the capital account. This is a result which ought to satisfy the most rigorous economist; and it may be confidently affirmed that no movement in the history of Methodism has been carried through with a more scrupulous oversight of expenditure than the Missionary Jubilee Thanksgiving Fund of the Primitive Methodist Church.

"Of the amount which was appropriated to the Missionary Fund one-third was given to the African, and two-thirds to the Home section. As there was some difference of opinion as to how best to utilize the amount available for Home-work, it was determined that each district should have returned to it its proportion of that section (one-sixth) to be devoted to objects within its own area."*

Mr. Mitchell is the energetic Secretary of the *Church Extension Fund*, established 1900. It is essentially missionary in character and since its formation has assisted Trustees in the payment of interest to the extent of £4823 6s. 6d.

Primitive Methodist Insurance Company, Limited.

The Connexional Insurance Company is the second of the strictly commercial houses established by the Primitive Methodist Church, the Book-Room alone claiming precedence over it in point of time. But it is the first limited liability company in the Church. It is rather remarkable that in a denomination almost entirely composed of the democracy, this institution should have come into existence at so early a period in its history. Quite a number of the Nonconformist Churches of England were without any arrangements for the insuring of their own property against fire at the close of the nineteenth century, some are without any such arrangements to this day, and even the great Baptist community did not succeed in forming a company till 1904, whereas, as far back as the year 1859, the following resolution appeared in the Minutes of Conference:—"The following persons shall form a Committee for drawing up certain preliminaries for instituting an insurance society, to be laid before the Conference of 1860,—W. Garner, J. Petty, W. Antliff, G. Lamb, R. Howchin, T. Bateman, T. Gibson, J. Fawcett, A. McCree, W. Hopper, and James Garner, secretary." That the Conference was impressed with the importance of the work it was putting into the hands of this Committee is evident from the names of the persons composing it, all of these, ministers and laymen, being at the time men of influence. Whether it proved difficult to obtain the needful information, or succeeding Conferences were diffident regarding the proposal, the records do not show. What is evident is that no reference to the matter is made in the Conference Minutes of 1860, and it was not till 1866 that the Company was actually formed, the Board of Directors being Henry Johnson

---

* See an interesting article in the *Aldersgate Magazine*, April, 1905, on the Jubilee Fund, by Rev. T. Mitchell.

McCulloch, engineer, York; Thomas Gibson, merchant, Sunderland; William Antliff, minister, London; William Stewart, merchant, Newcastle-on-Tyne; John Sissons, tailor and draper, Hull; Thomas Dearlove, Leeds; Thomas Newell, minister, York. The Rev. Richard Davies was the secretary, and Captain McCulloch, whose name is the first in the list of directors, was the treasurer. The articles of association provided for the issue of one hundred shares at a nominal value of one hundred pounds each, with only five shillings per share called up, but with powers to call up the whole amount should it be needed. At a later period the share-capital was increased to two hundred shares of one hundred pounds each, but the amount paid up remained at five shillings per share as before. For securing the full advantage to the Connexion no better arrangement than this could have been devised because, on the paid up capital, the amount belonging to each shareholder being so small, no interest or dividend is paid by the Company, and yet it would have enabled the Company, had an emergency arisen, to command twenty thousand pounds. The Company, however, has been unusually fortunate in the matter of losses by fire, hence no such emergency has arisen and now, with the large Reserve Fund it has built up, such an emergency is not likely to arise. The Company does not enter into competition with other Companies. It only insures chapels, schools, manses, colleges, and other buildings belonging to the denomination, making one exception to this in the matter of private property by insuring the personal belongings of Primitive Methodist ministers. From the first, the trust boards have manifested confidence in the Company, and gradually the amount of property insured by it has increased, so that now practically the whole of the property is insured by it. The growth of the business has been both rapid and steady. In 1876, ten years after the formation of the Company, the premium income amounted to £857; in 1886 it was £1,564; in 1896 it had reached £2,171, whilst the rate of increase was still more rapid in the nine years up to 1905, having in the last named year reached £3,033. In this year also the Reserve Fund had reached £31,960, and comparing this with the reserves of other Insurance Companies it is certain that in the matter of a reserve-fund taken in proportion to the risk, this is the strongest Company in the kingdom. Than this no higher compliment could be paid to the management. But this is not all. In 1884 the Reserve Fund had reached £10,000, and with the eighteen years' experience of probable loss, the directors that year felt justified in beginning to make grants out of the profits to help chapels in needy circumstances. That year the grant to the Chapel Fund was £500, and since then it has never in any year granted a smaller sum, though recently this amount has been divided between the two institutions, the General Chapel Fund and the Church Extension Fund. To help to float the Church Extension Fund also, it gave to that fund in the first four years of its existence the sum of £3,100. In addition to these

REV. ROBERT HIND.

grants to the institutions that have been established to assist chapels, the Company in 1889 began, to render assistance directly. In some instances, owing to special circumstances of various kinds, the properties have been placed in a most unfortunate position and, but for the substantial help the Insurance Company has given, it is to be feared that they would have been lost to the denomination altogether. Thirteen of these trusts have received sums varying from £250 to £516, and a much larger number have been assisted with smaller grants. The largest amount given in any one year was in 1903, when out of a gross premium revenue of £2,809, the directors disbursed to needy chapels £2,670. In all, the Company has disbursed in this way over £22,000 up to 1905. The present management consists of the following as the Board of Directors:—Messrs. John Coward, J.P., Durham (Chairman); Richard Fletcher, Silsden (Treasurer); Henry Adams, Sheffield; Joseph Smith, Hull; Elijah Jennings, Leicester; Revs. Robert Harrison (Deputy-Chairman), Thomas Newell, George Seaman, Edwin Dalton, and Robert Hind, Secretary. Preceding secretaries have been Rev. Richard Davies and Charles Smith, both of them superannuated ministers. But in 1894 the secretaryships of the Insurance Company and of the Chapel Aid Association were united in one office and the Rev. John Atkinson, an active minister in full work, was appointed to fill the office. At his death in 1899, Mr. Hind was made his successor in both the secretaryships. Under the present management the Company's affairs are as well conducted as they have always been, and the small expenditure in management, and larger income will doubtless enable the directors to render larger financial assistance to needy Connexional interests than at any former time. The chairman is an old servant of the Church, and by his special knowledge of limited liability law, is singularly well fitted to guide the Company in all the departments of its business. His interest in all that concerns Primitive Methodism is well known, and despite his years, his mind remains clear and acute. And this is only one of the ways in which he is serving the Church. For more than a quarter of a century he has been a member of well-nigh all the higher courts and committees of the denomination, and perhaps no layman has preached as many anniversary sermons as he. In all parts of the country, from Paisley in Scotland to Cornwall, he has rendered service in this way. The other directors are equally assiduous in attending to the business of the Company, and in the disbursement of grants manifest an impartiality and a sense of responsibility that are beyond all praise. No fees are paid to the directors, who give their services for their travelling expenses.

Primitive Methodist Chapel Aid Association, Limited.

The Primitive Methodist Chapel Aid Association, Limited, was established in 1889, the original directors having signed the Articles of Association on October 29th of that year. But the whole scheme had been worked out in detail by Mr. W. P. Hartley, the originator of the Company, fully ten years before that time, and it is remarkable, that when eventually the Company was launched, the rates of interest and other details were all those Mr. Hartley had originally proposed. In those days, however, Mr. Hartley's financial genius had not become recognised in the denomination.

He was known to be a successful industrial prince; but the financial statesmanship which combines in an almost equal degree originality, boldness, and safety had not then had the chance of being known beyond a limited circle. As a consequence when he first made his proposal it was regarded as impracticable by all the leading men in our Church with one exception. The exception was the Rev. Hugh Gilmore, who was in favour of the scheme from the day he heard it expounded by Mr. Hartley. On the whole it was not remarkable that there should have been hesitation and doubt. Since it has proved so great a success in our Church, the statesmen of other denominations have sought for information about it, but when the bolder spirits among them have proposed the establishment of a similar association, they have been met by exactly the same objections as were offered to Mr. Hartley. One of these objections was that the margin of profit allowed for the payment of expenses was too small; another that the people of our Church had no money to invest, and if they had they would not invest it in this company; another that trustees who borrowed would not feel the same obligations to pay promptly as though they had borrowed in the ordinary way— through a solicitor. All these objections have proved to be groundless, and even the expectations of Mr. Hartley, exaggerated as they seemed to be, have been greatly exceeded. The Chapel Aid Association is a kind of Banking Company. It accepts deposits, and pays thereon three and a half per cent. It also loans money to trustees of chapels under certain conditions at the rate of three and three-quarters per cent., having thus five shillings per one hundred pounds with which to pay working expenses. Mr. Hartley paid the whole of the expenses necessary for starting the Company, and, the facts of its history have more than justified Mr. Hartley's anticipations in every particular. After transacting business for sixteen years it has been found that the quarter per cent. has paid the working expenses, and left enough to build up a Reserve Fund of well over four thousand pounds, besides making grants to help to float the Church Extension Fund to the amount of twelve hundred and fifty pounds. The business-like manner in which deposits have been dealt with, and the promptitude with which the interest has been paid, together with other circumstances have created absolute confidence in the soundness of the Company as a mode of investment. And instead of the £250,000 which Mr. Hartley thought might ultimately be invested in it, already the deposits are considerably over £400,000, and the amount increases every year. The Company was fortunate when it started in having Mr. Hartley to assist it in this as well as in other respects, he placing a very large sum at the disposal of the directors as the first depositor. In 1905 there were about three thousand depositors. In this respect the Association has been of great advantage to many of the thrifty people in humble circumstances, in our Church, who have not known of good and safe investments in which to put their small savings. On the other side, loans are out to about eleven hundred boards of trustees of chapels, schools, and manses; as proof of the groundlessness of the fears entertained when Mr. Hartley made his proposals, it may be pointed out that in the sixteen years no bad debt has been made, and there are no arrears of interest due. The directors, however, exercise the greatest care in making loans. They require that one-half of the cost of the estate shall have been raised, or in some exceptional cases where the chapels are new, two-fifths. They also require that in addition to the interest a small proportion shall be paid off the loan each year. And before making the loan the directors ascertain whether the trust board, the membership of the church, and the congregation warrant the expectation that the payments will be made regularly. This care accounts for the satisfactory results in this section of the Company's business. The advantages to trustees are very great. It enables them to pay a small amount off their debt, whereas in the case of a mortgage they can only pay off in large sums. The total amount repaid during the sixteen years is about £240,000, and if a small part of this be taken off to account for cases where payments have been made for other purposes, it is certain that through the operations of the Chapel Aid Association, chapel debts have been reduced in that time by well over £200,000. It has come to be recognised, indeed, that this is by far the best scheme in the denomination for dealing with its temporalities effectively. The trustees get their loans at an easy rate of interest. And, one of the advantages obtained through this company, not originally contemplated, is the great saving in legal expenses. The total cost for effecting a loan, is at the rate of three shillings and sixpence per one hundred pounds, this being the amount paid to the inland revenue as stamp duty. The Secretary of the Company prepares all the legal documents gratis, and it is calculated that the saving to the Connexion in the matter of these particular legal expenses will be about two thousand pounds per year. Judging by communications that come to the office the Chapel Aid Association is the wonder and the envy of many leading men of other Churches. Its first directors were: Dr. Samuel Antliff, Mr. John Coward, J.P., Rev. James Travis, Rev. R. S. Blair, Mr. John Jones, Mr. John Caton, and Mr. W. P. Hartley. Next to Mr. Hartley the Association owes most to its first secretary, the Rev. John Atkinson. He was unceasing in his toil in its behalf in the first year of its history; for some time, when the business was comparatively small, doing the work without remuneration. The present directors, who give their services without fee or reward, are: Mr. W. P. Hartley, J.P., Liverpool (Chairman); Mr. John Coward, J P., Durham (Deputy-Chairman); Mr. W. Beckworth, J.P. (Treasurer), Leeds; Mr. J. Jones, Chester; Rev. J. Travis, Chester; Rev. T. Whitehead, London; Rev. R. S. Blair, Romford; Rev. J. Hallam, Leicester; Rev. T. Mitchell, London; Mr. B. Haswell, Gateshead; Mr. T. Robinson, Grimsby; Rev. J. T. Barkby, Harrogate; and Rev. Robert Hind, who has been the Secretary since the death of the Rev. John Atkinson. The uninterrupted success of the Company points to the conclusion, that the time will come when the whole of the chapel debts will be dealt with through this agency.

EPILOGUE.

A WORD ON LONDON EXTENSION.

W<small>E</small> cannot close without alluding to the remarkable extension of our denomination in London during recent years. What was the position of our Church in the Metropolis at the middle of the last century we have seen. In 1904 we had 47 Circuits, 9,827 Members, and 115 Chapels, of the estimated value of £284,308.* But for the inexorable limitations of space, we should have devoted a chapter to the purpose of showing how and to whom this remarkable advancement has largely been due. Such a chapter indeed we had written, but it cannot without a departure from our plan be printed here. The history of Primitive Methodism in London deserves and demands a book to itself, and by the time that the Centenary celebrations are upon us such a book should see the light.

All we can here do is to give the names and in some cases the portraits of a few of the men who by their long and efficient service have contributed to this remarkable extension. Amongst such must be named R. S. Blair (on whom the mantle of Hugh

REV. R. S. BLAIR.   REV. G. SHAPCOTT.   REV. R. R. CONNELL.

Campbell seems to have fallen), R. R. Connell, J. F. Porter, G. Shapcott, W. Mincher, J. Johnson, B. Senior, and his successors at Surrey—J. Tolefree Parr and James Watkin. Of younger men, still thinking of extension, T. J. Gladwin's success at Harringay and W. T. Clark Hallam's chapel enterprise at Leytonstone have been most creditable achievements.

The work of some of our London ministers has from the beginning commended itself to a few men of wealth who have stood by them and helped them in their efforts. Thus James Duncan, Esq., received the thanks of the Conference of 1886 for his

* The figures are given on the authority of Rev. W. Mincher.

additional gift of £1000 to Mr. Blair's erection at Canning Town, while Mr. and Mrs. Slater, whose portraits we give, have proved his friends in times of trial and difficulty. Many of our London adherents will be glad to see the likeness of Joseph Peters, Esq., who has for years been a most liberal supporter of our ministers in their work, especially of Revs. G. Shapcott, W. Mincher, and R. R. Connell. Mr. Edwin Tildesley has also nobly stood by Mr. Shapcott.

Of our London laymen probably Mr. E. C. Rawlings holds the foremost place. He was elected Vice-President of the Conference of 1905, has been President of the London Primitive Methodist Council, and he and his partner, Mr. S. Alfred Butt, who like himself is the son of a minister, fill the position of Legal Advisers to the Connexion, to which office they were elected on the demise of W. Lewis, Esq., in 1896.

MR. MARTIN SLATER.

MRS. SLATER.

EVANGELISM: MODERN PHASES.

In 1874 the Rev. G. Warner was set apart by the Conference as a Special Evangelist, and he laboured widely and unremittingly until 1886. He laboured assiduously to promote the experience of Scriptural Holiness, and as the annual gatherings of the Holiness Association bear witness he did not labour in vain. There is a link between the Association just named and the Evangelists' Home which we will let Mr. Odell describe in his own way.

The Evangelists' Home was commenced in September, 1888, in response to a deep conviction felt at the Holiness Convention held at Hainton Street, Grimsby, earlier in that year. The Institution was domestic, the Evangelists joining the home, and sharing the family-life of the founder. Mrs. Odell's participation in the movement was equally based on a Divine conviction. Her reply to the prospect held out of young men joining her family-circle and sharing her table was, "God has done so much for my boys that I am ready to do anything for any other boys that God may send to me." In this spirit the Home and Institution became one. It was felt that the Churches needed evangelistic labour. The demand was most imperative where the means of supply were the scantiest.

JOSEPH PETERS, ESQ.

THE PERIOD OF CONSOLIDATION AND CHURCH DEVELOPMENT. 541

There were rural circuits each with many chapels and only one minister—these chapels being, in many cases, closed on week-nights, even in winter, for weeks in succession. Then the Churches needed also the Prophet-ministry—pertinent and pressing; and, above all, evangelism was the national demand in order to meet the indifference, militarism, and growing materialism everywhere dominant.

From the commencement, the Evangelists' Home justified itself by its fruits. The principle of its support was commendable. There was no debt: there was to be none. Furniture came; funds also and friends. In six months the staff increased from two to twenty. The visits of the young men to rural districts produced favourable impressions, and imperishable fruit was gathered. In September, 1889, thirty young men were sent to needy fields. Many struggling stations were strengthened, decaying churches revived and large increases of members secured. The "signs" of Jesus Christ were continued during succeeding years. There is before us a volume of the

E. C. RAWLINGS.
Vice-President of Conference 1905,
and Legal Adviser to the Connexion.

S. ALFRED BUTT.
Legal Adviser to the Connexion.

reports of the young men and the records of struggle and success, together with some samples of service and conversions which read like modern "Acts of the Apostles."

The Conference of 1889, held at Bradford, requested Mr. Odell to go on and strengthen the work. It further recognised in his work the basis of a new order of workers after the manner of the New Testament Evangelists. In all this the guiding hand of God was evident. For successive years the young men kept the work advancing. There were notable instances of effective evangelism and glorious ingatherings.

The Evangelists' Home thus continued until June, 1904, when it was necessary that Mrs. Odell's work should cease and complete rest be secured. It was with reluctance that it was decided to discontinue the work as a Home. It was finished, as it commenced, without debt and without difficulty. It was, however, a great joy to recognise the absolute change in the trend and tone of the Connexion towards both the Home and the work. The Home did not close until the principle for which it stood was officially recognised by the Conference, and an Evangelist's order under the Missionary Committee fully established. Quite a considerable number of Mr. Odell's former staff are the evangelists now in charge of missions; while Mr. J. B. Bayliffe, a devoted son of the Evangelists' Home, stands with ministerial evangelists, and on equal terms with Mr. Odell in the new form of the work. It is evident the leaven has worked throughout the Connexion, and also beyond into other Churches, where evangelism has become the first arm of service.

More than 160 young men joined the staff of "Home-labourers." Of these 130 can now be traced to honourable spheres of toil, either missionary or in the pastorates of Churches. A great joy came to the founder and to the Mother of the Home, in the visitation of thirteen of these young men in the United States of America,—all in happy labour; some in influential positions and high command in the Church of God. During all these years the principle prevailed of—No debt. In sixteen years nearly £15,000 was received and expended, and to the end there was no debt. The young men at the end were placed in the work they loved; the books of the study were distributed by choice and selection amongst the latest members of the staff; the balance of funds handed to the last young man who assisted in the closing work; and the furniture placed in the new minister's house for the use of the Circuit.

We began with Evangelism, and with Evangelism we finish. While some of our most gifted ministers are going to and fro amongst the Churches, our Van Missionaries are carrying the Evangel to the villages which were too much in danger of being overlooked. We are getting back to the villages our fathers loved, while we are strengthening our hold of the towns.

Our task is ended, and we lay down our pen with thanks to God that we have had such a history to write. Also we breathe the prayer that whatever future developments may await our Church, they may be such as shall enlarge Christ's kingdom and bring greater glory to His name.

THE END.

INDEX.

Africa, Missions in, ii. 487—506.
Allendale missioned by Hexham and Barnard Castle, ii. 147; great revival in, 151.
Alresford, fierce persecution at, ii. 341. Connexional Orphanage at, 518—19.
Alston, great revival at, ii. 147—8; made a Circuit, 151.
America (United States), P. Methodism in, i. 436—7, ii. 446—9.
ANTLIFF W., D.D., his parentage and early life; enters the ministry when sixteen, ii. 376; his successful labours at Nottingham, i. 250, at Ashby-de-la-Zouch, 322; at Oldham, ii. 41; his influence in Conference, 376; an early advocate of Temperance, i. 472, in the Conference, ii. 376; Editor, 367, 395; twice President of Conference, '63 and '65. Principal of Theological Institute, 526 Probably the best known and most influential figure of the Middle Period, 375. *Portraits*; ii. 292, ii. 375.
ANTLIFF S., D.D., his home at Caunton, ii. 375; begins his ministry at Chesterfield, i. 498, in Newark Branch, 270; is late in getting to Conference, ii. 368, early advocate of Temperance, i. 472. G. M. Sec., ii. 373; Deputy Treasurer, etc., 405; Visits the Colonial Missions, 445. President, '73, 292; his great interest in Elmfield College, York, 523.
ASHWORTH JESSE, his call to the ministry in '37, *portrait*, ii. 49; his success in Peterborough and death, 423.
ATKINSON JOHN, his early life and usefulness at Kendal; Mr. McKechnie early discovers his "uncommon force of mind," ii. 138 G. M. Secretary, 373, 405. President, '86, 392; Sec. of the Insurance and Chapel Aid Cos., ii. 538.
Auditors, Connexional, appointment of, '43; Table showing the succession of, ii. 399—400.
Australian Missions, ii. 425—8, 431—440.
Auxiliary Fund, name given, '65, to Charitable Fund; A. F. abolished, '76, ii. 408—9.
Aylesbury, missioned by Shefford, ii. 314, made a circuit; missions Dunstable and Luton and takes over Buckingham, 352.

Barnard Castle, missioned from Darlington; becomes a branch of Hull, ii. 132—4; missions Weardale and Alston Moor, 143—7, Brough and Eden Valley, 149—51. One of the earliest Protracted Meetings held at, i. 455, *note*; made a circuit, ii. 151 takes charge of Kendal Mission, 138.
Barnsley. Sheffield sends W. Taylor to mission B., and the district; made a circuit; some early befrienders of the cause; circuits made from it, i. 486—7.

BATEMAN THOS., his early life and introduction to P. Methodism, i. 511—13; his labours at Chester, 551, on the Shropshire Station, ii. 284—5; his portraits i. 511, ii. 21, and Memorial, i. 557.
BATTY THOS., *portrait* and sketch of, ii. 117—8.
BECKWORTH, W. J. P., ii. 405, 518, 527; his connection with the S. S. Union, 531.
Bedford, its early history and progress, ii. 419—21.
Belfast, first Irish mission; its progress, ii. 281
BELLHAM W. G., his early life and ministry, i. 414; his rough usage at Daventry, *portrait*, i. 34'—4; at Witney and Oxford, 346—7; before the magistrate in Norfolk, ii. 219—20.
Belper, missioned by J. Benton, i. 182—4; made a circuit, 183; first missionary meetings at B. and Turnditch, 184; in a double sense our Antioch, 187—8; its extensions, continuity of its history, 525—37.
BENTON JOHN, his early relations with H. Bourne and the C. M. Methodists, i. 96—8; his Mission in London, ii, 250; is dissatisfied with the non-mission law and declines his plan; gets a hymn-book printed; his labours in East Stafford and Derbyshire, i. 190—2; missions Belper, 182—4; effects of Mercaston C. Meeting on him, 198; one of the main leaders of the Great Revival of '17-18, 233—40; at Grantham, 260—1; opens Leicester, 301—2; finances chapels, 317; his romantic marriage, 354—5; loses his voice at Round Hill C. M., 352—3; becomes "unattached"; his death, 356.
Berkshire Mission (Brinkworth's), J. Ride and J. Petty earliest pioneers; social and moral condition of the district, ii. 316—19; the Ashdown wrestle—"Lord give us Berkshire"; 320; toils and persecutions of the pioneers, 317, 319, 330—5.
Berwick, missioned by North Shields; labours of W Clough and W. Lister at; some notable early converts; some peculiarities of the circuit—freedom from persecution, a feeder of Churches, number of preachers pledged; *portraits* of Messrs. J. Brown and E. Jobson, ii. 175—7.
Beverley, J. Verity and W. Clowes at; W. Driffield arrested; first rooms; early cases of persecution; first chapel and its difficulties; i. 392—7.
Birmingham, origin and progress of P. Methodism in, ii. 472—8; view of chapels, 477.
Bishop's Castle, missioned by Shrewsbury; R. Ward overcomes hostility; useful workers raised up; *portraits* of J. Huff and Mr. R. Jones of Clun, ii. 279—80.
Blackburn, T. Batty's first sermon on dunghill, ii. 121; made a circuit; circuits derived from, 124.

Blaenavon, afterwards Pontypool; Oakengates' pioneer mission in South Wales, ii. 298; its subsequent extensions; *portraits* of J. Prosser and Ald. Parfitt, 307—10.

Bolton, great success of J. Verity and W. Carter at; made a circuit along with its daughter-circuit, Isle of Man; its chapels; some of its worthies, ii. 35—7; its offshoots, 41.

BONSER JAS. his conversion, i. 242; his arrest at Wolverhampton, 522; his labours in Manchester, ii. 17—18, Liverpool, 267, Oakengates, 274, imprisonment at Shrewsbury, 278; head of Western Mission, arrest at Bridgnorth and Tewkesbury, 295-6; reaches Stroud, 296, his retirement, 296—7, and death, 278.

Book-Room (1) Bemersley Period. Description of the locality and buildings; staff, ii. 5—7; interior economy, 7—8; personnel of the Book Committee, 3—5; functions, 4, 13, 381; the "Cross Providence," 13—14; close connection between Book-Room and Missions, 380. (2) *London Period.* Causes which led to its removal, 382—4; Sutton St., its acquisition, tenure, extensions, staff, with *portraits* of Mr. P. Brown and T. C. Eamer, 384—7. Removal to Aldersgate St., 385; Table showing succession of Editors, and Book Stewards, 390; *portraits* of Editors, 367, of Book Stewards, 370, 388; changes in the constitution of Book Committee, 398—9; T. Bateman on the advantages of removal, 393; gross amount of allocations, 395.

BOURNE H., *Career, chronological sequence of.* His birth, parentage, childhood, i. 7—10; conversion, 12; joins the Methodists, 15; is much about Mow on business, 15—16; the Christmas-day conversation-sermon, 22—7; his part in the Harriseahead revival and characteristics of that revival, 28—33; his first sermon in the open-air, 33—6; takes main part in building chapel, 37; revival checked—modern and primitive Methodism contrasted, 37—43; organizes and takes part in Mow Cop and Norton C. Meetings, 61-82; his strange experience at Lichfield, 151; he is unchurched; the real and the alleged ground of this discussed, 84—6; his relations with the Quaker and Independent Methodists, '44—6; he and his brother employ J. Crawfoo' as an itinerant evangelist, 147—9; is the head of the Camp-meeting Methodists, 113—15; meets with John Benton at Wyrley Bank, 96—8; takes part in weekly services in Mr. Smith's kitchen, Tunstall, 103—4; The Clowesites and C. M. Methodists unite, 129—35; works on the first Tunstall Chapel, 110; is General Superintendent of the body until '19, 281, 331. Drafts society rules, 169—172; establishes Tract Mission at Hulland, and Sabbath Schools, and employs Mary Hawkesley, 174—7; takes over Benton's circuit, 192, and Belper, 188; follows as overseer the tract of the Great Revival, 228; his editorship and frequent attendance at District Meetings, ii. 359—60; his superannuation by Conference of '42; the action of Conference discussed, 360; his circular on "High Popularity and Low Popularity," 361—2; goes out to U. S. A. and Canada, 446—7; his enthusiastic labours on behalf of Temperance, i. 472—3; his illness, death, and burial, ii. 363—4; Mr. Petty's estimate of him and comparison with W. Clowes, 364—5. *Portraits*, i. 7, 8, ii. 2; his tomb, 363.

———*Characteristics.* His morbid shyness, i. 7—8; his interest in the young, 10, 177, ii. 44—5; his belief in the power of the press, i. 12, preaching with hand before face, 34—5; *note;* no high views of ministerial office, 131; his scrupulosity in receiving favours or money from others, 87, 131; his forcible way of putting things, and his aptness at coining phrases, 140; his mysticism and complicity in "vision-work, 147—154; later attitude, ii. 288—9; his dislike of "speeching Radicals," i. 338—9; his incessant journeyings on foot, 154, ii. 153; his abstemiousness, i. 156; his practical idealism, 288 and *note*, 292.

———*Journals.* Psychological and historic value of, i. 136—7; side-lights on the period 1800—12 from, 138—156.

BOURNE JAMES, takes part in first C. Meeting, i. 65; momentarily wavers, but in the end resolves to stand by his brother, 80; specimens of his evangelistic labours, 154—5; first Book Steward, ii. 3; President, '26, 21; Conference reference to his death, 379, *portrait*, i. 155.

Bourne College, Quinton, establishment and progress of, ii. 524—5.

Bradwell, missioned by Sheffield; i., 503—6.

BRAITHWAITE W., the "Apostle of N. W. Lincolnshire," his character, i. 413—18; incidents of his mission, 419—21.

Bridlington, missioned by J. Coulson and W. Clowes; its early chapels; ii. 99—101.

Brinkworth. The Wiltshire Mission becomes Brinkworth Circuit, ii. 313; S. Heath's and R. Davies' experiences, 311—13; begins the Berkshire Mission, 316—21; some notable families, 335—6; resumption of missionary labours—Chippenham, Bristol, Malmesbury missioned, 315, 349—50.

Bristol, missioned by S. West and S. Turner; view of first and present chapels; influence of C. T. Harris; Conference of 1900 at, ii. 349—51.

Brough missioned by Barnard Castle; fruitless opposition of the "gentry"; the revival; view of old and present chapels, ii. 149—150.

Buckley, made a circuit from Chester; Gladstone gives an address in the Tabernacle (view of);

notices of worthies with *portrait* of E. Bellis, ii. 271 and 273.

Burland. How the Cheshire Mission became Burland Branch, i. 510—16.

Burnley replaces Clitheroe as head of circuit; its chapels; division and sub-division of circuit. Conference of '96 at; notices of worthies with *portraits* of J. Lancaster, Ald. Smith, and J. Clarkson, ii. 122—3.

Burton-on-Trent, S. Turner's labours at and neighbouring places; transferred to Nottingham district; its early chapels, i. 522—5.

Cambridge, notices of early P. Methodism in, ii. 225—7.

Camp-Meetings. Why there were none till '07, i. 56—8; their decline and revival on the new model, 196; tactical value of, 288; Wesleyan Conference recommends the practice of holding, 310; serious proposal to put them down, 311.

———*Some famous.* The first described, i. 63—7; the second in its relation to the Conventicle Act, 69—77; Norton the interdicted and crucial C M., 77—82; the Wrekin, 83—4; Nottingham Whit Sunday C. M., 210; C. M. Love-feast at Priest's Hill and its far-reaching effects, 254; Buckminster C. M. brings Wedgwood out of prison, 259—60; Woodhouse Eaves historic, 283—5; Hinckley, the first lantern-lighted C. M., 289—90; the "noisy" C. M. at Witney, 346; the "panic" C. M. at Round Hill, 352—3; Wrine Hill begins Cheshire Mission, 510; Oldham on the great C. M. Day, ii 41; Pickering, 87; Waterloo the decisive C. M. for So. Shropshire, 284—5; echoes in literature of some East Anglian C. Meetings, 240—1.

Canada. Establishment of the mission in, i. 438. Progress of until '84, ii. 449—53.

Cardiff missioned by Pontypool and made Circuit by G. M. C., *portrait* of Ald. Ramsdale, J. P., and J. P. Bellingham, ii. 309.

Carlisle, Clowes' invited mission to, ii. 137—9; missions Glasgow, Wigton, and Whitehaven, 139, 141.

Channel Isles, Sunderland and So. Shields' mission to; regarded as the stepping-stone to France, ii. 208—10.

Chapel Aid Association, its establishment and progress, ii. 536—8.

———*Building Era*, Hull leads the forward movement, ii. 458—63; facts and figures relating thereto, 456.

———*Committee, General*, its establishment, objects and constitution, ii. 458.

CHARLTON GEO., sketch of, ii. 193; *portrait*, i. 472.

Chartists, The, in Leicester, i. 334—6; in Loughboro', 339.

Cheltenham, its early history, ii. 414—16.

Chester, account of its first missioning by Burland; view of its chapels, and history of George St.; P. Methodism hereditary in families; has the Conferences of '66 and '94, i. 549—557.

Chesterfield missioned by Sheffield; account of its early chapels and view of present; numerical progress and stations made from it; *portrait* and sketch of Dr. Geo. Booth, i. 495—500.

CLOWES WILLIAM. *Career, Chronological sequence of.* His family and lineage; becomes a potter; his wild doings at Leek; his life in Hull; his anguish under conviction; his conversion and early usefulness at Tunstall, i. 45—55; exhorts at first C. Meeting, 66; present at the second, but labours little, 75; explanation of his holding aloof from C. Meetings for fifteen months, 87—9; is present at all the Ramsor C. Meetings, 89; he is "dealt with," 99—102; becomes the head of the Clowesites and a travelling evangelist, 102—6; the P. Methodist denomination formed, 111, 129—135; is Tunstall preacher until '19, but makes an excursion into Notts., 257—60, 264—7, and Leicestershire, 305—7, 463—4; is appointed to Hull, 363; missions York, ii. 53—5; Leeds, 67—8; Ripon and Hutton Rudby, i. 405—9; Scarboro', Whitby, etc., ii. 98, 104, 107—9; Darlington, 130—2; the Northern Mission, 168—72, 199—201, 164; Carlisle, 138—9; Whitehaven, 141; London, 253—5; Cornish Mission, 321—3, his superannuation, 359; last years in Hull, and death; funeral card and view of tomb, 362—3; Mr. Petty's estimate of him 364—5.

———*Characteristics.* Character simple not complex, i. 45; his magnetic power, 87, 102; the power of his eye and his thrilling voice, 258, 464; had a soul full of music, 161; his superb evangelizing gifts, 259, 409; took unkindly to the pen, 136; as much inferior to H. Bourne in legislative and administrative ability as he was superior to him as a speaker and evangelist, ii. 364—5.

———*Journals.* Defects and qualities of, i. 136.

Committees, origin of Circuit, i. 281; district, i. 323, ii. 458; General, and General Missionary, i. 377, ii. 401—3; General Chapel, 458.

CRAWFOOT JAS., sketch of; What, connexionally, do we owe him? i. 147—9; his mystic views—conflict of atmospheres, "taking the burden," the visionary power, 150—4; other references, 92, 110, 131.

Crisis, Connexional, '24—8, its signs, i. 434, 438—9; causes, and remedies applied, 435—6.

Cwm, the farm-house circuit—its missioning; its notable families, its missions, ii. 299—302.

Darlaston, when first visited; *portraits* of W. Carter, D. Bowen, Mr. and Mrs. Belcher;

M M

becomes a powerful and procreative circuit, the West Midland Dist. in embryo, i. 519—22.

Darlington. Clowes visits by invitation; subsequent labours of S. Laister, W. Evans, and W. Clowes at; Queen St. Chapel opened; Stockton, Wolsingham, Bishop Auckland, and Barnard Castle reached; view of chapels, ii. 129—134.

Daventry, G. W. Bellham's rough treatment at, i. 343—4; other references to, ii. 414, 417.

Deed Poll, read and approved, '31; explanation of the delay in its execution; names of the original members of, i. 438—40.

Derby, missioned by S. Kirkland, i. 195; Clowes' visits to Derby and neighbourhood, 198—200; view of the Armoury (200) and of Albion St., the first chapel in Derbyshire, 201; view of chapels, ii. 471.

Dewsbury, visited by W. Clowes, ii. 67; again made a circuit from Leeds, '57, 72—4.

Doncaster, early vicissitudes of, i. 500—1; its after prosperity; the Conference of '58 held at; 501—2; views of Duke St., and Spring Gardens Chapels, and *portraits* and notices of Rev. W. Leaker, Richd. Wadsworth, and Geo. Taylor, 501—3.

Dover. How the Mission became a Circuit; view of new church, ii. 410—11; G. Stansfield imprisoned in Dover Jail, *portrait*, 348.

Dow LORENZO, *portrait*, his strange character and movements; his visit to Staffordshire in 1807; the extent of the Dow factor in P. Methodism discussed, i. 58—61; on his last visit to England follows on the track of the Great Revival, 312—13.

Downham Market, formerly Upwell Circuit; its history outlined; its missions; view of chapel and *portrait* of J. Kemish, ii. 223—4.

Driffield, when visited; W. Clowes and J. Oxtoby at; its chapels past and present; usefulness of Mr. Byas; its long retention by Hull as a branch; made a circuit; its width and numerical strength; notices of various circuit worthies with *portraits* of Thomas Wood and Geo. Bullock, ii. 91—8.

Edinburgh, the first mission to Scotland: Messrs. Oliver and Clewer sent by Sunderland open their commission, '26; their house-to-house visitation; N. West heads a serious secession; Hull Circuit takes over the mission and sends J. Flesher; subsequent changes; some ministerial labourers at; missions Alloa and Dunfermline; gives J. Macpherson to ministry; Rev. J. Vaughan's success at; view of Victoria Terrace Chapel, ii. 206—8; the recent forward movement at E.; Livingstone Hall, ii. 516—18.

Education, Ministerial, growth of the sentiment in favour of; the successive institutions at York, Sunderland, and Manchester, with *portraits* of the Principals and Tutors, ii. 525—9.

Ellesmere Port, commanding position of the Denomination in; outline of its early history with *portraits*, ii. 271—3.

Elmfield College, York; its establishment and progress; its Governors and Head-masters, ii. 521—4.

Equalization Fund established by permissive legislation, ii. 409, *note*.

Fernando Po, the establishment and progress of the mission in, ii. 487—97.

Filey, change wrought by the Revival; John Oxtoby and other workers referred to; the hazards of the fisherman's life; *portraits* of Jenkinson and M. Haxby, ii. 102—7.

Flamborough and its fishermen; *portrait* of V. Mainprize, ii. 100—2.

FLESHER JOHN, unites with the Society, and begins his ministry, ii. 116—18; at Hull and Beverley, i. 395—6; is sent to save Edinburgh, ii. 207; and London, 255—7; the vindicator of the Connexion, i. 456, ii. 258; appointed Editor and gets the Book-Room removed to London, 381—4; prepares the Hymn Book, 371—2; his remarkable consolidation of the Minutes, 259; his immense influence in the transition period, 258; his eloquence—our "Chrysostom"—i. 368, 396; his humility, 485—6; his superannuation, later days and death, ii. 259; *portraits*, i. 396, ii. 257; memorial tablet, 259.

Forest of Dean, Oakengates' mission to, ii. 298; labours and persecutions in; circuits derived from the mission, 302—3.

Frome, reached by Tunstall's Western Mission; made a Circuit, and missions Bath, Dorset, and, later, Glastonbury, ii. 297.

Gainsborough, missioned by W. Braithwaite and T. Saxton; i. 413—16.

GARNER, the brothers, their early conversion and distinguished services, i. 242—5.

Gateshead, sketch of its early history and remarkable later development; view of Chapels; *portraits* of Messrs. J. Thompson, E. Gowland, G. E. Almond, ii. 197, 199—200.

General Committee, Secs. portraits of, ii. 404.

GILBERT JER., chief pioneer of the Sheffield group of circuits; i. 478—84; in North Shields Circuit, ii. 172.

Glasgow, Carlisle sends J. Johnson on a mission to, subsequent progress of, ii. 139.

Gloucester, its early missioning by Pillawell; J. Wenn's labours at; made a circuit by the G. M. Committee; *portraits* of J. Richards, J. Wellington, Levi Norris, ii. 414—16.

Grantham, J. Wedgwood's imprisonment at, i. 255—6, Mr. Lockwood arrested for preaching at the Cross, 256; *portrait* of S. Bayley, 259; J. Benton preaches from Sir W. Manners' pulpit, 260—1; Bottesford remissions Grantham, 262; chapel opened, 263, made a circuit, 264.

Grimsby, visited by Thomas King, i. 444—6; Farmer Holt proves himself a staunch friend, 446—7; early preaching-places, 448; the plan of 1820 analysed as to places and preachers, 448—60; view of present chapels, 461, and *portraits* of some leading officials, 460—3.

Halifax and neighbourhood missioned by Thos. Holliday; his arrest and imprisonment at Wakefield; made a circuit; view of first chapel and of Ebenezer; fifth Conference described; some early worthies, *portraits*, i. 488—92.

HARTLEY W. P., J.P., Gen. Miss. Treasurer, ii. 405; Vice-President of '92 Conference, 394; Founder of C. A. Association, 536-7; his financial genius; his great liberality and immense influence in the later development of the Connexion, 532—3.

Haverfordwest, a sketch of its history, ii. 306—7.

Hereford, early persecution at; view of old Chapel and present Church; *portraits* of Mr. T. Davies, J.P., Mrs. Davies, and Mr. T. A. King, ii. 303—5.

Hexham, commencement of a mission at, ii. 135; its extensive area and its missions; J. Spoor's labours on the Rothbury mission, 136; C. C. McKechnie's reminiscences of the circuit, 157—62.

HIGGINSON HENRY, his call to the ministry and labours at Swansea, ii. 308; joint-missioner of Luton and Dunstable, 352; anecdote and *portrait* of, 32.

High Wycombe, a Society at in 1811, ii. 250; visited by James Pole; taken over by Reading; resumes its status as a circuit, 352—4.

HODGE, the family of, in Holderness and Hull, i. 381—3.

Holderness, dark moral condition of, i. 388—9; Camp Meeting at Preston on Maudlin Sunday, 389—90; W. Clowes visits, 381, 390—2.

Hucknall Torkard, missioned by S. Kirkland, i. 230; the "Selstonite" split, 248—50; E. Morton re-missions it; subsequent prosperity, 251, 232.

Huddersfield, W. Taylor and Miss Perry imprisoned at; view of first chapel; made a circuit; *portraits* of John North, G. C. Treas., J. Rayner, and Samuel and Alexander Glendinning, i. 492—5.

Hull entered by invitation, i. 361—2; W. Clowes appointed in place of R. Winfield, 363; Jane Brown his precursor, 364; his first business the organizing of classes, 365—6; J. and S. Harrison appointed, 370; made a circuit, 370; the first plan of the circuit, 371; the building and opening of Mill Street Chapel, 373—7; some early Hull worthies, 377—385; Church Street chapel built, 382; Mason St. Chapel acquired, 386; divided into seven branches, 387; the circuit reaches from Carlisle to Spurn Point, ii. 139; the Stamp troubles, i. 456; Hull leads the way in chapel extension, ii. 458—63; views of its chapels, 459, 461.

Hutton Rudby, base of W. Clowes' North Riding Mission; made a circuit, '21; now included in Stokesley Circuit, i. 405—9

Hymn Books, earliest, ii. 2; pirated editions, 2, 10; the "Small" Hymn Book; the "Large," 10; Mr. Flesher's compilation, 369—71; the Hymnal, 371; On the character and influence of the early Hymns —their popularity with the masses, ii. 2, 11, 33—5, 380.

Isle of Man, early and typical example of a circuit mission, ii. 37; Bolton circuit sends J. Butcher and H. Sharman, 37—8; origin of the present stations on the Island; fluctuations in the membership accounted for; 39; *portraits* and references to early workers, 39—40.

JACKSON'S the three THOMAS, *portraits*, i. 182—3.
——— THOS. (1), the first superintendent of Belper, i. 183; holds the first Missionary Meetings at Belper and Turnditch, 184; meets with opposition at Kinoulton, 242, is put into the stocks at Cropwell Bishop, 238—9; and used with violence at Oakham. 240; missions Sandbach and Preston Brook, 543—6.
——— THOS. (3), his aggressive and social work at Walthamstow, Clapton, Whitechapel, and Southend, ii. 507-12

JERSEY F. N., assists W. Clowes at Darlington, ii. 132; his labours in Craven, 120; on the Kendal Mission, 137—8; is committed to Lancaster Castle for preaching at Dalton Cross, 137; in Weardale, 143; troubles of in Nottingham, i. 249.

JESSOPP CANON, quoted on the former condition of Mid-Norfolk, ii. 235—6; on the influence of P. Methodism in East Anglia, 242.

Jubilee Conference, and regulations for celebrating the Jubilee, ii. 377—9.
——— (Missionary), '92, 533—4.

JUKES RICHARD, *portrait*, the former popularity of his hymns, ii. 33; his early life, 283.

Keighley, ii. 119.

Kendal missioned by F. N. Jersey, ii. 137—8; its course till it became a circuit; its associations with John Atkinson and J. Taylor, 138.

KEY ROBERT, his conversion at Yarmouth, ii. 233; Mr. Goodrick's estimate of, 233—4; his toils and sufferings in Mid-Norfolk, 235, 237—9; his inner conflicts, 239; amongst the rick-burners, 241; his mission to Hadleigh, 245; walks to London District Meeting, 248; *portrait*, 237; his letter on Jubilee proposals quoted, 520.

KING THOS., connects himself with the Nottingham Society, *portrait*, i. 205—6; a member

M M 2

of the Preparatory Meeting, 378; visits Grimsby and other places in Lincolnshire, 443—8; walks to from the Tunstall Conference, 447; President of the '25 and '48 Conferences; Book Steward, ii. 390; preaches the Conference Jubilee Sermon, 378.

King's Lynn, early success followed by troubles at, i. 322, ii. 218; refounded by W. P. Belham; its missionary enterprise, 219—221; Conferences of '36 and '44 at; view of London Road Chapel, 221; *portrait* and notice of W. Lift, 222.

KIRKLAND SARAH, first female travelling preacher, i. 92; home and early life, *portrait* 176—7; pioneer visits to Derby, 194—5; Nottingham, 201—4, 206—7; enters the ministry and labours in Staffordshire and Cheshire, afterwards in Notts., 210, 226—34; and Hull Circuit, 370, 398—9, 402, ii. 55; her grave in Mugginton Churchyard, i. 175—6.

LAISTER S., a pioneer missionary to Driffield, ii. 93, Leeds, 71—2, in Craven, 117, Malton and Darlington, 131—4; see also i. 372.

LAMB GEO., joins the Society at Preston and is sent out to travel by H. Bourne; outline of his subsequent career, ii. 125; President of the Conferences of '66 and '84; Book Steward; Conf. Deputation to Canada, 452; Member of the Deed Poll, 125; his interest in the Temperance movement, *portrait*, i. 472. The "Lamb Scholarship," ii. 529.

Leeds, band of revivalists invite the P. Methodists, ii. 63—6; W. Clowes' visits, 67—8; troubles arise, 69—70; administrative changes, 72—4; Mr. G. Allen (*portrait*) on the origin of Leeds 2nd and 3rd, 74; view of Leeds chapels, 73; R. Davies, T. Batty, and Atkinson Smith at, 74—5; Conferences of '23 and '48 at, 72; *portraits* of J. Reynard, Mrs. Brogden, and J. Parrott, 70—1.

Leicester, John Benton enters, i. 298—303; first preaching-places, 304—5; Clowes' and Wedgwood's visits to, 305—7; John Harrison's ditto, 307—8; Robert Hall's and Daniel Isaac's attitude to our Church, 309—11; progress of the cause, 311—12; some early preachers, 312; the building of George Street Chapel—view of chapel and group of old officials, 324—8; Alexander St. Chapel acquired, 332; the Denmanite split, 333; building of York St. Chapel, 333—4, subsequent developments, 335; Chartists in Leicester, Thos. Cooper's "Lion of Freedom" goes down before W. Jefferson's "Lion of Judah," 335—6; *portraits* (with references) of early worthies, 326—8, 332—5.

"*Levellers,*" the; the Levelling System described; i. 218—224.

Lichfield, H. Bourne's travail of soul at, i. 150—1 S. Turner preaches at, 523; Darlaston and Birmingham's mission to; under the laborious R. Ward made a station, 523.

Lincoln, the early missioning of the district, i. 463; Clowes' rough reception at, 463—4; early preaching-places and ministers, 465—7; remarkable results of the City Mission, 468; *portraits* of W. R. Widdowson and W. Price, and views of first and second Portland Street Chapels, 467—9.

Liverpool, W. Clowes' early visit to, ii. 265—6 J. Ride's arrest and Jas. Role's rough reception, 266; made a circuit from Preston Brook, 267; Maguire Street Chapel and its memories, 267—8; the circuit's sympathy with missions, 268; its very recent development, 270; view of its chapels, 269; glance at some of the names on '34 Plan, 270—2.

London, H. Bourne and J. Crawfoot's excursion to, ii. 249. John Benton's labours in 1811, 250. The London Primitives of 1818, 250. Leeds Circuit sends P. Sugden and J. Watson, 251. Cooper's Gardens Chapel acquired, 252. J. Coulson walks from Leeds to take the place of Watson, 253. Hull Circuit takes over London Mission, and Clowes labours on it twenty months, 253—5. Made a Circuit of Hull District, 1826—7. 255. Transferred to Norwich District, 1828—1834, 255. Again a Mission of Hull, 255. Blue Gate Fields Chapel difficulties, 256. Sutton Street Chapel opened, 257. Importance of John Flesher's labours in London, 255—8. Elim Chapel, Fetter Lane, acquired, 260. Plan of the London Mission, 1847, described, 259—60. London becomes a circuit, 1847, 260. In 1853 three circuits, and London District formed 264. *Portraits* and notices of early London officials, 260—4. Its recent remarkable development, 539—40.

Loughborough missioned by J. Benton in a time of industrial agitation, i. 216—17; when made a circuit, 279—81 and 318, *note;* Loughborough section of the Nottingham Circuit Plan for 1818, 279; some of the places therein referred to, 281—7; plan of circuit for '22—'3, out of which eleven circuits have been carved, 278; history of Dead Lane Chapel, 314—18.

Louth, second place on the Grimsby plan of 1820, i. 449; made a circuit of wide area, 450; its advance under J. Coulson and J. Stamp, 451—2; J. Stamp leaves a legacy of chapel difficulties, 452; Mr. W. Byron lends valuable assistance; subsequent progress of the circuit, 454; view of chapel and *portraits* of J. Maltby, W. Byron, Mrs. Byron, 453, and Joel Hodgson and J. F. Parrish, 449.

Luddites and Luddism described, i. 212—18.

Ludlow, see Hopton Bank.

Luton, its missioning by S. Turner and H. Higginson, ii. 352; view of its chapels, 353.

INDEX.

Macclesfield, when and how missioned, i. 538—40; the early missionary zeal of the circuit, 540.
McKechnie C. C., early life at Paisley, "sung into the Kingdom," and his entry on the ministry, *portrait*, ii. 140; his experiences at Ripon, 82—3; his reminiscences of Hexham Circuit, 157—61; witnesses great Revivals in Weardale and Allendale, 151, and North Shields, 185—6; his references to Dr. W. Antliff and the Conference of '53, 376; his great interest in ministerial education, 397; Editor eleven years, 390, 395.
Magazines. For the serial literature of the Connexion, see i. 330—2, ii. 11—12, 395; for the P. M. Quarterly Review, 396—8.
Malmesbury, severe persecution at, ii. 312; successfully re-missioned by G. Warner, 315.
Malton, a branch of Hull—its wide extent and former religious condition—Canon Atkinson quoted, ii. 84—6; some of its first preachers, 86—7; circuit's history since '23, 89.
Manchester, when first visited, ii. 15—16; pioneer labours of Ann Brownsword, Bonser, Verity, and W. Carter, 17—19; S. Waller's imprisonment, 18—19; view of Jersey Street Chapel, 20; the Conferences of '27 and '40 held at, 23; made the head of a district, 1827, 22—3; great results from re-missionary labours, references to Jonathan Ireland, and other early workers, 23—6; view of present chapels, 27; Moss Lane Chapel and the origin of the second circuit, 26 and ii. 465—6; Higher Ardwick Church, ii. 26, 407, 466—7; Great Western Street, 467; the *College*, its establishment and successive enlargements, 527—8.
Market Rasen, J. Harrison's strange Sunday Service in the Market-place, i. 442; subsequent history, 440, 444.
Melton Mowbray, early history of, ii. 350—1.
Middlesbrough, its phenomenal growth, ii. 85, 478; view of its chapels, 479.
Middleton-in-Teesdale, J. Grieves establishes a Society at; extensions to Upper Teesdale and Eden Valley, ii. 148—9.
Milson Parkinson, *portrait* and estimate of, i. 426.
Minsterley, how P. Methodism was introduced into, ii. 281; made a circuit, 279.
Mitcheldever, made a mission by Shefford, ii. 341; Messrs. Ride and Bishop cited before the magistrates for open-air preaching at, 342; made a circuit, 341; successfully re-missions Winchester, 343.
Motcombe, missioned by Frome and made a circuit in '28, ii. 297; carries on extensive missionary operations in So. Wilts. and especially in Dorset, 297—8.
Mow Cop, a century ago and now, i. 15—22; the first and second Camp Meetings described, 62—9, 73—7; Jubilee Camp Meeting on, ii. 378.

Nelson Thomas, his extensive labours and usefulness in the North of England. ii. 170—1, 202.
——— John, *portrait*, fellow-labourer of Clowes on the North Mission, ii. 170—1; his experience on the Dorset Mission; retires under discouragement, 210—11.
Newark, Clowes and Wedgwood at, i. 267; fire-engine plays on Mr. Lockwood, 268; instances of retribution on persecutors, 269; its early vicissitudes; made a circuit, 269—70.
Newbury, heir and representative of Shefford Circuit, ii. 315—16,; view of manse and Church, 340.
Newcastle-on-Tyne, visited by W. Clowes and J. Branfoot, ii. 163—5; first class formed, 189; becomes a circuit, 189—90; Silver Street Chapel the centre for the first period, 190—2; Nelson St.—the chapel for the middle period—opened, 192; acquisition of the Central Church, 189, 192; glance at its later development, 196—7; references to notable adherents, *portraits*, 190—6.
New Zealand, establishment and progress of the mission to, ii. 440—6.
Northampton, on Welton plan of '24, i. 345; a mission of Burland; taken over by the G. M. Com.; made a circuit, its subsequent progress, ii. 416—19.
North Shields, Clowes' early visits to, ii. 168—9; Clowes' remarkable escape from death, 171; Union Street and Saville Street chapels, 172; Newcastle separated from it, 173; its missions in Northumberland—chequered history of Morpeth and Alnwick, 173—4; some early officials with *portraits*, 178—9; the missioning of Berwick its most notable achievement, 174; Cullercoats and the fisher-folk, 180—2; the mining villages—old Cramlington Missionary Meeting—imprisonment of Seaton Delaval P. M.'s—the Hartley Colliery Disaster—the Long Strike—the great revival, 184—6. Some worthies with *portraits*; influence of P. Methodism on the miners, 186—8.
North Walsham, its mission to Mid-Norfolk, ii. 235—40.
Norwich, view of the Lollard's Pit where first services were held, ii. 213; its first chapels, 214—15; its missionary labours, 214; reference to early officials, 216; view of Scott Memorial Church, 216.
Norwich District formed in '25, ii. 212—13; by '42 practically covered East Anglia, 213.
Nottingham, when and by whom missioned, i. 201—2; Factory in Broad Marsh opened, 203—4; Canaan St. chapel opened—origin of the name, 204—5; H. Bourne's visit to, 209; a base for further extension, 210; great Whit-Sunday Camp Meeting, 226; troubles arise and renewed prosperity, 249; Hockley chapel obtained, 250; *portraits*, and references to Jas Barker, 276, D. M. Jackson, John Spencer, 276, ii. 377; Circuit Committee first formed at, i. 280.

Oakengates, afterwards called Wrockwardine Wood, made a circuit from Tunstall, ii. 274; the story of Edgmond and Dark Lane Chapels, 275—7; offshoots of the circuits, 277—8.

ODELL JOSEPH, President of the Conference of 1900, ii. 483; takes charge of the church at Brooklyn, U.S.A., 448—9; his work in Birmingham—Conference Hall built and a new circuit created, 476—8; establishes the Evangelists' Home, 541—2.

Oldham, when visited, some famous Camp Meetings at, ii. 41; Peter Macdonald and other early officials, 43; some peculiar features of the revival of '29; H. Bourne's visit to, 44—5; early chapels and view of present, 42—3.

Oswestry, J. Doughty's arrest and imprisonment, *portrait*, ii. 284—5; Elizabeth Elliot, the girl preacher and her tragic fate, 286—7; a missionary circuit, 289; a secession and chapel embarrassments and the great service rendered by Messrs. E. Parry and S. Ward, *portraits*, 289—91; circuits made from it, 293.

Oxford, W. G. Bellham has a rough reception at i. 346; its subsequent re-missioning and made a circuit, ii. 352.

OXTOBY JOHN. Sketch of his life and character, with view of his grave, i. 365—70; his prayer on Muston Hill for Filey—the great Revival, ii. 104—6; is active in the Weardale Revival, 146—7.

Paisley, C. C. McKechnie and early P. Methodism in, ii. 139—40.

Pembrokeshire Mission begun, J. Petty's labours in, ii. 306—7.

Penzance, the missioning and subsequent progress of ii. 326—7.

Peterborough, the history of the circuit outlined, *portrait* of Isaac Edis, ii. 421—3.

PETTY JOHN, Editor, ii. 367; President of the Conference of '60, 292; first Governor of Elmfield College, 523; his conversion and early entrance on the ministry, 120—1, 123; his arduous labours in Pembrokeshire, 306 —7, i. 344; at Cwm, ii, 300—1, Northampton, 416—17, Sunderland, and Channel Isles, 208—9; builds Jubilee Chapel, Hull, 462.

Pickering, made a circuit from Malton, ii. 89; former condition of the North Riding, 85— 6; a famous Camp Meeting described, 87; reference to the families of Lumley, Frank, and Allenby, *portraits*, 90—1.

Pillawell, incidents connected with its missioning; persecution at Newnham; offshoots and partitions of the circuit, ii. 302—6.

Pocklington, missioned by S. Harrison and W. Clowes, i. 398.

Prees Green, originally Burland's Shropshire Station, made a circuit, ii. 287; some early worthies—Archdeacon Allen's high opinion of them, 288; offshoots of the circuit, 289.

Presidents of Conferences, *portraits* of, until 1859, ii. 21; from 1860 to 1874, 292; from 1875 to 1886, 392; from 1887 to 1897, 454; from 1898 to 1905, 483, 523, 498.

Preston (Lancs.), T. Batty and J. Harrison at, W. Brinning commences to travel at, *portrait*, ii. 121; a successful missionary circuit, 124—7; takes a foremost place in the Temperance cause, *portraits of* and reference to, some of the leaders in the movement; the "seven men of Preston," 128—9; view of Saul St. Chapel, 128.

Preston Brook, Thos. Jackson pioneer missionary to, i. 545; jubilee of the circuit celebrated, '69, 545; references to early Camp Meetings, 545—6; the circuit foster-mother to Liverpool, 546; in '32 sends F. N. Jersey to Ireland, 546.

Primitive Methodist, various uses of the word " primitive " illustrated by examples, i. 38—9; legitimately used as the antithesis of " Modern Methodism," 37—42; the name taken, 132.

Ramsor, early centre of Camp Meeting Methodists. First five Ramsor Camp Meetings referred to, i. 87—98; names and *portraits* of some early workers, 92—5.

" *Ranters*," origin of the nickname, i. 185—6 the name a stigma that marked the first period, 160, 186—7; yet the name contributed to extension, 187, 217, 221; the " putting down " of the " Ranters " seriously proposed in '20, 311.

RAWLINGS ED., *portrait*, ii. 349, 348.

Reading missioned by Shefford, ii. 344; its early chapels; made a circuit; costly case of persecution, 345; extensive missionary labours entered upon, 345; noteworthy Conference of '41 held at, 350—1; hands over its missions to G. M. Committee, 354; some Reading worthies—*portraits* of Mr. Jesse Herbert, Mary Bovaston, and Mr. E. Long, 344.

Redruth, W. Clowes' labours in the Cornwall Mission, ii. 321—3; great revival at, 323; view of chapel and *portraits* of Capts. Hosking and Bishop, 323—5; extensions of the mission, 325—7.

Rhosymedre, made a circuit from Oswestry; early labours of Mary Williams in, ii. 293.

RIDE JOHN, his conversion, i. 178; begins to preach at Mercaston Camp Meeting, 198; his return from America—flight to Burland, 518, 535; opens Wrexham and visits Chester, 551; what T. Bateman says of him, *portrait*, 518; arrested at Liverpool, ii. 265—6; is at Frome, 297; heads the main line of advance *via* Brinkworth, Shefford, and Reading, 314; the bout of prayer at Ashdown—" Lord, give us Berkshire ! " 320—1; his imprisonment at Winchester, 342—3; made visitor of Home Missions, 403; goes to Australia; his superannuation, 427.

Ripley, origin and progress of the circuit; *portraits* of J. Smith of Golden Valley, and E. Cox, i. 536—7.

Ripon, made a circuit—its very wide area and early importance, ii. 79; Clowes' visits to, 79—80; incidents in J. Spoor's ministry at, *portrait*, 81—3; *portraits* and references to T. Dawson, M. Lupton, and Mrs. Porteus, 80—1.

Rocester, facsimile and signatures of the deed of earliest chapel vested in trustees, i. 173—4.

Rochdale, missioned from Manchester and made a circuit; view of Packer Street, and reference to Drake Street Chapel; *portraits* and notices of some early workers, ii. 46—7.

ROLES JAS., early missionary to Liverpool, ii. 266; pioneer to Blaenavon, 299; Cwm, 299, Pillawell, 302; Pembrokeshire, 306.

Rugby, the interesting circumstances connected with its missioning, i. 347—8; heir and representative of Old Welton circuit, 346.

RUSSELL THOS., enters upon the Berkshire Mission—his toils and privations, ii. 319; the pleading on Ashdown, 320; his imprisonment at Abingdon, 331—3; his inhuman treatment at Wantage and Faringdon, 333—5; his experience in Hampshire, 338—9; at Longton, Stafford, 289; on Weymouth mission, 211.

Saffron Walden, missioned by Upwell—made a circuit, ii. 223.

St. Austell, visited by W. Clowes, ii. 322; great revival at; subsequent history, 325—6.

St. Day, visited by W. Clowes, ghostly experience alluded to, 322.

St. Ives, opened by Joseph Grieves, revival and progress; made a station, ii. 326—7; *portrait* and notice of A. F. Beckerlegge.

St. Ives (Hunts.), missioned by Cambridge, early preaching places; made a circuit by G. M. C., ii. 227.

Salisbury, missioned by Motcombe; made a circuit; its offshoots, ii. 297.

SANDERSON W., his conversion, eminence and success as a minister—ministers who were his spiritual children; *portrait*, i. 400—2.

Scarborough, society formed by W. Clowes and J. Coulson, ii. 107—8; N. West's and R. Abey's labours at, 109—10; its first home-made chapel, 110; *portraits* of early worthies, 113; the building of Jubilee and present Sepulchre Street Chapels, 112 and 114; view of chapels, 114.

Scotter, once the head of a district and centre of a wide evangelistic movement, i. 417; W. Braithwaite chief pioneer—also Miss Parrott, 417—18; incidents of village evangelization, 419—32; only rural village where a Conference has been held—significance of the fact, 433; Conference Chapel lost to the Connexion, 432—3; doings of the Conf. of '29, 436—8; a strong and aggressive circuit, 432.

Sheffield, J. Gilbert as Nottingham's missionary begins his pioneer labours, i. 479—84; building of Bethel Chapel, the audacity of faith, 485—6; *portrait*, group of early Sheffield worthies with personal references, 484—5; the Conference of '52 with a glance at some of the representatives, ii. 372—7; the recent development of P. Methodism in Sheffield, 468—71.

Shefford, made a circuit; its extensive missionary labours, ii. 314, 345; view of first meeting house, 311; See Berkshire Mission and Newbury.

Shrewsbury, Sarah Spittle and J. Bonser the pioneers; arrest of the latter for open-air preaching. ii. 278; made a circuit from Oakengates; conversion of Elizabeth Johnson, the mother of the Brownhills, *portraits*, 278—9; circuits deriving from, 79; establishes first mission to Ireland, 281; its Wiltshire Mission, 310—13.

Silsden, missionaries invited to; T. Batty's labours; references to early life of J. Flesher and J. Petty; *portraits* and notices of other early adherents, ii. 116—18, 120.

SMITH JOHN (1). Scholar in T. Bateman's Bible Class, i. 518. First superintendent of Chester, 556. Moves off to East Anglia, 518. His death and character, ii. 232—3. Portrait, i. 517. Anecdote of, 556.

——— ATKINSON, his early life, conversion, and ministry, i. 423—6; at Leeds, ii. 74—5.

South-East London Mission and its Social Ministries, ii. 513—16.

Southport, beginnings of P. Methodism in, ii. 126.

South Shields, J. Branfoot's pioneer visit to, ii. 165; first preaching-rooms and the building of the Glebe, 166—7; reference to early worthies, with *portraits*, 167—8; joint mission to Channel Isles, 209.

SPOOR JOS., *portrait*, incidents of his ministry at Ripon, ii. 81—4; on the Rothbury mission, 136.

Stanhope, great revival at, ii. 151.

Stanley, the question of the class at, discussed, i. 115—18.

STEELE JAS., claimed by W. Clowes as one of the founders of the Connexion, i. 1, ii. 22; becomes a "Revivalist," *portrait*, i. 45; his expulsion from the Methodist Society, 106—9; made the first Circuit Steward, 131; his death, ii. 22.

Stockport, early history of, *portraits* of S. Smith, J. Ashworth, W. Cheetham, sen., and view of present chapel, ii. 48—50.

Stockton-on-Tees, missioned by S. Laister, ii. 132; made a circuit, 201—2.

Sunday School Union established; *portraits* of Secretaries, ii. 530—1.

Sunderland, when first visited, ii., 199—201; Sunderland and Stockton Union Circuit formed—its wide area and successive partitions—its rapid growth, 202; the building of Flag Lane, 203; its influential officials, 204—5; the secession of, '77, 205;

its missions to Edinburgh, 205—8, Channel Isles, 208—10, Dorset, 210 ; view of chapels, 466 ; the first Theological Institute, 526.

Sustentation Fund established, ii. 409.

Swaffham and the district missioned by W. P. Bellham of Lynn, made a circuit, ii. 219—20.

Swansea, Blaenavon sends Henry Higginson to mission, ii. 308 ; Jos. Hibbs (*portrait*) first superintendent, 308—9.

Tadcaster missioned by N. West—its after history, ii. 77—8.

Temperance, the growth of sentiment in the Connexion in favour of, i. 469—76 ; the early efforts of Preston circuit in favour of, ii. 127—9 ; the appointment of Connexional Temperance Secretary, 531.

Tickets, Society, the origin of, i, 111, facsimiles of, 112.

Tunstall, revival at, i. 45 ; " Clowesites " preach in Boden's warehouse, 109 ; the first chapel built—view of, 110 ; first written plan of Tunstall circuit, 559 ; the second plan—its places and preachers, 114—29 ; Non-mission law prevails until '19, 187—9 ; end of the law, and resumption of aggressive policy, 507—10 ; Plan of the circuit for 1819, 508 ; Darlaston becomes a circuit and the rest divided into six branches, 510. Jubilee Conference at, ii. 378.

TURNER SAMPSON, his conversion, *portrait*, i. 169 ; enters the ministry, 510, 519 ; his labours in the Black Country, 519—20, Lichfield, 523, Burton-on-Trent, 524 ; T. Bateman's estimate, 516 ; missions Huxley, 549 ; at Macclesfield, 539 ; Northwich, 546 ; York, ii. 57—8.

———— SAMUEL, *portraits*, ii. 332, 343.

VICE-PRESIDENTS of Conference, *portraits* of, ii., 394, 480, 518, 541.

Wakefield, made a circuit, i. 477 ; reference to, 486.

Wangford, made a circuit from Yarmouth, early history of, ii. 245—6.

Wantage, Thos. Russell's severe persecution at, ii. 333—4.

WARD, ROBERT, a native of Swaffham Circuit, ii. 220 ; outline of his labours as a pioneer and planter of Churches in New Zealand, 440—5 ; *portrait*, 441.

WARNER GEO., successfully missions Malmesbury, *portrait*, ii. 315 ; his service as Connexional Evangelist, 540.

Weardale, labours of J. Ansdale, T. Batty, and others in—incidents in the great Revival, ii. 143—6 ; made a branch of Hull, 146 ; John Oxtoby in, 147 ; the revival spreads to Nenthead and Allendale, 147—8 ; some notable figures of the Dale, 143, 154—6.

WEDGWOOD JOHN, his early life and conversion, i. 164—5. Lost with Clowes on Morridge, 166—8. Travels with H. Bourne to Cannock Wood Camp Meeting, 169 Takes part in the great Revival in the Midlands, 251—4. First Primitive Methodist to be imprisoned, 255—7. Takes part in opening Leicester, 304—6. His labours on the Cheshire Mission, 510—13. Becomes a travelling preacher, 514. His funeral described, 514—15. His *portraits*, 163, 257.

Western Mission, geographical course of traced, ii. 295—8.

Westgate, story of the building of the Chapel at, ii. 154, see also under Weardale.

Weymouth, J. Nelson and G. Cosons, Sunderland's missionaries to, ii. 210 ; after history of, 211.

Whitby, Clowes and N. West visit, ii. 108—9 ; made a circuit, 110.

Whitehaven, when missioned. ii. 141 ; visited by W. Clowes and H. Bourne, 141, 153 ; J Garner and J. Oxtoby's labours—Mount Pleasant Church secured—circuits made from it, 141.

Winchester, struggle and success at, ii. 343.

Windsor, persecution on the mission, ii. 345—7.

Winster made a circuit, i. 525 ; its vigorous re-missionary efforts, 527—30.

Wisbech, early P. Methodism at ; some circuit worthies, ii. 224—5.

Witney, the noisy Camp Meeting at, made a circuit and transferred to Tunstall Dist., i. 346—7.

Woodley, its early history, the Stafford family (*portraits*) and the influence of J. L. Buckley, *portrait* and view of chapel, ii. 50—1.

Wolverhampton, opposition at to S. Turner, i. 519 ; J. Bonser imprisoned at, 522.

Wootton Bassett, persecution and success at, ii. 311—12, 335.

Worcester, T. Brownsword imprisoned at, i. 521—2.

Wrockwardine Wood, chapel built at, ii. 274—5 ; made the head of the circuit, 274 ; prosperity of, 275.

Yarmouth missioned by Norwich, ii. 228. Made a circuit, 228. Hayloft its first chapel, 228. First and second Tabernacles built on the same site, 228—9. Origin of the word " Temple " given to the present chapel, 229. Fatal accident to Mr. T. Kirk, 229. Yarmouth Sunday School, 230. Queen Street Chapel erected, 230. Five circuits made from Yarmouth, 231. *Portraits* and notices of prominent officials, 229, 232—3. Ministers who have gone out from the circuit, 232.

York, the strategic importance of, ii. 52 ; visits of Clowes and Mr. and Mrs. Harrison to, 53—5 ; Grape Lane Chapel, 56—8 ; severe persecution at, 57—8 ; made a circuit, 58 ; the building of Little Stonegate, 60—1 ; views of chapels and prominent early officials, 58—60 ; Elmfield College at, 521—4. Offices of Insurance Co. and Chapel Aid Association, 534—8.

YOUNG PEOPLE'S Society of Christian Endeavour, ii. 531.

FLETCHER AND SON, LTD., PRINTERS, NORWICH.